MANAGEMENT, WORK AND ORGANISATIONS

Series editors: **Gibson Burrell**, The Management Centre, University of Leicester
Mick Marchington, Manchester Business School
Paul Thompson, Department of Human Resource Management,
University of Strathclyde

This series of new textbooks covers the areas of human resource management, employee relations, organisational behaviour and related business and management fields. Each text has been specially commissioned to be written by leading experts in a clear and accessible way. The books contain serious and challenging material, take an analytical rather than prescriptive approach and are particularly suitable for use by students with no prior specialist knowledge.

The series is relevant for many business and management courses, including MBA and post-experience courses, specialist masters and postgraduate diplomas, professional courses and final-year undergraduate courses. These texts have become essential reading at business and management schools worldwide.

Published

Paul Blyton and Peter Tu
THE DYNAMICS OF EM   RELATIONS

Sharon C. Bolton
EMOTION MANAGEMENT IN THE WORKPLACE

Peter Boxall and John Purcell
STRATEGY AND HUMAN RESOURCE MANAGEMENT

J. Martin Corbett
CRITICAL CASES IN ORGANISATIONAL BEHAVIOUR

Keith Grint
LEADERSHIP

Irena Grugulis
SKILLS, TRAINING AND HUMAN RESOURCE DEVELOPMENT

Damian Hodgson and Svetlana Cicmil
MAKING PROJECTS CRITICAL

Marek Korczynski
HUMAN RESOURCE MANAGEMENT IN SERVICE WORK

Karen Legge
HUMAN RESOURCE MANAGEMENT: anniversary edition

Helen Rainbird (ed.)
TRAINING IN THE WORKPLACE

Jill Rubery and Damian Grimshaw
THE ORGANISATION OF EMPLOYMENT

Harry Scarbrough (ed.)
THE MANAGEMENT OF EXPERTISE

Hugh Scullion and Margaret Linehan
INTERNATIONAL HUMAN RESOURCE MANAGEMENT

Adrian Wilkinson, Mick Marchington, Tom Redman and Ed Snape
MANAGING WITH TOTAL QUALITY MANAGEMENT

Colin C. Williams
RETHINKING THE FUTURE OF WORK

Diana Winstanley and Jean Woodall (eds)
ETHICAL ISSUES IN CONTEMPORARY HUMAN RESOURCE MANAGEMENT

For more information on titles in the Series please go to www.palgrave.com/busines/mwo

Invitiation to authors

The Series Editors welcome proposals for new books within the Managment, Work and Organisations series. These should be sent to Paul Thompson (p.thompson@strath.ac.uk) at the Dept of HRM, Strathclyde Business School, University of Strathclyde, 50 Richmond St Glasgow G1 1XT

Series Standing Order

If you would like to receive future titles in this series as they are published, you can make use of our standing order facility. To place a standing order please contact your bookseller or, in case of difficulty, write to us at the address below with your name and address and the name of the series. Please state with which title you wish to begin your standing order.

Customer Services Department, Macmillan Distribution Ltd
Houndmills, Basingstoke, Hampshire RG21 6XS, England

Other books by the authors include:

P. Blyton   *Changes in Working Time: An International Review*

P. Blyton (with G. Ursell)   *State, Capital and Labour: Changing Patterns of Power and Dependence*

P. Blyton (with J. Hassard, S. Hill and K. Starkey)   *Time, Work and Organization*

P. Blyton and P. Turnbull (eds)   *Reassessing Human Resource Management*

P. Blyton (with A. Dastmalchian and R. Adamson)   *The Climate of Workplace Relations*

P. Blyton (with M. Noon)   *The Realities of Work*

P. Turnbull (with C. Woolfson and J. Kelly)   *Dock Strike: Conflict and Restructuring in Britain's Ports*

The dynamics of employee relations

Third edition

Paul Blyton
and
Peter Turnbull

First edition 1994
Reprinted once
Second edition 1998
Reprinted six times

Published 2004 by
PALGRAVE MACMILLAN
Houndmills, Basingstoke, Hampshire RG21 6XS and
175 Fifth Avenue, New York, N.Y. 10010
Companies and representatives throughout the world

PALGRAVE MACMILLAN is the global academic imprint of the Palgrave
Macmillan division of St. Martin's Press, LLC and of Palgrave Macmillan Ltd.
Macmillan is a registered trademark in the United States, United Kingdom
and other countries. Palgrave is a registered trademark in the European
Union and other countries.

ISBN–10: 0–333–94836–X
ISBN–13: 978–0–333–94836–1

This book is printed on paper suitable for recycling and
made from fully managed and sustained forest sources.

A catalogue record for this book is available from the British Library.

10   9   8   7   6
13   12   11   10   09   08   07

Printed in China

For our families

Contents

List of figures

List of tables

Preface to the third edition

In the early 1990s, when we originally planned the first edition of this book, we had two main questions in mind: could we write a book that held students' interest and could we write one that demonstrated the continuing importance of employee relations in contemporary industrial society? These questions continue to inform the structure and content of this third edition.

To address the first question, and make the subject matter more accessible, we have leavened the general analysis of trends, themes and issues with a series of case studies that depict both the realities of employee relations and their diversity. Employee relations occur wherever people work, be that in a hospital, office, garage, shop or factory. The cases we present reflect this diversity. They are drawn from a range of industries and types of employment: from civil servants to steel-workers, firefighters to shop assistants, supermarket workers to airline flight attendants. They are intended to give a flavour of the way that work and employee relations are organised in the public and private sectors, in manufacturing and services, and in manual and non-manual activities. Above all, they illustrate how employee relations embraces much more than the world of male-dominated industrial trade unions sat around the negotiating table with management, or manual labour in the factory, down a coal mine or on a construction site. Employee relations is as much about the customer care programme in the high street retailer or airline as the disputes procedure in the engineering factory, and is as much about the personal relations between management and staff in the small non-union office as the formalised union–management relationship in a large multi-divisional company. We hope that the cases will be used as a basis for seminar discussion, to provoke argument and debate.

As well as conveying the realities and diversity of employee relations, we have used the cases to introduce each of the themes in the central sections of the book, and we draw on them throughout the relevant chapter to illustrate and illuminate our argument. And an argument is what students will find when they read the book.

After many years of teaching, researching and writing on employee relations, we have formulated views which we believe it is important to set down. One view of a text is that above all it should be detached, providing information and summarising different arguments, while leaving readers to draw their own conclusions. We agree that it is important to have balance in any academic work. In addition, however, we also believe that there are some important things to say and lessons to be drawn from the current state of employee relations, not just for business organisations, public enterprises or state agencies but also for all those who sell their labour in order to subsist.

Employee relations are not just about the utilisation of human resources but the experiences and expectations of labour in the workplace and wider society. Thus, an overarching question in our minds when writing the book has been: what sort of employee relations do we want in ten or twenty years' time? This time frame reflects the fact that many students reading this book will probably hold senior positions by that time, formulating and implementing policies and managing people. How would you like to be managed at work? How can your employees improve the competitiveness and efficiency of your organisation? How can you enhance the working lives of the people who work for your organisation? How do you promote industrial democracy? How should conflicts of interest be resolved? These questions may be rather distant for many of our readers today, but they will no doubt loom large for them in years to come. We hope that by exploring relevant theoretical debates, analysing the empirical evidence and presenting our own assessment, readers will more readily appreciate the importance of employee relations in the twenty-first century.

We also address a broader range of contextual issues that shape the contours and conduct of contemporary employee relations. For example, to what extent, if at all, can management develop a highly committed and more flexible workforce in an economy widely characterised by low wages, low productivity, and low trust relations? Another set of problems are those facing trade unions in attempting to recruit and effectively represent employee interests in environments often hostile to union activity. All the evidence suggests that employees want a greater voice at work than they currently enjoy, so how can unions bridge this 'representation gap'? And what about the policies of the state? The state can play a crucial role in promoting industrial democracy and improving the conditions of work for millions of employees, both directly as the employer of public sector workers and through legislation and effective management of the economy.

In many ways, the central message of the book is the importance of appreciating the interdependent and reciprocal nature of employee relations. For example, within every organisation, relationships between management and labour will be characterised by conflicts of interest as well as co-operation between the parties. These relationships will impact on both organisational performance and employees' experience of work. In the modern world of work, organisations demand 'high commitment', 'continuous improvement', 'world class performance' and 'total quality'. But how will employees respond to the mantra of 'business efficiency' if this is constructed on the shifting sands of low trust, low skills and low wages? Throughout the book we highlight the many tensions and contradictions that characterise contemporary employee relations.

As the UK and its neighbours move towards greater European integration, as industry becomes more heterogeneous in its character and ownership, and as workforces become more diverse, it is all the more important to understand the nature of employee relations, the environments in which those relations take place, and the forces shaping their development. Moreover, in a society where too many workers experience long and unsocial work hours, discrimination, bullying, dissatisfaction and unreasonable work pressure; where job insecurity, redundancy and unemployment affect large numbers of the working population; where millions of employees work not only for wages that do not support a decent standard of living but also in jobs that provide only low quality work and poor protection; where affluence increases year-on-year but the fruits of human endeavour are more unequally distributed than ever before; where the economy generates more wealth but its workforce is no more satisfied with life – then something is wrong. Throughout the book we have sought to elaborate what the dynamics of employee relations mean for the individual employee – the 'missing subject' of so many texts in the management area. If we are to appreciate the importance of employee relations in modern society, what better place to start than the realities of people's working lives? If we can elucidate these arguments, hold students' interest as we do so, and encourage them to think more about the breadth and significance of employee relations, the factors that shape those relations and the issues that confront the people involved, we will be more than satisfied.

This third edition of *The Dynamics of Employee Relations* has been written in an employee relations climate significantly different from that prevailing when the first and second editions appeared in print (in 1994 and 1998). The first edition appeared after more than a decade of Conservative governments during which time the neo-liberal agenda pursued by Margaret Thatcher dramatically re-drew the landscape of employee relations. The decline of union membership, collective bargaining and strikes led some commentators to predict the 'end of institutionalised industrial relations'; but what seemed more remarkable at the time were the continuities with past practice, despite the onward march of Thatcherism.

The second edition of the book appeared shortly after the landslide victory of New Labour in May 1997. Mr Blair's government promised to steer a 'Third Way' between Thatcherism and the old-style socialism of previous Labour governments; but the policies of New Labour had not yet taken root and were too recent for us to assess with any degree of confidence. Indeed, as a political slogan, the 'Third Way' was rather imprecise, defined more in terms of what it was not rather than what it was or aspired to become. More than six years on, however, and well into Labour's second period of administration, we are in a much better position to evaluate the significance of changes that have occurred, highlight some of the main trends, including continuities with the past, and to make some judgements. What has become clearer in recent years is that while important changes have been introduced that have bolstered various individual and collective rights of employees (such as the introduction of a statutory minimum wage and signing up to the European Social Charter), other changes have as yet had only a modest impact (such as legislation relating to maximum working hours and trade union recognition rights and procedures), whilst in other areas restrictions introduced by the previous Conservative governments have remained firmly in place (e.g. legislation governing the conduct of industrial conflict).

Do these developments add up to a transformation of employee relations? The word 'transformation' conjures up an image of sudden and dramatic change. Taken in isolation, and making a comparison over a relatively short time period, many of the developments in the field of employee relations might appear rather innocuous and not add up to very much. But taken in combination, and over a longer time frame, the picture looks very different. Over the past decade, as we have worked on revised editions of this text, we have been increasingly struck by the magnitude and significance of the changes taking place in employee relations.

The question of change and transformation is therefore a central theme of this third edition of *The Dynamics of Employee Relations*, which incorporates all the most significant research findings in the field since the appearance of the last edition in 1998. We have updated earlier cases on British Airways and Marks & Spencer and written several new cases for this edition, including a study of union organising in London, the proposed privatisation of the Port of Belfast, management–labour partnership at Tesco, and the 2002–3 firefighters' dispute.

We would like to acknowledge the financial assistance of Cardiff Business School for providing the funds to allow us to undertake much of the research necessary for the new cases, as well as the Economic & Social Research Council and the Leverhulme Trust for their support of several research projects that we draw upon in the cases and elsewhere in the text. In addition, we would like to thank the many workers, managers, union leaders and government officials who have provided us with important insights, as well as our students whose comments on previous editions and early drafts of the current text have influenced the content and presentation of material. We are also grateful to Kate Bradbury and the library staff of Cardiff Business School for their assistance with secondary data used in several of the tables, as well as Penny Smith and Lesley Plowman for their assistance with the preparation of the manuscript. Finally, we would like to thank Sarah Brown and Ursula Gavin at Palgrave Macmillan for their encouragement and patience.

PAUL BLYTON
PETER TURNBULL

Acknowledgements

The authors and publishers would like to thank the following for permission to use copyright material:

Blackwell Publishing for Figure 5.2, reprinted from J. Kelly and E. Heery (1989) 'Full-Time Officers and Trade Union Recruitment' in the *British Journal of Industrial Relations*, **27** (2).

Blackwell Publishing for Figure 9.2, reprinted from P. Willman (1989) 'The Logic of Market-Share Trade Unionism: Is Membership Decline Inevitable?' in the *Industrial Relations Journal*, **20** (4).

Cornell University Press for Figure 3.1, reprinted from Harry C. Katz and Owen Darbishire, *Converging Divergences: Worldwide Changes in Employment Systems*. Copyright © 2000 by Cornell University. Used by permission of the publisher, Cornell University Press.

Thomas Kochan for Figure 4.1, reprinted from T. Kochan, W. Orlikowski and J. Cutcher-Gershenfeld (2002), *Beyond McGregor's Theory Y: Human Capital and Knowledge-based Work in the 21st Century Organisation*.

Palgrave Macmillan for Table 9.2, reprinted from Marek Korczynski: *Human Resource Management in Service Work*. Copyright © 2001 Marek Korczynski.

Pearson Education for Figure 4.4, reprinted from *Changing Patterns of Employee Relations in Britain* by M. Marchington and P. Parker, Pearson Education Ltd. Copyright © 1990 by M. Marchington and P. Parker.

Taylor & Francis for Table 10.2, reprinted from N. Millward, N. Bryson and J. Forth, *All Changes at Work: British Employment Relations 1980–1998, as Portrayed by the Workplace Industrial Relations Series*, published by Routledge. Copyright © 2000 by Millward, Bryson and Forth.

Every effort has been made to trace the copyright holders but if any have been inadvertently overlooked the publishers will be pleased to make the necessary arrangement at the first opportunity.

List of abbreviations

AA	Automobile Association
ABP	Associated British Ports
ACAS	Advisory, Conciliation and Arbitration Service
ACTT	Association of Cinematography, Television and Allied Technicians (now BECTU)
AEEU	Amalgamated Engineering and Electrical Union (now Amicus)
AEU	Amalgamated Engineering Union (now Amicus)
APEX	Association of Professional, Executive, Clerical and Computer Staff (now GMB)
ASLEF	Associated Society of Locomotive Engineers and Firemen
ASTMS	Association of Scientific, Technical and Managerial Staffs (now Amicus)
ATGWU	Amalgamated Transport & General Workers' Union
BA	British Airways
BALPA	British Airline Pilots Association
BASSA	British Airline Stewards and Stewardesses Association
BBC	British Broadcasting Corporation
BEA	British European Airways (now BA)
BECTU	Broadcasting, Entertainment, Cinematograph and Theatre Union
BETA	Broadcasting and Entertainments Trade Alliance (now BECTU)
BHC	Belfast Harbour Commissioners
BHPS	British Household Panel Survey
BIFU	Banking, Insurance and Finance Union
BOAC	British Overseas Airways Corporation (now BA)
BR	British Rail
BS	British Steel (now Corus)
BSAS	British Social Attitudes Survey
BSC	British Steel Corporation (now Corus)
BT	British Telecom
BTDB	British Transport Docks Board

CAA	Civil Aviation Authority
CAC	Central Arbitration Committee
CADCAM	computer aided design computer assisted manufacture
CBI	Confederation of British Industry
CCT	compulsory competitive tendering
CEGB	Central Electricity Generating Board
CEO	chief executive officer
CIPD	Chartered Institute of Personnel and Development
CME	co-ordinated market economy
CIM	computer integrated manufacture
COHSE	Confederation of Health Service Employees (now Unison)
CPSA	Civil and Public Services Association
CSEU	Confederation of Shipbuilding and Engineering Unions
CSU	Civil Service Union
CWU	Communication Workers Union
DGB	Deutscher Gewerkschaftsbund
DRD	Department for Regional Development (Northern Ireland)
DTI	Department of Trade and Industry
EA	Employment Act (2002)
EC	European Commission
EEF	Engineering Employers' Federation
EETPU	Electrical, Electronic, Telecommunication and Plumbing Union (now Amicus)
EMA	Engineers and Managers Association
ERA	Employment Relations Act (1999)
EPOS	electronic point of sale
ETUC	European Trade Union Confederation
EU	European Union
EWC	European Works Council
FBU	Fire Brigades Union
FDI	foreign direct investment
FMS	flexible manufacturing system
FTO	full-time (union) official
GATT	General Agreement on Tariffs and Trade
GCHQ	Government Communications Headquarters
GDP	gross domestic product
GMB	General, Municipal and Boilermakers' Union
GPMU	Graphical, Paper and Media Union
HCM	high commitment management
HCU	Hotel and Catering Workers' Union
HMSO	Her Majesty's Stationery Office
HP	Hewlett Packard

HR	human resource
HRM	human resource management
IBM	International Business Machines
ICD	Information and Consultation Directive
ICT	information and communications technology
IIP	Investors In People
IMF	International Monetary Fund
IPMS	Institution of Professional Managers and Specialists
IRSF	Inland Revenue Staff Federation
ISTC	Iron and Steel Trades Confederation
ITF	International Transport Workers' Federation
JCC	Joint Consultation Committee
JIC	Joint Industrial Council
JIT	just-in-time
LFS	Labour Force Survey
LME	liberal market economy
LPC	Low Pay Commission
LSB	lump sum bonus
LSC	Learning and Skills Council
M&S	Marks & Spencer
MDHC	Mersey Docks & Harbour Company
MDW	measured day work
MEBO	management–employee buy-out
MIDAS	Maritime Industrial and Distribution Activities
MSF	Manufacturing, Science and Finance
NALGO	National and Local Government Officers' Association (now Unison)
NAPE	National Association of Port Employers
NAS/UWT	National Association of Schoolmasters/Union of Women Teachers
NATFHE	National Association of Teachers in Further and Higher Education
NCU	National Communications Union
NDLB	National Dock Labour Board
NDLS	National Dock Labour Scheme
NEDC	National Economic Development Council
NEDO	National Economic Development Office
NER	non-union employee representation
NGA	National Graphical Association (now GPMU)
NHS	National Health Service
NIPSA	Northern Ireland Public Service Alliance
NJCCAT	National Joint Council for Civil Air Transport
NMW	national minimum wage
NUM	National Union of Mineworkers
NUPE	National Union of Public Employees (now Unison)

NUR	National Union of Railwaymen (now RMT)
NUS	National Union of Seamen (now RMT)
NUT	National Union of Teachers
NUTGW	National Union of Tailors and Garment Workers (now GMB)
NVQ	National Vocational Qualification
OECD	Organisation for Economic Cooperation and Development
Offer	Office of Electricity Regulation
Ofwat	Office of Water Services
ONS	Office for National Statistics
OPEC	Organisation of Petroleum Exporting Countries
PBR	payment by results
PCSU	Public and Commercial Services Union
PFA	Professional Footballers Association
PFI	Private Finance Initiative
PLP	Parliamentary Labour Party
POEU	Post Office Engineering Union
PPP	public–private partnership
PTC	Public Services, Tax and Commerce Union
R&D	research and development
RFU	Rugby Football Union
RMT	National Union of Rail, Maritime and Transport Workers
SBU	strategic business unit
SCELI	Social Change and Economic Life Initiative
SCPS	Society of Civil and Public Servants
SIC	Standard Industrial Classification
SME	small and medium sized enterprises
SOGAT	Society of Graphical and Allied Trades (now GPMU)
SPC	statistical process control
T&GWU	Transport & General Workers' Union
TASS	Technical, Administrative and Supervisory Section (now Amicus)
TNC	trans-national corporation
TQM	total quality management
TSB	Trustee Savings Bank
TSSA	Transport Salaried Staffs' Association
TUC	Trades Union Congress
UCATT	Union of Construction, Allied Trades and Technicians
UCW	Union of Communication Workers
UDM	Union of Democratic Mineworkers
UNCTAD	United Nations Council on Trade and Development
USDAW	Union of Shop, Distributive and Allied Workers
WERS98	Workplace Employee Relations Survey 1998
WIRS	Workplace Industrial Relations Survey

part **1**

The theory and context of employee relations

1

Employee relations

Introduction

Our point of departure in writing a book about employee relations can be summarised in a few short statements. First and foremost, *work dominates the lives of most men and women*. Aside from the domestic and voluntary work spheres, the vast majority of those who work are employees rather than employers. The terms and conditions under which they undertake that work are of central importance to them. These terms and conditions include both the 'market exchange' that they enter into with an employer and the 'managerial relations' to which they are subjected. The former evokes notions of fairness and equity in the exertion of effort and the remuneration of labour. According to an old Proverb, 'in all labour there is profit', but how much profit should the employer derive from the employee's labour? The latter, managerial relations, are equally important because 'there can be no employment relationship without a power to command and a duty to obey' (Kahn-Freund, 1972:9). Everyone is concerned about the authority of the employer to direct, use, and potentially abuse, their labour.

Secondly, *the management of employees, both individually and collectively, remains a central feature of organisational life*. Despite the competitive edge that may be secured from sources such as product innovation, technological change and the more efficient utilisation of energy and raw materials, the manner in which (and the terms under which) a workforce performs its functions will normally have a major bearing on the organisation's long-term success. As Alfred Marshall wrote in his *Principles of Economics*, 'the most valuable of all capital is that invested in human beings'. The modern-day versions of this truism, voiced by company directors and personnel managers alike, are that 'employees are our most valuable asset' or that 'people are the key to success'. The significance of the way that employees perform their roles is particularly visible in those service-related activities where employees interact directly with the public, the so-called 'pink-collar' occupations.

3

However, in manufacturing too, the social aspects of organisation remain a key feature on which organisational effectiveness turns (see, for example, Patterson *et al.*, 1997).

Thirdly, *within organisations a common interest between management and workforce cannot be assumed, willed, or 'managed' into existence.* On the contrary, the nature of employment relations, and the basic relationship between profit and wages, authority and compliance, creates a persistent (albeit often latent) tension between employers and employed, management and workforce. The objectives of employees at work – be they income, security, satisfaction, career, companionship – are not synonymous with the objectives of management or company shareholders. It is due to this underlying tension and potential source of conflict that the management of employee relations remains problematic. Conformity and consent cannot be assumed, however much reference is made by governments, employers and labour representatives to a desire for 'social partnership'. One indication of this comes from the British Social Attitudes Survey (BSAS), a nationally representative data set, which indicates that around 60 per cent of the workforce believes that 'Managers will usually try to get the better of employees if they get the chance', while less than 40 per cent agree with the statement: 'Managers at my workplace usually keep their promises to the employees'. The number of workers who report 'poor management–employee relations' increased from one-in-six in the early 1980s to around one-in-four by the mid 1990s. This is not to gainsay the importance of interdependence between capital and labour, rather to point out that interdependence does not equate with 'common interests'.

Finally, *it is misguided to assume that developments over the recent past such as the decline in trade union membership and collective bargaining coverage, the increased legal circumscription of industrial conflict and the greater prominence being given to human resource management (HRM) techniques of employee management, signal the demise of the collective aspects of the employment relationship* (see Blyton and Turnbull, 1992). Almost all work in contemporary industrial society is a co-operative endeavour. Individuals rarely work in complete isolation, and almost all rely on the work of others to complete their own tasks. Indeed, in many work settings the division of labour discerned by Adam Smith in *The Wealth of Nations* more than two centuries ago is even more in evidence today (see Braverman, 1974; and Noon and Blyton, 2002:142–70) creating a 'natural' interdependence and common interest among those who extract raw material from the earth, manufacture goods in the factory, or provide services in the office, shop, school, or bourse. The natural affinity and common interest of work groups give rise to forms of collective representation and action, expressed usually, though not always, through the medium of trade unions. Even where management seek to foster greater individualism among the workforce, the tension and conflict that is implicit in the relationship between capital and labour cannot be eradicated, nor can the (periodic) expression of that conflict through collective action.

At first sight these 'position' statements, reflecting the basic importance, problematic nature and contemporary significance of employee relations, may appear almost too obvious to warrant restating. We believe, however, that the tendency for them to be discarded or overlooked in much of the recent HRM literature and related fields (e.g. labour or personnel economics) may have led to a misconception about the continuing significance of employee relations in contemporary work organisations. Coupled with this conviction regarding the continuing importance of the subject, we believe it is essential to acknowledge the values associated with employee relations that are distinct from economic efficiency and that are rarely articulated in the prescriptive literature on HRM (see Osterman et al., 2001:3). Equity is the most obvious example, which is not only important in its own right but can also foster economic efficiency and more effective HRM (see Gunderson, 2001:446–8).

The same can be said of trust between the parties to a contract of employment. Indeed, it is increasingly recognised that trust is central to future economic and social prosperity (e.g. Hutton, 1997; and Korczynski, 2000:7–8). Trust can be defined as 'the confidence that the other party to an exchange will not exploit one's vulnerability' (Korczynski, 2000:2). Thus, the essence of trust is a belief that another party will continue to adhere to rules of fairness or reciprocity even in circumstances in which it might be advantageous to do otherwise. It follows, therefore, that trust cannot be based on self-interest alone – 'I trust you because it is in my interest to do so' is rarely a sufficient basis for mutual commitment – which is one reason why society places constraints on the pursuit of rational individualism (ibid; see also Streeck, 1997).

Other values that inform employee relations include ideas of work as a source of dignity (workers should not be treated as commodities), a 'fair day's pay' and a 'living wage' (to facilitate participation in society and the dignity of family life), solidarity or social cohesion (the pursuit of a 'good society' for its own sake and not simply for the achievement of economic benefits), and employee voice and the right to participate in decisions affecting one's work (and related non-work) activities (a system of industrial democracy to complement political democracy) (see Osterman et al, 2001:11–12). All employment relationships involve values as well as interests, ethics as well as economics – indeed, even the 'price of labour' is inherently invested with moral and political overtones (see Ackers and Wilkinson, 2003a:20; and Martin, 2003:162).

As we start a new millennium, however, there are concerns that the 'work based society' of the twentieth century, built on the idea of people gaining security and a sense of personal and social usefulness through gainful employment, has been seriously undermined by neo-liberal economic policies, labour market flexibility, new management practices, consumerism, globalisation and the like (see, for example, Ackers, 2002; Beynon et al., 2002:19–20; Forrester, 1999; Gorz, 1999; ILO, 2001; and Supiot, 2001). In this context, we believe it is important to restate the values traditionally associated with employee relations, to re-establish their moral grounding, and to integrate these values into our analysis, interpretation and prescription.

This approach may jar with those who believe that textbooks should be 'dispassionate' and steer clear of (political) policy debates. Even those who claim to be 'objective', however, are influenced by, and certainly influence, political debates, public policy and management practice. Much of the HRM literature, for example, as Bacon (2003), Kelly (1998), Legge (1995) and several other writers have demonstrated, follows an explicitly unitary and managerial agenda. As a result, workers' interests are all too often overlooked or are simply assumed to coincide with those of management and the organisation. Indeed, '[i]t is somewhat ironic that although HRM relates to the effective management of employees, we know remarkably little about how employees, as the subjects of HRM, react to its practice' (Grant and Shields, 2002:313). Labour economists, for their part, continue to separate market and non-market relations (see Turnbull, 2003) assigning priority to the former over the latter and denigrating any policies derived from institutional or other perspectives on employee relations or workers' interests (see, for example, Neumark, 2002:722–3). But what are the policy implications of a theory that advocates free market competition and the pursuit of rational self-interest? As Adams (1998:13) points out:

> It is one thing for the professional economist to assume economically maximizing behaviour: it is quite another for people to begin to relate to each other primarily as competitors for economic advantage. There is no problem with professional economists conceptualizing labour as a commodity with attributes of quantity and price. It is very problematic when the managers of human organizations begin to view their co-workers in the enterprise as little more than a cost on the balance sheet.

If employee relations is understood as 'an arena in which the contest between the pursuit of a "market society" and the defence of principles of "moral economy" is played out' (Hyman, 2001a:285), then it is impossible to separate 'market' from 'non-market' relations, economy from society, or the organisation from political economy. Equally, it is impossible to separate theory and practice, policy and prescription.

We also hold pedagogic views on the study of employee relations, and particularly the place of a core text within that scheme. It may be useful to outline these briefly, for a browse along library shelves and university bookshop displays reveals the presence of a number of other texts in this area. So, why another one? One reason is that many previous texts have tended to rely too much on aggregate information: there is an undue focus on overall patterns and trends in the various 'indices' of employee relations, such as the level of trade union membership, the number of strikes or general trends in collective bargaining activity. Clearly such approaches have value – indeed, we too will consider such trends. At the same time, at its core, employee relations is not about general trends, social aggregates or institutions but about *people*: people interacting with one another, pursuing objectives, reaching agreements, engaging in co-operative and conflictual behaviour. As such, an enquiry into the nature of employee relations will be significantly enhanced by examining specific cases as well as general trends and developments.

Many existing texts have sought to do this by reference to the findings of other studies. We feel, however, that this needs to be taken further. The dryness of texts which so many students complain about is not an inevitable or inescapable feature of industrial or employee relations. In some respects the subject has acquired 'a deserved reputation for being dull' (Nichols, 1980:12), but only because it has too often failed to relate in any meaningful way to the reality of people's working lives: what problems they experience, what options they have and what strategies they employ in attempts to change and improve their situation. In important part, it is a question of how one approaches the subject. The student is certainly no longer required to enter the field like a botanist, discovering facts and falling back on theory only when the relevant data are unavailable (McCarthy, 1992:2). In fact, from being a subject formerly criticised for its apparent (or at least explicit) absence of theory, there is now an entire literature on different theoretical approaches to the subject (see, for example, Ackers, 2002; Ackers and Wilkinson, 2003b; Adams and Meltz, 1993; Dabscheck, 1983; Edwards, 1995a; Giles, 2000; Guille, 1984; Kelly, 1998; Marsden, 1999; and Winchester, 1983b). Theory enables the student to understand and not just appreciate the complexity of a subject that, in reality, has few clearly defined boundaries (*pace* Edwards, 2003:29). What is needed, therefore, is a central focus around which to organise ideas, present data, and provide an explanation. The focus of this text is the *employment relationship*, which, as Fells (1989:471) points out, need not be an abstract notion but one of practical significance, being the basis of the parties' own interactions and the relationship upon which all other aspects of employee relations develop.

Even though there are now several routes over the 'mountains of facts' accumulated in the study of industrial and employee relations (Dabscheck, 1983), students nevertheless sometimes complain about the scenery *en route*, the way the facts are presented and the balance between the general and the specific. We have sought to overcome this in part by introducing each chapter in Parts 2 and 3 of the book with a case study. The cases have been chosen for the way they encapsulate some aspect of wider developments. Inevitably, the cases we present are not, and cannot be, wholly 'typical' of the developments under discussion; single cases alone can rarely convey all aspects of a broader pattern of development. Rather they have been chosen to illustrate, and in many respects exemplify, the way that broader issues operate in practice: to provide a more tangible feel for the different issues of employee relations. At various points in the text of each chapter, therefore, we refer back to, and elaborate upon, the opening case study to illuminate the argument and ground the analysis in a more concrete setting. Clearly, we cannot explain every nuance of the cases or explain them in great detail; to do so would require a separate book for each case. Given that such books or more detailed articles exist, we have sought to write these cases in such a way that they may be used as the basis for separate group discussions, with references to allow further exploration of the cases themselves.

One reason why case study material has not figured more prominently in previous texts is no doubt a simple lack of space. Typical conceptions of a text are that it should provide a comprehensive guide to a subject, summarising both its historical development and the different aspects of its current nature. In the present volume, it is true that by devoting a significant amount of space to the case studies, something else has had to be sacrificed in order to keep the book to a reasonable (and readable) size. In this instance it is some of the historical aspects of the subject which at times are sketched in less detail than we might have wished (although extensive references are provided throughout the text to enable readers to explore particular topics in more depth). Our emphasis is more focused on recent and contemporary developments, though at the same time we endeavour to provide sufficient historical context against which to judge the significance of more recent events. As Lyddon (2003:104) points out, historical study 'is not a luxury but a necessity ... to understand why the present is as it is'. That said, what really matters most is how we conceptualise historical processes rather than simply whether or not we provide sufficient historical detail (for the latter, see Fox, 1985; Hyman, 2003; Kessler and Bayliss, 1995:1–37; and Ursell and Blyton, 1988). A common aphorism is that 'history casts its shadow forward', but this does not mean that we must always live in the shadow of the past. To (mis)quote Karl Marx, people make their own history, albeit not exactly as they please.

Before embarking on our investigation, this introductory chapter needs to address two further questions. First, what do we mean by the term *employee relations* and how does it differ from other expressions applied to workforce management such as industrial relations, personnel management and the increasingly popular human resource management? Second, why are we concerned with the *dynamics* of employee relations? Over the last two decades, much discussion in the employee relations field has been dominated, implicitly or explicitly, by a debate couched largely in terms of change *versus* continuity. The adjective 'dynamics' is typically used to convey the idea of change and it is change, or transformation, that we seek to emphasise. This is not to deny the importance of underlying continuities in the employment relationship and the nature of employee and management interests. Rather, our aim is to highlight the degree of experimentation that is taking place and the opportunities this presents for practitioners, policy-makers, researchers and students (as future practitioners, policy-makers or researchers) to influence the immediate course of employee relations.

Why 'employee relations'?

Our title 'The Dynamics of *Employee Relations*', rather than 'The Dynamics of *Industrial Relations*', was chosen for a purpose. In one sense, we probably need hardly worry about the distinction for neither bears close scrutiny in terms of its literal meaning. Just as Hyman (1992:7) poses the question 'what is an industrial relation?' to highlight the vacuous nature of the actual label, the same question could also be asked of an 'employee relation'. However, while some authors use the terms 'industrial relations' and 'employee relations' interchangeably (e.g. Beardwell, 1996), and while we too should say at the outset that we see no hard and fast distinction between the two, there is nonetheless a tendency for each to place the subject's focus within somewhat different boundaries. In particular, industrial relations has, over time, acquired a particular set of meanings both in the sphere of work and among academics researching and teaching the subject (see Dunn, 1990). As Miliband commented, industrial relations traditionally represented 'the consecrated euphemism for the permanent conflict, now acute, now subdued, between capital and labour' (1969:80). Among the general public and much of the media, the typical view also seems to be that industrial relations is about trade unions, collective bargaining and strikes – a view no doubt reinforced by the recent firefighters dispute, which we discuss in Chapter 10. In an historical context, a popular (mis)conception of industrial relations is that the entire subject can be reduced simply to the Winter of Discontent (1978–9) and the year-long miners' strike of 1984–5 – constituting the zenith and nadir of trade union power in the UK – and the subsequent emergence of a new industrial order. Using the term 'employee relations' is a way of circumventing these prior (mis)conceptions of the subject, as well as a device to broaden that set of meanings in the light of significant developments which have occurred since the academic field of industrial relations was first mapped out.

A common criticism of industrial relations enquiry, for example, is that it has too strong a tendency to view the world of work *as if* composed of unionised, male, manual workers, working on a full-time basis. The proletarian stereotype was the muscular male hewing coal, hammering metal, assembling cars or swinging a docker's hook. As Wajcman (2000:185) points out, we still know far more about male manual workers than female clerical workers. More importantly, the tendency to treat workers as homogeneous, with this homogeneity based around male experiences, has resulted either in women's experiences being ignored altogether or analysed *in relation to* the male model, such that 'it is women who are marked as gendered, the ones who are different' (ibid:184).

The exclusion of women and other employee groups from the analytical gaze of industrial relations was compounded by a focus on the *institutions* of collective bargaining between trade unions and employers in manufacturing and extractive industries, such that the subject found less and less resonance with debates about the future of work and society (Ackers, 2002:3). As we illustrate in Chapter 3, changes in industrial structure and workforce composition are making this 'traditional' sub-set of employment a progressively less accurate index of the overall workforce, not that it ever was so (the UK, for example, has never had a majority of its workforce employed in the manufacturing sector). Using the term 'employee relations' represents an acknowledgement that 'industry' as it has been traditionally defined (i.e. goods production or manufacturing) is a progressively less prominent employer of labour (only one-in-five of the workforce are now employed in manufacturing). More than seven-out-of-ten of the workforce in Britain are now engaged in service sector activities; and the proportion is likely to grow even higher. Reflecting the nature of many service activities, the majority of the workforce is now employed in white-collar jobs in which, traditionally, their holders have been referred to as 'employees'. Furthermore, the 'standard' full-time job is in decline, with over one-in-five of the workforce now engaged on part-time contracts and a further one-in-fifteen working on a temporary basis (see Chapter 3).

Moreover, the majority (around seven-out-of-ten) of the UK workforce does not currently belong to a trade union. While in some sectors these non-members are 'free-riders' (not members of a union but covered by union-negotiated terms and conditions), in others – most notably in the private service sector – trade union recognition remains sparse. Yet it is precisely in some of these sectors, where many workers are poorly paid, face health and safety hazards and arbitrary and unjust disciplinary practices, that the need for adequate collective representation is at its most pressing (see Chapter 9). Hence, it is important to incorporate non-union as well as unionised settings into our analysis in a way which only a small number of texts have previously done (e.g. Beaumont, 1990) and more generally to reflect the diverse nature of contemporary work and employment. If nothing else, the analysis of non-union work settings illustrates that the determination of pay and conditions, and the direction of labour at work, is not solely achieved through collective bargaining. A feature of employee relations in many non-union firms, for example, is their highly personalised nature. Elsewhere, as the study of British Airways in Chapter 4 demonstrates, the control of labour can equally be sought through 'customer care' campaigns: a far cry from the popular image of the 'two sides' confronting each other across the negotiating table, locking the factory gate or manning the picket line.

In the USA, Kaufman (1993) identifies the changing structure of employment, the decline of collective bargaining and the concomitant rise of human resource management as contributing to a 'hollowing out' of industrial relations. Other factors contributing to the difficulties faced by the subject, which are also evident in the UK (Kelly, 1994), include the (deductive) science-building of related disciplines such as labour economics and organisational theory, which have 'encroached' on traditional areas of industrial relations research (see, for example, Lazear, 2000), and, equally important, the lack of any integrating theory in industrial relations itself. Echoing Kaufman's conclusion that industrial relations must return to the core focus of yesteryear, namely *all* aspects of the employment relationship, Paul Edwards (1995a:40) has argued that, 'In order to survive, industrial relations needs to change its focus to employment relations, examining not just institutions but how the employment relationship operates in practice, and exploring the outcomes for efficiency and equity'. A concern with efficiency and equity, and in particular the dependence of the former on the latter, is one of the features of our analysis in Part 3, which considers the various interactions and outcomes in employee relations. More immediately, Chapter 2 presents an integrated theory of the employment relationship which provides the foundation for the entire text.

Although we have forsaken the label 'industrial relations' in favour of 'employee relations', and although we are concerned to include non-union, 'non-traditional' workers in our analysis, it remains the *collective* aspects of relations between workforce and management that we take as our focal point. In this, employee relations is distinct from personnel management and human resource management, though again the distinctions reflect differences in emphasis rather than separate, watertight compartments (see Bacon, 2003:73–4). Most texts and courses on personnel management and HRM recognise the potential for collective action on the part of employees and the presence of trade unions, but they place their primary focus on the individual at work. Personnel management, for example, focuses principally on the ways that individuals are selected, recruited, trained, developed, supervised, motivated, rewarded, and retrenched. The way in which, and the extent to which, individual behaviour is influenced by group norms, custom and practice, or more proactive forms of collective action, is all too often overlooked.

The traditional distinction between personnel management and industrial relations was tolerably clear: the former dealt with individual aspects of the employment relationship while the latter addressed the collective aspects. In more recent times, the distinction between the two fields of study has become rather more blurred as a result of the attention claimed by HRM (Bacon, 2003), particularly since its rise in prominence has coincided (not unconnectedly) with a period of decline in trade union power (for an analysis of HRM see Blyton and Turnbull, 1992; Legge, 1995; and Storey, 2001). Whilst, as already noted, HRM contains certain 'collectivist' notions, its overall approach has been centred squarely on the individual and the way individuals may be managed to enhance the achievement of broader organisational objectives. As a result:

- HRM emphasises the *employer's* solutions to labour problems whereas an employee-relations approach also considers *workers* as well as *community* and *societal* solutions
- HRM focuses on forces *internal* to the firm whereas an employee-relations approach also considers forces *external* to the organisation such as markets, class and property rights

- HRM's primary goal is *organisational competitiveness* whereas an employee relations approach combines this objective with a concern for *employee well-being* (as well as a consideration of how the latter influences the former)
- HRM focuses on creating a *unity of interests* between employer and employee whereas employee relations focuses on the *generation and mediation of conflicting interests*
- HRM sees *management as the primary contributor* to positive employment outcomes, with unions and government as occasionally necessary (e.g. in relation to health and safety) but more often a burdensome constraint, whereas employee relations recognises the *limitations of management action* and the *propriety of trade union intervention and government regulation* (adapted from Kaufman, 2001:362).

Within the HRM literature, the role of trade unions and collective bargaining tends to be marginalised, if not denigrated, and the existence of conflicting interests scarcely acknowledged, if not ignored altogether (see Lewin, 2001). It is only in more recent years, for example, that researchers have explicitly considered employee experiences of, and responses to, HRM (e.g. Guest, 2002; Kelly, 1998; and Mabey *et al.*, 1998). Even when workers' interests are considered, however, they are all too often defined by a managerial agenda (e.g. motivation to work, willingness to participate in teams, commitment to the organisation and so on). There are still very few studies of HRM as 'a source of feelings of vulnerability, insecurity, tension, anxiety, conflict, anger, disenfranchisement, boredom, and apathy' (Bacon, 1999:1183; see also Grant and Shields, 2002). We seek to demonstrate that while the employment relationship comprises important individual aspects, it is only by recognising the simultaneous existence of collective dimensions in this relationship that an adequate picture can be constructed of how a workforce is constituted, and the nature of relations between managers and employees. The focus of HRM on the individual, and its general unwillingness to acknowledge the existence of distinct interests within the workplace, has created a picture of simple common interest among managers and managed, an interest supposedly centred solely on the organisation's success in the market-place. This is both too narrow and too simplistic an account, reflecting a managerial ideology rather than an objective summary of organisational reality. As such it needs to be countered in order to understand more clearly the dynamics of the employment relationship.

The dynamics of change and continuity and the transformation of employee relations

An overarching debate within employee relations has been whether developments post-1979 signify a fundamental change in those relations, or whether, and to what extent, underlying continuities from the past continue to exert a moderating or constraining influence. Richard Hyman, for example, suggests that the period since 1979 has witnessed the 'most radical changes in British industrial relations since the Industrial Revolution' (2003:38). But do these changes constitute a 'transformation' of employee relations? In contrast, Bill Roche claims that 'the level and pace of diffusion of practices associated with the new industrial relations have been substantially more moderate than predicted ... Much of the change which *had* occurred was piecemeal, ad hoc and fragile' (2000:265–6, original emphasis). If continuity is still the order of the day, why have all the management initiatives, state policies and broader developments in the economic, social and political context failed fundamentally to reconfigure employee relations?

To answer these questions, we need to consider what, and how, to compare, and over what time period. For example, should we focus on intentions or outcomes, structures or strategies? To what extent should we rely on nationally representative survey data such as the Workplace Industrial Relations Surveys (WIRS 1980, 1984 and 1990), the Workplace Employment Relations Survey (WERS98), British Social Attitudes Survey (BSAS), and the Labour Force Survey (LFS), or more in-depth case study research, and how do we reconcile any differences between these various data sources? Should we focus on a comparison between New Labour and Thatcherism, or compare the 1980s and 1990s with the earlier post-Second-World-War period (up to and including the 1970s)? Clearly, there are important temporal, methodological and substantive issues to address before we can proceed with any review of the dynamics of employee relations.

Any assessment of change and continuity in employee relations will involve a comparison between the 'here and now' and 'yesteryear'. But how do we determine our 'base year' or 'point of comparison'? Some textbooks begin with the immediate post-Second-World-War period and follow an historical narrative to the present day (e.g. Kessler and Bayliss, 1995). This suggests that we can understand the present as long as we can identify the appropriate starting point, or period of origin, and then trace developments over time to establish their contemporary imprint. This approach is often characterised as an 'event-driven' view of history, where 'the emphasis is on the unique and the unrepeatable' (Franzosi, 1995:371). This approach is usually contrasted with a 'structure-driven' view of history, where 'the emphasis is on regularities, patterns, repetitions, and sequences, with occasional disruptions and discontinuities conjecturally introduced by events of particular significance' (ibid). One such example of the latter is Kelly's (1998) account of the 'long waves' of capitalist economic development – prolonged periods of growth followed by equally prolonged periods of stagnation and even recession – and the association between developments in employee relations and particular phases of the 'long wave' (e.g. the increase in strikes that usually accompanies the end of an economic upswing, which we discuss in Chapter 10). This suggests that we can understand the present as long as we can identify the economy's current stage of development (upswing or downswing).

At the risk of oversimplification, the 'event-driven' approach can be characterised as linear, inasmuch as it focuses on progress (or more accurately progression) in employee relations, whereas the 'structure-driven' approach can be characterised as cyclical, inasmuch as it seeks to identify recurring patterns in employee relations over time. The juxtaposition of these two approaches has often led to a rather unproductive debate between those who see nothing but change and those who highlight continuities with past practice. This was certainly the flavour of much of the debate in the 1980s, with commentators drawing on different data to 'prove' their point. For example, surveys would often suggest continuity (in part as a result of their closed-ended questions that focused on structures or institutions) whilst case studies highlighted change and innovation, in part as a result of their open-ended approach to social processes and the meanings attached to various actions and outcomes by different actors. Thus, as Keenoy (1997:7) pointed out, while structural relationships may appear to remain unchanged, the new discourse of human resource management might signify 'that the character of the employment relationship, and what is expected of employees *is* different' (original emphasis; see also Hamilton, 2001). The first and second editions of this text provide an extensive review of these debates and the relevant data (Blyton and Turnbull, 1994 and 1998). Differences arising from different data sources are still evident in contemporary research (see Beynon *et al.*, 2002:297; and Erickson and Kuruvilla, 1998:6). However, both surveys (e.g. Cully *et al.*, 1999; and Millward *et al.*, 2000) and case-based research (e.g. Bacon and Blyton, 2001; Beynon *et al.*, 2002; and Brown *et al.*, 1998) now emphasise change rather than dwell on continuity.

Most considered discussions of employee relations seek to combine various sources of data and most resolve the continuity-versus-change debate through the concept of complexity or 'contingency as trend'. In brief, there is both change *and* continuity, making industrial and employee relations more diverse and complex than even the recent past (see Edwards, 2003), largely as a result of the decline of 'integrating institutions' or the 'national system' of employment regulation, thereby creating new contingencies at the firm and sector levels (Roche, 2000:278). In an international comparative context, this process has been described as 'converging divergencies' – different nations becoming more alike because of greater diversity *within* each country (Katz and Darbishire, 2000). Empirically, these accounts provide a more accurate picture of contemporary employee relations, but how do we conceptualise the changes taking place?

A useful approach, which we borrow from organisational theory (see Burrell, 1992; and Filipcova and Filipec, 1986), is based on the concept of 'spiral time'. The spiral can incorporate elements of both linear and cyclical time: movement along the spiral involves travelling away from the original point of departure but not in a simple linear fashion. The trajectory also contains cyclical elements or periods of reversal. By adopting the notion of a spiral, we may equip ourselves with a more adequate metaphor with which to understand the way employee relations develop over time – a development which simultaneously displays elements of change and continuity, progression and reversal. Through the concept of spiral time we avoid the trap of thinking too narrowly or having to choose between change *or* continuity as portraying the nature of employee relations in the recent past, present or future. It is the relative strength of change and continuity, rather than the presence of one and the absence of the other, which is likely to characterise a particular period. The concept of spiral time also allows short- and long-term patterns to be located within the same model – the short-term representing a single twist of a longer-term spiral. Thus, as we move along the spiral it is evident that historical continuities may help to define *but they do not determine* contemporary developments. Capitalist economies experience long waves of growth and stagnation/decline, but each wave is substantially different from the last.

The notion of spiral time, as a metaphor, helps us to understand how different views of history can be combined. But metaphors do no more than heighten our intuitive grasp of a particular phenomenon by comparing two 'objects' (in this case employee relations and a spiral) which are not normally associated with one another (for a discussion of the role and utility of metaphors in industrial relations, see Dunn, 1990; and Keenoy, 1991). The more important task is to combine effectively synchronic and diachronic analysis – describing a subject as it exists at one point in time, whilst at the same time incorporating the historical evolution of the subject. Theoretically, therefore, we adopt an inter-disciplinary approach, drawing on a range of (social science) disciplines such as sociology, economics, psychology, politics and history. Empirically, we seek to balance different sources of data (the general and specific, the survey and the case study). By doing this, we are better placed to offer a critical assessment of change and continuity in employee relations. In particular, we can evaluate whether recent developments add up to a 'transformation' of employee relations, or alternatively whether we are still in the midst of a period of transformational change and experimentation that will shape the future of those relations for years or even decades to come. The latter is certainly a view shared by many observers, and one with which we concur.

The late twentieth and early twenty-first century can be seen as a period of what Schumpeter (1950) called 'creative destruction', an 'epochal shift' characterised by new configurations of markets and social institutions, technological innovations (most notably in biotechnology, microprocessors and telecommunications) and organisational innovations (e.g. inter-firm relationships and networks), managerial initiatives in relation to work organisation and human resource management, new state policies in both the public and private sectors, and a liberalisation of the international economy (see, *inter alia*, Hall and Soskice, 2001:54; Hollingsworth and Boyer, 1997:5; and Kelly, 1998:86). These developments have had a profound effect on the 'social system of production', which includes the 'industrial relations system' but extends much further to incorporate:

- the system of training workers and managers
- the internal structure of corporate firms and their social responsibilities
- the structured relationships among firms in the same industry on the one hand and, on the other, firms' relationships with their suppliers and customers
- the financial markets of a society
- the conceptions of fairness and justice held by capital and labour
- the structure of the state and its policies
- and a society's idiosyncratic customs and traditions as well as norms, moral principles, rules, laws, and recipes for action (Hollingsworth and Boyer, 1997:2; see also Hall and Soskice, 2001:7; and Whitley, 1999).

This approach reflects a concern with society as well as economy, with equity as well as efficiency. As Beynon and his colleagues point out, recent changes to work and employment not only strike at the heart of the employment relationship – 'it seems we have moved to an era characterised by an unfair day's work for an unfair day's pay' (2002:261) – but also represent 'a deep and profound effect upon the sensibilities of our society' (2002:20). A fundamental maxim of industrial sociology was always that to understand what goes on inside the workplace it is necessary also to look outside, to the family, community and other facets of society (see, for example, Lockwood, 1966). The contemporary significance of this point is well made by Peter Ackers (2002:7) who demonstrates how the 'moral crisis' emanating from the economic system now pervades the whole of society and 'recoils back onto the employment relationship'.

Although many of the recent developments in employee relations might not deserve the label 'revolutionary', in many instances they do constitute 'discontinuous change' rather than 'evolutionary change'. The latter, which usually involves incremental changes, is less likely to result in a 'transformation' of employee relations, although revolutionary changes can often be traced to small decisions in the past which 'nudge' a system in one direction rather than another (Erickson and Kuruvilla, 1998:9). For example, most observers acknowledge the wider political significance of national miners' strikes in the early 1970s and in particular the mid 1980s. Indeed, the 1984–85 strike is widely regarded as a defining moment for Thatcherism (see, for example, Adeney and Lloyd, 1986). Yet the roots of this dispute could arguably be traced way back to the 1960s and the National Powerloading Agreement (1966), which gradually shifted the focus of industrial relations and strike activity from the individual pit to the national arena (see Chapter 10). Like most evolutionary accounts, however, such linear interpretations are not wholly convincing as they tend to collapse many years of human interaction into a few key events or prioritise particular structural forces that 'determine' subsequent outcomes. Consider an analogy with Darwinism whereby a lizard gradually evolves into a bird. At what point can a lizard be classified as a bird (When it has feathers? When it can fly?) and did the lizard consciously plan to become a bird? Although we might question whether, or to what extent, actors in employee relations behave strategically, especially management (see Chapter 4), they are certainly conscious of what they are doing (i.e. they behave intentionally) (see Erickson and Kuruvilla, 1998:9–10). Evolutionary accounts focus our attention on underlying structures and the processes of change, but all too often they pay insufficient attention to human agency.

An alternative (biological) theory to smooth evolution is 'punctuated equilibrium'. According to this account, the industrial relations system 'undergoes periods of apparent stability with only gradual and non-fundamental change punctuated by periods of rapid change when the network of mutually reinforcing basic assumptions and principles underlying that system comes under question' (Erickson and Kuruvilla, 1998:10). In other words, it is not just the industrial relations system that is subject to change and experimentation but the entire social system of production. This account is more consistent with developments in the UK over the past 50 years. In particular, the current period would appear to meet all three criteria that distinguish periods of transformational change:

1. a reconsideration (and ultimately change) of the 'deep structure' of industrial relations
2. change is more rapid by comparison with change during periods of relative stability
3. there is great experimentation, and an increase in speciation and diversity, as various new forms of organisation, workplace practices and public polices are tried out before dominant forms take root (ibid:11–12).

The data we present in the chapters that follow testify to the extent and greater urgency of recent employee relations changes in the UK. This is particularly evident in relation to the 'traditional system' of collective bargaining (see Chapter 7), new initiatives in employee involvement and participation (see Chapter 8), and 'initiative overload' in the public sector (Chapter 6), although whether this has led to more professional or effective human resource management or a sea-change in workers' attitudes is still an open question (see Chapters 4 and 5). One of the main conclusions from WERS98, for example, which is certainly consistent with the third criterion of (punctuated equilibrium) transformation, is that there is still no coherent system of HRM or industrial relations to replace the former reliance on collective bargaining (see Cully et al., 1999:246; and Millward et al., 2000).

The litmus test for change and transformation, of course, is ultimately the socio-economic outcomes that are most directly attributed to, or at least associated with, employee relations. Has employment increased and/or unemployment decreased? Is inflation stable and growth positive? Is labour productivity higher? Are profit margins greater? Is innovation more rapid? Is the organisation more competitive? Have earnings and living standards improved? Have accidents been reduced and occupational health improved? Has discrimination been addressed and income (re)distributed on a more equitable basis? Has job and life satisfaction improved? We must also acknowledge that even if economic outcomes remain the same, the social processes that create such outcomes may have undergone significant changes that carry important consequences for employee relations (e.g. productivity and earnings remain the same but management have reasserted their prerogatives and employees are less involved in decisions affecting their day-to-day working lives, which in turn affects their job satisfaction and sense of commitment to the organisation). This suggests that we need to consider both 'material outcomes' (e.g. profits, wages, un/employment) and 'cultural outcomes' (e.g. attitudes and meanings).

Figure 1.1 brings these elements together in a simple analytical framework. Unfortunately, we know surprisingly little about the interests of some actors, most notably workers (Kelly, 1998). In part, this reflects the managerialist agenda that has dominated much of the research in this field over the past 20 years. In addition, however, interests and intentions are often assumed rather than investigated. Economists, for example, typically assume that workers will behave solely on the basis of rational self-interest, seeking to *maximise their individual utility*. The latter is simply a positive function of the stock of goods or income enjoyed by the individual. Our own approach is more in tune with behavioural models, which typically assume that individuals seek to *satisfy their aspirations*. The latter will be influenced by personal perceptions as well as social norms, customs and traditions. In behavioural models, 'happiness', which is a broader concept than 'utility', is

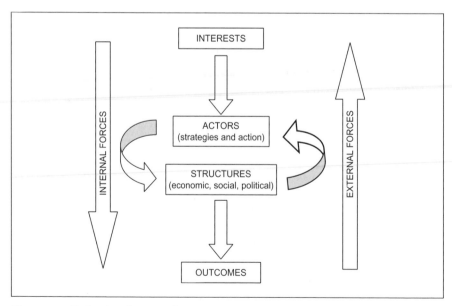

Figure 1.1 Evaluating change and continuity in employee relations

more often the focus of attention (see Kaufman, 1989 and 1999). Psychological research has demonstrated that happiness has a large 'relational' (or relative) component, such that even in the face of rising income the individual might not feel any happier if others are even richer. Habituation also plays a part – people compare what they have today with what they had yesterday and feel worse off unless they keep up with the current 'standard of living' – such that interests are in large part socially (and not just individually) constructed. Recent research does indeed suggest that despite economic growth and rising income, workers in the UK do not feel any happier (Blanchflower and Oswald, 2004; Layard, 2003; and Oswald, 1997). Indeed, only 49 per cent of the workforce look forward to going to work on an average day (Diamond and Freeman, 2001).

In addition to a desire to be 'happy', workers also have a strong interest in justice at the workplace. In fact, 'preferential treatment' by management is the biggest complaint at work, closely followed by 'unfair wages' (Diamond and Freeman, 2001). As a result, workers (collective) interests are often defined in terms of perceived *in*justice (see Kelly, 1998). For most workers, interests must be pursued on a collective basis if they are to redress the imbalance of power they face *vis-à-vis* their employer (see Chapter 2). This is no easy task, and one that is becoming more difficult with the decline of trade union organisation (see Chapter 5). Even those in positions of power, however, are not free to pursue their interests as they please. Management strategy (Chapter 4), or indeed any actor's choice of strategy, must be set in the context of the means needed to secure it (Crouch, 1982b:139).

Strategies and actions interact with, and on occasion reconfigure, the extant structural context (e.g. product, capital and labour markets, social and political institutions, statutory legislation and the like). These 'deep structures' embrace both markets and institutions, although markets are themselves institutions to the extent that while they may support relationships of a particular type (e.g. impersonal and contractual economic exchange) they are nonetheless sustained by institutional regulations (Wilks, 1996:538; see also Hall and Soskice, 2001:9). Institutions can be understood as a set of rules, or 'rules of the game', whether formal or informal, that actors generally follow (whether for normative, cognitive or material reasons) (North, 1990:3). Like all such rules, 'they constrain in order to enable' (Marsden, 1999:5), most notably by providing a mechanism 'to reduce uncertainty by establishing a stable structure for human interaction' (North, 1990:6). Deep structures are difficult, but not impossible, to change, as the UK's recent experience serves to illustrate. Indeed, Ackers and Wilkinson (2003a:14) contend that, '[t]he end of the social democratic consensus in 1979 has seen a restructuring of the *architecture* of UK workplace relations which is now irreversible' (emphasis added). While we concur on the first point (the profound impact of Thatcherism) we caution against the second (the irreversibility of change). This runs counter to the *dynamics* of employee relations and the scope for change and experimentation that currently pervades the UK.

One reason why change, and reversal, is possible is our political system – first-past-the-post voting, parliamentary sovereignty, and internally hierarchical political parties – which has led to very powerful, single-party governments. As a result, UK governments have enjoyed a degree of formal power unmatched anywhere in advanced industrial societies (Hennessy, 1994). This led to the implementation of more radical economic and social policies in the UK than elsewhere during the last period of Conservative government (1979–97). As a political project, Thatcherism was designed to transform the deep structures of our society and to produce very different socio-economic outcomes (see Wood, 2001:255–6), but these are not irreversible. To be sure, many of the policies that defined Thatcherism have since been maintained by New Labour, but there is also a significant new programme of legal reform and a discernibly different approach to economic policy and employee relations (see Chapter 6). These policies have already 'nudged' the UK in a different direction and while maybe not deserving of the label 'revolutionary' they certainly represent a 'discontinuity' when set against the project of Thatcherism.

Outcomes are the result of interaction between the principal parties to employee relations and may or may not reflect their original interests or intentions. The desire to effect change and create new or 'better' outcomes might be internally motivated (e.g. the desire to increase profits or improve earnings) or externally driven (e.g. competition from rival firms or price rises that erode real income). Some of the most notable outcomes in recent years include: the decline of trade union membership (Chapter 5) and collective bargaining (Chapter 7); the virtual disappearance of strikes, although not the eradication of industrial conflict (Chapter 10); and the increasing importance attached to employee involvement and participation (Chapter 8). Equally significant are outcomes that remain broadly the same, albeit in a very different context (Chapter 3), most notably the failure of management to embrace more sophisticated HRM or industrial relations policies (Chapter 4), the persistence of poor employee relations in most non-union firms (Chapter 9), and the failure of successive governments to transform the competitive performance of the UK economy despite, and in many respects precisely because of, the reform of employee relations (Chapter 6).

Utilising the framework set out in Figure 1.1, we demonstrate the interplay between change and continuity in employee relations in the remainder of the text. Our aim is to analyse the dynamic nature of employee relations and to establish that we are currently in a phase of development that has 'punctuated' the previous 'equilibrium'. To do this, we start by elucidating the *core* aspects of employee relations in the following chapter, thereby providing readers with a theoretical framework with which to understand the subject, and an empirical focus that informs the selection of data that we present in subsequent chapters. We advance the argument for a distinct approach to understanding the employment relationship and employee relations which recognises the need to return to basic questions such as: What is the *raison d'être* of firms in capitalist economies? What are management's overall objectives in the organisation? What are their specific objectives in managing labour? What responses are available to employees and their representatives? What interests do workers seek to advance? How does the state seek to influence employee relations, in both the public and private sectors, and to what effect? What power resources are available to the different actors? How is power exercised and to what effect?

Recognising that there is no *one* theory of industrial or employee relations, the main purpose of Chapter 2 is to establish a conceptual understanding of the subject by developing an integrated theory of the employment relationship. Any account of social life depends upon not only *what* one looks at but also *how* one looks. The 'answers', therefore, depend on the questions asked and the methods by which one 'solves' the questions. Put differently, the theoretical approach one adopts will determine, in large part, the questions to be asked, the way in which the solution is derived, and ultimately the construction of an answer. The central problematic of employee relations is the 'labour question' – the dual problems of social welfare (providing an adequate standard of living for all) on the one hand, and social order (the regulation of industrial conflict) on the other (Hyman, 1989a:3). Our concern, in other words, is not simply the efficiency of organisations, the control of labour and the resolution of conflict, but also the interests of workers, the conditions of their labour, and the remuneration of their effort.

The third chapter of Part 1 identifies the changing contexts in which employee relations are taking place. Of course, the nature and outcomes of employee relations cannot simply be 'read off' from the socio-economic context of a particular time and place, but equally cannot be understood other than in relation to those contexts (see Marchington and Parker, 1990:85). This requires a wide-ranging (though necessarily summary) review of developments in product and labour markets, including the changing fortunes of different sectors; the overall intensification of competition, including that stemming from globalisation; the changing character of the public sector; and changes in labour force composition, including the growth in female and part-time employment and the growing heterogeneity of work patterns. In reviewing contextual developments, however, account must be taken not only of the changes in the external and macro environment but also the significance of changes within the workplace itself, including changes in technology and the impact of developments in work process control (e.g. just-in-time production, total quality management, and customer care programmes) and in work organisation (e.g. the spread of team-working). Drawing together the implications of changes in the internal and external contexts, we consider the extent to which, in contrast to many European economies, a low-cost, low-productivity approach to securing competitive advantage continues to characterise the overall direction of change in the UK, and the implications this has for the character and conduct of employee relations.

Part 2 (Chapters 4–6) examines the principal actors in employee relations – management, employees and trade unions, and the state. The three chapters draw on three very different cases – British Airways, union organising in and around London, and the port of Belfast – in order to focus on the aims, objectives, strategies and actions of the different parties, especially their ability to exercise control over the other parties to achieve their desired goals. The actual exercise of influence and control is a major underlying theme of the four chapters in Part 3 (Chapters 7–10) on 'Interaction and Outcomes in Employee Relations'. The cases of Corus, Tesco and Marks & Spencer (together with one of its suppliers) are used to illustrate and assess three different approaches to employee relations, based on a restructuring of bargaining arrangements, the use of non-bargaining forms of involvement (based around consultation and 'partnership') and the operation of employee relations in the absence of trade union recognition. The final chapter in Part 3 (Chapter 10) examines the theme of industrial conflict, one of the most controversial 'outcomes' of employee relations. The case of the 2002–3 firefighters' strike is used to illustrate the issue and to highlight important themes such as the significance of industrial conflict in the public sector and the role that the media and public opinion can play in conflict situations.

Finally, in Part 4 (Chapter 11), we consider the future of employee relations in the UK, highlighting the increasing importance of European integration and noting the problems and potential of developing more inclusive forms of joint union–management relations. The final chapter also brings together some of the main arguments from earlier chapters and examines the case for a reconstitution of employee relations founded upon: greater equity, trust and reciprocity; enhanced employment standards, including a decent living wage for all and the right to work in a safe and healthy environment; greater employment security; greater access to work patterns that mesh better with employees' non-work commitments (most notably family life and community-based activities); a more robust system of industrial democracy; individual and collective employment rights enshrined in law; and a commitment to fostering a more inclusive and extensive system of vocational education, training and skills development.

2

The theory of
employee relations

Historical roots

The empirical roots of employee relations enquiry lie in the coincidence at the end of the nineteenth century of the two faces of the 'labour question': the issues of social welfare and social control (Hyman, 1989a:3). The theoretical roots of the subject can be traced principally to the clash between Marxian political economy and the emergent neo-classical economics at around the same time (Marsden, 1982:236–8). In terms of empirical enquiry, the problematic nature of the 'labour question' was epitomised at this time by two significant disputes: the Match Girls' strike of 1888 and the Great London Dock Strike of 1889. At that time, being a match girl 'rated somewhere practically below prostitution in the social scale' (McCarthy, 1988:57–8), their conditions of work were dangerous and unpleasant, their pay meagre. The match girls' victory in the 1888 dispute, however, secured with public opinion on their side, had a significance beyond the strike itself. It 'turned a new leaf in Trade Union annals ... It was a new experience for the weak to succeed ... [and] ... The lesson was not lost on other workers' (Sidney and Beatrice Webb, quoted by Stafford, 1961:79). The following year, the social convulsion sparked by the match girls at Bryant & May's reached the River Thames and the men who worked on the docks and wharves. The dockers' strike became the 'symbol of new unionism' that emerged at the end of the nineteenth century (Clegg *et al.*, 1964:55), not only a great victory for the dockers but a dispute that 'changed the whole face of the Trade Union world' (Webb and Webb, 1920:401). For radicals such as Henry Champion, one of the leaders of the strike, the dispute was won 'despite our socialism' (quoted by McCarthy, 1988:50), but for others such as Frederick Engels, lifelong companion of Karl Marx, the strike was,

> the movement of the greatest promise we have had for years ... If these poor downtrodden men, the dregs of the proletariat, these odds and ends of all trades, fighting every morning at the dock gates for an engagement, if *they* can combine, and terrify by

their resolution the mighty Dock Companies, truly then we need not despair of any section of the working class ... If the dockers get organised, all other sections will follow ... It is a glorious movement. (Marx and Engels, 1975:399, original emphasis)

The dockers, like the match girls, had attracted widespread public sympathy, and substantial financial donations, due partly to their own efforts during the strike itself but also to the work of social reformers such as Beatrice Potter (later Webb) and Charles Booth whose *Life and Labour of the People in London* demonstrated to the public and ruling classes alike not only the problems of poverty and degradation among casual workers such as the dockers, but also the wider threat to the stability of society from an 'underclass' deprived of a basic standard of life. The question of social welfare, it appeared, was inseparable from that of social control. Or more precisely, the latter appeared to be largely dependent on the former.

The theoretical origins of the subject can be traced to the 'Achilles Heel' of the emergent neo-classical economics, namely the analysis of labour and labour markets in general and the theory of wage determination in particular. The break between classical economic thought or political economy and neo-classical economics was marked by very different questions being asked about what constituted the subject matter of economics. Classical political economy was concerned, first and foremost, with the conditions that make possible the creation of an economic surplus (or as Adam Smith put it with *The Wealth of Nations*), and in particular how society had been transformed from a situation of subsistence to one of accumulation. Neo-classical economics, in contrast, is concerned with the allocation of scarce resources between competing ends, with the questions of supply and demand, pricing and allocation. As a result, the focus of economics shifted from the production of wealth to its consumption, from the division of labour and social relations between classes to the market mechanism and individual decision-making.

On the question of wages, classical economists such as David Ricardo (1817) had developed 'subsistence' theories to explain the remuneration of human labour. Wages would tend to remain at a level which sustained and reproduced human labour but did not provide that labour with any degree of affluence. Thus, although Ricardo allowed for the influence of 'custom and habit', such that the subsistence wage might increase to reflect what is deemed 'customary' or 'necessary' at any given time (the 'standard of living'), the theory nonetheless presented a rather bleak future for the financial well-being of the working class. Similarly, Marx (1976) also proposed a subsistence theory of wages, but with the added twist of the analysis being grounded explicitly in a theory of capitalism, wherein the wage labourer was subject to exploitation by the employer. Furthermore, even though the subsistence wage might increase over time, Marx put forward the notion of 'absolute impoverishment' for the working class, reflecting the progressive 'de-skilling' and 'alienation' of labour. For Marx, workers under capitalism would gradually, but inexorably, lose control over the process of production as greater division of labour created not only unskilled but highly fragmented work, with workers becoming, as a result, more and more estranged from the product of their labour. At the risk of over-simplification, the working class would thus cease to be a passive class *in itself* and become mobilised into a class *for itself*, ultimately seeking to overthrow capitalism and replace it with socialism.

But what has all this got to do with employee relations? Simply put, neo-classical economics sought to take the 'political' out of political economy by developing a theory of wage determination and income distribution based not on the social relations between classes but on the concepts of marginal productivity and individual choice. According to this new economics, wages were not determined by a (political) power struggle between classes but by the marginal productivity of the worker. To explain the theory, imagine a situation where capital (buildings, machinery and so on) is in fixed supply and the firm increases the number of workers employed. As more and more workers are engaged, there will be less capital per worker, and consequently the output of each additional worker will be less than that of the original workforce. In other words, the productivity of each successive employee to be hired (output per worker) will be lower. What matters is not whether total output is increasing but what the *marginal* increase to output is, because, according to neo-classical economics, it is the productivity of the final worker to be hired which determines the wage. To be sure, the last worker to be engaged adds less output than that created by the original workforce, but more than any future or potential workers because of declining marginal productivity. So, if any of the original workforce demanded a higher wage the employer could sack them and engage the marginal worker in their stead. Each and every worker is therefore worth to the employer only what the last (marginal) worker engaged can produce, and so the employer will continue to employ additional workers only up to the point where their cost (wage) is equal to the value of their marginal product. As each and every worker receives a wage equivalent to the amount of wealth he or she creates, there can be no exploitation. In short, the politics has been taken out of political economy, and the socialist movement theoretically defused.

Unfortunately for the new economists, as Alfred Marshall pointed out in his *Principles of Economics*, first published in 1890, marginal productivity is an incomplete theory of wages. In fact, it is not a theory of wages at all. Rather it is a theory of labour demand. It tells us how many workers an employer will hire at a given wage in order to maximise profits (suggesting that the higher the wage, the fewer the number of workers that will be employed, and vice versa). But what determines the actual wage that prevails? To complete the picture, the theory of wage determination requires an explanation of the supply side. Again, the theory is based on individual decision-making, this time the choices made by individual workers between income and leisure. Higher wages, up to a point, will induce workers to work longer hours (or sacrifice more hours of leisure), or alternatively will induce more people of working age to offer themselves for employment. The result is an upward sloping labour supply curve which intersects the downward sloping labour demand curve at what neo-classical economists call the 'market clearing wage' (that is, the wage at which there are neither shortages nor surpluses in the labour market, the wage at which every individual who wants to work can in fact find a job). The problem of wage determination has thus been solved without even a whiff of exploitation or a whisper of power. Or has it?

Even neo-classical economists, for all their heroic assumptions about the labour market, cannot ignore the presence of monopoly, combination and collective action on the part of both employers and employees. If the firm is a monopsonist (single buyer) in the labour market or if business organisations combine to form an employers' association, then neo-classical theory predicts that the firm will pay a lower wage than would prevail in a competitive market. On the other hand, if a trade union is a monopoly (single seller) in the labour market then it will seek a wage above the market clearing rate by restricting the supply of labour. Thus, in a situation of bilateral monopoly there will be no unique 'solution' to the problem of wage determination but rather a *range of indeterminacy* between what the union demands and what the employer is prepared to pay (for a formal exposition see Sapsford, 1981:102–4). In Marshall's words, 'if the employers in any trade act together and so do the employed, the solution to the problem of wages becomes indeterminate ... there is nothing but bargaining to decide the exact shares in which this [surplus] should go to employers and employed' (1930:627–8). For some neo-classical economists, such as Edgeworth (1881:20), the fact that 'contract without competition is indeterminate' meant that such matters were beyond the scope of economics. Not only had the 'politics' been removed from 'political economy' but the analysis of production, labour relations and social relations more widely were now matters to be left to other disciplines or specialist areas of social science research.

One such specialism was industrial relations, arguably founded by Beatrice and Sidney Webb. The Webbs have been credited with being the first to coin the phrase 'collective bargaining' (see Lyddon, 2003:97), for many years the central subject matter of industrial relations. The term itself, however, was clearly derived from Marshall, with whom they agreed 'absolutely in economics' (Marsden, 1982:237). Theoretically, therefore, the analysis and study of industrial relations largely grew out of a concern to explain the supply and sale of labour: 'The concern with collective bargaining did not materialize out of thin air, it was given by economics' (Marsden, 1982:238; see also Clegg, 1979:447). But henceforth it was to be an area of study largely *separate* from economics. As Hugh Clegg (1979:34) put it, there is 'not much to be gained by looking to economics for a theory of industrial relations if economists have to go outside economics to find an explanation for wage determination'. This separation not only narrowed the field of economics, it effectively forestalled the development of any political economy of industrial relations. Unfortunately, in this separation of industrial relations from economics, the work of the earlier classical economists and that of Marx was also ignored, arguably to the detriment of both economics and industrial relations (see Brown and Nolan, 1988; Gall, 2003a; and Kelly, 1998). A consequence of this was that one of the first explicit 'theories' of industrial relations, developed by the American labour economist John Dunlop (1958), centred on a (largely self-contained) 'system' of industrial relations which was *not* part of a society's economic system but a distinctive sub-system of its own, only partially overlapping the economic and political decision-making systems with which it interacts. The three sub-systems themselves were seen to be contained within an overall 'social system'.

The industrial relations system

For Dunlop, heavily influenced by the functionalism of Talcot Parsons (1952) and the core Parsonian question of how the elements of society interacted to produce social continuity, the industrial relations system is seen to be 'comprised of certain actors, certain contexts, an ideology which binds the industrial relations system together and a body of rules created to govern the actors at the workplace' (Dunlop, 1958:7). The actors include a hierarchy of management and their representatives, a hierarchy of non-management employees (workers) and their representatives, and specialised third party agencies such as governmental bodies. The environmental contexts which influence the decisions and actions of the actors include the technological characteristics of the workplace and the nature of the work community, market or budgetary constraints, and the locus and distribution of power in the larger society. Interaction between the parties within different environmental contexts is governed, in large part, by an ideology or common set of beliefs that 'defines the role and place of each actor and that defines the ideas which each actor holds towards the place and function of others in the system' (ibid:16). But the definition of industrial relations as 'the complex of interrelations among managers, workers and agencies of government' (ibid:v), as Marsden (1982:239) notes, was quickly and quietly switched to the formation and maintenance of the *rules* of the system: 'The central task of a theory of industrial relations is to explain why particular rules are established in particular industrial relations systems and how and why they change in response to changes affecting this system' (Dunlop, 1958:ix). Moreover, it was the *joint* determination of rules that commanded Dunlop's attention – his text contains virtually no reference to non-union employers or the philosophy and practice of management (see Kaufman, 2003:214–15).

At one level, systems theory might be viewed as a useful means of classifying variables relevant to industrial relations, but it is hardly an explanatory approach in its own right. If anything, it is 'more a set of questions than a theoretical statement' (Strauss and Feuille, 1978:267). Indeed, both theoretical and substantive criticisms of Dunlop's model abound (for a review, see Poole, 1981). As Poole (1988:13) in a later discussion argues, the relationship between variables in the framework are assumed to be interlocking and interactive, which runs counter to genuine explanatory analysis: it is very difficult to disentangle central from peripheral variables, to identify causal sequences, to isolate independent variables, and to attach explanatory weights to such variables. At best, systems analysis is a *description* of industrial relations, not a theory, an abstraction from the 'known facts' arranged into a coherent model or system (Marsden, 1982:239). More importantly, the very notion of a 'system' of industrial relations implies a functional integration of component institutions (Hyman, 1992:7), especially when a common ideology amongst the actors is assumed. When combined with a focus on rules, the implication is that 'what industrial relations is all about is the maintenance of stability and regularity in industry' (Hyman, 1975:11).

Subsequent expositions of systems theory (e.g. Craig, 1986) have considerably elaborated Dunlop's original schema and sought to introduce a far more extensive range of variables and a greater awareness of feedback relationships between variables over time. For example, management, unions and the state might be conceptualised as 'primary' or 'direct' actors while other actors not originally considered by Dunlop, such as consumers or other 'end users' of various goods and services, can be incorporated into the model as 'secondary' or 'indirect' actors. These end users might be involved in the industrial relations system as 'co-producers' or 'co-designers' (e.g. disabled groups who work with transport companies to facilitate access to vehicles, both in terms of vehicle design and route networks) or they may act as 'co-supervisors' of the employee's work (e.g. customer complaints or satisfaction surveys that are used increasingly in the service sector) (see Bellemare, 2000:390–8; and Heery, 1993). Thus, end users might influence day-to-day work routines, personnel policies such as supervision and discipline, and even collective bargaining strategies (e.g. legal action by customers in the event of a strike) (Bellemare, 2000:398). Expanding Dunlop's model in this way, however, calls into question his idea of industrial relations as a largely separate (sub)system (ibid:400). At the theoretical level, therefore, the model cannot accommodate a more diverse range of actors, which is tantamount to saying that the model cannot accommodate change or the emergence of new actors in industrial relations. As a result, the emphasis on order and stability remains.

The influence of Dunlop's systems analysis and the focus on stability and order in the study of industrial and employee relations is clearly evident in the work of prominent British academics in the field, most notably Allan Flanders, Hugh Clegg and (the early work of) Alan Fox, often referred to collectively as the 'Oxford School':

> Economics deals with a system of markets, politics with a system of government ... a system of industrial relations is a system of rules. These rules appear in different guises: in

legislation and in statutory orders; in trade union regulations; in collective agreements and in arbitration awards; in social conventions; in management decisions; and in accepted 'custom and practice'. This list is by no means exhaustive, but 'rules' is the only generic description that can be given to these various instruments of regulation. In other words, the subject deals with certain regulated or institutionalised relationships in industry. (Flanders, 1965:9–10)

Similarly, Clegg (1979:1) argues that industrial relations 'is the study of the rules governing employment, together with the ways in which the rules are made and changed, interpreted and administered'. The rules themselves 'cannot be under-stood apart from the organizations that take part in the process', namely trade unions, employers' associations and government/public bodies, and 'each of these organizations has its own sources of authority' (ibid:1). As a result, rules can be made jointly (through collective bargaining or custom and practice) or unilaterally (through managerial prerogative, trade union regulation or statutory imposition). But to define industrial relations as 'a study of the institutions of job regulation' (Flanders, 1965:10) is to conceive the subject in terms of relationships between agencies rather than between people, to ignore the real, active men and women whose activities *are* industrial and employee relations (Hyman, 1975:13; and Nichols, 1980:12). And there remains the over-riding concern with the 'problem of order', diverting attention away from the structures of power within the workplace and beyond. In sum, such a focus has relegated the problem of social welfare to the periphery, 'while the preoccupation with job regulation brought the problem of control to the centre of the agenda' (Hyman, 1989a:8).

Unsurprisingly, industrial relations became problem-focused, issue-driven, and policy-orientated (see Strauss and Feuille, 1978). In the UK, this was reinforced by governments in the 1960s identifying industrial relations as a 'problem', contributing to low productivity and increasing strike activity. This placed an emphasis on the practical need to study industrial relations institutions in order to recommend policy reform. The role of industrial relations academics in this was epitomised by many of the contributions to the Royal Commission on Trade Unions and Employers' Associations (Donovan, 1968), and in particular in most of the research papers written to inform that Commission.

Research on the subject was thus predominantly empirical, characterised by the aphorism attributed to the Oxford School of 'a pound of facts and an ounce of theory' (Cappelli, 1985:91). To study industrial relations was to be a detective, for as Sir Arthur Conan Doyle wrote in *The Memoirs of Sherlock Holmes*, 'it is a capital mistake to theorize before one has data'. Hugh Clegg made this orientation quite clear in his book on *The Changing System of Industrial Relations in Great Britain*. Having described 'what appear to be the main elements of, and developments in, British industrial relations', it is 'only after that have explanations been offered – where they were available, and as they seemed to fit in' (1979:446). The question of theory was in fact left until the final chapter of his book, with the reader presented with the option in the introduction of reading the final chapter either first or last – for Clegg it made no difference.

Methodologically, the approach of the Oxford School, and indeed industrial relations research dating from the Webbs (Brown and Wright, 1994:155–8), can be characterised as essentially one of induction, where 'theories or rules are suggested by behaviour in specific examples and are used to make inferences about the general case' (Cappelli, 1985:91; see also Whitfield and Strauss, 1998 and 2000). The classic example of this approach was Allan Flanders's (1964) investigation of *The Fawley Productivity Agreements*, a single case study which suggested that the structure of collective bargaining could have a powerful influence on the conduct of industrial relations at the plant level, and on the behaviour of management and trade unions. This analysis, and the prescription that followed, was then extended to much of British industry in the form of 'productivity bargaining'. But as Cappelli warns, the inferences generated by induction do not follow logically or necessarily from the phenomena to be explained. They are 'at best probable explanations that must be supported by empirical arguments in order to be judged reasonable' (1985:91). Empiricism is therefore perpetuated, but more importantly there is a tendency for any general laws to come from the same level of analysis that is employed, which in turn is largely determined by the questions being asked. Put differently, if the focus is 'the institutions of job regulation', an inductive theory will place a heavy emphasis on institutional detail, frequently to the detriment of other levels of analysis or explanatory variables, consequently leading to an emphasis on order rather than disorder in employee relations.

An important illustration of the shortcomings of this approach was the work of the Donovan Commission (Donovan, 1968) which, as already noted, was heavily influenced by the Oxford School. Prior to the Royal Commission it was widely believed that Britain had only a single system of industrial relations, based on a formal system of collective bargaining between trade unions and employers' associations, conducted largely at the national level (see, for example, Flanders and Clegg, 1954). Reality proved to be somewhat different, but rather than abandon the idea of an industrial relations system the Royal Commission's approach was to describe an additional one, an informal system of negotiations involving workers, shop stewards and management at the workplace level. The prognosis was that the informal system was in conflict with the formal system, or more precisely the former had undermined the stability of the latter. But to say that the formal and informal systems were in conflict was 'equivalent to saying that systems theory cannot explain reality, fact is in conflict with reality' (Marsden, 1982:242). In order to maintain the integrity of the system, Lord Donovan's prescription was inevitably to bring about a closer integration of component institutions in order to curtail 'disorder'. More elaborate, formalised, systematic procedures at the local level were deemed necessary, as were stronger industrial relations management and a closer integration of shop stewards into (official) trade union structures. These recommendations not only reflected the failure of systems theory to adequately explain the problems of British industrial relations, but also highlighted the hold which the pluralist perspective, as propounded by the members of the Oxford School, had gained.

Pluralism and industrial relations orthodoxy

Pluralism is far from being a homogeneous body of analysis and prescription (see Hyman, 1978 for a discussion), but the central tenets of the dominant influence in British industrial relations enquiry – what might be termed 'institutional pluralism' – can be briefly stated. Organisations are viewed as 'a miniature democratic state composed of sectional groups with divergent interests over which the government tries to maintain some kind of dynamic equilibrium' (Fox, 1966:2). Today, these ideas find expression through the discourse of 'stake-holding', with the organisation and its managers presumed to be accountable to the workforce, customers, suppliers, environmental groups, and the general public, rather than just the owners or shareholders. A recent large-scale survey of members of the Institute of Management certainly indicates that many managers subscribe to this view: 'modern managers do now perceive their organisations in terms of a variety of stakeholders having a legitimate stake in the goals and objectives of their organisations' (Poole *et al.*, 2001:29). What, then, are the implications of this approach?

Recognising the reality of separate interests within industry and society, and the legitimacy of their organised expression, pluralists argue that a stable 'negotiated order' will develop from the organisation of competing interests. In other words, conflict is accepted as both inevitable and legitimate within any organisation, but the dominant preoccupation of pluralists is with establishing structures and procedures within which those legitimate conflicts of interest can be contained and prevented from damaging the interests of all. As Brown (1988:49) notes, this 'institutionalisation of conflict' requires a recognition of both the existence and legitimacy of conflicting interests; the effective representation of those interests; some flexibility of objectives and central direction of policy; a climate where sectional interests can be realised; a semblance of power balance between the parties; and, as a second line of institutional defence, a system of mediation and arbitration. In short, not only must management be prepared to *recognise* and *accept* a conflict of interests with their workforce, but be prepared to *negotiate* with independent trade unions in a climate of 'give-and-take'.

Pluralism is usually contrasted with unitarism, where the organisation is viewed as a team 'unified by a common purpose' (Fox, 1966:2), namely the success of the organisation. With a single source of authority (management) and all participants sharing the same goal, harmony and co-operation are the predicted outcomes. For

76656

unitarists, conflict is not inevitable but pathological, the outcome of misunder-standing or mischief. Either management has failed to communicate its goals effectively, causing temporary friction until the message 'gets home', or there must be trouble-makers deliberately stirring up problems where none would otherwise exist. Writing in the mid-1960s, Fox held that the unitary approach 'has long since been abandoned by most social scientists as incongruent with reality and useless for the purpose of analysis' (1966:4), but the view is still widely held by many British managers (Poole *et al.*, 1981:82–3; and Poole and Mansfield, 1992 and 1993) and underpins many of the recent developments encapsulated in the term 'human resource management' (see Blyton and Turnbull, 1992; Legge, 1995; Redman and Wilkinson, 2001; and Storey, 2001). Consequently, the unitary view of organisations and employment relationships 'is not simply to be dismissed. It is important to try to understand why practitioners hold the views that they do instead of treating them as wrong' (Edwards, 1986:20–1). But then we must treat unitarism as a *perspective* rather than a theory. The same can be said of pluralism.

Although pluralists recognise that there is an imbalance of power within organisations, and that no single interest group will be able to dominate totally all other interest groups, when it comes to employee relations where there are essentially only two main parties (management and labour) there is nonetheless a tendency to assume (at least implicitly, if not explicitly) that an approximate balance of power exists, with the state acting as a neutral referee. As a result, many pluralists very quickly move from a statement that conflict is natural, rational and inevitable to an assessment of how conflict is organised, channelled and ultimately 'managed'. In other words, a pluralist approach 'does not tackle the problem of the nature or the basis of conflict, and merely concentrates on what happens when organizational expressions of conflict have already been articulated' (Edwards, 1986:24). Hence, the focus is on the *resolution* of conflict rather than its *generation*, or in the words of the pluralist on 'the institutions of job regulation'. This in turn 'encourages a segregation of industrial relations as an area of analysis from the underlying social relations of production, and hence facilitates an uncritical orientation towards managerial priorities of cost-effectiveness and technical rationality' (Hyman, 1978:35). Thus, issues of social control tend to predominate over those of social welfare.

Furthermore, by asserting the autonomy of industrial relations (Hyman, 1978:20) and rejecting existing theories derived from the social sciences in preference for an inductive approach (Bain and Clegg, 1974:107), pluralist industrial relations has simply replicated many of the problems of systems analysis. There cannot be a coherent theory of industrial relations when almost every situation is believed or portrayed to be a 'special case', to a greater or lesser extent, inexplicable by existing laws and therefore requiring detailed empirical, institutional analysis. For it is a truism, not a theory, that conflict is inevitable. Pluralism offers no comprehensive explanation for such conflicts, beyond acknowledging that different interests prevail in the workplace. In fact, by failing to elaborate the bases of conflict within organisations, pluralism serves more to mystify than to illuminate. As Richard Hyman has argued,

> understanding would be better assisted by a radically different approach: a sensitivity to the contradictory dynamics of capitalist production, the antagonistic structure of material interests within the labour market and the labour process, and the consequent and persistent generation of conflict and disorder within the very institutions and procedures designed to bring order and stability to employer-employee relationships. (1978:35)

Hyman is one of a number of Marxist theorists who have posed broader questions about the nature of the employment relationship, and in doing so have rejected the accepted orthodoxy of British industrial relations and its tacit support for the *status quo*.

Marxism and the issues of control and resistance

Just as there is no homogeneous body of pluralist thought, the same is true of Marxist analysis. In particular, because Marxism became a movement, there has been a tendency to focus on the political agenda derived from Marx's writings, rather than what he contributed to our understanding of society. As capitalism has not been superseded by socialism, many writers assume this to be sufficient to dismiss Marxist thought outright. Thus, Farnham and Pimlott (1990:16–17) write,

> To Marxists, industrial relations are essentially politicized and part of the class struggle ... the Marxist stress on the inevitable and polarized class struggle in industry and society between capitalist and proletariat, whilst probably a valid interpretation of nineteenth-century Victorian capitalism, does little to explain the complex, economic and social conflicts of late twentieth-century Britain.

However, this is to miss the point and to ignore the insights that can be derived from Marx's analysis of the nature of capitalism and how these illuminate aspects of the relationship between employers and employed. To focus on the Marxist *movement* rather than Marxist *thought*, and to reject the theory out of hand (as Farnham and Pimlott seem to advocate), is to throw the baby out with the bath water. If nothing else,

> the major contribution of Marxists has been as much in the questions asked as in the answers given or the methods of their attainment. It is the framework of what is taken for granted or what is regarded as problematic that most clearly differentiates Marxists from conventional 'industrial relations' analysts. (Hyman, 1989a:128)

For Marxists, industrial and employee relations can *only* be understood as part of a broader analysis of (capitalist) society, in particular the social relations of production and the dynamics of capital accumulation (Hyman, 1994:171). That is why there can be no such thing, strictly speaking, as a Marxist 'theory' of industrial relations: the project is a contradiction in terms (Marsden, 1982:245). As Hyman notes, for Marxists, 'the activities of employers and unions are to be construed in terms of such concepts as relations of production and class struggle; the term industrial relations is at worst vacuous and at best incoherent' (1989a:124). What Marxian analysis offers is a different perspective to understand society, a theoretical approach which emphasises totality, change, contradiction and practice (Hyman, 1975:4). Totality reflects the idea that all social phenomena are inter-related, and that no one area can be analysed satisfactorily in isolation. Unlike systems analysis, however, Marxists not only seek to construct a political economy of industrial relations, in which industrial relations are *integrated with* and not *separated from* the political and economic spheres, but also to assign causal priority to the social relations of production – that is, 'the way in which economic activity is organised in any society' (Hyman, 1975:4). In other words, the material, productive base of society will shape political institutions, legislation, modes of thought, even the nature of the family. As Marx himself put it, 'the mode of production in material life determines the general character of the social, political and spiritual processes of life' (1972:11).

An emphasis on stability is rejected by Marxists in favour of change and contradiction. Social relations are judged to be not only dynamic but characterised by the opposing interests of different classes. These contradictions present opportunities for change, but actual changes reflect the choices made by the different actors – what Marx refers to as *praxis*. In Marxist analysis, the material features of social life, especially the economics of production, limit the possibilities available for the organisation of human existence, but do not determine behaviour. A dialectical, not a deterministic process takes place.

It is this broader approach to the study of employment relations that most usefully distinguishes Marxism from systems theory, pluralism and unitarism, and it is through this approach that Marxists have sought to dig beneath the surface elements of employee relations such as collective bargaining, management decision-making, legislation, trade union regulations and workplace custom and practice. It is important to emphasise that this is not simply a question of different 'levels of analysis' – the 'individual' or 'unified organisation' in unitarist analysis, the 'sub-system' in the functionalist analysis of pluralism, or the 'system as a whole' in Marxist analysis – but rather how we conceptualise employment relationships (see Martin, 1999:1213–14). Thus, in contrast to any implicit or explicit assumptions about a balance of power in industry, Marxists emphasise the *asymmetry* of power between employer and employee, derived primarily from the ownership or non-ownership of capital. That is, at the most basic level, an employer is able to survive longer without labour than the employee can survive without work. Of course, the employee has a degree of freedom to choose the employer for whom he or she wishes to work but, as Marglin (1974:37) points out, 'it is a strange logic of choice that places its entire emphasis on the absence of legal compulsion'. The employee, by definition, must sell her or his ability to work in order to subsist.

Ownership acts as a source of power and control, bestowing on employers not only the 'right' to hire and fire labour but also to direct that labour in the process of production. Moreover, if employers can convince employees that they not only have a legitimate (property) right to control certain decisions but a moral right or duty, they exercise not only power but authority (see Gospel and Palmer, 1993:189–97). For Marxists, the exercise of power and the achievement of authority is a key dynamic in all employment relationships, because the employer can never secure total control or achieve complete authority. The capacity to work may be bought and sold in a (labour) market like any other commodity, but the object that is sold (the physical, mental and emotional capabilities of individuals) cannot be separated from the subject of the actual exchange (the individuals themselves). When the employee agrees to work for so many hours per week at a given wage, that is not the end of the matter but the start. Unlike other 'factors of production', the precise nature of the labour input, or more accurately the precise tasks the worker is expected to perform, both in a quantitative and qualitative sense, can never be perfectly specified in advance by the employer. The labour input involves 'a continuous bargain every day and hour, renewed either in the prices that are to be paid or the amount of product that the worker turns out' (Commons, 1919:24). The 'wage-effort bargain' is therefore contended and in a continuous state of flux, 'an invisible frontier of control ... which is defined and redefined in a *continuous* process of pressure and counterpressure, conflict and accommodation, overt and tacit struggle' (Hyman, 1975:26, original emphasis). For Marxists, then, the 'negotiation of order' is an unceasing power struggle between capital and labour: the frontier of control, at any point of time, 'represents a compromise unsatisfactory to *both* parties' (ibid:27, original emphasis).

Since first elaborated against the backcloth of nineteenth century capitalism, many subsequent events have challenged aspects of Marx's anticipated development of capitalist society. For example, the growth of a substantial proportion of the labour force occupying 'intermediate' positions in the occupational structure – administrative, middle managerial and professional positions, for example – is not easy to square with Marx's prediction of the general polarisation of the two principal classes within capitalism. Moreover, because much of Marx's analysis was directed at the societal level – identifying the basic nature of capitalism and the sources of its instability – the concepts which he developed often prove in practice somewhat blunt instruments for analysts seeking to understand the nature of employment relations within different work contexts. For example, to what extent, and to what effect, do power relations within organisations display a degree of autonomy from wider social class relationships? Marxism tends to deal with individuals only as bearers of economic class, such as 'labour' (workers or employees) and 'capital' (owners or managers), and the theory fails to provide adequate tools for understanding how 'alienated social relations' are subjectively experienced and acted on by the individual (Thompson and McHugh, 2002:383; see also Martin, 2003:173). There is certainly evidence to suggest that many UK workers *are* alienated from the system (e.g. BSAS data reported by Kelly, 1998) but it is unclear how this affects their behaviour (see Martin, 1999:1212). As Korczynski (2002:155) points out, 'it is conceptually inappropriate to draw conclusions about the subjective experience of work from arguments about the objective nature of labour in capitalism'.

Nevertheless, it is the questions which the Marxian analysis poses, and the situating of employee relations within a broader conceptual framework, that represents its significance to contemporary enquiry. With its emphasis on the 'unceasing power struggle' between capital and labour, it follows that 'industrial relations is the study of *processes of control over work relations*' (Hyman, 1975:12, original emphasis), both inside the workplace and beyond. But the distinctiveness of this definition, and that of the Marxist approach to the subject, is often lost. Clegg (1979:450–2), for example, tries to play down the differences between Marxism and pluralism in both a literary and theoretical sense. By contrasting the definitions of Flanders ('the institutions of job regulation') and Hyman ('the processes of control over work relations'), Clegg concludes that:

> 'Job regulation' is to be preferred *for its greater elegance and precision*, but if students of industrial relations had to rub along with 'processes of control over work relations' they would probably manage fairly well. (1979:452, emphasis added)

In terms of their theoretical approach, Clegg suggests that since both are concerned with conflict and stability, and as both regard conflict as inevitable and seek to explain how it is contained, students adopting either approach 'will come to much the same conclusions at the end of the day' (ibid:452). The divergence, if any, is 'to be found mainly in their attitudes' (ibid:455). Here again, therefore, we are back to a focus on Marxism as a movement rather than a theory. Not only is this a misrepresentation of the different theoretical approaches to the subject, it presents a persistent and significant source of confusion for students. This confusion is compounded by tendencies to draw on different elements of the various perspectives in a generally *ad hoc* manner, resulting in a lack of theoretical coherence and clarity. Such coherence is critical if we are to traverse successfully the 'mountains of facts' and penetrate beneath the surface of the day-to-day activities that make up the practice of industrial and employee relations.

A theory of employee relations

Industrial relations has always been a specialist area of study. From its origins in the late nineteenth century it has been studied predominantly as a separate, autonomous area of material life. But as the industrial relations 'system' in the

UK was seen to disintegrate in the 1960s it was necessary to cast the subject's net more widely, to incorporate the informal as well as formal processes of industrial relations. Pluralists suggested that the UK had two systems of industrial relations, but following the dramatic changes of the 1980s and 1990s (as outlined in the following chapters) very few commentators would insist that there are two identifiable systems in the UK today, let alone one. The traditional focus on male, manual workers is equally unsustainable (Wajcman, 2000), as is the failure of many scholars to look at how life 'beyond the factory gates' and 'office doors' has influenced industrial relations (Ackers, 2002). These issues are addressed throughout this text.

Just as the boundaries and content of the subject have changed in response to events and circumstances, it also responded to theoretical criticism. John Kelly (1998) for example, has drawn attention to the theoretical neglect of workers' interests and power relations in industrial relations. By focusing on 'injustice' and how workers mobilise their interests through collective action, Kelly has considerably deepened our understanding of some of the key questions in industrial relations (for example, whether employees are now less 'collectivist' and more 'individualistic' in orientation, how and why union power has declined in recent years, and by how much, and to what extent this decline can be attributed to the different actors in industrial relations). Yet despite new empirical lines of enquiry and important theoretical developments, the very term 'industrial relations' has been brought into question, as have the underlying assumptions that inform much of the research and teaching in the area (see, for example, Ackers and Wilkinson, 2003b; and Edwards, 1995a:40). Work organisations and corporate managers increasingly use the term 'human resource management' instead of industrial relations, the government displays a preference for 'employment relations' (e.g. www.dti.org.uk), and even those who stick to the title of 'industrial relations' admit that 'employment relations' might be the best label if we were starting from scratch (Edwards, 2003a:1).

Using terms such as employee relations rather than industrial relations reflects part of the redefinition of the boundaries of the subject to include *all* employment relationships, rather than ones only involving unionised male manual workers, but also the underlying assumptions that now inform theoretical perspectives on the subject. Thus, it is possible to discern a growing tendency to focus on, and define the distinctive characteristics of, the *employment relationship*; to locate that relationship within the *broader nature of economic activity*; to analyse the *structural bases* of conflict and accommodation between employer and employee; to consider the influence of the *wider society*; and to develop an *inter-disciplinary approach* using concepts and ideas derived from sociology, economics, psychology, history and political science.

It has become commonplace, for example, for academics in the field to argue that the jurisdiction of industrial and employee relations embraces 'all aspects of the employment relationship' (Strauss and Feuille, 1978:275; see also Fells, 1989; and Kaufman, 1993). Strauss and Feuille (1978:275) go on to argue, however, that

> this is much too broad because the 'employment relationship' encompasses such diverse fields as selection and testing, health and safety, equal employment rules, career paths, government labor market programs, and the entire field of organizational behavior. Pulling this conglomeration together under a single head would be intellectually meaningless.

But this would only be the case if research followed the traditionally empirical, inductive approach of earlier generations of writers. As it is impossible to ignore these diverse factors, the question becomes how to order, prioritise and understand such a complex range of variables, rather than how to limit the subject to a manageable range of analysis. In other words, having defined the boundaries of the subject, it is necessary to assign priority to particular variables or relationships, to identify causal links and to produce (testable) hypotheses. On the latter point we concur with Thompson and McHugh (2002:19) who argue that, 'any critical theory not testing its ideas through empirical investigation or practical intervention is ultimately arid'.

To focus on the employment relationship has the advantage of homing-in on the (material) basis of the interaction between employer and employee, and the relationship from which all other aspects of employee relations stem. As already noted, to focus on a system of rules or the institutions of job regulation is to ignore the foundations underpinning such rules and regulations in the sphere of production, to run before learning to walk (and without an adequate map of which direction to run). So what is the nature of the employment relationship? What do management and workers seek from such a relationship? And how does each party attempt to achieve its goals?

At its most basic level, every employment relationship is an *economic exchange*, an agreement between employer and employee over the sale of the latter's capacity to work (commonly known as labour power). But the employment relationship is also a *power relationship* as the worker, by definition of being an employee, agrees to submit to the authority and direction of the employer. The exchange of labour power is therefore unlike that of any other 'commodity'. As Brown (1988:55–7) points out, the employment relationship is a *continuous relationship*, not a 'one off' exchange; the employment contract itself is *open-ended*, in that the wage might be agreed in advance but effort is not, and cannot be, specified explicitly or exactly; the employment relationship is necessarily an *authority relationship* between super- and sub-ordinates, where the employee agrees to accept and follow the 'reasonable' instructions of those in positions of authority; the parties are *interdependent*, creating patterns of both conflict and co-operation; but the employer is in possession of greater power resources than the employee, creating an *asymmetrical* relationship between the parties. Each of these points warrants further elaboration as they provide the foundations upon which a theory of employee relations can be built.

The demand for labour, to borrow a term from economics, is a 'derived demand' because the employer is not interested in labour *per se* but in the contribution of the employee to the production of goods and services. In other words, the employer has no commitment towards the talents and needs of the employee except, and unless, they are useful in the process of production or the delivery of services. But what the employer purchases in the labour market is the *capacity* of men and women to work (labour power), whereas what the employer is actually interested in is the *performance* of work (physical, mental and in many cases emotional labour). As Edwards (1986:35) notes, 'in the labour contract what the employer wants is not a capacity but its exercise'. This creates an on-going relationship between the parties, but also a pattern of conflict and accommodation because while the wage may be agreed the level of effort is not. Even if workers are paid by the piece or for every sale they complete, their diligence and/or the quality of the product/service is invariably difficult, if not impossible, to specify precisely in the contract of employment. As Mike Emmott (2001a:vii) of the Chartered Institute of Personnel and Development (CIPD) has pointed out, 'few organisations seek to define in advance what is a reasonable level of effort or application'.

In a capitalist economy the emphasis will inevitably fall on the economic aspects of the employment relationship, but there are also important social and ethical issues to consider (Ackers, 2002:12). In fact, all employment relationships reflect a tension between the economic and the social, or between contract and status (see Hyman, 2001a). Conflict will thus emerge from the 'exploitation' of labour, but as Edwards (1986:31–2) argues, exploitation does not exist solely because the employer takes part of the product but also because of the way the product is actually produced. The 'right to manage' must be exercised in a 'reasonable' manner, which in large part will be determined by 'customary' and 'socially acceptable' standards of behaviour. To reiterate, employment relationships are not just 'economic contracts' – there is also a 'psychological contract' between the parties, which for employees involves 'a form of evaluation ... of management policy and practice with particular reference to fairness, trust and delivery of promises' (Guest, 2001:110).

As already noted, the employer hires the mental and physical attributes of employees, not the employees themselves. In effect, therefore, labour bears no market price, because it is *labour time* and not work itself that is purchased. Put differently, paid working time is not necessarily equivalent to time worked. What determines efficiency (and profitability) is not simply the (technical) combination of different 'factors of production' but also the degree of congruence between potential and performed labour. Since the latter depends, in large part, on the power and authority of the employer over the employee, firms can be expected to organise work in a way that reproduces the authority and control of capital over labour (Bowles, 1985; Gordon, 1976; and Marglin, 1974). This may result in, for example, improvements in productivity being sought via changes that involve work intensification, the sub-division of operations, the de-skilling of jobs and outright job losses, all of which are likely to invoke worker and/or trade union opposition (Turnbull, 1991b:141). Employees may submit to the authority of the employer but will always retain a very strong interest in the (ab)use of their labour. Indeed, the study of work group behaviour shows how workers combine and co-operate with each other not only to bargain over wages and working conditions but also to control or influence the pace of work, to create meaning in otherwise alienating work processes, and to protect themselves not just from 'overwork' but particularly from 'unremunerated overwork' (Turnbull, 1988a:101). As Marsden (1999:3) points out, '[t]he key to the employment relationship is that is enables management to decide detailed work assignments after workers have been hired ... however, few workers would agree to giving their employer unlimited powers over work assignments'.

Clearly, the use of labour power within the process of production encapsulates within it important sources of potential conflict (see Edwards, 1986:35). The task of management in this process is not to hope or assume that worker and union interests coincide with those of their own, but rather to structure workplace relations in a manner most conducive to the attainment of higher productivity, lower unit costs and improved profitability (Turnbull, 1991b:141). Those holding a unitary perspective of work relations simply assume that the only goal of the employee is furthering the profits of the firm, such that management need only apprise the worker of the 'needs' of the organisation to elicit worker co-operation and optimum performance. This approach characterises much of the recent writing on HRM (see Lewin, 2001). Pluralist writing, which continues to dominate mainstream industrial relations research, accepts a 'conflict of interests' between the parties but rarely explores the material base of those conflicts, preferring instead to focus on the resolution of conflict. Instead, the reality faced by management is how to reconcile the two problems of securing workers' co-operation and a surplus product (Nolan, 1983:303).

It is in this respect that the concept of interdependence plays a crucial role. The interests of capital may dominate the organisation of work, and employers will hold the balance of power in any employment relationship by virtue of their ownership of capital and the authority this imparts. But, ultimately, it is the workforce that actually performs the detailed activities of the work process. Service workers, for example, often play well-defined roles and follow carefully scripted lines but they still hold the power to 'fluff' those lines and reveal the inauthentic nature of the service encounter (see Korczynski, 2002; and Sturdy et al., 2001). Likewise, even unskilled manual workers hold the power to frustrate the efficiency and profitability of the organisation by failing to co-operate actively in the work process (see Delbridge, 1998; and Scott, 1994). The required level of co-operation needs to go beyond mere compliance with rules if work is to be performed efficiently. Indeed, a common form of worker insubordination is 'working to rules', whereby employees are able to undermine the work process merely by doing exactly and precisely as they are required, rather than exercising a level of discretion not covered by the rules. Consider, for example, a service industry setting where employees work 'without enthusiasm' or simply refuse to smile 'genuinely' at the customer – such action might well dull the corporate message of 'service quality' and 'customer care'. Essentially, then, management want workers to follow the spirit, not the letter of the rules. Employers cannot rely on coercion or even compliance to secure high performance; they also need to secure active employee consent and co-operation.

Power is typically understood as the ability of one party to compel another party to do something which they otherwise would not undertake of their own volition. In the employment relationship, employers seek to enjoin *and entice* workers to comply with their demands and co-operate with their instructions. To do otherwise would run the risk of overt conflict between capital and labour. For their part, one reason why workers do not simply resist management control is that they identify with, and define themselves in relation to their work: indeed, the majority of British workers have long-term commitments to their organisation, even though they may be not be particularly satisfied with their work (Diamond and Freeman, 2001). The fact that many people seek intrinsic reward from their work indicates that there is likely to be at least a latent degree of co-operation with management. The nature of the employment relationship, then, is not simply one of (management) control *versus* (worker) resistance, but a more problematic mix of dissent and accommodation, conflict and co-operation. In the past, one of the major criticisms of industrial relations research, and in particular the juxtaposition between pluralism and Marxism, was that 'industrial relations writings, overall, seems polarized around the two problematics of how is order achieved and why is disorder not rampant' (Guille, 1984:486). But in reality,

> It is not a matter of employers gaining what workers lose, or vice versa, but of the coming together of the two sides in a relationship which is inherently contradictory: employers need workers' creative capacities, but cannot give them free rein because of the need to secure a surplus and to maintain a degree of general control; and workers, although subordinate, do not simply resist the application of managerial control. (Edwards, 1986:6)

It is these features of the employment relationship – *the creation of an economic surplus, the co-existence of conflict and co-operation, the indeterminate nature of the exchange relationship, and the asymmetry of power* – not the institutions of trade unions, employers' associations or government agencies, that makes the subject matter of employee relations distinctive. The activities of institutions, such as collective bargaining or other 'rule-making' processes, in fact *arise from* the employment relationship and cannot be understood in isolation from it. Thus, trade union activity, first and foremost, is the organised expression of the grievances, deprivations and wider interests of employees that arise from their (subordinate) role in the process of goods production or service provision. Given the asymmetry of power that exists, collective action is invariably necessary if employee interests are to be represented effectively (see Kelly, 1998). Likewise, the need for management control derives from the tensions that exist between employer and employee within the employment relationship, giving rise to the development of a variety of control strategies. These activities can be grounded in a theory of the employment relationship, which has the added advantage of accommodating both sides of the labour question, namely the achievement of social welfare on the one hand, and social control on the other.

Having emphasised the distinct nature of the employment relationship and the process of creating surplus value, it is also important to acknowledge that the employment relationship does not take place in a vacuum: work organisations are not islands, workers are not automatons. What occurs in the workplace is also influenced by the wider society. Indeed, it is a maxim of industrial sociology that to understand what goes on inside the workplace it is also necessary to look at what goes on outside it, to consider such factors as the structure of power in society, the nature of communities and the degree of occupational solidarities (Lockwood, 1966). The labour forthcoming from a worker depends, in addition to biology and skills, on such factors as states of consciousness, degrees of solidarity with other workers, labour market conditions, and other societal influences such as schooling, welfare provisions and family life (see Gintis, 1976; and Lazonick, 1978). Thus, workers 'learn to labour' (Willis, 1977) and generally enter the workplace with a 'work ethic', a respect for private property, and a general willingness to accept authority:

> explaining the nature of the employment relationship necessarily involves considering the culture, the values and norms of the wider society and the institutional arrangements which ensure that appropriate normative obligations are internalized, and developed and reinforced by each generation. (Brown, 1988:61)

In a modern-day 'consumer society', for example, management increasingly adopts the role of 'champion' for the customer, enjoining workers to internalise the demands and desires of the customer (e.g. 'treat the customer as you yourself would like to be treated', 'the customer is always right'). The consumer is a source of authority in contemporary society. Some commentators go so far as to suggest that people now define themselves by what they consume rather than what they produce, such that a 'consumer discourse' in the workplace can provide management with an important source of legitimacy for their actions (see Korczynski, 2002). Appeals to the 'imperatives of the market', 'competition from rivals', or the ubiquitous forces of 'globalisation' can all provide an equally powerful source of authority for management and the state. The discourse of 'modern business needs' plays an integral, not an accidental role in shaping the relationship between employers and employees.

This framework of analysis is set out in a simplified form in Figure 2.1. As illustrated, the core of our analysis is the employment relationship. At the most general level, the nature of economic activity has a direct bearing on the essential structure of this relationship: the ownership or non-ownership of capital gives rise to an authority relationship characterised by hierarchy and control. But this cannot be achieved simply by using the coercive power that ownership imparts. Thus, in order for management to achieve their objectives they must secure the co-operation and consent of the workforce. The outcome is one of contest and accommodation, as those employed seek to improve the wages and general conditions of their employment. The end result is the many and varied employment relationships that we observe in the real world. Again, however, interaction is a dialectic rather than a deterministic process, as indicated by the influences (arrows) in Figure 2.1 flowing out from, as well as into, the employment relationship.

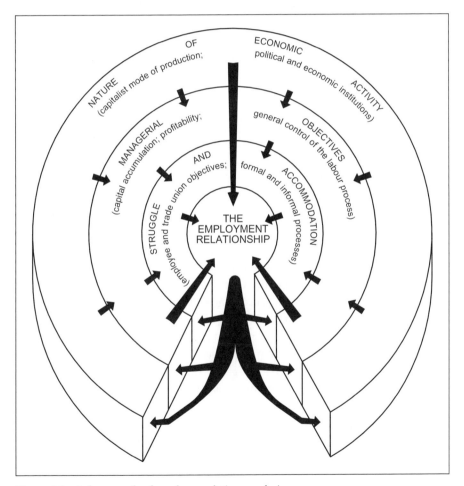

Figure 2.1 A framework of employee relations analysis

Rather than attempt to illustrate all the possible influences on the employment relationship in Figure 2.1, we have sought to portray only the central elements of our framework. What should be apparent from our discussion thus far, however, is that any political economy of employee relations must be holistic (i.e. involving a systematic analysis of the workings of the economy as a whole). In addition, this approach:

- takes social and economic structures and relations as its starting point, thereby placing emphasis upon class and stratification more generally (the economy is 'embedded' in society and the polity)
- brings notions of power and conflict to the fore, how they are forged and how they are exercised, not least through the state
- explains systemic tendencies and processes, such as globalisation and uneven development, primarily on the basis of the imperatives of profitability and capital accumulation (see Fine, 2002:197).

While these are generic features of the political economy of capitalism, there is still the question of any specific British characteristics of employee relations that deserve particular attention. After all, the very study of industrial relations as a *separate* field divorced from political economy is an anglophone peculiarity, largely the result of employment regulation in the first part of the twentieth century having developed in the absence of direct and systematic intervention by the state (Hyman, 2003).

Employee relations and varieties of capitalism

All employment relationships are 'embedded' in a particular social system of production and bear the imprint of specific national institutional forms (see Hollingsworth and Boyer, 1997). These institutional forms are heavily influenced by the state, especially as the state plays a major role in determining, and enforcing, the 'rules of the game'. For example, the state protects private property rights, upon which all employment relationships are ultimately founded; manipulates fiscal and monetary policy, thereby establishing the general economic context of employee relations; and may engage directly, to a greater or lesser extent, in production and exchange relations (ibid:13; see also Hall and Soskice, 2001:15). In an historical context, the principal characteristic of the British state was seen to be the 'insignificance' of its role in employee relations (e.g. Kahn-Freund, 1954:44). However, what was unique about the British system was not the absence of state intervention but the form of state regulation in key areas such as employment legislation (Ewing, 2003:141). We discuss these issues in more detail in Chapter 6. At this point it is more important to highlight the British state's historic reliance on markets rather than institutions. This reliance was heightened by the neo-liberal policies that defined Thatcherism.

Over the past 20 years or more, in the UK and many other advanced industrialised economies, the political and economic consensus was that markets are the most efficient method for co-ordinating business activities, with any public intervention more likely to cause harm than do good. According to neo-liberals, the role of the state is to ensure free and unfettered competition in product, financial and labour markets. Thus, the clarion call of Thatcherism was 'competition where possible, regulation only when necessary'. However, one of the basic features of modern economies is the growing importance, and arguably greater effectiveness, of co-ordinating mechanisms *alternative to* the market (see Gerlach, 1992; and Hamilton and Biggart, 1988). The market might be efficient when it comes to impersonal forms of contractual exchange, where prices provide sufficient information for all parties. Yet many relationships in business and employee relations depend on co-operation rather than competition, trust rather than opportunism, equity as well as efficiency, altruism rather than self-interest, reciprocity instead of indifference. Moreover, at some threshold, as the UK has discovered, 'the domination of the market rationale tends to challenge the viability of other institutional arrangements: the values of community, the family, and other authority systems can be eroded under the pursuit of private interests by each individual' (Boyer and Hollingsworth, 1997:445–7).

It was the failure of Thatcherism that led New Labour to seek a 'Third Way' between the 'invisible hand' of the market and the 'heavy hand' of the state. Nonetheless, there are still far fewer 'constraints' on business and the market in the UK in comparison with most other advanced industrialised economies and the Labour Government is still wedded to the idea that '[e]ffective markets and competition are the best means of ensuring that the economy's resources are allocated effectively' (HM Treasury, 2000:28). As a result, the UK is typically characterised as a 'liberal market economy' (LME), along with the USA, Canada, Australia and Ireland, in contrast to the 'co-ordinated market economies' (CME) of continental Europe (e.g. Austria, Belgium, Germany and the Netherlands), Scandinavia (Denmark, Finland, Norway and Sweden) and Japan. The key difference between these economies is the extent to which firms in a LME rely on the market mechanism (e.g. relative prices) to co-ordinate their endeavours, as opposed to forms of institutional intervention or non-market mechanisms in CMEs (see Hall and Soskice, 2001:33). The latter might include business associations, trade unions and (multi-employer) collective bargaining, cross-shareholding (firms holding shares in their suppliers), industry-wide vocational training programmes, and 'deliberative institutions' such as company-based works councils or national (tripartite) consultation bodies. Such institutions are designed to reduce uncertainty and build credible commitments between various stakeholders, thereby increasing the capacity of firms to develop long-term (strategic) behaviour. This contrasts sharply with the short-term (maximising) behaviour of firms in LMEs (ibid). The implications for employee relations are both manifold and profound, as we document in subsequent chapters. At this point we highlight just one issue by way of illustration, namely job insecurity.

In a business system where firms are (over)reliant on capital markets to finance their activities, as in the UK, they will invariably seek to maintain profits (rather than market share, for example) as this will influence the firm's future access to capital and its ability to resist hostile takeover bids. If revenue or profitability decline, firms will seek to lay off workers, in part to appease the City and bolster the share price as the following, not untypical, report from the *Financial Times* (20 December 1993) bears witness: 'Fisons, the troubled pharmaceuticals and scientific equipment group, is planning plant closures and large scale redundancies *in a bid to restore confidence in the company*' (quoted by Beaumont, 1995:103, emphasis added). It is no coincidence that UK workers enjoy, or rather endure, much weaker statutory employment protection than their European counterparts: firms in a LME demand such 'flexibility' (see Estevez-Abe *et al.*, 2001:163–7; Morgan *et al.*, 2001; OECD, 1999; Purcell *et al.*, 1999:1; and Turnbull and Wass, 2000). In a CME such as Germany, in contrast, firms can sustain a decline in returns because the financial system provides them with access to capital independent of current profitability. Moreover, one reason why German firms seek to retain market share is because labour market regulations demand a social as well as an economic case for any restructuring, making it difficult for firms to shed labour in the short run simply to maximise profits (see Bosch, 1990; and Casey, 1992:428–9). It is hardly surprising, therefore, that UK workers report a much stronger sense of insecurity than their European counterparts (see Burchell *et al.*, 1999; Heery and Salmon, 2000; and ISR, 1996).

Moving from a (somewhat abstract) discussion of the capitalist employment relationship to the specific national context of employee relations represents the first step towards more concrete levels of analysis that enable us to understand the reality, variety and dynamics of employee relations. We elaborate on the national context of employee relations in some detail in the following chapter, set within the international dynamics of global capitalism. We also look at broad trends across different sectors of the economy in Chapter 3 (e.g. manufacturing and services, public and private sectors). Likewise, in Part 2 we consider broader national trends and developments in relation to the organisation and activities of employers (Chapter 4), trade unions (Chapter 5) and the state (Chapter 6). More importantly, we combine macro (national) level analysis with the meso (industry) and micro (organisation) levels in each of these chapters. Thus, we discuss the case of British Airways in the context of both UK employee relations and broader developments in the domestic, European and global civil aviation industry (Chapter 4); we focus on the organising activities of the GMB and T&GWU in different industrial sectors, drawing on evidence from specific firms and relating these to broader developments in both unions and the trade union movement as a whole (Chapter 5); and we discuss the proposed privatisation of the Port of Belfast in relation to the port's function as a maritime, industrial and distribution area, as well as in relation to local and national political developments (Chapter 6).

The cases presented in Part 3 – Corus, Tesco, Marks & Spencer (and one of its suppliers) and the UK fire service – follow a similar method of analysis. Each case represents an example of the varied nature of employee relations and patterns of interaction with wider society. We start with this level of analysis as it is the most immediate and most accessible. However, a deeper understanding of the issues and processes covered in each of these chapters can only be derived from the higher, more abstract levels of analysis which have been identified in this chapter, and which underpin our approach throughout the remainder of the book. This theoretical framework informs the questions we pose, the structure of the analysis, the inferences drawn and the conclusions reached in each of the remaining chapters.

3

The dynamic context of employee relations

Introduction

Employee relations do not exist in a vacuum. They are located within, influenced by, and in turn impact upon many other aspects of the work organisation and wider society. Factors such as the size and structure of companies, the technologies they use, their patterns of ownership and control, and the character of their product markets have increasingly been recognised as important influences on the processes and outcomes of employee relations. Just as significant is the nature of the workforce and the composition and conditions prevailing in the broader labour market from which individual workforces are drawn. Important changes have been occurring in the composition of the labour force in the UK and elsewhere, the types and location of industries that the labour force is employed in (or, if unemployed, excluded from) and the patterns of ownership, organisational structures and inter-organisational linkages existing in those industries.

In addition, many companies find themselves operating in very different market conditions from those prevailing two decades ago as a result of far-reaching political and economic changes. Intensified levels of competition in the private sector have also been mirrored by greater financial stringency in the public service sector, as the state has sought to commercialise, and in many cases privatise, public sector organisations (see Chapter 6). Within organisations, too, changes have been taking place at an accelerated pace in the way jobs are designed and performed. Ways of working that typified many industries in the twentieth century, based on extensive division of labour, narrow job boundaries, close supervision and a separation of powers between those controlling tasks and those carrying them out in the office or on the shopfloor, are giving way to work systems based more on devolved responsibilities, flatter hierarchies and broader job boundaries. New technologies, coupled with operational techniques emphasising production and service provision which is 'just-in-time', reflecting 'customer service', 'total quality management' and 'right first time', are also contributing to significant changes in what jobs are undertaken, in what way, at what pace, by how many people, and in what kind of relationship with one another.

It is not possible here to rehearse in full all the changes that have been taking place in industrial societies over the recent period that impact on the experience of work. Further, the significance of particular developments, such as the changing role of the state in influencing labour market conditions and the growing role of the European Union (EU), will be dealt with in more detail in later chapters. What is necessary at this point, however, is to note some of the most pertinent developments taking place at society, industry and organisational levels, and highlight their significance for the analysis of employee relations. In order to bring into focus some of the many contextual developments impacting upon employee relations, this chapter begins by noting some of the key changes in the broader political and economic contexts. This is followed by sections considering developments in the nature and composition of the labour force and changes occurring within individual work organisations. These are then combined to demonstrate the practical interaction, and theoretical integration, of product and labour market processes.

Globalisation and the national economy

There are few developments in contemporary society that are not, in some way, linked to globalisation. Even universities, according to the Department for Education and Skills, 'exist to enable the British economy and society to deal with the challenges posed by the increasingly rapid process of global change' (*Times Higher Educational Supplement*, 9 May 2003). In many instances, of course, reference to globalisation as the root cause of contemporary changes to the economy, society and employee relations is simply 'globaloney'. But it is increasingly difficult to deny the impact of economic, social and political changes at the international level, despite the best efforts of some sceptics to pour cold water on globalisation (e.g. Hirst and Thompson, 1996; and Kleinknecht and ter Wengel, 1998). Acknowledging the impact of globalisation, however, does not mean that one has to accept that it is now a 'fact of life' or a *fait accompli*. Globalisation represents the latest stage of capitalist economic development, or more precisely 'the extension of the capitalist mode of production to virtually every corner of the planet' (Giles, 2000:182). As such it is a *process* authored by certain actors – most notably transnational corporations (TNCs) and the nation state, acting through international agencies such as the European Commission, World Bank, International Monetary Fund (IMF), and World Trade Organization (WTO) – and effected through (de)regulatory changes at the national and international levels. Thus, globalisation is not a 'natural' or 'inevitable' process, nor is it uncontested, as the 'battle of Seattle' and demonstrations at other meetings of the WTO have served to demonstrate.

The 146 countries that belong to the WTO account for well over 90 per cent of world trade and together they have agreed a range of measures to open up market access and promote competition, continuing the work previously undertaken through the General Agreement on Tariffs and Trade (GATT) (see Milberg, 1998). In 1997, for example, 69 governments agreed to wide-ranging liberalisation measures in telecommunications; 40 governments agreed tariff-free trade in information technology products; and 70 countries concluded a financial services deal covering over 95 per cent of trade in banking, insurance, securities and financial information (see www.wto.org; and OECD, 2000a:152). Even basic services such as water supply and public transport, in many countries the preserve of the public sector, have been opened up to international market forces. These and other developments at the national and international levels have facilitated the more rapid expansion of world trade, faster and larger capital flows, and a massive increase in foreign direct investment (FDI).

The defining characteristics of globalisation are the ever closer integration of spatially separate locations around the world into a single international market and the functional integration of internationally dispersed business activities (see Dicken, 1998). World trade grew at more than 6 per cent per annum during the 1990s, which throughout the decade represented a much higher rate of growth than total output (in terms of gross domestic product (GDP)) (see Bank of England, 2000:234; and WTO, 2002:10). This growth is set to continue (Pain et al., 2000:34). Of the world's 100 largest 'economies', 51 are now global corporations rather than countries (much of the world's trade is in fact trade within and between TNCs) (see Clausing, 2000:190). Between 1991 and 2000, a total of 1185 regulatory changes were introduced to national rules and regulations governing FDI, of which 1121 (95 per cent) were in the direction of creating a more favourable environment for FDI. During 2000 alone, 69 countries made 150 regulatory changes, of which 147 (98 per cent) were more favourable to foreign investors (UNCTAD, 2001:12). Not surprisingly, FDI has increased massively in recent years. For example, combined FDI inflows and outflows increased from US$94 billion in 1982 to US$437 billion in 1990 and US$2421 billion in 2000 (at current prices) and foreign affiliates employed well over 45 million workers worldwide in 2000 (compared to just under 24 million in 1990 and 17 million in 1982) (ibid:2). FDI now reaches many more countries in a more substantial manner than in the past, and for the first time three companies from developing countries (Hutchison Whampoa, Petróleos de Venezeula and Cemex) are among the world's 100 largest TNCs. Hutchison owns the port of Felixstowe, the UK's largest container port, and with its interests in Rotterdam is now the largest container handler in Europe (see Turnbull, 2000).

These developments hold important implications for employee relations. For example, organisations increasingly 'benchmark' their activities against interna-tional 'best practice', especially in sectors most exposed to global competition such as civil aviation (see Blyton et al., 2001). As globalisation has been driven, in large part, by (cost) competition this has often translated into an 'international race to the bottom' in respect of wages and workers' terms and conditions of employment (ibid; see also Brecher and Costello, 1994; and Wiseman, 1996). Within the EU, the process of TNCs moving production to Member States with lower wages, weaker employment protection and a less comprehensive system of employment rights is usually referred to as 'social dumping'. The Social Chapter, which we discuss in Chapter 11, is designed to combat this process. However, in an interdependent international economy it is increasingly difficult for any one country to stay aloof while others are liberalising their markets and subjecting their workforce to the pressures of global competition (see Streeck, 1998:432).

Like many other developments in employee relations, as we indicated in Chapter 1, there are elements of both continuity and change at work. For example, UK firms have always traded goods and services on world markets and many have operated subsidiaries around the globe for over a century. Likewise, American subsidiaries operating in the UK can be traced back as far as the 1860s (Ferner, 2003:82) and in key sectors such as vehicle production they have played a dominant role for more than half a century. However, taking both quantitative and qualitative measures, recent changes represent a break with the past, or to use the terminology deployed in Chapter 1 constitute 'discontinuous change' that has 'punctuated' the previous 'equilibrium'. For example, competition is now more intense across a much wider range of industries (DTI, 2001:15); UK firms invested more overseas than any other country in 1999 and the UK is the second largest recipient of FDI (ibid); the UK attracts a disproportionate share of Japanese FDI within the EU as well as investment from other Asian countries; foreign companies in the UK accounted for over 80 per cent of the rise in capital intensity of UK manufacturing between 1984 and 1997 (CBI/TUC, 2001:9); and the UK now has one of the highest shares of foreign research and development (R&D) as a proportion of total R&D in the OECD (DTI, 2002:18). Foreign ownership of UK-based establishments more than doubled during the 1990s (Millward *et al.*, 2000:32–3) and by the end of the decade foreign-owned firms employed over 1.82 million workers in the UK, including over 855 000 in manufacturing and a total of over 760 000 in the trade and financial services sectors. Foreign-owned manufacturing firms now account for around a third of the UK's manufacturing output (see OECD, 2003).

As well as foreign firms establishing independently in the UK, there has been continued growth in acquisitions by foreign-owned firms, cross-national mergers and joint ventures. The latter involves foreign and domestically-owned firms joining forces to gain such advantages as shared research and development costs, combined marketing activities and a stronger market position. Recent joint venture growth has been particularly evident in the communications sector (such as between BT and Yahoo, and BT and Microsoft), in civil engineering (such as Balfour Beatty with the support services group WS Atkins), along with a variety of joint ventures between pharmaceutical and biotechnology companies. Deregulation makes acquisition, mergers and joint ventures much easier today than in the past, but these business ventures often fail to deliver the anticipated benefits, with employment, human resource management and cultural factors often proving to be highly problematic (see, for example, Hubbard and Purcell, 2001:17–19).

Foreign companies bring with them to the host country their own ideas and methods of production and labour management, the result of which is not only a greater diversity of employee relations practice but also pressure on indigenous firms to adopt similar 'best practice'. Thus, the Ford Motor Company brought more formalised collective bargaining procedures to the British motor industry than those being practised by domestic manufacturers at the time (Beynon, 1984). More recently, McDonald's has brought its own brand of low wage non-unionism to the UK's shores, and beyond (see Ritzer, 1996; and Royle, 2000). Other non-union American TNCs practice a more sophisticated pattern of HRM, which is distinct from the Japanese-oriented system associated with Japanese automotive and electronics companies. These companies have brought to the UK a variety of employee relations practices ranging from single-union and no-strike agreements to company uniforms and a morning work-out (accompanied in some cases by the company song) (see Delbridge, 1998; and Oliver and Wilkinson, 1992). German and Swedish firms are different again, often associated with a joint team-based system (although in the absence of an appropriate national regulatory framework this model appears not to travel as well as the Anglo-Saxon and Japanese systems of work and employee relations) (see Dickmann, 2003; and Ferner and Varul, 2000). Figure 3.1 summarises these patterns of work and employee relations, based on the international comparative study by Katz and Darbishire (2000) of two industries (autos and telecommunications) in seven countries (UK, USA, Japan, Australia, Sweden, Italy and Germany) (for a more general discussion of foreign-owned firms, see Edwards et al., 1999; Ferner, 2003; and Marginson and Sisson, 1996).

TNCs are attracted to the UK by a combination of (internationally) low labour costs and a 'business friendly' regulatory environment, especially in relation to labour market flexibility. As Figure 3.2 demonstrates, the UK is a low wage economy and has much lower non-wage labour costs (e.g. social security charges, compulsory pension contributions and health insurance) compared to other G7 countries (the G7 countries are the UK, USA, Canada, Japan, Germany, France and Italy). Measures of labour market regulation indicate that the UK now has weaker employment protection than other advanced industrialised economies, with the exception of the USA (Estevez-Abe et al., 2001:163–7; and OECD, 1999). In the 1970s, 'poor industrial relations' was seen as a brake on FDI. Today, the Government lauds the UK's 'relatively healthy industrial relations' (DTI, 2001:22), as indicated by historically low levels of strike action (working days lost). But is it a coincidence that UK employment law no longer adequately protects union members/strikers and is in breach of internationally accepted standards (see Hendy, 2000)? Is it any surprise that business leaders look favourably on the UK's

Low wage	HRM	Japanese-oriented	Joint team-based
Managerial discretion with informal procedures	Corporate culture and extensive communication	Standardised procedures	Joint decision-making
Hierarchical work relations	Directed teams	Problem-solving teams	Semi-autonomous work groups
Low wages with piece rates	Above-average wages with contingent pay	High pay linked to seniority and performance appraisal	High pay with pay-for-knowledge
High turnover	Individualised career development	Employment stabilisation	Career development
Strong anti-union animus	Union substitution	Enterprise unionism	Union and employee involvement

Source: Katz and Darbishire (2000:10).

Figure 3.1 Four patterns of workplace practices

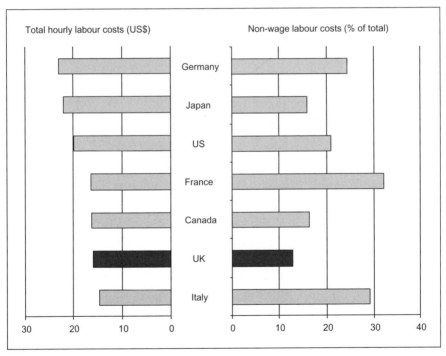

Source: Calculated from US Bureau of Labour data.

Figure 3.2 Hourly labour cost and non-wage labour costs (production workers) G7 comparison, 2000

regulatory environment? The international Institute of Management Development conducts regular surveys of business leaders in 46 countries and asks whether they regard labour market regulations as 'too restrictive' or 'flexible enough'. The results suggest that, across the full range of employment legislation, the UK labour market has a regulatory environment that is perceived as significantly 'better' (i.e. more flexible) than other major European countries, and on a par with the USA (DTI, 2001:23). The same survey reveals that business executives perceived the UK to be the most 'lightly regulated' of the G7 economies in 1996/97 in terms of 'government regulation' and 'bureaucracy', and is still ranked second (behind Canada) in the latest survey (ibid:24; see also DTI, 2002:35–6).

Notwithstanding the advantages to inward investors of comparatively low labour costs and an attractive regulatory environment, TNCs do not base their business and employee relations strategy in the UK purely on the foundations of cost minimisation and labour flexibility. Indeed, to do so would be a serious mistake in a competitive environment that demands high productivity, service reliability, world-class quality, technological innovation, knowledge transfer and the like. On the contrary, foreign companies operating in the UK have often been more innovative in terms of work organisation and employee relations, they have invested more heavily in plant and capital equipment, and recorded much higher productivity and profitability than comparable UK-owned firms (see, for example, DTI, 2001:74; Dunning, 1976; and Turnbull, 1991a:169–71). A study by Oulton (2001) of comparable foreign and domestic owned firms found that the former operate with 50 per cent more capital per worker (see also CBI/TUC, 2001:9). In a study of innovative work practices such as just-in-time (JIT), total quality management (TQM), integrated computer-based technology (e.g. CADCAM, CIM, FMS) and 'people practices' such as empowerment, learning cultures (i.e. development opportunities beyond immediate task training) and total productive maintenance involving shop-floor employees, Clegg *et al.* (2002) found that UK-owned firms have adopted fewer practices than their foreign-owned counterparts operating in the UK. Moreover, UK companies operating overseas have adopted fewer of these practices than comparable host country firms or other foreign-owned companies in that country. A further indictment of UK-owned firms is that they report less success with these practices than comparable foreign-owned firms.

Thus, in addition to bringing new models of work and employment to the UK, FDI has exposed the widespread deficiencies of British management. These deficiencies have been highlighted in a number of recent studies (e.g. Bosworth, 2000; CBI/TUC, 2001; EEF, 2001) and are now a major concern for the Labour Government (DTI, 2002:25). Of course, this problem is not a new phenomenon. As Nichols (1986:168) put it almost 20 years ago, 'it does seem that British managements have not been doing their jobs very well'. Williams *et al.* (1988:22) were equally forthright: 'The British management problem is that, within their area of discretion, British managers consistently take poor decisions about the priority of different problems and execute their strategy in a way that is generally inept'. In the most comprehensive study ever conducted into the supply and demand for management and leadership capability in the UK, the recently created Council for Excellence in Management and Leadership (2002) described current management and business leadership development as a 'dysfunctional system' which is holding back the UK's economic performance (see Chapter 4 for a more detailed discussion of management).

For many years, the UK's poor productivity performance, which is still very much in evidence, was attributed to poor labour relations and the 'British worker problem' (see Nichols, 1986). Some of these problems are still apparent. For example, strike action may have declined to historically low levels but this does not equate with more co-operative employee relations or indeed the eradication of industrial conflict (see Chapter 10). Skills are still a major problem – there are 7 million adults who are functionally illiterate in the UK, which translates to 20 per cent of adults reading less well than the average 11-year-old – and the skills gap is particularly acute at the intermediate/vocational level (see DTI, 2002:9; HM Treasury/DTI, 2001:33; and Keep and Rainbird, 2003). (We discuss these deficiencies in more detail below.) To what extent, if at all, can these problems be laid at the feet of the workforce? Even when workers might appear to be 'at fault', as is often assumed to be the case in a strike situation, the causes (and causality) of employee relations 'problems' might be very different:

> the lack of sophistication in management organisation both in relation to labour relations and the more technical aspects of production ... not only led directly to low productivity, but also exacerbated industrial relations problems ... To a significant degree, therefore, rather than poor labour relations leading to production problems, production problems lead to poor labour relations and low productivity. (Batstone, 1986:41)

Improving labour productivity is the main priority of the current Labour Government (DTI, 2002:3) and it is not difficult to understand why. Productivity is the main determinant of living standards and the key to rising long-term prosperity – if the UK could match US labour productivity (based on 1999 figures) then output per head would be over £6000 higher (HM Treasury/DTI, 2001:1). For firms too, labour productivity 'is the touchstone against which every new human resource policy ought to be evaluated' (Boxall and Purcell, 2003:8). But on any standard measure of productivity the UK is still a long way behind other advanced industrial economies (DTI, 2001:74–5). The Government has identified five key areas to drive up productivity, namely investment, innovation, skills, enterprise and competitive markets. These are areas where the Department of Trade and Industry (DTI) is believed to have most influence, but the emphasis of Government policy is on encouragement and facilitation rather than co-ordination and compulsion. Markets are still given preference over institutions, which is only to be expected in a liberal market economy.

Responses to competitive pressures

Despite some variation over specific periods, both liberal and co-ordinated market economies seem capable of providing satisfactory levels of long-run economic performance (Hall and Soskice, 2001:20–1).The economic performance of the USA (a LME) and Germany (a CME) serves to illustrate this point (see DTI, 2001). The UK's problem is that it is unable to match the performance of the more successful LMEs or CMEs – at best the UK's performance is average, at worst it is a weak performer. Even some of the so-called strengths of the UK economy, such as its 'flexible and lightly regulated labour market', would no doubt be viewed as a source of weakness by some actors, most notably workers who find themselves in low-paid jobs with little or no prospect of training or promotion. In fact, one of the most disconcerting features of LMEs such as the UK, USA, Canada and New Zealand is that they have a far more unequal distribution of income than CMEs (see Hall and Soskice, 2001:21–2).

Having been implored by Mrs Thatcher to 'glory in inequality', by the mid-1990s the UK was the most unequal country in the western world (United Nations, 1996). Using the Council of Europe's 'decency threshold', which measures whether countries are complying with Article 4 of the European Social Charter to provide 'fair remuneration', by the early 1990s the UK contained over 10 million employees on adult rates (6 million of whom were women) below the decency threshold (the figure is calculated as 68 per cent of all full-time mean earnings) (Pearson and Quiney, 1992:1). This represented nearly a quarter of all Europeans living below this threshold, *and almost half (47 per cent) of the working population in Britain*. Unlike neo-liberals, who believe that, '[t]here needs to be fear and greed in the system in order to make it tick' (Hutton, 1996:173) – the former to prevent dependency and the latter to encourage enterprise and efficiency – New Labour is committed to reducing poverty, most notably through its introduction of a National Minimum Wage (NMW) in April 1999.

Together with other policies designed to combat poverty and social exclusion, the NMW has arrested the trend towards greater inequality. But many workers are still paid 'poverty wages' as defined by the Council of Europe (around a third of all full-time employees), 330 000 jobs were paid below the NMW in April 2002 (compared to 1.42 million in April 1998), and an estimated 2 million adults were paid at or just above the NMW (see Palmer *et al.*, 2002). In 2000/01, there were still 13 million individuals (including 3.9 million children) living in homes with incomes below the Government's own poverty threshold (defined as 60 per cent of the median household income after deducting housing costs). This was 1 million fewer than in 1996/97 but was still almost double the number 20 years earlier (ibid; see also www.jrf.org.uk). Contrary to standard economic theory, the evidence suggests that low wages do not create jobs, the NMW has not reduced employment, and growing inequality actually hinders economic growth, amplifying the boom and slump of the economic cycle and destroying social cohesion (see Hutton, 1996:175–81; and OECD, 1996). As CMEs have discovered, equality and efficiency are complements, not alternatives.

Despite comparatively low wage and non-wage labour costs (Figure 3.2), and a significant number of workers (especially women, part-timers and some ethnic groups) employed on poverty wages, unit labour costs are significantly higher in the UK than most other advanced industrial economies because of poor productivity (see Neale, 1992). The UK's productivity performance is significantly below the USA and both the EU and OECD average, and this shortfall is common to both the manufacturing and service sectors and is apparent right across the size distribution of firms (DTI, 2001:74). The best UK firms are able to match the best in the world (HM Treasury, 2000:19; and Owen, 1998:36), which suggests that intra-organisational developments (e.g. the introduction of new technology, the adoption of new work process and new people policies) and inter-organisational developments (e.g. sub-contracting, supply chain integration, joint ventures or vertical re/disintegration) can have a significant impact on performance. These developments are discussed in more detail in a subsequent section. At this point it is more important to note that the UK's 'world class' companies tend to be small and few in number, which suggests that we need to look first at national (macro level) factors that account for poor performance before looking at industry- or firm-specific factors (the meso and micro levels).

Comparing the UK with the world's leading LME (USA) and CME (Germany) reveals a productivity gap (output per worker) of 45 per cent and 11 per cent respectively (there is a 20 per cent gap with the former West Germany) (HM Treasury, 2000:1). Analysis of this productivity gap highlights the structural weaknesses of the UK economy and the potential danger of a 'third way' between markets and institutions that might simply consign the UK to continued mediocrity. Most notably, low investment in physical capital is the main source of the productivity gap between the UK and Germany (accounting for more than half the difference). Investment accounts for almost a third of the USA's lead over the UK, but innovation and research and development is a more important source of the trans-Atlantic productivity gap (accounting for almost two-thirds of the difference). Innovation and R&D is also an important factor underpinning Germany's lead over the UK (accounting for 17 per cent of the difference) (see Crafts and O'Mahoney, 2001).

Although the causes of low investment and poor investment decisions are many and varied (see, for example, House of Lords, 1985:25–6), two factors are particularly worthy of note. First, UK companies fail to re-invest profits, preferring instead to make dividend payments. During the 1980s, investment increased by 2 per cent per annum compared to profits which rose on average by 6 per cent per annum and dividends which jumped by 12 per cent per annum (Hutton, 1996:8). Between 1992 and 1997, dividend payments increased by 67 per cent compared to a rise in capital investment of 27 per cent (TUC, 1999). Second, low wages serve to perpetuate low investment as many firms are able to remain (cost) competitive by holding down labour costs (Fine, 1990:140; Fine and Soskice, 1988; and Rubery, 1994). This simple 'fact' of economics – the relative price of capital and labour encourages firms to hire (cheap) labour rather than invest in (expensive) capital, whereas higher wages would encourage firms to substitute capital for labour – appears to have eluded successive UK governments.

Although skill levels play no part in accounting for the superior productivity of the USA compared to the UK, they are a significant factor behind the superior performance of German firms (higher skills accounting for 14 per cent of Germany's productivity lead over the UK) (see Crafts and O'Mahoney, 2001). More widely, new evidence demonstrates that improvements in the quality of labour, measured by educational attainment, directly contributed to labour productivity growth in virtually all OECD countries (Bassanini and Scarpetta, 2001). Figure 3.3 indicates that the UK compares well against Germany (and indeed most other CMEs) in terms of higher educational qualifications (degree level and above) but is well behind the USA (this accounts, in part, for differences between the UK and USA in terms of innovation and entrepreneurship, as more highly educated workers are more likely to succeed when setting up their own business; see Bates, 1990; and West *et al.*, 1999). Like the USA, the UK has a significant proportion of the workforce with low skills. The demand for low skilled labour has fallen dramatically in recent years – in 1979, unskilled male inactivity rates in the UK were less than 4 per cent compared to over 30 per cent by 1998 (DTI, 2002:23) – which further highlights the importance of the yawning skills gap at the intermediate/vocational level between the UK and Germany (see also Keep and Rainbird, 2003:399).

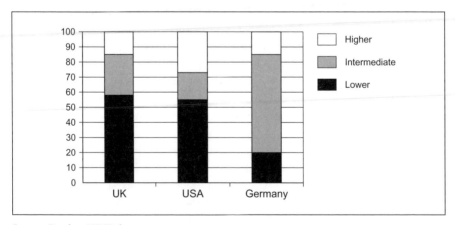

Source: Based on NIESR data.

Figure 3.3 Skill proportions by country (1998–9)

After 1979, successive Conservative governments progressively dismantled any legislative backing (compulsion) for training and abandoned any notions of social partnership or tripartite control of training design and delivery (see Keep and Rainbird, 2003:395–7). Consequently, the UK reverted to a market-based, largely employer-led training system which not only fails to produce sufficient levels and quality of training, but effectively encourages firms *not* to train: in the absence of compulsion, a rational policy is to minimise training investment (and associated costs) and simply poach skilled workers when market conditions demand it (see Hutton, 1996:187–92). One consequence was that the UK became trapped in a 'low skill/low quality equilibrium' (Finegold and Soskice, 1988; and Stevens and Mackay, 1991). Since 1997 the Labour Government has given greater priority to education and training through, *inter alia*, the expansion of student numbers in further and higher education, the further development of the national vocational qualification (NVQ) system, the continuation of City and Guilds qualifications, and the training requirements of the Investors In People (IIP) initiative. This has contributed to an increase in the volume of educational and training activity taking place. Question marks remain, however, about the impact of these (countless) initiatives. For example, on average, training practice is better in IIP-accredited workplaces but a large minority of accredited workplaces fail to engage in good practice – for them, IIP 'is just another plaque on the wall' (Hoque, 2003). As Keep and Rainbird (2003: 406) conclude, despite often substantial progress in some areas of vocational education and training provision, 'the overall prognosis remains gloomy'.

There are still deep structural problems to address in relation to skills and workforce training (Mayhew, 1991:5), most notably the demand for skills which is limited by the growth of small firms and part-time work, the erosion of skilled manual employment, and the structure of customer demand within the economy (i.e. large numbers subsist on relatively low incomes, which encourages firms to concentrate on cheap goods and a cost-centred competitive strategy) (Keep and Rainbird, 2003:415). As Bryan Sanderson, Chairman of the Learning and Skills Council (LSC) commented, 'many employers are unaware of the skills needed, not only to improve their performance but to enable them to move into higher value added markets' (LSC Press Release, 10 February 2002, www.lsc.gov.uk; see also LSC, 2003). Existing skills deficiencies are estimated to cost the UK economy as much as £10 billion per annum (e.g. as a result of poor quality, lost orders, poor communications with customers, and reduced scope for internal promotions) (CBI/TUC, 2001:20–1; see also LSC, 2003). The failure to address structural and strategic training issues in the immediate future will cost the economy and its workforce considerably more.

Performance data for the UK suggest some improvement during the late 1990s, which has continued in the new millennium (www.statistics.gov.uk). In fact, the UK's growth in GDP per head has recently been faster than other G7 economies. However, this owes more to improved labour market performance (an increasing proportion of people in employment) than the productivity of those in work (DTI, 2002:7–8). GDP per person can increase simply as a result of those in employment working longer hours – the UK has some of the longest working hours in Europe (Kodz et al., 2002) – even though the increase in physical output per employee is slowing down, as is currently the case (O'Mahoney and de Boer, 2002:31–5). Other changes in the labour market and composition of employment can also have a statistical effect on productivity. For example, the UK's underlying productivity performance is generally better in more traditional industries where non-price factors such as quality and innovation are less important (Smith, 1986) compared to ICT producing/using sectors (O'Mahoney and de Boer, 2002:29). However, the former are shrinking (under the pressures of global competition) while knowledge-based industries continue to grow, fuelling GDP growth as they do so (OECD, 2002c). Thus, whereas aggregate economic growth is typically led by manufacturing growth – generally referred to as 'Kaldor's Law' (Kaldor, 1966; and Cornwall, 1977) – the long-term decline of manufacturing in the UK, both in absolute terms and in relation to the composition of the sector, has adversely affected national economic performance (Aldington, 1986:7). The service sector may provide more jobs, but there is even greater dispersion of productivity between firms in this sector (i.e. a longer tail of poor performers) (see Oulton, 1996) and it would take a massive increase in services to compensate for the revenue losses arising from a further decline of the nation's manufacturing base (for example, every 1 per cent fall in manufacturing exports requires a 3 per cent rise in services to compensate, given the greater revenue and employment generating effects of manufacturing). These developments not only affect the aggregate performance of the UK economy but the employment opportunities and living standards of the workforce.

Changes in employment and the labour force

Broad shifts in employment can be identified in all mature industrial societies. Many aspects of these developments have been occurring over a long period, though the conditions prevailing over the past two decades appear to have fuelled the pace of change along several dimensions. Consequently, it is in discussions on the labour market that one encounters directly the question of whether or not recent changes amount to a 'transformation' of the labour market from what prevailed before, in the UK and elsewhere (for a discussion of these developments in the USA, see Osterman et al., 2001; for Germany, see Hassel, 1999 and 2002; and Klikauer, 2002). For example, manufacturing employment in the UK has declined dramatically since the early 1980s, there has been a significant increase in the number of part-time workers over the past two decades, and there are many more women in the labour market today. These data suggest that the labour market 'equilibrium' of the 1950s and 1960s, based on the idea of a 'male breadwinner' working full-time and earning a 'family wage', has been punctured. Those who emphasise continuity, however, would no doubt retort that the manufacturing sector has been in relative decline since 1966 (Thirlwall, 1982), part-time employment has always been a feature of the UK's industrial landscape, and female participation rates have been increasing since the end of the Second World War. But even these accounts must recognise that the labour market has 'evolved' into something rather different – to return to the analogy used in Chapter 1, the lizard now looks much more like a bird. While not ignoring continuities with the past, we highlight six aspects of change that are particularly noteworthy:

- the decline of employment in production industries and rise in service sector employment;
- the increasing participation of women in the labour force;
- the growing level of part-time work;
- changes in the location of production and employment;
- the level and changing nature of self-employment;
- the incidence of unemployment, redundancies and job insecurity.

Employment in manufacturing and service industries

Throughout the industrial world, a shift in employment from primary and secondary sectors to the tertiary, service sector has been pronounced. In the OECD countries as a whole, two-thirds of employees worked in the service sector in 2000. In eleven of the thirty OECD countries, over seven employees in every ten work in services (OECD, 2000b). Back in 1971 the proportion of employees in OECD countries that worked in service industries was five-out-of-ten, and in 1961 the proportion was just over four-in-every-ten (Blyton, 1989:137).

In the UK, in the thirty one years up to 2002, while the number employed in the service sector rose by almost nine million (an increase of almost four-fifths), the total employed in manufacturing fell by almost four-and-a-quarter million, or over half (Table 3.1). Thus, by 2002, more than five times as many people in the UK were employed in service industries than in manufacturing. When all industries are taken into account (agriculture, forestry and fishing; mining and quarrying; electricity, gas and water utilities; and construction; as well as manufacturing and services) the proportion of employees engaged in the service sector in the UK in 2002 stood at almost four-fifths (79.4%), up from just over one-half (52.6%) of all employees in 1971 who worked in services. In contrast, manufacturing employment by 2002 had fallen to one-in-seven (14.3%) of the total in employment.

Within the service sector, employment in some industries has grown significantly more rapidly than in others. Between 1992 and 2002, for example, wholesale and retail trade, hotels and restaurants, real estate, and particularly computer-related services, showed a much faster growth rate than, for example, transport and finance

Table 3.1 Changes in employment in UK manufacturing and services, 1971–2002 (thousands)

Year	Manufacturing	Services
1971	7 890	11 388
1981	6 107	13 102
1991	4 215	15 802
2001	3 834	20 216
2002	3 668	20 375
Actual change 1971–2002	− 4 222	+ 8 987
% change 1971–2002	− 53.5%	+ 78.9%

Source: Adapted from: *Employment Gazette* Historical Supplement 4 (October 1994); and *Labour Market Trends* (December 2002).

(*Labour Market Trends*, December 2002). Similarly, the continued decline in manufacturing employment during the 1990s was far more marked in certain industries (most notably the manufacture of clothing, textile and leather products which declined by over 48% between 1992 and 2002) than in others (such as chemicals, paper and food products). This shift in the industrial composition of employment affects not only employment opportunities but also the nature of work and living standards. For example, employment for many workers in the service sector involves a three-way relationship between the employee, management and the customer, rather than the dyadic management–worker relationship. Turning to income levels, average gross weekly pay is much higher in mining and quarrying (£567 in April 2001), the utilities (£509), construction (£444), and manufacturing (£436), and even higher in specific areas of manufacturing such as pharmaceuticals, medicinal/chemicals and botanical products (£610), compared to hotels (£290), retail outlets (£280–90), bars (£289), and restaurants (£265), although some service sector jobs are very well paid (most notably activities auxiliary to financial intermediation, except insurance and pension funding, with average gross weekly pay of £923 in April 2001; other financial intermediation, £704; software consultancy and supply, £700; radio and television activities, £599; advertising, £584; scheduled air services, £572; and education, £438) (Jenkins, 2002:134).

Male and female workers

The increasingly dominant position of service sector employment is also reflected in the changing composition of the workforce, particularly the proportions of male and female employees (and as we see in the next section, full-time and part-time employees). From the 1950s, but particularly from the 1970s, a growing proportion of the workforce has been female. Within the EU, 6 million of the 10 million additional jobs created between 1997 and 2000 were taken by women (European

Table 3.2 Number of females and males in employment in Britain, 1959–2002 (thousands)

	1959	1979	1992	1999	2002
Females	7 174	9 435	10 395	12 253	12 509
Males	13 817	13 176	10 911	12 607	12 674
TOTAL	20 991	22 611	21 307	24 860	25 184
Proportion of females in total (%)	34.2	41.7	48.8	49.2	49.7

Sources: *Employment Gazette* and *Labour Market Trends*, various dates.

Commission, 2001). As Table 3.2 shows, women's share in the workforce in Britain grew from just over one-third at the end of the 1950s to near parity with the numbers of male workers by 2002. Women are expected to fill more than four-fifths of the extra jobs created over the next decade (HM Treasury/DTI, 2003:8), giving the UK one of the highest female employment rates in the EU (behind Denmark and Sweden). Around 69 per cent of working age women are now in employment, compared to around 65 per cent in 1992 (ibid). Other countries outside the EU (e.g. Canada, Norway, Switzerland and the United States) also have high female employment rates, though by a significant margin the highest female employment rate is found in Iceland where almost nine-out-of-ten women of working age are in employment or seeking work (OECD, 2002d:67).

As the participation rate of women continues to rise, it may not be long before the majority of the total working population is female. In some geographic regions this is already the case. For example, the 1993 Census of Employment in Britain identified twenty-five counties and Scottish regions (out of a total of sixty-six) where the number of female employees outnumbered males (Thomas and Smith, 1995:369). In some industries and occupations, women have traditionally filled the majority of jobs. Today, over two-thirds of jobs in sales and customer service occupations, over three-quarters of jobs in administrative and secretarial occupations and over nine-tenths of caring jobs, are held by women (Duffield, 2002:615). More than half of all women in employment work in catering, cleaning, hairdressing and other personal services, or in clerical and related jobs. These tend to be low paying jobs (of the one and a half million workers whose pay was increased to £3.60 as a result of the NMW, two-thirds were women) (Low Pay Commission, 2000). The horizontal and vertical segregation of women into particular jobs is a major factor behind the inequality of pay between the sexes (average gross hourly earnings, excluding overtime, for full-time women in the UK was 81.6 per cent of the equivalent amount for men in April 2001, compared to 63 per cent in 1970) (Jenkins, 2002:129–30). Even at the same grade, the pay gap between men and women is 18 per cent.

When employment structures were organised primarily on the basis of full-time hours undertaken by male 'breadwinners', then work organisations could operate *as if* the employee was unhindered by non-work responsibilities (Beck, 1992; and Crompton, 2002). To a significant extent this remains the case, but a new, class-type polarisation in labour market situations has emerged. When they enter the labour force, young men and women now have similar levels of educational attainment, which are strongly influenced by their parents' socio-economic positions. Partnerships form and both partners continue to work until the first child is born when a new dynamic emerges. Most jobs in the UK have relatively long and inflexible hours, at least by European standards (HM Treasury/DTI, 2003:10–11) and child-care is often expensive or simply unavailable. So parents can either pay for (expensive) child-care or at least one parent must work part-time or withdraw completely from the labour force. In almost all cases where child-care is unaffordable, the woman withdraws. This reduces her work experience and accumulated human capital, certainly in relation to that of her male partner (women who return to employment after a one year gap receive a wage which is on average 16.1 per cent less than the one they had before, a wage penalty that is more than double that faced by men) (HM Treasury, 1998). As a result, it becomes economically rational for men to work (Gershuny, 2002) and the woman's role as the carer is reinforced as men work longer hours – male full-time workers in the UK are twice as likely to work long hours (over 48 hours per week) than their EU counterparts, almost 11 per cent of employees work 60 hours or more a week (typically men in professional and managerial jobs), and over a third (37 per cent) of men working full-time in couple households with dependent children work 49 or more hours a week (around one-in-seven work more than 60 hours a week) (DfEE, 2000; and HM Treasury/DTI, 2003:10–11). So as Patricia Hewitt, Secretary of State for Trade and Industry, put it, 'women suffer from the pay gap – and men suffer from the time gap' (speech to the Work Foundation, 29 May 2002). The exception to this pattern is amongst women with fathers who had relatively high levels of 'human capital' (i.e. educational qualifications and work-based skills). They are nowadays likely to have high human capital themselves and their partner is also more likely to have invested in human capital. As they can afford child-care, both parents are more likely to continue their careers in parallel (Gershuny, 2002).

The rise in women's paid work activity – and in particular the increase in dual earner households and lone parent employment – has given greater importance to policies and practices to reconcile the competing demands of work and family life. Further, given the widespread refusal, reluctance or tardiness that the majority of men have shown to shoulder a fairer share of family and household responsibilities (see OECD, 2001; and Sullivan, 2000), these 'family friendly' or 'work-life balance' issues have a particular significance for women seeking or currently in paid employment. For example, a survey by the recruitment agency Reed, as part of the DTI's Work-Life Balance Campaign, found that 46 per cent of job seekers cited flexible working as the benefit they would look for most in their next job, a third would prefer flexible working to £1000 extra pay per annum, 68 per cent wanted the chance to work flexibly when necessary, and 77 per cent of parents with children under the age of 6 years said work-life balance was an important factor in deciding on a new job (www.dti.gov.uk). Another survey found that 92 per cent of non-working mothers said that flexible working arrangements would be either 'essential' or 'important' to help them back into work. Around 63 per cent of women in employment at the time of child birth returned to work at the end of their maternity leave (this figure rises to 74 per cent 12 months after the birth) (Women and Equality Unit, 2001).

In terms of the employing organisation, work-life balance issues currently fall mainly into three categories:

- policies providing time off for child-bearing, emergency child-care and/or career breaks,
- arrangements to create shorter and/or more flexible work schedules that allow work and non-work time demands to be reconciled more easily (for example via part-time working, flexible work hours, term time working, working at or from home, and job sharing), and
- workplace provisions to support parents such as child-care facilities or subsidies (Glass and Estes, 1997; and Thornthwaite, 2002).

The first category is the most highly regulated, particularly in relation to maternity and parental leave. The Employment Act 2002, for example, gave further support to maternity leave via an increase in entitlement from 18 to 26 weeks paid and a further 26 weeks unpaid maternity leave, and increases in the standard rate of Statutory Maternity Pay and in the Maternity Allowance from £75 to £100 (or, if less, a weekly rate equal to 90 per cent of the woman's average weekly earnings). In addition, in line with the European Parental Leave Directive, men are now entitled to 2 weeks paid paternity leave; adoptive parents are now entitled to 26 weeks paid and a further 26 weeks unpaid leave; and from 6 April 2003, for the first time, mothers and fathers of young children under 6 years, or disabled children under 18 years, have a right to request a flexible working arrangement. Employers have a statutory duty to consider such requests seriously and according to a set procedure, and they are only be able to refuse requests where they have a clear business reason.

In terms of other flexible and family-friendly arrangements, the WERS98 employee survey found that whilst almost one-third of employees indicated they had access to flexitime and just over one-quarter to parental leave (this survey was undertaken prior to the legislation mentioned above) far smaller proportions perceived that they had access to job-sharing or the facility to work at or from home, and just one-in-twenty-five workers indicated they had access to a workplace nursery or child-care subsidy. Perceived access to all these arrangements was higher in the public than in the private sector, in larger than smaller organisations (Cully *et al.*, 1999:143–6), and in unionised workplaces (Fernie and Gray, 2001). Data from the British Household Panel Survey (BHPS) 1998 reveals that 36 per cent of men in full-time jobs and over 40 per cent of women in full-time jobs would prefer to work fewer hours at the prevailing wage (just over 9 per cent of men in part-time jobs and just under 10 per cent of women in part-time jobs want fewer hours). Less than 7 per cent of men in full-time jobs and just over 4 per cent of full-time women wanted more hours (Böheim and Taylor, 2001).

Although examples of family-friendly policies are increasingly well publicised, enhancing the support and choice for families requires a shift in the UK's working culture (see HM Treasury/DTI, 2003). The Government is therefore keen to disseminate 'best practice' and highlight the benefits to business as well as employees of family friendly policies (ibid; and DTI, 2003). Examples of 'best practice' in the retail sector, where firms are heavily dependent on female staff, include:

Asda
- childcare leave allows parents to stop work for a short period during the summer holidays, returning in term-time with continuous service and maintained benefits
- store management positions are available on a job share basis to enable staff to manage their work and home commitments
- a shift swapping scheme enables colleagues to be absent from work for specific family or domestic reasons.

Marks & Spencer
- there are flexible working, home and part-time working, job-share, educational sponsorship, secondments, career leave and flexible retirement options
- a confidential employee helpline is available to advise and support staff on work-life balance issues
- parents are able to take time off to attend appointments during pregnancy and IVF treatment
- time off is available for foster carers
- mothers going back to work following maternity leave have a range of options, including gradual return and term-time working, and a 'child break' scheme is in place for those who do not wish to start work again immediately.

Sainsbury's
- career breaks, job sharing, dual store contracts are available
- leave for fertility treatment and time off for emergencies are given
- employees are able to suggest to their line manager a working pattern that would suit them, and as long as there is a strong business case and it fits in with colleagues, it will be seriously considered.

Employers with flexible working and HR policies that support employees' work-life balance choices report a range of benefits. These include an improvement in staff morale and a decrease in absenteeism and turnover, retention of skilled staff and improved returns from training, and fewer recruitment problems (shortages) and a reduction in recruitment costs (HM Treasury/DTI, 2003:20). In addition, family-friendly work practices are associated with above average financial performance, labour productivity and other measures of organisational performance (Dex and Smith, 2002; and Gray, 2001a and 2001b). However, both case study and survey evidence suggest that employees who reduce their working hours in order to accommodate their family life still experience a negative impact on their career prospects, which might also mean that potential performance is lost to their employer (see Gray, 2001a and 2001b). The proportion of women returning to work part-time following maternity leave rose from 29 per cent to 42 per cent between 1988 and 1996 (the proportion returning to work full-time increased from 15 per cent to 24 per cent over the same period), and the majority of women in couples with young children and a partner in full-time work tend themselves to have part-time rather than full-time jobs (HM Treasury/DTI, 2003:16). To a large extent, the predominance of part-time working reflects choice – almost 73 per cent of women working part-time say they do not want a full-time job (Eurostat, 2000) – but this does not equate with adequate support for working women, especially as many part-time jobs are poorly paid.

Part-time employment

Alongside the growth in service sector employment and the proportion of the workforce that is female, the majority of developed countries have experienced a significant increase over the last two decades in the number of employees working part-time. Across the OECD industrial countries as a whole, and similarly among the EU members, approximately one-in-six employees worked part-time in 2000 (OECD, 2002b:18). However, this proportion varies considerably from country to country – in the EU, for example, as few as one-in-nineteen workers work part-time in Greece, while almost one-in-three employees work part-time in the Netherlands (Table 3.3).

In the UK, the incidence of part-time working among female employees has remained fairly stable in recent years (Duffield, 2002) although among men the incidence of part-time working has been rising, albeit from a much lower base. A similar rise in the proportion of men working part-time is also evident in the majority of EU countries (Table 3.3), but in all EU countries women's share of total part-time employment far exceeds that of men. On average, just under four-out-of-five (79%) of all part-time jobs in the EU were held by women at the turn of the twenty-first century (OECD, 2002b:19). In the UK, the vast majority (over nine-out-of-ten) of part-time jobs are located in the service sector. Industries particularly

Table 3.3 Part-time employment in the EU, 1990–2000 (persons usually working < 30 hours per week in their main job)

| | Part-time employment as a % of total employment | | | | | |
| | Men | | Women | | All | |
Country	1990	2000	1990	2000	1990	2000
Austria	n/a	2.6	n/a	24.4	n/a	12.2
Belgium	4.6	7.1	29.8	34.5	14.2	19.0
Denmark	10.2	8.9	29.6	23.5	19.0	15.7
Finland	4.7	7.1	10.6	13.9	7.5	10.4
France	4.4	5.3	21.7	24.3	12.2	14.2
Germany	2.3*	4.8	29.8*	33.9	13.4*	17.6
Greece	4.0	3.0	11.5	9.4	6.7	5.4
Ireland	4.2	7.7	20.5	32.2	9.8	18.4
Italy	3.9	5.7	18.2	23.4	8.8	12.2
Luxembourg	1.6	2.1	19.1	28.9	7.6	13.0
Netherlands	13.4	13.4	52.5	57.5	28.2	32.1
Portugal	3.1	4.8	11.8	14.7	6.8	9.2
Spain	1.4	2.7	11.5	16.5	4.6	7.8
Sweden	5.3	7.3	24.5	21.4	14.5	14.0
UK	5.3	8.4	39.5	40.8	20.1	23.0
EU average	4.2	6.0	27.0	30.0	13.3	16.3

Note: * Former West Germany only
Source: Adapted from OECD, 2002b.

reliant on part-time working include retail distribution, hotels and restaurants, health and social work, and education. Within individual occupational groups, the highest rates of part-time working are to be found among cleaning workers and bar staff. Across the economy as a whole, more than one-in-five workplaces now employ a predominantly part-time workforce (Cully *et al.*, 1999:32–3).

While the amount of part-time working among women has continued to increase in many countries, it is not necessarily correct to assume that this trend will continue in the long term. Some writers have suggested, for example, that a high level of part-time working among women may be a transitional phase between a 'male breadwinner' model of the labour market and a labour market where men and women's participation is more equal, at least in terms of volume (see Bosch, 2001). In the UK, however, the dominant pattern of household work organisation is for men to work full-time and women part-time, and more couples would like to follow this pattern (if stated preferences were realised the 'single earner' household model would fall by over half and there would be fewer households where both men and women worked full-time) (HM Treasury/DTI, 2003:6–7). Some 36 per cent of people in work have a dependent child but this figure rises to 56 per cent for women in part-time work (compared to 28 per cent for women in full-time work) (ibid:9).

As the economic activity of women with dependent children continues to grow the demand for 'less than full-time' employment increases (ibid; and Desai *at al.*, 1999). It is interesting to note that in countries with stronger employment rights and a more extensive range of 'family friendly' work practices that facilitate the combination of full-time jobs and child bearing/rearing activities, as found in several Scandinavian countries, the incidence of part-time working among women has fallen in the last decade (see Table 3.3).

Changes in the location of employment

As well as shifts in the gender composition and proportions of part-time and full-time employment, there have been changes taking place in the locations where people work. In particular, the decline in the proportion of workers employed in traditional manufacturing industries has been reflected in more overall employment growth taking place outside the main industrial conurbations. Not only has much service sector employment tended to have been located elsewhere, but many new manufacturing developments have tended to locate outside traditional industrial areas than hitherto, preferring to develop new economic activity on 'greenfield' sites, in semi-rural areas. This decline of industrial conurbations accelerated in the 1980s and 1990s but has been occurring for over a generation. Between 1960 and 1978, for example, the level of manufacturing employment in Britain located in rural areas (districts in which all settlements have less than 35 000 people) increased by 38 per cent; this contrasts with a fall of over 26 per cent in manufacturing employment in the six major industrial conurbations over the same period (Massey, 1988:61; see also Sayer and Walker, 1992). Parallel declines have occurred elsewhere, such as in parts of northern France and northeastern USA (Hoerr, 1988; Hudson and Sadler, 1989). Thus, not only are the arenas of employee relations increasingly likely to be located in service sector activity rather than in manufacturing, those arenas are also increasingly likely to be found away from those industrial regions which contain more extensive trade union traditions than the semi-rural districts in which 'greenfield' and other developments are being increasingly located.

The regional distribution of jobs has a major impact on recruitment and retention, especially in the public sector where national pay scales apply. The forces of supply and demand dictate that pay will be higher in regions with a higher employment rate, lower unemployment, and fast growing industries. Average gross weekly pay in April 2001 was £594 in London compared to £381 in North East England; in South East England, weekly pay was £473 compared to £382 in Wales. The National Health Service and the education sector face particularly acute recruitment problems in London and the South East. University lecturers, for example, are paid according to a national salary scale with a London Allowance for those living in the capital. This Allowance has remained unchanged for the past 10 years (at just £2134 per annum) while property prices have soared by 145 per cent since 1992 and the cost of travel in London Zones 1–3 has increased by 53 per cent over the same period. Newly appointed lecturers on a salary of just over £20 000 per annum can no longer afford housing within the 'golden triangle' of London, Cambridge and Oxford. Those with qualifications in science and engineering, business and economics, computing and statistics, can command much higher salaries in the private sector. Thus, relative wage levels have a major impact on employment across the regions and between the public and private sectors within those regions.

At the micro level, another significant development, at least for a minority of the workforce, is the opportunity to work from home (see Felstead and Jewson, 2000). One of the main areas of growth in homeworking in recent years has been the expansion of teleworking. Teleworkers are defined as those who undertake some paid or unpaid work in their own home and who use both a telephone and a computer. This definition includes both people who always or mainly work from home and those who work occasionally (at least one day per week) from home. In 2001 there were 2.2 million teleworkers in the UK, comprising over 7 per cent of the total in employment (Hotopp, 2002). This number has been increasing rapidly in recent years (up by two-thirds between 1997 and 2001) and is expected to continue growing. Two-thirds of teleworkers are men and a high proportion is self-employed (over two in five, compared to just over one in ten of the labour force as a whole). Around three-quarters of teleworkers are employed in the private sector, particularly in professional, managerial and technical occupations. In comparative terms, the UK stands just above the EU average for the proportion of its labour force engaged in teleworking, but overall the EU has a much lower level than the United States, where one study indicates that as many as 21 per cent of the labour force are engaged in teleworking (see Hotopp, 2002:316).

Self-employment

Up to now in this chapter we have focused on changes taking place among the employed workforce. In the UK, this group represents around four-fifths of the total labour force. The remaining fifth comprises those who are unemployed (see below); those who are serving in the armed forces (204 000 in September 2002); those on government training programmes (91 000); unpaid family members (95 000); and the self-employed. Self-employment increased only slightly between 1961 and 1981, but during the 1980s the number of self-employed rose by one-half to over 3 million by 1990 (Table 3.4) as high levels of unemployment, limited job vacancies and state support for those moving from being unemployed to self-employed, stimulated a growth in self-employment. Some industrial relations texts exclude the self-employed because they are not engaged in a direct employment relationship with a capitalist employer (e.g. Edwards, 2003:2), but the data indicate that these workers play an increasingly important role in the activities of 'mainstream' work organisations. In recent years, for example, many companies have terminated employment contracts with some groups of their workforce (often those operating outside the main workplace, such as service engineers and drivers) offering instead commercial contracts that have required these former employees to alter their status to being 'self-employed', even though many are still almost entirely dependent on their former employer for 'business' (see Evans, 1990 for an analysis of this pattern in the construction industry). A recent survey of entrepreneurship in the UK found that one in every hundred people in the UK start up a business (become self-employed) because they have no better choice for work (called 'necessity entrepreneurs') (Harding, 2002:4).

During the 1990s, the level of self-employment stabilised at around one-in-nine of the labour force. In comparative terms, the UK's rate of self-employment is slightly below both the EU average (where self-employment represented 13.6 per cent of total employment in 2000) and the OECD average (14.3 per cent). However, rates of self-employment vary considerably from country to country, and are far higher where agriculture and small family businesses remain major sectors of activity (such as Greece where over 30 per cent of the labour force were self-employed in 2000) in contrast to more industrial countries such as the United States where just over 7 per cent of the labour force were self-employed in 2000 (OECD, 2002c:19). A significant difference between the UK and other EU countries is the higher levels of human capital among the self employed in other Member States (Cowling, 2003).

Men comprise around two-thirds of the self-employed in Britain. Just under four out of five (78 per cent) of self-employed worked full-time in 2002, with self-employed women more likely to work part-time than men. The gap between men and women has narrowed in recent years, but is still greater in the UK than many other industrialised economies (Harding, 2002:5). Most (over two-thirds) of the self-employed operate with no employees (Campbell and Daly, 1992) and many do not 'own a business' (many are 'labour-only sub-contractors' whose employers have simply shifted their job from 'employee' to 'self-employed' status in the manner noted above) (see Cowling, 2003; Dale and Kerr, 1995:462).

Self-employment is often equated with 'entrepreneurship' (defined as 'any attempt at new business or new venture creation'), which is one of the

Table 3.4 Changes in the level of self-employment in Britain, 1961–2001 (thousands)

	1961	1971	1981	1991	2001
Number of self-employed	1 665	1 953	2 058	3 066	3 205
Total labour force	24 221	24 637	26 028	27 614	28 871
Percentage of labour force which is self-employed	6.9	7.9	7.9	11.1	11.1

Sources: Department of Employment Gazette, Labour Market Trends, various issues.

Government's key competitiveness indicators (DTI, 2001). Survey data suggest that 4-in-every-100 people who start up a business in the UK do so because of an opportunity, with entrepreneurial activity highest among Asian people (who are twice as likely to be involved in autonomous start-ups as their white counterparts) and in the East of England, London and the South East (Harding, 2002:4–5). Despite a favourable environment for the self-employed (HM Treasury/DTI, 2001:9), entrepreneurial activity in the UK is poor by international standards (DTI, 2001), ranking 23rd out of 37 countries in a recent international study (Harding, 2002).

Temporary work

The extent of temporary work has increased in several industrial countries over the past two decades (for example France, the Netherlands and Spain) (OECD, 2002c) and is one factor used to support arguments that paid work is becoming more insecure (see below). Essentially, temporary employment contracts provide employment flexibility in those countries with strong employment protection for permanent workers. The experience of the UK is somewhat different as weak employment protection has been associated with a lower and more stable percentage of the workforce in temporary jobs (Booth *et al.*, 2002a).

There are several different forms of temporary work, including agency jobs (often referred to as 'temping'), fixed-term contracts, casual work and seasonal work. In the UK, temporary workers increased as a proportion of total employees in the first half of the 1990s, but this has not been sustained in more recent years (see Table 3.5). In certain sectors, however, temporary work continues to grow apace. Higher education is perhaps the best example – in 2000/01, 42 per cent of total staff were employed on fixed-term contracts and 73 per cent of the 20 000 new entrants were hired on temporary contracts. This pattern is repeated elsewhere in the public sector, which makes greater use of fixed-term contracts than the private sector (Cully *et al.*, 1999:35).

Within the overall group of temporary workers in the UK, the 1990s saw a growth in the number of temporary agency workers ('temps'), stable levels of those

Table 3.5 Temporary working in the UK, 1992–2002

	1992	1994	1996	1998	2000	2002
Temporary employees (thousands)	1304	1492	1671	1748	1733	1546
Total as % of all employees	5.9	6.8	7.4	7.4	7.1	6.4

Source: *Labour Market Trends*, various issues.

on fixed-term contracts, and declines in the number of seasonal workers and other forms of temporary work (OECD, 2002c:134). According to the UK Labour Force Survey data, of those working on a temporary basis in 2002, just over one quarter (27 per cent) were doing so because they could not find a permanent job, and a further 30 per cent were working in a temporary job because they did not want a permanent job (the remainder were working in temporary jobs for some other reason).

Employment agencies play an increasingly important role as major employers (or suppliers) of temporary labour, on both a national and international scale. Manpower Inc., for example, is now the largest firm worldwide in terms of the number of people on its books (2.7 million in 2000) (Boxall and Purcell, 2003:207). Labour Force Survey figures for the UK reveal that the number of temps increased from 50 000 in 1984 to 250 000 in 1999. Temps constituted 1.1 per cent of the employed labour force by the end of the 1990s (Forde, 2001:631). Although one function of agencies is to provide employers with temporary labour that might subsequently be selected for direct employment by the client organisation, Forde's study of employment agencies in Leeds and Telford reveals how the provision of 'repeat workers' and other strategies pursued by agencies to build relationships with client firms can exacerbate the contingent and insecure nature of temping. This is one reason why the Government has sought to make the employment agency responsible for providing basic employment rights for temps.

Although temporary contracts are often regarded as an important source of labour market flexibility, in the UK and other LMEs employers have a range of other options open to them including (less regulated) part-time work and the greater ability to lay-off permanent workers. Moreover, many employers have found problems with temporary labour in terms of low levels of motivation and retention of such staff (Purcell et al., 1999). There are also considerable costs to employees who work on temporary contracts. A survey of 200 unionised workplaces by the TUC (2001), for example, found that half of firms paid temporary workers different rates from permanent workers, 70 per cent did not offer the same access to occupational pension schemes, 25 per cent did not give access to contractual sick leave, and 14 per cent did not give paid holidays (see also OECD, 2002c). Using longitudinal data from the British Household Panel Survey (1991–97), Booth et al. (2002b) found considerable wage penalties for workers who previously held temporary jobs. Even with 10 years experience, having held one seasonal/casual job has a wage penalty of 12.3 per cent for men and 8.8 per cent for women. The penalty arising from one fixed-term contract, again after 10 years experience, was 5 per cent for men. Women who previously held fixed-term contracts, in contrast, were able to catch up with their permanent counterparts within a period of 7–10 years. At least for this group, temporary contracts might be a 'stepping stone' to permanent employment in good jobs, rather than just 'dead end' jobs with poor pay and prospects.

Unemployment, redundancy and job insecurity

Even though unemployment levels have fallen significantly in recent years, unemployment levels over the past two decades in the UK have been far higher than during the previous thirty year period. Precise comparisons are hindered by the many changes that have been made to the basis on which unemployment figures are compiled. Bearing this qualification in mind, official unemployment increased steadily following the oil price rises and resulting economic setbacks in the mid 1970s. By the late 1970s the average level of unemployment was around 1.25 million, 5.6 per cent of the workforce (Table 3.6). However, a marked acceleration in unemployment occurred in Britain during the early 1980s (peaking eventually at 3.21 million unemployed in February 1986). In the latter 1980s, unemployment levels fell steadily, yet despite substantial economic growth during this period they only fell to around 1.5 million (in June 1990) before commencing to rise again as economic recession reappeared and subsequently deepened. By January 1993 more than 3 million people were registered unemployed, equivalent to over 10 per cent of the workforce. Despite falls in unemployment in recent years, by the beginning of 2003 there remained almost 1 million people (998 000) officially registered as unemployed in the UK, and among certain groups (such as the young and ethnic minorities) unemployment rates are persistently much higher. In the UK and many other industrial countries, for example, the youth unemployment rate (that is, for those under 25 years) is double the rate of general unemployment (OECD, 2002b).

Table 3.6 Unemployment rates in the UK, 1945–2002 (five-year averages)

Year	Yearly average (%)
1945–49	2.1
1950–54	1.7
1955–59	1.7
1960–64	1.9
1965–69	2.1
1970–74	3.1
1975–79	5.6
1980–84	11.1
1985–89	9.7
1990–94	8.7
1995–99	7.1
2000–02	5.2*

* Three-year average
Sources: Calculated from Denman and McDonald (1996), and *Labour Market Trends*.

In reality, however, levels of unemployment are much higher than the official figures (unemployed benefit claimant count) suggest. The basis of unemployment statistics is the number of people who are out of work and claiming benefit from Employment Service offices; since May 1979 the basis of these statistics has altered over thirty times. Groups who are jobless but who are excluded from the unemployment figures include: women who have no call on means-tested benefits because they have a working partner; men over the age of 60 who do not have to register as job seekers; recipients of sickness or invalidity benefit; and those who have exhausted their entitlement to the Jobseekers' Allowance and fail to qualify for income-related allowance. The higher official rate of unemployment in recent years compared to the period before the late 1970s is also despite a marked reduction in the number of young people entering the labour market, as a result of both demographic trends and an increased tendency for young people to remain in full-time education.

It is important to appreciate that unemployment is not a 'stagnant pool' of workers unable to secure gainful employment but a constantly changing mix of people moving into and out of un/employment. However, the experience of unemployment can damage the worker's chances of securing long-term employment. Data from the BHPS, based on the work histories of 7000 people, reveal that individuals who find work after being unemployed are four times more likely to become unemployed compared to workers who enter a new job directly from another job. One in five men and women re-enter unemployment within 12 months of starting a job (less than half the jobs that follow unemployment last for 12 months or more). There are two main causes of short job tenure: those who have previously been unemployed are more likely to take up temporary jobs; and they are also more likely to be laid off (ISER, 2001:9). It is easier, and less expensive, to dismiss short-tenure employees who do not qualify for statutory employment protection (those with less than 1 year's service) or for statutory redundancy payments (those with less than 2 years' service).

Between 1990 and 2000 over seven million redundancies were declared in Britain. Whilst redundancies have always been part of the experience of paid work, what is new in the recent period are some of the causes of redundancy. In the past, redundancies have been a consequence of economic difficulty, as Cappelli (1995b:577) comments: 'Firms clearly laid off workers because of cyclical downturns or other situations where their business declined, but reductions in other situations were extremely uncommon'. However, it has become increasingly common for employers to announce redundancies as a cost-cutting measure even at times when the business and the economic outlook are buoyant. 'Workforce reductions are increasingly strategic or structural in nature as opposed to a response to short-term economic conditions' (ibid:577). Recent experience in the UK demonstrates this tendency: firms announce redundancies when they are doing badly *and* when whey are doing well, with the constant reduction in workforce totals being used as a method of cost control. WERS98 data indicate that while a third of establishments reduced employment because of falling demand, 40 per cent said that job cuts were also part of a cost reduction programme and as many again cited reorganisation (Turnbull and Wass, 2001). A key reason for this is that outside the organisation – and particularly among shareholders and investment markets – cutting workforce levels has come to be taken as a sign of restructuring, efficiency-saving and likely improvement in profitability (see Turnbull and Wass, 2000). The upshot is that redundancy announcements can improve share prices, especially in the days immediately following lay off announcements (ibid; see also Cameron, 1994:183–4; and Worrell et al., 1991).

One of many examples of this in the UK came in February 2001 when Corus, the Anglo-Dutch steel-maker, announced over six thousand redundancies in Britain – more than one-fifth of its UK workforce. The job cuts involved the ending of steel-making at one of its two South Wales plants, the closing of two finishing plants, and reductions in workforce numbers at several other plants. On the day of the announcement, the company's share price, which had been falling in the previous period, immediately jumped by over 9 per cent in its value (see also Chapter 7). At the same time, however, evidence suggests that the effect of redundancies on stock market values is no more than a short-term palliative (companies rarely if ever shrink their way to success). As an editorial in the UK's *Management Today* magazine put it in the mid 1990s:

> Too many companies today are preoccupied with the benefits to the bottom line that can come from paring away at fixed costs. This has become an obsession, like anorexia. Management eyes the already feeble corporate frame, and continues to slash at yet more pockets of what it perceives to be fat. (February 1995)

As a result, downsizing is rarely 'lean', in terms of being part of a *systematic* programme to improve organisational performance through just-in-time, total quality management, team working and the like, but it is often 'mean', with adverse effects on employees (both victims and survivors) and organisational performance (see Kinnie et al., 1998).

Managers have also been the 'victims' of corporate restructuring. A recent survey of members of the Institute of Management found that managers who survive a reorganisation programme with redundancies are more likely to report lower levels of morale, motivation and loyalty to their company. They are also more likely to report the emergence of a 'blame culture' in their organisation, a general decline in morale, and less importance attached to employees or human resource management (i.e. managers are less likely to view employees as the organisation's greatest asset) (see Worrall et al., 2000:659–64).

Over the past decade, the redundancy rate (measured as the number of redundancies per annum for every 1000 employees) has gradually declined, although, as Table 3.7 illustrates, it is much higher in manufacturing than services.

Table 3.7 Redundancy rate (number of redundancies per 1000 employees)

Year	Manufacturing	Services	Other	All
1992	15	8	26	11
1993	14	7	15	9
1994	11	6	16	7
1995	10	7	13	8
1996	11	6	19	8
1997	10	6	18	7
1998	12	6	10	7
1999	16	5	17	8
2000	16	5	11	7

Sources: Labour Force Survey and Office for National Statistics.

'Other industries' include construction which in 1992 had a redundancy rate of 30 per 1000 employees. In Spring 2002 the aggregate redundancy rate was just 8.1, which has led some commentators to ask why so many employees report feelings of 'job insecurity' – if just 0.8 per cent of employees experience redundancy, why do opinion polls and other surveys regularly report that somewhere between 25–50 per cent express a 'fear of redundancy' (Doogan, 2001:435–6)? In the first instance, this fear stems from inadequate employment protection for many (short-service) employees, the ease with which employers in the UK can declare redundancies on economic grounds alone, and the ability of the employer to control selection (i.e. to decide who goes and who stays) (see Turnbull and Wass, 2000). It is interesting to note that even when the firm has a formal policy of 'guaranteed job security' or 'no compulsory redundancies' it is no less likely to experience job losses and its employees are just as likely to report feelings of job insecurity (Cully *et al.*, 1999:189). Second, even though relatively few *individuals* may experience redundancy, 40 per cent of *establishments* responding to WERS98 reported redundancies (Turnbull and Wass, 2001). Thus, many more employees will have been touched by redundancy in some way. Third, the fear this creates is compounded by anxiety over the consequences of unemployment, which is evident even amongst those who are confident about keeping their job (see Burchell *et al.*, 1999). This anxiety is understandable when one considers that the costs of unemployment facing British men in terms of real wage losses have increased by 40 per cent over the past two decades (Nickell *et al.*, 2002). As a result, full-time workers in the prime of their career feel most insecure (especially those with children) (Cully *et al.*, 1999:167–8). Finally, the government's role must not be overlooked, most notably in terms of promoting labour market flexibility, the 'marketisation' of public services, and the further 'opening-up' of the economy to international competitive pressure. These policies serve to 'manufacture insecurity':

Insecurity is the outcome of a conscious strategy of government that arises from attempts to increase the productivity and competitiveness of the economy ... it serves to discipline the workforce through a variety of means, by altering the atmosphere in which wage negotiations take place, by changing the environment in which the terms and conditions of contracts are specified, and dampening public expectations of what the state should provide by way of social protection. (Doogan, 2001:439)

Those who lose their job are most likely to experience an 'irregular' pattern of work – periods of employment punctuated by spells of unemployment – and as a result are more likely to experience feelings of job insecurity (see Burchell *et al.*, 1999; Gregg and Wadsworth, 1995:74; Heery and Salmon, 2000). For these workers, employment has became 'a much more precarious affair with insecurity, redundancy, temporary contracts and unemployment contributing to an overall experience of a fragmented, rather than a unified, working life' (Noon and Blyton, 2002:45). In the 1970s, the 'average' person had six to seven jobs in their working lifetime; by the 1990s this average had risen to eleven to twelve jobs. However, long term employment with one employer is still the experience of a substantial minority of workers – in 1999 a third of the workforce in the UK had worked for the same

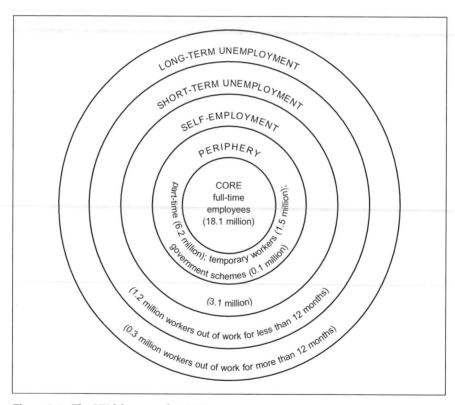

Figure 3.4 The UK labour market 2002

employer for ten or more years (Doogan, 2001:423–7) – which is indicative of further polarisation in the labour market alongside temporary/permanent jobs, full-time/part-time employment, work rich/work poor households, time rich/time poor jobs, family-friendly/unfriendly organisations, and high-paid/low-paid jobs.

These various developments in the labour market – growth in the proportions of female, part-time, and self-employed in the workforce, increasing proportions working in service rather than manufacturing activities, away from the traditional industrial heartlands, the persistence of high levels of unemployment even in periods of economic growth, and increasing job insecurity – indicate the extent to which the context of employee relations in the UK has altered from that prevailing a generation ago. Not only has the typical arena changed, but the nature of the typical employee constituency has also altered significantly, with that constituency bringing to the fore new employee relations priorities such as the need for practices to improve work-life balance. Moreover, the widespread experience of redundancy, unemployment, and job insecurity impacts considerably on how employees view work, the employment relationship, and their relations with employers. The structure of the UK labour market is depicted in Figure 3.4, which sub-divides the labour force into three broad categories: a core of full-time employees, a periphery of part-time and temporary workers together with the self-employed, and finally, those out of work, differentiated between the short- and long-term unemployed.

As well as the broader economic developments and overall shifts in labour market activity which we have identified above, important changes in the intra- and inter-organisational context have also been taking place. Indeed, the former are intimately related to the latter. It is to these organisational developments that we now turn.

Organisational changes

Several developments relating to the structure of organisations, to inter-organisational relations and to the nature of production processes, impact directly upon the contexts within which employee relations take place. First, in terms of patterns of *ownership and control*, we have already noted certain prominent trends such as the expansion of trans-national operations and different forms of joint venture activity. One of the employee relations issues raised in later chapters is the extent to which trans-national 'transplants', such as the expansion of Japanese companies in the UK, have acted to stimulate more widespread changes in managerial approaches to employee relations. Further, as Beaumont (1992a) comments, where joint ventures involve organisations from different countries, this raises significant questions not only concerning the ability of venturers to accommodate different employee relations 'styles' but also the extent to which joint venturing may stimulate change in the parties' approaches to those relations (see also Boxall and Purcell, 2003:220–6).

Other changes in the ownership and control of organisations are also highly relevant to the analysis and experience of employee relations. As companies have sought to position themselves more effectively in their existing product markets, or enter new ones, any resulting concentration or diversification strategies, and any related acquisition and/or divestment activity, creates not only greater uncertainty among employees regarding the form of ownership and control, but in many cases has resulted in the breaking of previously long-standing ownership relations. One effect for employees is that their representatives are increasingly faced with dealing with new management cadres and employers, whose main business may well lie in other spheres of activity, frequently in another country. Nor is this a situation faced only by workers in large organisations such as Jaguar employees following the purchase by Ford, Asda employees after its purchase by Wal-Mart, or ICL taken over by Fujitsu. For example, the experience of the two hundred or so employees at a plant manufacturing industrial components just outside Cardiff is not untypical of thousands of employees in similar work contexts elsewhere. Having been part of a UK business for several decades, the employees in the Welsh plant found themselves taken over, hived off and taken over again in the space of three years, the second time by an American company whose main activity was brewing beer! Take-over activity is far greater in the UK than other comparable economies: in the 1980s, for example, three-quarters of all hostile take-overs in the European Community occurred in the UK.

To date, structures of ownership and control have been studied more by those concerned with corporate strategy and organisational analysis than those specially focusing on employee relations – though notable exceptions include the work of Purcell (1991; and Purcell and Gray, 1986), the surveys conducted by researchers at Warwick University (Marginson et al., 1988 and 1993; and Purcell et al., 1987) and the case studies on new organisational forms by researchers at UMIST (Rubery et al., 2002). But earlier research on employee relations indicates that many of the dominant forces for change during the decade were *beyond* the traditional boundaries of the subject (e.g. Ahlstrand and Purcell, 1988; Hendry, 1990; and Marchington and Parker, 1990). As Purcell (1991:38) notes, developments in business policies and corporate strategies concerned with the structure, shape and control systems of the firm have forced personnel and industrial relations managers, often reluctantly, to restructure collective bargaining arrangements and other traditional methods of managing the workforce. This is especially so among the large companies which dominate the UK economy, where there has been a devolution to profit centres within the organisation and a focus on 'strategic business units' (SBUs). But the process is one of both disintegration *and* integration, as operations are often broken down into smaller units but within the context of large firms retaining overall control and command (Amin and Dietrich, 1990; and Blackburn, 1990). In other words, although large firms still dominate the economy, 'what has changed is the *way* in which they dominate'

(Turnbull and Weston, 1993a:118). Instead of controlling productive activity through vertical integration, for example, many large firms have sub-divided their core operations into SBUs and moved towards a system of 'quasi-vertical integration' (Turnbull, 1991a). As Purcell notes,

> [SBUs] have tougher requirements to meet in terms of performance targets. The emphasis is placed on performance and productivity within the business unit and greater monitoring of results from corporate and divisional head office through the performance control systems. (1991:38)

The latest WERS98 data in fact indicate a substantial reduction in the decision-making capacity of workplace managers during the 1990s, especially in relation to the use of any financial or budgetary surplus (Millward *et al.*, 2000:78–9).

The effects on employee relations from decentralisation, therefore, are likely to be pressures for both quantitative and qualitative improvements in performance under the more watchful eye of corporate management. These pressures are likely to be particularly acute in those industries where product market competition is most intense, such as civil aviation (Blyton *et al.*, 2001) but similar pressures are evident in the public sector as a result of financial management initiatives, external quality audits, centrally imposed performance standards and cash limits (see *inter alia*, Bach and Winchester, 2003; Bailey, 1994 and 1996; Beaumont, 1992b; Corby and White, 1999; Ferner, 1989; Foster and Scott, 1998; and Pendleton and Winterton, 1993).

Intra-organisational developments such as these represent a shift to *organisation-based* employment systems, rather than an industry or occupational basis (Dore, 1989; and Katz and Darbishire, 2000). Essentially, the organisation is seeking to insulate itself from the external labour market but *not* from the product market. For some this represents 'the replacement of class struggle with the struggle for markets. No longer us workers against them management, but us Company X against them Company Y people' (*Financial Times*, 7 September 1985). Greenfield sites are an extreme example of this broader-based development, where companies such as Nissan and Toyota have sought to reach an agreement with a single trade union before production even begins, and therefore before any workers are even hired, in order not only to dictate terms but to create a *firm-specific* relationship with the union in question. In general, as Purcell (1991:41) cautions, it is difficult to judge how extensive or how effective the development of organisational-based employment systems will be, but what is clear is that managerial *intentions* are markedly different from the past. This is perhaps best illustrated by management attempts to engender a form of psychological as well as economic dependency from employees (ibid:40). The emphasis is on winning the 'hearts and minds' of the workforce, epitomised by the attempt of human resource management initiatives to engender greater employee commitment (see Appelbaum *et al.*, 2000; Blyton and Turnbull, 1992; Legge, 1995; and Chapter 4).

In addition to changes in the structure of individual organisations, the last decade has seen significant change in inter-organisational relations. We have already noted the presence of joint venture activity as organisations join forces to spread risk, share research and development costs, rationalise production and marketing activities, and strengthen market position. Also important is the expansion of organisational networks incorporating for example, agencies, outsourcing, franchising, and public-private partnerships, which are generating growing numbers of situations where employees share a common work location but are employed by several different employers (Rubery *et al.*, 2002). Arrangements such as franchising allow franchiser organisations to secure a greater presence in a market without incurring significant capital outlay to fund expansion or increases in direct employment (Felstead, 1993). Much comment has also been made on the growth of sub-contracting arrangements to undertake both service activities (such as catering, cleaning and transport) and production-related work. Sub-contracting is one of the factors believed to account for the growth of small firms during the past two decades and is generally viewed as being functional for larger companies, who are able to dominate and to a large extent determine the environment faced by small firms. As a result, pay and conditions of employment are likely to be inferior at smaller firms. Size, however, is secondary to the relationship with the client company and the wider economy (Curran, 1990:130; and Chapter 9). Thus, Holmes (1986:89–95) suggests that sub-contracting can be used to accommodate not only structural and temporal instability in product markets, but also establish different levels of 'minimum efficient scale', and respond to the structure and nature of different labour supply conditions. The last has understandably been the main focus of research in employee relations, where sub-contracting arrangements are used to minimise and control labour costs; to ensure that labour is a truly variable rather than fixed cost of production; to enhance managerial control over the labour process, as the withdrawal of a commercial contract is arguably more potent a weapon than the termination of an employment contract; and to ensure an adequate supply of labour, especially where reserves of labour not normally available can be mobilised.

The use of sub-contracting arrangements has increased to the point where, in 1998, nine out of every ten workplaces in Britain reported that they contracted one or more services, most commonly building maintenance, cleaning, training and security (Cully *et al.*, 1999: 35). Of all workplaces that were more than 5 years old at the time of the WERS98, 28 per cent had contracted out some services that 5 years earlier had been performed by direct employees (either on site or by the parent company) (ibid:36). As a result, for a significant number of people, their physical place of work is not coterminous with their direct employer. Important employee relations issues arise in such situations, in particular questions of comparability, representation and job security (see Keenoy, 1985:1–26). At a number of points in later chapters (for example, in the Corus case in Chapter 7) we also see how the threat of putting additional work out to sub-contractors has had a direct bearing on employee response to managerial initiatives over recent years.

Shutt and Whittington (1987) have summarised these intra- and inter-organisational changes as processes of decentralisation, detachment and disintegration (which are not necessarily mutually exclusive). The first refers to operations that are broken up into smaller units but are retained under the same ownership. Detachment refers to those situations where large firms cease to own units directly but still maintain commercial links with them through some form of franchising or licensing agreement. Finally, disintegration arises where large firms cease to own units of production but maintain control through market or contractual power (e.g. sub-contracting) and/or the ability to re-purchase. As with decentralisation and detachment, this need not imply a loss of control, often quite the opposite. In each case, product market developments play a key role, but the importance of employee relations cannot be overlooked. In Britain's docks, for example, new ownership structures and intra- and inter-organisational relations can only be explained as part of a process through which capital has sought to regain or strengthen control over the labour process and to offset the (highly variable) costs of fluctuating labour demand in the port transport industry (Turnbull and Weston, 1993a). Similar conclusions have been drawn from construction (Evans, 1990), steel (Blyton, 1992 and 1993; and Fevre, 1986) and civil aviation (Blyton et al., 1998 and 2001).

As well as these general developments in organisational ownership and control and inter-organisational relations, more specific developments in *production* and *work processes* are noteworthy, for these encapsulate a range of issues relevant both to the context and content of employee relations. The spread of microelectronic technologies into a broad range of manual and non-manual work in both goods and service production has had (and continues to have) both a quantitative and qualitative impact on jobs, though it is clear from the many studies now conducted that the actual effects have varied considerably between different work contexts (see Clark, 1993; Daniel, 1987; Noon and Blyton, 2002; and Ramsay et al., 1992). In quantitative terms, the issue has been the extent to which jobs have disappeared and/or been created as a result of technological changes in both products and work processes. Qualitative issues, on the other hand, have focused primarily on questions of skill and control. Earlier debates on whether new technology results in de-skilling or enskilling (e.g. Wood, 1982) have been superseded by subsequent empirical studies indicating a less clearly defined reality (for a review, see Noon and Blyton, 2002). While clear cases of de-skilling and enskilling can be found, as can cases of simultaneous de-skilling and enskilling affecting different groups within an organisation, it is evident that in many cases, as Ramsay et al. (1992:176) conclude, 'the evidence on skill is largely indeterminate', not least because 'jobs are often just different, gaining and losing skill elements in ways that are not readily commensurable' (see also Geary, 2003).

Similarly, the extent to which the introduction of new technology is associated with any change in the level of control (either towards greater centralisation or decentralisation) is influenced by a number of possible factors, including the extent to which employees or work groups exercised control prior to the technological change and the degree to which in practice the technology performs to specification or requires additional operator intervention (Ramsay *et al.*, 1992). While in some cases it is apparent that new technology entails a transfer of control from supervisors to work groups, in others – for example check-out operators using electronic point-of-sale (EPOS) equipment, clerical employees working on computer terminals, or the growing number of call centre employees – the new technology enables greater centralised monitoring of time-keeping and performance.

As well as issues of skill and control, new technology has wider relevance for employee relations, for example in relation to the nature of its planning and implementation, and the potential for different technological developments to alter patterns of work organisation by combining former discrete tasks into single jobs, thereby undermining traditional job boundaries. This last aspect can be particularly significant for those trade unions that have traditionally organised their recruitment along occupational or skill lines, basing their power on exclusive representation of an individual craft or occupation (see Chapter 5).

New technologies have also influenced developments in production control techniques, most notably in terms of using more powerful information systems to achieve a closer integration of different stages of service provision and goods production. In manufacturing, for example, key aspects of this process have been the closer matching of customer order to manufacture, and an improvement in work-flow, with materials and components being delivered just-in-time to be incorporated into products, which are in turn completed and delivered just-in-time to the market place. Improved information on production processes, together with the closer integration of different production stages, enable management to reduce stocks of materials and work-in-progress and remove reserve 'buffer' stocks of part-finished items within the system. Just-in-time (JIT) operation, however, requires a high level of employee co-operation to maintain the work-flow and prevent production bottlenecks. Moreover, the tendency to link JIT with teamworking and a search for total quality based on both minimising resource waste (human, capital and energy) at every stage of production and a maximising of output quality, further heightens the degree to which contemporary production systems rely on a high level of worker compliance with managerial objectives and an active co-operation within the production system itself (for a discussion of the nature and growth of teamworking, see Proctor and Mueller, 2000; see also the discussion of teamworking in Chapter 7).

The need to secure employee co-operation with JIT and total quality management (TQM) systems indicates the relevance of employee relations for production developments. Indeed, these developments highlight not only management's need to use those relations to ensure minimum disruptions in work-flow, but also employees' potential power stemming from the relative vulnerability of JIT systems to disruption (see, for example, Delbridge, 1998; Turnbull, 1988b; and Wilkinson and Oliver's, 1990 account of a strike at Ford). Moreover, the disruptive power of labour extends well beyond the immediate work process to distribution and supplier networks. A recent dispute at all 29 US West Coast ports in October 2002, for example, cost the US economy a staggering US$2 billion per day.

The integration of product and labour markets in liberal and co-ordinated market economies

Although it is now commonplace for commentators to note the importance, and occasionally the interaction, of product and labour markets, this is rarely integrated into the analysis of employee relations. A key feature of product market pressures in the UK and other liberal market economies (LMEs) is that they are mainly transmitted through price, 'and when this is adverse the employers simply lay off workers' (Wilkinson and White, 1994:126). In other words, where market pressures are manifest through price competition rather than non-price competition (e.g. quality, design, reliability, after sales service), firms will tend to 'reap' instead of 'sow', to cut assets (capital and labour) rather than grow or diversify the business (e.g. identify new markets, invest in new products and/or processes, improve the quality and performance of products and services, and of course invest in the education, training and development of human resources) (see Hamel and Prahalad, 1994). The firm's employee relations policies will therefore be a product *and also a determinant* of wider business strategies through which the organisation seeks to compete (Marchington and Parker, 1990).

To understand the potential interaction of product and labour markets, consider a situation where firms are faced with flexibility in their access to the external labour market but must accept strong rigidities with respect to internal (re)deployment and (re)training. Such a combination is characteristic of the UK and other LMEs such as the USA: firms can hire-and-fire with comparative ease (Emerson, 1988:791), and increasingly employ labour on short-term, part-time, temporary or sub-contracts which can more easily be terminated, but in the internal labour market employees have traditionally sought to protect their status, and secure a degree of employment security, by preserving job boundaries, staffing levels and working methods. When combined with low levels of training and development, as previously noted, the result has been only modest strides in the area of greater functional or skill flexibility, particularly in achieving more advanced forms of flexible work organisation (Geary, 2003). Firms rely instead on temporal and numerical flexibility (i.e. long working hours, part-time, temporary work and sub-contract labour). Indeed, the search for external flexibility now extends right into what were traditionally regarded as 'core' jobs within the organisation (Cully *et al.*, 1999:35–8). Moreover, WERS98 data reveals that firms' use of external flexibility is negatively correlated with the use of internal forms of flexibility (e.g. task/job rotation and team-working) suggesting that firms tend to use one approach rather than the other (ibid). Boyer (1988) and others have characterised the pattern of flexibility pursued in the UK and other LMEs as essentially defensive and short-term, representing reactions to market fluctuations. In contrast, extending the skill range of employees is viewed as a more long-term, offensive flexibility strategy by creating a more adaptable labour force, capable of responding to longer-term changes in job requirements.

Flexibility in the external labour market combined with rigidity in the internal labour market is better suited to the (mass) production of standardised goods and services (Streeck, 1988:417–18; see also Hollingsworth, 1997). As already noted, it is precisely in those industries characterised by low research and development intensity, and the preponderance of price factors, where UK firms have traditionally been more successful (Smith, 1986; see also Matraves, 1997; and Porter, 1990). Under such circumstances, where firms compete predominantly on the basis of price, management will continually seek to 'strip out' labour costs in order to remain competitive, which reinforces the UK's low skill, low wage, low productivity equilibrium. This combination of flexibility and rigidity, and its association with particular product market strategies is depicted in Figure 3.5, where it is contrasted with flexibility in the internal labour market and rigidity in the external labour market.

Where employees have a rigid 'entitlement' to employment security, whether as a result of legislation (as in Europe) or social obligation (as in large Japanese corporations), it is more difficult for firms to simply hire-and-fire whenever

| | | EXTERNAL LABOUR MARKET | |
		Flexibility	Rigidity
INTERNAL LABOUR MARKET	Flexibility	*Anomic conflict* (e.g. increasing number of UK and US firms)	*Diversified quality production* (e.g. Germany and Japan)
	Rigidity	*Standardised production* (e.g. UK and US firms prior to the 1980s)	*Uncompetitive firms* (e.g. some UK firms in the 1970s)

Source: Adapted from Streeck (1988:417–18).

Figure 3.5 Rigidity and flexibility in the internal and external labour market

product market demand dictates (see Turnbull and Wass, 1997a:42). In many co-ordinated market economies (CMEs) however, where management's recourse to the external labour market is more rigid, the 'trade-off' is invariably greater flexibility in the internal labour market: workers who enjoy a rigid or institutionalised entitlement to job security are more prepared to concede greater flexibility in adapting to new technology, new working methods, changing job requirements, retraining and even relocation (see Dore, 1986, 1988 and 2000; and Streeck, 1988). As rigidity and flexibility, like equity and efficiency, are not mutually exclusive but rather part-and-parcel of the same organisational and economic dynamic, the key question is how different combinations of rigidity and flexibility in the internal and external labour markets shape and constrain different outcomes, and whether particular combinations are more or less effective given prevailing economic and social conditions. According to Streeck (1988), as illustrated in Figure 3.5, flexibility in the internal labour market and rigidity in the external labour market is more conducive to serving volatile markets with diversified, high quality products. Under these conditions, exogenous shocks (e.g. a sharp decline in product demand) are generally diffused, rather than magnified, because firms are required to keep workers on the payroll and are therefore encouraged to devote resources to 'reconversion' (that is, producing new, differentiated, high quality products utilising the functionally flexible skills of the workforce, who are well paid and highly productive).

Many employers, and certainly the Thatcher and Major governments of the 1980s and 1990s, argued that UK firms were uncompetitive in the 1970s because they were enveloped in both external and internal labour market rigidities. Consequently, 'rigidities' in both markets – especially those 'imposed by' or 'attributed to' trade unions – were a prime target for Conservative government reforms (Chapter 6) and a succession of management initiatives in recent years (Chapters 4 and 7). Many of these initiatives have continued apace under New Labour, especially in the public sector. However, trying to impose greater flexibility in both labour markets 'involves firms in unending anomic conflict as it deprives workers of both employment security and the protection offered by standardized work roles and the external tradability of associated skills' (Streeck, 1988:417). The clearest indication of anomie, already alluded to, is the growing insecurity and associated stress now regularly reported by UK workers in countless studies (e.g. Burchell et al., 1999; CBI, 1997; Demos, 1995; Heery and Salmon, 2000; and ISR, 1996). Anomie frustrates the successful adaptive behaviour of individuals and organisations alike, as workers have no incentive to form skills and employers no incentive to offer training. Instead, management relies on outmoded techniques, or bastardised versions of the latest initiatives in production control or service provision, combined with a poorly paid and inadequately trained labour force, to produce standardised, low quality goods. Not surprisingly, the UK's performance is weak or at best average in relation to knowledge-based industries, information and communications technology, R&D, new product development and the like (see DTI, 2001). The organisational and economic dynamic which ensues, as subsequent chapters will demonstrate, is inherently *ill*-suited to prevailing economic and social conditions.

Conclusion

The foregoing analysis has highlighted a number of important developments in the context of employee relations. These include more intense product market competition, changes to the ownership and control of organisations, the changing balance between employment in goods and service production, the growing prominence of women in the workforce, the persistence of unemployment, redundancies and insecurity, and developments in technology and production techniques. Together these represent the intricately woven back-cloth against which the day-to-day interactions which comprise employee relations must be assessed. These developments, of course, should not be seen as *determining* the precise nature of those relations but they have helped to *shape* those relations and, as a result, a full understanding of employee relations can only be obtained by incorporating these broader contextual changes into the analysis. Many of these facets of the world of work have traditionally been seen as beyond the remit of employee relations enquiry. This chapter has demonstrated both their interaction and integration with employee relations. As subsequent chapters show, employee relations can *only* be understood in relation to, and not in isolation from, these broader developments in industrial society.

part 2

The actors in
employee relations

4

Management and employee relations

The management of employee relations in British Airways

'Living the brand' – emotional involvement in customer service

'Living the brand' is a short-hand term for getting staff to understand and commit themselves emotionally to the product or service provided by the organisation. The idea, 'in a nutshell, is that companies can't afford to have a mismatch between what they promise in their advertising and what customers experience in real life' (Gofton, 2000:29). As a result, employees must continually ask themselves the question: 'Am I on brand?' (ibid:30). For British Airways (BA), the brand revolves around customer service: as the logo on the company's coat of arms boldly proclaims, 'We Fly to Serve'. This means that staff must 'treat every single customer as though the entire airline is at his or her service, as indeed it must be' (Sir Colin Marshall, quoted in Corke, 1986:91). To quote BA's former Chief Executive again, 'Anyone can fly aeroplanes, but few organizations excel in serving people' (quoted in Prokesch, 1995:103). Prior to the appointment of Colin Marshall in February 1983, BA's reputation for customer service was 'bloody awful' (Campbell-Smith, 1986:8). In a survey conducted in 1980 by the International Airline Passengers Association, 33 per cent of customers put BA at the top of the list of airlines to be avoided at all costs, ahead of Aeroflot, Nigerian Airways and even teetotal Arab carriers (ibid:11).

'Living the brand' was central to BA's transformation during the 1980s from a state-owned, loss-making transportation company to a customer-focused, highly profitable private enterprise. As Dr Nick Georgiades, a former Director of Human Resources at BA and previously a professor of industrial psychology at the University of London made quite clear,

We are maintaining a commitment to customer service which transcends merely being nice. It demands more than a plastic smile and 'have a nice day' ... As well as using their brains, they are going to need to use their hearts and engage in what we call 'emotional labour'. (quoted in Corke, 1986:114)

This involves front-line workers managing their appearance, demeanour and feelings during any interaction with customers, such that customers receive the service that the company promises in its advertising. Although BA does not 'sell girls' in the same way that Singapore Airlines (SIA) differentiates its brand (Chan, 2000a and b), the company was recently criticised for its 'sexy' cabin crew uniforms designed by Julien Macdonald (*Western Mail*, 17 May 2001). Moreover, BA tried to ensure svelte staff by insisting that uniforms would not be available above size 14 and it maintains strict height/weight limits, some up to 9lbs below levels recommended by the Department of Health. According to a company spokesperson, these limits are set to ensure staff are up to the rigours of the job: 'if you are a beanpole or a fatty you are probably going to flag out' (quoted in the *Daily Express*, 11 October 1996).

By the end of the 1980s, BA could truly claim to be 'The World's Favourite Airline', not just by virtue of flying more international passengers than any other airline but as a result of meeting, if not exceeding, customer expectations. In 1990, for example, BA was voted the 'world's best airline' in the independent *Business Traveller* survey, a position it held until 1996. The company was certainly a favourite of the City and its shareholders. By the time it was privatised in 1987, BA was making pre-tax profits of £162 million, compared to losses of over £140 million in 1981, and in 1996 the company surpassed SIA to become the world's most profitable airline. According to BA managers, and indeed many other commentators, the company's transformation epitomised the 'necessary compatibility of pleasure and profits' (Georgiades and Macdonell, 1998; see also Grugulis and Wilkinson, 2002), or what the burgeoning literature on service sector management describes as a win:win:win scenario – job satisfaction for workers leads to a better service for customers and higher profits for the organisation (for a critical review of this literature, see Korczynski, 2002:19–41).

By the late 1990s, however, there were clear signs that not everyone, or more precisely nobody, was winning. BA's pre-tax profits were falling at an alarming rate (from a high of £640 million in 1997 to £225 million in 1999), employee satisfaction (as measured by BA's own annual workforce survey) was in freefall, and this was dragging down customer satisfaction (according to BA's own passenger surveys). In fact, for every 1 per cent decline in employee satisfaction there was a corresponding 0.24 per cent decline in customer satisfaction (Lebrecht, 1999). In a staff opinion poll conducted in 1999 called 'Its Your Shout', returned by 54 per cent of all employees, the lowest scores registered by staff concerned the directors of BA. In particular, employees doubted their ability to manage costs effectively without sacrificing quality, their desire to communicate openly and honestly, and the extent to which they cared about employees (Barsoux and Manzoni, 2002:11). As one of BA's seasoned cabin crew put it at the time, 'Customer service and good employee relations go hand-in-hand. But all BA want is the customer service, they've dismissed the idea of good employee relations' (quoted in Turnbull *et al.*, 2001). For Robert Ayling, then BA's Chief Executive Officer (CEO), it was time to reassess the company's business strategy and 'Put People First – Again', following the ructions caused by the company's Business Efficiency Programme (BEP).

BEP – Business Efficiency or Beginning of the End?

In a liberal market economy such as the UK's, management often finds it easier to implement major restructuring programmes, if only because of their ability to hire-and-fire with impunity (see Chapter 3; and Turnbull and Wass, 1997a and 2000). This was certainly the case with BA during the 1980s when there were large scale redundancy programmes and major management shake-ups (Blyton and Turnbull, 1998:70–1; Campbell-Smith, 1986:27–8; Colling, 1995a). More importantly, under the guidance of Lord King and Sir Colin Marshall, BA's senior management were able 'to orchestrate the organizational experiments and firm-internal power shifts needed to undertake radical innovations and break with the conventional industry configuration' (Lehrer, 2001:362). As a result, power shifted from the technical to the commercial side of the airline (from operations to marketing) (ibid:368–9) and BA secured 'first mover' advantages over its rivals through a market-led strategy that involved redefining the market, both in terms of the service that passengers could expect (and rival carriers would now have to match or exceed) and as a point of reference for employees (which management used to legitimise the restructuring of the airline).

The new rhetoric of the market – global competition, the enterprise culture, the sovereign customer, etc – was grounded in far-reaching developments in the civil aviation industry, most notably the commercialisation and privatisation of national (state-owned) flag carriers and the liberalisation and deregulation of market access (see Blyton *et al.*, 1998). Initially, BA was well placed to exploit these developments, being the first major European flag carrier to be fully privatised and having experience of operating in more competitive aviation markets than many of its rivals (see Martínez Lucio *et al.*, 2001). Indeed, BA was instrumental in pushing for deregulation measures that would give it greater access to the European market (Dobson, 1995:191). But once the industry stabilised in the mid-1990s, BA's major rivals were able to catch up, emulating many of BA's commercial innovations and customer-service initiatives (see Lehrer, 2001:362; and Turnbull *et al.*, 2001). In addition, BA now faced competition in its 'domestic' (i.e. European) market from low cost airlines such as Ryanair (which switched to a low-fare structure in 1991) and easyJet (which started operations in 1995). With a cost-per-seat kilometre that was less than half that of BA, and even less compared to other European flag carriers, low cost airlines have expanded rapidly in recent years, making significant in-roads to the market share of national airlines (see AEA, 2002:I4–I5).

These developments exerted strong pressure on (labour) costs. Although BA's market-led strategy of the 1980s and 1990s focused heavily on customer service, with major training initiatives such as 'Putting People First' (PPF), 'Managing People First' and 'A Day in the Life' (see Corke, 1986:112–15; Goodstein, 1990; Grugulis and Wilkinson, 2002:183–5; Höpfl, 1992 and 1993; and Höpfl et al., 1992), there was always close attention to costs. As one senior BA manager made clear, 'Don't be deluded into thinking the change was about being nice to each other. It was about effectiveness, performance and survival' (quoted in Höpfl et al., 1992:34). In fact, the company was only able to remain cost competitive with major European airlines such as Lufthansa and KLM as a result of lower input prices, most notably labour costs (see Oum and Yu, 1998). Employee relations were therefore central to BA's business strategy in terms of costs, efficiency and customer service.

Into this increasingly turbulent milieu stepped the new CEO, Robert Ayling, in January 1996. His first official act was to slim down the company's 'top heavy' executive team from 25 to 14 and reorganise the management structure (e.g. the HR Director, whose background was in customer services, was replaced by a new Director with a background in finance, and several Departments, including Human Resources, no longer reported directly to the Chief Executive) (see Barsoux and Manzoni, 2002; and Turnbull et al., 2001). This reorganisation was part-and-parcel of Mr Ayling's stated intent to rid BA of any complacency or lingering public sector attitudes, and his very public declaration to make BA the 'best managed' company in the UK by 2000. The centre-piece of his strategy was to be an ambitious £1 billion cost-reduction programme. The Business Efficiency Programme (BEP) was announced in May 1996 and coincided with the publication of record profits (£585 million in the year to 31 March 1996). At the time, employees were expecting a 'pay back' for all their efforts over the previous years, not an assault on their terms and conditions of employment which many construed as a pay cut.

Although BEP was portrayed in the press as a simple cost-cutting exercise, employees and union officials recognised it as an attempt to control the future cost structure of the airline. For example, BA's expenditure on key operational groups such as cabin crew was 48 per cent higher than domestic rivals such as British Midland and 90 per cent higher than Virgin (CAA, 1996). Under BEP, new cabin crew recruits would be hired on lower rates of pay (30 per cent below existing rates) with much slower progression up the salary scale. More importantly, as a senior BA manager pointed out, 'BEP is not just about costs, it's about what businesses we should be in' (quoted in Turnbull et al., 2001). Under Ayling's stewardship, being 'market-led' was reinterpreted as paying no more than the 'market price' for any activity. This was defined as the price at which the same or better quality of service could be purchased elsewhere, to be determined by a process of 'benchmarking'. If internally-provided activities or operations could not match the cost/quality of external providers then it would be out-sourced or franchised (e.g. a BA route might be operated by another airline using its own aircraft, albeit painted in BA colours, and employing its own staff, albeit wearing BA uniforms and performing to BA standards of service). As a senior BA manager put it, 'We do not want to pay more for a job or a function than the market rate. We do not want to have an internal cost for doing a job which is higher than someone on the outside can do it for' (quoted in *Airline Business*, August 1997). BA managers talked about a 'virtual airline' that concentrated on selling seats and operating flights – the company would employ only a core of 'back office' staff and 'front line' employees who interact with customers; all other functions would be externally provided (see Blyton *et al.*, 1998:10–11; and Eaton, 2001:189).

To suggest that BEP caused disquiet among BA staff would be an understatement. Management sought to reassure employees that they would be no worse off under BEP, but for many this was the last straw, the beginning of the end:

> It may say BA on the plane but it's not BA. BA is becoming a brand, the virtual airline. (Female cabin crew, quoted in Turnbull *et al.*, 2001)

> Rather than try to improve the efficiency of the business, they look to outsource it. That's not management, that's not taking responsibility for the business. They're selling off everything, that's the reality of the virtual airline. (Male engineer, quoted in Turnbull *et al.*, 2001)

Discontent erupted into a succession of disputes with staff, most notably pilots (see Turnbull *et al.*, 2002) and cabin crew (see Turnbull *et al.*, 2001). The latter proved to be a particularly bitter affair, described in the press as the 'last kick of Thatcherism' (*The Guardian*, 7 July 1997; and *Financial Times*, 10 July 1997) as BA management sought first to impose the BEP and then caution staff about the consequences of any strike action (an internal bulletin issued to staff warned them of the loss of all travel allowances and promotion prospects for 3 years, possible dismissal, and even being sued for damages arising from any losses incurred by the company in any dispute) (see Barsoux and Manzoni, 2002; and Turnbull *et al.*, 2001). A 44-year-old female cabin services director with 25 years service with the company summed up the feelings of many cabin crew:

> We know there are cost savings that can be made, but these have to be negotiated. The management just want to walk all over us. The climate has really changed. When Lord King was in charge, he did unpopular things, but we felt he liked us. With Ayling, we feel he despises us and would rather get in cheap labour from overseas ... No one wants a strike. But people feel that if we give in now, we're not going to have a job that's worth doing. (*Daily Telegraph*, 9 July 1997)

Mr Ayling soon realised that he needed to apologise for appearing 'heavy handed or clumsy' (*The Times*, 10 July 1997), and after concluding an agreement that secured the desired cost savings from cabin crew operations he declared that: 'today is the day when I put a stake in the ground and re-involve everyone in this company' (*Daily Telegraph*, 23 September 1997). The HR Department, now re-established as a separate department reporting directly to the Chief Executive, would champion this process through a programme called 'Putting People First – Again' (PPF-A), 'designed to remind staff what the brand stands for and involve them in its evolution' (Gofton, 2000:29). But management soon realised that PPF-A would have only a limited impact:

> The first time around, in the 1980s, PPF [Putting People First] was like ploughing a fallow field with a shiny new plough, so it was easy to make a big difference. Now the field is already ploughed, and overgrown in places, so all you can do is try to make it look better, tidy things up, which is very difficult. (Senior BA manager, quoted in Turnbull *et al.*, 2001)

More importantly, PPF-A jarred with the more intense working environment in the wake of BEP and the attitude of some BA managers towards staff – 'If it wrecks them physically and they only last 3 years, then so be it. We've got 16,000 people who want a cabin crew job with BA' (BA manager, quoted in Turnbull *et al.*, 2001).

Trade unions were also to be 're-involved' in the company, but the new relationship did not get off to the best start:

> We were called to a meeting, a presentation by Ayling, where he listed the top priorities of the company – customer service, greater efficiency, route networks and all that. Eventually he got to point number eight, or whatever it was, 'Putting people at the *top* of the agenda!' (T&GWU official, original emphasis, interview notes)

Working with (or against?) trade unions

During the 1980s, while BA management developed a whole range of employee relations initiatives directed towards the individual, such as PPF and Customer First Teams (quality circles), collective bargaining structures were maintained intact. These structures dated from the days of state ownership and BA's statutory duty under the British Airways Board Act 1977 to negotiate the terms and conditions of its employees through collective bargaining. As the major employer in the civil aviation industry, BA was the principal actor on the employers' side of the National Joint Council for Civil Air Transport (NJCCAT). The NJCCAT agreements covered such areas as statutory holidays and payments during sickness and absence. Negotiations on other items were covered by National Sectional Panels (NSPs), where separate agreements would be reached for different occupational groups within different airlines. However, while structures remained intact after privatisation, there was an increasing tendency to play-down collective relations, and on several occasions BA management by-passed the usual trade union channels and sent letters direct to each employee's home to explain the company's position on key issues. But this did little to avert a succession of disputes during the 1980s (see Blyton and Turnbull, 1998:74). Moreover, latent discontent among *all* grades of staff was revealed in a survey conducted by BA which indicated that while employees were certainly committed to the company, many felt that the 'World's Favourite Airline' did not care about *them* as much as it should (*Financial Times*, 2 December 1991; see also Höpfl, 1992).

A key element in BA's strategy during the mid-1990s was the reorganisation of collective bargaining. Ideally, the company wanted 'to write the unions out of the system, by-pass and marginalize them' (BA manager, quoted in Turnbull *et al.*, 2001), but the first stage was to dismantle national bargaining arrangements. The unions 'boxed clever', however, by opposing the abolition of the NJCCAT in order to preserve effective national level bargaining through the NSPs, which in the words of one union official 'we'd die in a ditch to defend' (interview notes). The NJCCAT was scrapped in the summer of 1996 but the role and responsibilities of five NSPs – representing pilots, cabin crew, ground/support services, clerical grades, and management – were redefined and reinforced. But this did not mark the end of BA's assault on organised labour. During the pilots' dispute in 1996 the company threatened to replace pilots if they went on strike. Then, during the cabin crew dispute the following year, BA threatened to 'derecognise' the T&GWU. Although the cabin crew dispute only involved members of the British Airline Stewards and Stewardesses Association (BASSA), an affiliated union of the T&GWU, at a meeting between Robert Ayling, Bill Morris (General Secretary, T&GWU) and George Ryde (Civil Aviation Secretary, T&GWU), BA managers produced a computer printout listing all T&GWU members employed by the company and paying their union subscription by 'check-off' (i.e. deduction from their wages by the company paid directly to the T&GWU). Ayling threatened to 'press a button on the computer and delete the entire membership roll' (George Ryde, quoted in Turnbull *et al.*, 2001), which would no doubt have adversely affected subscription income and possibly even membership levels. It was widely known that Ayling argued privately that unions had no place in the airline business (Eaton, 2001:189).

Following the dispute with pilots, BA and the British Airline Pilots Association (BALPA) negotiated a new 'partnership agreement' designed to reconstruct the relationship between pilots and management, based on ten 'guiding principles' related to the responsibilities of each party, accountability, appropriate behaviour, information exchange, communications, flexibility, problem-solving, and general 'good practice'. But this agreement failed to transform (adversarial) relationships between the parties (see Turnbull *et al.*, 2004). BA also sought a more co-operative, partnership-based approach with the other major unions (MSF, AEU, Cabin Crew '89, GMB and T&GWU) but no formal agreement was signed. As George Ryde explained:

what was needed was a buy in from our representatives at the very least and just as important was the understanding and acceptance of the membership. As a result, Bill [Morris, T&GWU General Secretary] didn't sign and eventually we got BA to accept that there was still too much distrust right down to the 'shop floor' that it was not as simple as five General Secretaries signing for motherhood and apple pie ... This was important because for the first time BA accepted that the behavioural problems ... went right down to the lowest level of supervision. In other words we had a real cultural problem. (quoted in Turnbull *et al.*, 2004)

At the heart of this 'cultural problem' was BA's inconsistent, and at times contradictory, approach to employee relations, at both an individual and collective level. As already highlighted, the company's approach towards staff alternated between 'hard' and 'soft' human resource management, or in the words of one BA manager, between 'killing people one minute and loving them the next' (quoted in Turnbull *et al.*, 2001; see also Colling, 1995a; and Grugulis and Wilkinson, 2002). Such inconsistencies also characterised the company's approach to unions and collective bargaining – seeking to marginalise unions one minute and then talking about partnership the next. There was certainly no strategic use of collective bargaining to generate pacts on employment or competitiveness that might underwrite the company's customer service approach, unlike the partnership agreements developed by several major European airlines (see, for example, Arrowsmith, 2001; and Bruch and Sattelberger, 2001).

The 'best managed' company in the UK or just an ailing airline?

In March 2000, after BA recorded its worst annual financial results for 18 years, Mr Ayling 'resigned'. The City breathed a sigh of relief and the company's share price immediately surged by 14 per cent (the shares eventually closed 2.1 per cent up on the day). BA staff were also relieved: 'Normal service has been resumed after 4 years', quipped one check-in employee (*The Independent*, 11 March 2000). But when BA announced the departure of its Chief Executive, the Board maintained that the company's business strategy was still the right one; Mr Ayling was simply the wrong man to implement it (*Financial Times*, 11 March 2000). The Board was forced to acknowledge, however, that 'there is a need for greater emphasis on the employee relations side of the business' (BA Press Release, 11 March 2000). As the former General Secretary of BALPA pointed out, 'You can't have a strategy based on reducing everything to the core activities, and then fail to manage these people effectively. You need to manage these people without risk of disruption, not alienate them and drive them to distraction' (interview notes).

Contrary to the Board's announcement of 'no change', there has been a discernible shift in the company's business strategy under Rod Eddington, the new CEO (e.g. bringing various activities and routes back in-house and reorganising the short-haul network) and union leaders report a change in their relationship with the company, although some remain sceptical: 'We're now told what's happening at the same time, or sometimes even before the City and the shareholders, instead of reading about it the next day in the press. But we're still not involved in the real decision-making processes' (interview notes). More importantly, for many employees, the company still appears to be ailing. Major job losses were announced in both 2000 and 2001, prior to the events of 11 September. The terrorist attacks on New York have hit the industry particularly hard, sending many airlines into a tailspin (see Harvey and Turnbull, 2002; and Turnbull and Harvey, 2001). The outcome has been further job losses and a renewed assault on employees' terms and conditions of employment. In the words of Shane Enright (2002), Aviation Secretary at the International Transport Workers' Federation (ITF), airlines are once again 'using the workforce as the primary shock absorbers to manage the economic cycle'.

The management of labour: control, confrontation and competition

As this account of BA indicates, despite the importance traditionally ascribed to collective bargaining, strikes and other activities of trade unions, the principal actor in employee relations is in fact management. Indeed, the employment relationship is fundamentally an *individual* exchange between employer and employee. Further, the importance of management must be acknowledged if only because management is ubiquitous whereas trade unions in the UK have at best organised only a little over half of the working population. Unions themselves are in fact 'secondary' organisations, as their members have already been engaged and organised into distinctive groups and relationships by employers (Offe and Wiesenthal, 1980:72). In this respect, employers exert a strong influence over both individual and collective relations with employees. More importantly, management holds the 'balance of power' by virtue of its control over the means of production and the authority this imparts (see Chapter 2). And yet the analysis of management played little part in industrial relations texts until after the Donovan Report in the late 1960s (see Chapter 7). Today, no textbook on employee relations would be complete without at least one chapter devoted to management.

The change was partly brought about because management, at the behest of the Donovan Commission and leading authorities on industrial relations such as Allan Flanders, were adjured to take responsibility for the much-needed reform of industrial relations in the UK. For Flanders (1975:62), for example, the most important lesson from his influential study of *The Fawley Productivity Agreements* was that management must accept full responsibility for the human aspects of its job, or what is now increasingly called human resource management (HRM).

Subsequent research, however, indicated that company directors in particular devoted little attention to employee relations issues (Winkler, 1974:197–202; see also Hickson *et al.*, 1985:30; and Hill and Pickering, 1986). Even today, CEOs are found to be sceptical about the potential benefits of HRM. As Marchington and Parker (1990:56–7) concluded,

> Serious though the labour control problem may appear to senior managers, it tends to take a back seat in comparison with other issues at most times, at least in its *explicit* contribution to strategic decisions ... managers operate in a manner which implicitly expects labour to conform to management plans, chosen in the 'best' interests of the company. (original emphasis)

The interests of the company are increasingly equated with those of the shareholders, and while changing conditions (outlined in the previous chapter) have provided managers with new choices, 'these very same conditions have allowed management to fall back on an almost atavistic preference for the assertion of its prerogatives at the workplace' (Kessler and Purcell, 2003:314).

In the light of extensive research over the past two decades, Clegg's (1979:164) assertion that 'the study of management in industrial relations is in a primitive state' could nowadays be rejected, but the argument that management *strategies* in employee relations remain in a primitive state would doubtless occasion considerable support. For most managers, 'industrial relations only becomes a consideration when it becomes a problem' (Keenoy, 1992:97). The absence of any coherent, let alone strategic approach towards the management of labour is often noted (e.g. Boxall and Purcell, 2003; Hyman, 1987a:25–6; Kessler and Purcell, 2003; Purcell, 1987:545–6; and Sisson, 1989:3), and yet so too is the importance of management control over the actions and activities of labour. If control is so important, why is it that most UK firms are characterised by a pragmatic, opportunistic, and *ad hoc* approach towards labour? Three reasons are commonly cited. First is the weight of history and key structures inherited from the past (Sisson, 1989:3). In combination, early industrialisation, growth by merger and acquisition, the late development of professional personnel management, greater importance attached to the finance function and the control of large share-holdings by investment trusts which demand immediate returns, 'constitute a major barrier to managements in Britain investing in the long term and, in particular, in people' (ibid:16; and Edwards *et al.*, 1992:20). The persistence of these features in the UK economy today represents an on-going (but not insurmountable) problem for effective management control.

A second and more important factor is the 'dynamic of confrontation ... a dialectical interplay between control and resistance' (Storey, 1985:196), which Hyman (1987a:28–30) simply refers to as contradiction. Contradiction exists both within and between the various managerial specialisms, as well as between capital and labour. Given the open-ended, indeterminate nature of the wage-effort bargain, firms organise work in ways which reinforce and reproduce the authority and control of management over labour. But here is the rub:

> Control has to be constructed in a fashion which also 'manufactures' consent ... however imbalanced the distribution of power, the controlled always have some leverage on the terms of exchange. No matter how extensive the controls, in the final analysis, management is reliant on employee co-operation. (Keenoy, 1992:93–5)

Capital owns and has the 'right' to control both the means of production and the labour it has hired, but at the same time capital must 'surrender' the means of production to the control of the worker for their actual use in the labour process (a good example is in-flight services provided by cabin crew). 'It is precisely because capital must surrender the use of its means of production to labour that capital must to some degree seek a cooperative relationship with it, unite labour with the means of production and maximise its social productivity and powers of co-operation' (Cressey and MacInnes, 1980:14; see also Burawoy, 1979). It is this underlying contradiction inherent in management control over labour that 'creates potential for worker initiative in ways which further adapt and qualify the strategies of management' (Hyman, 1987a:49).

Thirdly, management must continually respond to the external environment, in particular the pressures of competition. Almost every new development in employee relations in recent years appears to have been initiated, if not justified or explained, by reference to more intense (international) market competition. In reality, of course, employee relations are not simply, automatically or directly adjusted in line with contingent circumstances. To be sure, some firms appear to be purely reactive, adapting their business and human resource policies in order to minimise competitive uncertainty (e.g. minimising fixed costs by increasing the proportion of temporary or contract labour that can more easily be laid off whenever market conditions 'dictate'). Other firms, however, are more innovative, creating new cost-quality-service-productivity combinations that previously did not exist. These firms play an important role in shaping their economic (and social) environment. Indeed, the trajectory of monopoly capitalism has been for large firms to secure ever greater influence over markets, rather than simply respond to them. As Lazonick (1991:148) points out, 'in an international economy dominated by powerful organizations, behind every competitive challenge is an enterprise with superior organizational capabilities'. Of course, this is not to gainsay that management no longer responds to market signals, nor to suggest that they are able to control product and labour markets. As demonstrated in the previous chapter, it is the *interplay* of these different forces that must be considered, where management action is 'viewed as both a cause and a consequence of environmental influences' (Marchington and Parker, 1990:99).

Each of these three factors has played an important part in the unfolding pattern of the management of employee relations in both British Airways and the UK economy as a whole. To continue with the example of BA, the company has grown historically through a process of merger and acquisition, the most significant being that between BOAC and BEA in 1972 which created BA. At the time it was said that two airlines had been amalgamated into three, as not only did the merger bring together two companies with very different histories and cultures, which carried over into the 1980s (Campbell-Smith, 1986:10), but management itself was not fully integrated until four years after the merger (Corke, 1986:60). BA's acquisition of British Caledonian in 1988 presented further problems, not least that created by the formation of a break-away union, Cabin Crew '89, from the T&GWU cabin crew section (BASSA) which gave rise to considerable animosity and ill-feeling among the crew, especially as BA decided to recognise the new union. Cabin Crew '89 agreed the contract changes proposed by BA which led to the 1997 strike by BASSA, adding a further (inter-union) twist to the dispute.

More recent take-overs (e.g. Dan Air and Brymon) and franchising agreements (e.g. deals with GB Airways, Maersk, Logan Air, Comair and Sun-Air) presented additional problems for BA (not least industrial action in 1993 and the grievance at the centre of the pilots' dispute in 1996) and in some respects have undermined the corporate identity that BA has worked so hard to create. In addition to these internal developments, a succession of financial crises arising from the 1991 Gulf War, September 11, and the recent war in Iraq, and of course the progressive deregulation of the industry, have all created strong environmental pressures. In order to weather the storm of competition, and exert greater influence over its product market, BA created (and later divested) its own low cost airline (Go) and established a global airline alliance called **one**world (in co-operation with Aer Lingus, American Airlines, Cathay Pacific, Finnair, Iberia, LanChile and Qantas). As a result of all these developments, management policy towards labour has changed markedly over the course of the last two decades, if not in purpose (to make a profit) then at least in practice. And yet doubts are still expressed about the success of past policies and the prospects for the future.

These doubts apply with equal force to the UK economy as a whole. The failure of UK management to secure control of the labour process, to develop a coherent approach to the management of employee relations, to respond effectively to competitive and other environmental changes, and ultimately to develop a high-productivity, high-investment, high-wage, high-growth economy, are the key themes in the remainder of this chapter. Following a review of various management control strategies, a number of distinctive management styles, and how these have changed over recent years, are identified. Noting that most UK companies adopt an essentially pragmatic and opportunistic style of employee relations management, relying largely on compliance rather than more effective forms of co-operation, the key factors that account for the failure of management are examined.

The management of control

One point on which both the Confederation of British Industry (CBI) and Trades Union Congress (TUC) are agreed is that UK companies are over-controlled and under-managed (CBI/TUC, 2001). For some organisations, control appears to be the *sine qua non* of all management action. Michael Edwardes's account of his chairmanship of British Leyland (now Rover) is a case in point:

> The real problem was that management was still striving to get into the driving seat, having been out of it for many years ... we needed to re-establish management authority ... We could either regain control of the company, or in the event of failure, concede that closure was the only viable option. (1983:78–85)

Usually, however, labour is only one of several management problems, and arguably not even the most important (Wood and Kelly, 1982:77). Having produced goods and services in a cost-effective manner, firms must then sell those goods and services on the market in order to realise a profit. For British Leyland/Rover, this proved to be a continuing problem after Edwardes's departure, as product design, marketing and other aspects of the management function had been woefully neglected (Williams *et al.*, 1987). Thus, employee relations are often characterised as a 'third order' or 'downstream' decision, following 'first order' choices over the company's general mission or purpose and second order choices over organisational form and related control mechanisms (see Kessler *et al.*, 2000:18; and Purcell, 1989). Many authors would argue, however, that herein lies the problem: 'HR should not merely be affected in a knock-on manner, but be located much further up the business strategy process' (Redman and Wilkinson, 2001:13; see also Miller, 1987:348). In other words, employee relations should be *part of*, rather than flowing from, the organisation's business strategy.

As organisations and their managers are ultimately judged in the only terms which count in a capitalist economy, namely a good return on capital, some have argued that management is not interested in control *per se* (Littler and Salaman, 1984:64). According to the former Personnel Director of Nissan Motor Manufacturing (UK) Ltd, 'companies are not in the employee relations business they are in business to sell profitably a product desired by the consumer' (Peter Wickens, quoted by Marchington and Parker, 1990:55). While this statement is self-evidently correct, management control of labour is nonetheless a *precondition* for the production and subsequent sale of a product or service desired by the consumer. Some authors go further, suggesting that management will actually forgo technically superior methods of production unless they maintain, and preferably reinforce, management control over labour and the process of production (see Gordon, 1976; and Marglin, 1974). If profits are based on the exploitation of labour, as Marxists suggest, then this statement is equally self-evident (see Chapter 2).

In liberal market economies such as the UK and USA, as distinct from the co-ordinated market economies of Western Europe or Japan, pre-eminence is usually afforded to shareholder interests. But the emphasis on profitability, and the consequent neglect of employee and other stakeholder interests, has arguably intensified in recent years (see Coates, 2000; and Hutton, 1996). ICI, for example, described itself in the company's 1987 Annual Report in the following terms:

> ICI aims to be the world's leading chemical company, serving customers internationally through the innovative and responsible application of chemistry and related sciences.

> Through achievement of our aim, we will enhance the wealth and well-being of our shareholders, our employees, our customers and the communities which we serve and in which we operate.

As John Kay (1997:22) points out, however, following Hanson's abortive attempts to buy ICI the company's description of itself changed significantly:

> Our objective is to maximise value for shareholders by focusing on businesses where we have market leadership, a technological edge and a world competitive cost base.

Whereas the 1987 statement emphasised *operational* activities, recognising all *stakeholders* in the company, the new portrait emphasises *financial* activities and recognises only *shareholders*. With this reorientation ICI is no longer forward looking, seeking instead to restrict activities to what it is already doing, and profit is no longer a means but an end in itself (ibid:24). Evidence suggests, however, that companies which embrace a stakeholder rather than a shareholder view of their business actually perform better (Wheeler, 1997), and for very good reasons. As Kay (1997:23) argues, an emphasis purely on shareholder interests undermines the very factors – trust, commitment, and flexibility – that have been central to the competitive advantage of many successful firms such as ICI. British Airways is another case in point.

For BA, management control over employee behaviour, or in management's terms the exercise of 'emotional labour', was identified as a key element of corporate reorganisation and cultural change. As in all industries, but more so than most, management in the airline industry is highly dependent on employee initiative, co-operation and ultimately autonomy if work is to be performed quickly, efficiently and to the required standards. Unlike the provision of physical goods, however, where standards can be defined according to *technical* dimensions, in the service sector, where the level of involvement with customers is much greater, quality and other standards tend to be defined in *functional* and *expressive* terms. In fact, the technical dimensions of the service are almost taken-for-granted: customers expect the plane to fly and to be conveyed to their chosen destination, along with their baggage! But what about reliability (did the plane depart/arrive on time?); the responsiveness of the staff (are they willing to help customers?);

assurance (the knowledge and courtesy of staff and their ability to instil confidence and trust?); and of course empathy (do staff provide caring and individualised attention?). These factors tend to be the key determinants of service quality in 'high contact' industries such as hotels, catering and air transport, and each provides a measure of customer perception or satisfaction with the service. Of particular significance in the service sector are 'system failures' or 'critical events' and how employees handle such incidents, because every service encounter has the potential to lead to a satisfactory experience for the customer. Should a passenger develop acute appendicitis on a flight from London to Sydney, for example, and have to be taken off the plane in Bangkok for an emergency operation, then a negative event can be turned into a positive experience if the airline provides medical support, rearranges flights, and arranges hotel accommodation for convalescence (for a discussion of service quality, see Bitner *et al.*, 1990; Lewis, 1999; and Parasuraman *et al.*, 1991). Clearly, the role of front-line personnel (cabin crew, airport administrative staff, airline doctors, etc.) becomes critical in such situations, one of the everyday events that airline chief executives describe as 'moments of truth' (Carlzon, 1987).

In a detailed study of Delta Airlines, the US carrier with a world-wide reputation for service quality that BA and other airlines have sought to emulate, Hochschild (1983) describes in great detail the pressures on customer contact staff. In fact, the term 'emotional labour' as sometimes used by BA is derived from Hochschild's study, defined as the management of feelings to create a publicly observable facial and bodily display. Such labour involves 'acting', but 'it is not a resource to be used for the purposes of art, as in drama, or for the purposes of self-discovery, as in therapy, or for the pursuit of fulfilment, as in everyday life. It is a resource to be used to make money' (ibid:55). Emotional labour, in other words,

> requires one to induce or suppress feelings in order to sustain the outward countenance that produces the proper state of mind in others ... This kind of labor calls for a co-ordination of mind and feeling, and it sometimes draws on a source of self that we honor as deep and integral to our identity. (ibid:7)

Maintaining a difference between feeling and feigning over long periods inevitably leads to strain, especially among female flight attendants who, in addition, face sexual harassment perhaps partly as a result of their own status (or lack of it) (ibid:90–4), but more notably as a result of expectations created in the past by company promotional campaigns (Continental Airlines, for example, hired Playboy bunnies for a short period, while a naked woman implored customers to buy cheap Virgin Airline tickets in a Danish TV commercial) and airline advertising ('Fly me, you'll like it' and 'We really move our tails for you to make your every wish come true' are just two of the slogans previously used by carriers) (see Noon and Blyton, 2002:197–8). Female cabin crew are not only required to deploy skills and abilities that they are deemed to posses simply by virtue of their sexual difference from men

– principally 'caring', physically and emotionally, for others and presenting themselves as 'feminine' and aesthetically pleasing – for which they are not fully remunerated (see Taylor and Tyler, 2000; and Tyler and Abbott, 1998), but expectations of submissiveness and deference from female front-line staff systematically informs customer perceptions of service quality (Korczynski, 2002:52).

Flight attendants are just one of an increasing number of 'pink-collar' workers (around a third of all employees, the majority of whom are women), who must exercise emotional labour at work. Check-out operators in a major supermarket chain, for example, are confronted by a sign as they walk onto the shopfloor which reads 'Smile, you are going on stage', and a major UK food retailer issues each employee with a plastic card which summarises key points for action:

> Acknowledge eye contact and smile at your customer.
> Say Hallo/Good Afternoon etc.
> Be smart. Impress your customer.
> Thank your customer and say Goodbye.
> Remember! Customers always have a choice.
> (Marchington and Harrison, 1991:294)

At another store, one check-out operator complained that 'there are times when I just want to look up angrily and tell [customers] to shut up but I have to be busy and keep smiling' (Ogbonna, 1992:91). If they fail to exercise emotional labour, employees are reprimanded by supervisors: 'We are able to detect when a check-out operator is not smiling or even when she is putting on a false smile ... we call her into a room and have a chat with her' (ibid:85; see also Noon and Blyton, 2002:189–90; Ogbonna and Wilkinson, 1988 and 1990). Along with the 'stick' of surveillance and discipline, one high street retailer offers the 'carrot' of store gift vouchers for 'best grin of the day' (see Turnbull and Wass, 1997b).

BA employed management consultants and appointed a professor of industrial psychology to effect the desired changes in employee behaviour. Generally, management scientists consider the problem of labour control in terms of employee motivation, involvement and job satisfaction. In contrast to the assumptions of Taylorism (scientific management) – that employees have an inherent dislike of work and must therefore be coerced, controlled, directed and threatened with punishment if they are to exercise the required level of effort, with financial reward acting as the only motivator – Maslow (1943) and other psychologists suggest that individual behaviour is determined by a 'hierarchy of needs' ranging in ascending order from physiological need, safety, love, esteem and self-actualisation. The quest for fulfilment of these needs is governed by a ratchet mechanism, such that once individuals have secured basic physiological needs such as food and shelter (or when employees have secured acceptable physical working conditions), they then seek higher-order needs. In a similar vein, Douglas McGregor (1960) distinguishes three major classes of need, namely physiological, social and self-fulfilment, arguing that self-fulfilment is especially important but that conventional organisation structures and practices totally ignore it. Thus, managers tend to assume that employees dislike work, are passive, unambitious, indolent and resistant to change, and will therefore prefer to be directed (follow orders and obey the rules) rather than be self-directed at work. Managers therefore reap what they sow: such an approach is self-defeating, bringing about resentment, dissent and resistance to change.

This approach, which McGregor calls 'Theory X', is contrasted with 'Theory Y' which is based on very different assumptions about human motivation and behaviour. In effect, Theory Y is the reverse image of Theory X. Employees are assumed to welcome self-direction and self-control at work and to be capable of personal psychic development. Thus, there is perceived to exist a reservoir of creativity to be harnessed by management towards the goals of the organisation. Narratives on the future of work and employment often refer to Theory Y as one of the core assumptions of the twenty-first century organisation, as depicted in Figure 4.1.

Unfortunately, for most workers the idealised twenty-first century organisation depicted in Figure 4.1 is a mirage that exists principally at the level of managerial rhetoric (see, for example, www.leeds.ac.uk/esrcfutureofwork). Theory Y, for example, is better understood as a prescription for change rather than a description of management attitudes towards employees or even a framework for under-

Contrasting assumptions in twentieth and twenty-first century organisations		
Assumptions about:	Assumptions characterising twentieth century organisations	Assumptions characterising twenty-first century organisations
People	Theory X: people are a cost that must be monitored and controlled	Theory Y: people are an asset that should be valued and developed
Work	Segmented, industrially-based and individual tasks	Collaborative, knowledge-based projects
Technology	Design technology to control work and minimise human error	Integrate technology with social systems to enable knowledge-based work
Leadership	Senior managers and technical experts	Distributed leadership at all levels
Goals	Unitary focus on returns to shareholders	Multi-dimensional focus on value for multiple stakeholders

Source: Kochan et al. (2002).

Figure 4.1 Organisations of the future

standing employee behaviour and management action (see Rose, 1975:189). Most notably, there is a fortuitous concurrence between individual and organisational needs: if management adopt structures and practices that facilitate self-fulfilment, employees will work harder, efficiency will improve and profits rise (ibid:193). As a result, there is a very narrow interpretation and understanding of industrial conflict. As we argued in Chapter 2, these conflicts are inherent in the very structure of the employment relationship.

A more fruitful approach is to follow labour process theories of management control which actually *start* from the structured antagonism between capital and labour. As with the motivational theories of McGregor, a range of possible control/ motivation strategies are identified as available to management. Friedman (1977), for example, distinguished between 'direct control' and 'responsible autonomy'. The former conforms to the principles of scientific management and is characterised by the fragmentation of tasks and the de-skilling of work accompanied by close supervision and tight discipline (what is sometimes referred to as the '3B' system of 'Bark, Bollock and Bite'). Responsible autonomy, on the other hand, is characterised by managers' attempts 'to harness the adaptability of labour power by giving workers leeway and encouraging them to adapt to changing situations in a manner beneficial to the firm' (ibid:78; see also Melman, 1958). In other words, employers grant discretion but surround this with policies designed to encourage the employee to identify with the goals of the organisation, a policy clearly evident in BA's 'Putting the Customer First' programme.

Other control strategies have been identified in the labour process literature, such as Richard Edwards's (1979) distinction between simple/direct control (via close supervision), technical control (achieved through technology and the production process itself) and bureaucratic control (adherence to rules and administrative procedures). The problem with Edwards's analysis, however, like that of Gordon *et al.* (1982), is that these different control strategies are linked to different stages of capitalist development, suggesting that, at any given time, there is a single, or at least predominant, strategy of control which will ensure continued accumulation of capital (these 'structure-driven' or 'cyclical' approaches are discussed in Chapter 1). More importantly, the different control strategies identified in the labour process literature draw predominantly from the manufacturing sector, which as we have already noted (Chapter 3) is a minority and declining sector of employment. In the service sector, customers are increasingly involved in the management of employment relationships (see Bellemare, 2000; Heery, 1993; and Ogbonna and Harris, 2002), and this can create an even more fragile social order at work (Korczynski, 2002:95). Companies such as BA need to be both efficient and customer focused, they must appeal to the utilitarian sense of the customer (i.e. the desire for reliable, safe, on-time flights) but also enchant the sensibilities of the customer (i.e. offer a personalised service, empathy and assurance). In the 'customer-oriented bureaucracy',

Taylorism is coupled with 'Tailorism'. The routinising logic of standardising procedures is married to the logic of dealing with variable and unpredictable customers. The need to improve efficiency by cutting costs is joined as an organisational imperative by the need to deliver high-quality service. (Korczynski, 2002:65–6)

The five attributes of service sector work that distinguish it from manufacturing are: (i) *intangibility* (service is not a physical object); (ii) *perishability* (service is temporally specific, it cannot be stored); (iii) *variability* (service depends on who delivers it and the customer's perception); (iv) *simultaneous production and consumption* (during the service encounter the worker produces and the consumer consumes); and (v) *inseparability* (the customer 'takes part' in the service work process) (see Lewis, 1999; and Korczynski, 2002:6). These attributes allow a range of different types of service work to be distinguished. For example, to what extent do customers actually 'take part' in the service encounter? In a fast food restaurant, the focus is on the product rather than on the process of service delivery and workers are simply a 'buffer' between production and consumption. Hence the rather routine interaction in McDonald's, Burger King, or similar outlets – 'What can I get you today', 'Would you like to eat in or take-away', 'What drink would you like with your meal', and so on. At the other extreme, the service interaction *is* the product (e.g. psychiatric consultation). Here the focus is on the process of interaction, rather than on the 'back stage' production of a separate product. Airlines fall somewhere in between these two extremes – the service encounter is clearly an important part of the product being delivered, but the company must also ensure an efficient back stage operation (e.g. scheduling, baggage handling, catering, maintenance, and fuelling) (see Korczynski, 2002:11). Thus, instead of a choice between alternative strategies – direct control versus responsible autonomy, Theory X as opposed to Theory Y, direct supervision or self-managed teams – many organisations are faced with the tensions, and at times outright contradictions, of applying *different* systems of control to the *same* workers. These tensions are thrown into much sharper relief in the service sector, but they apply to a greater or lesser extent in all capitalist firms.

Although managers face the problems of labour control on a daily basis, all too often the analysis of control within organisations tends to cast management in the role of monolithic, omnipotent, omniscient strategist (Thompson and McHugh, 1990:157 and 2002:70). 'Managers too often are simply regarded as essentially unproblematic agents of capital who dispatch their global functions of capital in a rationalistic manner' (Storey, 1985:195). Yet conflicts between different management groups have already been noted (see Armstrong, 1984; and Whipp and Clark, 1986:213), as has the variety of 'means of control' which co-exist at any one time (see Storey, 1985:198). Furthermore, the presence of any particular strategy, such as 'responsible autonomy', may reflect management neglect (allowing control to drift away) rather than a deliberate policy of ceding control to the workforce to elicit co-operation, motivation and self-actualisation. Reality, as Paul Edwards (1986:41) illustrates, is far more anomalous:

> Firms will develop their practices of labour control with whatever materials they have available. They are unlikely to have explicit strategies and more likely to react to particular circumstances as best they can. Even when they have fairly clear goals they are unlikely to follow a policy which conforms to an ideal-type: they will proceed according to their own needs. In particular, they are likely to use a variety of means of controlling the labour process and tying workers to the firm. Reliance solely on arbitrary power or technology or rules would be a very limited and dangerous approach.

Labour control is therefore of crucial importance, but management are not simply confronted with a (strategic) choice between different types of control. Ultimately, choice is not entirely in their hands, because control is the product of past and present struggles within the social relations of production (see Child, 1997). Because of such *constrained choice*, a contradictory array of structures and practices is invariably the outcome. In particular, as Storey (1985:201) notes, managers frequently want both to use labour instrumentally and to tap co-operation and initiative. In other words, 'employers require workers to be both dependable and disposable' (Hyman, 1987a:43), which in the case of British Airways produced both internal tensions (e.g. reducing staff numbers, cutting pay and conditions and intensifying the work process while at the same time imploring staff to be polite, patient and courteous towards passengers) and external contradictions (e.g. selling a brand based on high quality service delivered by an increasingly disgruntled and embittered group of front-line workers) (see Turnbull *et al.*, 2001). The result, in BA and many other organisations, is a Theory X structure and Theory Y management. This combination often involves a separation of individual and collective relations with labour, where managers pursue an array of employee relations policies to elicit individual co-operation and commitment, while at the same time referring to external organisations such as trade unions to handle the inevitable conflicts of interest that arise from the very structure of the employment relationship itself (as discussed in Chapter 2).

Given the limits to any rational choice of a coherent 'means of control', and the tensions inherent in the very purpose of management control, namely to secure the co-operation of labour and at the same time make a profit, it is hardly surprising that most firms display a distinctly *un*strategic approach towards employee relations. In general, management practices are found to be 'opportunistic, habitual, tactical, reactive, frenetic, *ad hoc*, brief, fragmented and concerned with fixing' (Thompson and McHugh, 1990:137). To return to employee relations in British Leyland and the account of Michael Edwardes, management 'were still fire-fighting, running from dispute to dispute without tackling the root of the problem' (1983:80). British Leyland was not alone in its approach, as the account of British Airways clearly demonstrates. Nor was either company alone in its determination to change its style of management during the last two decades of the twentieth century.

The management of employee relations

There are two fundamental dimensions to the management of employee relations. First, there are the terms on which labour is hired, the substantive terms such as wages and hours of work that are adjusted periodically to reflect changes in both the external environment (such as inflation and the relative pay of other workers) and internal conditions (in particular, profitability or the 'ability to pay'). The determination of these terms and conditions in union and non-union environments is discussed elsewhere (Chapters 7 and 9 respectively). Secondly, there is the general control and direction of labour exercised by management on a day-to-day basis. Frequently referred to as 'managerial relations' or the company's employee relations 'style', this second dimension can be seen 'as a set of proposals and actions which establishes the organization's approach to its employees and acts as a reference point for management' (Brewster et al., 1983:62). Alternatively, it is simply managements' 'preferred way of dealing with employees individually or collectively' (Purcell and Gray, 1986:213). This will be heavily influenced by managements' 'frame of reference', which might be unitary or pluralist (Fox, 1966; see Chapter 2). In general, however, the vast majority of managers display a pronounced preference for unitarist values (Bacon and Storey, 2000:424; Goodman et al., 1998:547; Poole et al., 1981:82–3; and Poole and Mansfield, 1993). This is only to be expected, as such values 'have been strongly inculcated in their own training and development, they are uncomplicated in their implications, and they are self-reassuring' (Purcell and Sisson, 1983:113).

One group of managers who might be expected to differ in this respect, however, are personnel or HR managers, and they might also be expected to play an important role in determining the organisation's employee relations 'style'. But personnel representation at the board level has declined in recent years, albeit due largely to the changing composition of workplaces (Millward et al., 2000:76–7), and the majority of workplaces (around 70 per cent) do not employ a personnel/HR specialist (Cully et al., 1999:49–50). To be sure, many more establishments have 'access' to a personnel/HR specialist elsewhere in the organisation (ibid:51–2) and there is evidence that those responsible for employee relations (both designated personnel/HR specialists and non-specialist managers) are increasingly likely to have attained some form of 'personnel' qualification (see Millward et al., 1992:35–7; and Millward et al., 2000:52–6), but more UK firms have an accountant/finance specialist in charge of employee relations than a specialist 'human resources' manager. This matters, because accountants are more likely to see labour as a cost than a resource and there is evidence that these managers adopt a less sophisticated approach to people management (see Hoque and Noon, 2001:17). This was very much in evidence in our case study of British Airways.

Given the potential impact of personnel/HR managers on a company's employee relations, typologies have been developed to classify a range of possible approaches.

For example, HR/personnel managers might be strategically or tactically oriented, and might enjoy a high or low degree of discretion in overall management policy (Storey, 1992:167–8). Storey's classification of personnel roles is empirically grounded in the 'problematic reality' of employee relations (Caldwell, 2003:988), unlike the 'prescriptive vision' offered by Ulrich (1997) which is based on whether the manager in question is strategic or operationally focused and whether she is people or process oriented (the majority of employee relations specialists in Britain are now women) (Millward *et al.*, 2000:60). Nonetheless, there are striking similarities in the resulting (ideal-typical) roles of HR/personnel managers identified by both authors, and these are therefore combined in Figure 4.2.

In the right-hand quadrants of Figure 4.2, personnel/HR managers, or those with designated responsibility for employee relations, are depicted as either advisers/ strategic partners or hand-maidens/administrative experts. In both cases they play a largely reactive role focused on processes rather than people. Consider the HR Department in BA during Mr Ayling's tenure as CEO, which appeared to oscillate between these two roles. HR was *supposed* to act in an advisory role to line managers who were afforded greater responsibility for employee relations. But many line managers were 'poor people managers and were all too often reluctant to call the HR Department for help. To do so, they thought, would be seen as a sign of failure on their part' (BA manager, quoted in Turnbull *et al.*, 2001). Instead of immediate advice and a partnership role in the development of the company's business strategy, the HR Department was often left to 'hold the line manager's hand' and walk him/ her through the appropriate administrative procedures invoked by omission, neglect or simple incompetence (e.g. grievance and disciplinary procedures).

The 'regulators' depicted in Figure 4.2 are more interventionist, but they operate within a more traditional industrial relations paradigm as the 'managers of

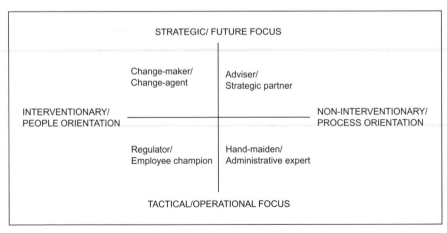

Sources: Based on Storey (1992:168) and Ulrich (1997:24).

Figure 4.2 Types of personnel manager

discontent', seeking order through temporary, tactical truces with organised labour (Storey, 1992:168–9). This was a role that senior HR managers at BA were frequently 'dragged into', despite their attempts to separate these 'fire-fighting' activities into a sub-section of the HR Department called Collective Relations. In other large organisations it would appear that fewer and fewer HR specialists now regard regulatory activities as their primary role, although many more recognise the need to champion the rights and protect the interests of their workforce. As a personnel manager responding to Caldwell's (2003:999) survey pointed out,

> If you give management a total free hand the workforce will get screwed ... I see myself as a countervailing force against the short-termism of the business. In the long-run the people are the business.

In contrast, the change-makers or change-agents have higher ambitions, seeking to put relations with employees on a new footing, namely the 'needs of the business'. Typically, this means eschewing the regulative approach in favour of a management style which engenders employee commitment and a willingness to 'do the extra mile' (Storey, 1992:169), or in the words of British Airways management 'use their hearts'. Storey's (1992:186–7) research evidence, drawn from fifteen British 'mainstream' organisations, indicated that this particular approach was rare, but more and more personnel/HR specialists now regard the management of change as the most important part of their job (see Caldwell, 2003:999–1000). As for BA, the HR Department has yet to assume the role of change-agent, as one of the company's HR managers complained:

> There was practically no input from HR in the Size and Shape Review [BA's latest corporate reorganisation published in February 2002] as well as in the design of the new organisation. There were five general managers who conducted the whole review but no one from the HR Department. So the discipline of having strategic HRM disappears entirely. Good people management is lacking, for example the process of headcount reduction and the whole selection process, and of course the role of trade unions and the style in which BA is approaching it, i.e. adversarial rather than a partnership approach. (BA HR Manager, personal communication)

The change-maker or change-agent role is often associated with the rise of human resource management. In the late 1980s, HR specialists were a rarity (Guest and Hoque, 1993; and Sisson, 1993:201), but the number of establishments employing an HR specialist has increased significantly in the 1990s (from less than 1 per cent of workplaces with 25 or more employees in 1990 to 7 per cent in 1998) (Millward *et al.*, 2000:52–3). The distinction between 'personnel' and 'human resource' managers is important because many practitioners believe there is a difference between personnel and HR (Grant and Oswick, 1997); those who identify their primary role as 'managing change' are more likely to be 'HR' as opposed to 'personnel' managers (Caldwell, 2003:999); and job titles appear to be a proxy for different specialist roles, with very different outcomes in terms of the management of employee relations (Cully *et al.*, 1999:80–2). Using WERS98 data, Hoque and Noon (2001:17) found that:

- HR specialists are more likely to hold a formal related qualification than personnel specialists
- Workplace level strategic plans are more likely to emphasise employee development in workplaces with an HR specialist rather than a personnel specialist
- HR specialists are more likely to be involved in the development of strategic plans than are personnel specialists
- Devolution of responsibilities to supervisors for pay and grievance handling is more likely in workplaces with an HR specialist than a personnel specialist
- Supervisors are more likely to have authority over hiring and firing in workplaces with an HR specialist rather than a personnel specialist
- Personality tests, attitude surveys, off-the-job training and performance related pay are more likely to be found in workplaces with an HR specialist
- No-compulsory-redundancy policies are less likely in workplaces with an HR specialist.

Despite these differences, the emergence of the 'HR Manager' is not necessarily indicative of a new approach to employee relations within particular companies, and is certainly not indicative of a shift towards more progressive forms of employee relations in the UK as a whole. Within specific firms, HR/personnel managers now perform an increasingly complex, multi-layered role (see Caldwell, 2003; and Gennard and Kelly, 1997) which no doubt helps to account for the 'mixed messages' emanating from many of the UK's personnel or HR departments (see Bacon, 1999:1182). In fact, such confusion is inherent in the very role of personnel/HR management (Hart, 1993), as Legge (1995:14) explains:

> The fact that personnel specialists oscillate between the 'personnel' and 'management', between 'caring' and 'control' aspects of the function, can be attributed to their role in mediating a major contradiction embedded in capitalist systems: the need to achieve both the control *and* consent of employees. (original emphasis)

For the UK as a whole, HRM is still a *minority* activity, at least in terms of a coherent or commitment-based system of people management characterised by high levels of employee involvement (see, *inter alia*, Cully *et al.*, 1999:295; Edwards and Wright, 2001:569; Guest and Conway, 2001:7–10; Kessler and Purcell, 2003:314; and Legge, 1995). This is a rather disconcerting finding, as research evidence suggests that HRM is not only associated with more 'favourable' employee attitudes and 'better' employee relations (e.g. higher work and life satisfaction, perceptions of co-operation, lower absence, fewer quits) (see Cully *et al.*, 1999:284–91; Guest, 1999 and 2002) but is also positively associated with superior organisational performance.

Although the empirical evidence on HRM and performance is somewhat mixed and not entirely convincing (see Edwards and Wright, 2001; Guest *et al.*, 2003; and Legge, 2001), the majority of studies to date conclude that HR practices, albeit measured in different ways, are positively associated with measures of organisational performance (see Delaney and Godard, 2001:405–7; Guest, 1997; Wood, 1999; and Wright and Boswell, 2002). Debate has focused on questions of generalisation (most of the research is based on manufacturing rather than services); research methodology (most studies are based on surveys rather than in-depth case studies); data reliability (most information comes from a single management respondent who provides data on both HR practices and various measures of organisational performance); data compatibility (workplace-based or even work group HR practices are usually correlated with company-wide performance measures); and causality (cross-sectional survey data can only reveal associations between variables, raising the possibility of 'reverse causality' whereby successful firms can afford to invest time and money in sophisticated HR policies, rather than investment in HRM leading to higher profits and superior organisational performance). The latter is the most important point of contention because it raises questions about precisely *what* HR practices give rise to higher performance and more pertinently, precisely *how*?

Confusion often arises as a result of commentators conflating HRM as a *generic* term simply denoting *any* approach to employment management, and HRM as a *specific* approach to the management of employee relations (see Storey, 2001:5). The latter, of course, is of most interest as it denotes both a different approach to traditional forms of management in general and personnel management in particular. To qualify specifically as 'HRM', most commentators agree that the organisation's HR policies must be internally coherent and externally consistent. BA's attempt to promote emotional labour while simultaneously intensifying the work process and seeking to erode the pay and benefits of core staff is clearly an example of *in*coherent HR polices that were *in*consistent with the business strategy of high quality service. Commentators are divided, however, on whether cost as opposed to resource-based approaches qualify as HRM. Redman and Wilkinson (2001:11), for example, label strategic approaches that treat people as a resource as 'HRM', but a strategic approach combined with treating people as a cost is labelled 'not HRM' (see also Edwards, 2003:26). Defining a particular approach to the management of employee relations in the negative (i.e. what it is not) is bound to cause confusion. Take the example of McDonald's, which clearly follows a strategic, *cost-minimisation* approach to HRM (see Ritzer, 1996 and 1998; and Royle, 2000). To describe this as 'not HRM' is not particularly illuminating. As depicted in Figure 4.3, a more usual (and more useful) distinction is between 'hard' and 'soft' versions of HRM (see, for example, Blyton and Turnbull, 1992; Legge, 1995; and

	Strategic	Non-strategic
People as resource	HRM – Soft	Personnel
People as cost	HRM – Hard	Traditional management

Source: Adapted from Redman and Wilkinson (2001:11).

Figure 4.3 Managerial approaches to people management

Storey, 1989). Both hard and soft approaches are strategic and therefore qualify for the label 'HRM', but one approaches people as a cost to be minimised while the other seeks to develop people as a resource. The former achieves high performance through labour control whereas the latter seeks high performance through employee commitment (see Ramsay *et al.*, 2000).

Managerial prerogative prevails under 'traditional' forms of employee relations (the bottom right-hand quadrant of Figure 4.3). Workers face a take-it-or-leave-it choice, if it can be called a 'choice', in relation to pay and conditions of service, and firms will rely heavily on their 'right' to hire-and-fire at will (see Kessler and Purcell, 2003; Purcell and Sisson, 1983; and Purcell and Gray, 1986). Although this approach evokes images of the 'dark satanic mills' of nineteenth century industrial towns in the north of England, there are still many firms whose approach to employee relations can best be described as a 'black hole', characterised by the absence of formal personnel policies or employee voice mechanisms (see Cully *et al.*, 1999:295; Guest and Conway, 1999; Sisson, 1993; and Chapter 9).

Where more formal policies are in place the label 'personnel management' is typically applied, but the approach is rarely strategic (top right-hand quadrant of Figure 4.3). Many textbooks on personnel management – before they were re-titled 'human resource management' – advocated a strategic approach to employee relations but such normative models fell short of the reality of personnel practice. As Legge (1995:27) points out, personnel management is characterised by a 'vicious circle' wherein the absence of board level representation, inadequate status or simply the non-involvement of personnel managers in the planning process leads to poorly formulated business/HR policies (the absence of external integration); this in turn leads to people management problems (e.g. grievances, poor performance and even strikes) which the personnel department is held accountable for and expected to resolve; any response to these problems is almost inevitably reactive and *ad hoc*, with the personnel department thereby cast in the role of 'firefighters'; this further tarnishes the image and status of the personnel function with other senior managers, making board level involvement and a strategic approach even less likely. Clearly, personnel managers are not entirely to blame – from their unitary perspective, most senior managers assume that employee relations are unproblematic until events prove otherwise, such that the importance of people management tends to vacillate over time (see Purcell and Sisson, 1983:116). BA's experience is clearly a case in point.

A strategic approach to employee relations is intended to counter, if not pre-empt, such problems. But if HRM holds the key to industrial harmony and superior organisational performance, why have so few companies embraced this latest management approach? Almost every organisation these days will proclaim: 'People are our most valuable asset!' But why do so few firms translate words into deeds?

Many of the problems that beset 'strategic personnel management' also impede the adoption of HRM, such as the costs of investing in human resources, the desire of (senior) managers to maintain their authority and control, and the scepticism of CEOs (see Guest *et al.*, 2000; Kessler and Purcell, 2003:331; and Sisson, 2001). Others have questioned whether UK managers possess the skills to make sophisticated forms of HRM work (Delaney and Godard, 2001:414–15; and Sisson and Marginson, 2003:169–71), a view that was recently echoed by the Council for Excellence in Management & Leadership (2002). Where labour represents a significant proportion of total operating costs, as is often the case in the service sector, firms may be particularly reluctant to invest in their human resources – minimising costs is preferred to maximising productivity. As a result, some authors have questioned the propriety of a 'high skills' strategy in the UK given the existing skills base, low labour costs and other features of the economy as described in Chapter 3 (see Keep, 2000). Others have argued that while a shift from 'traditional management' to 'good personnel practice' will bring significant benefits in terms of employee relations and organisational performance, any additional benefits from 'best practice HRM' may not outweigh the additional costs of investment in training and development, new payment systems, single status benefits and the like (see Boxall and Purcell, 2003: and Delaney and Godard, 2001:414–15).

In addition to questioning whether HRM is appropriate in the UK, there is the question of whether strategic HRM is even possible. Two important factors stand out. First, any empirical correlation between HRM and employee co-operation or organisational performance is typically based on 'high commitment management' (HCM) (i.e. *soft* HRM), which is extremely rare in a liberal market economy (LME) such as the UK where there are strong *dis*incentives to invest in human resources or indeed any approach to labour management that treats people as a resource to be developed. What incentives are there for firms to invest in human capital when they know that their rivals can, and will, poach their most highly trained workers? In 1996, for example, Tesco recruited a complete buying team from Marks & Spencer (we discuss these companies in Chapters 8 and 9 respectively). Data from WERS98 suggests that, at best, only 14 per cent of workplaces pursue a strategic HCM approach (Cully *et al.*, 1999:295).

Jeffrey Pfeffer (1998:29), one of the best-known advocates of 'universal best practice' and high commitment management, attributes the limited take-up of

HCM to the '$\frac{1}{8}$ rule' – half the people will not believe the connection between HCM and profitability, half of those who do believe will try a single (one-shot) solution rather than a systematic approach, and only a half of the firms that do make systematic changes will persist long enough to see the difference ($\frac{1}{2} \times \frac{1}{2} \times \frac{1}{2} = \frac{1}{8}$) (note that $\frac{1}{8}$ is just shy of the figure from WERS98, i.e. 12.5 per cent compared to 14 per cent). Given that managers in LMEs enjoy greater freedom of choice when it comes to employee relations, it is perhaps unsurprising that Pfeffer attributes the low take-up of HCM to managerial attitudes. Nor is it surprising that he seeks to rectify this situation by trying to persuade managers of the 'business case' for HCM (in the same way that a 'business case' is advocated for equal opportunities policies or family friendly policies in the UK and other LMEs) (see Dickens, 1994 and 1999). But as Marchington and Grugulis (2000:1120) ask, will self-interest alone be sufficient to persuade managers to choose HCM over cost-based approaches? As Streeck (1992 and 1997) demonstrates, the root problem is not simply a question of managerial attitudes or a deficiency of incentives to choose HCM, rather the absence of regulations that prevent firms opting for a cost minimisation strategy.

Social or institutional regulations, which are typically classified (and denigrated) as constraints on 'free enterprise' or 'managerial prerogative' by neo-liberals, can in fact be highly productive or beneficial, not just for workers but also for organisations. Indeed, Streeck (1992 and 1997) uses the nomenclature 'productive constraints' or 'beneficial constraints' to denote the *necessary* regulations that should be placed on self-interest and market forms of exchange in a capitalist economy. These 'beneficial constraints' might include a high wage floor (e.g. a national minimum wage that encourages firms to invest in training and development in order to increase productivity and reduce *unit* labour costs, thereby ensuring 'value for money'); economy- or industry-wide collective bargaining that standardises substantive terms and conditions of employment (e.g. basic rates of pay, hours of work, health and safety provision, sickness schemes, pensions and the like) as well as training provision (which thereby discourages poaching by firms or job-hopping by workers); a comprehensive system of statutory employment protection (e.g. making it more difficult for firms to declare redundancies, especially for short-service workers, which might encourage a more considered approach to recruitment and selection whereby firms only hire the most suitable candidates whom they can employ in the long term rather than until the next short-term downturn); and an effective system of employee voice at work via co-determination, works councils or trade union representation (workers who know they will still be around to enjoy the fruits of their endeavours are more likely to be willing to commit effort and ideas to the organisation, but they need appropriate channels of communication, involvement and participation to make their voice heard). The absence of 'beneficial constraints' not only helps to explain the sparsity of HRM but the prevalence of traditional management and non-strategic personnel practice.

The second factor that limits the possibilities for HRM is simply the nature of capitalist employment relationships and the conflicts that arise from *any* attempt to secure workers' co-operation and an economic surplus from their labour (see Chapter 2). This suggests that the distinction between hard and soft HRM is less palpable than is often implied. Typologies such as Figure 4.3 present different approaches as (hermetically sealed) alternatives, but these are 'normative models' rather than 'descriptive-functional' or 'critical-evaluative' categories (see Legge, 1995; and Truss *et al.*, 1997:54). As already noted, managers need workers' co-operation as well as control over their labour, such that HR strategy is all too often an inconsistent mix of hard and soft policies. As in the case of BA, managerial rhetoric often accords with soft HRM while the reality smacks of hard HRM (see, for example, Mabey *et al.*, 1998; and Truss *et al.*, 1997). Even the Director General of the Chartered Institute of Personnel & Development (CIPD) has acknowledged that most UK firms are pursuing cost-driven strategies (quoted in Storey, 2001:12–13), despite the CIPD's attempts to promote softer forms of HRM. Conflicts inevitably arise when management promise one thing but deliver something else or whenever they treat labour as nothing more than a cost on the corporate balance sheet. As a result, instead of working with commitment, employees work without enthusiasm, which in a customer-oriented business can prove particularly detrimental to performance and profitability. In organisations where employees and trade unions are well organised, as in BA, the result can be official strikes or other forms of collective resistance (e.g. the unofficial mass walk-out by BA ground staff at London Heathrow in July 2003).

Figure 4.3, like much of the literature on HRM, is silent on the role of trade unions or the management of employees on a collective rather than an individual basis. This omission is unsustainable, if only because HCM is more likely to be found in unionised as opposed to non-union workplaces (Cully *et al.*, 1999:110–11). To be sure, this is largely because HCM practices are more widespread in large, private sector workplaces and the public sector, where unions are more likely to be recognised (see Chapter 5), but this does raise a number of interesting possibilities. As Kelly (1998:22) asks, is the co-existence of unions and HCM indicative of partnership and compatibility or the exact opposite, namely an anti-union strategy that is more likely to be found in unionised workplaces because managers are using more sophisticated human resource management policies to undermine union organisation?

Different management 'styles' with respect to employee relations are usually categorised along two dimensions, namely individualism and collectivism. The former expresses the extent to which the firm gives credence to the feelings and sentiments of each employee and seeks to encourage each employee's capacity and role at work, while collectivism indicates the extent to which management recognise the collective interests of employees, their collective involvement in the decision-making process and the legitimacy accorded to the collective by management (see

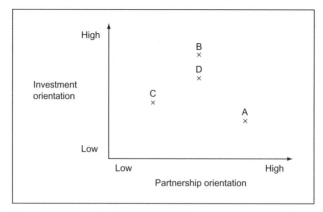

Source: Marchington and Parker (1990:238).

Figure 4.4 Mapping management style in employee relations

Purcell and Gray, 1986:213). Alternatively, individualism can be (re)interpreted as the extent to which management is prepared to invest in employees and collectivism can be (re)interpreted as the extent to which the firm is prepared to work in partnership with trade unions (see Marchington and Parker, 1990: 235–8). As an individualism/investment orientation and a collectivism/partnership orientation are not opposites but rather two facets of the managerial belief or value system towards employees, this allows different or changing management styles to be represented graphically as in Figure 4.4. In the case of BA, for example, management's approach shifted from somewhere in the region of point A (late 1970s) towards point B (by the mid 1980s), then towards point C during Robert Ayling's early years as CEO and then towards point D by the late 1990s (clearly, these points represent broad rather than precise movements).

In defining management style, Purcell (1987:533) suggests that it is 'a *deliberate choice* linked to business policy' (emphasis added). Consequently,

> Pragmatic, reactive responses to labour problems cannot be classified as management style. Style implies the existence of a distinctive set of guiding principles, written or otherwise, which set parameters to and signposts for management action in the way employees are treated and particular events handled. Management style is therefore akin to business policy and its strategic derivatives. (ibid:535)

In other words, management style must not only be deliberate but ubiquitous, coherent, integrative, consistent and long term (see also Poole, 1986:43). Some firms meet these criteria and have become the stock examples of particular and distinctive management styles (see Blyton and Turnbull, 1998:88–9; Purcell and Sisson, 1983), although many have changed their approach to employee relations in recent years. Hewlett Packard, for example, whose approach is typically classified as 'sophisticated human relations' (high individualism/investment orientation, low collectivism/partnership orientation) now employs an increasingly large proportion of its workforce on fixed-term contracts, largely in response to events in the external environment that have had an adverse effect on the company's management style and employees' experience of work (see Purcell, 1999:30; and Truss, 2001:1144). Marks & Spencer, another company that traditionally followed a 'sophisticated human relations' style, has faced similar difficulties (see Chapter 9).

Most UK firms, however, do not follow a coherent or consistent approach to employee relations, and neither HRM nor partnership agreements with trade unions (discussed in Chapter 8) add up to a new management 'style' as defined by Purcell (1987:535) (see, for example, Bacon and Storey, 2000:422). As a result, these initiatives are 'like the seed on stony ground', having only 'a short life because there is no underlying accepted standard of treatment for employees beyond pure short-run commercial logic' (ibid:567). As at British Airways, then, the management of employee relations in the UK continues to wax and wane in the light of changing circumstances, invariably in a reactive rather than proactive manner. The question that remains is whether the mis-management of employee relations is inevitable.

Competition, confrontation and the failure of British management

Throughout the 1980s and 1990s, management was glamorised, even lionised, in much of the academic and popular writing on business and organisations. While this was largely a reflection of a 'second managerial revolution', namely the reassertion of managerial prerogative (Clarke and Newman, 1993), the idea that managers possess 'special insights' which qualified them to pronounce on a broad range of issues was actively promoted by neo-liberals and was subsequently accepted by New Labour (e.g. private sector managers have been drafted in to help construct the National Curriculum, rescue failing schools, reorganise the National Health Service, and even take charge of leading universities). As Fournier and Grey (2000:11) argue,

> New Right and New Labour have joined forces in constructing the iconic status of management, a status legitimised on ontological grounds (managers as the bearers of the real world), epistemological grounds (management as the embodiment of expert knowledge), and moral grounds (managerialization being equated with greater justice, public accountability, democracy and quality in public services).

Robert Ayling, for example, was not only CEO at British Airways but Chairman of the Millennium Dome Company. His resignation from this post, six weeks after his departure from BA, was set as a condition by the Government to agree a £29 million cash lifeline for the Dome (in addition to the £509 million of lottery cash already absorbed by the project).

In general, senior managers in the UK, as in other LMEs, enjoy much greater autonomy and face fewer constraints on decision-making than their counterparts in CMEs. Major management shake-ups in BA, for example, in both 1983 and 1986, were implemented with little advance warning and were decided by a small elite. Robert Ayling continued this practice (see Barsoux and Manzoni, 2002). This certainly gave BA an advantage over its rivals inasmuch as it enabled the airline to effect a more rapid shift of control from operations to marketing, giving the company an important 'first mover' advantage (see Lehrer, 2001:373–4). But other airlines were able to emulate many of BA's initiatives (e.g. frequent flier programmes and customer service initiatives) and to do so with the support of their staff (ibid; see also Arrowsmith, 2001; Bruch and Sattelberger, 2001; Martínez Lucio et al., 2001; and Turnbull et al., 2001). The absence of dissenting (but well-founded) voices in BA arguably contributed to the employee relations problems encountered by the company (see Wheatcroft, 2000:33).

Prior to his resignation as BA's CEO, Robert Ayling appeared to blame the company's declining fortunes on everything from the economic crisis in Asia and rising fuel prices, to North Atlantic over-capacity, the value of sterling and cut-throat pricing (Flint 1999:5). In contrast, the press, the City of London, and eventually the BA Board of Directors blamed Mr Ayling (see Harper 2000; and *The Economist*, 16 October 1999). This episode encapsulates two opposing views on corporate strategy and organisational decision-making: the first casts management in a largely responsive role as 'slaves of the market' ('environmental determinism') while the second draws attention to the active and decisive role of leadership groups, casting management in the role of 'captains of industry' ('action determinism') (see Whittington, 1989). In practice, of course, consideration must be given to both positions – the nature of the organisational environment, and the role of agency and choice within the organisation – as well as the relationship between organisational agents and the environment (Child, 1997:43). As Child (1997:44) demonstrates, management strategy should be understood 'as a *political process*, which brings together agency and structure into tension and locates them within a significant context' (original emphasis).

Although managers tend to view employee relations as being subordinate to the market, especially at the plant or workplace level, considerable research exists which illustrates the importance of (strategic) management choice (Marchington and Parker, 1990; Worrall and Cooper, 2000). In the civil aviation industry, for example, global and local competition (from international alliances and low cost carriers) is propelling airlines to cut (labour) costs (Blyton et al., 2001), but this has not produced a uniform management response (see Arrowsmith, 2001; and Martínez Lucio et al., 2001). In the USA, for example, cost-cutting and 'hard bargaining' (e.g. Eastern Airlines and Continental pre-1993) proved far less successful than a 'high commitment' strategy (e.g. Southwest Airlines and Continental post-1993) and to a lesser extent 'joint governance' via employee share-ownership plans (e.g. Northwest and United Airlines) (see Hoffer Gittell *et al.*, 2001; and von Nordenflycht, 2002). In the case of Southwest Airlines, however, consistently the most profitable and successful US carrier (measured by customer satisfaction), managements' approach to employee relations cannot be divorced from the company's business strategy which is based on a 'no frills', point-to-point domestic service. Major carriers such as Northwest, United, Continental, and American Airlines, in contrast, operate a 'hub-and-spoke' system in the US domestic market and a 'network' configuration linked to their alliance partners for their international routes (e.g. American is a member of the **one**world alliance and United is a member of the Star Alliance which also includes Air Canada, Air New Zealand, All Nippon Airways, British Midland, Lufthansa, Mexicana, SAS, SIA, Thai Airways, and Varig). These market configurations are illustrated in Figure 4.5.

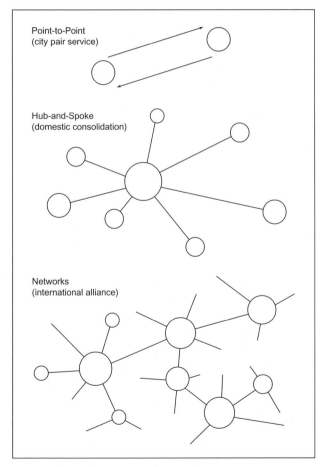

Source: Adapted from Yergin *et al.* (2000:37).

Figure 4.5 Market configurations in the civil aviation industry

The idea that organisations should strive to achieve a 'strategic fit' between their business and HR policies can be traced to the seminal work of Fombrum *et al.* (1984) and attempts to identify appropriate HR policies to 'match' different competitive strategies (e.g. Schuler and Jackson, 1987). Theoretically, such arguments make sense: surely a firm's business strategy will be more effective if HR policies ensure that employees are able and willing to deliver the kind of service that customers expect? Poorly constructed HR policies are certainly a source of competitive *dis*advantage (Purcell, 1999:38) as BA found to its cost in the late 1990s. Empirically, however, while there are examples of business strategy informing HR polices and employee relations, there is little evidence of the reverse, even at so-called 'blue chip' companies with a reputation for good people management (Truss *et al.*, 1997:67–8; see also Boxall and Purcell, 2003). In fact, the idea of matching HR polices and employee relations to the organisation's business strategy is limited by the impossibility of modelling all the contingent variables that might affect the business and its workers, as well as the difficulties of demonstrating the inter-connections between these variables (Purcell, 1999:31). More importantly, 'multiple fits' are required (most organisations must satisfy the demands of several stakeholders, in addition to their primary objective of meeting shareholder expectations) and strategy itself is multi-faceted (e.g. many firms need low costs *and* high quality *and* a product or service that they can differentiate from rival firms) (see Boxall and Purcell, 2003:54–5).

In the rush to proclaim the importance of HR policies and employee relations to business strategy, there has been a tendency to overlook the operational performance of people in the work environment (Purcell, 1999:33), which is fraught with tensions, conflicts and contradictions. In fact, although the employ-ment relationship is an important component of what Child (1997:44) describes as the 'significant context' of management strategy, as well as an important variable in determining the success (or more likely the failure) of the organisation, it is largely overlooked in most accounts of management strategy (see Bacon, 2001b:367–8; and Turnbull *et el.*, 2001). What are workers' experiences of HRM and other management practices? We have already noted (Chapter 1) that BSAS data indicates a deterioration in management-employee relations in the 1990s and data from WERS98 reveals that workers are far less likely than management to report 'good' or 'very good' employee relations in comparison to management respondents (Cully *et al.*, 1999:277; see also Bryson, 2001c) (recall that most data on HRM and performance comes from management respondents). While undertaking in-depth case-based research, Beynon *et al.* (2002:296) found that when they discussed customer orientation, performance management or other new work practices, they were 'often speaking to conscripts rather than converts'. The problems of 'conversion' have actually led some authors to suggest that it might be easier to find a new business strategy to go with the company's existing employee relations than to develop new HR practices and employee competencies to 'fit' a new business strategy (see Cappelli and Crocker-Hefter, 1996; and Wright and McMahon, 1992).

In many organisations, senior managers appear not to be in control of events; 'they are buffeted this way and that, dealing with uncertainty and risk by displacing it down the organisation – most normally through adjustments of employment practices' (Beynon *et al.*, 2002:299–300). Whether or not they are in control of events, managers often appeal to the market or wider environment to increase their power within the organisation. Indeed, managers in both the private and public sectors increasingly use the rhetoric of market forces to expedite changes in both collective bargaining arrangements and working practices: the argument is usually that unless changes are made, the company or service will become uncompetitive, and orders, customers and jobs will be lost. It is often difficult, therefore, to disentangle the dialectics of structure and agency. In general, however, the 'power' of product markets over the employer, and therefore the extent to which employers, on balance, are reactive or proactive in their policies towards labour, will be influenced both by competitive pressures (the degree of monopoly power) and customer pressure (the extent of monopsony) (Marchington and Parker, 1990:240–6).

In the civil aviation industry, for example, the overall level of demand is obviously beyond the control of individual carriers, although the low cost strategy of easyJet, Ryanair and other 'no frills' airlines has 'created' a new market for cheap (and sometimes cheerful) travel that is more akin to catching a bus or a train than a plane. Moreover, the pattern of demand in the industry is *pro*-cyclical, such that the demand for air travel generally expands (contracts) with increased (reduced) economic growth *but at a much faster rate*. This creates recurrent problems as airlines add capacity and jobs in the boom and then subsequently reduce flight frequency, rationalise route networks, and shed jobs during the inevitable downturn that follows. As a result, the expectations of management and labour are often 'out of sync' with respect to current or future market conditions. For example, during any downturn or crisis, when airlines suffer a more significant decline in demand than most related businesses, costs will be tightly controlled and employees are often expected to make 'sacrifices' to safeguard the financial position of the airline. When business picks up, airlines still tend to be cautious on costs, knowing that traffic might be lost to rivals in an increasingly competitive and deregulated aviation market, or adversely affected by any future downturn. Employees, in contrast, anticipate improvements in pay and benefits in line with business prosperity as well as an element of 'catch up' for previous sacrifices. This 'mismatch' is most apparent, and potentially most explosive, at the peak of the business cycle when employee expectations are still rising but airlines anticipate, or actually face, falling demand (e.g. a decline in advance bookings). This was precisely the situation at BA in the mid to late 1990s.

But airlines are not simply victims of the market. Major airlines in particular still control the majority of prime take-off/landing slots at the hub airports, which partially insulates them from competition, and they have strengthened their market position through computer reservation systems, integrated route networks and international alliances (the four major international alliances controlled over 50 per cent of the world market by the late 1990s). Thus, even though low-cost carriers have made significant in-roads into the European market in recent years, most industry experts anticipate progressive concentration around just a handful of major carriers (see Doganis, 2001). This would mirror the situation in the United States where the four largest carriers accounted for 45 per cent of total miles flown in 1983 and 64 per cent in 1999. Of the 58 new start-ups established between 1978 and 1990, only America West is still operating. Monopoly power is very much in evidence and customer pressure has been largely ineffective. As a result, critics argue that:

> Airline service has gone to hell ... We are herded aboard aerial slums, served cardboard food, overbooked, bumped, and misconnected. Our luggage is routed through the Twilight Zone, never again to be seen during our natural lives. Business and small town travellers pay several hundred dollars more than the vacation travellers seated next to them. The market gives us a choice, of course. We can either spend an arm and a leg or sleep in a strange city on a Saturday night. (Dempsey, 1989:251)

The power of individual organisations over their product and labour markets is clearly a key variable in determining whether or not a distinctive 'style' towards employee relations will emerge and persist over time. This is quite different from financial success which, as Purcell and Sisson (1983:116) note, is insufficient to explain whether or not firms will have a specific management style. Firms with a distinct and coherent management style tend to be either market leaders or major (oligopolistic) players in their respective product markets. Obviously, not all firms can secure oligopolistic control over their product markets. Equally, however, not all oligopolistic organisations display a uniform, consistent and coherent management style. British Airways is a case in point.

Where companies grow through merger and acquisition, as in BA's case and most other major UK firms, rather than 'organically', management will doubtless be faced with a wide variety of traditions, practices and approaches to employee relations throughout the organisation. Consequently, 'it is not difficult to understand why most of them opt for pragmatism' (Purcell and Sisson, 1983:117). But this is the symptom rather than the cause of the problem: 'British companies not only suffer one of the highest cost of capital in the world, but the febrile stock market compels them to earn a very big mark-up over even that cost of capital to fend off the threat of take-over and keep their shareholder base stable' (Hutton, 1996:157). Thus, companies aim to keep their financial returns high in the short term, principally by maintaining downward pressure on pay and other terms and conditions of employment, to ensure that the company is a predator rather than a victim in any hostile take-over bids (ibid:327). In LMEs, the booms and slumps of the business cycle tend to be amplified by the demands of financial capital and, as a result, human resources are invariably treated as a cost rather than an investment on the accountant's ledger. It is hardly surprising, then, that so few UK companies are able to establish or maintain a clear and consistent management style.

Nonetheless, some organisations clearly do have a recognisable management style, which Purcell and Sisson (1983:116–17) attribute, in the first instance, to the presence of strong personalities at an early stage in the company's development. The 'founding fathers' often establish a pattern which continues to influence subsequent developments, such as 'Cadburyism', the 'HP Way' or being an 'IBMer'. But then it is very difficult for other companies to imitate the management style of these successful companies. The case for 'people as a source of competitive advantage' is often grounded in resource-based theory (Barney, 1991) which identifies people as a resource that is difficult for competitors to imitate, cannot be easily substituted by other resources (e.g. technology) and which 'adds value' to the product or service. But competitive advantage does not derive from human capital *per se* (firms can always poach outstanding people from other organisations) or particular HR practices (firms can readily introduce team-working or a profit-sharing scheme). What matters are human processes (Boxall, 1996:66–7) or what Mueller (1996:757) calls 'the social architecture that results from ongoing skill formation activities, forms of spontaneous co-operation, the tacit knowledge that accumulates as the unplanned side-effect of intentional corporate behaviour'. This architecture will emerge 'slowly and incrementally over time, and may even predate the tenure of current senior management' (ibid). Len Peach, the former personnel director of IBM, when asked how other companies could emulate IBM's personnel style, replied, 'you start thirty years ago' (quoted by Bassett, 1986:170). Even when key management figures emerge or are appointed, therefore, their ability to impose an over-riding approach or style is constrained both by what has gone before (Purcell and Sisson, 1983:117), and by the resistance that is almost inevitably encountered (to a greater or lesser extent) from other managers, but especially from labour.

Given these factors – market uncertainty, internal management factions, and worker opposition – it is not unreasonable to question whether management can *ever* take rational, strategic decisions. As a former BA manager commented,

> no change process lasting several years can be mapped out in advance at the top and then adhered to by those below. It meanders along a course that responds to the various pressures, energy levels, ideas, past experiences and new hires and promotees encountered along the way in the system. (Tate, 1991:111)

As Tate continues, however, 'To satisfy our need for rationality, we fabricate the pieces of the jigsaw puzzle after admiring the finished picture' (1991:111). To impute, *post hoc*, rational intent to all management action is clearly fallacious, but that does not mean that managers always act without strategic intent. As Tate makes clear in the case of BA, it is invariably the *implementation* and actual *practice* of employee relations policy on the shopfloor (or in the aircraft) that creates a disparity between intentions and actions (see, *inter alia*, Bacon and Storey, 2000; Boxall and Purcell, 2003; Marchington and Parker, 1990:258; Purcell, 2001:72–3; Kessler and Purcell, 1995:347; Storey, 1985:203; and Storey and Bacon, 1993:669).

Over the past two decades, the predominant response of UK managers to more intense international competition has been to intensify the work process rather than attempt to raise the skills and functional flexibility of the labour force – working harder rather than smarter – and noisily to reclaim the prerogatives they had given up (often willingly) in the 1960s and 1970s (Beynon *et al.*, 2002; Edwards and Whitston, 1991; Elger, 1990; Green, 2001; Neale, 1992; Nichols, 1986; and Waddington and Whitston, 1995b). However, not only has work practice reform been too narrowly focused to reverse the UK's relative economic decline, but even the policy of cost-cutting itself has been pursued in an opportunistic (non-strategic) fashion (Hakim, 1990:168–78; and Rubery, 1988:271). In the 1970s, trade unions in general, and strong workplace union organisation in particular, were widely regarded as the primary source of 'restrictive practices' and the comparatively poor international performance of UK firms. Today, it would not be unreasonable to argue that management prerogatives are the new restrictive practices – managers enjoy too much power which they have too often exercised to the detriment of the workforce. It is hardly surprising that managers in companies such as BA and countless others have failed to win the 'hearts and minds' of their employees (see for example, Beynon *et al.*, 2002; Mabey *et al.*, 1998; and Scott, 1994). The failure of UK managers to secure the most basic of all objectives – the active co-operation of the workforce as distinct from mere compliance or coerced consent – arises from the fundamental tension that exists, and persists, between employer and employee. Ultimately, there is no 'one best way' to manage these conflicts, 'only different routes to partial failure. It is on this basis that managerial strategy can best be conceptualised: as *the pragmatic choice among alternatives none of which can prove satisfactory*' (Hyman, 1987a:30, original emphasis).

Conclusion

Under capitalist employment relations, management are the predominant, though by no means the exclusive, agents in the determination of employee relations. Thus, central to an understanding of the employment relationship is an appreciation of the needs and objectives of management. Simply put, management need to secure a productive and cost-effective workforce. But control and compliance is often insufficient to secure the rate of return on capital that management (and shareholders) demand. Increasingly, this requires the active co-operation and commitment of the workforce. At BA, for example, the difference between compliance and commitment was reflected by the quality of a smile or the courtesy and patience displayed by employees towards the customer. Whether such emotional labour appeared 'forced' or 'genuine' was seen to be a critical aspect of a broader competitive strategy.

Management face a variety of options and routes to secure their aims. Throughout the 1980s and 1990s, the decline of union membership and the policies of both Conservative and Labour governments appeared to offer UK managers a unique opportunity to reconstitute the bases on which they structured and conducted employee relations. But as the example of BA and countless other organisations aptly demonstrates, the majority of UK firms are still characterised by a style of employee relations management based essentially on pragmatism and opportunism, rather than any coherent philosophy or standards of behaviour. The piecemeal adoption of HRM is just one illustration of this.

Of course, while the previous two decades provided an opportunity for managers, the period also imposed severe constraints on management action and the development of any long-term strategy. Economic recession, heightened international competition, and the demands for improved quality all militated against long-term policies. More important, management seemed unable to break out of the low-trust dynamic that has been an enduring feature of employee relations in the UK (see Fox, 1974). This in part stems from feelings of job insecurity among many workers and from the fact that the UK remains a comparatively low-wage, low-productivity economy where investment in employee skills and training have been woefully neglected (see Chapter 3). Equally important, however, is the 'dynamic of confrontation' between capital and labour. Not only do workers continue to resist management attempts to intensify the work process and shift the wage-effort bargain in management's favour, but trade unions continue to provide collective support for employee resistance. It is to the activities of trade unions that we now turn.

5

Unions and their members

Organising the Capital

Working for union

'We came out of the workplace, and I just thought, YES! What a feeling', enthused Louise Chinnery, 'there's nothing else like it. We've enabled people to change their lives, to look after themselves at work. There's no other job I know of where you get that kind of feeling' (interview notes). Louise was working for the T&GWU in Region 1 (South East and East Anglia) as a Women's Recruiter, having previously worked as an Assistant Development Manager at Homes for the Homeless People in Luton after graduating from Essex University with a degree in History and Politics. Along with Karen Hannant, who previously worked for Britannia Airways and was a shop steward at Servisair, Louise's job was to recruit and organise non-union workers, especially women and young workers. During the first 5 months of their one-year contract with the T&GWU, Louise and Karen recruited 187 new members, 65 per cent of whom were women and well over half were under 30 years old. Of course, the process of recruitment was by no means automatic: 'It's a myth that just because we're women that we'll automatically be able to recruit other women. It's not just a case of showing your face and expecting people to sign up. If anything, they're rather surprised when we turn up – I don't think they expect people from the Union to look like us' (Karen Hannant, interview notes). Karen and Louise found that speed of response, being sensitive to workers' problems, active listening, understanding, sympathy, imbuing confidence, and organising around issues were all vital to recruiting new members to the Union.

The London Region of the GMB has also been actively organising and recruiting new members in the Capital, especially in the East End clothing sweatshops, where many workers are still paid less than the national minimum wage (NMW), and light industries in North and West London that support the service economy (e.g. sandwich and croissant makers, the fast food pizza and curry producers). Many of these companies employ first generation immigrants, presenting additional problems of language and communications. Two Asian women who lost their jobs after a prolonged union organising campaign at their own workplace, in which they played a leading role and were dismissed as part of the 'settlement' to the dispute, were hired by the GMB to recruit in these sectors of the economy where workers are 'one bounce from the bottom' (interview notes). These women have built close relationships with community leaders to win the trust, confidence and support of local people. They have used 'mapping' techniques to identify all employees at the target workplace, and then rated each worker in advance of recruitment in terms of their propensity to join the union, with particular emphasis on workers who hold the respect and trust of fellow workers. In some cases, the organisers have also taken jobs in non-union firms to build membership and organisation 'from the inside', a technique known as 'salting' (see Fiorito, 2003:194; and Heery and Simms, 2003:12). Between 2001 and 2003, the London Region of the GMB recruited 30 000 new members, including 15 000 part-time women and 5000 black and Asian workers.

There is little doubt that both the T&GWU and the GMB, like most other unions in the UK, desperately need to recruit more women, part-timers, young people, and minority ethnic workers in order to turn back the tide of falling membership. Total membership of the T&GWU fell by 59 per cent between 1979 and 2001, while membership of the GMB declined by 38 per cent over the same period. Membership decline has been stemmed in recent years, however, and both unions have been more successful in the Capital. The GMB's London Region, for example, increased its membership by over 7 per cent in the year to October 2002. This success is based on the 'six Cs' of union organising:

- *Campaign* – the union must be a campaigning organisation that seeks to get members involved ('the union' is not the activities of the national officials)
- *Credibility* – the union needs to establish what the issues are for the particular workforce in question (rather than impose its own agenda)
- *Commitment* – the union needs a sustained organising programme to support workers (not a 'balloons and buses' tour of the local shopping centre with recruiters handing out leaflets and membership forms)
- *Contact* – face-to-face contact is essential, using the techniques of mapping and 'like-recruits-like' (e.g. women recruit women) to establish a positive image of the union (very few members are directly recruited by full-time officers, most are asked by activists or fellow workers to join)
- *Communicate* – unions need to use a variety of media to improve their internal communications and external image, including one-to-one contact (rather than rely on the union journal or newsletter)
- *Collective* – unions should emphasise collective issues at work and seek to build a strong and self-sustaining organisation at the workplace (rather than simply recruit individuals on the basis of membership services).

Many of these organising principles are embodied in the TUC's Organising Academy, established in 1998 to train a new cadre of (young) union organisers who would not only recruit new members and build collective organisation at the workplace, but also help to change the culture of the union movement (see Heery *et al.*, 2000 and 2003a). The Academy offers a 12 month training programme to organisers who are employed jointly by the TUC and individual sponsoring unions. Lousie Chinnery was one of the first recruits to the new Academy, though she was sponsored by the CWU rather than the T&GWU. Neither the T&GWU nor the GMB have sponsored trainees at the Academy, preferring instead to develop their own organising initiatives. Within particular geographical areas and/or particular industrial sectors this has proven to be very successful, but the 'organising agenda' has yet to be diffused throughout these unions or indeed the labour movement as a whole.

Diffusion or confusion?

By the early 1990s, most trade unions accepted that structural changes in the labour market – the shift from manufacturing to services, full-time to part-time, male to female (see Chapter 3) – were 'here to stay'. Within the T&GWU, this was formally recognised at the 1995 Biennial Delegate Conference where the Union determined to 'Organise for Strength', initiating 'a rolling programme of activities to enhance recruitment, organisation and ultimately the industrial and political strength of the T&G' (T&GWU, 1995b:15). The strategy was based on:

- the identification of potential areas of membership growth
- training programmes for both lay members and full-time officers (FTOs) designed to enable them to recruit and organise with confidence and professionalism
- the development of regional recruitment teams, both lay and full-time, with clear objectives and local and regional accountability
- the exploitation of information technology to improve membership records and develop a database of companies with recognition agreements as well as non-union employers
- the regeneration of branches as campaigning centres throughout the Union
- more positive coverage of recruitment and organising activities in Union publications
- a programme of recruitment among temporary, fixed-term, casual, and contract workers
- the provision of adequate resources to effect the strategy.

Of particular importance was the development of a new culture within the Union that prioritised the delivery of a strategy for recruitment and organisation, 'recognising the sometimes different needs of those workers who have not automatically seen the T&G as a natural home' (ibid:14). This, for one full-time union official at least, was the root of the Union's membership crisis:

> We can talk about the new strategy, everyone can agree on the primacy of organising, and we've put the framework in place, but all we've really done is create an *atmosphere* in which people are now taking recruitment and organising seriously. This doesn't represent a *cultural* change. (interview notes)

Previous T&G initiatives had foundered on the inability of the Union to effect an 'organising culture', a situation in which 'organisation and recruitment are second nature to us, a part of the day-to-day life of the Union' (T&GWU, 1996:2). The Unions 'Link Up' Campaign, for example, launched in February 1987, foundered on the rocks of (dis)organisation, disillusion and opposition – from both employers and union officials. At the height of Thatcherism, most new workplaces excluded trade unions and there was a growing trend in some sectors of the economy towards *de*recognition (see Gall, 2003c:11–12; and Chapter 9). Within the T&GWU, the Link Up Campaign was seen as a top-down, short-term initiative, rather than a long-term strategy for growth and union renewal. This gave the impression, in the words of Ken Fuller (then Regional Organiser, South East and East Anglia), that 'we expected Officers and lay activists to dash about with application forms in their hands for two or three months and then revert to normality' (T&GWU, 1996:2). 'Normality' for many full-time officials (FTOs) was not to do *any* recruitment or workplace organising, and their response to the Link Up campaign was at best 'patchy' (Snape, 1994:227). Even if they have the inclination, most FTOs rarely find the time to undertake sustained recruitment and organising initiatives, and the majority prioritise other work (see, for example, Heery *et al.*, 2000; and Kelly and Heery, 1989 and 1994:103–4). Moreover, for most FTOs, whose job revolves around negotiation and servicing the existing membership, targeting part-time or temporary workers was regarded as too difficult, excessively time-consuming, and ultimately cost-ineffective (Snape, 1994:227). As no additional officers were recruited for the Link Up campaign, one of the main effects was to simply increase the workload of FTOs, which many resented.

In order to address these problems, Region 1 of the T&GWU established a separate Organising Support Unit to focus on recruitment activities and assist members and specialist organisers seconded to the Unit on a short-term basis (Louise Chinnery and Karan Hannant were the first trainee organisers to work with the Unit). Region 1 has also initiated several high profile, and highly successful, recruitment campaigns, most notably the organisation of all the Kwik-Fit tyre and exhaust outlets in the London area. While the company sought a nation-wide union recognition ballot, knowing that its outlets outside the Capital were less well organised by the Union and would therefore outweigh any pro-union vote in London, the T&G was able to persuade the relevant authorities (the Central

Arbitration Committee and the courts) that a regional (i.e. London-based) ballot was appropriate. These organising initiatives, however, have not been uniformly embraced and often met with less success in other Regions of the T&G.

The same is true of the GMB. Within its London Region, the GMB now employs twelve dedicated organisers and provides all its own training for these officials (although two of the organisers graduated from the TUC's Organising Academy). The Region's commitment to organising and recruitment, in the words of a senior official, was 'a risky decision. Even with falling membership our existing officers had their hands full with servicing, so we had to decide whether to manage decline or take the decision to invest in recruitment and create growth' (interview notes). So far, the risk has paid off. But while the London Region displays impressive growth, other Regions of the GMB have continued to decline.

Problems of co-ordination and commitment to organising might be expected in large general unions characterised by a diverse membership; considerable autonomy within particular regions, occupational groups and even individual workplaces; and the (self-)interests of existing members that prevail over potential members (current members will usually prefer union funds to be spent on services to them rather than the recruitment of 'outsiders'). Nonetheless, FTOs in both T&GWU and GMB now report a range of organising activities to be 'one of the most important parts of my job', including the identification of new sites for recognition campaigns, direct recruitment, and supporting recruitment (Heery *et al.*, 2003a:15). This finding applies to FTOs in many other unions as well, suggesting a progressive and cumulative diffusion of the organising agenda throughout the labour movement (ibid). But there are different ways to recruit new members and not all unions, and certainly not all FTOs, are convinced that organising, as opposed to servicing, is the best way forward. Equally, some unions and many FTOs favour partnership over organising (i.e. the recruitment of employ*ers* rather than employ*ees*).

Servicing or organising?

Both Region 1 of the T&GWU and the London Region of the GMB have embraced the 'organising model' of trade unionism, which is essentially 'a new name for a back to basics grassroots organising, using the methods which built unions in the first place. It recognises that genuine organisation and collectivism are still the best ways of winning justice and dignity for workers' (Organising Works, 1995:3). The central tenet of this model is that rank-and-file members *are* the union, and as such they should be empowered to recruit other workers (on the basis that like-recruits-like), generate their own agenda, and resolve as many of their own problems as is practicable. The first law of organising is: 'Never do for others what they can do for themselves'. In its *Organisers' Manual*, for example, the T&GWU warns that, 'the workplace must never get into dependency mode ... Self-organisation shouts to members: It's your Union, you are the Union, take control and get involved'

(T&GWU, 1995a:35). In the words of Martin Smith, a full-time official with the GMB, 'If you do something for someone they will ask you to do something else for them. If you show them how to do it for themselves, they will show someone else' (personal correspondence).

Under the organising model, the objective is no longer recognition but organisation (the former is simply one element of the latter). As one T&GWU lay organiser explained:

> We work around recognition. The priority is self-organisation, helping people to look after themselves. Tactically it can be fatal to go for recognition, especially if you lose. Much better to organise around an issue like health and safety, win an improvement, then go for the next issue. Success breeds success. More people join and the organisation gets stronger. If the workers are looking after themselves, if *they are* the Union, what does it matter if the T&G has formal recognition? (interview notes)

To achieve (self-)organisation, an 'organising cycle' is set in motion where employees/members, with the assistance of lay organisers and/or full-time officials, identify an *issue* that affects and is of concern to most people in the workplace, and most importantly is winnable. *Organisation* is built on the back of this issue, setting in place structures or networks to communicate effectively on a one-to-one, face-to-face basis with every employee in the workplace. Organisation is used to *educate* each worker on the issue that concerns the workforce and what can be done, through *unity*, to redress the problem. When members understand the issues they can then be asked to become involved in collective *action* to win changes at work. The organising cycle,

$$issue \longrightarrow organisation \longrightarrow education \longrightarrow unity \longrightarrow action$$

is designed to build union consciousness, encourage membership participation, and foster rank-and-file leadership.

The organising model, then, is not just about recruiting new members but (re)building a new form of participative unionism. This approach is often contrasted with a 'servicing' approach (i.e. improving the quality and range of benefits offered to existing and potential members), which the GMB London Region has explicitly rejected:

> we don't see ourselves as an institution that offers services to individuals in return for a monthly fee. That's the job of insurance companies. We see the Union as a permanent workplace-based campaign for legal rights, justice and respect. We are very close adherents to the social justice model of union organising – and this both reflects and informs our work in organising workers who are 'one bounce from the bottom'. So the organising agenda and the organising policies we have adopted are central to our understanding of who we are – a permanently moving campaign that invites workers to get involved rather than an institution that does things for people. (Martin Smith, GMB, personal correspondence)

Within the T&GWU, organising is likewise part of a broader agenda to re-establish both the industrial and political strength of the Union, as the latter depends ultimately on the former (T&GWU, 1995b:15). As one Union official put it,

> The Union was always large numerically but small ideologically. We didn't educate the members. All we had was a 'factory gate' culture, and because we've been 'institutionalised' industrially we've relied far too heavily on employers – you know, check-off [for the payment of union dues], union-management [closed shop] agreements, and facilities provided by the employer. (interview notes)

Many union officials within both the T&GWU and the GMB, however, along with may other FTOs in other unions, are still 'beguiled by partnership' with employers, which has lessened the impetus to organising (see Frege and Kelly, 2003:20).

Organising or partnership?

Just as individual unions and the labour movement (through the TUC's Organising Academy) embarked on a concerted drive to consolidate existing membership (via the systematic recruitment of non-union 'free-riders' at workplaces where unions have recognition, known as 'in-fill' recruitment) and more importantly diversify into new job territories, a Labour government was elected promising a statutory union recognition procedure and a new 'partnership' approach to employee relations (see Chapters 6 and 8). This presented unions with something of a dilemma as the case for organising is the 'opposite' of partnership: 'It rests on an interpretation of contemporary capitalism which stresses not the transition to a new and relatively benign state, but the return of old ills as the postwar settlement in welfare and industrial relations unravels' (Heery, 2002:29). At the risk of oversimplification, organising is based on union militancy, partnership is based on union moderation (see Kelly, 1996).

In some unions, initial enthusiasm for organising has been eclipsed by other priorities, including partnership with employers (see Carter and Cooper, 2002:717). Even at the highest levels within the TUC, running alongside the Organising Academy, is a Partnership Institute, which promotes: a joint commitment to the success of the enterprise; mutual recognition of each party's legitimate interests and a commitment to resolve differences in an atmosphere of trust; a commitment to employment security; a focus on the quality of working life; transparency and the sharing of information; and mutual gains for unions and employers, delivering concrete improvements to business performance, employee involvement and terms and conditions (www.tuc.org.uk/partnership). To date, however, genuine partnership agreements that meet these criteria are rare.

Where workers are subject to poor terms and conditions of employment, both the T&GWU and the GMB have found that organising is a more appropriate, and successful, strategy. Where the unions have a more established relationship with both the workforce and the employer, however, a more co-operative approach is often more attractive. For unions to embrace both organising and partnership, either separately (organise the 'bad' employers and offer partnership to the 'good' employers) or sequentially (start with an organising campaign and then develop a partnership over time) is problematic. Each strategy makes very different assumptions about the employment relationship in terms of the balance between conflict and co-operation; each requires a very different discourse to legitimise union activity; and each demands very different policies and tactics to implement effectively (Heery, 2002:31–2). What is clear, however, is that workers should only enter partnership agreements from a position of strength (see, for example, Kelly, 1999; and Turnbull *et al.*, 2004). Otherwise, any 'partnership' is unlikely to be a 'relationship of equals'. As a result, partnership is dependent on organising, but not vice versa. If an organising agenda has been diffused throughout the union, then 'Partnership might then be constructed on the collective power of workers within the firm, rather than being offered as an alternative to that power' (Heery, 2002:33).

Trade unionism in the twenty-first century

The questions confronting the trade union movement in the new millennium are at the same time simple yet momentous. How seriously has the power base of the union movement been eroded since the 1970s? Has that former influence, as McIlroy (1988:42) and others (e.g. Coates, 1980:59; and Hyman, 2001b) suggest, been exaggerated, such that any decline in power since 1979 has similarly been exaggerated? To what extent has any decline been due to cyclical or more deep-seated structural factors? If cyclical factors are diminishing trade union influence, how long are the cycles? Has there been a decline in 'collectivist' attitudes among the workforce and is there now greater 'individualism'? What policies have trade unions adopted in efforts to rectify their position? With what success? Can unions regain their former position of influence, or are they a spent force?

Overall, the future health of the trade union movement rests, as it always has done, on securing the twin (and closely interconnected) goals of, on the one hand, workers who are willing to join, participate in union activities, and remain union members, and on the other hand, employers who are willing to recognise trade unions as bargaining or representative agents for their workforce. The key question, of course, is how unions might best secure these inter-related goals. What should be the basis of the relationship between the union and its members, and the union and employers? Should unions seek to improve services for existing members, in anticipation that non-union members will be attracted by such benefits, or alternatively seek to empower their members and encourage greater participation to make the union more relevant to both current and potential members? Should the union seek co-operation with employers via 'social partnership' or new-style agreements, or confront employers and define the interest of their members in opposition to those of management? For example, the organising model embraced by many unions in recent years, which is very much in evidence in the activities of both the T&GWU and GMB, is based on a 'participative' rather than a 'transactional' (servicing) relationship between the union and its members. Moreover, rather than the union being a 'third party' in the eyes of rank-and-file members, and especially management, the organising model seeks to establish that there are just two parties to the employment relationship: the employer and the workforce who are united in their union.

In contrast to this approach, many unions have emphasised new union benefits, such as insurance schemes, free legal advice, credit facilities and the like. Others have negotiated single-union agreements with 'no-strike' clauses giving primacy to consultative over collective bargaining arrangements (see Blyton and Turnbull, 1994:96–103; and Gall, 2003b:91–2). Part of the thinking behind such initiatives is that because the climate of employee relations is believed to have changed 'irreversibly' since the 1970s, most notably as a result of new management practices that seek to undermine any perceived need for collective representation, trade unions must in turn respond by offering new services to members and new procedural arrangements to employers. But is this in fact the case? Does this prognosis apply to all workers or just to those in particular sectors of the economy? Put differently, just why do workers join trade unions? Some unions, such as the T&GWU and GMB, clearly believe that both current and potential members' interests remain basically unchanged: essentially the protection of employment rights and the improvement of pay and conditions, which can best be secured through membership participation (collective action). These different approaches – 'managerial unionism' versus 'participative unionism' (Heery and Kelly, 1994) – are a central focus of this chapter. Before considering these, however, it is necessary first to review the extent to which the position of trade unions has changed since the 1970s, the factors contributing to that change and the scale of the task facing the union movement in securing a greater degree of influence at both local and national levels in the immediate future. In sum, what has happened to trade union power in recent years?

Batstone (1988) suggests that the power resources of labour include *scarcity value* in the labour market, *disruptive capacity* in the production process, and *political influence* within the political arena. The scarcity value of any worker's labour will clearly depend on his or her skills and the availability of other (alternative) sources of labour. One means by which workers attempt to control the supply of labour, and enhance their power, is through union organisation. Thus, union membership is an indicator (or more accurately a prerequisite) of trade union power. The disruptive power of labour within the production process will depend on a range of factors including technology, interdependencies between processes, stock levels and the nature and extent of work-related changes being introduced. It will also depend on union organisation within the workplace, including the extent of union recognition, the scope of joint regulation, and the strength of shop steward or representative organisation. Finally, the political power of trade unions rests, among other things, on the political party in power, the relationship with the government of the day, union involvement in national (and increasingly international) policy-making bodies, and the content of labour-related legislation.

In order to establish a broad picture of trade union influence it is useful, therefore, to consider both aggregate information relating to union membership as a whole, more localised information regarding union presence and activity at the workplace, and wider political activities. Some indicators such as the changing relationship between unions and the state and the nature of industrial action are dealt with separately (see Chapters 6 and 10). The present chapter proceeds by reviewing the current state of trade unionism, the responses that have been made by the unions themselves, and the prospects for the future development of the union movement. Without pre-empting all the argument, our assessment points to the propriety of more participative forms of trade unionism and the need for greater inter-union co-operation, which in turn should enhance the role and influence of trade unions in the UK.

Union membership

Unlike other indicators of union power, union membership totals are readily accessible, though not always wholly accurate (see Kelly and Bailey, 1989), but the extent to which a change in membership size affects the degree of influence that a union can exert, or the way it may affect employer reactions to trade union claims, calls for much more localised and detailed enquiry. Nonetheless, it is the aggregate level of trade union membership – or more specifically overall trade union density (that proportion of the potential membership who are actually trade union members) – which tends to be used as the main bellwether of overall trade union influence. In terms of the numbers belonging to trade unions in the UK, the recent picture has been one of persistent decline. In fact, the fall in membership from 1979 to 1997 was the longest continuous decline on record. This contrasts sharply with the 1970s which saw a major rise in union membership, primarily reflecting the increased unionisation of white-collar workers. Between 1968 and 1979 total union membership rose by 3 million and union density increased from 44 to 55 per cent. During the years of Conservative government between 1979 and 1997, however, the number of trade union members fell by over 41 per cent (Table 5.1), and the density of unionism dropped from over half to less than a third of the workforce. The losses of the 1980s and 1990s more than wiped out any gains accumulated during the previous 30 years (see Waddington, 2003b:220).

The decline in membership was particularly sharp between 1979 and 1983, during which time total membership fell by over 2 million or 15 per cent. However,

Table 5.1 Membership of trade unions, 1974–2000

	Total membership at end of year (000s)	Change in membership since previous year (%)
1974	11 764	+ 2.7
1975	12 193	+ 3.6
1976	12 386	+ 3.0
1977	12 846	+ 3.7
1978	13 112	+ 2.1
1979	13 289	+ 1.3
1980	12 947	− 2.6
1981	12 106	− 6.5
1982	11 593	− 4.2
1983	11 236	− 3.1
1984	10 994	− 3.2
1985	10 821	− 1.6
1986	10 539	− 2.6
1987	10 475	− 0.6
1988	10 376	− 0.9
1989	10 158	− 2.1
1990	9 947	− 2.1
1991	9 585	− 3.6
1992	9 048	− 5.6
1993	8 700	− 3.8
1994	8 278	− 4.9
1995	8 089	− 2.3
1996	7 938	− 1.9
1997	7 801	− 1.7
1998	7 852	+ 0.7
1999	7 898	+ 0.6
2000	7 779	− 1.5

Source: Certification Officer of Trade Unions and Employers' Associations.

a reduction in membership was recorded during every year of the 1980s, leading some commentators to conclude that the high-water mark of trade unionism in the UK had been reached in 1979 and was unlikely ever to be eclipsed. This pattern of membership decline continued into the 1990s, although there was some recovery and growth by the end of the decade. By 2000, union membership stood at just 7.8 million, which was the lowest total of the post-Second-World-War period. Union density levels estimated from annual Labour Force Surveys (LFS), based on workers in employment, showed a decline from 39 per cent of employees in 1989 (when these data were first collected) to less than 29 per cent in the first two years of the twenty-first century.

For much of the 1980s and 1990s, the analysis of trade unionism in the UK focused on the causes of decline rather than any prospects for growth. The latter seemed a very distant proposition for much of this period. However, with the election of a Labour government, and more importantly a change in strategy by the TUC and many individual trade unions, analysis shifted to the question of union renewal (see, for example, Fairbrother, 2000). But any assessment of these strategies, such as new organising and recruitment techniques or partnership agreements with employers, must still be informed by a careful analysis of the causes of trade union decline. Consider, for example, the prospects for union growth if decline was attributable solely or primarily to legislative changes introduced by successive Conservative governments during the 1980s and 1990s (see Chapter 6) as opposed to deep-seated structural changes in the economy and labour market (see Chapter 3). In the former case, union fortunes might be more easily reversed by a change of government and a more supportive legislative framework. The latter, in contrast, would demand a more far-reaching reappraisal of the role of trade unions in the 'new economy'. As John Monks, former General Secretary of the TUC, acknowledged, there is a general assumption among non-union workers that 'unions are for blue collar workers with problems, not white collar workers with opportunities' (Monks, 2001). Our first task, therefore, is to consider the causes of union decline before we offer any evaluation of the prospects for growth.

Various arguments have been put forward to account for the decline of trade unions since 1979. While some have noted the interaction of several factors, others have sought to identify *primary* influences, including changes in workforce composition, macroeconomic variables, and the influence of labour legislation. Green (1992), for example, concentrates on the significance of structural shifts (specifically in regard to the industrial context and the composition of the workforce) in accounting for the decline in union density. According to Green's calculations, around 30 per cent of the decline in density in the latter 1980s was due to compositional factors such as changes in industrial and occupational structures, establishment size and proportions of different groups in the labour force. Sometimes referred to as the 'mountain gorilla hypothesis', as the unions' natural habitat, like that of the mountain gorilla, is seen to be gradually dying out, this argument points to the adverse structural conditions facing trade unions in the 1980s and 1990s, including a decline in employment in heavily unionised industries such as coal-mining, dock work, shipbuilding, and steel-making, and a growth in service sector employment, particularly in the private sector, where density levels are typically far lower. In wholesale and retail trade, for example, overall union density in 2001 was 12 per cent, in real estate and business services it was 11 per cent, and in hotels and restaurants just 5 per cent of the workforce were union members (Brook, 2002:348). Further, as Green (1992) notes, union membership levels are higher overall for men than women, for full-timers than part-timers, and those working in larger rather than smaller establishments. The figures in Table 5.2 bear this picture out (see also Chapter 9).

Table 5.2 Distribution of union density in Britain, 1990–2002

Year	1990	1992	1994	1996	1998	2000	2002
All employees[a]	38.1	35.8	33.6	31.2	29.6	29.4	28.7
Male	43	39	37	33	31	30	29
Female	32	32	30	29	28	29	29
Full-time work	43	40	38	35	33	32	32
Part-time work	22	22	21	20	20	21	21
Manual workers	42	38	35	31	30	29	[b]
Non-manual workers	35	32	33	31	30	30	[b]
Production	43	38	36	32	31	29	27
Services	37	36	34	32	30	31	30
Less than 25 employees	19	18	17	16	15	16	15
25 or more employees	47	45	42	39	37	36	36
Public sector	n/a	n/a	64	61	61	60	60
Private sector	n/a	n/a	23	21	19	19	18

Notes:
[a] includes all employees except those in the armed forces
[b] data for the Manual/Non-manual split are no longer available due to the move to the Standard Occupational Classification 2000

Source: Employment Market Analysis and Research, DTI (analysis of the LFS).

The problem with the compositional argument, however, is that it is a *description* of what has happened to union membership, not an *explanation* of trade union decline. As Kelly (1990:34–5) pointed out, there is no reason why a decline in manufacturing or the growth of female employment should automatically signal a decline in union membership. After all, in the 1970s union density among females rose faster than among males. Similarly, during the 1980s the fall in density was faster among males than females (Waddington, 1992:292–3). The net membership fall of 211 000 between 1980 and 1990, for example, represented a net fall of 210 000 among male union members and just 1000 among females (Bird *et al.*, 1992:188). In the 1990s, membership has fallen less slowly among female employees, part-timers, non-manual workers, and service sector employees, compared to male, full-time, manual, and production sector workers (see Table 5.2).

More significant, perhaps, is the fact that *intra*-establishment union density declined in the 1980s (Andrews and Naylor, 1994) and 1990s (Millward *et al.*, 2000:180). In other words, even where unions are recognised they still lost members, which composition effects clearly cannot account for. As far as Kelly (1990:34) is concerned, the compositional argument 'is a perfect example of a plausible but specious correlation, which begs numerous questions but answers hardly any'. One such question is why unions managed to increase membership in the 1970s when the changing composition of the labour force was 'averse' to union growth, but failed so conspicuously to do so in the 1980s? Another question is why nearly all the membership growth of European unions in recent years has come from an increase in the recruitment of women, *with the exception of the UK* (and Austria) (see Visser, 1998a:117–18)?

A more convincing argument is the effect of cyclical changes which affect the *incentives* and *opportunities* for workers to join trade unions, and for employers to resist unionisation. Rising real wages, for example, reduce the incentives for workers to join, while high levels of unemployment provide employers with an opportunity to resist unionisation. Equally, many unemployed union members believe that trade unions do not cater for those on the dole and so have little incentive to retain their membership (Gallie, 1996:169–70; and Lewis, 1989:274–5). These macroeconomic variables are highlighted by Disney (1990) in his account of membership decline in the 1980s (see also Carruth and Disney, 1988). One of the most important incentives for management to resist unionisation was government action (and example) in the public sector, where management were able to secure the goodwill of its government paymaster by 'taking on' the unions (see Ferner, 1989; and Pendleton and Winterton, 1993). This approach has 'softened' somewhat under New Labour (see Fairbrother, 2002:61; and Chapter 6), although the Blair Government has not balked from confrontation with public sector unions (see Chapter 10). Union membership is still much higher in the public sector (60 per cent) compared to the private sector (18 per cent) (see Table 5.2).

One reason why workers are less likely to support trade unions today is that they are uncertain about whether unions can 'deliver' (see Diamond and Freeman, 2001). In fact, WERS98 data indicates that only a minority of members (46 per cent) believe that 'unions make a difference to what it is like to work here' (Cully *et al.*, 1999:212–13). A major factor behind such a pessimistic assessment was the impact of legislation that undermined both individual and collective employment rights. Not only did individual workers feel more vulnerable at work, but the ability of trade unions to protect their members via collective action was significantly eroded during the 1980s and 1990s (WERS98 was conducted before the legal changes implemented by New Labour, which we discuss in Chapter 6, so it gives a clear indication of the impact of 18 years of Conservative government).

Freeman and Pelletier's (1990) analysis focuses directly on the importance of the legal environment for employee relations, and in particular the decline in union density due to the labour laws passed in the Thatcher years. Analysing movements in union density between 1948 and 1986, controlling for macroeconomic and compositional variables and comparing movements in union density in the UK with those in Ireland where different labour legislation has prevailed, the authors argue that membership levels respond to the degree of favourable or unfavourable legislation towards trade unions. Among other impacts, the 1980s legislation undermined union security based on the closed shop and weakened ACAS's role in supporting union recognition (see the Appendix to Chapter 6). But is legislation the *cause* of union decline and membership losses the *effect*, or the other way around? After all, Conservative governments adopted a step-by-step approach to legislative reform as unions declined (see Chapter 6), and the decline of union density slowed after 1983 (see Table 5.1) when one would expect, according to the legal argument, that it would accelerate (see Andrews and Naylor, 1994:415; and Waddington, 1992:310–11). Research data from the Social Change and Economic Life Initiative (SCELI) suggested that the Conservative governments' privatisation programme 'may have constituted a greater threat to the unions' longer-term influence than its specific legislative programme for industrial relations reform' (Gallie and Rose, 1996:64; see also Gallie, 1996:153–5).

These foregoing studies attempt to go beyond those commentaries which simply list a range of influencing factors without assigning weights or priorities either to the different factors or the various interactions between them. The lack of agreement on the relative importance of different factors, however, indicates the difficulties of achieving a satisfactory conclusion (see Mason and Bain, 1993; and Waddington, 1992 and 2003b). Not least this reflects the fact that the decision to join a union is influenced by several variables including, most obviously, the presence of a union to join and the attitude of the employer towards union membership. Green (1990), for example, using data from the General Household Survey, found that overall less than 30 per cent of female part-timers were trade union members, but where a trade union was available to join the figure rose to over 60 per cent. In the SCELI study, Gallie (1996:166–7) discovered that the attitude of employers to union organisation was one of the most important predictors of union membership. Many authors have identified the employer's attitude to trade unions, and in particular the employer's willingness to recognise unions as the bargaining agent for a group of employees, as a crucial influence on actual membership decisions (e.g. Bain, 1970; see also Gall, 2003c:6–7; Gospel and Wood, 2003; and Chapter 9). One indication of the importance of employer attitudes is that throughout the 1980s and 1990s, newly established workplaces were far more likely to remain non-union, with the sharpest falls in union recognition among private manufacturing establishments set up after 1980 (see Machin, 2000).

According to Metcalf (1991:19), 'recognition is the fulcrum on which the health of the labour movement turns'. Fulcrums are points of balance, and in identifying the need for unions to balance their appeal to both employees and employers, Willman (1989:263) notes that:

> unions operate as mediating organisations between employers who see some benefit either in the granting of recognition or its maintenance ... and employees who seek various forms of insurance and representation. It follows that, to succeed, they must appeal to both sets of interests.

In much of the single factor arguments, the role of the individual employer is omitted or under-emphasised, whereas in practice the interaction between individual propensity to join, the presence of a suitable union and the employer's attitude, are closely interlinked. The individual factors contribute to an understanding of this relationship but do not in themselves fully explain it.

Further, the championing of single factor arguments can act to obscure the changing influence of different factors in different periods. Millward *et al.* (1992:101–2), for example, argue that in the first half of the 1980s the demise of large, highly unionised manufacturing plants played a key role in the decline in union membership. In the second half of the decade, however, weakened support for unionism among employees, various government measures constraining unionism and antipathy amongst a growing number of employers, are judged to have played a greater role in the continuing decline in union membership levels. In the 1990s, declining support for trade unions among members appeared to be more important than employer hostility to unionism (Millward *et al.*, 2000:180). Beaumont (1986:33–4) in fact suggests that employer opposition to unions will pass through several phases, starting with a reduced influence for existing joint structures (less regular meetings, less well attended, and so on), the development of new structures to by-pass trade unions, stronger opposition by management towards the possible unionisation of any uncovered groups (e.g. white-collar staff), and finally derecognition of existing unions. During the 1980s and early 1990s this indeed appeared to be the trend, with an increasing number of (reported) cases of union derecognition (Gall, 2003c:11) and the rout of trade unions in some sectors of the economy such as port transport (see Turnbull *et al.*, 1992). The introduction of a statutory union recognition procedure (Employment Relations Act 1999) appears to have put paid to outright and aggressive derecognition cases (Gall, 2003c:11) but not employer opposition to new union organising and recruitment campaigns, with increasingly sophisticated ('union busting') techniques being employed in several cases (see Gall, 2003b; and Heery and Simms, 2003).

Returning to the more recent past rather than the prospects for the future, Metcalf (1991) argues that the emphasis on particular factors has served largely to exclude other influences. According to Metcalf (1991:22), union membership and density are determined by the interaction of five factors: the macroeconomic climate, the composition of jobs and the workforce, the policy of the state, the attitude and conduct of employers and the stance taken by unions themselves. Waddington (1992:311–14) suggests a similar cocktail. What is significant about parts of Metcalf's list and both the 'macroeconomic factors' and 'legislation' arguments, is their degree of cyclical character (the cycles turning on economic and/ or political change). Even Green's (1992) analysis of structural changes in industrial and workforce composition only 'accounts' for a minority of the decline in union density, and there are no *a priori* reasons why these compositional factors should be associated with lower membership levels. Successful periods of union organising (the 1890s, 1910–20, 1933–45, and 1968–79) are closely associated with 'long waves' (Kondratieff cycles) of capitalist economic development, when unions have been able to satisfy employee demands for protection and advancement at work (see Kelly, 1998 and Kelly and Waddington, 1995). As Boyer (1995:552–3) notes,

> waves of unionization are linked with general movements about social values which shift back and forth from individualistic to more holistic and solidaristic: trade unions prosper after dramatic episodes of economic collapse and build upon the high values attached to collective action.

In the longer term, therefore, union density among currently low unionised sectors, occupations or groups could increase. Indeed, in many job categories or among particular groups of workers, membership levels *have* increased in recent years. Moreover, the fact that unions appear to have 'stemmed the tide' of falling aggregate membership suggests that earlier talk of the demise of collectivism in general, and trade unionism in particular, was premature. However, sufficient industrial, economic and political change has occurred to guarantee that any revival of union membership is unlikely to flow automatically from, for example, a fall in unemployment, a reduction in real wage increases or even the election of a pro-union government. As Gall (2003c:9) points out, 'new members are not falling into the arms of unions: they are, in the main, being fought for, albeit under more favourable public policy'. This suggests that a single twist of the temporal spiral, to use the metaphor introduced in Chapter 1, is unlikely to bring the union movement back to the position of the mid to late 1970s. If nothing else, the more favourable influences on union growth are unlikely to coincide: the political climate is 'permissive' rather than strictly 'supportive' of union membership (see Chapter 6), industrial restructuring continues apace (see Chapter 3), and management continue to pursue more 'individualised' forms of employee relations (see Chapters 4 and 9).

As a result, the scale of structural change in the pattern of economic activity and workforce composition requires trade unions to develop different approaches to membership organisation and representation than were adopted in previous decades. Yet as various writers have pointed out, such adaptation is not a new phenomenon for the trade union movement (see, for example, Bain, 1986; Fairbrother, 2000; and Kelly 1988 and 1998). Indeed, despite the various images of the trade union movement as a mountain gorilla faced with an ever-shrinking habitat or a lumbering cart-horse unable to adapt to changed circumstances, in practice, at different points in their history, trade unions have demonstrated considerable versatility, for example in gaining acceptance among the growing non-manual workforce in the post-war decades and particularly during the 1960s and 1970s (Bain and Price, 1983). Put differently, unions are not simply the *object* of 'external' factors, as economists typically assume (e.g. Disney *et al.*, 1995:417–18; for a critique of recent economic studies of trade unionism, see Turnbull, 2003). Trade unions are also the *subject* of their own history, capable of determining, to a significant extent, their own fate (see Gallie *et al.*, 1996; Heery *et al.*, 2003b; Hyman, 2001b; Mason and Bain, 1993:333; Undy *et al.*, 1981).

This fact is evident during the current period, as the actual pattern of union membership change is far more complex than the figures in Table 5.1 would suggest. These figures show net change but this summary statistic fails to reflect the degree of flow into and out of trade unions. For the picture since 1979 has not been simply one of union members 'flowing out' of trade unions. On the contrary, even during the very difficult years of the 1980s, trade unions continued to be active recruiters (though some critics would argue, not sufficiently active in the circumstances). For example, the shopworkers' union USDAW recruited and lost roughly a quarter of its members each year, reflecting the lack of employment stability in much of the retail sector (in 1987, USDAW recruited 108 444 new members, but recorded an increase of membership of only 5223) (see Metcalf, 1991:22; and Waddington, 1992:313). Thus, while a majority of TUC unions lost members during the 1980s, in particular most of the larger unions listed in Table 5.3, a number actually registered a net gain, and in several other cases the drop in membership was contained to less than 5 per cent of the total (see Kelly,

Table 5.3 Membership of major TUC-affiliated unions, 1979 and 2001

Union	1979	2001	% change 1979–2001
T&GWU	2 086 281	858 804	−59
AEEU[a]	1 661 381	728 211	−56
Unison[b]	1 657 926	1 272 470	−23
GMB	1 096 865	683 860	−38
MSF[c]	701 000	350 974	−50
USDAW	470 017	310 222	−34
PCSU[d]	445 329	267 664	−40
UCATT	348 875	114 854	−67
CWU[e]	334 453	284 422	−15
GPMU[f]	313 000	200 008	−36
NUT	290 740	286 245	−2
NAS/UWT	152 222	255 768	+68
UNIFI[g]	131 774	160 267	+22

Notes:
[a] formerly AEU and EETPU, merged with MSF in 2002 to form Amicus
[b] formerly NALGO, NUPE and COHSE
[c] formerly ASTMS and TASS, merged with AEEU in 2002 to form Amicus
[d] formerly SCPS, CSU, IRSF and CPSA
[e] formerly NCU and UCW
[f] formerly SOGAT and NGA
[g] formerly BIFU, Unifi and NatWest Staff Association. 1979 figure for BIFU only

Sources: TUC Annual Reports and Certification Officer.

1990:32). Several non-TUC affiliated unions, most notably the Royal College of Nursing, also recorded significant membership gains. Excluding the Police Federation, non-TUC affiliated unions and associations increased their membership from 363 000 in 1978 to over a million by the early 1990s (Farnham and Giles, 1995:13). Thus, while the net outcome has been an overall decline in membership levels, unions continue to attract new members. A picture depicting only a scene of dwindling membership, with employees unwilling to become union members, is in reality a gross over-simplification.

What is not yet clear is to what extent the 1970s and 1980s were unusual decades for trade unionism in the UK, the one characterised by conditions particularly conducive to growth, the other by the conjunction of several factors anything but conducive to growth. Indeed, it was the conjunction of these factors that progressively transformed the landscape, and the practice, of employee relations (see Chapter 1). By the late 1990s, membership levels had been significantly depleted compared to where they stood in 1979, but as membership 'bottomed out' it became evident that the losses by no means constituted a rout of trade unionism from the workplace. At the same time, it is also evident that the road to membership revival may be far harder for trade unions than in previous periods, not least because of the number of employers who appear to be more inclined to question both the need to locate trade unions at the heart of employee relations and the propriety of dealing with employees on a collective rather than an individual basis. It is to the presence of trade unions at the workplace that we now turn for a further view of the contemporary state of trade union influence.

Unionism in the workplace

Data from the latest Workplace Employee Relations Survey (WERS) (Cully *et al.*, 1999; Millward *et al.*, 2000) reveal the extent to which the overall fall in union membership levels has been associated with both a decline in the number of workplaces with a union presence and in the number of establishments where unions are recognised by employers as bargaining agents. Between 1984 and 1998, the proportion of establishments which had any union members fell from 73 to 54 per cent (Millward *et al.*, 2000:85). Almost all of this decline took place in the private sector – public sector workplaces, virtually without exception, continued to have union members. A similar decline is evident in relation to average union density. Between 1984 and 1998, overall union density in the sample organisations fell from 58 to 36 per cent, though with continued marked variations in density levels between public and private sectors: in 1998, union density in the public sector stood at 57 per cent, compared with 26 per cent in the private sector (ibid:88).

Union recognition by employers for negotiating pay and conditions also fell during the 1980s and 1990s. In 1984, two-thirds (66 per cent) of establishments recognised trade unions for some of their workforce; by 1998 this had fallen to just over two fifths (42 per cent) (ibid:96). The fall in recognition has been most pronounced in the private sector where the proportion of establishments recognising trade unions fell from 48 to 25 per cent between 1984 and 1998 – one of the clearest indicators of a significant decline in trade unions' presence within the UK economy. This decline in recognition has been particularly marked in smaller organisations: by 1998, for example, only 13 per cent of private sector organisations with less than 100 employees recognised trade unions, down from 30 per cent in 1984 (ibid:98; see also Chapter 9).

Part of this reduction is due to explicit derecognition strategies by employers, especially in the 1980s and early 1990s (Gall, 2003c:11; and Gall and McKay, 1999) and particularly in specific industries such as provincial newspapers (Smith and Morton, 1990), docks (Turnbull and Weston, 1993b:185–6) and oil (where examples of derecognition have included BP, Esso, Mobil, and Shell). However, other factors accounting for the decline in recognition include the failure of unions to secure recognition where companies open new, greenfield sites. Where a multi-plant company recognises a union in some (well-established) plants but refuses recognition in other (newer) plants, this situation is known as 'double-breasted' arrangements, a term borrowed from the US construction industry (Beaumont and Harris 1992). Non-union establishments in the UK are more likely to be foreign-owned, to have recently changed ownership, and to employ a relatively higher proportion of non-manual workers, all of which are on-going trends within the economy (ibid:281). At present, however, more significant than either derecognition or double-breasting are new (single site) employers refusing to accept union recognition and the ending of industry bargaining not being replaced by bargaining activity in many small companies (see Disney *et al.*, 1995; Millward *et al.*, 2000:84–5; and Chapter 7). In fact, the aggregate fall in union presence at the workplace between 1990 and 1998 is almost wholly attributable to the lesser penetration of unionism in new workplaces, especially in the private sector (Millward *et al.*, 2000:84–5). The WERS data also identifies a fall in union presence and recognition in the public sector, but this fall is almost entirely accounted for by the government's unilateral withdrawal in 1987 of pay negotiation machinery for teachers in state schools in England and Wales and its replacement by a pay review body (ibid:97).

Taken together, the decline in the number of establishments with union members, the drop in union density levels and the fall in the number of workplaces recognising unions for purposes of negotiation, signal a significant weakening of the position of trade unions in the UK over the past two decades. Nevertheless, the point is worth underlining that the trade union movement in the UK still entered the twenty-first century with most of the public sector and a majority of larger establishments in the private sector recognising trade unions as the bargaining agents for at least part of their workforce.

Just as union membership and recognition levels fell in the 1980s and 1990s, so too did the proportion of employees covered by collective bargaining, from 70 per cent of employees in 1984 to 40 per cent in 1998 (Millward *et al.*, 2000:197; see also Chapter 7). This fall is evident in both private and public sectors; in the latter, where coverage fell from 95 to 62 per cent of employees between 1984 and 1998, this was accounted for mainly by the loss of negotiating rights among teachers and nurses, together with the contracting-out of services in local government and the civil service, which has been accompanied by a reduction in the role of trade unions. Potentially, however, these developments, could represent an *opportunity* for trade unions: 'Paradoxically, contracting may also provide exactly the stimulus to expanded forms of workplace unionism, and increasing levels of activity, that have been missing to date' (Colling, 1995b:137). Opportunities, of course, must be seized (via collective organisation), which in the context of previously neglected workplace structures in the public sector is not an easy task (ibid:143; see also Fairbrother, 1996:110–11 and 2000; and Terry, 2003:272).

A further aspect of the union presence at the workplace that did change substantially in the 1980s relates to the closed shop. In 1979, at the peak of union membership and density, almost 40 per cent of all trade unionists (23 per cent of all workers) were covered by a closed shop (Gennard and Dunn, 1984:15). In terms of workplaces, the second WIRS revealed that, in 1984, 36 per cent of establishments with recognised trade unions operated closed-shop arrangements. By the 1990s, however, following the 1980s legislation making it progressively more difficult for closed shops to operate lawfully (see Chapter 6), coverage had fallen dramatically (to 8 per cent of establishments with recognised unions in 1990, and to 2 per cent by 1998) (Millward *et al.*, 2000:147), although informal arrangements remained in some work contexts, especially for manual and craft workers (Wright, 1996). More importantly, following the logic of Hyman's (1989a:179) argument that member-ship gains in the 1970s were often obtained *without* securing the ideological commitment of the workforce, as membership was often a condition of employment (the closed shop) and involved limited interaction between the union and the membership (due to check-off arrangements; see below), these develop-ments might paradoxically foster a more committed, if numerically much depleted, membership in the future.

Yet, notwithstanding the marked changes in union membership, recognition, the coverage of collective bargaining, and decline of the closed shop, further evidence of both the resilience of workplace organisation and the opportunities for union renewal abounds. There has been little change, for example, in agreed time-off arrangements for union representatives, while union representatives' access to office facilities has also remained broadly the same. Similarly, in 1984, 80 per cent of establishments recognising trade unions reported check-off arrangements (mem-bers' union subscriptions deducted on behalf of the union through the employer's payroll administration); in 1998 this proportion had fallen only slightly, to 75 per cent (Millward *et al.*, 2000:151). Likewise, in terms of the number of shop stewards (elected representatives of trade union members at the place of work where they are themselves employees), while the number of establishments with on-site representation by shop stewards or equivalent fell in the latter 1980s (from 82 per cent of establishments with recognised unions in 1984 to 71 per cent by 1990) this proportion stabilised during the 1990s (and stood at 72 per cent in 1998) (ibid:152–3). Much of the 1980s decline was concentrated in smaller workplaces with fewer than 100 employees (Millward *et al.*, 1992:110). Over a longer time period, Terry (2003:259) notes that the actual number of shop stewards may have fallen from over 250 000 in the late 1970s to around 218 000 by 1998.

The presence and activity of shop stewards was one of the most important characteristics of the UK trade union movement during the 1960s and 1970s. In the full employment years of the post-war period, when employers faced relatively 'soft' (Commonwealth) product markets, informal bargaining with shop stewards proved to be a flexible and effective method of handling a whole range of employment issues at the workplace (see Chapter 7). For the unions, the reliance on shop stewards proved to be very cost-effective, but the growing influence of shop stewards arguably led to a loss of authority (and control) for the unions' district committees, executives and even branches (the basic units of organisation of virtually all trade unions). During the 1960s, this presented relatively few problems for the union movement. In fact, shop steward activity not only proved to be an effective method of securing improved pay and conditions at work, but played an important role in 'democratising' a number of highly autocratic unions (most notably the T&GWU). But the growth of shop steward organisation, an increasing number of whom were paid by management to work full-time on union activities (see Terry, 1983), proved in many respects to be a 'fair weather' unionism. In the 1980s, when the chill wind of Thatcherism began to blow, many shop stewards found themselves isolated: members were fearful of losing their jobs and were unwilling to support shop stewards victimised by management, while the unions were unable to provide sufficient (full-time officer) support. Not surprisingly, many managers took the opportunity to by-pass shop stewards (e.g. Brown, 1983; and Chadwick, 1983), as reflected in the marked decline in workplace bargaining in the first half of the 1980s over issues ranging from physical working conditions, redeployment, staffing/manning levels, and redundancy/redundancy payments (Millward and Stevens, 1986:248).

The 1990s, however, saw this pattern stabilise, with the result that in relation to some issues, the joint regulation of non-pay conditions of employment in establishments with recognised unions has remained substantial. In 1998, for example, four out of five such establishments bargained with union representatives over physical working conditions, three-quarters over the reorganisation of working hours, and two-thirds over internal redeployment (Millward *et al.*, 2000:168; see also Chapter 7). Hence, while the proportion of establishments recognising trade unions has declined significantly over the 1980s and 1990s, as has the level and density of union membership, in those establishments where unions continue to be recognised the degree of joint regulation over a range of issues appears to have remained fairly stable. This is very important for trade unions because, in order to retain members, they need to protect workers' interests and 'make a difference' in the workplace (see Bryson, 1999:81; and Diamond and Freeman, 2001:19). As a recent study undertaken by the TUC (2003a) concluded, 'there is no substitute for having workplace representatives who can communicate effectively with members and respond rapidly to problems and complaints'.

The comparatively unique dependence of UK trade unions on workplace organisation in general, and shop stewards in particular, is likely to continue, given the decentralisation of collective bargaining (see Chapter 7). In this context, the propriety of participative forms of trade unionism is immediately apparent. As Fairbrother (1996:136) argues:

> No longer is it possible for unions to organise on the assumption of relatively remote and inactive memberships, involved in union activity at the behest of national leaders or regional officers ... Instead, a premium is now being placed on forms of collective organisation that are rooted in the workplace in ways that were not necessary in the past.

For active workplace unionism to be effective requires workplace representatives who are 'leaders' rather than 'populists' (Batstone *et al.*, 1977). The former display a much higher commitment to trade union principles and the larger union, act as representatives of rank-and-file members rather than simply delegates, initiate workplace issues, and help create, and perpetuate, a strong trade union ideology among the workforce (ibid: 34–5). Not only are management more likely to develop a stronger bargaining relationship with stewards who are both willing and able to lead the membership (ibid:176–7), 'leaders' display greater success in securing increased wage levels, in maintaining various forms of worker control, and in manipulating consciousness in favour of trade union principles (ibid:250; see also Darlington, 1994).

For unions to realise the potential of (participative) workplace organisation they must develop supportive relationships between shop stewards and the union bureaucracy on the one hand, and empower rank-and-file members on the other. In recent years, however, many unions have concentrated their efforts on developing a 'managerial servicing' relationship where members are regarded as passive consumers of union benefits rather than active participants in union activities (see Bacon and Storey, 1996; and Heery and Kelly, 1994:7–10). A servicing relationship clearly sits more comfortably with management-union co-operation, and many unions have made overtures to employers in the form of new-style agreements or company-based partnership agreements. These initiatives merit critical scrutiny. First, however, the political influence of trade unions is considered. Throughout the years of Conservative government in the 1980s and 1990s, many unions, and many commentators (e.g. McCarthy, 1991:19; and Waddington and Whitston, 1995a:192), argued that the labour movement would only be revived with a change of government and a new legal framework for union recognition. In other words, union renewal was dependent on political as well as industrial activity.

Beyond the workplace:
unions and politics

All trade unions are involved in political activity, by virtue of necessity (Crouch, 1982b; and Hyman, 2001b:6). Trade unions in the UK have always maintained a clear, and some would argue too rigid a separation between their industrial and political activities (Hyman, 1989a:167–9), but as Flanders (1975:30) argued, unions have been compelled, at a minimum, to seek to establish a legal and economic environment which allows them to flourish as industrial organisations. But unions' political activity extends well beyond sectional (or vested) interests, for they must take on broader social issues, such as housing, transport, education and health care, if they are to broaden their appeal (what Flanders described as the union's 'sword of justice'). Thus, at national level, the trade union movement in general, and the TUC in particular, gradually extended its involvement with government bodies in the 1960s and 1970s. In part this reflected an increased tendency for governments to take soundings on economic and industrial policy from both employer and union organisations. This led to union membership of bodies such as NEDC (National Economic Development Council) which, together with the little 'neddies' concerned with particular sectors, were established to secure tripartite discussions over national and sectoral economic issues. Other bodies on which trade unions gained a presence were the Industrial Training Boards, the Manpower Services Commission, the Health and Safety Executive, the National Enterprise Board and the Council of ACAS.

By 1975 there were over 2000 trade union nominees sitting on tripartite bodies at national and local level (McIlroy, 1988:44). In addition, the pact established between the unions and the 1974–9 Labour government (the Social Contract) increased the degree of union involvement in the government's economic management (see Chapter 6). However, although this period is regarded as the high point of union political influence, it must be recognised that the historical separation of politics from industrial relations left the union movement with no overall vision of trade unions' role in society. In addition, political involvement in the 1970s was based less on a corporatist ideology (discussed in Chapter 6) but on the pragmatic needs of governments to come to terms with the industrial power of trade unions which might disrupt (however unintentionally) national economic policy (Hyman, 1989a:169–73). Thus, as McIlroy (1988) has pointed out, the amount of influence which the trade unions had in the tripartite arrangements and under the Social Contract can easily be inflated (see also Coates, 1980; and Hyman, 2001b). Many of the tripartite bodies, for example, were consultative rather than decision-making in character, allowing the government to take soundings rather than committing them to joint decision-making. Similarly, the breadth of the Social Contract, and the powers it gave to trade unions, must not be exaggerated. In practice, the Social Contract,

> increasingly became simply an instrument for the control of wages. There was no open and formalised bargaining between the state, capital and labour, where broad social objectives were articulated, analysed and bargained over. (McIlroy, 1988:43)

The point here is that the degree of influence enjoyed by trade unions over the state in the 1960s and 1970s can easily be overstated: greater involvement there certainly was, but the extent to which this translated into real influence is more questionable. Coates (1980:59) even goes so far as to argue that 'the visibility of trade union leaders in the process of policy making was less an index of their power than of their subordination'. One possible consequence of this tendency towards overstatement is that any subsequent perceived decline in that influence is also likely to be exaggerated. It is true that during the 1980s the union presence on national bodies was reduced or removed altogether (see Crouch, 2003:120–1). Tripartitism lost favour in the Thatcher years. Yet it is probably more accurate to represent this as a reduction in access to national *consultative* arrangements with the state, than as a removal of unions from joint *decision-making* bodies. Moreover, this decline in involvement was under way before the 1979 Conservative electoral victory: the Social Contract had effectively broken down well before the 1974–9 Labour government left office. What is more, the subsequent success enjoyed by the Thatcher government in circumscribing union influence at national level in the 1980s may be seen as attesting, in part, to the restricted nature of that union influence – and certainly its fragility – during the preceding decade.

There is no doubting, however, the political problems that afflicted the labour movement in the 1980s and early 1990s, and the consequent decline of political influence. In particular, the relationship between the trade unions and the Labour Party, and the decline of electoral support for the Labour Party even among trade unionists, proved particularly problematic. Initially, the Labour Party and the trade unions, through the TUC, were united in their opposition to the first Thatcher government (1979–83), with the TUC leading political campaigns and demonstrations against the new government. The unions actually increased their influence within the Labour Party at this time: in addition to holding the majority of seats on the Party's National Executive Committee (either directly or indirectly), a new electoral college system for the election of Leader and Deputy Leader of the Party gave the trade unions 40 per cent of the vote, the Parliamentary Labour Party (PLP) 30 per cent, and the constituencies 30 per cent (previously the PLP elected both Leader and Deputy Leader). This change, however, along with the Conference block votes held by the larger unions which were no longer overwhelmingly passed in support of the right of the Party, led to the break-away of more than twenty Labour MPs to form the Social Democratic Party (in March 1981), which effectively split the labour vote. This split, combined with the failure of past Labour governments' economic policies, the unattractive image of bureaucratic state socialism (inefficient public services and costly nationalised industries), and the growing influence of the militant left within the Labour Party, led to a second General Election defeat in 1983 (see Hyman, 1989a:175–7). Of course, the Falklands War also played a major part in the 1983 election, but less than 40 per cent of trade unionists voted for Labour in 1983, fewer than ever before.

Union policy then changed from political opposition and the hope of a return to 'the good old days' under a Labour government, to 'new realism'. The idea of collaboration with both employers and the Tory government had taken root (Kelly, 1990:58–9). The labour movement was now split on both industrial and political fronts. However, members continued to support *their* union, even on politically contentious issues such as the closed shop (the unions won 82 per cent of the 111 ballots on the closed shop between 1982 and 1986) (ibid:44), and union political funds (see Leopold, 1986; and Chapter 6). Such limited support failed to prevent two subsequent General Election defeats for Labour, which clearly exacerbated the political problems facing the labour movement. The 1987 defeat, however, focused the attention of a number of unions on recruitment activity as the prospect of a Labour government being returned seemed an ever more distant prospect, as proved to be the case in the 1992 election.

In 1997, the incoming Labour government promised the unions 'fairness, not favours', continuing to distance itself from the labour movement (for example, 'one member, one vote' was passed at the 1993 Labour Party Conference, further eroding the unions' influence within the Party, and the 1995 Conference abandoned Clause IV of the Labour Party's constitution which committed Labour to public ownership) (see McIlroy, 1995:299–304 and 410–11). As one senior union official remarked, the relationship between the unions and New Labour became rather like that between parents and their teenage offspring: 'You can drive me to the disco, pay for my booze, but park round the corner so my mates can't see you' (*The Independent*, 6 September 1996). For the Labour Party, an accommodation with neo-liberalism and modified acceptance of the Thatcherite landscape, based on a distancing of Party from unions, was essential for electoral success. Union politics obviously differed from those of New Labour, accepting modernisation but demanding important revisions to employment legislation, increased public spending, a developmental state, EU integration and an enhanced role for trade unionism (McIlroy, 1998:558). These differences have caused on-going tensions, and occasional (overt) conflict (see Chapters 6 and 10), but 'ultimately the accumulated weakness of a trade unionism in decline motivated acquiescence' (McIlroy, 1998:559).

Politically, therefore, trade unions and the TUC face a number of difficult choices in relation to the economic, employment and legislative policies of the Labour Government. For example, New Labour has prioritised links to employers and is keen to promote 'business interests' through partnership (see Chapters 6 and 8). But most employers display an 'entrenched antipathy to significant *social* partnership' (McIlroy, 1998:559, emphasis added), preferring *company-based* forms of partnership or *no* formal involvement for trade unions (see, *inter alia*, Ackers and Payne, 1998:541; Heery, 2002:25–6; IPA, 2001; Kelly, 1999; and Turnbull, 2003:509–10). For partnership to be effective, there must be trust between the parties. In co-ordinated market economies such as Germany, trust is developed through deliberative institutions with statutory backing (e.g. works councils and collective bargaining) (see Rogers and Streeck, 1994; Wever, 1995). In the absence of such institutional support, unions in the UK must 'persuade' or 'compel' management to provide employees with information, consult them over business decisions, and provide opportunities for workers to participate in various decisions that affect their working lives. To do this, they need strong workplace organisation: where unions are present in UK workplaces, trust in management is higher where the union has sufficient power to challenge management and where employees perceive the union to be effective (Bryson, 2001b). In this institutional context it is 'rational' for employers to resist union organisation, because unions could also use this power to increase wages and other benefits: the union wage premium or 'mark-up' over non-union or market wage rates has all but disappeared in recent years (see Hildreth, 1999; and Millward *et al.*, 2001) *except* where unions retain high levels of membership density (in excess of 70 per cent) or where they represent 'sectional' interests in a multi-union workplace (see Booth and Bryan, 2001; and Forth and Millward, 2000). As a result, the TUC and individual unions are faced with a 'choice', or more accurately a dilemma, between 'responsible' forms of partnership advocated by the Government, or more aggressive forms of recruitment and organising (see, for example, Heery, 1998:348). As McIlroy (2000:14) concludes,

> Playing the social partner where the state and capital have no intention of engaging in more than minimal exchange may achieve the worst of all worlds: the suppression of mobilisation, without its reciprocal benefits. Restraint appears unlikely to transform the current situation.

Union recognition is another example of the 'uneasy alliance' between unions and the Labour Government. Prior to Labour's election, the absence of a statutory union recognition procedure was widely regarded as the 'biggest obstacle to a restoration of union membership' (Waddington and Whitston, 1995a:192). New Labour has introduced such a procedure (Employment Relations Act 1999), demonstrating the influence of the TUC and the political clout of the labour movement (see McIlroy, 2000). But this is not exactly the procedure the unions or the TUC wanted as it is deficient in important respects (e.g. the exclusion of firms with 20 or fewer workers, the requirement to have a majority vote *and* 40 per cent of the eligible workforce in favour of recognition, and the restriction of statutory recognition agreements to just pay, hours and holidays) (see Chapter 6). More importantly, it is clear that the new statutory recognition procedure, when set alongside the Conservative employment laws that New Labour has *not* repealed (e.g. restrictions on the closed shop, secondary action, picketing and strike action) is designed to preserve the economic advantage of employer over employee in the labour market. For example, under the Employment Relations Act, the 'bargaining unit' for any recognition vote must be 'compatible with effective management', thereby reinforcing the trend towards decentralised collective bargaining (see Chapter 8). Furthermore, the Central Arbitration Committee (CAC) cannot accept an application for a ballot where recognition already exists, which not only works against multi-unionism (recall that unions are more successful in raising wages and other benefits when they operate in a multi-union setting) but also presents employers with the opportunity to 'pre-empt' a vote or any determined organising campaign by granting 'voluntary' recognition to another, more compliant union. As Gall (2003b:91) notes, single union and 'sweetheart' deals are now back in vogue. Not surprisingly, the TUC (2003d) has demanded significant changes to the Employment Relations Act to bolster the unions' ability to represent members and potential members more effectively.

Even with a statutory recognition provision in place, therefore, trade unions must not only persuade a clear majority of the workforce to join, but more importantly the union must be able to mobilise its membership to engage in collective action (see Kelly, 1998). Without such mobilisation, unions will find it increasingly difficult to deliver improved benefits or protect even the basic employment interests of their members. For many, but not all workers, statutory recognition is a necessary condition for union organisation and collective action, but it is by no means sufficient. Put differently, membership, organisation, and the exercise of collective strength must still be 'achieved'. Political influence may be inseparable from the industrial power of trade unions, but the former is invariably dependent on the latter, and the latter is ultimately in the hands of the unions themselves.

Trade union responses

Trade unions have not been passive victims of membership decline. It has already been noted how the overall net decline in membership contains within it significant (though insufficient) recruitment, to the point where a number of unions have recorded an increase in membership and the union movement as a whole appears to have stemmed the tide of membership losses. Trade unions have various options to secure new members. On the one hand, for example, they might simply decide to 'sit tight' and wait for the external environment to improve (unemployment to fall, manufacturing to recover, firms to grow in size, etc.). On the other hand, they might undertake a series of initiatives to recruit new members, wherein leaders might develop new strategies, recruitment drives are targeted at specific groups, and the effectiveness of the organisation improved. Many unions have sought to offer new services, both to employers and employees, while others have stuck with a more traditional approach, emphasising the role that trade unions can play in protecting employee rights, raising pay and improving conditions of work. Finally, there are choices, and constraints, facing both individual unions and the labour movement as a whole as a result of the structure of different unions, their respective job territories, and the authority of the TUC. Formerly, some unions, such as the old craft-based unions like the NGA, had a closed membership base while others, most notably the two major general unions (the T&GWU and GMB) and a number of ex-craft based unions that now recruit more widely, such as Amicus, are engaged in competition for members across broadly similar job territories. In recent years the TUC has attempted to regulate such competition more closely, as well as the signing of single union agreements, but Congress has very limited power over its affiliates (expulsion, for example, the TUC's ultimate sanction, can actually *increase* competition between unions as the excluded union is no longer bound to respect other unions' membership territories, and vice versa). Figure 5.1 summarises these possibilities.

On the more specific question of recruitment, unions face several options. They can seek more members in areas where they already have recognition; they can attempt to recruit in areas where no recognition agreement exists (in the hope that as membership grows, recognition will be afforded to them); they can merge with another body and thereby increase not only their membership but also their recruitment base; and they can try to secure recognition (single-union) agreements with employers at non-union or greenfield sites which will then act to 'deliver' a membership from among those employed at the site (Willman, 1989; see also Heery and Adler, 2004). While the first two options involve the recruitment of individual members, the last two involve the organisation of groups of members. As Willman (1989) argues, this will typically make the options of merger or employer agreement much more cost-effective recruitment strategies than seeking individual members, particularly in areas where employers are hostile to unionism (see also Visser,

	OPTIONS		
Possibility to increase membership	Environment	*vs*	Union initiatives
Union policy to attract new members	Extended services	*vs*	Traditional unionism
Recruitment territories and job boundaries	Inter-union competition	*vs*	Regulation

Source: Adapted from Mason and Bain (1991:36–7).

Figure 5.1 Options for trade union renewal

1998a:126; and Willman, 2001). Given the financial constraints facing many unions (Willman, 1989: 266), which have not been reversed in recent years despite continued reform of financial management systems within trade unions (Willman and Morris, 1995), the more cost-effective means are likely to hold sway, even though this will tend to result in greater inter-union competition for members in certain areas (what Willman terms 'market share' unionism) rather than a more 'expansionary' recruitment drive into the virgin territory of the private services sector. These options, which for most unions are concurrent if not always complementary strategies, are explored in more detail.

Union mergers

The tendency towards 'market share' unionism has been clearly evident in the heightened merger activity that has characterised the UK labour movement over the past generation. In the recent period, most of the biggest unions have been involved in merger discussions or have completed a merger. This pattern is not new: there has been a steady fall in the number of unions since 1920 (see Table 5.4). What is new, however, is the pace of decline in the number of unions, largely brought about by increased merger activity and the resulting disappearance of many of the nation's smaller trade unions. The 1980s recorded the steepest decline of any decade with the number of unions falling by over one-third in the ten-year period; the 1990s saw a further fall of almost one-quarter. The increasing concentration within the trade union movement is indicated by the fact that in 2000 the eight largest unions (each with 250 000 or more members) accounted for over 72 per cent of all union members. Less than 10 per cent of all unions now account for almost 87 per cent of all union members.

Table 5.4 Number of trade unions in Britain, 1900–2000

Year	Number of unions	% change over previous period
1900	1323	–
1910	1269	– 4.1
1920	1384	+ 9.1
1930	1133	– 18.1
1940	1004	– 11.4
1950	732	– 27.1
1960	664	– 9.3
1970	543	– 18.2
1980	438	– 19.3
1990	287	– 34.5
2000	218	– 24.0

Sources: Certification Officer and Office for National Statistics.

Mergers can take different forms, most notably amalgamations (where two or more unions join together to form a new union) and transfers of engagements (where one union is subsumed by another and loses its legal status) (see Bird *et al.*, 1992; and Undy, 1999b). Among the most prominent mergers in recent years have been: the merger in 2002 of the Amalgamated Engineering and Electrical Union (AEEU) with Manufacturing, Science and Finance Union (MSF) to form Amicus; the merger in 2001 of the Institution of Professional Managers and Specialists (IPMS) and the Engineers and Managers Association (EMA) to form Prospect; the merger in 1999 of the Banking, Insurance and Finance Union (BIFU) and NatWest Staff Association to form UNIFI; and the merger in 1993 of the white-collar local government union NALGO, the public sector manual union NUPE, and the health service union COHSE to form Unison. With over 1.2 million members in 2001, Unison is now Britain's largest trade union. Further, at different times, discussions have been held concerning the possible merger of the two largest general unions, the T&GWU and GMB, which if successful would then become Britain's largest union with over 1.5 million members. In general, however, more unions seek merger than actually achieve it (Willman, 1996).

A significant feature of many of the more recent mergers is that, unlike *defensive* mergers of the 1970s, where small unions sought the protection of bigger unions in order to avert serious financial problems or membership decline (see Undy *et al.*, 1981), a more *consolidatory* or *aggressive* approach to mergers is in evidence in the 1980s and early 1990s (see Buchanan, 1992; and Undy, 1999b). The former typically involve two relatively strong unions in a given industry or occupation that decide to pool their resources for mutual advantage. Recent examples include NGA/SOGAT (to form GPMU), and ACTT/BETA (to form BECTU). More aggressive mergers, designed to protect relative membership share and expand trade union job territories as the basis for further growth, include Amicus and Unison. Merger activity, then, may be driven by the problems of membership decline, but it is not an entirely defensive act – indeed, in some cases it may be just the opposite. As Waddington (2003b:222) notes, however, to date there is no consistent evidence that merged unions have successfully expanded into new areas of membership growth.

Whatever the 'urge to merge', the outcome has *not* been to simplify the historically complex structure of British unions, or significantly to reverse membership decline (Waddington, 1995). Early unions were (closed) craft based organisations that, over time, opened their membership to less skilled workers in order to survive (e.g. the AEU). These unions were joined in the late nineteenth century by the first mass organisations of unskilled workers that recruited any and all workers, although they usually had a strong base in particular industries. The roots of the T&GWU, for example, formed out of the amalgamation of more than a hundred separate organisations, were the docks and wharves where strong local unions had developed (see Coates and Topham, 1991). The original founders of the GMB were gas stokers in East London who, in the 1890s, were excluded from craft-based unions. Boilermakers, municipal workers, airport staff, teaching assistants, minicab drivers, night club bouncers, roadies at music festivals, and even sex workers (following the recent incorporation of the International Union of Sex Workers) can now be counted among the ranks of the GMB. Many unions, therefore, can (historically) lay claim to similar 'job territories'. As present trends continue, the union movement will soon be dominated by just four or five 'super unions', but their membership base will be even more diverse and they will no doubt continue to compete for members (Waddington, 1995:214). Thus, while centralised financial control may improve the administrative efficiency of these 'super unions', problems of representative effectiveness may actually be exacerbated (see Visser, 1998a:126; and Willman and Cave, 1994:405).

Two of the more innovative 'solutions' to such problems are 'single-table' and 'single-union' agreements, but these arrangements typically involve changing the relationship with *employers* in the first instance (although there are important implications for the relationship between the union and its members). The non-union sector, in contrast, 'is attacked by several expansionist unions, apparently with limited success, whose efforts are competitive' (Willman and Cave, 1994:406). As Willman and Cave (1994:407–10) demonstrate, inter-union co-operation (joint ventures) would probably be more effective than further mergers, and may be easier to co-ordinate between the 'super unions'. Returning to Figure 5.1, the conclusion is that regulation, whether by the TUC or joint ventures between major unions, is essential to increase significantly the level of union membership.

Recruitment through employer agreements

Just as mergers deliver whole groups into a union, albeit either from a staff association or another union, so too the signing of a single union agreement with an employer can ensure a substantial number of members for the union concerned. Hence, despite the costs of making approaches and presentations to employers, the potential pay-offs are considerable – not only recognition but a 'captive' workforce from which to recruit. Further, with employer recognition typically comes other benefits for the union – in particular union subscriptions being collected at source via check-off arrangements, as well as facilities for trade union representatives such as time off for union activities and office facilities.

For trade unions, the experience with single-union agreements over the past fifteen years displays some similarities to, but also a number of important differences from, what has gone before in terms of union recognition and member representation. Many other worksites, for example, have representation by a single union. In the recent WERS98 study, more than two-fifths (43 per cent) of establishments with recognised unions had only a single union (Cully *et al.*, 1999:91) compared to 36 per cent in 1990 (Millward *et al.*, 1992:81). In the vast majority of establishments (72 per cent) where management recognised only one union, this was the result of a formal single union agreement rather than it 'simply having worked out that way' (Cully *et al.*, 1999:93). If anything, this will become more common in the future as a result of the new statutory union recognition procedure (see above and Chapter 6). But like anywhere else, trade unions who have signed single union agreements at greenfield or non-union sites must still convince a potential membership that it is worthwhile actually to belong to the union, rather than 'free ride' under the umbrella of the recognition agreement. Research on greenfield sites in the early 1990s, for example, found that employees still demonstrated a propensity to join a trade union, even where they benefit from company-specific training, single status, and extensive communications and consultation, all of which supposedly 'negates' the need for trade union membership (Newell, 1993). At the plants studied by Newell, workers displayed high levels of dissatisfaction with management, as do workers in Britain generally (BSAS data reveal that the majority of workers do not trust management, most believe that 'managers always try to get the better of employees', and one in five respondents describe management-employee relations as 'poor'; see also ISR, 1996). But what are the benefits from union membership under a new-style, single-union agreement?

It is important, in the first instance, to distinguish single-*union* from single-*table* agreements. The latter, which are also on the increase, represent a 'coming together' (co-operation) of unions who negotiate together with the employer around the same table, thus saving time and resources for the company, increasing flexibility, and precluding 'leap-frogging' pay claims (Gall, 1994). In 1998, among workplaces with two or more unions present, around 60 per cent conducted joint negotiations (single-table bargaining) with all of the unions (Cully *et al.*, 1999:94). Like single-union agreements, single-table bargaining is often associated with single status, more integrated pay schemes (including performance-related pay), multi-skilling and teamwork. The key difference is that single-table agreements are negotiated at 'brownfield' sites where unions are typically well established, whereas the distinctive feature of many single-union agreements is that unions only *begin* their recruitment of members *after* recognition has been granted, rather than secure recognition as a result of building up a strong, and committed, membership base. In the early 1990s, at some greenfield sites, it was not uncommon for agreements to be signed even before any employees were engaged (IRRR, 1992 and 1993). Thus, in a very real sense, in these cases trade unions in the first instance were recruiting *employers* rather than employees. In reality, however, it would be more accurate to say that the initial recruitment process works the other way round: employers choose the union which they are prepared to recognise. This presents the union movement with the problem of inter-union competition (what some have dubbed 'beauty contests') and individual members with inadequate representation and protection.

Although the incidence of single-union agreements in the late 1980s and early 1990s was small, and the number of workers covered by such agreements was arguably insignificant (see Gall and McKay, 1994:446; and IRRR, 1993:10), there has been a revival of interest in such deals as a result of the Employment Relations Act 1999. As Gall (2003b:91) notes, some employers have recognised that the question they face is not one of granting or not granting recognition, but to which union should recognition be granted and with what type of deal (recall that the new statutory recognition procedure encourages voluntary agreements which can be used by employers to 'pre-empt' an organising drive by a 'militant' union simply by offering recognition to a more 'moderate' rival union). TUC figures indicate that around a third of all recent recognition agreements were the result of an approach by the *employer* (www.tuc.org.uk/organisation). It is not clear how many of these agreements are 'sweetheart' deals, but it is clear that,

> employers are attempting to set the terms by which recognition is granted whether this be with an 'appropriate' or 'inappropriate' union in order to lessen the influence of the union and maintain managerial prerogative. This may take the form of a weakened union presence where the union is unable to deliver membership benefits, the membership is passive, and the union lacks independence and has to continually struggle to assert its legitimacy. (Gall, 2003b:91)

Past experience highlights the potential divisions that might erupt as a result of the revival of sweetheart agreements. The explicit 'business unionism' of the electricians' union (EETPU) in the 1980s, for example, caused a serious rift within the union movement, leading to the expulsion of the electricians from the TUC in 1988 (see Blyton and Turnbull, 1994:101–3). Once a union 'breaks ranks', this acts to create a process of 'whipsawing', as the Americans call it, where unions compete to 'do business' (sign deals) with employers and in the process sign away employees' rights and union responsibilities. The EETPU's agreement with Hitachi in South Wales, for example, included a joint commitment to: pendulum arbitration rather than industrial action to settle unresolved issues; complete job flexibility; single status; and discussions on pay and conditions routed initially and primarily via a consultative Company Members Board rather than through separate union-management negotiations (ibid). The precise terms of a single union deal will obviously vary from one agreement to the next (see Garrahan and Stewart, 1992; IRRR, 1993; and Yeandle and Clark, 1989:39), but in each and every case there is arguably a much diminished influence for the trade union. Not only do such agreements approximate to a new form of 'enterprise unionism', virtually excluding *external* trade union influences and any wider social, economic, political or legal agendas that the union, let alone the union movement, might be involved in, but the union also has a greatly reduced internal role. Management have effectively usurped many of the traditional functions of the union, and it should come as no surprise that union membership under many single union agreements is extremely low. As we have already noted, where union density is low, unions find it difficult to deliver benefits to their members.

The typical response of the unions involved in such agreements is that the alternative would be non-unionism. What many unions have ended up with, however, may in fact be little better. From the point of view of the union movement, and certainly the individual employee, would it not be better for a union to win the support of the workforce and then secure recognition from the employer, rather than the other way round? After all, unions have had to do this in the past, and have done so with considerable success, especially in the manufacturing sector at larger workplaces where most of the single union deals are to be found. The problem for the union movement, then, is not the apparent *need* for 'new realism', but the *opportunism* of individual unions caught up in a struggle over a declining membership base and the failure in many such instances to address the real needs of the workforce. As Kelly and Waddington (1995:424) argue, 'It is fallacious to suggest that unions must satisfy employers; a more rewarding approach, albeit more difficult to achieve, is to find ways of making employers tolerate a trade union presence'. The organising model embraced by the TUC and now widely adopted by many unions, including the T&GWU and GMB but more notably by GMPU, ISTC, MSF, TSSA, Unison and USDAW, seeks to achieve both objectives: to meet the needs of employees and command a hearing from employers.

Recruiting new members

In recent years a great many unions have devoted resources to recruiting new members, albeit with variable success (see, for example, Carter, 2000; Carter and Cooper, 2002; Heery *et al.*, 2003a and 2003b; Turnbull, 1997; Waddington and Kerr, 2000; and Wills, 2003). For some unions, such as multi-occupational industry unions (e.g. NUM) and single-occupation, single-industry unions with an already high union density (e.g. ASLEF), the potential to recruit new members is virtually non-existent. The greatest scope exists for the general unions (e.g. T&GWU and GMB) or those in areas of employment growth where union density is low (e.g. UNIFI in finance and USDAW in retail distribution). As Kelly and Heery (1989) illustrate, recruitment *targets* will vary significantly for different unions, depending on the proximity of the job territories of potential members to those already organised (to varying degrees) by the union, and the coverage of recognition agreements among the target groups. In some instances (close consolidation), the union might simply be involved in a 'mopping-up' exercise of non-union members within the union's existing job territories where collective agreements are in place (usually referred to as 'in-fill' recruitment). Much of the T&GWU's recent recruitment activity, for example, is directed towards '100 per cent' or '100 per cent plus' campaigns (which include sub-contractors such as cleaning, catering and security). In other situations (distant consolidation), the union might have a recognition agreement for the industry or specific companies, but organisation is poor and union density is low, perhaps because establishments are small and difficult to organise and/or labour turnover is high. Data from the Labour Force Survey suggest that around 3 million employees who are not union members work in an establishment with union recognition, which gives some indication of the massive potential for membership consolidation (see Monks, 2001). Not surprisingly, most union organising is directed towards consolidation (see Heery *et al.*, 2003b:61). Other potential membership groups, however, are not covered by a recognition agreement (usually higher level or management grades) but work in organisations where union density is already high (close expansion). Finally, the most difficult groups to recruit (distant expansion) are those in job territories where the union has neither recognition agreements nor (successful) experience of organisation to build on. It is among such groups (discussed in more detail in Chapter 9) that the potential for membership growth is greatest but union organisation is most difficult. Figure 5.2 provides a summary of these different recruitment targets.

Identifying potential membership targets, or what unions often refer to as 'mapping' (building up a detailed profile of the workplace, workforce, company policies, existing terms and conditions, etc.), is simply the first step of a recruitment and organisation strategy. The most important question a union must ask when recruiting new members is: 'Why should workers sign up?' Many unions, for example, have sought to attract new members by offering a wider range of services to the *individual*, based on the assumption that:

> individualism now outweighs collectivism in what union members want, and if individualism is the clear direction being pursued by employers in their relations with their employees, trade unions need to examine their supply side ... to meet the new individual demand. (Bassett and Cave, 1993:8)

| | | **Proximity of target terrritories** | |
		Close	*Distant*
Coverage by recognition agreements	*Yes, Consolidation*	Non-members in organised establishments covered by recognition agreements, e.g. civil service.	Non-members covered by company/national agreements but in weakly/non-organised establishments e.g. retail distribution.
	No, Expansion	Non-members in organised establishments not covered by recognition agreements, e.g. white collar staff in manufacturing.	Non-members in un-organised establishments without recognition agreements, e.g. insurance, hotels.

Source: Kelly and Heery (1989:198).

Figure 5.2   Typology of union recruitment

The new 'role models' for trade unions, according to Bassett and Cave (1993:17), should be the Automobile Association or BUPA, reconstituting trade unions 'as businesses – private-sector organisations engaged in providing a range of services for people who wish to buy them'. This form of 'passive consumerism' is evident in the provision of union credit cards, insurance schemes, legal advice, trade discounts and a range of other private benefits (see Fairbrother, 2002:73–5).

The shortcomings of this approach, however, are legion. For example, it overstates the extent of 'individualism' adopted by employers in their 'human resource management' policies (see, for example, Gallie and Rose, 1996:63; Legge, 1995; and Chapter 4), and more importantly the extent to which employees have embraced individualism or, more specifically, now place individual benefits over and above collective protection in their reasons for joining a trade union. Given the extent of social injustice, inequality of income and opportunity, work intensification, and employment insecurity in the UK today (see Chapter 3), it is hardly surprising that new union members cite 'support if I had a problem at work' as the principal reason for joining, along with 'improved pay and conditions'. Very few new members cite non-work related services such as trade discounts, financial packages and the like (see, for example, Charlwood, 2002:486; Sapper, 1991; Waddington and Whitston, 1997:521; and Whitston and Waddington, 1994:37). In short, 'Individualism was not central to union decline, and collective issues remain at the core of workers' demands of unions' (Waddington and Whitston, 1995a:197).

The central problem for trade unions is not so much the assumed growth of individualism as a discernible shift in the balance of power in favour of employers, which makes it more difficult for unions to 'deliver' on day-to-day workplace issues (Kelly and Waddington, 1995:421; McIlroy, 1995:399; and Turnbull, 2003). Put differently, how do unions translate collective demands into concessions from employers? Kelly's (1996:79) assessment is that 'militancy is likely to prove a better guarantor of union survival and recovery'. Moderation, as Kelly (1996:95–6) demonstrates, has brought unions only meagre returns and subjects the union to greater dependence on the 'goodwill' of the employer (see also Turnbull, 1997). This is the inherent danger of a 'servicing model' of trade unionism which is contrasted with the 'organising model' in Figure 5.3. In the context of an 'organising cycle' (issue ⟶ organisation ⟶ education ⟶ unity ⟶ action), however, 'militancy' is a method rather than an aim, with the emphasis, first and foremost, on *solidarity* as opposed to *strike* action (the former might include wearing badges or T-shirts emblazoned with workers demands, petitions, boycotts, sit-downs, or phone-ins) (see Organising Works, 1996:118–20). Whereas the servicing union expects its members to ask no more than 'What can the union do *for me*?', the organising union asks 'What can *we* achieve *with* the union?' The organising union depends upon membership being of value *in itself*, because through the act of membership workers should be able to generate their own issues, organise to solve their own problems, and satisfy their aspirations on a collective

A servicing union means ...	An organising union means ...
The union is seen as a third party. It enters the workplace to increase membership or solve problems.	Members own the campaign to unionise their workplace.
Unions tell members how they can solve their problems.	Members generate own issues and organise to solve them together.
Relying on employer to provide lists of names and workers to union official.	Mapping the workplace and staff attitudes are crucial – names and information are provided by workers.
Relying on workplace access and employer co-operation.	Initial organising can be done outside work – in workers' homes and other places.
Cold selling union membership by organisers.	Establishing initial contacts and finding natural leaders to help recruit.
Selling the union for services and insurance protection.	Workers empowered to do it for themselves through education and support.
Relying on full time officials to recruit and solve problems.	An internal organising committee formed and workers encouraged to build the union through one-to-one organising.
Recruiting is seen as a separate activity.	Recruitment and organising are integrated.
Results are achieved, but they are likely to be short term.	Results obtained through sustained efforts – more likely to be permanent.
The union is blamed when it can't get results.	Members share decisions and solve problems together with union leaders.
Members complain they pay fees and the union does nothing.	Members make a real contribution to union struggles and identify with the union. An attack on the union is an attack on themselves.
Organisers resent members for not coming to meetings or participating.	The image of the union is positive and active.
Management acts, while the union reacts and it is always on the defensive.	The union has its own agenda with members involved and it keeps management off balance.

Source: Organising Works (1995).

Figure 5.3 Servicing and organising models of trade unionism

basis. If all union members defined their own interests in isolation, and then simply looked to 'the union' to service their needs, not only would the costs prove prohibitive, but the very basis of organisation and unity would be precarious and ultimately ephemeral. In short, there would be no union.

The organising model is clearly based on 'participative' forms of union organisation. Indeed, the basis of 'self-organisation' is that workers recruit their fellow workers (like-recruits-like), generate their own agenda, and solve as many of their own problems as is practicable. In the present context of employee relations in the UK the propriety of the organising model is readily demonstrated (see Turnbull, 1997 and 2003:502–12). For example, recent survey data reveal that 'made contact myself' and 'approached by shop stewards' or other members are the most prevalent forms of union recruitment (Whitston and Waddington, 1994:37). Very few members are recruited by FTOs (ibid), which suggests that a more appropriate role for officials is one of support and co-ordination of lay activists or full-time organisers rather than direct recruitment. This is precisely the structure established by individual unions such as the T&GWU and GMB, as well as the rationale behind the TUC's Organising Academy (see Heery et al., 2000). By the end of 2002, the Academy had trained 120 organisers, who were predominantly women aged below 30 years. During their training, these organisers targeted more than 1200 employers, added nearly 40 000 new members and identified nearly 2000 new activists (Heery et al, 2003a:9). But the more important role of these organisers is to act as 'points of expertise' who can develop and diffuse new ways of organising that can be adopted by other union officers and lay activists, as well as to lead special projects that require planned organising activity (ibid:18). In addition, these organisers have brought a new language to the workplace to challenge the rhetoric of HRM, a language based on justice, respect, dignity, fairness and equity (see Heery, 2002:27–8).

The organising model has now taken root in many unions, although these tend to be smaller or medium sized unions such as Connect, GMPU, ISTC, TSSA and USDAW (see Heery et al., 2000:411–13, 2003a and 2003b). Thus, while organising strategies have made a significant contribution to smaller unions, or particular regions or occupational groups within larger general unions such as the T&GWU and GMB in London, it has done no more than help to stabilise aggregate union membership in the UK (Heery and Adler, 2004). Many union leaders are still cautious about the organisation and financial implications of an organising strategy (i.e. the impact on union hierarchy and decision-making, the costs of more intensive recruitment activities, and the reaction of current members if they experience a reduction in the services they enjoy from the union). In addition, greater co-ordination by the TUC is needed, both to diffuse the organising agenda more widely throughout the labour movement and to forestall competition and duplication of effort by affiliates in their quest for new members (ibid). For most unions, therefore, as well as the TUC, organising is likely to be just one of several methods to rebuild the labour movement's membership base, their bargaining power *vis-à-vis* employers, and their political influence with the government of the day. As Heery et al. (2003b:75) conclude, 'Unions, it seems, are assuming multiple identities and are pragmatic not principled in the methods they use'. Unfortunately for the labour movement, the plurality of methods they adopt – moderation and militancy, partnership with employers and independent workplace organisation, servicing and organising – are all too often contradictory.

Conclusion

The difficulties facing the trade union movement in the new millennium are certainly considerable, yet at the same time not insurmountable. Membership continues to decline, but unions continue to attract new members and most workers, union and non-union, hold positive views about trade unions (see Diamond and Freeman, 2001). More importantly, there are clear indications that many more workers would join a union given either the opportunity or the incentive. For workers to have the opportunity to join, unions must actively recruit and organise in the workplace. For workers to want to join they must be convinced that through collective action they can change their working lives and not simply buy cheap insurance or secure discounts on a range of (private) benefits. In both the workplace and beyond, however, trade unions have seen their industrial and political influence eroded. But if it is borne in mind that, contrary to the popular accounts of the halcyon days of the 1960s and 1970s, the union movement has always been characterised by differentiation, division and disunity (Hyman, 1991), then the present-day dilemmas facing trade unions are, in part at least, aspects of longer-running problems. Thus, as in the past, unions currently possess an area of strategic choice in responding to the changes and challenges they face:

> There are opportunities for policies which appeal to new working-class constituencies (or often, old sections whose interests have hitherto been neglected); for initiatives which address members' interests outside the workplace, and thus provide a fertile basis for transcending particularistic employment identities; and for programmes which link workers' interests as producers and consumers (as, for example, in demands for the improvement of public health care) so as to enable the construction of new types of encompassing and solidaristic alliances. (ibid:16)

Of course, given the changes to the composition of the workforce, economic policy, and the political context, the future role of trade unions within the economy, while significant, will be very different from that of the past. More strategic union policies designed to reverse their fortunes, most notably the emphasis on recruitment, organisation and participation, are reflections of this. Although not a perfect substitute for 'exogenous' changes more favourable to union organisation, the development of strategic union initiatives based on the organising model are at least less dependent on changes in labour market and trade union legislation, economic revival or a warmer political climate. The fact that unions now operate in such a climate, with much lower unemployment and a new recognition procedure in place, indicates that the outlook for trade unions is better than it has been for more than 20 years. However, not all state policies are conducive to a revival of the labour movement, in many instances quite the opposite. It is to the general role of the state in employee relations that we now turn.

6

Employee relations and the state

Privatisation of the Port of Belfast

Peace and prosperity

On 25 May 1999, Chancellor Gordon Brown announced a £315 million investment package that was intended to provide a 'framework for prosperity' in Northern Ireland. This would dovetail with the 'mechanism for peace' established by the Belfast (Good Friday) Agreement 1998. As the Chancellor made clear:

> The future of Northern Ireland, its prosperity, requires stability and there is absolutely no doubt that the most prosperous economies throughout the world are those that have managed both political and economic stability ... The mechanism for peace that has been set in place is now matched by this new framework for prosperity. It is a serious attempt to address every single problem that the economy faces. (Gordon Brown, quoted by *The Irish News*, 16 May 1999)

These problems include equality and human rights, especially in relation to religious discrimination in the workplace (Dickson, 2003). Of course, equality and social cohesion are desirable aims in their own right, beyond any economic rationale, but if Northern Ireland is to become a modern high technology economy, functioning at high levels of efficiency, then workplace and wider social relations must be characterised by equality, respect and cohesion (see Bradley and Hamilton, 1999).

The 'Chancellor's Initiative', as it became known, followed 'comprehensive soundings' in the business and political communities, including the trade union movement, to determine how to invest the £315 million. The improvement of housing estates, education and training, and 'welfare to work' (job opportunities for the unemployed) were to be targeted. Infrastructure investment was also high on the list of priorities, especially improvements to road transport. Everything in the

Initiative was 'new money', with the one exception of funds to be raised from the privatisation of the Port of Belfast (estimated to generate somewhere in the region of £70–90 million). This part of the package was hailed by Belfast Harbour Commissioners (BHC), the public body responsible for the management of the port, as 'an opportunity for the port to realise its full commercial potential and enable it to play its full part in driving forward the economic expansion of the area' (*The Irish Times*, 26 May 1999). But the trade unions greeted the announcement with dismay (ibid). As Bumper Graham of the Northern Ireland Public Service Alliance (NIPSA) subsequently remarked, 'It's an absolute con. The Treasury gave nothing to the peace process. Now they're saying, "Sell your port and we'll give you some of your money back". It's an absolute bloody con' (interview notes, April 2000). Port users were also opposed to the sale:

> If it ain't broke, don't try to fix it! In the past 30 years of the troubles, not much worked in Northern Ireland. But the port worked very well. It's well managed, generates a good surplus and offers an efficient service. Why sell it off? (Ian Webb, Belfast Harbour Users Group, interview notes, April 2000)

Other ports in Northern Ireland also expressed their opposition, most notably Warrenpoint and Londonderry, because they believed that a privatised Port of Belfast would be able to exploit its dominant market position (Belfast handles over 60 per cent of the Province's sea-borne trade) without any 'checks and balances' imposed by the state (neither port users nor rival ports believed that the Competition Act 1998 was sufficiently robust to protect their interests). But more important than the opposition of trade unions, other ports and port users was the opposition of local politicians. In fact, the proposed sale united all the major political parties of Northern Ireland, from Sinn Fein to the Democratic Unionist Party (DUP), in opposition to privatisation.

A question of trust

The Port of Belfast is one of many 'trust ports' in the UK that are managed by an independent board of trustees or commissioners appointed by the government and charged with acting in the interests of the port and all relevant stakeholders (e.g. users, operators, port-related businesses such as transport and distribution, environmental groups, local communities, and employees who work directly or indirectly for the port). Any surpluses generated by the port must be ploughed back into improving facilities, operations, conservancy and the like (see Saundry and Turnbull, 1997). Thus, trust port status was seen as a vehicle for ensuring administrative independence from particular interests, even though some of these interests might be represented on the board of trustees or commissioners (port users, for example, were traditionally represented on the Board of BHC, as were the trade unions).

Other ports in the UK were municipally owned (e.g. Bristol) and many 'railway ports' (e.g. Ayr, Cardiff, Grimsby, Hartlepool, King's Lynn, Port Talbot and Southampton) were brought into public ownership in 1947 (initially with railways under the British Transport Commission and later as a separate British Transport Docks Board) (see Turnbull, 1993:188). Most ports were therefore firmly located in the public sector, with the notable exceptions of Manchester, Liverpool (from 1972) and Felixstowe. State involvement also extended to the employment of dock workers who un/loaded cargo in the major UK ports (under the National Dock Labour Scheme), although Belfast was excluded from this particular employment Scheme (see Blyton and Turnbull, 1998:141–4; and Turnbull *et al.*, 1992). Thus, the state was (directly or indirectly) the owner, operator and regulator of many activities in the nation's ports, including, at one time, the employment of around 250 000 port workers (including port management, dockers, pilots, mooring staff, maintenance workers and port police) who were subject to both general and industry-specific legislation (see DETR, 2000).

The ports operated by the British Transport Docks Board (BTDB) were an early target for privatisation under the Conservative government of Mrs Thatcher (sold in February 1983). Following the abolition of the National Dock Labour Scheme in 1989 and the mass redundancy of registered dockers, one of the most militant and well-organised groups of workers in the country (see Turnbull and Wass, 1994; and Turnbull *et al.*, 1992), the next privatisation target for the Conservatives was the major trust ports. The Ports Act 1991 allowed trust ports with an annual turnover in excess of £5 million to opt for (voluntary) privatisation, with provisions for the government to compel trust ports of this size to privatise after 1993. Six trust ports were voluntarily privatised between 1992 and 1997 (Clyde, Dundee, Forth, Sheerness, Teesport and Tilbury) and Ipswich was compulsorily privatised. The Ports (Northern Ireland) Order 1994 provided legislative authority to enable trust ports in the Province to transfer to the private sector. When New Labour came to power in 1997, a final decision on the compulsory sale of the Port of Tyne was outstanding. Ministers decided that this should not be pursued and instead initiated a review of trust and other ports (see DETR, 2000). This marked a significant departure from the 'market-based' approach of the previous government – when asked to describe the Conservative government's ports policy the former Minister for Shipping, Lord Brabazon, famously declared that 'The policy is as such no policy' (quoted by Turnbull *et al.*, 1992:209) – but New Labour left the Ports Act 1991 intact.

With a combination of public and private sector organisations operating in the same industry, port transport offers a unique opportunity to compare the efficiency and other outcomes of privatisation in both a contemporary and historical context (i.e. to compare the current performance of public and private ports and to compare the performance of private ports pre- and post-privatisation). The data indicate that privatisation failed to deliver the anticipated benefits in terms of investment, employment and port efficiency, and many public sector ports continue to out-perform their private sector counterparts (see Barton and Turnbull, 1999; Saundry and Turnbull, 1997; and Turnbull, 1993). What privatisation *did* deliver, however, was massive salary increases for port managers and 'windfall profits' when ports were subsequently resold to the highest bidder. The Chief Executive of Clydeport, and his Deputy, became instant millionaires when their port was floated on the stock exchange in December 1994, but this pales in comparison to the £12 million in cash and shares realised by Peter Vincent of Medway Ports (Sheerness) when the business was sold to Mersey Docks and Harbour Company (MDHC) for £103.7 million in September 1993 (the port was privatised for just £29.7 million in March 1992). More than 200 dockers unfairly dismissed by Medway Ports, during a dispute over the unilateral imposition of longer working hours and a reduction in pay, were forced to sell their shares back to the company for just £2.50 per share, six weeks before MDHC paid £38 per share. Not surprisingly, the people of Northern Ireland were extremely wary about the sale of their major port. Awareness of the downside of privatisation was further heightened after the sale of Northern Ireland Electricity left customers in the Province paying more for their electricity than almost anywhere else in Europe; while the privatisation of Belfast Airport – sold to its managers for £34.75 million in 1994 and resold 2 years later to TBI, the airports group, for over £107 million – netted three senior managers a £6 million windfall (on an investment of just £50 000 each).

Belfast Harbour Commissioners had already dismissed rumours that the port would be privatised under a management-employee buy-out (*The Irish Times*, 21 January 1999) but was ready with a public-private partnership (PPP) proposal in response to the Chancellor's Initiative. With a 'golden share' held by the government, the PPP was designed to provide a degree of protection from any hostile take-over or managerial profiteering (similar to arrangements at BAA, British Aerospace, British Energy, Cable & Wireless, National Grid, National Power, Rolls-Royce, PowerGen, Scottish Power and Scottish Hydro), which BHC claimed would also 'safeguard the existing rights of employees, port users, customers, tenants and the local economy' (Ann McLaughlin, BHC, quoted in *The Irish Times*, 26 May 1999). However, as a local senior civil servant with the Department for Regional Development (DRD) later reflected, somewhat ruefully, 'Belfast might be a trust port, but there was a lot of *dis*trust of BHC. The Commissioners certainly didn't enjoy the trust of local politicians' (interview notes, April 2003).

Under the existing legislation, namely the Ports (Northern Ireland) Order 1994, there is only limited opportunity for consultation with interested parties, so in the face of mounting opposition, and no doubt with one eye on the Belfast Agreement, Mo Mowlam, then Secretary of State for Northern Ireland, decided that the Northern Ireland Assembly should have the final say on the proposed sale of the Port of Belfast. The Assembly established an Ad Hoc Committee to consider a range of options, including:

- the status quo, i.e. continuation of the port's existing trust status
- a trust port with extended powers, most notably greater commercial freedom to borrow money, develop property on port land, and integrate both vertically and horizontally into port and related businesses through joint ventures
- a new semi-state port under the management of a Port Authority of Belfast together with a Port Development Corporation, thereby separating the port's cargo-related operations and land/leasehold developments
- a trade sale to the highest bidder, with all the port land included in the sale to make the sale more attractive and realise the Chancellor's target of at least £70 million
- a public-private partnership with a golden share option to enable the DRD to veto any unwanted take-over, prevent any particular group of shareholders from exercising undue control, and ensure fair charges to port users, and
- a public-private corporation with a Port Authority responsible for regulatory duties relating to navigation, safety, pollution control and environmental protection, and a Private Corporation responsible for both the commercial operation of the port and its land bank.

The Ad Hoc Committee favoured a separation of the commercial port operations (cargo handling, passenger traffic, storage, distribution activities and the like) from the port's landbank. The Committee proposed a trade sale for the former and public ownership for the latter, which would be managed 'for the benefit of all the people of Northern Ireland' (Northern Ireland Assembly, 1999:20). This was unacceptable to the Harbour Commissioners, however, who were prepared to give up some land but certainly not all its non-port operational land. The total amount of land under the control of BHC is 1950 acres, of which 855 acres is used directly for cargo handling, passenger terminals and related activities. Some land is reserved for nature conservation (90 acres) but the rest is either leased (e.g. 300 acres to Harland and Wolff and 460 acres to Bombardier Shorts, including Belfast City Airport) or is ripe for re-development. This has created numerous 'conflicts of interest' between different parties (e.g. BHC, leaseholders, property developers, and community groups) (see BHC, 2002:5; and *The Irish Times*, 25 June 1998). In particular, local communities were keen to protect the many jobs that are still located within the port estate (ERM Economics, 1999:9) and they were determined to ensure their voice was heard and their interests represented in any future re-development.

Working on the waterfront

BHC employs fewer than 140 workers, comprising operational staff, pilots, maintenance workers, management, and port police, but like many other ports around the world, the Port of Belfast is a magnet for maritime, industrial and distribution activities (MIDAS) (see Barton and Turnbull, 1999). In fact, the port has one of the highest concentrations of industrial and commercial activity on the island of Ireland (ERM Economics, 1999:9). This 'MIDAS touch' has lost some of its shine in recent years with the decline of several traditional industries, most notably shipbuilding and dock work, but there are still over 15 000 people employed within the port area (ibid).

Competition and technological change have taken their toll on employment in and around the port. Harland and Wolff, for example, which built the *Titanic* and more than 1700 other vessels, struggled to compete with shipyards in the Far East and elsewhere. A workforce that once numbered more than 35 000 had dwindled to less than 200 by the time the yard's last ship was completed in March 2003. But there were indications that, in some sections of the community at least, there was not much sympathy for the plight of the company or its workforce:

> For most of its existence, [Harland and Wolff's] workforce was overwhelmingly Protestant, leading nationalists to condemn it as a bastion of sectarian discrimination. Its two giant cranes, Samson and Goliath, are plainly visible across the city from areas of high unemployment in Catholic west Belfast. (McKittrick, 2003)

The unemployment rate of Catholics in Northern Ireland is twice that of Protestants (Equality Commission, 2000; and Murphy and Armstrong, 1994).

Opposite the shipyard is the main cargo-handling area of the port. In days gone by, several thousand dockers worked in the port, reporting every day to various 'corners' (designated streets or areas of the port) where they would be 'schooled' (hired) by the 'gangers' and foremen who worked for local stevedores or the major shipping lines. Today there are less than one hundred dockers involved in cargo handling. John Campbell, a former casual docker, described the impact of technological change in a poem written in 1980:

BELFAST DOCKS
When I was young I took the road that those who came before me strode.
I stood with the crowds in the cobbled pen where the gangers schooled the casual men
The work was tough, the conditions bad, and it didn't help to be a lad,
for the ganger's eyes would pierce and scan as he probed the school for an all-round man
who could sling and stow or drive a winch. With skills like these you'd be a cinch
to work each day in the ship or shed, but now it seems those times have fled.
Forklift truck and container box ... you've torn the life from Belfast Dock ...
...
Now I muse as I watch the scenes of ships unloaded by huge machines,
Stripping hatches in record time. Sometimes progress can be a crime.
More work done by fewer men, most are left in the schooling pen.
Mechanical shovels scooping bulk. It's enough to make a bagman sulk
for bag-boats used to be ten-a-penny, now you'll find there's hardly any
as these giant monsters clear the quay, quick as you'd drink a cup of tea.
Dieselled horses working 'round the clock, you've torn the life from Belfast Dock.
Empty berths and cranes a'waiting. Flattened sheds and tarmacked basin.
Forklift ... Shovel ... Bulk and Block ... you've torn the life from Belfast Dock.
(Campbell, 1997:73–4)

Any cargo that was 'swung and hooked' in the Port of Belfast was handled by Protestants who were members of branch 11/10 of the Amalgamated Transport & General Workers' Union (ATGWU). Any cargo handled by 'bucket or shovel' was claimed by Catholic dockers who belonged to branch 11/9 (this work was particularly arduous, invariably dirty, and often dangerous) (see Campbell, 1999). Foremen and gangers could easily identify different dockers by the different 'buttons' (branch union badges bearing the numbers 11/10 or 11/9) worn on the lapel of their jackets. Any unfilled jobs would go to 'second preference' men (who wore a red button with the initials 'SP') and when demand for work was at its peak 'outsiders' would be hired. These men might eventually get a 'blue' button (both 11/10 and 11/9 buttons were blue), but they would often be 'passed over'. As one former docker remarked, 'I was a docker's son, so I got a blue button. Second preference men might have worked in the port for years but family members would always get the 11/10 buttons, you could forget about equality' (interview notes).

Employment opportunities are therefore inextricably linked to religion and the Northern Ireland conflict. Religion affects whether employers offer particular workers a job, whether the unemployed accept a particular job, or indeed whether they even apply for a particular job in the first place (see Shuttleworth *et al.*, 1996). It also colours individual attitudes towards fair employment and equality. According to McVey and Hutson (1996:3), the core nationalist view of fair employment and employment equality,

> is likely ... to commence with the belief that the creation of the Northern Ireland state was a means by which an artificial sectarian statelet was created wherein their rights were of little or no importance ... a Protestant state for a Protestant people.

The core unionist view of fair employment, in contrast, would challenge the nationalist assumption that partition created division rather than reflected it, and would claim that 'discrimination in Northern Ireland, if it existed at all, was not as great as has been asserted and was perpetrated by both sections of the community (thus nullifying its significance)' (ibid). Not surprisingly, neither community was prepared to vest control of the Port of Belfast to the management or shareholders (many of whom would no doubt be London-based financial institutions). With high levels of unemployment and a large proportion of young people in the working population, it is estimated that Northern Ireland needs to create 130 000 new jobs by 2010 (DED, 1999; EDF, 2002). Both Protestant and Catholic communities believed that a publicly accountable Port of Belfast could regain its MIDAS touch.

Trust and accountability

The impasse created by the political process left all parties with little option but to accept a continuation of trust status, albeit with greater commercial freedom. As a result, BHC can now borrow up to £45 million (the previous limit was £8 million) and there are no restrictions on the source of borrowing. In addition, vertical and horizontal integration is now possible as BHC is allowed to set up subsidiary companies. But investment outside the Port area is still prohibited, as is investment in non-port activities (e.g. residential property development). Other commercial powers will probably not come into effect until 2005 or 2006. In the interim, BHC has agreed a Memorandum of Understanding with the DRD under which the Commissioners are obliged to notify and consult with the Department prior to any change in land use or the disposal of any lands within the harbour estate. These measures are reinforced by a 'power of general direction' designed to safeguard fully the public interest – BHC can determine what is in the best interests of the port but the Assembly will judge whether this is also in the public interest.

To consolidate these changes, the new composition of the Board of BHC reflects the political climate in Northern Ireland. The number of Commissioners has been increased from ten (formerly the Chairman, one trade union representative, one City Council representative and seven Commissioners from the business community) to fifteen (instead of just one City Council representative there is now one Commissioner from each of the four main political parties, namely Social Democratic and Labour Party, Sinn Fein, DUP and Ulster Unionists, as well as two community representatives). According to the Director of the Air & Sea Ports Division of the DRD, the Port of Belfast is not only subject to greater public accountability, 'but probably more so than any other UK port' (interview notes).

Although BHC is a comparatively small employer, certainly in relation to total employment in the Port of Belfast, whether or not these workers remained in the public sector assumed huge political significance. As in many other areas of public sector employment, the involvement of the state, and the interests of different stakeholders, extends well beyond the immediate terms and conditions of employment of public sector workers (which in this case would have been protected under the Transfer of Undertakings Regulations had the port been privatised). With employee relations issues even further complicated by the Northern Ireland conflict, virtually all interested parties preferred a more robust system of public accountability to the discipline of the market or the financial interests of shareholders and City institutions.

The state and the employment relationship

Not only in the nation's ports but throughout the economy, the influence of the modern state permeates every aspect of people's working and non-working lives. First and foremost, economic policy and the (in)efficient management of the economy will have a major bearing on the number and type of jobs available. If a worker is unemployed, the state provides unemployment benefit. To improve their chances of obtaining work, the unemployed can enrol on government-sponsored training schemes. When actually seeking work, the employer cannot (by law) unfairly discriminate against applicants on grounds of either sex or race (in Northern Ireland, discrimination on the grounds of race was made illegal for the first time as late as 1997, compared to 1976 in Great Britain). When in work, women who perform work of equal value to that of their male counterparts must (by law) be paid an equivalent wage. Health and safety standards in the workplace are also determined, at least in part, by the state. In addition, legislation governs the possible breach of an employment contract by the employee, as during a strike, or the termination of such a contract by the employer, as in the case of redundancy or dismissal. Workers' pay will be settled, in part, by reference to the rate of inflation and the 'cost of living', which is a key outcome of government economic policy. More directly, just under one-in-five of the nation's workforce is employed by the state, either in central government (e.g. the Civil Service), the NHS, local authorities (including education, housing, social services, the police and fire service), or in the (ever shrinking) public corporations (e.g. the postal service, BBC, and the Royal Mint). This illustrates the fact that 'the state' is not simply 'the government'. The latter is one element of the former (albeit a crucial one), which also includes the administrative agencies of the nation, the judiciary, and the legitimate agencies of violence (the police and army). Thus,

> More than ever before men [*sic*] now live in the shadow of the state ... It is for the state's attention, or for its control, that men compete; and it is against the state that beat the waves of social conflict. (Miliband, 1969:1)

Given the pervasive influence of the state on all aspects of society, it is inevitable that any theory of the state is also a theory of society and the distribution of power within that society (ibid:2). Thus, the state can be conceptualised as 'an institutional complex which is the political embodiment of the values and interests of the dominant class' (Parkin, 1971:27). As was demonstrated in Chapter 2, capitalist societies are characterised, above all else, by an asymmetry of power between capital and labour. In this context, state intervention in the economy in general, and the employment relationship in particular, is inseparable from the nature of the capital–labour relation. Put simply, in a capitalist economy we have a capitalist state, wherein the capitalist class might not govern but it certainly rules (Miliband, 1969:55). In general, then,

> What the state protects and sanctions is a set of *rules* and *social relationships* which are presupposed by the class rule of the capitalist class. The state does not defend the interests of one class, but the *common* interests of all members of a *capitalist class society*. (Offe and Ronge, 1982:250, original emphasis, quoted by Edwards, 1986:148–9)

This is not to suggest, however, that the state will always and everywhere act in the interests of the capitalist class. The latter is itself an extremely heterogeneous group, and what may be in the interests of financial capital may be contrary to the interests of industrial capital, just as the interests of small-scale capital may not be best served by policies designed to improve the stability or profitability of large-scale capital. The dominance of financial interests over those of manufacturing, for example, is a major factor in the poor performance of the UK's industrial capital documented in Chapter 3 (see also Coates, 1994 and 2000; and Hutton, 1996). The privatisation of many of the nation's ports, for example, boosted the profits of the port authorities (the owners of the ports) but created more intense, often cut-throat, competition between small stevedoring companies and labour agencies who vie for cargo handling contracts in a more deregulated transport market.

Given the divergence of capitalist interests, this introduces a degree of autonomy for state action. Moreover, state action is not always unified by a common set of values and behaviour, which not only results in contradictory tendencies within state policies but also in state action that is not directly beneficial to capital (at least not in the short term). A commonly held perspective on the mid to late 1970s, for example, is that the interests of labour prevailed over those of capital. Not only were trade unions believed by many people to be 'above the law', enjoying an 'unrivalled position in the courts with the sole exception of the Crown itself' (Minford, 1985:109), but unions appeared to have virtually unlimited access to political power: industrial disputes were settled over 'beer and sandwiches' at Number 10, union representatives sat on a variety of tripartite bodies such as the National Economic Development Council (NEDC), and Jack Jones (then General Secretary of the T&GWU) was thought by many people to be the most powerful man in the country. Ultimately, however, labour and the unions did not seriously challenge the hegemony of the capitalist class. As Crouch (1979:19) argued at the time, the greater role afforded to trade unions 'is best regarded as a strategy pursued by capitalism when it cannot adequately subordinate labour by preventing its combination and allowing market processes to work'.

From 1974 to 1979 the unions had a Social Contract with the Labour government, which represented a major departure from earlier post-war arrangements based on 'voluntarism' or what, in a legal context, Kahn-Freund (1959:224) described as 'collective *laissez-faire*'. The three key features of voluntarism were: a preference for collective bargaining rather than state regulation as a method of settling wages and other terms of employment; a preference for a non-legalistic form of collective bargaining; and a desire among the parties for complete autonomy in their relations (Flanders, 1975:174). In short, there was a preference for *industrial self-government* rather than statutory regulation or state intervention. The 1970s, in contrast, have been characterised as a period of 'corporatism', which Panitch (1981:42) describes as 'a system of state-structured class collaboration'. During the period of the Social Contract, the trade unions offered wage restraint under the Labour government's incomes policies, in return for a protective code of individual employee rights and an extension of trade union immunities from the common law consequences of collective organisation and industrial action. Thus, for many the state was perceived to be acting in the interests of labour rather than capital.

The term 'immunities', according to Lord Wedderburn (1989:5), is a rather unhappy one, or more poignantly for the trade union movement a rather unfortunate one, as it implies that strikers are in some way 'privileged' or 'above the law' (Welch, 1991). This could not be further from the truth, 'rather as if an Act that gives slaves an immunity against recapture were interpreted as necessarily granting them a privilege' (Wedderburn, 1989:5). During the period from 1871 to 1906, trade unions secured the 'liberty of', rather than a 'right to', collective organisation and industrial action: statutory protections provided only a minimum basis of *social* rights to organise and act collectively, and took the *legal* form of 'privileges' (the immunities that British unions enjoyed from the law were the equivalent of what in other countries took the form of positive rights to organise and to strike guaranteed by legislation or by the constitution) (Wedderburn, 1972:272–3). Thus, the immunities of British unions did *not* place them above the law, in fact quite the reverse as 'the law retained a restrictive function: the freedom to take industrial action was always qualified by the possibility of legal remedies to restrain the unlawful consequences of such action' (Lewis, 1983:363). This was not how the situation was portrayed, however, either by the media or the Conservative Party, both in opposition (1974–9) and government (1979–97).

In 1979, Keith Joseph MP, arguably the architect behind much of the 'New Right' thinking on trade unions and the Thatcherite programme of the 1980s, suggested that unions were 'uniquely privileged' and that the previous Labour government had enacted a 'militants charter', which he derided as 'a charter for the systematic destruction of law-abiding, job-creating, free enterprise, in the name of socialism' (1986:103). Even in the 1990s, this view was continually reiterated and reinforced. In the 1991 Green Paper on *Proposals for the Further Reform of Industrial Relations and Trade Union Law*, the Conservative government argued that,

> It was a widely held view in the 1960s and 1970s that the severity and damaging consequences of Britain's industrial relations problems were exceeded only by their intractability ... The balance of bargaining power *appeared to have* moved decisively and permanently in favour of trade unions. In many cases union leaders *were seen to be* both irresponsible and undemocratic in exercising their industrial power. (Department of Employment, 1991:1, emphasis added)

It is then but a short step from the rhetoric of popular opinion to the assertion that 'the law gave trade unions virtually unlimited protection to organise strikes and other forms of industrial action' (ibid). The importance of such rhetoric should not be overlooked, since a key function of the state, in addition to assisting the process of capital accumulation, is to legitimise the system of dominance which characterises the capitalist mode of production (Edwards, 1986:147). Thus, 'Thatcherism' was not just a political project to create a new 'enterprise culture', but was, 'fundamentally, an ideological project intended to realize a new moral, organizational and social order' (Keenoy and Noon, 1992:561).

New Labour is equally adept at the 'rhetorical turn'. While Thatcherism was based on an ideological preference for, and dogmatic attachment to, the market, Labour's advocacy of 'market solutions' and 'minimal government' is presented as a technical necessity in terms of macroeconomic policy and a practical necessity in terms of industrial policy and the delivery of public services. Tony Blair and his Ministers have repeatedly deployed the rhetoric of 'globalisation' – specifically the mobility of capital and the international interdependency of financial markets – to justify an anti-inflationary macroeconomic policy (see Watson and Hay, 2003). As Gordon Brown made clear in a speech to the CBI in 1997, 'We understand that in a global market place, traditional national economic policies – corporatism from the old left – no longer have any relevance' (ibid:296). But if New Labour is to promote the interests of business and improve the nation's competitiveness in world markets, then (market facilitating) political intervention is still necessary. The DTI (2002), for example, has identified five 'drivers' of productivity – investment, innovation, skills, enterprise and competitive markets – where the state can play an active role. This is the essence of a 'Third Way' between markets and institutions, which is perhaps best illustrated by the Government's approach to the public sector. New Labour has not reversed the privatisation of major public utilities such as gas, electricity, water and transport, including ports, and the Government is enthusiastic about importing private sector management practice into the public sector (for example, in schools and hospitals). But there is also an evident shift away from ideological dogmatism and towards pragmatism, emphasising that 'what counts is what works' (Boyne et al., 2001:1).

In order to understand the role of the state in employee relations, it is essential to evaluate different political projects – specifically voluntarism, corporatism, Thatcherism, and the Third Way – in the context of the central spheres of state activity, namely the state's role as economic manager, legislator and employer. As with other chapters, our primary interest is the contemporary development of employee relations, but this is set within a very clear historical context. The 'social Darwinism' of the Thatcher project, for example, represented a complete rejection of the post-war 'settlement' or 'consensus' built around full employment, the involvement of trade unions in government decision-making bodies, an acceptance by all major political parties of the separation of industrial relations and political controversy (keeping politics out of the workplace and collective bargaining), and a similar commitment to the welfare state (Crouch, 1982a:19). The politics of Thatcher's economic programme can only be understood in relation to the abandonment of the post-war settlement, which the New Right condemned as being too *dirigiste*.

Tony Blair essentially endorsed this view in a speech to business leaders in Singapore in 1997 (see Watson and Hay, 2003:296), but while New Labour has no intention of reverting to the (failed) corporatist policies of the 1970s, it recognises the failure of neo-liberalism to create a high investment, high skill, high productivity economy. In the case of the port transport industry, for example, Ministers are adamant that 'It is not Government's job to run the ports industry' (DETR, 2000:1.1.8), but they also recognise the need for an integrated transport policy and the impact of market failures on investment, jobs, health and safety, the environment, public accountability and the like (ibid:1.1.10). Institutional regulation is therefore unavoidable, but the aim is to 'make regulation add value rather than unnecessary cost, ensuring that different regulators co-ordinate their overall demands' (ibid:1.2.2; see also Boyne *et al.*, 2001:1).

In its role as legislator, the policies of the Conservative governments of the 1980s and 1990s were out of step with both previous philosophies of statutory employment regulation and those currently prevailing elsewhere in the European Union. Individual workers in the UK came to have fewer rights as employees than they did as citizens. For trade unions, by the mid-1990s their activities were circumscribed to an extent not witnessed since the nineteenth century. Under New Labour, there has been some movement towards an extension of individual employment rights, albeit in several areas somewhat reluctantly under pressure from the European Union. The bargaining position of trade unions has been enhanced by the introduction of a statutory recognition procedure, although the terms of the new procedure have limited its impact, and the Government advocates 'partnership' at work (see Chapter 8). But the restrictive laws on strikes remain in force and Labour is keen to maintain a flexible labour market where the balance of power lies with employers rather than labour.

Finally, as an employer the state has massively reduced its involvement in the public sector over the past 20 years, through a process of rationalisation, commercialisation, and privatisation. Privatisation of Britain's major ports, for example, combined with the deregulation of employment, led to massive job losses and the re-emergence of casual forms of employment more akin to the pre-Second-World-War period (see Turnbull, 1993; Turnbull and Wass, 1994; Turnbull *et al.*, 1992). The state still plays an important regulatory role in the port transport industry (see DETR, 2000), but its ability to steer the future course of the industry has been diminished by its withdrawal from ownership and operational activities (see Barton and Turnbull, 1999 and 2002). But state intervention along other dimensions has increased or simply changed in character in recent years (e.g. pay determination for public sector workers) as successive governments sought to 'stiffen the sinews' of public sector managers, 'regardless of union and workforce opposition and any resulting disruption to public services' (Ferner and Colling, 1991:393–4). New Labour has adopted a more emollient approach to public sector workers than previous Conservative governments, but is nonetheless determined to 'modernise' public services and confront organised labour if necessary (as we discuss in relation to the recent fire-fighters dispute in Chapter 10). Public sector workers have been subjected to a barrage of reforms designed to reduce costs, increase productivity and improve service provision, and yet despite – some would argue *because of* – these policies, there are still on-going problems of low morale among the workforce and a growing perception among the electorate that public sector reforms have 'failed to deliver'.

The state as economic manager

The post-war settlement constructed by the Labour government of Clement Attlee was an inclusive programme based on need rather than ability to pay and underwritten by Keynesian demand management policies. The state would 'pump prime' the economy to set in motion a multiplier effect – one employee's wages, initially paid for by the state, would become another employee's source of income, as wages were spent on consumer or other goods, creating further spending and income, and so on – and this would ensure full employment. Beyond this, however, the state played a relatively limited role in the affairs of British industry. Even in the nationalised industries any planning was unambiguously *indicative* rather than *dirigiste* in character. Instead, the state supported the philosophy of industrial self-government. But this 'liberalist' system contained inherent weaknesses, not least the problem of maintaining the magic triangle of Keynesian demand management: full employment, price stability and a balance of payments surplus. Deficits on the foreign account, for example, put pressure on sterling and forced the government to damp down domestic demand. But this led to rising unemployment and pressure from labour and the unions to restore full employment. The latter, when combined with a system of free collective bargaining (that is, without state regulation), led to rising wage demands and wage drift (discussed in Chapter 7) and put pressure on costs and therefore prices. If prices rise, UK goods become more uncompetitive on world markets, leading to balance of payment problems, and so on. Debate raged about the source of this instability in the UK economy (see Coates and Hillard, 1986), but while the state equivocated, the magic triangle became ever more elusive. The result was a continual cycle of stop-go economic management.

The most expedient solution to the UK's economic ills, for many post-war governments, was wage restraint. Initially, incomes policies, if they could be called that, were informal, largely *ad hoc* arrangements, such as the February 1948 *Statement on Personal Income, Costs and Prices* or Harold Macmillan's call for a 'price plateau' in May 1954 to promote price and pay stability. Selwyn Lloyd introduced a temporary 'pay pause' in 1961–2, but the Conservative government's subsequent incomes policy recommendation of 2.0–2.5 per cent was ignored by unions and employers. These policies were, in effect, the prelude to formal restraint under the Labour governments of 1964–70 (see Davies, 1983), which marked a significant change in the government's role in employee relations – direct intervention, if only on an intermittent basis, signalled the end of free collective bargaining. But incomes policies ran aground on the rocks of rank-and-file militancy, with trade union leaders unable to control membership demands for higher wages in the face of rising prices. Moreover, in the public sector – where the government could enforce pay norms more effectively and where there was limited scope for self-financing pay increases above the norm as a result of productivity improvements – incomes policies not only upset established pay comparisons with private sector employees but also destroyed the façade of government neutrality in management-employee relations. This 'politicisation' of public sector employee relations was a key factor in the growing unrest of the 1970s (see Chapter 10).

The 'quasi corporatist' project of the 1960s gave way to a 'bargained corporatism' in the mid to late 1970s, when again the trade union leadership promised wage restraint in exchange for a 'share' in economic policy-making. But they failed to secure the latter or deliver the former, with rank-and-file rejection of Prime Minister Callaghan's 5 per cent pay maximum under Phase IV of the government's incomes policy playing a major role in the explosion of industrial conflict during the so-called Winter of Discontent (1978–9). But what stands out during the entire period from 1945 to 1979 is the 'extraordinary passivity and incapacity of the state in the face of growing economic difficulties' (Rowthorn, 1986:264). The state

> has never seriously pursued a concerted modernising strategy … The hesitant and ineffectual character of government policy since the war is the outcome of a particular balance of class forces in Britain during the period. Capital has in general been opposed to a policy of vigorous planning and detailed state intervention in industry, whilst the working class has lacked the consciousness or unity of purpose to impose such a policy. (ibid)

In other words, each of the three major actors in employee relations – management, labour and the state – 'found it easier to guard their own mutual autonomy' than to press home radical reform (MacInnes, 1987:16), such that the power of each party over the other was of a negative rather than a positive order (see Fine and Harris, 1985:17; and Harris, 1986:261–3).

> Employers, unions, and the state were all strong enough to maintain defensive positions while too weak to organize radical departures from the tradition of compromise and muddling through. (Edwards *et al.*, 1992:6)

In short, nothing united the different parties in a way that might make possible a national economic and industrial strategy, 'since the only thing that really brought them together was their incapacity for strategy' (Crouch, 1995:236).

Mrs Thatcher sought to change all this. Of course, the New Right did not define the root of the 'British disease' to be the deadlock of social relations and institutional arrangements between capital, labour and the state, but the inordinate power of labour and the excessive intervention of the state itself in all aspects of

		Position of trade unions	
		Strong	**Weak**
Nature of the system	**Liberal**	Free collective bargaining	Neo *laissez-faire*
	Co-ordinated	Bargained corporatism	Corporatism

Source: Adapted from Crouch (1982a:201).

Figure 6.1   Typology of state–union interaction

social and economic life. As Crouch (1982a:118) argued, the new liberal philosophy of the Conservative government had strong antecedents in the nineteenth century and a long tradition within the Tory Party itself. But the idea of rolling back the welfare state, reducing government intervention in industry, abandoning any kind of (formal) incomes policy, breaking off all relations between Ministers and trade unions, allowing unemployment to rise to contain inflation and union power, and ultimately letting the market reign, had been shunned within a Conservative Party committed to compromise and accommodation (at least from 1945 to 1979). Under Mrs Thatcher, however, such ideas were now government policies, while 'the kind of relationship between a Conservative government and trade unions of which Churchill and Monckton boasted was seen as an object of shame by her' (ibid). As Figure 6.1 illustrates, the 'neo *laissez-faire*' policy of Mrs Thatcher's Conservative Party was grounded in the liberal tradition of the past but was predicated on a weak trade union movement.

The objective of government policy in the 1980s can be simply stated: namely to encourage enterprise through the deregulation of markets, especially the labour market. Thus, the economic foundations of Thatcherism can be found in the writings of free market economists such as Milton Friedman and in particular Friedrich Hayek. Indeed, Lord Wedderburn has argued that the 'mixture of market forces and strong government' of the Thatcher years, 'displaying a determination to put down those who might disrupt the spontaneous order, is quintessentially Hayek' (1989:15). Of the UK economists in this genre, the work of Patrick Minford (1985) is illustrative. Minford argued that trade unions used their 'monopoly power' (derived from their legal 'privileges') to raise wages above the market rate. As a result, employers hire fewer union workers, which swells the ranks of the unemployed. According to neo-classical economics, therefore, unions not only increase (wage) costs and thereby inflation, but cause unemployment, a more unequal distribution of income within society, and in the process reduce the efficiency of both individual firms and the economy as a whole through the imposition of restrictive practices, demarcations and the like. In short, unions are a 'public bad' (IEA, 1978).

According to this argument, therefore, one way to reduce unemployment, and in the process improve efficiency and equality, 'is to reduce the power of unions to raise wages. As union wages fall, the demand for union labour rises, people are withdrawn from the non-union sector, non-union wages rise and more people are prepared to work in it' (Minford, 1985:104). This became a primary focus of government policy throughout the 1980s and into the 1990s, and was successful in terms of reducing trade union bargaining power and the ability of unions to 'mark-up' wages above the equivalent non-union wage, but was not successful in terms of job creation or improving labour productivity (see Turnbull, 2003). The main method used to reduce union power was the law, withdrawing the immunities of trade unions in relation to strike action and undermining union influence within the workplace by, for example, outlawing the closed shop. These developments are discussed in more detail in the following section. At this point it should also be noted that along with legislation to weaken union bargaining power the Conservatives sought to deregulate the non-union sector of the economy, effectively forcing the (voluntarily) unemployed (as Minford defined them) back into work through such measures as raising the disqualification period for unemployment benefits from thirteen weeks to six months for those who 'voluntarily' quit their job; specifying that all claimants (re-labelled as 'Jobseekers') must not only be available for, but also actively seeking work (and provide proof to that effect); stipulating that claimants can be disqualified from benefit if they refuse employment on the grounds of the (inadequate) level of remuneration; reducing the real level of benefits (to the lowest level in Europe when calculated as a percentage of the average weekly wage); undermining (and ultimately abolishing) the powers of wages councils; and eroding the protections afforded to individuals for unfair dismissal, redundancy, maternity leave and the like. Qualification for unfair dismissal protection, for example, was raised from six months to one year (in 1979) and then two years (in 1985). In the deregulated labour market of the 1980s and 1990s it was not uncommon for employers to routinely dismiss staff (with no obligation to pay redundancy) literally weeks or even days before they completed two years service in the job. Not surprisingly, such practices were, and still are, most prevalent in the non-union sector (see NACAB, 1993; and Chapter 9).

The Conservatives proclaimed that their policies had secured an 'economic miracle' in the 1980s, but as the economy sank into an even more prolonged recession in the early 1990s than that of the early 1980s, the economic miracle appeared more like a mirage. By the turn of the millennium, all the principal actors in employee relations acknowledged the poor performance and structural weaknesses of the UK economy (see, for example, CBI/TUC, 2001; and HM Treasury, 2000), although opinion was still divided on the most appropriate course of action to reverse the nation's poor international performance. Under New Labour, trade unions were no longer blamed for the economic ills of the nation, but nor were they regarded as necessarily part of (or partners in) the solution. In other words, the Government had no intention of reverting to a system of bargained corporatism or free collective bargaining, as depicted in Figure 6.1. The former would entail the promotion of institutions over markets, which would be unacceptable to capital and especially the City (see Crouch, 2003), and no doubt the key electoral constituency of 'middle England' (Watson and Hay, 2003:302). The latter would entail much stronger statutory support for trade unions, collective bargaining and employee voice than the Government was prepared to countenance, let alone concede.

Labour's economic strategy for international competitiveness is founded on macroeconomic stability, thereby giving companies the confidence to invest, and microeconomic reform to remove barriers to the functioning of product markets, to promote enterprise and innovation, and encourage investment in human capital (education and skills formation) (see, for example, HM Treasury, 2000; and HM Treasury/DTI, 2001). Both pillars of New Labour's economic strategy are firmly grounded in the market mechanism. Indeed, the Government is unequivocal on this point:

> Effective markets and competition provide the best means of ensuring that the economy's resources are allocated efficiently ... All markets in the economy – in products, capital and labour – have an important part to play in promoting aggregate economic growth. (HM Treasury, 2000:28)

Thus, whereas previous ('Old Left') Labour governments sought to replace the market in some areas of the economy (e.g. through nationalisation) or at least correct 'market failures', New Labour seeks to facilitate the market (see Watson and Hay, 2003:297). On a continuum of government-market relations, as depicted in Figure 6.2, this implies that while the Labour Government has rejected the dogmatic attachment to, and glorification of, markets that characterised government economic policy in the 1980s and 1990s, they still favour markets over regulation.

New Labour's assessment of industrial relations and current labour market regulation (or more precisely the absence thereof) is very positive. Indeed, these are two areas where the Government believes that the UK enjoys a competitive advantage over, or is on a par with other leading G7 countries (Canada, France, Germany, Italy, Japan, and the USA) (see DTI, 2001:22–3). As a result, the Labour Government has been reluctant to initiate any major reform of industrial relations and is keen to retain and extend various forms of labour market flexibility introduced during the 1980s and 1990s. But the measures used by the Government to demonstrate 'good industrial relations' are simply days lost in industrial disputes

| Replace | Correct | Facilitate | Glorify |

Figure 6.2 Continuum of government–market relations

and managers self-reporting of 'good' or 'very good' employee relations (based on WERS98 data). Other evidence, however, suggests that conflict at work has not abated (see Chapter 10), managers' assessment of 'good' (or 'bad') employee relations is hardly the most reliable indicator of the general climate of management-labour relations (see Dastmalchian *et al.*, 1991), and other evidence (e.g. BSAS data) contradicts this assessment, including data from WERS98 (see Bryson, 2001c; Cully *et al.*, 1999:283; and Stirling, 2000).

According to the Government, 'Direct measures of the degree of labour market regulation are not available' (DTI, 2001:23), so two indirect measures are used instead: non-wage labour costs, indicating the 'burden of government intervention in the labour market', and whether business leaders perceive labour market regulations to be 'too restrictive or flexible enough' (ibid). Leaving aside the question of whether non-wage costs used to pay for health, pensions and other social benefits should be defined simply as a 'burden on employers', rather than a 'beneficial constraint' that actually improves organisational and economic performance (see Streeck, 1997), the reliability, and relevance, of business leaders' opinions must be questioned (the government cites data from an international survey of less than 5000 business executives in more than 50 countries, so fewer than 100 managers in the UK are asked to put into international perspective the characteristics of their local environments) (see www.imd.ch, *World Competitiveness Yearbook*). More objective measures of labour market regulation *are* available, such as indicators of the relative strength (or weakness) of employment protection legislation, which leads to a similar international ranking for the UK as an economy with a 'flexible' labour market (see, for example, Morgan *et al.*, 2001). But instead of

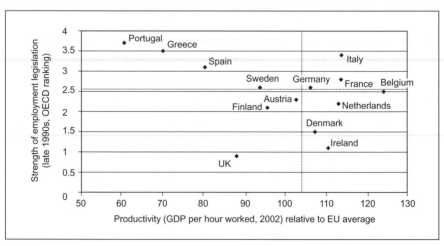

Sources: Eurostat and OECD.

Figure 6.3 Productivity and labour market regulation in European countries

a 'positive business spin' we now have a 'negative employee experience' as our principal indicator. Using these data to graph the relative position of European countries (Figure 6.3) exposes the UK as a low protection/low productivity economy. To be sure, some European countries have a combination of lower productivity and a more highly regulated labour market with stronger employment protection, as illustrated in Figure 6.3. But the policy of deregulation, as advocated by previous Conservative governments, is clearly not the route to high productivity. Equally, what route does the 'Third Way' follow?

A system of labour market regulation that guarantees workers' employment protection is clearly not incompatible with high productivity. In most countries, this system also extends to workers' rights to representation, which we discuss in Chapters 7 and 8. Industrial democracy in the UK has been systematically undermined alongside employment protection, leaving a yawning 'representation gap' and chronic insecurity in many workplaces that only concerted action by the state might conceivably begin to close. New Labour has not been averse to statutory measures that go some way to addressing these issues, but the focus has been very much towards individual rather than collective employment rights and the Government has been keen not to compromise the interests of business.

The state as legislator

Just as the elusive goals of Keynesian demand management slipped further and further out of reach in the late 1960s, so too did the consensus that supported legal abstention in employee relations. The tradition of non-intervention was based on the principle that 'the peaceful exercise of collective economic sanctions in the field of industrial conflict should be completely lawful' (Auerbach, 1990:12). As Lord Wright put it in the case of *Crofter Hand Woven Harris Tweed v. Veitch* (1942), the right to strike was 'an essential element in the principle of collective bargaining' (quoted by Lewis, 1991:61). Thus, there was perceived to be 'no incompatibility between the public interest and a *degree* of trade union power, whether economic, social or political' (ibid:62, emphasis added). But this benign view of trade union power was severely damaged by rising strike rates in the 1960s (see Chapter 10).

Despite calls for greater statutory intervention in employee relations, the Donovan Royal Commission (1968) proposed a voluntary programme of reform (outlined in Chapter 7), although the Report did recommend removing the legal immunity of unofficial strikes in some situations. The major political parties were less patient, however, and while Labour's proposals contained in the White Paper *In Place Of Strife* (1969) were withdrawn in the face of trade union opposition, the Conservative Party's proposals from *A Fair Deal at Work* (1968) were effectively implemented as the Industrial Relations Act 1971 under the new government of Edward Heath. This Act transformed the legal regulation of employee relations in

Britain, introducing a comprehensive, restrictive legal code to curb the activities of trade unions (including legal penalties on strikes, the creation of several 'unfair industrial practices', and outlawing the closed shop). More importantly, its introduction demonstrated, yet again, that legal abstention in Britain was always *conditional*. When labour and the unions challenged the interests of capital, the state (either the government or the judiciary) intervened. For example, having been granted immunity from criminal law conspiracy in the 1870s, and following the emergence of militant 'new unionism' among the semi-skilled and unskilled workforce in the 1880s, the judiciary used the civil wrong (or tort) of conspiracy to restrict union organisation and industrial action. This was reversed by the Trade Disputes Act 1906, which gave unions protection from action for civil conspiracy if acting 'in contemplation or furtherance of a trade dispute' (the so-called 'golden formula' of trade union immunity), but the state imposed direct controls on strike action during both world wars when disruption to production could not be tolerated, and again after the General Strike of 1926 (the Trade Disputes and Trade Union Act 1927). Judicial bias against the unions was again in evidence in the 1960s and late 1970s in a number of cases (see Griffith, 1981:72–84). In *Duport Steels Ltd v. Sirs* (1980), Lord Diplock even went so far as to declare that union immunities were 'intrinsically repugnant to anyone who has spent his life in the practice of the law', openly affirming that their effects 'have tended to stick in judicial gorges' (quoted by Wedderburn, 1989:7).

The Industrial Relations Act, therefore, was not a temporary aberration but the explicit expression of an underlying tension that ran right through the voluntarist tradition. But the most notable thing about the Act was that it was a spectacular failure. It was unwieldy (with 170 Clauses) and poorly drafted. Ultimately, the Act 'foundered on the rocks of union opposition and employer indifference' (ibid; and Weekes *et al.*, 1975). The latter was particularly important, as 'the draconian strategy of the Heath government did not match the perspectives of important sectors of British capital, whose aim was to enlist the voluntary co-operation of union representatives in imposing greater shopfloor discipline' (Hyman, 1981:133). In this instance, then, the relative autonomy of the state was clearly at odds with the interests of capital.

The Industrial Relations Act was repealed by the incoming Labour government in 1974, returning the legal *status quo* to the position first established in 1906. Individual employee rights were strengthened and extended by a number of Parliamentary Acts, as were the collective immunities of the trade unions. Significantly, the intentions behind the legislative programme of the mid 1970s were 'a far more accurate reflection of the role that the parties wanted the law to play in industrial disputes than the policy underlying the Industrial Relations Act' (Elgar and Simpson, 1993:71–2). Regulatory or reformist law that grants workers, as a collective, a 'right' to strike and, as individuals, a 'floor of rights', is not necessarily anti-capitalist. In fact, such laws can promote more effective and professional management. Communications might improve, for example, and employers would no longer be able to victimise employees or rely on an arbitrary, and unjust, system of 'hire and fire'. Equally, the laws of the mid 1970s were, in many respects, in the interests of capital (although not necessarily in the interests of all capital*ists*). In any event, they

> were characterised by a gap between aspiration and reality. They were supposed to be a great extension of worker and trade union rights ... In practice, these rights secured workers and unions only limited benefits. (Lewis, 1986:34–5)

The overriding concern was to modernise employee relations, not to effect a redistribution of power between capital and labour, as evidenced by the fact that there were only weak sanctions attached to the new rights. The key question was always, and still is, how to strike a balance between the interests of capital and the rights of labour. In the Conservative Party, there have always been two schools of thought on this issue. James Prior MP, Conservative Employment Secretary from 1979 to 1981, argued in the House of Commons debate on the Employment Bill (1979) that

> The law should always give full recognition to the inherent weakness of the individual worker *vis-à-vis* his employer, to the need for him to be organised in a union and to the need for his union to have such exceptional liberties as may be necessary to redress the balance. (quoted by Wedderburn, 1989:3)

For Prior, the major lessons from the experience of the Heath government (1970–4) was the need for legislative reform to be limited and specific, to respond to the mood of 'public opinion' and, above all, to be subject to full consultation, even with the unions (see Auerbach, 1990:19–20). This was reflected in the content and objectives of the Employment Act 1980 (details of this Act, and the other main labour laws passed since 1980, are given in the Appendix to this chapter).

Others in the Conservative government of the 1980s, however, saw the failure of the Industrial Relations Act as a strategic and tactical lesson – there was nothing wrong, in principle, with the content and objectives of the Act. Heath was judged to have simply gone about things the wrong way, injecting a massive dose of legalism overnight, and then backing down ignominiously when the going got tough. The 'Iron Lady', in contrast, was 'not for turning'. Moreover, Mrs Thatcher favoured the notion of 'freedom of contract' between employer and employee, drawing on the ideas of Hayek (1979) who argued that, 'the unions are destroying the free market through their legalised use of coercion ... There can be no salvation for Britain until the special privileges granted to the trade unions three-quarters of a century ago are revoked' (Hayek, 1984:55–8; see also Hanson and Mather, 1988:89–90). An alternative view, of course, is that freedom of contract is 'a legal fiction to legitimise the superior strategic strength of the employer who could dictate the terms to the individual employee' (Lewis and Simpson, 1981:7).

Legislative reform accelerated after 1982 following the arrival of Norman Tebbit at the Department of Employment. His appointment

> signalled a clear and deliberate shift in the Government's rhetoric with regard to trade-union immunities. The regulation of industrial conflict was not to be seen as simply a matter of striking an equitable balance between the strength of employers and employees, and of tackling the worst and most destructive abuses of trade-union power. It was also to be presented as an important arm of the Government's economic, and in particular, labour market, policy at a much wider level. (Auerbach, 1990:75)

In short, legislative reform in the 1980s became integrated with, and was a major instrument of, economic policy. The most significant elements of the Employment Act 1982 were, first, the redefinition of industrial disputes, where such action had to 'relate wholly or mainly' to industrial (and certainly not political) matters, thus abandoning the 'golden formula' of legality if such action was 'connected with' action 'taken in contemplation or furtherance of a trade dispute'. The Employment Act 1982 thereby 'denie[d] legitimacy to many disputes which [were] clearly about industrial relations issues' (Simpson, 1986:192). Secondly, trade unions were given a 'legal personality' through the removal of their immunities from the civil courts, such that unions could be sued for a wide range of unlawful activities. Given that a union with over 100 000 members could be required to pay £250 000 in damages for unlawful action, it would only take a few court cases to bankrupt even the most financially secure trade unions.

The restrictions imposed on strike activity were just one, albeit the most draconian, constraint on union activity designed to weaken the influence of trade unions *vis-à-vis* the employer and the state. Although a right to strike is seen by many as a fundamental human liberty, by the 1990s such action was:

> liable to be unlawful if it is secondary or sympathetic, concerns a union membership or recognition issue, involves persons picketing away from their place of work, lacks the support of a majority of those involved in a ballot, or possibly one of a set of ballots, is regarded as politically inspired, or otherwise falls outside a narrow range of legitimate topics for dispute. (Auerbach, 1990:2)

Furthermore, the position of the British striker became one of 'extreme vulnerability' (Ewing, 1991:vii):

> The legal position of the British worker engaged in a labour dispute is quite remarkable. A strike, for whatever reason, is a breach of contract; any form of industrial action short of a strike can lead to the total loss of pay; those engaged in industrial action may be dismissed with impunity (regardless of the reason for the industrial action); there is no right to unemployment benefit; and strikers and their families are penalized by social welfare legislation, even when the dispute is the singular fault of the employer. (ibid:141)

'The short point', according to Elgar and Simpson (1993:106), 'is that English law does not recognise an individual right to strike' (see also Hendy, 2000).

Other measures designed to weaken the bargaining power of trade unions included the progressive restriction, and ultimately the illegality, of the closed shop; the removal of all measures designed to support collective bargaining (such as commercial contracts that specify the employment of unionised labour); and the requirement to hold ballots to establish a fund to finance political (as opposed to industrial) activities (e.g. financial support for a political party) (see the Appendix to this chapter).

The legislative attack on trade union immunities through the 1980s and early 1990s also sought to restructure the internal relationship between trade unions and their members. The emphasis was on giving precedence to the rights of the individual *over* the collective, or in the Conservative government's rhetoric 'giving the unions back to their members' (see Martin *et al.*, 1995). For example, as well as unions no longer being allowed to 'unjustifiably discipline a member', which includes those who refuse to take part in a lawful strike (i.e. disputes sanctioned by the majority in a ballot) or who encourage others to 'scab', union membership complaints against trade unions attracted special legal support. Underlying the legal regulation of unions' internal affairs was the assumption that union officials were more militant than their rank-and-file, which was reflected in the Conservative government's preference for individual, secret, and fully postal ballots.

What the Tory government envisaged was that individual decisions reached through a postal ballot would be more *moderate* – there would be fewer strikes, more moderate union leaders elected, and political activities rejected (see Fairbrother, 1983; and Hyman, 1987b). In all these areas, however, the legislation backfired. In union leadership elections, for example, the vast majority of General Secretaries secured re-election. As Smith *et al.* (1993:380) concluded, 'the legislation has singularly failed to initiate a transformation in the political complexion of union leadership or a reorientation of union policy in a moderate direction' (see also Martin *et al.*, 1995:150) (more recent union leadership elections confirm this point, with the election of several left-wing leaders to major unions, dubbed the 'awkward squad' by the media). One adverse effect of the new balloting system, for both government and the unions, was that participation in union elections was *reduced*, which is hardly indicative of democratising the unions or 'giving them back to their members' (ibid; *Labour Research*, May 1990; and Leopold, 1997:296).

The failure of the legislation on balloting was the result of an inadequate conception of democratic practice in contemporary British trade unionism and the capacity of trade unions themselves to negotiate the context of their constitutional processes and the resulting political outcomes, regardless of formal statutory requirements (Smith *et al.*, 1993). Of particular importance was that the Trade Union Act 1984 allowed workplace ballots, which gave union officials the opportunity to address members *within a collective context* which, if anything, strengthened the relationship between union representatives and the rank-and-file. Moreover, ballots had the effect of legitimating, in the eyes of many members, the process of union decision-making without effectively changing its character. Thus, 'far from undermining collective consciousness, ballots have been adopted in ways which largely reinforce it' (Martin *et al.*, 1991:198). Union success in strike ballots (see Chapter 10), for example, indicates that union members may be *more* willing to strike, and that solidarity may actually be enhanced as NO voters 'have no means of knowing who their fellow opponents are – it would be an unusual trade unionist indeed who would defy a majority vote and cross a picket line alone' (ibid:206; see also Brown and Wadhwani, 1990; and Dunn and Metcalf, 1996:84).

Conservative support for 'minority dissidents, even single voices' (Dunn and Metcalf, 1996:73) within trade unions was not matched by support for non-unionists. In fact quite the opposite. By the mid 1990s, for example, a third of the workforce lacked protection for unfair dismissal from unscrupulous employers (McIlroy, 1995:401), while among young workers (aged less than 24 years) the proportion without such protection was over 70 per cent (TUC, 1996b:6). Constructing an 'index' of employment rights based on the legal regulation of working hours, fixed term contracts, minimum wage legislation, and legal rights to representation in the workplace, the OECD in the early 1990s placed the UK next to bottom among the industrialised nations of the world, with only the USA below them (OECD, 1994; see also Figure 6.3). Under the legal fiction of 'freedom of contract',

> The legislative assault on collective organization and collective bargaining created a space filled less by statutory determination of terms and conditions of employment than by unilateral employer decision. The legal principles promulgated since 1979 have been compatible with, and encouraging of, increased scope for the exercise of managerial prerogative. (Dickens and Hall, 1995:296)

In sum, then, the Conservative laws designed to undermine the bargaining power of trade unions also had the effect of reinforcing the diminution of individual employment rights at work, which served only to sour employee relations in many workplaces and widen the representation gap in many more firms (see also Chapters 7 and 8). The UK was increasingly 'out of step' with the rest of Europe with respect to employee rights, reinforcing trade union demands for any incoming Labour government to address questions of fairness and equity at work. Even managers no longer believed that trade unions were too powerful or were acting against the economic interests of the country (see Poole *et al.*, 2001:43–4).

The election of a Labour Government in 1997 marked a substantial, though not a fundamental shift in the approach of the state to employee relations, with the introduction of *specific* rights at a *minimum* level rather than a radical programme of legislative reform. Prior to its election, Labour indicated that its employee relations agenda would be focused on three main areas: the introduction of a minimum wage, signing up to the EU's Social Chapter (thereby reversing the

Conservative government's earlier 'opt-out' position) and the creation of additional rights for employees and trade unions (Undy, 1999a:326). A review of the principal pieces of legislation highlights three important aspects of the Government's approach: first, *individual* employee rights have been significantly extended, reversing the approach of the previous Conservative governments, partly through nationally-derived legislation and also through the translation of EU Directives into national law; secondly, the *collective* rights of trade unions have also been extended, but to a more limited extent; and thirdly, important areas of existing legislation introduced by Conservative governments in the 1980s and 1990s, in particular that relating to the legality of industrial conflict, have remained untouched by Labour, and look set to remain so. The consequence of the last, coupled with the modest extension of collective union rights and the minimal way in which European social policy has in practice been embraced by the UK government, is that whatever benefit the Labour government has brought to employees and their representatives through recent employment legislation, it has not fundamentally altered the relative power positions of labour *vis-à-vis* capital. To reiterate, legislative change post-1997 is substantial but has not fundamentally redirected the prevailing currents of employee relations. A brief consideration of the main aspects of Labour's legislative programme serves to demonstrate this point.

First, for many of those undertaking the poorest-paid activities in the UK economy, the most significant change that the Labour Government has made has been the introduction of a national minimum wage (NMW). This is all the more significant given the growing income inequality that has characterised the UK in the last two decades, in part resulting from the decline of collective bargaining and a rising proportion of low-paid workers (Rubery and Edwards, 2003:449; see also Chapter 3). Throughout much of the twentieth century, various (though far from all) low wage groups in the UK had received some protection and quasi-collective bargaining under a system of Wages Councils that effectively established minimum wage levels in different sectors of employment (at their peak in the 1950s, Wage Councils covered around 3.5 million workers). However, these Councils were progressively weakened under the Conservatives after 1979, and were finally abolished in 1993.

The introduction of a national minimum wage in Britain in 1998 brought it into line with many other industrial countries such as Australia, France, Belgium, Canada, Japan, Netherlands, Spain and the USA (Metcalf, 1999:185). This was achieved in two stages. First, the Government established a Low Pay Commission (LPC), comprising individuals representing employers, trade unions and independents, and chaired by Sir George Bain, Vice Chancellor of Queen's University Belfast (who was later involved in the Government's response to the 2002–3 firefighters' dispute; see Chapter 10). The LPC gathered evidence and presented a report and assessment to Parliament in 1998 (for a discussion of the activities of the LPC, written by one of its members, see Metcalf, 1999). The Government accepted most of the LPC's recommendations, including the initial level for the NMW of £3.60 per hour, though it modified the Commission's recommendations on the age at which the NMW should apply (22 years not 21), and the lower rate applying for younger (18–21-year-old) workers. Since the introduction of the National Minimum Wage (NMW) Act in July 1998, and following recommendations by the LPC, there have been several increases to NMW levels; in October 2003 the main (adult) rate for workers aged 22 years and over was £4.50 per hour, with the 'development rate' for workers aged 18–21 years (and for those aged 22 and over during their first six months in a new job and receiving training) of £3.80. The rates are planned to rise further to £4.85 and £4.10 in October 2004.

Although the NMW applies to all sectors (though agriculture has its own minimum wage machinery) some sectors have been more affected than others because of the uneven distribution of low paying jobs. First, as Metcalf (1999:182) has pointed out 'Low pay is overwhelmingly a private sector phenomenon'. Individual sectors most affected include: retail; hospitality; cleaning; security; social care; childcare; the manufacture of textiles, clothing and footwear; and hairdressing (see Arrowsmith et al., 2003; and Gilman et al., 2002). The NMW raised the pay of around 1.7 million workers, two-thirds of whom were women, of whom two-thirds worked part-time (Rubery and Edwards, 2003:464; see also Metcalf, 1999:182–3). Though compliance is not total (for example, compliance in respect of home-workers remains patchy) the vast majority of employers appear to be complying with the new regulation (see Low Pay Commission, 2000).

Initially, employer bodies expressed opposition to a proposed national minimum wage, arguing in accordance with neo-classical economic theory that it would raise costs and as a result cause job losses. However, partly because of the wage level set (£3.60 was significantly below what some supporters of a NMW hoped for) and partly because of the lower youth rate for 18–21 year olds, employer opposition in practice has been muted, and any effects on employment appears to have been 'indirect and probably small' (Rubery and Edwards, 2003:465). This is because most small firms operate with sufficient 'slack' and 'indeterminacy' to allow them to absorb the cost of the NMW (Gilman et al., 2002:54). Thus, firms can still compete on the basis of (labour) costs. Even where employer costs have increased substantially as a result of the NMW, it is envisaged that as they will be forced to compete more effectively on the basis of higher productivity and the quality of their products or services, this may actually reduce unit labour costs. As a result, the NMW can be seen as 'facilitating' market competition and not simply 'correcting' (i.e. raising) the market wage to a socially acceptable level.

The second main legislative change, and the cornerstone of the Government's 1998 *Fairness at Work* White Paper, was the creation of a statutory union recognition system, together with a significant extension of individual employment rights (DTI, 1998). On the former, the Employment Relations Act (ERA) 1999 established a statutory recognition procedure that the Minister for Competitiveness,

Alan Johnson (a former trade union leader) championed as 'fair, workable and balanced':

> It is fair because it gives individual workers the right to be collectively represented where a majority of them wants it. It is workable because it gives maximum scope for parties to resolve their difference voluntarily at every stage. And it is balanced because it safeguards the legitimate interests of business. (DTI, 2000:1)

In practice, the legislation sets out three routes to union recognition. The first is a voluntary route: a stated intention of the Government in putting the Act on the statute book was to encourage the parties to reach voluntary recognition agreements to obviate the need for unions to enter a process for securing statutory recognition (Wood and Godard, 1999:204). There is some evidence that the Act had this effect prior to its coming into effect in 2000 and this trend has continued (e.g. 450 of the 470 new recognition agreements signed between November 2000 and October 2001 were voluntary) (see TUC, 2001). The second route involves a ballot of employees in those situations where employers and unions cannot reach a voluntary agreement. A public body, the Central Arbitration Committee (CAC) oversees the ballot of employees. In the ballot the union seeking recognition must secure a majority in favour of recognition, and that majority must also equal at least 40 per cent of those employees eligible to vote for recognition to be awarded. In cases where recognition is awarded following a ballot, issues of pay, hours and holidays become subject to collective bargaining. The third route for recognition, referred to as the 'automatic' route, is where recognition may be awarded by the CAC without a ballot if more than half the workforce are members of the union(s) applying for recognition.

Given the similarities with US legislation (see Wood and Godard, 1999), however, where employers have used union recognition procedures to increasingly contain and even derecognise trade unions (see Adams, 1995:56–7; Friedman and Wood, 2001:588; and HRW, 2000), it could be anticipated that employers in the UK might use the legislation to similar effect. The terms of the Employment Relations Act are in fact designed to limit recognition to designated bargaining units; each claim for recognition is treated as an individual case, with no automatic implications for other parts of the company or sector. This is both consistent with employers' efforts to decentralise employee relations issues over the past two decades (see Chapters 4 and 7) and ensures that any spread of recognition will be piecemeal rather than wholesale. More importantly, the Act follows the 'institutional' (American) version of workers' rights to freedom of association in that it is based on a majority vote in a democratic election. The 'prerogative' (European) right to association, in contrast, is based on the principle that no majority should have the power to stop a minority from acting collectively (see Compa, 2002:119; and Leader, 2002:130–1). The institutional threshold for recognition in the UK (the majority rule and the 40 per cent rule) is clearly an arbitrary (restrictive) rule designed to limit union membership, as is the exemption of all firms employing 20 or less employees (e.g. a 9–8 vote in favour of the union will secure recognition in a company with 21 employees but even if *all* workers in a company with 20 employees wanted union membership they are denied statutory recognition). As we demonstrate in Chapter 9, many workers in small firms want, and need, union representation. This rule automatically excludes around 4.6 million workers from the statutory right to union representation for collective bargaining (see Towers, 1999:87; and TUC, 2003d).

To date, most employers in the UK have not been overtly hostile to the new legislation (see, for example, Heery and Simms, 2003). However, the are numerous examples of employer activity to avoid and subvert union recognition campaigns (Gall and McKay, 2001) and the recent successful anti-union campaign by T-Mobile, using the expertise of a US union-busting consultancy, may be a portent of future employer tactics. Moreover, securing recognition is only half the battle. In the USA, even after they win a recognition election, a third of newly-certified unions fail to achieve a first contract, despite the obligations on employers to 'bargain in good faith' (Brody, 2001:602). In the UK, the restricted range of bargaining areas that recognition following a ballot gains for trade unions – pay, hours and holidays – is a further indication of the Government's attempt to contain union influence and appease the business community.

Thus, few believe – and the evidence of the immediate period following the ERA coming into effect supports this – that the statutory recognition process will lead to a rapid expansion in union membership or collective bargaining coverage. With trade unions in a much weakened state in terms of membership and recognition than they were in the 1970s (see Chapters 5 and 7), their road to recovery, including the securing of union recognition, will prove a time-consuming and costly one. In practice, and at least initially, it makes sense for unions to focus their attention on contexts where they already have significant membership and in companies where they already have recognition in some parts (Oxenbridge *et al.*, 2003: 320). As we discuss in Chapter 5, much will depend on the unions' ability to sustain and intensify their recruitment and organising activities. One important factor in their favour, however, is that while the impact of the recognition provision may be slow to be felt on overall union strength and influence, the ERA may prove significant in what Smith and Morton (2001:133) call a process of 're-legitimising' trade unions in the eyes of potential members. If this then affects employer perceptions of union membership (i.e. employers become more willing, over time, to cede recognition), then the prognosis for the labour movement looks very different (see Turnbull, 2003:508–12).

In addition to the statutory recognition provisions, the ERA 1999 contained a number of extensions to individual employment rights relating, for example, to the right for part-timers to be treated equally to comparable full-time employees in the same organisation, increases in maternity and parental leave, and substantial uprating of maximum unfair dismissal compensation (in a separate change, not part of the ERA, the qualifying period for unfair dismissal protection was also reduced from two years to one) (see Brown, 2000:301).The ERA also gave a right to employees to be accompanied by a fellow worker or union official during disciplinary and grievance hearings. Significantly, this applies to all workplaces, including those with less than 20 employees (where statutory recognition procedure does not operate). For trade unions, this offers a further opportunity to gain access to workplaces and demonstrate their value in supporting workers with problems (Dickens and Hall, 2003:141).

The 'family-friendly' provisions (on maternity and parental leave) in the ERA are further extended in the Employment Act (EA) 2002, most notably the enhanced entitlement to maternity leave and maternity pay, and the introduction of paternity leave for working fathers. The EA also bolstered the rights of fixed-term workers not to be treated less favourably than similar permanent staff working for the same employer. Equality of opportunity has been especially important in Northern Ireland, not simply in the workplace but as part of the political peace process (see Dickson, 2003; and Harvey, 2001). The Fair Employment (Northern Ireland) Act 1989 broke new ground in UK legislation by placing a duty on Northern Ireland employers to monitor their workforces and undertake regular reviews of their employment composition and practices. The Northern Ireland Act (sec. 75) places a duty on public authorities in Northern Ireland, such as BHC, to have due regard to the need to promote equality of opportunity between persons of different religious belief, political opinion, racial group, age, marital status or sexual orientation, between men and women generally, between persons with a disability and persons without, and between persons with dependants and persons without. Without prejudice to this duty, public authorities must also have regard to the desirability of promoting good relations between persons of different religious belief, political opinion or racial group (www.ofmdfmni.gov.uk/equality).

Many of the current provisions for equality of opportunity in Northern Ireland and the rest of the UK reflect the incorporation of most of the substantive provisions of the European Convention of Human Rights into the law of the UK (under the Human Rights Act 1998). The influence of European law is evident in many other areas. For example, the provisions in the Employment Act 2002 on parental leave and fixed-term workers represent the translation into national law of EU Directives covering these aspects of employment. In the same way, the provisions on part-time work in the ERA were introduced to comply with an earlier EU Directive on part-time workers (see Dickens and Hall, 2003:132; and McKay, 2001:294–5). The translation of these and other EU Directives (notably on European Works Councils; see Chapter 11) follows the Labour Government's signing of the EU Social Chapter of the Maastricht Treaty in 1997. European influences now permeate many aspects of employee relations in the UK, and this will continue with the implementation in 2005 of the Information and Consultation

Directive (see Chapter 8), as well as forthcoming Directives on discrimination on grounds of disability and age.

At the same time, just as the 'business-friendly' nature of recent employment law relating to the minimum wage and union recognition have been noted above, so too the way that EU Directives have been opposed or diluted by the UK government has reflected what has been termed a 'grudging acceptance' (Oxenbridge *et al.*, 2003:317) by Mr Blair's Government:

> Although it has formally signalled its support for European social policy [by signing up to the Social Chapter] in practice the Labour government has complied with the European proposals in a minimalist fashion, never exceeding what the European legislation required. On the contrary, it has proposed or introduced measures that appeared to fall short of the full requirements specified under EU law. (McKay, 2001:291)

This stance, in turn, reflects employer opposition towards many aspects of EU social policy, the Government's concern not to antagonise the City, and more specifically an objective of the Government to minimise the impact of European regulation on UK business (Waddington, 2003a:342).

The desire to remain 'on-side' with business is enshrined in the Government's constant references to promoting 'flexibility' (that is, minimum restrictions on employer action) and is perhaps most evident in the reluctance of New Labour to make any changes to the law on industrial action. To be sure, certain changes to the strike laws have been implemented by Labour – most notably the introduction of an eight-week protection from unfair dismissal for workers taking lawful strike action – but these changes serve only to underline the fact that the main legal circumscriptions of industrial action, introduced by the previous Conservative governments, have remained firmly in place. As Undy (1999a:330) points out, 'the existing balance of bargaining power, which favoured the employer, was seen as appropriate [by the incoming Labour government], otherwise the Conservative's anti-union legislation would have been subject to more radical changes'.

As a legislator, therefore, Labour's approach, which has 'maintained the essential characteristics of the flexible labour market sought by previous Conservative governments' and thereby 'enabled the government to sustain close working relationships with employers' (Waddington, 2003a:353), is clearly consistent with the Government's economic strategy elaborated in the previous section. That is, New Labour has sought to facilitate the market rather than significantly re-shape market relations. This is not to deny the importance of many of the recent legislative changes for individual employees (e.g. the low paid and working mothers). Rather, the key point is that the path of employee relations along the 'Third Way' is closer to Thatcherism and the neo-liberalism of the 1980s and 1990s (as depicted in Figure 6.1) than either free collective bargaining or corporatism associated with 'old Labour', or indeed the more co-ordinated (social market) approaches that characterise many European countries.

The state as employer

The state's role as an employer in the public sector is fundamentally shaped by its broader understanding of what the public sector is for, what should be its overall size, how it should be organised and controlled, and its activities financed. Countries vary substantially on whether, for example, they operate with 'big' government (that is where a high proportion of GDP is devoted to public expenditure, and where a comprehensive range of public services is financed by comparatively high rates of taxation) or with 'small' government (where public service provision is more restricted, public expenditure levels lower, and additional services provided by the private sector). Even within specific countries, the public sector will be more or less important to different regional economies (Northern Ireland, for example, has a much higher dependency on the public sector than other areas of the UK). Similarly, there are differing approaches to the extent to which the state should directly own and operate commercial activities, such as airlines and railways, or alternatively whether such activities are better placed in the private sector. Different approaches are summarised in Figure 6.4 according to whether (or how) the state is involved in the ownership, operation and regulation of particular economic activities. For example, the state may hold a 'golden share' and insist that management operates on a commercial (private sector) basis, but ultimate control still rests with the public sector. Alternatively, the state may prefer private sector ownership and operation but regulatory control is retained in the public sector (either directly, under a Government department or ministry, or indirectly, under an 'independent' body appointed by the state).

Throughout the industrialised world there has been a shift from nationalisation to commercialisation and privatisation in recent years, especially in industries such as transport (see Turnbull, 1999). However, co-ordinated market economies (CMEs) such as the Scandinavian countries still operate with significantly higher public expenditure levels, and as a result a more comprehensive public service sector, than liberal market economies (LMEs) such as the UK and USA. The current approach of the UK Government towards the public sector echoes its approach to economic management and employment legislation: the mantra is to 'modernise'

	Ownership	Operation/Management	Regulation
Nationalisation	Public	Public	Public
Commercialisation	Public	Private	Public/Independent
Privatisation	Private	Private	Independent

Figure 6.4 Models of state involvement in economic activity

public services based on a more pragmatic approach 'to what people want' (Cabinet Office, 1999:9), which has involved extensive intervention in the public sector, but in ways that still reflect, and in many respects is still driven by, the market. Thus, rather than a simple break with Thatcherism, the Third Way is characterised by important continuities with past practice. In order to situate recent developments in the state's role as an employer of public sector workers, therefore, it is necessary first to consider the legacy created by the previous Conservative government's approach to the public sector.

Under the four Conservative governments of the 1980s and 1990s, the public sector was portrayed as the very antithesis of the 'enterprise culture' that the Conservatives sought to foster: it was portrayed as bureaucratic, inefficient, ineffective, inflexible, unresponsive to customer needs, and highly unionised. In his biography of Mrs Thatcher, Hugo Young (1989:35) observed that she had always said, when asked to crystallise the essence of the British Disease, that the nationalised industries were the seat of it:

> where monopoly unions conspired with monopoly suppliers to produce an inadequate service to the customer at massive cost to the tax-payer. They were, she thought, two sides of the same debased coinage. The nationalised industries, which should have virtue on their side, were hopelessly distorted and confined by state control and the absence of market competition. The unions, who were beneficiaries of these monopolies were accomplices to the most scandalous inefficiencies, and had to be stripped of power.

In economic terms, the Conservatives argued that the public sector was too big, not only for the state to finance but for the economy itself to sustain. Private enterprise was seen to be 'crowded out' by the rise of public expenditure, which in the mid 1970s accounted for almost half the nation's GDP: this was seen by the Conservatives in particular to be putting an ever-increasing strain on an only slowly growing industrial base. Public sector policies in the 1980s and 1990s therefore focused on rationalisation, commercialisation, deregulation, decentralisa-tion, and ultimately denationalisation (i.e. privatisation). The post-war consensus in the public sector was largely jettisoned.

Although there is great diversity across the public sector in terms of the nature of work, occupational structure, composition of the workforce, and so on, there were a number of common characteristics that could be identified, many of which still help to differentiate public from private sector employee relations today. Pendleton and Winterton (1993), for example, identified the following features:

- a formal separation of political and operational control, with industry boards responsible for day-to-day management, operations and administration, while government Ministers are empowered to give general direction to the board
- an 'obligation' to be a 'model employer', setting a 'good example' to the private sector in respect of health and safety, welfare, and in encouraging trade union organisation and supporting collective bargaining (which under the

Nationalisation Acts was a statutory obligation) and offering a high degree of job security

- formalised and (largely) centralised collective bargaining procedures, with explicit provision for arbitration
- high levels of union membership (and invariably a multi-union structure) with well-developed systems of workplace representation
- hierarchical, and bureaucratic, management structures with internal promotion, a uniform approach to employee relations, and an emphasis on keeping services running.

For much of the post-Second-World-War period, the most notable outcome of these structures and procedures was relatively low levels of industrial conflict (although the coal mining industry was a notable exception, as demonstrated in Chapter 10, illustrating again the problems of generalisation across the public sector). Industrial peace was secured through the institutionalisation of conflict, as disputes or grievances were resolved through well-developed procedures and a commitment by all parties to maintain consensus and keep the trains running, the lights on, the water flowing, and so on.

In addition, consensus rested on the relative absence of market pressures, allowing the development of greater stability in employee relations. That consensus was certainly not attributable to industrial democracy. In the post-war reconstruction and nationalisation of many sectors of British industry, the Labour government flinched from conceding any more than nominal worker involvement in the running of industry. Nor was any consensus reflective of industrial planning. On the contrary:

> the nationalised industries have been used as a mechanism for regulating the private economy rather than providing the basis upon which the economy as a whole can be planned ... The development of individual nationalised industries, as well as co-ordinated planning amongst them and the rest of the economy, has been subordinated to macroeconomic objectives such as the reduction of inflation or reducing public expenditure. (Fine and O'Donnell, 1985:157)

As voluntarism gave way to corporatism, and as legal abstention gave way to statutory regulation, industrial peace in the public sector gave way to rising levels of conflict. Indeed, during the period of most intense conflict during the post-war period, from 1970 to 1974, the public sector accounted for over 40 per cent of the 70 million working days lost (Winchester, 1983a:167). Industrial militancy was a direct result of incomes policies, or as Fine and O'Donnell (1985:157) put it, the subordination of public sector management and employee relations to the macroeconomic objective of reducing inflation. Incomes policies invariably have a more direct, and often arbitrary and unjust effect on public sector workers, which upsets the established practice of pay comparability between the public and private sectors. It is hardly surprising, therefore, that 'virtually all episodes of incomes policies in Britain have been broken, at least formally, by public sector strikes, with groups of public sector employees spearheading the resulting pay explosion' (Beaumont, 1992b:125). Small wonder, then, that the Conservative Party castigated public sector unions as the 'enemy within'.

The scale of rationalisation in the public sector during the 1980s and 1990s is indicated by the decline of both employment and public expenditure as a proportion of GDP. Employment in the public sector has declined from around 30 per cent of the total working population in the late 1970s to around a quarter by the late 1980s and just under one-fifth by the mid 1990s (19 per cent in 2002). As Table 6.1 illustrates, employment increased by 5 per cent between 1962 and 1982, but declined by over 29 per cent between 1982 and 1997. Likewise, public sector expenditure as a percentage of GDP, which had stood at over 48 per cent in the mid 1970s, fell to less than 40 per cent by the late 1980s, and averaged just over 39 per cent between 1997 and 2001 (Bach and Winchester, 2003:291). The reduction in employment has been achieved predominantly through privatisation, as the decline of employment in public corporations clearly illustrates (employment in the public corporations fell by 79 per cent between 1982 and 1997).

Although privatisation was a key component of Conservative government economic policy, it was the culmination of a much broader policy of commercialisation within the public sector. In addition, it was not a prominent issue on the agenda of the new government in 1979. Instead, attention focused on cash limits to control public sector spending (a policy in fact inherited from the previous Labour government, introduced in 1976) and of course pay. As such, cash limits operate as an incomes policy 'by the back door', but they are far more flexible in that they allow for variability around the 'norm', and selective discrimination can

Table 6.1 Changes in public sector employment 1962–2002 (thousands)

Year	Central government[a]	Health	Local government[b]	Public corporations[c]	Total
1962	1255	785	2652	2009	6701
1972	1184	821	2771	1929	6705
1982	1173	1227	2865	1756	7021
1987	1100	1212	3062	985	6359
1992	1091	1231	2899	562	5783
1997	792	1199	2593	370	4954
2002	818	1360	2741	379	5298

Notes:
[a] Includes HM Forces
[b] Includes Education, Social Services, and the Police
[c] Includes nationalised industries

Source: Adapted from Black *et al.* (2003).

be built into the policy in order to avoid confrontation with particular groups. The miners, for example, were 'paid off' on several occasions in the early 1980s, while cash limits in the steel industry made the 1980 strike almost inevitable (see Docherty, 1983; and Chapter 7), as planned in the infamous Ridley Report (*The Economist*, 27 May 1978). In addition to cash limits, Conservative Ministers repeatedly called for 'responsible' wage behaviour in the public sector, and from 1981 to 1986 announced a pay provision figure for central government services in an attempt to limit pay increases (see Beaumont, 1992b:172). At the operating level within the civil service, the introduction of the Financial Management Initiative saw the reorganisation of departments around cost centres to shift the emphasis towards 'ability to pay' (defined by the government's own cash limits) rather than comparability. The *Next Steps* report (Ibbs, 1988) recommended the creation of 'executive agencies' in the civil service to create a closer synergy between policy and the efficient management of services. By 1993 these agencies employed around 60 per cent of all non-industrial civil servants, the largest being the Social Security Benefits Office (with 62 000 staff) and HMSO the first to pull out of national collective bargaining and adopt its own pay and grading system (in 1990). John Major's government maintained the downward pressure on public sector pay by imposing a 1.5 per cent 'ceiling' on the wage bill in 1993 and then 'freezing' the pay bill in subsequent years by only allowing increases financed by 'efficiency savings', cuts in services, and job losses (see Bailey, 1994:119–31 and 1996; and Goodman, 1996:155–6).

While the emphasis of Conservative government policy was clearly focused on decentralisation and directing management attention towards labour costs (which were both consistent with broader Conservative government economic policy and the very high proportion of operating costs accounted for by labour costs in the public sector) (see Ferner and Colling, 1991:397), there was also a very clear attempt to change public sector management and set a very different example as the 'model employer'. For management, the emphasis became one of: a more professional approach with clearer assignment of accountability; attention to outputs rather than procedures, with explicit standards of performance; the promotion of internal competition; a decentralisation of decision-making authority; a shift in financial responsibility from the centre to individual operating units; and greater flexibility, and efficiency, in the management of human resources (Ferner, 1991:3; and Winchester and Bach, 1995:316–17). In addition, management's approach, and certainly that of the Conservative government, towards employee relations became more confrontational rather than co-operative and was implicitly, if not explicitly, anti-union. For example, managements were encouraged to withdraw from unilateral arbitration procedures, to move away from national pay bargaining, and no longer to encourage trade union membership. Union recognition was withdrawn from some groups (e.g. senior management staff in British Rail) and collective bargaining for nurses and teachers in England and Wales was abolished by the government to be replaced by statutory pay review bodies. In addition, the government denied trade union membership to 8000 civil servants at the Government Communications Headquarters (GCHQ) in 1984 (a decision reversed by the in-coming Labour Government in May 1997). In effect, then, the relationship between public and private sector employee relations was turned on its head: rather than set a 'good example' (as defined above) to the private sector, Conservative governments in the 1980s and 1990s gave a different lead through a more confrontational approach in the public sector. As Fredman and Morris (1989:29) concluded at the time, 'For those who support the promotion of employment protection and collective rights, the abandonment of the traditional good employer model is highly regrettable'.

The growing penchant for flexibility in the public sector, as practised in the private sector, especially in terms of numerical and temporal flexibility, led to a massive growth in sub-contracting, ranging from office cleaning, land and building maintenance and laundry work in central government, to Compulsory Competitive Tendering (CCT) imposed on local authorities under the Local Government Act 1988 (e.g. initially for refuse collection, street cleaning, school catering, and the maintenance of grounds and vehicles, and subsequently for a variety of other activities including leisure services and sports-field upkeep). The effect of such policies was not only a decline in pay and conditions, and of course union membership (Beaumont, 1992b:63; and Ferner, 1991:15), but also a deterioration of service (Ascher, 1987). However, unions had some success in resisting contracting-out and prevented any deterioration in employees' terms and conditions of employment in many cases (see Colling, 1995b). The extension of Transfer of Undertakings (Protection of Employment) legislation to the public sector, such that under CCT the successful bidder was required to hire public sector employees on their existing terms and conditions, further strengthened labour's position. In fact, in many areas of the public sector, many contracts were secured by in-house bids (Beaumont, 1992b:67), illustrating yet again elements of continuity in employee relations in the face of, and contrary to, Conservative government policy and intentions.

Of course, this is not to deny the scale of change that took place in the public sector under the Conservatives, only to suggest that, within an extremely diverse area of employment such as the public sector, elements of traditional employee relations survived, in some areas with remarkable tenacity. Specific indicators, such as reduced employment and major improvements in productivity (Beaumont, 1992b:177; and Pendleton and Winterton, 1993), reflect the extent of change, as does the remarkable shift in the boundary between public and private sectors. Over thirty organisations and industries were returned to the private sector after 1980, as Table 6.2 illustrates.

Once a nationalised industry or corporation is privatised, the government obviously loses direct political control over its objectives and behaviour, as the

Table 6.2 Privatisations

Year	Organisation/industry	Year	Organisation/industry
1981	Cable & Wireless	1990	National Girobank
1982	Britoil	1990	Electricity distribution
1982	National Freight Company	1990	Liverpool Airport
1983	Associated British Ports	1991	Electricity generation
1984	British Telecom	1991	Trust ports
1984	British Shipbuilders	1992	British Technology Group
1984	Jaguar	1993	East Midlands Airport
1986	British Gas	1993	Northern Ireland Electricity
1986–88	National Bus subsidiaries		Service
1987	British Airports Authority	1994	British Coal
1987	British Airways	1994	London Regional Transport
1987	Rolls-Royce	1995	Bournemouth Airport
1987	Royal Ordinance	1995	Cardiff Wales Airport
1987	TSB	1996	British Rail
1988	British Steel	1996	British Energy
1989	Water	1996	HMSO
		1997	Birmingham Airport
		1997	Agricultural Development Advisory Service (ADAS)
		1999	Department of National Savings
		2001	National Air Traffic Services*

Notes: * Partial privatisation

privatised company is now expected to satisfy shareholders and financial markets rather than political paymasters (Ferner and Colling, 1991:393 and 1995:493–5). Even following transfer to the private sector, however, the government is able indirectly to influence management policy, as regulatory agencies for industries such as gas, electricity and telecommunications use pricing formulae which hold price increases below the retail price index by an amount that takes into account the potential for efficiency gains (see Figure 6.4). This creates continued pressure on management to cut costs, including labour costs (see Ferner, 1991:13–14). In the water industry, for example, where a natural (regional) monopoly exists based on the river basins of each of the ten privatised water plcs in England and Wales, competition is 'engineered' through a price formula based on the Retail Price Index plus 'k', where the 'k factor' is assessed separately for each water company on the basis of investment requirements, operating costs, revenues and efficiency targets. Crucially, Ofwat, the industry regulator, makes comparisons *between* water companies to determine k and inject 'yardstick competition' into the industry (see Ogden, 1994:69–70 and 1995:209). This has introduced strong cost competition between operators, which invariably falls on labour, one of the largest and more easily varied operational costs.

Throughout the 1980s and 1990s, then, change in the public sector was managed more through competition and confrontation than consensus and co-operation, resulting in a series of set-piece industrial disputes which invariably ended in defeat for the unions and an after-taste of resentment among the workforce. The Conservatives, of course, pointed to improved productivity and other indices of efficiency to vindicate its approach, and as Ferner (1991:19) argued at the time, it was important not to lose sight of the need to improve efficiency given the squeeze on public resources. But the ability of public sector and recently-privatised company managements to deliver such efficiency improvements in the absence of employee commitment, rather than mere compliance, must always be open to doubt (especially when directors award themselves massive pay increases unrelated, or at best only weakly related, to company performance) (see Conyon, 1995; and Ogden and Watson, 1996). Given that the state effectively abandoned control over large sectors of British industry which, were they in the public sector, might have been used as the basis upon which to build a long-term economic strategy, the privatisation programme of successive Conservative governments 'was the culmination of the British state's long abdication from the real planning of production and accumulation even in the nationalised industries' (Fine and Harris, 1985:18).

Under Labour, there is evidence that the state's approach to public sector employee relations has been revised, although certainly not reversed. For example, after initially sticking to the previous Conservative government's spending plans during its first two years in office, continuing the squeeze on public sector finances (and public sector pay), Labour significantly increased expenditure, and employment consequently increased, particularly in health and education (see Table 6.1; also Black et al., 2003; and Hardwidge, 2002). The Government also abandoned CCT and (the rhetoric of) the internal market in the NHS. A more positive approach to trade unions and human resource management in the public sector was also instigated (see Bach and Winchester, 2003:292; and Fairbrother, 2002:61). Indeed, given that the 'core values' of the Third Way are equal worth, opportunity for all, responsibility and community (Blair, 1998), the public sector was always likely to be an important site of, if not a vehicle for, a more progressive approach to people management. As with other areas of state activity, however, the market is never far below the surface.

Consider Labour's approach to privatisation. Although this has not been actively promoted, it has not been abandoned (e.g. the controversial privatisation of the National Air Traffic Services or the attempt to privatise the Port of Belfast). More importantly, Labour accepted its predecessor's policy that most new capital projects should not be funded by the Treasury (under the Private Finance Initiative introduced by the Conservatives, private sector bids are considered for contracts to finance, design, build and operate public facilities such as roads, schools, hospitals and prisons, with the Treasury making an agreed annual payment for the duration of the contract, typically 25–30 years) (see Bach and Winchester, 2003:288). These contracts are often couched in the language of a Public-Private Partnership (PPP), but for public sector workers and their unions, this is effectively privatisation under a different guise and by a different route. Consequently, these contracts have been an important source of conflict in the public sector, although a more important source of unrest has been low pay (relative to the private sector) and greater work pressure. This has resulted in low morale and poor service quality in many areas of the public sector. Thus, an alternative interpretation of the Government's approach to HRM in the public sector is that it is conflict and competition in the labour market (e.g. chronic problems of recruitment and retention, especially in South-East England), rather than the core values of the Third Way, that lie behind many of the new initiatives such as family friendly policies. In fact, as Bach and Winchester (2003:296) point out, there is a widespread belief amongst public sector workers that 'the government, management and the public do not sufficiently acknowledge the value of their work' (see also Emmott, 2001b).

Although generalisation across the public sector is problematic given the diversity of jobs and conditions of employment that prevail, it would be fair to say that most who work in the public sector are suffering from 'reform fatigue' (Bach and Winchester, 2003:309). Public sector workers regularly report low morale and work intensification (see, for example, Emmott, 2001b; and Green, 2001) and this lies at the heart of simmering discontent and industrial conflict (see Chapter 10). While Labour might be prepared to see the public sector expand, unlike the previous Conservative government, it has continued many of the market-based approaches to how the public sector should be organised and financed. It has also intensified market-based forms of control through measures of 'best value' and performance targets for everything from the educational attainment of 7-year-old schoolchildren to how long an old-age pensioner should wait for a hospital bed. To be sure, these measures are not simply based on market price and cost control, but they have a similar effect on public sector employees in terms of work pressure, stress, and 'control from above'. There has also been an important redefinition of what the public sector is for, inasmuch as patients, passengers, students, home-owners, and others are all defined as 'customers' (see Korczynski, 2002:13–14). As a result, public sector workers are subject to many of the management control techniques discussed in Chapter 4. The ethos of customer choice creates additional pressures on public sector workers as a form of 'control from below', compounding low morale and exacerbating the on-going problems of public sector employee relations.

Conclusion

In many respects, Thatcherism, as a political project, was defined by its approach to labour and employee relations in general, and the public sector in particular. Whole swathes of the public sector were privatised, with market relations infused into what was left. In addition, a more confrontational style of management was fostered, with Conservative governments abandoning the 'good employer' model of public sector employee relations. Public sector trade unions were a particular target for many of the legal restraints imposed on trade unions during the 1980s and 1990s (e.g. laws relating to picketing, secondary action, union leadership elections and political funds). These polices have been central to the transformation of employee relations in the UK over the past 20 years. Ultimately, however, Thatcherism failed to transform the international competitiveness of the UK economy, destroying any justification for growing levels of poverty and low wages, an ever-widening gap between rich and poor, and the systematic erosion of workers' individual and collective employment rights.

New Labour, in contrast, appears to recognise the capacity of the state to express the 'common good' and not simply individual self-interest (see Blair, 1998). As Hutton (1996:25) notes, 'The extent to which the state embodies trust, partnership and inclusion is the extent to which these values are diffused through society at large'. At the same time, however, the capitalist state faces strong pressures to deliver policies that are congruent with prevailing business strategies, which in the UK are biased heavily towards cost-based forms of competition, labour market flexibility, and a strong preference for unitarist forms of management. This presents something of a conundrum for the Labour Government. For while it has the *capacity* to effect radical change – like Mrs Thatcher's governments of the 1980s, Mr Blair has enjoyed large majorities in the House of Commons during his first two administrations – the *ability* of the Labour Government to pursue 'labour friendly' policies is heavily constrained.

Over time, of course, the progressive strengthening of individual employment rights, even if this comes under duress from the European Union, might give a very different complexion to employee relations, especially in the public sector where unions enjoy higher membership. Similarly, collective aspects of employee relations, in both the public and private sectors, may increasingly be affected by union recognition procedures, especially if more and more employers come to respect the legitimate (statutory and human) right of employees to act collectively. The uncertainty surrounding the future of employee relations in the UK therefore is a reflection of New Labour's reticence to abandon Thatcherism and radically re-cast the balance of power between management and labour. But if we are indeed in the midst of an 'epochal shift' characterised by new configurations of markets and social institutions, as we argued in Chapter 1, then current state polices are likely to shape the future of employee relations for many years to come.

Appendix: Major UK employment legislation since 1980

Employment Act 1980

- Significant reduction of employee rights under the unfair dismissal provisions
- Maternity rights to re-instatement reduced
- Restrictions on the closed shop (non-membership allowed on grounds of strongly held personal convictions)
- Any new closed shop requires the support of over 80 per cent of the workforce (or 85 per cent of those voting)
- Repeal of trade union recognition procedure
- New restrictions on picketing (and a new code of practice)
- Secondary picketing outlawed
- New limitations on 'secondary' and sympathetic strikes
- Extension of grounds for refusal to join a trade union

Employment Act 1982

- Reinforcement of restrictions on the closed shop (protection and compensation for non-membership)
- Ballots on closed shops extended to all existing arrangements
- 'Union labour only' commercial contracts illegal
- Selective dismissal of strikers now legal
- New definition of a trade dispute
- 'Political' strikes now illegal
- Removal of trade union immunities from the civil courts

Trade Union Act 1984

- Ballots to be held every five years to elect (voting) officials to the union's National Executive Committees
- Secret ballots before industrial action (not more than four weeks before the action is to take place)
- Ballots to establish political funds (and to reaffirm every ten years)
- Redefinition of 'political objects' on which the political fund could be spent

Wages Act 1986

- Wages councils are only allowed to specify a single minimum rate of pay and a single overtime rate
- Workers under the age of 21 years are no longer covered by minimum wage protection

Sex Discrimination Act 1986

- Removed exception for small firms (five or less employees) from complying with the Sex Discrimination Act 1975
- Restrictions on women's working hours and other conditions removed
- Discriminatory clauses in collective agreements void

Employment Act 1988

- Union must hold separate ballots for industrial action if those who are likely to take part in such action have different places of work
- Ballot papers must ask whether the member is prepared to take part in a strike or action short of a strike
- Members have a right not to be 'unjustifiably disciplined' by their union
- Ballots for union officials extended to all National Executive Committee members (whether or not they have the power to vote on the NEC or not)
- New Commissioner for the Rights of Trade Union Members
- Post-entry closed shop 'illegal' (unenforceable)

Employment Act 1989

- Right to time off for trade union duties narrowed
- Equal access for men and women to employment, vocational training, and promotion and working conditions

Employment Act 1990

- Pre-entry closed illegal
- Union vicariously liable if any of its officials (including shop stewards) call for industrial action
- Restrictions on unofficial strike action
- Employers given greater freedom to dismiss any employee taking unofficial industrial action
- Further restrictions on secondary action

Trade Union Reform and Employment Rights Act 1993

- Union members to be given the right to decide which union they join
- Fully postal ballots before any strike
- Unions must provide employers with at least seven days' notice of official industrial action
- Union members to authorise (and re-confirm every three years) the collection of union subscription by automatic deduction ('check-off') from their pay packet
- Abolition of the 26 wages councils
- Removal of ACAS's requirement to encourage collective bargaining

National Minimum Wage (NMW) Act 1998

- Establishes adult national minimum wage (NMW) rate for workers aged 22 years and over
- A lower, 'development' rate created for 18–21 year olds and workers aged 22 years and over during their first 6 months in a new job with a new employer and who are receiving accredited training
- NMW applies to all sectors of employment, though agriculture has its own minimum wage machinery
- The NMW is enforced in two ways. The Inland Revenue acts to secure enforcement and acts on complaints. Individuals also have a right of redress to an Employment Tribunal

Employment Relations Act (ERA) 1999

- Establishes a statutory procedure for union recognition in organisations employing 21 or more workers
- Ballots held to determine support for recognition must achieve a majority in favour of recognition, and that majority must be equal to or greater than 40 per cent of all workers eligible to vote
- Where a majority of the workers are already members of the union seeking recognition, the Central Arbitration Committee may award recognition without a ballot
- Part-time workers to be treated no less favourably than their full-time colleagues
- Increases in maternity and parental leave provision
- Workers granted the right to be accompanied by a fellow worker or trade union official during disciplinary and grievance hearings
- Made unfair to dismiss workers taking lawful industrial action lasting less than eight weeks
- Regulations introduced to prohibit the compilation, dissemination and use of lists recording individuals' trade union membership and activities
- Several minor changes to the law on ballots for industrial action

Employment Act (EA) 2002

- Extension of statutory maternity leave to 26 weeks paid and a further 26 weeks unpaid
- Introduction of 2 weeks paid paternity leave for working fathers
- Mothers and fathers of young children have the right to request a flexible working arrangement. Employers will only be able to refuse requests where there is a clear business reason
- Right for fixed-term employees not to be treated less favourably than similar permanent staff working for the same employer
- Limits imposed on the use of successive fixed-term contracts
- Introduces minimum internal disciplinary and grievance procedures

part 3

Interactions and outcomes in employee relations

7

Collective bargaining and joint regulation

Re-casting employee relations in Corus plc

An industry transformed

Back in 1978, annual crude steel production in the UK stood at just under 21 million tonnes. Most of the 165 000 employees involved in producing that steel worked for the nationalised British Steel Corporation (BSC). In that year it took BSC 15.3 man hours to produce each tonne of liquid steel. A decade later in 1988, the output of the UK steel industry was just over 19 million tonnes, 8 per cent lower than the 1978 level. Employment in the industry, however, had been cut by a massive 67 per cent to a little over 55 000. BSC's productivity levels had correspondingly risen dramatically (to 5 man hours per tonne) and as a result BSC had gone from being a comparatively high cost producer of bulk steel to one of the world's lowest-cost producers.

After 1988, the year BSC was privatised and renamed British Steel plc (BS), rationalisation continued as management made further cuts and concentrated activity at the most efficient works. During the 1990s, these trends continued; in 1999, the company's output of crude steel was just under 17 million tonnes and its overall productivity levels had improved further to below 4 man hours per tonne. Employment costs, which had been 30 per cent or more of total costs in the late 1970s, had fallen to 21 per cent by the end of 1999. This fall in labour costs during the 1990s, coupled with other factors such as investment in newer and larger-scale technology, was increasingly reflected in the company's profits, which rose to over £1 billion in 1995–6. After this date, however, increasingly difficult trading conditions in the world steel sector resulted in the company experiencing several years of losses: the £1 billion profit of 1995–6 turned into a £1 billion loss in 2000. By this time, British Steel had merged with the Dutch steelmaker Hoogovens to form Corus plc. In response to the losses, job cuts in recent years have been severe, particularly in the UK operations, with the closure of entire plants (such as the Ebbw Vale works in South Wales) and the radical slimming down of other plants (such as the Llanwern works, also in South Wales). By the end of 2002 the Corus Group as a whole employed 50,900 people, but of these only 25,400 were in the UK (Corus, 2002).

Behind these bare statistics lies the story of an industry transformed, and continuing to transform, not to mention the severe impact wrought on numerous steel communities and tens of thousands of people formerly dependent on the industry for their livelihood. Inside the industry, the process of steel-making, little altered for over half a century, has undergone radical changes in scale and technology. A notable feature, too, is the way the process of transformation has been inextricably linked with major changes in work organisation and the structure and process of collective relations between management and trade unions. Given the stability of employee relations structures in the steel industry up to 1980, the extent and pace of developments thereafter beg a series of questions: What factors were central in the change process? What have been the major aspects of employee relations change? Why did the changes apparently occur so rapidly compared to what had gone before? And what have been the main implications of the changes for the different parties involved?

In order to understand contemporary employee relations developments in the steel industry, it is necessary to look back to the late 1970s and a critical period of change focused on the 'Slimline' plan. The problems facing BSC at this time were clear: principally, large-scale obsolescence due to inadequate investment and a failure to modernise over several decades, coupled with enormous over-capacity due both to a stagnant world market for steel and declining competitiveness in the domestic market. It is true that in response to these problems some rationalisation of the Corporation had already taken place during the 1970s. BSC had closed entire plants, as well as shutting down parts of plants, in order to concentrate bulk steel-making activity and other processes on fewer sites. In the face of mounting economic crisis and financial losses, however, the extent and pace of this rationalisation programme was seriously inadequate. The upshot was both a new rationalisation programme announced in 1979 and moves to alter fundamentally the character of employee relations. The latter was to be achieved, in large part, through the re-casting of collective bargaining arrangements in the industry.

As with the rationalisation of plant and production processes, some attempts at reforming the character of employee relations had been made in the 1960s and 1970s, principally through forms of productivity bargaining (see Blyton, 1993; and Owen Smith, 1971). Negotiations in BSC at this time were characterised by a substantial degree of centralisation; pay rates in the industry were negotiated nationally and separately with each union, while other terms and conditions (for example, hours and holidays, shift and overtime premiums) were negotiated nationally between BSC and a combined union committee comprising the main production union, the Iron and Steel Trades Confederation (ISTC), together with the various craft and general unions with members in the industry. With this national structure in place, the secondary role of local bargaining was to supplement national agreements in such aspects as tonnage bonuses and 'abnormal conditions' payments connected to working in conditions which were, for example, unduly hot or dusty.

Attempts at employee relations reform before 1980 marginally increased labour productivity via agreed redundancies and locally agreed changes in working practices involving increased flexibility both among and between production and craft tasks. The overall extent of work reform, however, was limited. Inter-union differences, rigid demarcations, a lack of monitoring of change and the varied nature of craft work proved significant obstacles to the development of new work practices. Given the slow pace at which rationalisation had been proceeding before the late 1970s, and the degree to which the structure of negotiations and pattern of work organisation were resilient to change, the twelve months from late 1979 were thus all the more remarkable for the developments that occurred and the ways these laid the basis for a refashioning of employment relations in steel on a scale hitherto unknown in the history of the industry, and one that continues to be reflected in those relations today.

'Slimline' and the national strike

In 1979, BSC published its emergency Slimline plan against the background of mounting economic crisis and the newly-elected Conservative government's instruction to stem losses and reach break-even by 1980–1. The plan was based on a cut in output by a quarter to be achieved by total and partial plant closures, and concentrating activity at more efficient works (see Blyton, 1992 and 1993 for more details). The most visible outcome over the next three years was a scale of redundancies unprecedented in the European steel industry (Harris, 1988; and Houseman, 1991).

At the same time, BSC also announced its intention to reduce the prominence of national pay bargaining and increase the degree to which earnings were tied more directly to local performance. This was consistent with the Thatcher government's economic policy, an important part of which was based on cash limits to the public sector and the requirement for pay awards to be self-financing. The first outcome of this was the BSC management's 1980 pay offer which was one based on local performance bonuses with no provision for a national, across-the-board increase. This refusal to make a national offer, coupled with job insecurity surrounding possible further plant closures, culminated in a protracted national strike in 1980, the first official national strike in the industry since 1926 (for accounts of the strike itself, see Docherty, 1983; and Hartley et al., 1983).

The outcomes of the thirteen-week strike, involving almost one hundred thousand workers, are far from easy to quantify, not least because the effects on management and worker attitudes continued to be felt in the industry long after the dispute was over. In several ways the strike acted as a watershed. As one manager put it, 'while the strike was on, we [the managers] sat down and said what we are not going to stand for when it was over' (interview notes). From the unions' perspective, the strike failed either to shift government policy on the funding of the industry, or bring about any reconsideration by BSC of its closure programme. In terms of the wage settlement, a Committee of Inquiry (the Lever Committee), set up under the auspices of ACAS, recommended an improved pay offer which was accepted. A significant part of this increase, however, was to be made up of local bonus payments negotiated at district level.

The move to local negotiations

In the aftermath of the strike, the centre of gravity of employee relations shifted down to the local level. Though national negotiations continued, their role and significance were increasingly circumscribed. Rather than negotiating basic pay rises, the national bargaining machinery came predominantly to function as the mechanism for reaching framework agreements for local negotiations and for consolidating elements of previous local bonuses into basic rates.

Central to the development of local union-management relations was the introduction of a works lump sum bonus (LSB) scheme which tied a significant element of potential earnings (initially up to 18 per cent) to the achievement not only of plant performance targets (including output and quality levels) but also to the acceptance of change by the workforce, including manpower reductions, the introduction of sub-contractors, alterations to work practices, and technical change. By putting a monetary value on co-operation, the LSB scheme, based on multi-union committees at works level, was to play a crucial role in assisting management to fulfil its rationalisation programme in the coming years.

Worker co-operation took three main forms. First, by making job cuts one of the LSB targets, management were able to define job losses as essentially local issues, outside the remit of national industrial relations machinery. The offer of comparatively good severance terms for those made redundant, coupled with tying reduced manning levels to bonus payments for those remaining, combined to diffuse much local union opposition to the redundancy programme. At the same time, national unions were effectively excluded by what they saw as this 'divide and rule' policy by BSC, executed through local employee relations. This exclusion also reflected the unions' diminished power due to membership losses and the difficulties of remounting campaigns against closures so soon after the national strike.

Second, the financial incentive of the LSB payments reduced opposition to other changes which in the past had been resisted by trade unions both locally and nationally. The most significant of these changes was the increased use of sub-contract labour to undertake a wider range of activities within the steelworks (see Fevre, 1987). In addition were specific agreements on technological change and job enlargement involving not only craft and production workers but also non-manual staff. Through job enlargement and increased sub-contracting, coupled with increased automation, BSC management sought to cover the huge reductions in manpower which occurred at sites which continued in production (reductions of more than two-thirds of total employment were implemented at major plants such as Teesside in the North-East, and Port Talbot and Llanwern in South Wales).

Third, tying bonus payments partly to achieved performance acted to stifle any oppositional activity which might affect output. With high levels of inflation prevailing in the early 1980s, securing increases in income was a high priority for those remaining in work. With the LSB potentially worth almost one-fifth of earnings, this was an important source of income for those still employed in the industry. Moreover, the significance of the LSB was further strengthened from 1984 onwards when BSC management made the payment of any national increases conditional on the successful conclusion of local LSB negotiations within a six-week 'window' from the signing of a national agreement (Avis, 1990). Thus, both local and national pay improvements were made to hinge on the acceptance of manpower change and performance improvements at local level.

Privatisation of BSC in 1988 exerted a further pressure on the decentralisation of employee relations. The establishment of four separate business divisions within the privatised British Steel (General Steels, Strip Products, Stainless and Diversified) led to the termination of any remaining national bargaining and its replacement by business level and increasingly local level negotiation machinery. In this way, BS mirrored the creation of strategic business units involving the devolution of financial responsibility to the individual businesses, through the devolution of employee relations machinery (Avis, 1990).

The Future Employment Package and teamworking

Throughout the 1980s and much of the 1990s, LSB negotiations remained a crucial element in the company's relations with its workforce. Only in the late 1990s did the emphasis change again, partly reflecting the impact of declining profits on the scale of bonus payments. In its place, management introduced a twin bargaining approach, much of this again focused at local level. First, in 1998 management and unions agreed what became known as the British Steel Future Employment Package (FEP) which contained two core elements: (i) conditions of employment would be harmonised between manual and non-manual grades, improving manual workers' sick pay entitlement, their holidays, removing clocking on/off for manual grades and introducing a 36.5 hour working week for all grades, and (ii) these changes would be introduced on a stepped basis, once certain 'milestones of improvement' had been agreed. The milestones for implementing the FEP were directed at local level change and included performance improvement targets and particularly the conclusion of local teamworking agreements, followed by the full operation of teamworking practices. Following the merger with Hoogovens, the local (works and departmental-level) negotiating of teamworking has been the main focus of employee relations in the majority of Corus's UK plants.

The importance given to teamworking is part of a longer standing emphasis in the company on changing working practices and progressively eliminating the distinctive occupational categories of 'craft maintenance' and 'production' workers, replacing these, where possible, with single categories of team members comprised of both former production and former craft workers. An important step towards this was the introduction in the 1990s of craft restructuring, under which the former complex craft structure was simplified into two general craft disciplines (broadly covering the mechanical and electrical areas) thereby reducing or eliminating many of the traditional demarcations surrounding particular skills (Blyton and Bacon, 1997).

Teamworking involves a number of fundamental changes to work organisation, including: termination of the seniority system of promotion for production workers (under which the longest serving employees obtained the most senior positions in work crews) and its replacement by managerial selection of team leaders; the integration of former production and craft workers into single teams; a reform of pay and grading structures in the move to teams; and widespread changes in job responsibilities and patterns of work allocation. Levels of work effort and work pace have also risen significantly though this reflects not simply teamworking but also the widespread employment reductions that have accompanied the introduction of teamworking (Bacon and Blyton, 2003a). The extent and detail of the changes – in employment levels, working practices, pay and working time systems, selection and promotion criteria and so on – coupled with the very different conditions prevailing in the different parts of steel works (for example around a blast furnace compared to a rolling mill or a dispatch area), and the need for commitment to the teamworking model (with its various training and work re-organisation implications) meant that the new system required detailed local negotiations.

In Corus's Constructional and Industrial Steel business, for example, centred on its Scunthorpe and Teesside plants, the introduction of teamworking initially involved two plant-level 'enabling' (framework) agreements signed in 1998. These established the 'principles and framework' within which local teamworking negotiations would take place. These enabling agreements set out the principles of five shift working to accompany teamworking, the selection criteria for team members and team leaders, and the general principles of pay structures within teams. These agreements also included an early retirement programme with a full pension from 55 years of age. This was central to departmental managers meeting a requirement from corporate management that the introduction of teamworking should also deliver a 20 per cent manning reduction in each department, to cut costs.

The plant-wide enabling agreements were followed by 22 separate departmental agreements, some of which were negotiated quickly and with high levels of co-operation, whereas others were much more protracted and gave rise to a much greater degree of conflict (Bacon and Blyton, 2003a). Departmental negotiations agreed precise team composition (for example, the mix of former craft workers in different production teams), the nature of the five shift system (some departments opting for 12–hour shifts, others maintaining an 8–hour pattern); and the specific pay levels for team leaders and team members (see Bacon and Blyton, 2003b).

The outcomes of decentralised bargaining

Through this process of local bargaining, management have achieved several of their aims with respect to reducing employment levels and increasing efficiency. Other desired outcomes, however, such as the creation of fully flexible teams with a high degree of job rotation, remain more elusive. Though the types of teamworking that have been introduced vary significantly, with some approaching more advanced, 'high road' forms of semi-autonomous teams, the more typical are somewhat restricted, 'low road' forms of teamworking where levels of discretion, flexibility and autonomy are relatively low (Bacon and Blyton, 2000). These differences have significant effects on team performance.

More generally, the latest wave of local teamworking agreements demonstrates the marked shift in emphasis in the conduct of employee relations in British Steel (now Corus) during the past two decades. Although elements of change were visible earlier, the conjunction of several factors in the 1980s and thereafter fuelled both the depth and pace of change. Market pressures, government policies and the outcome of the national strike combined to create a context in which management were not only forced into making substantial changes to the industry's operations, but were also provided with the conditions conducive to a refashioning of employee relations. In particular, this involved a diminution of centralised bargaining machinery and national trade union influence, and an increase in the significance of local agreements. The upshot was the creation of a system that has proved highly amenable to the pursuit of a managerially-defined agenda for change. Unlike the earlier experiments with productivity bargaining, the LSB scheme allowed management to assert greater control over labour in a context in which the latter was generally weakened by broader labour market conditions, and specifically weakened by the market conditions for steel and the failure of the national strike to bring about any reversal in state or employer policy towards employment in the industry. From management's point of view, greater control has continued to be exercised by maintaining decentralised employee relations and tying improvements in terms and conditions to fundamental changes in work organisation such as the introduction of teamworking. At one level, the result has been a widespread acceptance of change with little organised resistance and a closer linking of earnings to local performance. Yet, while the change to more localised employee relations has helped management to keep the focus on a performance-specific *agenda*, this has not automatically meant that management have achieved all the desired *outcomes* that they have sought from that agenda. Whatever their weakened position, steel unions have still been able to *negotiate*, rather than simply *accept* change and in so doing, win important changes and concessions from management.

The pattern of collective bargaining

In Corus, as in various other sectors of industry, collective bargaining and negotiated agreements remain important features of contemporary employee relations. Historically, for a large part of the post-1945 period, collective bargaining has acted as the principal mechanism for the determination of pay rates and other basic terms and conditions for the majority of the workforce, and more generally has represented a key arena for the conduct of collective relations between managers and managed. By the early 1970s, collective agreements covered over 80 per cent of all male and over 70 per cent of all female manual workers in the UK, and over 60 per cent of the non-manual labour force (both male and female).

Developments since the mid 1980s (set out in more detail below) however, have raised important questions about the future role and significance of collective bargaining in the UK. While for several million employees, collective bargaining remains the principal mechanism by which their trade union representatives exert influence over terms and conditions of employment, for many other workers this mechanism has been far less significant over the past two decades. In fact, the majority of workers are no longer covered by collective agreements and for those workers, any impact is therefore marginal and indirect (e.g. union wage agreements might establish the 'going rate' or act as a 'benchmark' for non-union workers). This contraction of collective bargaining coverage could be read by some as a signal of the ultimate demise of collectivism and negotiated agreements as mechanisms for determining changes in terms and conditions of employment (pay, working hours, holiday entitlement, and so on). Indeed, it is one of the key indicators marking the transformation of employee relations in recent years (see Chapter 1). But it is too early to write off collective bargaining and other forms of joint regulation as core elements in future employee relations. The recent stabilisation of union density levels in the UK (see Chapter 5), the introduction of statutory instruments to support union recognition procedures (see Chapter 6), as well as the priority given by trade unions to collective bargaining activity, are all testament to the continuing importance of collective bargaining and joint regulation. Moreover, in some sectors of the economy, most notably the public sector and significant parts of manufacturing, collective bargaining still occupies centre stage in management-union relations.

Of greater concern, however, is the drift from joint regulation to managerial prerogative. Collective bargaining has not been supplanted by individual negotiation – skilled and articulate workers negotiating a pay and benefits package that best suits their personal needs and career aspirations, ensuring high levels of motivation, commitment to the organisation and maximum productivity – but by managerial fiat (see Brown *et al.*, 2000:615). As we have already noted (Chapter 4), and as we demonstrate in the case of non-union workers (Chapter 9), management have failed to replace collective bargaining and joint regulation with sophisticated forms of human resource management (in fact, HRM is more often found in unionised workplaces). This is one reason why the UK economy continues to under-perform (see Chapter 3). As with so many other aspects of employee relations, the UK is again 'out of step' with much of Europe, where collective bargaining coverage is typically over 80 per cent (despite very low levels of union membership in countries such as France and Spain or comparable levels of density in countries such as Germany and the Netherlands). Many firms in co-ordinated market economies (CMEs) employ production systems or service strategies that rely on a highly skilled workforce given substantial autonomy and encouraged to share any information acquired from the work process with management (e.g. potential quality improvements or customer feedback). This approach carries risks, however, for management and workers.

In a CME, the firm is vulnerable because workers may withdraw co-operation in order to back up demands for higher pay or improved benefits, and skilled workers might be 'poached' by rival firms. For employees, sharing the information they gain at work with management exposes them to potential exploitation (i.e. unremunerated effort). As Hall and Soskice (2001:24–5) point out, CMEs need employee relations institutions capable of resolving these problems. These include multi-employer (national and/or industry-based) collective bargaining which standardise pay, benefits, training provision and the like, thereby reducing the incentives for firms to poach labour; and company-based systems of co-determination (e.g. works councils composed of elected employee representatives endowed with considerable influence over employment policies within the firm) which provide both the mechanisms and security that workers need to share information with management. We discuss the latter in more detail in the following chapter. In this chapter we explore the benefits (and costs) of multi-employer bargaining, which previously played an important role in collective relations between management and labour in the UK, the impact of decentralisation where firms have retained collective bargaining, and the implications for employee relations arising from the recent demise of collective bargaining for the majority of the UK's workforce.

A necessary, but by no means sufficient condition for a 'knowledge-based' or 'learning economy' founded on high skills, high productivity and high wages is a supportive institutional framework for the determination of pay and other conditions of employment (most notably training provision). We therefore begin by considering the nature of collective bargaining in more detail, together with some of the salient features of its historical development. Contextualising recent developments historically and internationally highlights both the scale of the 'representation gap' in the UK (Towers, 1997b) and the deleterious consequences of recent developments for industrial democracy, social justice and economic performance.

What is collective bargaining?

John Goodman (1984:145) succinctly describes collective bargaining as 'a process through which representatives of employers and employee organisations act as the joint creators of the substantive and procedural rules regulating employment'. 'Substantive' rules relate to aspects of the *substance* of the employment relationship, such as the wage rate, the length of the working day or week, holiday entitlement, sick pay and the like. 'Procedural' rules, on the other hand, establish the *procedure* by which, or how, substantive agreements are to be reached (how negotiations are to be conducted, by whom, how any disputes which may arise should be handled, and so on). In other words, collective bargaining is not only a *market* process, affecting the sale of labour power, but also a *political* process which, as a rule-making activity that involves power relations between the parties, serves to define rights, duties and obligations (Flanders, 1975:220). In the words of Slichter (1941:1), collective bargaining is a system of 'industrial jurisprudence' or, as Flanders (1975:236) put it, 'an institution for regulating labour management as well as labour markets'. In this respect, collective bargaining can be regarded as a form of 'industrial government' and a means to 'industrial democracy' (ibid).

Others have argued that the outcomes of collective bargaining can usefully be seen as not just a set of substantive and procedural agreements, but more generally as a means of management control (i.e. a managerial process). At first sight this argument may seem curious, since one of the defining features of collective bargaining is that it is a process in which issues are subjected to *joint* control. So how can it act to augment management's control? The argument here relates both to the consequences of trade unions participating in collective bargaining activity, and the possible repercussions of the absence of bargaining relations. On the former, the joint establishment of the basic terms on which labour is sold will conceivably vest those terms with greater legitimacy in the eyes of the workforce (and are thus less likely to be challenged by that workforce) than where the terms are set unilaterally by the employer:

There are numerous ways in which a positive acceptance of the union, an effort to integrate it into the administrative structure of the enterprise instead of treating it as a thing apart, can contribute to efficient management ... This sort of relationship, in which union and management officials not only accept each other's existence but support each other's objectives, is frequently referred to as 'mature collective bargaining'. (Reynolds, 1956:176–7)

The establishment of legitimacy is part of a broader issue, however. As Sisson (1987) argues, by entering into a collective bargaining relationship with employers over some aspects of the employment relationship, employee representatives not only demonstrate their willingness to reach compromises with employers over those aspects, but by implication also signal a broader acceptance of managerial rights in other areas and, more generally, the respective roles of management and labour within the status quo. Thus, in the historical development of the rule-making process that constitutes collective bargaining,

relatively few of these rules were (or have become) the subject of joint regulation; in most cases only a framework of minimum pay and conditions was involved. In fact much more important was the legitimacy that trade union involvement in the rule-making process gave to the employers' right to manage. For collective bargaining involves *mutual* recognition. In agreeing to make some rules subject to joint regulation, employers were requiring that trade unions should recognize the employers' right to make other rules unilaterally. In a number of cases ... this trade-off was explicit ... the exercise of managerial prerogative [was] the *quid pro quo* for the employers' willingness to negotiate over pay and other conditions of employment. (Sisson, 1987:12, original emphasis)

No wonder Harbison (1954, quoted by Jackson, 1991:162) has called collective bargaining 'one of the major bulwarks of the capitalist system'. By entering bargaining relations with trade unions, employers simultaneously 'gained an additional source of supervision over worker behaviour and an institutionalised means of pay settlement' (Ursell and Blyton, 1988:94). In addition, there are areas of workplace activity where, if anything, control rests with the work group rather than with management. Hence, for management, collective bargaining may represent an attempt to establish a degree of joint control where formerly they did not even have that. This strategy underpins much of the development of productivity bargaining in the 1960s and flexibility bargaining in the 1980s and 1990s, in which management sought to gain a greater degree of influence over 'job control' issues such as demarcation, the organisation of work and overtime hours.

As well as according legitimacy to both the specific areas of joint agreement and, following the argument above, to wider areas of managerial action, collective bargaining also represents a potential source of managerial control in the way in which it institutionalises conflict by channelling the power of organised labour into a mechanism which, while acknowledging that power, at the same time circumscribes it and gives it a greater predictability. 'By collective bargaining,' wrote Dahrendorf (1956:260), 'the frozen fronts of industrial conflict are thawed.' Thus, while collective bargaining clearly does not lead to a *cessation* of industrial conflict, the existence of negotiation machinery will tend to act to *temper* that conflict and reduce the chances of it fundamentally threatening the basic existence of the enterprise. Thus in the case of Corus prior to 1980, for example, the extensive national bargaining structures acted as an important contributor to the absence of large-scale strikes in the industry.

This is not to suggest that employers have welcomed collective bargaining with open arms or (as we discuss below) have not sought to diminish its role when given the opportunity to do so. Evidence suggests that, recent legislation notwithstanding (see discussion of Employment Relations Act 1999 in Chapter 6), it has become harder than ever for unions to gain recognition in new companies, new sites, or in those industries where recognition has always been difficult to achieve (Brown *et al.*, 1995:140–1; Gall, 2003b; Gall and McKay, 1999 and 2001; and Millward *et al.*, 2000:95–108). There are strong historical precedents for such resistance. The early period of trade unionism in the UK and elsewhere is replete with examples of embryonic unions fighting for recognition with employers highly averse to conceding *any* part of their prerogative to joint control. Faced with growing craft union organisation within the workplace, however, together with increased militancy among the newer unions of semi-skilled and unskilled workers, employers found themselves in a position where yielding to collective bargaining over basic pay and conditions was the lesser of two evils. In so doing, employers ensured that much of the conflict between capital and labour became institutionalised, the basic legitimacy of the system was tacitly acknowledged and union power became accommodated within the broad status quo.

Sisson (1987) and others have pointed to specific historical incidents, such as the industrial unrest in the iron and steel industry in the 1860s and the 1897–8 strike and lock-out over a shorter working day in the engineering industry, as critical events in the formation of particular bargaining arrangements. It is also important, however, to avoid treating these events in isolation. Part of the broader explanation of why employers in the UK did not demonstrate more concerted opposition to the growth of trade unionism, for example, and why they ceded recognition rights relatively early, may lie in the apparent complacency which gripped many employers in the late nineteenth century (see Gospel, 1992). Easy access to colonial materials and markets lowered competitive pressures which might otherwise have fuelled a stronger employer zeal to minimise labour costs by destroying union organisations (Ursell and Blyton, 1988:94). Moreover, the nature of early trade union growth in the UK among the 'labour aristocracy' of craft workers – a unionisation designed to maintain a separateness from, rather than a solidarity with, the growing class of semi-skilled and unskilled workers – meant that employers were 'anxious to avoid giving succour to a more militant unionism by rejecting the extant version' (ibid:94). Thus, in extending recognition and joint regulation to a union movement initially dominated by skilled workers, employers were seeking to accommodate a brand of unionism which shared many of the individualist values of *laissez-faire* capitalism. As we discuss below, the state also came to share this view that the institutionalisation of conflict within collective bargaining accorded a greater degree of stability. As a result, for more than half a century, the state both directly and indirectly supported the development of collective bargaining arrangements (see Ewing, 1998).

Though often discussed as if it were a homogeneous and comparatively simple entity, in practice collective bargaining is both a complex and diverse process. Walton and McKersie (1965) have observed that bargaining encapsulates negotiations occurring within, as well as between, the major parties, and incorporates attempts to structure attitudes as well as establish agreements over the terms of the employment relationship. In addition, collective bargaining exhibits considerable variation in:

- the *level(s)* at which bargaining activity takes place and the linkages between different levels
- the *coverage* of bargaining across different work groups, usually referred to as the bargaining *unit*, which may be few or many, wide or narrow
- the range or *scope* of topics subject to joint regulation
- the *processes* which constitute collective bargaining
- the extent or *depth* of union influence within bargaining activity, and the degree to which union representatives and managers become involved in the interpretation and application of rules and practices
- the *forms* which bargained agreements take, whether they are written or unwritten, formal or informal, precise or flexible (see, for example, Clegg, 1979:115; and McCarthy *et al.*, 1971:3–5).

It is clear that in the recent period significant changes have occurred along several of these dimensions. It is to a consideration of these changes, and the consequences for the parties involved, that we now turn, for it is evident that the type of changes evidenced in the Corus case are far from unique. And, as the steel example illustrates, these changes, such as in the level of bargaining and the nature of representation, can have a significant bearing on the kinds of issues included in (and excluded from) collective bargaining and the resulting outcomes stemming from that bargaining activity.

To this end, the remainder of the chapter examines changes occurring in patterns of bargaining and assesses the extent to which workers have 'lost their voice' at work. Following an historical review, the significance of the period since 1979 is emphasised. One issue of note is the fact that despite a tradition of 'free collective bargaining' in the UK, the outcomes of the bargaining process were foreclosed on numerous occasions in the past as a result of incomes policies (see Chapter 6). In contrast, the past two and a half decades represent one of the longest sustained periods of 'free' collective bargaining in the post-war years. This recent period has also witnessed many significant changes in the structure and content of collective relations between employer and employees, not least the historically unprecedented withdrawal from collective agreements by many companies in general, and the decline of multi-employer collective bargaining in particular. These developments have permitted a marked increase in wage inequality and a decline in perceived 'fairness' at work (see Brown et al., 2003:210; and Millward et al., 2000:137). It is not only industrial democracy and social justice that suffers as a result but also economic performance.

The historical development of collective bargaining structures

Early collective bargaining activity tended to be local in character, as individual or neighbouring groups of employers struck bargains with the representatives of local work groups. In the UK, both early trade unions and employer bodies organised on the basis of individual localities or districts: for both parties, national organisation only came later, and in some industries, only much later. To continue our iron and steel example, employers' associations in the industry maintained their regional organisation until comparatively recently; in 1925, twenty-five separate employers' associations were functioning, and by the time of the 1967 nationalisation, ten iron and steel employers' associations remained in existence (Owen Smith, 1971:39). In industries such as engineering and shipbuilding, the localised character of collective bargaining was reinforced by the early development of shop steward organisation before and after the First World War (Hinton, 1973).

In the early decades of the twentieth century, however, local arrangements for collective bargaining became increasingly overlaid by national, industry-wide collective bargaining arrangements involving (by now, nationally-organised) trade union organisations and national industry associations of large numbers of employers. The upshot was the growth of industry-wide agreements on pay and other basic terms and conditions (covering issues such as hours, holidays and overtime rates). Where industries comprised many employers, pay agreements tended to establish *minimum* or 'standard' pay rates, while in the public sector, national pay determination involved setting *actual* rates and scales.

Various factors contributed to the growth of industry-wide bargaining. First, in different ways it served the interests of all the parties to concentrate their bargaining activity at the national level. For employers, this meant a more concerted response to growing trade union organisation, particularly as unions began to expand significantly among semi-skilled and unskilled workers, became more militant (e.g. strike waves in 1912 and 1921) and developed as national organisations. As Traxler (1999:345) notes, '[h]istorically, employer organisations emerged no earlier than in response to the spread of unions which had acquired so much power that collective action in the labour market became an unavoidable ingredient of employer strategies.' Under national or industry-wide bargaining arrangements, individual employers in particular districts and localities became less vulnerable to trade union pressure in the form of 'whipsawing' whereby unions play off one employer against another (e.g. seeking to extend concessions wrought from more vulnerable employers to other employers in the same industry or locality on the basis of 'comparability'). National bargaining also allowed small employers to reduce the amount of time and resources they devoted to negotiating with trade unions. More significantly, perhaps, it kept unions out of the workplace, or at least neutralised their impact (Sisson, 1987:188).

For the expanding trade unions, national bargaining arrangements allowed them to rationalise their bargaining activity and marshal their meagre finances to service more effectively a small cadre of negotiators. It also underlined the role of trade unions within an industry, improving their possibilities for recognition and increasing membership growth (see Bain, 1970; Bain and Elsheikh, 1980; and also Chapter 5). In addition, national bargaining provided some protection against whipsawing by employers (i.e. a 'race to the bottom' in respect of pay and conditions of employment as one employer after another demands concessions to match those secured by their rivals) and enabled unions to wield the 'sword of justice' (standardisation is one route to fairness and greater equality).

Finally, for the state, the extension of collective bargaining represented an important institutionalisation of conflict and both an important counter to bouts of industrial unrest and a mechanism for promoting industrial co-operation, especially during wartime and economic crises. During the First World War, for example, the introduction of industry arbitration under the terms of a Treasury Agreement (subsequently incorporated into the 1915 Munitions of War Act), coupled with the taking of certain industries directly under state control for the period of the war, encouraged a centralisation of employee relations. More generally, the importance of state support for co-ordinated, multi-employer bargaining should not be underestimated as there is always an (economic) incentive for employers to renege on these agreements or their membership of the employers' association. This is because the employer's greatest power resources (e.g. investment decisions) are exercised *outside* its association, unlike workers whose power resources are most effectively mobilised *within* the trade union, such that the individual employer will always perceive some advantage to non-co-operative behaviour, for example setting wages just below the agreed industry rate in order to secure a cost advantage (many UK employers' associations formally recognise this problem through a 'non-conforming member' category which frees the individual employer from certain obligations of ordinary members) (see Traxler, 1999:345–6). More important for the state is the fact that individual employers are unlikely to take account of any 'negative externalities' in terms of the impact of their wage agreements on price inflation or unemployment, as their individual settlement is unlikely to have any noticeable impact on the economy as a whole. In combination, however, a succession of individual (inflationary) wage agreements, with each settlement higher than the last, can have serious economic repercussions in terms of (un)employment, interest rates and growth. As Traxler (2003:198) points out,

> Effective macrocoordination is beyond the capacity of formal institutions based on the principle of free collective bargaining. As an implication, the two sides of industry can arrive at such coordination only when receiving support from a third party. There is no possible party other than the state which can provide this support due to its imperative role in society.

In combination, these factors resulted in the progressive extension of national and/or industry-wide bargaining during the twentieth century in most industrialised economies. In the UK, national bargaining covered at least a third of the employed labour force and over half the total trade union membership by 1917 (Clegg, 1985:168). In that year the government established a Committee of Inquiry (under the chairmanship of the deputy-speaker, J.H. Whitley), and in a total of five reports issued over the next two years the Whitley Committee recommended the establishment of industry-wide collective machinery for all industries, centred on national Joint Standing Industrial Councils (JICs) supported by joint committees at district and works levels. The national committees were rapidly established in many industries and in the public sector; by 1921 seventy-four JICs had been set up (Ursell and Blyton, 1988:115). Though many fell into decay during the recessionary years of the 1930s, there was a revival of interest in industry-wide collective bargaining during the Second World War, again stimulated by government taking direct control of some industries and looking to secure peaceful industrial relations and co-operation with wartime production requirements in others. The upshot was that by the end of the war, 15.5 million employees out of a total workforce of 17.5 million were covered by some form of national bargaining machinery (Jackson, 1991). This proportion rose further as the nationalisation Acts of the late 1940s brought hitherto unorganised groups (particularly non-manual workers) within the scope of national collective agreements.

Throughout this period, a degree of local bargaining activity continued, in some industries more than others, concerned with the application of national agreements, the supplementing of those agreements in particular areas and the establishment of local work rules. The Whitley model also advocated the establishment of works committees to discuss local issues. While these always remained less prominent than the national JICs, they became well established in certain industries, particularly in the growing public sector. Further, during the Second World War, the government promoted the establishment of factory-wide Joint Production Committees: by mid 1943 there were over 4000 of these in the engineering industry alone, dealing with a range of issues from technical matters to levels of absenteeism and the application of 'dilution' agreements (the introduction of workers into skilled jobs who had not completed the normal apprenticeship) (Clegg and Chester, 1954:338; and Currie, 1979:156). Similar committees were established in shipbuilding, mining and construction. While the emphasis was on consultation rather than negotiation, these and similar committees nevertheless contributed to the maintenance of local collective relations at a time when most attention was being given to the development of joint machinery at national level (see Chapter 8 for a discussion of joint consultation).

From the mid 1950s onwards, however, there was a reassertion of local bargaining activity in the private sector, which gained further momentum during the 1960s. Industry-wide agreements remained in place but were increasingly subject to elaboration and extension at local level. Following Sisson (1987), local bargaining in large parts of manufacturing moved from 'supplementing' national agreements to 'supplanting' them. The shop steward movement grew from an estimated 90 000 in 1961 to between 250 000 and 300 000 by the late 1970s (see Terry, 1983), as did the degree of job control that work groups exerted over aspects of work pace and effort. Explanations for this growth in workplace bargaining have been sought mainly in labour market and economic conditions. The general argument runs that labour shortages, coupled with improved union organisation within the workplace, provided both a power base and a means for unions and work groups to mobilise that power to force wage concessions. The spread of piecework and bonus schemes are seen to have provided increased opportunities for bargaining to take place over rate-fixing for particular jobs. The general conditions of economic growth are further seen to have encouraged employers to secure local settlements in order to avoid disruptions to production and retain scarce skilled labour. As Boxall and Purcell (2003:177) point out, '[t]he old industrial relations were about control and stability: gaining agreements to keep the production system going and avoiding disruptive conflict.'

Sisson (1987) has analysed the significance of the relative weakness of most industry agreements in the UK, compared to their counterparts elsewhere in western Europe. In Europe, the broader range of substantive issues covered by national agreements resulted in local bargaining activity remaining an essentially administrative activity *vis-à-vis* the national agreements. In the UK, on the other hand, the narrower range of coverage of industry agreements meant that local collective bargaining developed a more substantial and independent role, filling larger gaps left by the national settlements. While national minimum rates were agreed at industry level, negotiations (often informal) at local level increasingly took place over issues such as piecework rates and bonuses, as well as demarcation issues and other working practices such as manning levels (Cliff, 1970). Thus, the relative weakness of national industry agreements in the UK gave trade unions significant room for bargaining at local level, and left individual employers faced with the need to establish rules and agreements in those areas insufficiently covered by the industry agreement. As Ogden (1982:170) notes, the variety and complexity of collective bargaining arrangements at that time were 'generally seen to be unsatisfactory not least because they are highly fragmented, encourage the pursuit of comparisons, breed competitive bargaining, are a major source of disputes, and produce dissatisfaction which fuels inflationary wage claims'.

The overall outcome was that by the time of the review of industrial relations undertaken by the Royal Commission on Trade Unions and Employers' Associations in the mid 1960s, it was not only judged that those relations were operating with a considerable degree of, or more precisely too much, informal workplace bargaining activity, despite the widespread retention of national industry agreements, but also, and of greater importance, that this bargaining was 'ineffective' (Donovan, 1968). The existence of this dual system, and in particular the informality, autonomy and fragmentation displayed by the workplace activity, was judged partly to blame not only for the increased numbers of strikes (see Chapter 10), well over 90 per cent of which were 'unofficial' (Durcan et al., 1983:109–10), but also the relative decline in productivity and wage drift (that is, earnings substantially exceeding nationally negotiated base rates). The significance of local bargaining on earnings levels by the late 1960s is illustrated by Cliff (1970:39). For example, while the nationally agreed standard rate for engineering fitters in 1968 was under £13 per week, in practice average earnings for fitters at that time, excluding overtime but including local agreements, was almost £23 per week, over 75 per cent higher than the national minimum rate (see also Donovan, 1968:9).

Essentially it was the *form* of collective bargaining in the UK that was identified as the problem. Collective agreements were basically 'gentlemen's agreements', and as such were not legally enforceable. This is in stark contrast to many other countries where there is a substantive agreement on all matters currently subject to joint regulation, the agreement runs for a fixed term, and is legally enforceable. During the period of the contract there is a procedure in operation to settle disputes arising over the interpretation of the agreement, but disputes outside the agreement must await termination of the contract itself, when amendments or extensions may be negotiated. Industrial action is only permitted at the end of the contract as a means of reaching a new agreement. Clegg (1979:116–17) classifies this as the 'statute law' model of collective bargaining, which he contrasts with the 'common law' model which is more reflective of (some areas of) British industry. Under this model there is again a disputes procedure, but *any* dispute can be referred to the procedure. In other words, there is no distinction drawn between disputes of right under the existing agreement, and disputes of interest concerning the terms of a new agreement. Industrial action is allowed whenever a procedure has failed to resolve a dispute. Substantive issues can be regulated by as many agreements as the parties choose to make.

Clegg (1979:117) suggests that the common law model has fitted the public sector reasonably well, but points out that in the private sector in particular, negotiation and administration associated with collective bargaining has often been more noticeable by its absence. Moreover, in some key areas such as disciplinary codes and redundancy arrangements there is often no direct trade union involvement, while formal agreements are often rare. More characteristic were *ad hoc* arrangements, custom and practice and unwritten status quo agreements. This 'primitive' or 'basic' model of collective bargaining, as Clegg (1979:123) labels it, is underpinned by a tacit agreement to disagree and an acceptance that there are areas where joint regulation is unwelcome. Both parties have the right to make rules and take industrial action to impose them on the other side, although agreed rules are made wherever possible to avoid anarchy and disruption. Under such arrangements, the action/reaction of one party will be shaped by expectations about the other party's likely response, leading to what Walton and McKersie (1965) describe as 'attitudinal structuring' and a continuous state of flux in employer-employee relations.

Although workers and local union organisation might gain from this pattern of bargaining, the authority of national union officials was perceived to have been undermined and employers faced ever stronger incentives to withdraw from multi-employer bargaining. The former is an example of what Traxler (2003:196–7) calls the 'vertical problem' of bargaining co-ordination (e.g. securing agreement from all parties within an organisation or interest group, such as trade union leaders, local activists and rank-and-file members) whilst the latter is an example of the 'horizontal problem' of co-ordinated bargaining (e.g. securing the agreement of all employers and trade unions who are signatories to the collective agreement). These problems heightened, and according to some analysts were a root cause of the UK's deteriorating economic performance in the late 1960s (most notably wage/price inflation and poor labour productivity). By the end of the 1960s, both major political parties favoured legal reform of industrial relations via the adoption of something akin to the statute law model.

For Donovan, however, the solution to the shortcomings of the dual system lay not in greater centralisation and co-ordination but in the extension and formalisation of local bargaining arrangements around more comprehensive agreements, drawn up and administered by an enhanced industrial relations management function. In other words, the *form* of collective bargaining was to change, and its *scope* extended. Thus, formal bargaining at the plant or company level was envisaged as expanding beyond its traditional subject areas to encapsulate a wide range of job control issues, such as staffing levels, demarcation and work rate, which had hitherto been determined by 'custom and practice'. In addition, payment-by-results (PBR) was to be replaced by measured day work (MDW) or other payment schemes to reduce wage drift. The introduction of job evaluation would reduce the problems of fragmented bargaining and comparability claims, and new dispute procedures would help to reduce strikes. Underlying these recommendations was the criticism that negotiations had traditionally been 'a one-sided affair' (Donovan, 1968:85) with employers failing even to secure concessions on working practices in return for wage increases. Under the expanded version of collective bargaining, however, wage rises would be *exchanged* for agreements over job control issues.

An influential model informing these recommendations, and much quoted in the Donovan Report itself, was the productivity agreement reached earlier at Esso's Fawley refinery (Flanders, 1964). In this highly detailed, book-length agreement, Esso management sought to regain control over labour costs and secure productivity improvements by entering into an agreement with local trade unions which exchanged a (substantial) pay increase for detailed changes in working arrangements involving, among other things, reduced overtime working, greater job flexibility and a simplification of the pay structure. For members of the Royal Commission and others, Esso's 'Blue Book' agreement, and productivity bargaining more generally, became a model of how collective bargaining might be better organised.

Initial enthusiasm for productivity agreements soon evaporated, not least because most failed to deliver significant increases in productivity, due in part to many being used more as a way to by-pass the government's incomes policies in operation at the time. However, workplace bargaining continued to develop in importance during the 1970s, with shop steward organisation spreading among non-manual groups and beyond manufacturing into public service settings such as local authorities (Nicholson *et al.*, 1980). In the decade after Donovan some formalisation of local bargaining did occur (see, for example, Marsh, 1982), partly as management responded to growing shop steward organisation and an increased number of strikes (see Turner *et al.*, 1977). But on the shopfloor, control over working practices by individual work groups if anything increased, although the extent to which this hindered managerial control has been fiercely debated (see, for example, Hyman and Elger, 1981; and Kilpatrick and Lawson, 1980). The growing influence of shopfloor groups may, in part, have been due to employers' lack of investment in newer technologies at that time, which allowed work groups to retain and reinforce the informal rules devised around older, non-automated equipment (see, for example, Belanger, 1987). More generally, it must be acknowledged that the managerially-led reform of collective bargaining proposed by Donovan not only discounted trade union resistance, but assumed that the 'formalisation of the informal' was in the best interests of *both* parties. As Ogden (1981 and 1982) and others have demonstrated, this was simply not the case. As a result,

> Even though trade unions may not positively challenge managerially determined arrangements regarding the levels at which bargaining takes place, trade union power acts as a significant constraint on what choices management may make. Consequently, decisions about bargaining structure may represent defensive responses by management as well as offensive initiative. (Ogden, 1982:182)

Of equal importance, however, were the shortcomings of management. Under the Donovan proposals, the onus was placed upon management to implement change, albeit by consent and through the process of joint regulation. The prescription, as Ogden (1981:31) notes, was that 'if management accepted their responsibility, embraced the opportunities collective bargaining offered, and took advantage of the techniques available such as job evaluation ... they could regain control where they had lost it and improve efficiency and productivity'. But management failed to carry through the Donovan programme for at least three reasons (in addition to the problems of union or work group opposition).

First, managers valued the informality and flexibility of the existing system. Thus, while there were considerable changes in the nature and conduct of bargaining over *market* relations, there was little change so far as *managerial* relations were concerned (Sisson and Brown, 1983:137). As a result, by the end of the 1970s a dual structure of pay bargaining had developed, with multi-employer, industry-wide agreements still prevalent in industries with a large number of small firms, relatively low capital requirements and ease of entry, while elsewhere there was a move towards a formal, single employer pay bargaining system (Sisson and Brown, 1983:147–8). As for managerial relations, however, the scope of collective bargaining appeared 'as hazy as it ever was. It is massively variable from industry to industry and from workplace to workplace, heavily dependent upon the form of management controls and the relative power of the protagonists' (ibid:149–50).

Secondly, many managers had neither the capacity nor the expertise to exercise sufficient (formal) control over industrial relations at the plant or company level (Ogden, 1981:39 and 1982:181). As Michael Edwardes, former Chairman of British Leyland (now Rover) made clear in his autobiography *Back From the Brink*, ten years of vacillation by plant management in employee relations had left them with little credibility or authority (1983:78). But as Nichols (1986:165–6) illustrates, this was not so much a case of workers gaining control as of managers losing it. When combined with the failure of many firms to organise productive activity effectively, this undermined workers' respect for management and led to deterioration in employee relations (see Chapter 4; and Batstone, 1986:41).

Thirdly, in following Allan Flanders's famous dictum that management should 'regain control by sharing it', Donovan not only assumed that management were prepared to share control, but that they would be willing to change their attitude towards trade unions in general and shop stewards in particular. As Ogden (1981:36) notes, however, 'the idea of giving them [shop stewards] more by sharing power was complete anathema to them [management]'. Despite Fox's (1966) critique, most managers still hold a unitarist perspective on employee relations (see Chapter 4). Not surprisingly, the effort 'to educate management of the need for change in attitudes – from unitary to pluralist frames of reference, from management by prerogatives to joint regulation – deemed essential in the programme of reform has generally met, with some exceptions, little success'

(Ogden, 1981:37). In short, management did not seek to share power, but to restore their prerogative.

Thus, by the end of the 1970s, there was still a very complex and varied pattern of collective bargaining in the UK, in terms of each of the various dimensions identified (level, form, scope, depth, and so on). According to Hugh Clegg, the draftsman of the most influential chapter in the Donovan Report, that on collective bargaining,

> the true disciples of the Royal Commission have been those managers of British companies who have carried through a reconstruction of their industrial relations at workplace level along much the same lines as the Commission's report had recommended, with considerable increases in productivity and a substantial decline in strike activity. (1990:6)

But the more widely accepted view, and certainly that of the incoming Thatcher government, was that the Donovan prescription had failed, certainly in its intentions to deliver a higher rate of productivity growth which would reverse the relative economic decline of the UK economy (for an exposition of this view see Metcalf, 1989). Not surprisingly, then, the 1980s and 1990s were to witness more dramatic change, as the experience of Corus and many other organisations clearly illustrates.

Decentralisation and decline of collective bargaining

Since the early 1980s to the present, the pattern of collective bargaining in the UK has exhibited three main trends: (i) a substantial reduction in the proportion of employees covered by collective bargaining arrangements, (ii) a growing tendency for those arrangements to be local rather than national in character, and (iii) a narrowing of the scope of collective agreements. The contraction in coverage and scope of collective bargaining, combined with the decentralisation to lower levels, add up to a fundamental change in the character and conduct of employee relations in the UK over the past two decades.

In the early 1980s, over two-thirds of employees in Britain were covered by collective bargaining arrangements. In only a decade and a half, this slumped to just two-in-five of all employees (Millward *et al.*, 2000:197). What makes the decline in coverage particularly significant is that it is evident across all sectors of employment: public and private sector, manufacturing and service activities (see Figure 7.1). If smaller workplaces were included in these calculations (i.e. those employing fewer than 25 workers) then collective bargaining coverage would be further reduced.

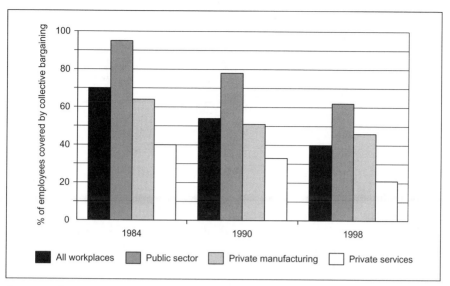

Source: Millward *et al.* (2000:197).

Figure 7.1 Changes in overall coverage of collective bargaining activity in Britain 1984–98

As Figure 7.1 demonstrates, there remain substantial variations between sectors, both in the degree of coverage and in the rate of change. For example, in the 1990s the rate of decline of bargaining coverage in private sector manufacturing was far less than the rate in the public sector, while in private sector services the fall in the 1990s was particularly marked. Similarly, there are variations within sectors with some (such as energy and water, and metal goods and engineering) maintaining similar levels of coverage throughout the 1990s (Millward *et al.*, 2000:198). Overall, however, the picture is one of very substantial decline in bargaining coverage during the 1980s and 1990s. Statistically, this decline reflects two important trends. First, the growing number of workplaces where no unions, and thus no collective bargaining, are present (this trend is not so much attributable to union derecognition, although this has been important in specific industries, rather to the tendency of newly established workplaces not to recognise trade unions). Secondly, even where a trade union has recognition, collective bargaining coverage has declined: in 1998, 69 per cent of employees in workplaces with recognised unions were covered by collective bargaining compared to 90 per cent in 1984. This decline has been particularly evident where union density levels are fairly low, indicating that managers have used low union density as a pretext for withdrawing from collective bargaining for pay determination and other issues, to be replaced by unilateral (i.e. managerially-determined) pay setting. Both trends, of course, are not simply the result of a failure on the part of unions to organise new workplaces or to maintain an active membership where they have recognition, but represent an important shift in management strategy away from joint regulation.

If recent developments are viewed from the perspective of management control, then decentralisation is more readily understood. In many cases, of course, multi-employer agreements have simply been replaced by unilateral pay determination by management (half the workforce now have their pay set by management, a figure that rises to two-thirds in the private sector) (see Brown *et al.*, 2000:615). Where bargaining still takes place, there is a tendency within larger companies for bargaining activity to be devolved to the level of individual divisions, units, establishments and/or profit centres where market forces and internal pressures are more keenly felt. In this way, management seek to diminish the influence of 'comparability', the 'going rate', 'standardisation' or other 'outmoded' concepts of pay determination.

Unfortunately, there is a tendency for some authors to discuss this latter development simply in terms of 'decentralisation', which can be misleading for two reasons. First, many firms and industries were already characterised by highly decentralised workplace and workshop bargaining arrangements (see above). Secondly, and more importantly, in positioning collective bargaining more clearly at the establishment level, what the pattern of change has simultaneously involved has been a decentralisation of bargaining activity from corporate level and an attempt to diminish the role of informal shopfloor bargaining by shifting the focus of local joint regulation from the individual section and department up to more formal activity at establishment level. As a result, 'much of the decentralization that has taken place is an illusion. Things may happen at local level, but they are not decided there' (Storey and Sisson, 1993:212; see also Sisson and Marginson, 1995:105–6). As management retain greater (centralised) control of decentralised bargaining, the resulting bargaining activity at the establishment level is generally of a more formalised nature than that criticised by the Donovan Commission in the 1960s. In the local teamworking agreements at Corus, for example, all aspects relating to the new work structures (grades, pay levels, job responsibilities, working patterns and so on) were formally set out in detail within each departmental agreement. In addition, however, key parameters for those departmental agreements – most importantly, the requirement to reduce employment numbers by a fifth, as part of the move to teamworking – were decisions made by corporate management.

The continued move away from multi-employer to single-employer bargaining has been documented by the series of workplace industrial relations surveys undertaken between 1980 and 1998 (Millward *et al.*, 2000:186–96; see also Brown and Walsh, 1991:49; Gregg and Yates, 1991; Howell, 1995:161–2). In private sector manufacturing, the proportion of workplaces where multi-employer collective bargaining was the dominant mode of pay determination declined from 21 per cent in 1984 to just 6 per cent in 1998. In private sector services the corresponding figures were 17 per cent and 3 per cent (Millward *et al.*, 2000:187–93). As one might expect in the private sector, changes have often been driven by market forces, reflecting the fact that:

The overwhelming desire by managers has been to get employees to work harder and more efficiently in return for pay increases ... Decentralized bargaining has allowed bargaining over market relations to be linked to bargaining over managerial relations. (Jackson et al., 1993:161–2)

However, unlike the 'productivity bargaining' of the 1960s and 1970s (see McKersie and Hunter, 1973), or the 'flexibility bargaining' of the 1980s (see Dunn and Wright, 1994; Ingram, 1991; and Marsden and Thompson, 1990), 'The usual rules of bargaining no longer apply. For one thing, the items placed on the negotiating table become too numerous, too complex and too interwoven for classic trade-off deals' (Boxall and Purcell, 2003:177).

As bargaining has been decentralised, management have sought to narrow the scope of joint regulation. Survey evidence and case-based research often conflict on this point, reflecting different measures of presence (i.e. where any bargaining takes place) and process (i.e. whether workers or their representatives have any real influence on bargaining outcomes). As the coverage of pay bargaining began its seemingly inexorable decline after 1979, surveys initially indicated a corresponding decline in bargaining over non-pay issues. WIRS90, however, suggested far less change in non-pay bargaining between 1984 and 1990 (Millward et al., 1992:249–53). More detailed case studies, in contrast, identified a more sustained and substantial reduction in the trade unions' bargaining role (e.g. Morris and Wood, 1991), as did a longitudinal case study conducted over a ten-year period (Kinnie, 1992). These findings accord with our own experience at the time of researching in a variety of work contexts including steel, port transport, engineering, electronics, airlines and the automotive industry: unions maintained a bargaining role on certain issues but this was increasingly augmented by management handling work-related changes outside the bargaining framework.

Evidence from case-study research conducted in the mid 1990s suggested not only a continuation of these trends (i.e. a substantial reduction in the scope of collective bargaining in companies that continued to recognise unions) but a narrowing of the bargaining agenda to the point where this was tantamount to 'implicit or partial derecognition' (Brown et al., 1998:iii). By the end of the 1990s, even surveys indicated that the scope of joint negotiation at the workplace was quite modest (Cully et al., 1999:103–4). To be sure, where unions were still well organised and membership levels were high, management were more likely to negotiate (ibid). In these organisations there is evidence of very little change in the scope of bargaining over non-pay issues (see, for example, Millward et al., 2000:167–73). But this should not detract attention from the overall decline in pay bargaining or the much narrower scope of joint regulation at the workplace.

At first sight, one possible exception to these developments might appear to be the public sector, where collective bargaining is still the dominant form of pay determination (see Figure 7.1) with 39 per cent of establishments still covered by multi-employer pay bargaining (Millward *et al.*, 2000:194). Moreover, although this is far fewer than in 1984 when 82 per cent of public sector workplaces were covered by multi-employer bargaining, this decline has been partially offset by two factors: (i) an increase in multi-site, single employer bargaining (unlike the private sector where this form of bargaining has declined in recent years) (ibid:187–96) and (ii) the introduction of pay review bodies (in place of national bargaining) for nurses and midwives (in 1983) and schoolteachers (in 1991) which simultaneously took almost one million employees out of collective bargaining machinery for their pay determination, but at the same time maintained a national system for pay settlement for these groups (Bach and Winchester, 2003:298). Thus, the institutional structure of collective bargaining in the public sector still (potentially) supports an element of standardisation across workplaces.

The dominant trend, however, is still a marked shift away from centralised bargaining systems, reflecting the policy of successive governments, both Conservative and Labour, to 'commercialise' large sections of the public sector and to 'proxy' market forces through compulsory competitive tendering, local management of schools, GP fund-holding, NHS hospital trusts, Next Step agencies in the civil service, and a range of other initiatives (see Chapter 6). As Bach and Winchester (2003:299) note,

> As managers were given greater responsibility for budgets in which labour costs were the most significant component, the relevance of national pay and conditions arrangements was increasingly questioned. The restructuring and organisational fragmentation of public services, and the growing interest in private sector management 'best practice' added further weight to the arguments in favour of a more decentralized system of pay determination.

As in the private sector, therefore, trade unions are now far less likely to be involved in pay bargaining, and in particular multi-employer pay bargaining, than they were in the past. The same conclusion holds for non-pay bargaining issues such as staffing levels, redeployment, training, physical working conditions, the re-organisation of working hours, and equal opportunities. As the scope of joint regulation has narrowed across the economy, with private and public sector workers alike increasingly subject to market forces and managerial fiat, workers are routinely excluded from decision-making at their place of work. This has deleterious consequences for industrial democracy, social justice and economic performance.

Effects of changes in collective bargaining

Collective bargaining in the UK, as in other liberal market economies (LMEs) such as the USA, is employer dependent (see Osterman *et al.*, 2001:101; and Turnbull, 2003:508). Without provision for the extension of collective agreements beyond the unionised bargaining unit – either by statutory regulation or more extensive membership of employers' associations (wherein some members of the association apply union-agreed contracts, even though they may be non-union firms or have much lower levels of union density) – then joint regulation is inherently firm-specific.

The UK has always had a 'voluntary' system of industrial relations, but collective bargaining was previously supported by the state, especially in the public sector. Between 1979 and 1997, however, any auxiliary measures to support and encourage collective bargaining were progressively dismantled by successive Conservative governments (e.g. the Fair Wages Resolution, repealed in 1983, which extended the terms of collective bargaining agreements to firms not directly involved in such agreements, and the removal of the duty 'to encourage collective bargaining' from the terms of reference of ACAS in 1993). Concurrently, membership of employers' associations collapsed in the rush to single-employer bargaining (Millward *et al.*, 1992:45–6). Despite some revival in employer association membership during the 1990s (Cully *et al.*, 1999:228) there is no longer a sufficiently robust or extensive membership base through which employers might co-ordinate or standardise collective bargaining in the UK. Even the statutory union recognition procedure introduced by New Labour (Employment Relations Act 1999) is explicitly company, or more precisely bargaining unit specific (50 per cent of employees must vote in favour of recognition, which must represent at least 40 per cent of the relevant bargaining unit). As Towers (1997a:303) points out, 'although effective rights to trade union recognition and a consequent duty for employers to bargain in good faith are important instruments of industrial democracy through collective bargaining, they do nothing for those who are without representation, by choice or circumstance'. Whereas collective bargaining used partly to reflect a national agenda for industrial democracy, income (re)distribution and greater equality, it now more singularly reflects employers' firm-level concerns with productivity and efficiency (see Thelen, 2001:71).

As the Corus case clearly illustrates, changes to the level, scope and processes of collective bargaining, together with the depth of union involvement, have been important instruments driving the restructuring of industry in recent years. When job losses are on the agenda it is much easier for management to secure change, and as we have already noted these job losses have often been associated with work intensification in a process of 'distributive' (win-lose) as opposed to 'integrative' (win-win) bargaining. Employers have certainly been able to secure greater control over staffing levels, demarcation rules, working hours and the like, but this is not always reflected in superior competitiveness. Certainly at the aggregate level, any advantages secured from more decentralised bargaining have been insufficient to close the productivity gap between the UK and other leading industrial economies (see Chapter 3). Moreover, while for many companies the move away from multi-employer bargaining reflected a desire to shake off the constraints imposed by the annual wage round, cost-of-living increases, and what they saw as 'outmoded' concepts such as 'comparability' and the 'going rate', many of these 'outmoded concepts' of wage setting remain very much in evidence. 'After 15 years, the emphasis on freer markets appears to have left much of the institutional operation of the wage-setting process intact' (Ingram *et al.*, 1999:35).

Unions have always sought to standardise pay across workers, leading to a compression of income distribution and greater equality in society, as well as to increase the pay of their members relative to non-members or the 'market rate' (an increase usually referred to as the union mark-up or wage premium). In the 1980s, the union wage premium held up remarkably well, despite the adverse economic and political climate (Stewart, 1991 and 1995) but by the early 1990s there were clear signs of an erosion of the premium enjoyed by trade unionists (Hildreth, 1999). By the end of the 1990s the wage premium for male trade unionists had all but disappeared (Machin, 2001) and any remaining wage differential was confined to women (ibid) or union members in workplaces with high bargaining density (in excess of 70 per cent) or multi-union recognition (Forth and Millward, 2000; see also Booth and Bryan, 2001). The latter no doubt partly accounts for the decline of multi-union recognition and the move towards 'single-table bargaining' (i.e. all unions negotiating together, rather than in succession as the latter is more likely to encourage competitive pay claims or 'leap-frogging') (see Millward *et al.*, 2000:199–205). As Millward *et al.* (2001) conclude, trade unions now affect the *process* of pay determination in the UK more than the *outcome*.

Decentralisation led to a greater dispersion of pay settlements (Ingram *et al.*, 1999:36–7) and has certainly permitted rising income inequality (Brown *et al.*, 2003:209–10), but employers have been unable to insist on purely internal determinants for pay setting (e.g. profitability, the firm's 'ability to pay', productivity, individual performance and the like). Residual notions of fairness and equity make it difficult for firms to ignore the going rate or cost of living. Failure to account for these variables can serve to heighten the 'trust gap' that exists between management and labour in the UK (see Kessler and Undy, 1996) and undermine employee morale and motivation (BSAS data reveal that approaching half the working population no longer regard their pay as 'reasonable', a similar proportion perceive the gap between high and low incomes at their own place of work to be too large, and almost 90 per cent now believe the gap between high and low incomes within the economy as a whole to be too large). Likewise, comparability, or what is now usually referred to as 'pay benchmarking', also continues to exert an important influence on pay determination. In fact, comparability is inevitable in a decentralised wage-setting system if firms are to recruit good workers or avoid costly labour turnover (see Ingram *et al.*, 1999:41).

Unfortunately, the absence of complementary institutions to support decentralised collective bargaining renders 'high road' production or service strategies unstable. At a minimum, decentralisation requires 'deliberative institutions' to facilitate information sharing, knowledge transfer, trust and co-operation between the parties; and financial institutions that allow the development of long-term business strategies. Without such institutions, employers will more often than not fall back on the 'low road' route of cost-cutting and further deregulation (see Thelen, 2001:74). As a result, attempts to forge greater co-operation with labour, or more precisely the 'core' workforce of the organisation, will usually be based on a strategy of segmentation and strong internal controls (e.g. in-house training and company-based participation schemes, which we discuss in the following chapter) which clashes with trade union principles and national or industry-based collective bargaining structures. Hence, firms prefer to pursue these strategies *without* trade unions, or at least attempt to 'cut off' the local union from the national union where the company retains recognition (ibid:78). But in the process of abandoning centralised pay-setting, employers have also jettisoned any possibility of co-ordinated bargaining (and in doing so have thrown the baby out with the bath water).

Numerous studies have demonstrated the benefits of co-ordinated bargaining, including superior performance in terms of wage moderation, lower unemployment and inflation, and improved international competitiveness (see, *inter alia*, Hall and Soskice, 2001; Soskice, 1990 and 2000; Storper, 1995:155; Traxler and Kittel, 2000; and Traxler *et al.*, 2001). Where collective bargaining is co-ordinated, for example, the union mark-up tends to be lower and a higher level of union membership appears to be less of an obstacle to any employment adjustment (Morgan *et al.*, 2001:65). Union wage policy will more directly affect aggregate employment in economies where collective bargaining coverage is much higher and unions are therefore willing and able to 'exchange' wage restraint for tax and welfare benefits that advance social justice (see Visser, 1998a and 1998b). This is not to deny that markets can, in some instances, improve co-ordination among private sector actors, rather to highlight the fact that employers in the UK have 'missed a trick' by surrendering the ability to co-ordinate collective bargaining and by retreating from more extensive forms of joint regulation that guarantee a higher coverage of more standardised terms and conditions of employment.

It is important at this point not to confuse (or equate) centralisation with co-ordination, where the former refers to the level of collective bargaining and the latter the degree to which bargaining and collective agreements are concerted across the economy (at whatever level) (see Traxler, 2003:195–6). Multi-employer bargaining is generally a precondition for macro-co-ordination and the benefits that ensue, as found in Western Europe, but Japanese companies have reconciled single-employer settlements with co-ordinated bargaining by concentrating all bargaining activity within a very limited time period each year (the 'Spring Wage Offensive' or *shunto*) which is co-ordinated through very strong inter-firm networks (ibid:204 and 207). Even under the UK system of unco-ordinated, single-employer bargaining, joint regulation can still deliver significant benefits. For example, workers are more likely to trust management where their company supports union membership and the union has sufficient power to challenge the employer (Bryson, 2001b and 2001d); management perceptions of the employee relations climate tend to be poorer where unions have higher membership but this relationship does not hold where unions have 100 per cent membership (Bryson, 2001c); and although workplace closures are more likely among unionised manufacturing plants compared to their non-union counterparts, the one exception is plants with a more comprehensive collective bargaining agenda (in particular, where unions are directly involved in negotiation over recruitment and staffing levels, the chances of closure are no different from non-union plants) (Bryson, 2001a; and Millward *et al.*, 2001).

In general, however, the wider benefits of co-ordination rely on the leading role of peak associations or more direct forms of state intervention (see Traxler, 2003; and Traxler *et al.*, 2001). In the UK, neither the CBI nor the TUC is in a position to concert the bargaining activities of its affiliates (ibid; see also Traxler, 1999:350; and Chapters 4 and 5) and the current Labour Government shows little sign of adopting a more supportive or interventionist role in collective bargaining. Somewhat more promising are the forthcoming EU regulations on information and consultation, which will require an employer to set up a works council if a written petition is received from at least 10 per cent of its employees (or 250 of them, whichever is the lower) (see Chapter 8). Notwithstanding this development, however, the assumption that collective bargaining is the most effective way of conducting employee relations no longer runs through public policy (Wood and Godard, 1999:237).

Employer support and state backing for collective bargaining in the UK has always been conditional on its ability successfully to regulate industrial conflict, facilitate industrial restructuring, and deliver higher productivity. Regardless of whether these outcomes ensue, this should not detract from, and certainly should not be allowed to negate the primary democratic role of collective bargaining. As the Donovan Commission (1968:54) pointed out, 'properly conducted, collective bargaining is the most effective means of giving workers the right to representation in decisions affecting their working lives, a right which is or should be the prerogative of every worker in a democratic society'.

Conclusion

For much of the twentieth century, collective bargaining was the cornerstone of employee relations in the UK. Collective agreements covered the majority of the workforce and joint regulation was widely regarded as the most effective way to resolve conflicts of interest, manage employment contracts, and involve workers in decisions that directly affected their daily working lives. Today, only 40 per cent of the workforce is covered by collective agreements. More workers now have their pay set by management. The picture with regard to non-pay issues is even more alarming, with very little negotiation (joint regulation) in the majority of workplaces. To be sure, more workers are now 'consulted' or 'informed' about changes to their conditions of employment, training and development, staffing levels, health and safety, performance appraisal and the like, but as we document in the following chapter this often falls well short of any real opportunity for workers and their representatives significantly to influence outcomes.

Given the considerable advantages of joint regulation, which are still evident even in the UK context, some commentators admit to being rather puzzled by management's lack of support for trade unions and collective bargaining (Bryson, 2001b:103). After all, the evidence categorically indicates that employees are more likely to trust management, report that the workplace is better managed, and have a more positive view of the firm's employee relations climate where management support union membership and joint regulation (ibid). However, opposition to unionism and collective bargaining appears to make sense, from the employer's perspective, when we recall that positive employee attitudes and effective union voice depend on high levels of union density and the union's ability to challenge managerial authority (see Chapter 5). Just as employers behave opportunistically in their dealings with labour, unions might use their bargaining power to mark up wages, insist on job demarcation rules, the retention of higher than necessary staffing levels and the like. Employers might be more willing to support collective bargaining if their rival firms would do the same – either via co-ordinated bargaining through an employers' association or statutory requirements enforced by the state – but these conditions do not apply in LMEs (indeed, this is one of the defining characteristics of such economies). As a result, managers know that other firms may choose to reduce costs by cutting back their expenditure on information sharing, management-union meetings, employee involvement and other forms of joint regulation. This in turn will lead many firms to adopt an irrational employee relations strategy (chopping away at the foundations of mutual trust, labour co-operation, and high productivity) for rational reasons (the demands of shareholders for a quick return on their investment, competition with other firms, and traditionally adversarial relationships with employees).

Regardless of the economic arguments for and against different systems of collective bargaining, the democratic role of joint regulation should not be overlooked. As collective bargaining has declined, no effective alternative has yet been implemented to address collective interest representation (see Chapter 8). Employees want, and deserve, a more effective system of representation at work (see Diamond and Freeman, 2001). The current 'representation gap' is an affront to the principles of a democratic society. Management may have 'regained control', 30 years after the Donovan Report, but in most cases not by sharing it. In the process, the protection of employee rights, the representation of their collective interests and the fair remuneration of their labour have, in many industries and firms, been severely eroded.

8

Employee involvement and participation

Management–Labour Partnership at Tesco

Working Better Together

In 1998, Tesco, the UK's largest food retailer, and the Union of Shop, Distributive and Allied Workers (USDAW) signed a 'partnership agreement'. The agreement was seen as crucial for both parties: Tesco needed to improve communications with staff and more effectively involve both employees and union representatives in the day-to-day affairs of the business; USDAW needed to retain recognition and more effectively represent its members in any negotiations or other dealings with the company. Tesco employed over 170 000 people in 729 UK stores in 2002, a rise of over 20 000 full-time equivalent employees since 1998 (Tesco, 2002). Seventy per cent of Tesco staff are female and 65 per cent work part-time (Haynes and Allen, 2001:174). Involving such a large group of workers, with diverse needs and aspirations, and more importantly securing their active participation, is a major challenge for management. For USDAW, Tesco workers represent the largest single cohort of union members in the UK private sector (the Union has a sole recognition agreement with the company and a membership level of around 58 per cent of all staff).

If partnership agreements are to work effectively, they require dense and reciprocal communication networks with enhanced information sharing, greater trust between the parties, more effective problem-solving processes, and constant attention to constituent interests (see Heery, 2002; Rubinstein, 2000; Walton *et al.*, 1994). The Tesco-USDAW partnership agreement, entitled *A Real Partnership: Working Better Together*, created a three-tier structure of consultation involving, at local levels, both union and non-union representatives. Under the terms of the agreement, staff forums have been created in every Tesco store. These forums are made up of representatives of store management (the Store manager and Personnel

248

manager), a union representative and elected employee representatives. The latter are elected on the basis of one employee representative per fifty employees, with a minimum of five representatives per store and a mixture of grades/jobs to cover the whole store, such as checkouts, night-team and fresh food.

Elected representatives receive training in, among other things, holding effective meetings and giving briefings. The staff forums meet four times a year and discussion focuses mainly on store performance, ways to improve how the store operates, implementing change, local store issues and points raised by staff (quoted from Tesco managers' briefing pack on the partnership agreement). Further, as the briefing pack distributed to managers made clear, Tesco and USDAW also agreed what the staff forums were *not* about: a company propaganda route; a one-way communication channel; another meeting run by managers; or the way to get personal grievances sorted out (see also Suff, 2000:20). These local forums also do not discuss employees' terms and conditions of employment. However, in addition to company performance and competitor activity, the agreement *did* envisage areas for consultation as including health and safety, pensions, and issues relating to redundancies, transfer of undertakings or acquisitions (IDS, 1998:29) – issues clearly relevant to core terms and conditions of employment.

In addition to their local meetings, the individual store forums in turn send representatives to one of three regional forums, held three times a year. At these regional forums USDAW divisional officers and area organisers are also represented, along with five management members including company regional managing directors and regional HR managers. These forums consider regional and corporate issues (including those issues passed up from store forums) and also hold a secret ballot on the annual pay review negotiated at a separate national-level forum (see below). These regional forum ballots have replaced the former national ballot of all union members in Tesco on the annual pay offer.

The regional forums appoint three representatives to attend the national forum, on which USDAW national and divisional officers and senior Tesco management, including the Retail Managing Director and Retail Human Resources Director, also sit. The principal activities of the national forum, which also meets three times a year, include an annual review of employees' terms and conditions, consultation over major corporate issues and a review of the overall partnership structure.

As with other partnership agreements in the UK, there are two possible interpretations of how the Tesco-USDAW agreement came about and two very different ways of interpreting the actual agreement. The 'benign' interpretation of partnership is that it reflects a shift towards high commitment management (HCM) and more flexible working practices. Unions are often in a strong position to support, if not champion, such developments and will be intimately involved in the direction, if not the determination, of change. The 'management opportunism' interpretation, in contrast, sees partnership as a short-term response to business or employee relations problems, with the emphasis on stripping out (labour) costs rather than expanding the collective bargaining agenda or intimately involving employees in the future of the organisation (Heery, 2002:24–5). The differing influences behind different partnership agreements are reflected in their content and practice. The 'nurturing' approach is often based on informal relationships, rather than a formal agreement, and is usually found in organisations with a high level of unionisation and active workplace representatives. The 'containment' approach, in contrast, is more likely to be characterised by a formal agreement that accords minimal or reduced rights to unions (Oxenbridge and Brown, 2002:272–3). The motivation behind the Tesco-USDAW agreement appears more benign than opportunistic but it displays strong elements of containment.

Why work in partnership?

Traditionally, Tesco was associated with a 'pile 'em high, sell 'em cheap' ethos, which was also reflected in the company's employee relations (e.g. low wages and high labour turnover, or what is sometimes called a 'high sacrifice' HR strategy). As Tesco sought to compete more effectively in the retail food sector, by raising quality and customer service whilst retaining a competitive pricing strategy, the company has systematically improved pay and conditions and sought to involve employees more intimately in their work and the business of the company (i.e. serving the customer).

For example, Tesco has introduced a range of 'parent-friendly' HR policies similar to those of rival retailers (see Chapter 3) as well as a profit-sharing scheme with profit-related bonuses as high as 14 per cent of salary in some stores (see McCall, 2002:57). In 2001, Tesco made the largest share release in UK corporate history, distributing £123 million of shares to 33 000 staff (ibid). In combination with higher wage levels, this has resulted in the company becoming one of the best paying employers in UK food retailing, which has been instrumental in reducing staff turnover. Improving customer service demanded a much stronger commitment from employees than that required simply to perform the physical labour (passing the goods through the bar code reader, stacking shelves, and so on) (see Rosenthal *et al.*, 1997). For example, high-quality customer service requires employees to do much more than learn particular 'scripts' (making eye contact, smiling, saying hello/goodbye, offering to help with the packing) but to deliver this emotional labour 'sincerely' (see Noon and Blyton, 2002:186–8). Further, it became evident early on in the development of service delivery in supermarkets that unchanging scripts were not regarded by many customers as sincere interactions. As a result there has been increased discretion introduced to vary the script according to the situation to give a greater sense of 'authenticity'.

While low pay will certainly de-motivate staff, it has long been recognised that higher pay will not necessarily deliver high levels of employee commitment (Herzberg, 1966; and Maslow, 1943) or levels of customer service demanded by retailers in the 'consumer society' (see Korczynski, 2002). Tesco's new strategy therefore accords particular importance to improved channels of communication, consultation, and the opportunity for staff to become more involved in the company. Existing union–management relations were widely regarded as inadequate for this purpose. These relations were centred nationally on the annual negotiation of the Retail Agreement covering employees' terms and conditions of employment (the outcome of the negotiations being put to a ballot of members to accept or reject) together with local level activities centred mainly on representing members in discipline and grievance cases. Neither was seen as adequate to foster greater involvement and consultation (IDS, 1998:27). The Union recognised this too, noting that 'for some time ... our established ways of working have not really delivered ... meeting together once a year to talk about wages, balloting our members and reaching a settlement' (quoted in IDS, 1998:27). Haynes and Allen (2001:174) note that dissatisfaction with the structure and process of union–management relations was brought to a head for management during the mid 1990s by the question of Sunday trading over which management felt that Union policy was being determined by USDAW members and representatives in other companies and sectors, and also that management were keen to consult with Tesco staff by means other than the union channel.

Working Better Together can therefore be seen as part of, if not a vehicle for, a broader approach to shifting relations with employees from a detached, arm's length relationship (exemplified by high labour turnover, low levels of communication, minimal union–management interaction) to a more engaged relationship (lower quit rates, higher levels of communication and consultation with both employees and trade union). As with all partnership agreements, however, the 'devil is in the detail'.

Nourishment or containment?

The word 'partnership' denotes a relationship of equals. Management might seek greater control over communications and the mechanisms through which employees are given some say in decisions affecting their daily working lives, but employees and their representatives should be able to challenge managerial authority and question the propriety of management action. Some of the more successful partnerships are precisely of this ilk (Oxenbridge and Brown, 2002) and there is more general evidence that employees are more likely to trust management, believe that their workplace is better managed, and have a more positive view of the firm's employee relations climate where managers support union membership (Bryson, 2001b:103). This is formally recognised in the Tesco-USDAW agreement, which states that one of its five aims is: 'to enable USDAW to challenge management'. This is essential if the Union is to 'act as the company's conscience, informing Tesco if it fails to live up to its values and commitments' (Marchington,

2001:12). The other four aims of the agreement are: to secure high quality representation for staff; to allow USDAW to understand and promote Tesco's business goals; to guarantee co-operation; and to allow Tesco to remain flexible enough to retain its leading market position (Allen, 1998).

There is considerable evidence that partnership agreements 'pay off' for management by improving business performance, but whether such agreements deliver mutual or indeed any benefits for employees has been questioned (Guest and Peccei, 2001; Kelly, 1998 and 1999; TUC, 2002; and Turnbull *et al.*, 2004). At Tesco, the Union was highly supportive of the partnership agreement, which was strongly endorsed in a membership ballot (by 4-to-1 in favour). The General Secretary of USDAW (Bill Connor, elected in 1997, a year before the agreement was signed with Tesco) has been a supporter of partnership agreements as a way of increasing union involvement over a broader agenda and gaining more effective consultation over issues such as in-store technology. At the time, the General Secretary commented that the partnership with Tesco would offer 'the opportunity for more involvement, more dialogue and more consultation than ever before' (quoted in IPA, 1998:2), and enable the union to be 'at the centre of the business, rather than on the sidelines raising grievances' (quoted in Allen, 1998:41). In introducing the partnership proposals in an explanatory pack for USDAW representatives, the General Secretary set out his vision for the future relationship:

> Partnership is the key word. We're looking for a whole new way of working with Tesco in which communication and involvement are key. A culture in which people from top to bottom feel valued, respected and included in all key decision-making. (USDAW, 1998)

However, like many unions and employees that have entered into formal partnership agreements with management, USDAW and its membership in Tesco faced some very stark choices. One possibility that the Union had to contend with was de-recognition should it not support the partnership proposal. Other alternatives the company considered were union recognition for individual representation only (as is the situation at rival supermarket J. Sainsbury) or the creation of a staff association as an alternative to union representation (IRS, 1999:5). Clearly, with such a large number of union members within Tesco, de-recognition would have been a disaster for the Union (Haynes and Allen, 2001:175). As one USDAW delegate at the Union's 1998 Annual Delegate Meeting succinctly put it in relation to the 'social partnership strategy': 'This is how it has had to be' (quoted in Haynes and Allen, 2001:180).

Since that time, the partnership agreement has attracted a degree of criticism from within the Union: at its annual conference in 2000, for example, some USDAW delegates called for a review of the agreement, concerned at a perceived loss of negotiating powers, and commenting that the Union had been 'taken for a ride' by the company (quoted in *People Management*, 27 April 2000). In general, however, criticism of the agreement, or more generally the shift in the nature of employee relations that the forums and other aspects of the agreement represent, has been muted. This can be attributed, in large part, to Tesco's continued business success and profitability, which in turn has boosted employee earnings through its profit-sharing scheme. As with most other partnership agreements in the UK, which to date 'seem to represent union accommodation to an employer-dominated process of reform' (Heery, 2002:25), it seems likely that *Working Better Together* will only be nourished if management continue to realise some (commercial) advantage from the agreement.

Participation and employee relations

At different points in the development of employee relations, the question of the extent to which employees and/or their representatives should take part in decision-making has been a recurring issue. Indeed, examples of different participatory arrangements stretch back a century or more. In unionised workplaces, however, participation has often occupied a marginal rather than central role within employee relations policies and practices, certainly when compared to collective bargaining. Some non-union employers, as we discuss in the following chapter, have developed highly sophisticated forms of employee involvement and participation, but these firms remain in the minority. In fact, throughout the UK, the majority of managers acknowledge that employees are *not* involved in decisions made by the organisation that affects their jobs (Guest and Conway, 2001:ix). The historic failure of UK firms, and the state, to institute a formal and effective system of employee involvement and participation has exacerbated the 'representation gap' identified in the previous chapter (see also Towers, 1997b).

In recent years, however, there has been renewed interest in various forms of employee involvement and participation, in part reflecting the desire of the Labour Government to promote 'partnership' and the influence of the European social agenda (most notably the implementation of the EC Information and Consultation Directive throughout the European Union by 2005; see below). Thus, the development of new staff forums and consultation at Tesco can be seen as part of the latest wave of interest in employee involvement, participation and partnership. Yet, whether, and to what extent, these latest initiatives will afford employees or their representatives any greater say in decision-making, remains to be seen. It is arguable that pre-existing obstacles to the effective development of participation remain: not least a general opposition within management to relinquishing decision-making prerogative; a continuing trade union ambivalence, both towards accepting greater responsibility within organisational decision-making, and towards the extension of participatory forms which provide not only very limited influence but also entail the direct involvement of individual employees rather than their trade union representatives; and a lukewarm and minimalist state approach to extending statutory support for participation.

It is this issue of the contemporary significance of employee participation or 'involvement' initiatives that gives rise to the core questions of this chapter. To what extent is the current interest in 'employee involvement' and 'partnership' significantly different from previous interest in 'workers' participation' and 'industrial democracy'? To what degree do forms of involvement represent any real sharing of decision-making power? How do employees respond to involvement and participation initiatives? What are management's objectives in introducing different forms of involvement? Are there continuing obstacles to the development of effective participation? More generally, what implications does the current interest in employee involvement and partnership have for the broader fashioning of employee relations in coming years?

To address these questions, we must begin first by briefly situating the current developments within a broader conceptual and empirical framework. This involves reviewing the nature of employee participation, the different forms that it takes, the attitudes of the different employee relations parties towards participation, and the historical pattern of development of participation prior to the latest wave of interest. In this way, it will become clearer to what extent the recent developments share both similarities with, and are distinct from, previous periods of interest in employee participation. Having examined the arguments and evidence we will also be in a better position to assess the depth, robustness and implications of the latest changes. Our overall view is that despite the outwardly convincing language of Human Resource Management, Employee Involvement, Total Quality Management and the like, towards the importance of building commitment through more open styles of decision-making, we remain somewhat sceptical that the latest period marks any sea-change in the trajectory of participation. Not only is there an unwillingness, as in the past, to tackle issues which have inhibited the development of participation, but many of the changes of the past two decades owe more to the attempts of management to exert control over labour than they do to any desire to involve or empower employees.

The nature of participation

At one level, the notion of employee participation is straightforward. For Wall and Lischeron (1977:38), for example, participation refers to 'influence in decision-making exerted through a process of interaction between workers and managers'. As soon as we begin to interrogate such a definition, however, the complexities start to appear. Marked variations are possible, for example, in the degree or *depth* of participation, the range or *scope* of decisions subject to participation, the *form* that participation structures might take, the organisational *level(s)* on which participation occurs, and the *purpose* and *outcomes* of such activity. In combination these various sources of diversity give rise to a concept and a range of activity which is heterogeneous rather than unified – indeed so heterogeneous that the validity of the concept itself is brought into doubt. Further, the conceptual confusion has been exacerbated by the many expressions used to denote aspects of the activity – for example 'industrial democracy', 'participation', 'involvement', 'empowerment' and now 'partnership' – and the tendency for these to be used interchangeably, despite the very evident gap in the power-sharing implications of what formerly travelled under the heading of 'industrial democracy' and what now marches under the banner of 'employee involvement'.

The *depth* of participation refers to the degree to which employees, or their representatives, influence the final decision (Marchington *et al.*, 1992:8). Participatory activity may be seen as forming a continuum rather than as an absolute, with points on the continuum signifying different levels of employee involvement and influence (elsewhere, Marchington and Wilkinson, 2000:343 have referred to an 'escalator' of participation). At one end of the continuum, illustrated in Figure 8.1, the minimum level of involvement is represented by the receipt of information from management, with no active involvement in any decision-making process. Further along the continuum (moving from left to right in Figure 8.1), employees and/or their representatives have the opportunity to exert advisory power, based on joint consultation. Studies of joint consultation indicate that, in practice, various activities take place under the guise of consultation (see, for example, Blyton 1981; and Marchington, 1989 and 1994). In general, however, consultation primarily involves management discussing production, service delivery or other issues with representatives of the workforce, seeking comments and suggestions, while retaining authority over the final decision-making process. The remit of the Tesco staff forums, with their emphasis on local store operations, together with discussion of (non terms and conditions) issues raised by employee representatives, is typical of local consultative activity.

The main distinction along the continuum lies between consultation and joint decision-making, for under the latter, employees (or their representatives) formally secure access to exerting *influence* rather than simply being *involved* in the decision-making process. For some observers, it is only at this point that true participation occurs, with everything to the left of this point representing 'pseudo' or 'phantom' participation (Ramsay, 1980). Finally, at the right-hand end of the continuum,

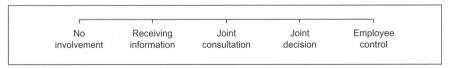

Figure 8.1 A continuum of employee participation

employees themselves enjoy full control over decisions. Where this exists in traditional enterprises, it is likely to be confined to areas of task arrangement, for example craft workers controlling the way their craft is practised. In terms of higher levels of decision-making, employee control is largely confined to workers' co-operatives, although even here workers may control the immediate labour process but little else (Mellor *et al.*, 1988:81–2; and Turnbull and Weston, 1993a).

Clearly, the implications for management of participatory forms from the left-hand side of the continuum (information and consultation) are markedly different from those reflecting the principles of the right-hand side (joint decision-making and employee control). This diversity has allowed *all* parties in employee relations – employers, employees, trade unions and the state – to express support for participation, although in practice this has entailed giving support to quite different principles and practices and with distinct – and to a degree, opposing – objectives in mind. As discussed below, the recent managerial (and state) interest in involving employees has been focused squarely on those forms located on the left side of the participation continuum: management have been more concerned to 'tell and sell' and get their employees 'on side' than to promote a redistribution of decision-making power.

The diversity arising from variation in the depth of participation is also reflected in the multitude of *forms* that participatory activity can take. These cover a broad spectrum, from suggestion schemes to worker co-operatives, from briefing groups to board-level representation. As well as the different degrees of involvement and influence they bestow upon employees and their representatives, these different forms can also be classified in terms of the extent to which they are *formal* or *informal* activities. A further important distinction – particularly given the recent pattern of developments in the UK – is whether the activities entail employees participating *directly* in discussions, or whether participation is achieved *indirectly* via the election of representatives (and if the latter, whether these representatives are union or non-union members). Typically much of the involvement or participation activity which occurs at the lowest levels of the organisation – involving, for example, team meetings to discuss the organisation of individual tasks and discussion of production schedules – takes place directly. Involvement in decisions away from the immediate work task, on the other hand, typically takes place via representative forms of participation (such as Tesco's partnership forums).

Variation also exists in the different *levels* at which participation can occur. As we see below, most recent attention has been concentrated on extending the degree of involvement at lower levels within the organisation. This contrasts with the 1970s when the emphasis was more on the extension of participation at higher levels through board-level representation. In a more general analysis, Clegg (1976) examined the pattern of development of participation and industrial democracy in six countries, identifying the structure of collective bargaining as a major influence on the level and form of participation typical in a country. Where bargaining structures were identified as being stronger at workplace level – as in the UK – much of the need for local-level participation was seen to be met by the presence of local union–management machinery. The result was a low level of development of participation at that level other than as secondary to the bargaining machinery. However, where collective bargaining was focused away from the workplace at industry or national level – which has been the case in Sweden until recently, for example – this was seen by Clegg to leave a vacuum for employee 'voice' at the local level, which stimulated a greater development of other participatory activity at the local level. For Clegg this was an important factor in accounting, for example, for the greater interest in direct forms of participation in Sweden in the 1960s and 1970s, such as job enrichment schemes, compared to the UK where participation has in the past been more characterised by limited indirect participation via joint consultation.

A further source of variation lies in the *scope* of different participation mechanisms, that is the range of decisions which employees or their representatives participate in. This scope may vary between 'immediate' level decisions such as work allocation, 'medium' level decisions such as process changes, and more 'distant' level decisions such as major technological change, product changes, investment plans and so on. The growth of financial forms of involvement over the recent past – through, for example, employee share-ownership schemes – has further added to the possible scope of participatory activity.

Overall, the range or scope of issues subjected to participation will depend on a variety of factors. These include the attitudes of the parties involved (particularly management's predisposition to making issues available for participation); the extent of experience (and competence) among employees and their representatives to engage in participation; the degree of stability in product markets, which influences the time for participatory activity to occur; the nature of ownership and organisational characteristics, including the size of organisations and the degree to which decision-making is a centralised or decentralised activity; and the extent to which participation is based on statutory requirement (as is the case, for example, in Germany and Scandinavia) or voluntary agreement. In a landmark, twelve-country study in the 1970s, the Industrial Democracy in Europe (IDE) research group highlighted the importance of two factors – statutory support and managerial attitudes – as the central factors explaining variations in levels of industrial democracy between countries (IDE, 1981). Participation tended to be higher in those countries where it was underpinned by legislation (such as the German and Swedish Co-determination Acts) but also where managerial attitudes were more supportive of co-operation and openness in decision-making. However, the comparatively low overall level of participation identified by this study, and the variations between different enterprises within a single country, is understandable only by taking account of the many other variables which can influence the depth and scope of participation.

Perspectives on participation

Variations in perspective on the *purpose* and *outcomes* of participation are evident in the way various groups have supported participation at particular points in history. We have already referred to the tendency for different actors to use different terminology when discussing participation. This contrast in language is significant; it reflects fundamentally divergent views about the nature and purpose of participation. For managers, support for 'involvement' stems largely from the principles of Human Relations management, which draws attention to the importance of the social aspects of organisation in general, and the connection between, on the one hand, communication and consultation between management and workforce, and on the other, increased worker commitment, higher job satisfaction and motivation, and reduced resistance to change (Mayo, 1933; McGregor, 1960). Greater involvement of employees in the planning and particularly the implementation of change is viewed as a means of breaking down resistance, gaining acceptance for change, and improving the overall level of worker integration into the process of service provision and goods production. Improved communication also affords management a greater opportunity to dispel rumours, correct 'misunderstandings' and 'get its message across', a factor which has been particularly emphasised in the latest period of interest in employee involvement. Participatory mechanisms have also been viewed as a means used by management (and the state) at different points to 'head off' calls by organised labour for a greater redistribution of power and reward in industry (Ramsay, 1977). For Ramsay and others, this explains why managerial interest in participation tends to move in cycles, growing at times of increased labour power and labour unrest, only to diminish later when labour power weakens. We return to this issue again below.

The Human Relations view is consistent with a managerial orientation which is strongly unitarist in perspective (see Chapter 2 for a discussion of unitary and pluralist perspectives). More than this, however, management's advocacy of certain types of participation represents an acknowledgement that employee commitment needs to be actively *secured* rather than passively assumed, and that involving employees in decision-making is a means of achieving this. Management's support for (some forms of) participation is also an acknowledgement of the potential contribution of employee knowledge to the management of the organisation – in particular, tapping valuable worker experience and benefiting from their suggestions regarding the way work tasks are organised and performed. More generally, this management orientation is an acknowledgement that many employees seek not only financial recompense from work but also a more extensive engagement with the institution in which they spend a large proportion of their waking hours.

Many of these aspects of management's orientation to participation show up in attitude surveys, as well as other studies of the responses of line managers and supervisors to participation (Marchington and Wilkinson, 2000:355–7). Overall, these studies demonstrate a considerable positive disposition among managers towards *certain* forms of participation. Specifically these are the forms which Clegg *et al.* (1978:5) have characterised as being 'soft on power' – that is, those forms which focus on day-to-day operational issues, which involve no *significant* transfer of decision-making power from management to workers, and thus no disruption of the hierarchical structure of managerial authority. These 'soft' forms contrast with 'harder' or more 'power-oriented' forms of participation which focus on major organisational decisions and involve joint decision-making rather than retention of managerial prerogative. The establishment of the store forums under the partnership agreement at Tesco, for example, is clearly a reflection of the former rather than the latter type.

This pattern of support for unitary forms of worker involvement, extending, at most, advisory and consultative rather than joint decision-making powers to employees, is clearly evidenced in the studies of managerial attitudes conducted by Poole and his colleagues over the past two decades (Poole *et al.*, 1981; Poole and Mansfield, 1992; Poole *et al.*, 2001). In both the 1980 and 1990 surveys of British managers for example, general support was expressed for greater employee participation in the respondent's own organisation. In the 1990 survey, only just over a quarter (26 per cent) of the managers disagreed with the view that there was a need for greater employee participation in their organisation (Poole and Mansfield, 1992:203). Specific support was also evidenced for such forms of participation as regular meetings between work groups and their supervisors, joint consultation and particularly, financial participation through employee shareholding (ibid:203 and 205). In both the 1990 and 2000 surveys, for example, over three-quarters of managers were in favour of profit-sharing and employee shareholding schemes (Poole *et al.*, 2001:55). In contrast, the managers in these surveys have been much less willing to endorse more power-oriented forms of participation based, for example, on extending collective bargaining or worker directors (Poole and Mansfield, 1992:204). This pattern was repeated in a subsequent survey of managers' attitudes to HRM (Poole and Jenkins, 1996:35–6). As Poole and Mansfield (1992:207) comment,

> Managers appear to support most employee involvement practices so long as these do not radically affect their control function within the firm. In other words they tend to prefer a unitary rather than a pluralist approach to employee participation in decision-making.

This pattern is repeated in other liberal market economies (LMEs) such as the United States: managers are unwilling to share power and 'Many oppose programs that would keep them from making the final decisions about workplace governance' (Freeman and Rogers, 1999:7).

The general orientation of trade unions towards participation has been different from that of most managers. First, trade unions in the UK have in the past been distinctly wary of: forms of participation which imply an integration of employees and their representatives into the management of the enterprise; forms which extend only very limited (advisory) powers to employees and/or their representatives; and forms which establish alternative (and competing) lines of communication between workforce and management to that represented by the trade union organisation (Hyman and Mason, 1995:151–5). These views have manifested themselves historically in such ways as (i) a critical, or at best lukewarm, trade union reaction to those forms of participation which are 'soft on power', viewing these as fettering employees with responsibilities but without any commensurate influence; (ii) a preference for increasing participation via the extension of collective bargaining, thereby securing participation based on negotiation and joint decision-making activity, executed via the trade union channel and undertaken using a mechanism in which union negotiators have a recognised competence; and (iii) an equivocal response to certain other forms (such as worker directors and company-level councils) which, while more power-oriented, nevertheless are seen as potentially compromising the union's independent negotiating position (Ursell *et al.*, 1980; and Ursell, 1983). The lack of unity over worker directors, for example, was evidenced in the 1970s in the different union responses to the recommendations of the Bullock Report (1977) concerning worker directors in larger corporations. While the TUC supported worker directors, many individual trade unions were far less enthusiastic, fearing that their negotiating position would be compromised if union representatives sitting as members of a board of directors were party to decisions which subsequently became the focus for negotiations (Elliott, 1978). Likewise, more recently, trade unions have been divided in their approach to 'partnership'. While the TUC has explicitly supported partnership initiatives, the response of individual trade unions, and sections within those unions, has been more variable (Waddington, 2003a:348).

In (partial) contrast to trade union views, studies of employee attitudes over a long period towards participation point to a predisposition for greater involvement and participation, particularly in decisions with a direct bearing on their own jobs and working environment (for an early discussion of this see Wall and Lischeron, 1977). While more direct participation is generally desired over these immediate-level decisions, attitude surveys have revealed a weaker desire for participating in higher-level decision-making (such as over planning and investment) and a greater preference that any participation at this level should be effected through representatives rather than involving employees directly (ibid).

As the UK and the USA are exceptions to the usual pattern of 'dual channel' representation (i.e. collective bargaining and company-based works councils) found in most advanced industrialised economies (Rogers and Streeck, 1994), and as employee relations in both countries is characterised by a clear 'representation gap' (Towers, 1997b), it is instructive to review two recent surveys of employee attitudes towards involvement and participation. In their US study of *What Workers Want*,

Freeman and Rogers (1999) found strong evidence that employees want more say in their workplace than they currently enjoy. The authors found that workers desired more influence both as individuals and as part of a group – that is, they supported the extension of both direct and representational forms of participation. Reasons cited for wanting more say included not only to improve the quality of their working lives, but also because many felt that it would make their organisation more productive and successful. The difference between how much influence workers say they have over decisions affecting them, and how much they would prefer to have, is just one measure of the 'representation gap' (see also Osterman *et al.*, 2001).

Following this US study, Freeman undertook a similar study in the UK (Diamond and Freeman, 2001). As expected, this revealed a number of similarities. Asked about current and desired level of influence in six areas of decision-making, the UK study found that the participation gap was relatively small over how people do their work (the question asked about 'deciding how to do your job and organise work') and the gap was only modest over 'setting the pace at which you work'. A much wider gap was evident, however, in such areas as 'deciding how to work with new equipment or software', 'setting working hours including breaks, overtime and time off', and particularly 'deciding what kind of perks and bonuses are offered to employees' (ibid:6).

Other studies of worker response to direct and indirect forms of participation indicate that while involvement in direct forms of participation can have a measurable impact on employee attitudes and behaviour (for example, being associated with higher job satisfaction and lower levels of absenteeism), the existence of indirect forms of participation tends to elicit no equivalent response among employees (see, for example, Rubenowitz *et al.*, 1983). Over time, however, there is a tendency for the effects of even direct forms of participation on attitudes to diminish, as they become more of a routine and less of a novel activity (Wall and Lischeron, 1977). Positive attitudes are also likely to diminish if participation is not perceived to be achieving results: in particular if management are seen to be failing to act on ideas raised by employees in the participation forum (see Collard and Dale, 1989; Hill, 1991; and Hyman and Mason, 1995:160–1). It is one thing for organisations such as Tesco to establish employee involvement structures. It is quite another, however, for those involved to maintain these as meaningful activities over the long term, once the initial novelty and enthusiasm has passed.

Several studies in the past, conducted on both sides of the Atlantic, have also pointed to a tendency for higher-grade workers to favour consultation activity and the development of joint co-operative programmes with management, to a greater extent than their lower-level counterparts (Cook *et al.*, 1975; Dyer *et al.*, 1977; and Ponak and Fraser, 1979). In part, this may reflect the existence of a greater 'participatory competence' among higher-level employees. Pateman (1970), for example, argues that participation is a learned capacity: only by experience do employees gain the necessary skills, and thus a greater predisposition towards participation. Not least these include the social skills of learning to function in group settings, including the ability to overcome inhibitions stemming from members holding very different statuses outside the group (e.g. manager and shopfloor worker) (Blyton, 1980; and Blyton *et al.*, 1981). More senior-grade employees are not only likely to have higher levels of education (and thereby may be able to articulate ideas more easily), but many may also be more experienced in working in small groups as part of their work roles. We return to this issue of participatory competence again below.

At various junctures, the state too has advocated forms of employee participation. At times, the explicit motive for this has been to win workforce co-operation and reduce expressions of conflict. During the twentieth century this was particularly evident during wartime. In the First World War, the creation of increased consultation in the munitions industries was reinforced towards the end of the war by the recommendations of the Whitley Committee. This Committee had been established to devise ways of dissipating growing labour militancy reflected in increased strike levels, support for workers' control and the growth of shop steward organisation (Ursell and Blyton, 1988:111; see also Chapter 7). Its recommendations had a long-term influence on the approach taken to industrial relations in the UK. The principles of Whitleyism – embodied in its recommendations for joint committees at national, district and local levels in each industry – included not only support for collective bargaining but also that relations between employers and employees should be based on joint co-operation and collaboration. Increased consultation was viewed as resulting in,

> the better utilisation of the practical knowledge and experience of the workpeople . . . [a] means of securing to the workpeople a greater share in and responsibility for the determination and observance of the conditions under which their work is carried on . . . [and] co-operation in carrying new ideas into effect and full consideration of the workpeople's point of view in relation to them. (para. 16, Interim Report, quoted by Charles, 1973:104–5)

The upshot of the Whitley recommendations was a rapid take-up of the Joint Industrial Council (JIC) model. As with many later forms of joint committee, however, the initial enthusiasm for JICs subsequently waned and many fell into disuse during the interwar period, together with much of the local Whitley structure (Charles, 1973; and Cole, 1923). A significant revival did occur during the Second World War and support for consultation also became a statutory feature in the nationalisation Acts in the latter half of the 1940s. In addition, the Whitley model of joint committees became prominent in the Civil Service and local government as well as in the newly formed National Health Service (Ursell and Blyton, 1988:144). Only in recent years has this Whitley structure been at least partially superseded by other structures following the re-organisation, for example, of much of the Civil Service and NHS (see Chapter 3; and Bach and Winchester, 2003).

Over the past three decades, the pattern of state support for participation has reflected the markedly divergent attitudes of different governments towards trade unions and employee relations. In the 1970s, for example, individual government ministers not only supported the establishment of worker co-operatives (Coates, 1976) but also established a Committee of Inquiry (the Bullock Committee) to examine ways to introduce worker directors into larger companies. Disagreement within the Bullock Committee was evident right from the outset, however, for while the government set the Terms of Reference to address *how* a worker director system could be introduced, the employer representatives on the Committee wanted it to examine the question of *whether or not* worker directors were an appropriate means of extending participation. Thus it was no surprise when the Committee was divided in its recommendations, issuing Majority and Minority Reports reflecting disagreement, among other things, on the nature and extent of worker representation at board level, and whether this representation should take place within a single-tier or two-tier board structure. In the face of considerable employer opposition, a diluted version of the Majority Report's recommendations was translated into a government White Paper in 1978, but action on this was dropped following the change of government in 1979.

In the 1980s and first half of the 1990s, Conservative government support for employee participation was markedly different. Specifically, support came in the form of legislation to provide tax relief for approved employee share-ownership and profit-related pay schemes. In the WIRS studies, the proportion of industrial and commercial establishments with profit-related pay schemes rose from 19 per cent in 1984 to 44 per cent in 1990. However, during the 1990s, the trend for greater financial participation did not continue. While the proportion of establishments with profit-related pay schemes rose very slightly to 46 per cent by 1998 (Millward *et al.*, 2000:214), the incidence of employee share-ownership (which had also increased during the 1980s) fell back. Overall, the proportion of workplaces with at least one of these two forms of financial participation declined from 54 per cent in 1990 to 50 per cent in 1998 (ibid:217).

The Conservative governments' interest in promoting financial participation, reflected an emphasis on the *individual's* involvement (having a financial stake) with the company. In this way the Conservative governments sought to promote material rather than participative-democratic forms of employee involvement. Individualism was also echoed in the Conservatives broader attack on collectivism and collective aspects of employee relations during the 1980s and 1990s through, for example, a reduction in union involvement in national policy-making bodies and restrictions on the closed shop and the taking of industrial action (see Chapters 5 and 6). As well as supporting financial participation, the government in the early 1980s (in Section 1 of the 1982 Employment Act) also made it a requirement for companies of over 250 employees to report annually on developments in employee involvement (see Hibbett, 1991, for a study of stated employee involvement practices in companies' annual reports; see also Hyman and Mason, 1995:70–3). While overall the impact of this measure appears to have been limited (Marchington and Wilkinson, 2000:341), it has probably contributed to a raised awareness of employee involvement issues and reinforced the notion of employee involvement as 'good management practice' (Marchington *et al.*, 1992:53).

Since its election in 1997, the Labour Government has been keen to promote 'partnership' at work, but unlike European systems of *social* partnership (European Commission, 1997; and Wever, 1995), Labour's vision of partnership is confined to voluntary arrangements within the firm or the workplace, bound by unitarist images of individual interest within a united team (see Ackers and Payne, 1998:539). The Government is certainly elusive on the role that unions should play (ibid:540), and it is perhaps unsurprising that most partnership agreements are more akin to a 'productivity coalition' between management and 'insiders' (i.e. core workers seeking to protect their jobs and conditions of employment by participating in a management-led agenda for restructuring, cloaked in the language of 'partnership') (see Heery, 2002:22). Concrete examples of 'genuine' partnership are rather thin on the ground (ibid) – the TUC has only endorsed around sixty 'real' partnerships and the Involvement Participation Association around fifty – with most employers seeking to narrow rather than expand the collective bargaining agenda (see Millward *et al.*, 2000:121–6; and Chapter 7).

In contrast to the sterility of domestic policy, more promising developments have emerged from the European Social Chapter (which the Labour Government has endorsed). These include the adoption of the European Works Council (EWC) Directive in the UK, entailing the establishment of an EWC in those multinational corporations operating in more than one EU Member State (see Chapter 11), and the EC Information and Consultation Directive (ICD) which establishes the basis for a works council-style system in UK domestic organisations by the middle of the present decade (see below).

The extent of consultation and communication

Just as the previous chapter traced a considerable shift in the pattern of collective bargaining in the UK over the past two decades, so too the pattern of employee participation and involvement has undergone significant alteration during this period. From the various workplace industrial relations surveys and other studies that have been undertaken since 1980, two contrasting trends are evident in relation to indirect and direct forms of employee participation and involvement:

- a decline in the coverage and change in the form of indirect participation, particularly joint consultation arrangements;
- a growth in direct forms of communication between management and employees.

We will examine each of these in turn.

The proportion of workplaces with a joint consultation committee, and the proportion of employees covered by joint consultation machinery, has fallen significantly since the mid 1980s, though less dramatically than the coverage of collective bargaining. In 1998, 29 per cent of workplaces had a consultative committee compared with 34 per cent in 1984 (Millward *et al.*, 2000:109). However, a distinction can be made between 'functioning' committees that meet at least once every 3 months and other consultative committees that meet less frequently. In the WIRS 1980, 1984 and 1990 surveys, this definition excluded less than 10 per cent of the total number of joint consultation committees from the 'functioning' category, but in 1998 it excluded nearly 20 per cent. So there is a more substantial decline in the proportion of establishments with a functioning joint consultation committee (from 31 per cent in 1984 to 23 per cent in 1998). The proportion of employees in workplaces with a functioning consultative committee fell from 50 per cent in 1984 to 43 per cent in 1998 (ibid).

Joint consultative committees (JCCs) remain most common in larger establishments: two-thirds (66 per cent) of workplaces of 500 or more employees reported having some form of workplace JCC in 1998, compared with 41 per cent of establishments with 100–200 workers, 30 per cent of workplaces with 50–100 employees and 19 per cent of workplaces of 25–49 employees (Cully *et al.*, 1999:99). Workplace JCCs continue to be more prevalent in public compared with private sector establishments (39 per cent of workplaces in the former, compared with 24 per cent in the latter) and were more than twice as likely to be present in workplaces where a union is recognised compared with non-union workplaces (ibid:100). In respect of the activities of workplace consultation committees, in 1998 the most common issues for discussion were working practices (discussed in 88 per cent of committees), health and safety (86 per cent) welfare services and facilities (83 per cent) and future workplace plans (83 per cent) (ibid:101).

Three further points are worth noting in regard to the recent pattern and future development of consultation arrangements. First, within the consultation structures, there appears to have been a significant shift in the relative importance of union and non-union representatives. As union membership and recognition has fallen, there has been a significant replacement of union by non-union representatives (Millward *et al.*, 2000:114–15). In this regard, the developments at Tesco, where the staff forums have been introduced on the basis of *both* union and employee representatives – replacing a system where local union representatives had acted as the sole channel of representation – is typical of this 'broadening out' of the basis of employee representation beyond trade unions. In some organisations, this represents a genuine attempt on the part of management to involve all employees in organisational decision-making, but in others it represents an attempt to further undermine union organisation at the workplace.

Second, whilst there has been an overall decline in coverage of consultation committees during the 1980s and 1990s, the number of higher level (i.e. multi-workplace) committees has grown, reflecting partly the introduction of the European Works Council (EWC) Directive, adopted in the UK in 1997 (see Chapter 11). In 1998, 56 per cent of workplaces belonging to a larger organisation reported the existence of a higher level consultative committee in their organisation, compared with 50 per cent in 1984. We can expect that this proportion has risen further since the WERS98 survey. At the same time, a recent study by Kerckhofs (2002) indicates considerable scope for further growth, given the tardiness of some firms to comply with the EWC Directive. Kerckhofs estimates that in the UK only just over one-third of multinationals (479 out of 1200) falling within the scope of the Directive have so far established EWCs. Similar rates of non-compliance are also evident in the majority of other Member States (ibid).

Third, and in a similar way to the effect that the EWC Directive is having on the growth of higher level committees, we can anticipate a further expansion of workplace consultative arrangements following the implementation of the EC Information and Communication Directive (ICD) in 2005. The ICD sets out minimum requirements for employers to consult with or inform employees over a range of issues. Under the framework of the Directive, information and consultation will cover:

- information on the recent and probable development of the undertaking's or the establishment's activities and economic situation;
- information and consultation on the situation, structure and probable development of employment within the undertaking or establishment and on any anticipatory measures envisaged, in particular where there is a threat to employment;
- information and consultation on decisions likely to lead to substantial changes in work organisation or in contractual relations
  (from Article 4 of the Information and Consultation Directive).

Member States have until March 2005 to comply with the Directive, though in the UK and Ireland, where no statutory system for information and consultation exists (unlike in other Member States), smaller undertakings have up to a further three years to comply. Individual Member State governments can choose whether the Directive applies to all undertakings of 50 or more employees, or to all establishments of 20 or more employees. (The Labour Government's draft regulations, issued in the summer of 2003, propose that the Directive will apply to employers with over 150 employees in March 2005, those with more than 100 in

2007, and those with over 50 in 2008; employers with fewer than 50 employees will not be covered.) The Directive gives employees rights to information and consultation; the employer is only obliged to inform and consult, however, where employees exercise this right by requesting the employer to do so. (Labour's draft regulations propose that an employer will be required to set up a works council when it receives a written petition from at least 10 per cent of its employees, or 250 workers, whichever is the lower.)

As Sisson (2002) points out, the ICD is particularly significant for the UK given the absence of statutory requirements for providing information and/or consulting with employees (other than over certain specific issues such as redundancy). Dundon *et al* (2003:4) make a similar point in relation to Ireland, another LME, commenting that the impact of the Directive on 'the Irish industrial relations landscape cannot be over-stated'. What the Directive means in practice is that 'the UK will have to make provision for a universal right to employee representation so far as the undertakings or establishments covered' (Sisson, 2002:5; see also Hall *et al.*, 2002). This shifts the emphasis away from the existing voluntary nature of information and consultation – a voluntarism which Sisson (2002) and others argue has failed to deliver effective information or consultation in many workplaces. For Brendan Barber, the new General Secretary of the TUC, 'The proper implementation of the Information and Consultation Directive is the key to unlocking the potential of UK employees and business. The Government's [economic] programme depends on it' (TUC, 2003b).

Clearly, the Directive will require many companies to establish greater provision for informing and consulting with employee representatives than is currently the case. What remains open to question, however, is the extent to which the Directive will contribute to fuller and more effective participation, rather than engender a minimalist response where companies minimise their informing/consulting responsibilities towards their employees. The experience of European Works Councils is relevant here, for it is evident that EWCs reflect a range of practice from substantial to negligible consultation (see Chapter 11). Also, as the decline in the number of JCCs makes clear, there is no sign yet that we live in a 'consultation culture' or that its appearance will necessarily follow the implementation of the ICD.

Sisson (2002:11) argues that the state has a crucial role to play in creating a climate for the full development of consultation: 'leaving it to the parties to do as they think fit simply does not work in a context where the corporate governance pressures to pursue short-term profitability are so powerful'. But to date, the UK government has not shown a strong lead in this area. As Truter (2003:30) and others point out, for example, the fact that the UK government supported a diluted rather than a more extended version of the ICD does not provide grounds for optimism of a strong lead on participation from the UK state. In other countries, such as Germany, the works council system is effective precisely because: it is embedded in a broader statutory framework of participation and collective representation; that for at least three decades most trade unions and many employers have shown a willingness to actively engage in workplace-based participation; and that works councils have been given sufficient statutory rights to maintain an independence from management (see Truter, 2003; and Wever, 1995). None of these conditions currently prevail (or are on the horizon) in the UK. Thus, Truter's (2003:28) conclusion is that while the ICD provides a real opportunity to extend participation and influence in the UK, in itself 'the Directive is not sufficiently empowering of workers to allow it to play a pivotal role in the construction of a German-style social partnership model'.

Turning to direct forms of communication, it is well-established that such forms of 'involvement' have increased in recent years, not only in the UK but also cross-nationally (Markey et al., 2001). Marchington and Wilkinson (2000:345) usefully distinguish between two forms of direct communication: 'downward communication', where management inform staff about particular issues through written documents or face-to-face interaction, and 'upward problem-solving' which 'incorporates a range of techniques which are designed to tap into employee knowledge and ideas' (ibid:346). Clearly, the latter contains much more scope for employee participation than the different forms of downward communication.

Both downward and upward forms of direct communication increased during the 1980s and 1990s. In 1984, for example, managers in 55 per cent of workplaces in Britain reported that they provided information to their employees or their representatives on the financial position of their workplace, and in 27 per cent of workplaces information was given about investment plans. By 1998, these proportions had risen to 66 per cent and 53 per cent respectively (Cully et al., 1999:231). A significant exception, however, is evident in relation to staffing plans: management in fewer workplaces in 1998 reported that they provided information on staffing, compared to their counterparts in 1984 (61 per cent in 1998 compared with 67 per cent in 1984) (ibid). Given the recent impact of redundancy and other staffing arrangements such as temporary work and sub-contracting (see Chapter 3), this can only add to employees' growing sense of insecurity in the UK and will no doubt compound low trust relationships between management and labour.

In terms of upward communication involving employees and management, this again shows a significant increase during the 1980s and 1990s. For example, in relation to regular meetings between senior managers and all sections of the workforce, these were reported to be taking place in just over one-third (34 per cent) of workplaces in 1984, but almost one-half (48 per cent) of workplaces by 1998 (Millward et al, 2000:118). The existence of problem-solving groups involving employees also showed a marked increase (from 35 to 49 per cent of workplaces between 1990 and 1998) (ibid), whilst 'briefing groups' or 'team briefings' demonstrated an even sharper rise from just over one-third (36 per cent) of workplaces in 1984 to nearly two-thirds (65 per cent) by 1998 (ibid:118, 120).

This last development partly reflects the significant growth of different forms of team-working since the 1980s. The scale of team-working practices and the changes that team-working implies for traditional patterns of work organisation, makes it an important factor in assessing the development of direct employee participation in decision-making. The period since the mid 1980s has witnessed considerable interest in team-working practices on both sides of the Atlantic and beyond, and led to much debate on whether, or under what conditions, team-working creates more interesting and involving jobs, or alternatively more intensified and stressful work (Geary, 2003).

In the UK, surveys have found as many as two-thirds of workplaces reporting the use of team-based working (Cully et al., 1999:43), though it is evident that what constitutes team-working is often defined very loosely (see Geary, 2003). For example, while 65 per cent of workplaces report team-working for the largest occupational group, this falls to 62 per cent when only 'teams where members work with one another' are included and 54 per cent where they also 'have responsibility for a specific product or service' (Cully et al., 1999:43). If an additional criterion of the team 'jointly deciding how work is to be done' is included then team-working falls to just 35 per cent of all workplaces (ibid). For most people, at a minimum, team-working evokes the image of team members having some responsibility for immediate work-related decisions, such as the organisation and allocation of work. In practice, however, the extent to which team-working extends employee involvement is highly variable (see, for example, Bacon and Blyton, 2000; Sewell, 1998; and van Amelsvoort and Benders, 1996).

Reflecting this variation in the forms that team-working can take in practice, Marchington's (2000) conclusion on the impact of team-working on levels of employee involvement is that the latter cannot be assumed simply from the existence of the former. If a 'high road' model of team-working is followed, involving more rather than less of the elements of a full team-working model (e.g. flexible or no job titles, multi-skilling, peer involvement in team leader selection, and a significant devolution of powers), the impact on the level of employee involvement will be far greater than if more restricted, 'low road' forms of team-working are introduced (see Bacon and Blyton, 2000). It has been found, in some cases, that the adoption of team-working does indeed increase employees' sense of influencing decisions (see, for example, studies by Edwards and Wright, 1998; Geary, 1993; and Wilkinson et al., 1997). Likewise in their study of team-working, Bacon and Blyton (2000:1146–7) found that delayering of management and decentralising some decision-making power to teams were key to team-working delivering benefits to organisations and employees. In more restricted forms of team-working, however, where existing hierarchical forms of control are left in place, team-working is likely to have little if any impact on levels of employee involvement (both real and perceived).

Further, as Marchington (2000) points out, the features of team-working and the extent to which they contribute to greater employee involvement will in turn be influenced by the context in which team-working is introduced. Important ingredients in this context will include, for example, the degree of senior management support for and commitment towards team-working, and the existence of other human resource policies which support (or undermine) the development of greater employee participation through team-working, such as single status and harmonisation, employment security and career development (Marchington, 2000:75). Notwithstanding these important differences in terms of the various forms and functions that team-working might embrace, some form of team-based working is widely regarded as an important component in the development of high involvement or high performance work systems (see, *inter alia*, Appelbaum *et al.*, 2000; Becker and Gerhard, 1996; Ichniowski *et al.*, 1996; Lawler, 1986; and Proctor and Mueller, 2000) and as such is likely to remain an important focus of attention in work re-organisation initiatives in coming years.

Cycles or waves of participation?

Debate surrounding the history of participation epitomises the broader issue in employee relations as to whether its development is best characterised by a line or a circle: has there been a development of participation over time or is it characterised by a series of cycles, with no overall forward movement? Or, alternatively, can the notion of a spiral (see Chapter 1) be profitably employed again here, with the development trajectory of participation demonstrating both linear and cyclical characteristics? Some authors have argued that there is a recognisable growth of participation over time, stimulated by factors such as increased average levels of education, or the growth in technological sophistication. As regards the latter, for example, an argument runs that as technology increases, workers using that technology gain a particular competence which acts to undermine the prevailing authority structure. Specialist knowledge is held more and more by those away from the top of managerial hierarchies. 'Little by little,' argues Goldman, 'technological progress demands that hierarchy be replaced by co-operation' (quoted by Brannen *et al.*, 1976:259).

In contrast, Ramsay (1977 and 1983) has persuasively argued that the history of participation can be viewed as a series of cycles, with periods of development followed by periods of decay, with little or no overall change in the extent to which decisions in industry are subject to joint influence and control. In the twentieth century, periods of heightened interest in participation included the two world wars (see above), together with the 1970s which witnessed both increased interest in worker directors, and an apparent resurgence of interest in joint consultation (Marchington, 1987, and 1992:20). According to Ramsay, these periods of interest in participation reflected particular conditions: labour shortages, industrial unrest, a desire by employers to accommodate labour power and – in two of the periods –

the wartime needs of the state to secure co-operation. Once these conditions abated, however, either as a result of labour power weakening or wars ending, the participation structures are seen to fall into decay. Ramsay cites this as evidence of their function only as a temporary means of accommodating potentially disruptive labour power, rather than any underlying employer or state commitment to greater worker participation in decision-making.

For at least one group studying the more diluted forms of participation in the recent period, however, this 'cycles of control' argument about how, why and when interest in participation develops, does not seem to fit. In seeking to account for the level of interest in employee involvement in the 1980s, Ackers *et al.* (1992) point to the absence of pressures during that decade to accommodate labour power. In the 1980s, most managers transparently had little need to incorporate union representatives, and if the cycles of control argument held, the weakening of organised labour after 1979 'should have seen participation fade from the scene' during the ensuing decade (ibid:272–3). The fact that this has not happened as far as employee involvement initiatives are concerned (and WERS98, together with our opening case study of Tesco, show the continued popularity of such initiatives) is used as the basis for rejecting the 'cycles' analysis of participation after the 1970s, and replacing it instead with an argument based on 'waves of interest' in participation. While recognising that interest in participation 'ebbs and flows', in using the notion of waves rather than cycles the authors seek to avoid both the assumption that a common set of circumstances (that is, strong labour power) has given rise to interest in participation at different points in time, and also that there is an all-embracing theory which applies in the same way in all workplaces. In practice, argue Marchington *et al.* (1992:26),

> waves come in different shapes and sizes, and last for different lengths of time in different organisations. Some may endure for long periods while others fail to gather momentum or break soon after formation. Further, although waves may appear to be losing strength, they may increase in intensity again due to an extra push or drive from managers.

As Marchington and Wilkinson (2000:343–4) note, factors accounting for the nature and strength of different waves will vary – and not the least important of these factors is likely to be the self-interest of managers seeking to make a name for themselves and advance their career through the launching of 'involvement' and other employee relations initiatives.

However, while for Marchington and Wilkinson (2000) and others, the circumstances giving rise to this latest interest in employee involvement are distinct from earlier periods (which Ramsay identified as characterised by increased labour power and unrest), our own view of the developments over the last two decades draws somewhat closer links between the present and earlier waves of interest in participation. We concur that the 'participation as control' argument places too much emphasis on management's need to secure *control* and gives insufficient consideration to participation as a means of securing active labour *co-operation*. For, as discussed in Chapters 2 and 4 above, managers rely on achieving not only a controlled workforce, but also one that actively engages with the labour process in order to increase the efficiency of that process. It is this desire to secure the workforce's active co-operation which represents an abiding theme in the managerial interest shown in participation – particularly those forms of participation which provide employees with a significant degree of involvement but comparatively little real influence. And, of course, co-operation and control are not opposites but complementary. A management that has gained the active co-operation of its workforce has in practice increased its level of control.

That this need for active co-operation is not something attaching only to recent initiatives in employee involvement is evidenced in the extract quoted earlier from the Whitley Reports with its references to securing 'the better utilisation of the practical knowledge and experience of the workpeople' and 'co-operation in carrying new ideas into effect'. For a state embattled by war, the Joint Industrial Councils were more than a means to re-assert control, they were also a vehicle to gain the active involvement of employees in improving the production process and a means of bolstering collaboration behind the war effort and its aftermath. It is in this respect, of participation as a vehicle for securing the active co-operation of the workforce, that the latest period has similarities with the past. What is different from, say, the development of participation in the 1970s, however, is that in the more recent period, the influence of strong labour power has been absent. This has enabled management to shift the focus of participation completely away from any power-oriented forms of participation towards those forms which are both soft on power and which match most closely managers' own attitudes and orientations. Comparing the 1970s-style industrial democracy and 1990s-style employee involvement, Marchington (1995:282) comments that: 'Employee involvement starts from the assumption that managers might see the advantages of *allowing* employees to become involved, whereas industrial democracy has its source in the *right* of the governed to exercise some control over those in authority' (original emphasis). The same holds for many of the initiatives over more recent years, most notably the promotion of company-based partnership agreements where the emphasis is all too often on communication and consultation rather than joint decision-making (see, for example, Heery, 2002; and Kelly 1999).

While diminished labour power may explain the particular direction that participation has taken, the factor which appears to have driven much of the interest in participation *per se* is the intensified level of competition evident since the 1980s, and in particular the managerial approaches (such as the 'excellence' movement and Human Resource Management) together with Japanese-style production techniques (such as Just-in-Time and Total Quality Management) which that greater competition has occasioned. Within most versions of HRM, for example, emphasis is placed on the importance of achieving greater employee commitment, not least via the use of employee involvement, 'as an important component of an organization's attempts to create a positive employee relations policy' (Marchington, 1992:176; see also Blyton and Turnbull, 1992; and Chapter 4). Beyond HRM, however – which has only been adopted by a small number of organisations, though elements have been adopted more widely (see Chapter 4) – the production pressures created by JIT, TQM and more generally by lower staffing levels and more intensive work systems, have increased the need for active workforce co-operation. The absence of buffer stocks under JIT systems, for example, and the need to secure continuous improvements under TQM, results in a management *dependency* on labour co-operation in a way that was less apparent when, for example, banks of stocks and higher levels of work-in-progress provided management (and workforce) with a greater degree of insulation from short-term disruptions to production. Part of this dependence involves management securing an active labour contribution: that is, not simply management's need to 'get the message across' but also to harness employee knowledge in the task of continuously improving the production process (Delbridge, 1998; and Delbridge and Turnbull, 1992).

Thus in the latest period, while labour market pressures have diminished, product market pressures have brought about a managerial re-assessment both of the potential contribution of employees to quality improvement and the significance of employee commitment for overall productivity. The result has been a variety of initiatives – including employee involvement schemes – designed to secure workforce co-operation. This is not to argue that product market pressures were absent during former waves of interest in participation, nor that questions of controlling labour power are irrelevant to understanding current developments in employee involvement (in fact quite the opposite). Rather, the balance between the two is different today compared to the 1970s.

Future prospects for participation

A continuing management need to secure active co-operation and employee contribution, together with the growth of various forms of downward communication and upward problem-solving machinery, point to the likelihood of forms of employee involvement and participation remaining significant features of employee relations in coming years. The introduction of the Information and Consultation Directive, and the spread of team-working will reinforce this. At the same time, the extent to which individually and collectively these developments amount to a significant extension of employee influence is much more debateable.

An additional development over the last two decades further underlines this point. The increased attention being paid to Total Quality Management (TQM) from the 1980s onwards has been identified by some as significantly enhancing the prospects for employee participation (Hill, 1991). TQM is an approach to managing which gives primacy to quality, continuous improvement and customer satisfaction as the central tenets of the organisation. For the leading exponents of TQM (Deming, 1982 and 1986; Juran, 1979 and 1988; Oakland, 1989), its adoption requires a fundamental cultural change within organisations in order to support the changes in attitudes and behaviour necessary to realise the goal of continuous quality improvement and the primacy of customer satisfaction. More importantly, exponents talk of 'worker empowerment' and 'mutual dependency' between management and labour. For Hill (1991:555), key aspects of the cultural change in TQM involves more open communication, more extensive involvement of a wider range of people in decision-making, and the creation of high-trust relations. Among those companies adopting TQM, he argues that

> decentralization and participation represent a major change in the style of managing for most companies, a shift from individual decision-taking and authoritative, top-down communication towards a more collective style with greater two-way communication and less emphasis on giving and receiving commands. (Hill, 1991:561)

For Hill, the cultural change encapsulated in TQM means that senior and middle management are more committed to the change and to both greater shared involvement in decisions and the creation of more space for devolved decision-making. However, he rightly cautions against assuming too much from the participation activity: most participation is limited to work task and work organisation issues. This is in fact a key feature of such activities. Real autonomy for the workforce is largely cosmetic, as production decisions and all quality targets are dictated either by management-decreed goals and regulations or 'customer needs' (Delbridge et al., 1992:102). External customers (consumers on the street) determine the quantity of output and demand ever improved quality, while customers inside the organisation (fellow workers 'on the line') dictate the pace of work and monitor the quality of other employees' work. Not surprisingly, therefore, workers tend to experience TQM as a 'low-trust' activity (Klein, 1989:64), and as a system of 'information and control' rather than genuine participation (Taylor et al., 1991; see also Dawson and Webb, 1989:236; Legge, 1995:208–46; Sewell and Wilkinson, 1992; and contributions to Wilkinson and Willmott, 1995). Essentially,

> Responsibility is devolved to the shopfloor but not control, which remains highly centralized in the hands of management. Employees are only required to participate in incremental improvements to product quality and process efficiency, which simply incorporates workers in the projects of capital without extending any real control or collective autonomy to the workforce. (Delbridge and Turnbull, 1992:65–6, original emphasis)

Many service sector workers' experience of quality initiatives – typically articulated through 'customer care' programmes – has been equally repressive in terms of limiting genuine autonomy but holding employees accountable for any sub-standard service encounter (see Harris and Ogbonna, 2002; and Korczynski, 2002).

Notwithstanding the various developments at organisational, national and international levels, ranging from teamworking and Total Quality to EC Directives – suggesting prospects for an extension of employee involvement and participation – a number of significant obstacles remain to the general development of participation. Above all, in the vast majority of cases, organisations remain rigidly hierarchical, with an overriding emphasis on individual responsibility and accountability, top-down decisions and a strict adherence to a hierarchically-ordered chain of command. Both the CBI and TUC concur that UK companies, on the whole, are over-controlled and under-managed (CBI/TUC, 2001), which is hardly conducive to encouraging real and effective employee participation. These (hierarchical) structures and (control-oriented) practices simply do not lend themselves to responding to bottom-up ideas: the result is that information made available to participation groups is almost inevitably inadequate, and insufficient attention is paid to ideas and suggestions emanating from these groups. The consequence is very likely to be a gradual disillusionment with the participation mechanism among those involved.

The experience of different participation and involvement initiatives is replete with the waning of initial enthusiasm and the decay of particular mechanisms. This disillusionment is all the more likely where the organisation's decision-making processes are ill-equipped to incorporate participatory activity. Where management operate a 'fire-fighting' approach to decision-making, perhaps justifying this on the basis of product market volatility, little time is (made) available for participation to occur (Marchington, 1980). More generally, if senior and middle management are not fully supportive of participatory activity, insufficient space is likely to be incorporated into decision-making processes to allow effective consultation and participation to take place. The result, in many cases, is consultation taking place *after* decisions have been made, the exercise then becoming one of management *selling* decisions rather than *consulting* over them. In the past, too much participatory activity has been simply 'bolted-on' to existing decision-making structures without due regard to the need to adapt structures to allow decisions to be influenced from below. This unwillingness to modify organisational structures is an additional factor encouraging the development of consultative rather than joint-decision-making forms of participation: the former can be accommodated into existing decision-making processes far more easily than the latter.

Further, as we have seen, much of what is currently being offered by employers is *involvement* rather than full participation based on a sharing of *influence*. Hence, one obstacle to the development of participation is the limited nature of its current manifestations, and the inability of employees to secure more joint decision-making rights. There is no automatic movement along the participation continuum (Figure 8.1) over time (Bate and Murphy, 1981). On the contrary, one effect of the current developments in involvement may be to stifle rather than (re)kindle demands for more extensive participation. As noted above, one way this may occur is by extensive management communication with employees acting to marginalise the role of the trade union and the shop steward. In addition, as Pateman (1970) has pointed out, the gaining of a participatory competence is a vital ingredient in the extension of effective participation and democracy. It could be argued, however, that contemporary employees are gaining merely an 'involvement competence' which does not adequately prepare them for a greater role in decision-making. This is certainly the case in non-union firms (Terry, 1999:25; and Chapter 9).

Finally, it remains to be seen to what extent recent developments in employee involvement form part of a concerted effort by management to move out of the low-trust dynamic which has been recognised as characterising much of British employee relations (Fox, 1974). As Crouch (1982a:216) notes,

> It is usually employers' representatives who bemoan the idea of 'two sides of industry' and who call upon workers to co-operate in the common good. But it was not workers who instituted the rigorous distinction between those who make decisions and those who receive instructions. Or, to put it another way, how can responsibility be demanded from those to whom responsibility is not given?

This has led the TUC (2003b and 2003c) to identify managers as being a barrier to high performance because they do not trust workers with decisions and do not respect the people they manage.

Participation is, by definition, a higher-trust and potentially positive-sum activity, where emphasis is placed on the shared resolution of issues to the mutual benefit and gain of those involved. However, over the longer term, such activity can only be sustained if it is nourished by other indications of higher-trust relations. Just as participation mechanisms cannot be satisfactorily bolted onto existing organisational decision-making structures, so too the values of positive-sum, high-trust relationships cannot be bolted onto an organisational climate otherwise characterised by low-trust relations. The latter, as illustrated in Chapter 4, are pervasive characteristics of the majority of UK firms. In such a context, employee involvement and diluted forms of participation appear to trade unions, and indeed to many workers, as forms of management control rather than opportunities to influence management policy and decisions.

Conclusion

Employee participation has traditionally represented the Cinderella of employee relations in the UK. In part, this probably reflects the extent of development of workplace trade union organisation and bargaining activity since the 1950s, as well as a more widespread failure to secure commitment towards participation among the parties involved. For McCarthy (1967), a secondary role for joint consultation was the inevitable outcome of the development of workplace trade union organisation and workplace bargaining. Once these aspects grew in significance, unions would understandably seek to shift as many of the important issues as possible from the consultative to the bargaining forum, in order to exercise joint decision-making influence rather than merely advisory power.

The recent period, in contrast, has been characterised by a management-led (and since 1997, a government-encouraged) interest in forms of employee involvement and partnership designed to enhance worker integration, co-operation and contribution. The weakened state of the trade union movement and managerial philosophies emphasising the significance of employee commitment and contribution, have acted to support the development of employee (rather than trade union) centred forms of involvement. European integration – and the social polices which stem from that – may act to bring collective aspects of participation into closer consideration, but unions and employees would be unwise to pin too much hope on Europe. Many of the underlying obstacles to participation remain, not least the unwillingness of management to relinquish hierarchical control and decision-making power, the low-trust relations obtaining between many managements and workforces, the lack of opportunity of many employees to gain the participatory competence necessary to mount a significant challenge to existing decision-making structures and processes, and, more generally, the underlying tension of interests between employers and employees. It may indeed be true that the current context of weakened unions and decline in bargaining coverage is one in which non-bargaining forms of employee–management interaction thrive. However, for the representation gap to be closed and participation to attain its full potential in employee relations, these obstacles to its development need to be more satisfactorily addressed than has hitherto been the case. Put differently, if collective bargaining can no longer ensure the effective right of representation for employees in the decisions affecting their working lives, as the evidence presented in Chapter 7 seems to indicate, but society still values participation as a democratic right of all workers, then urgent and concerted action by the state, employers, employees and their trade union representatives, is called for.

9

Managing without unions

Marks & Spencer: a manufacturer without factories?

Good jobs and bad jobs

In an industrial town on the outskirts of the Greater Manchester conurbation, Marks & Spencer (M&S) has a well-placed, and invariably busy store. In this respect the town is like many others, as virtually every desirable high street in the country plays host to the UK's most renowned retailer. Every week, 10 million customers pass through the doors of M&S stores, buying the *St Michael* branded goods that have a deserved reputation for quality and value for money (see Kumar, 1997:823). Inside the stores, 67 000 employees (70 per cent of whom work part-time) are well looked after. The proverb 'Do as you would be done by' (Sieff, 1990:84) has long been the golden rule of the company's *human* relations policy – so-called because, as the former Chairman Lord Sieff (1984:28) explained, 'we are human beings at work not industrial beings'. Any policy derived from the 'law and the prophets' carries with it a strong moral obligation, as Lord Sieff makes clear (ibid:55 and 118). Indeed, the extensive provision of welfare and medical benefits such as subsidised meals, hairdressing, chiropody and dental check-ups, 'is an act of faith. When asked why the company spends so lavishly on the health of its employees managers reply that it feels right to do so' (*Financial Times*, 30 April 1991). Lord Sieff was always less speculative: 'Good human relations at work pay off; they are of great importance if a business is to be efficiently run' (1990:56). The latter was certainly true of Marks & Spencer, a company hailed by Peter Drucker (1974:98) as one of the most efficient companies in the world, and previously voted Britain's 'best managed company' by a panel of institutional investors, captains of industry and business journalists (*Financial Times*, 19 March 1997).

Less than two miles away from the M&S store is a family-run business, Sew & Son (a pseudonym), making ladies' underwear and nightwear for M&S. Like many of the small and medium sized enterprises (SMEs) who supply clothes and other goods to M&S, the company has 'sold its soul to St Michael', as the *Sunday Times* (6 June 1983) once put it, on the basis of no more than a batch-by-batch contract (see Rainnie, 1984:149). The same could be said of Sew & Son's employees. Although they enjoy a subsidised canteen, conditions of work are almost the opposite of those enjoyed by M&S staff. Lines of sewing machines buzz with continuous activity. Conversation is difficult above the noise, and costly. Payment is by the piece, and the pace of work is intense if the women are to earn a decent wage. On the M&S lines in particular, 'Everything is all speed' (interview notes). As the supervisor elaborated,

> On the M&S work, women either stick it or leave. They're always coming and going. The M&S work can make you ill, it's so fast. It has to be. You only get a few pence for every dozen ... Marks & Spencer tell you how to organise the work. A man from their technical division came in and sorted it all out. And the quality has to be just right. If M&S find even one or two that are not right they send the whole lot back – could be as many as 200 dozen. They turn up any time to check quality. They're like ghosts in the factory – they don't own us, but they're always there. (interview notes)

As another woman commented somewhat ruefully, 'I'd much rather work for Marks & Spencer than make the work for them' (interview notes).

Not surprisingly, Marks & Spencer has been described as a 'manufacturer without factories' (Tse, 1985:4). As such, the relationship between M&S and its factories (suppliers) is of critical importance, not only to the reputation and financial success of M&S but to the continuation of small, low-technology firms in the clothing (and other) industries. Marks & Spencer pays for the welfare benefits of its own employees out of such dependency. In contrast, small textile firms often pay little heed to employee needs or their employment rights.

Who needs a union anyway?

Ever since the late 1960s, the non-union 'Marksist' approach to human relations (Tse, 1985:173–4) (not to be confused with Marxist!) has been popularised as an alternative to the collectivist, institutionalised approach to employee relations based on the Whitley and later the Donovan model (see Chapter 7), as Lord Sieff (1986:182) points out in his memoirs. When employees are recruited to Marks & Spencer they receive a 'Welcome Pack' which gives information on the company and its principles. These include the company's policy to:

- Sell merchandise of the highest quality and outstanding value
- Provide the highest standard of customer care in an attractive shopping environment
- Improve quality standards continually throughout our operations
- Support British industry

- Pursue mutually rewarding long-term partnerships with suppliers
- Minimise the environmental impact of our operations and merchandise
- Ensure that staff and shareholders share in our success
- Nurture good human relations with customers, staff and the community.

For M&S, 'the newest recruit is in a sense the most important person in the company at any given time since by definition he or she is the least educated and experienced and therefore the most likely to fall below the company's standards' (Sieff, 1990:123). Thus, 'A good firm will make its philosophy of good human relations clear to its employees from the moment they join the company' (ibid:81). A second booklet, 'Facts for New Staff', gives details of employees' conditions of employment. These include competitive rates of pay, non-contributory pensions, profit sharing, and extensive medical care. Female employees, for example, are offered breast and cervical screening, while male employees can view a video and read a company leaflet on testicular self-examination. Everyday health and safety is covered in another booklet, 'The Right Move' (which advises on such matters as the lifting of heavy boxes), while 'Personal Safety' offers employees advice on going to and from work (see Sieff, 1990:81–3). As with other HR policies, the company's recently launched 'work-life balance' package (see Chapter 3) is 'not only about being seen as caring. It makes sound commercial sense to offer policies that attract and retain the best people' (M&S spokesperson, quoted in *People Management*, 27 September 2001).

According to Lord Sieff (1984:28), good human relations is not just about wages and conditions but also moral fortitude and a deeper understanding of employee needs. For this reason, Tse (1985:118) argues that it is a misrepresentation simply to label the 'Marksist' approach to human relations as paternalism (*pace* Turnbull and Wass, 1997b). The company's human relations policy, according to Tse (1985:119), also includes a respect for the individual, attention to the problems of individuals at work, full and frank communications, the recognition of people's effort and contribution, and continuous training and development. In other words, attention is paid not only to those factors which, according to Herzberg (1966), (dis)satisfy employees (wages, amenities, physical working conditions) but also those that motivate employees (achievement, recognition, responsibility, advancement). In the words of Lord Sieff (1990:121 and 176),

> good human relations have a most beneficial effect on the morale of the employees and their performance ... The key fact about a policy of good human relations at work is that it is not *primarily* concerned with the nature of the work which the employee does but with the state of mind, the spirit in which he or she does it. A policy of good human relations at work is not about jobs, it is about people. (original emphasis)

Of course, policy statements and 'good intentions' are one thing, implementation is another. In all organisations there is invariably a 'gap' between aspirations and outcomes, between the espoused management style and the reality of personnel practice (see Purcell and Ahlstrand, 1994:177). An important litmus test of actual policy would of course be employee perceptions, attitudes and experiences of work, but there is a dearth of such information for non-union workers. Management (e.g. Sieff, 1984, 1986 and 1990) and managerialist (e.g. Davies, 1999; and Howells, 1981) accounts of M&S, however, claim that the rhetoric of 'good human relations' is matched by the 'reality' of employees' experience:

> the company not only looks after the staff well, but, more importantly, the staff feel they are being treated as individuals; that they are given opportunities continuously to train and develop themselves; that management is on their side, not against and above them; and that they see very little gap between what top management preaches and what is being practised. (Tse, 1985:118)

Effective implementation is proclaimed to be the result of top management commitment, the importance attached to the personnel function, and the unremitting zeal with which the policy is effected on a day-to-day, day-after-day basis. To quote Lord Sieff again,

> Good human relations cannot be legislated for ... Good human relations develop only if top management believes in and is committed to their implementation and has a genuine respect for the individual. This is not something tackled from time to time but demands continuous action. (1984:29)

In short, 'good human relations owe more to example than precept' (Sieff, 1990:82). The example starts with the personnel function which is heavily staffed and strongly represented on the board of directors. The strategic importance attached to personnel is a key feature of M&S (Tse, 1985:130), but the emphasis is very much on an organic relationship with line management (see Turnbull and Wass, 1997b). In fact, the company's philosophy is that 'good human relations is not something that can be left to the personnel department' (Sieff, 1984:29). Rather, 'personnel work – in the broadest sense of the term – is conceived of not so much as a function but as a way of life, and as such it permeates the entire organization, from the board room to the sales floor' (Tse, 1985:141). Responsibility is therefore delegated to line and store management, who deal directly, and at times generously, with all personnel issues (Sieff, 1986:159). All local managers were told, 'if you are going to make a mistake, err on the side of generosity' (Sieff, 1984:30). Issues that cannot be resolved at this level are taken to the Welfare Committee, first established in the early 1930s, which meets and attempts to resolve issues on a weekly basis. Speed is of the essence.

As far as trade unions are concerned, Marks & Spencer's approach can best be described as 'pre-emptive' (Tse, 1985:122), straightforwardly *non*-union rather than explicitly *anti*-union. Put differently, the approach is one of substitution rather than suppression of union activity (Beaumont, 1987:130). Anybody who works for M&S can join a trade union, but the company 'cannot guarantee an audience' (Sieff, 1990:84). To ensure that an 'audience' does not convene, M&S provides *collective* channels of employee involvement and representation. Thus, in addition to direct communications and employee publications such as 'On Your Marks' that aim to keep individual workers up to date with company developments, M&S also operates business involvement groups (Bigs) at the store, area and national levels. Employees elect representatives to the store Big; there are forty-three area Bigs with representatives drawn from the store Bigs; and the national Big is composed of eight representatives from the area Bigs, two from head office, and one from the company's Burnley Print facility. Like the company's European Works Council, however, Bigs were established largely in (a pre-emptive) response to the European Union's Directive on workplace information and consultation (see Higginbottom, 2003). It is well established that non-union employee representation (NER) systems are more likely to be developed, and to be effective, when there is a real threat of unionisation (Kaufman and Taras, 2000). Otherwise, NER is little more than a 'cosmetic exercise', or as Terry (1999:27) puts it, 'managerial emanations subject to managerial whim'. Union representatives who sit on consultative committees or company councils in unionised firms, for example, will usually be trained in advocacy and negotiating skills whereas 'non-union representatives are less able, trained, expert, or more nervous than their union counterparts (and hence less likely to press management)' (ibid: 25). M&S has provided training for Big representatives, but as the company's Chief Executive has made quite clear, their role is 'making sure that you help your colleagues understand important work issues' (Roger Holmes, quoted in Higginbottom, 2003:33).

Ultimately, union substitution at M&S is based on good pay and conditions of employment, rather than opportunities for employee voice or sophisticated NER (see Turnbull and Wass, 1997b). As the company's former Director of Personnel has pointed out, M&S 'appreciate that in companies that are unwilling or unable to provide more than the basic terms and conditions for their employees, trade unions do have a valuable role to play in negotiating for their members' (Salsbury, 1993:569), but with such care and attention lavished on the promotion of good human relations, 'unionism simply finds it difficult to flourish in St Michael soil' (Tse, 1985:122). As a union official from the building industry commented to an audience of employers after a speech by Lord Sieff at the 1983 annual meeting of the National Federation of Building Trades Employers, 'If you all followed a policy similar to that about which Lord Sieff has spoken I would be out of a job' (quoted by Sieff, 1986:223). As Lord Sieff himself put it, 'I suppose that so few [M&S employees] join because they feel the management provide them with as much and perhaps more than an active trade union would' (1990:84). The same cannot be said, however, for the management of many of the suppliers who manufacture for Marks & Spencer.

You can't have a union!

At Sew & Son, not all the factory's output was earmarked for *St Michael*. While the majority of the women worked on the underwear section for M&S, a group of sixteen women worked on the ladies outerwear section, producing skirts, jackets, trousers and suits for mail-order catalogue companies. This work was 'make-through', with payment based on ten complete items, and was therefore much more highly skilled. However, 'The boss didn't like outerwear, the make-through section', recalled one woman, 'there was no hum, no buzz. The women liked it. It was well paid and it was interesting work, there was some involvement' (interview notes). But work on this section declined and the women were transferred to M&S work, at first making T-shirts (until this work was transferred to a factory in Cheshire), and then on women's night-dresses. For the women, events had taken a turn for the worse. Under the work system designed by Marks & Spencer for the night-dresses, the garment was broken down into twenty-one separate sections/operations. Not only was the work de-skilled, but the women who had been transferred from outerwear were now earning a third less. At first they were paid an average wage (based on their earnings on the outerwear section) until they had become accustomed to the work, but as the supervisor recalled,

> When they were transferred to the night-dresses they'd already lost heart. When they went on to piece-rates it was too much. Fifteen of them left in the end, all top machinists. So we took on young kids. We'd start ten on Monday morning and there'd only be four left by Friday. But it didn't seem to matter. You didn't have to be skilled, just fast. And young. They wouldn't start any older women. They still had to be trained, but only how to do the job fast. It wasn't a skilled job. (interview notes)

Prior to the transfer onto the M&S work there had been some union recruitment activity in the factory. The women on the outerwear section had been receptive to the idea and nominated one of their number to act as their representative. The response from management, however, was distinctly hostile. The women were called into the owner-manager's office and told outright: 'We don't want a union in here. They only cause trouble' (interview notes). Instead, he suggested promoting the women's representative to the position of supervisor over the outerwear section. This proved to be acceptable to the women, especially as the supervisor kept a close check on the distribution of work between machinists (to ensure equality) and the prices of every item. As she later recalled, 'I always kept the price tickets. With it being catalogue work you got a lot of variety, so I always kept the tickets. When new work came in, management would try to set a lower price, but we wouldn't have any of it. We had the tickets, and they had to pay us' (interview notes). The cut in wages on the M&S work, alongside the de-skilling of the work, therefore proved to be a particularly bitter pill to swallow. Even then, 'If they'd given us a few coppers more we might have got the girls moving, but the money was just too tight' (interview notes). Several women took their case to an Industrial Tribunal, but lost. Shortly after, the supervisor left as well, as did her sister. As for the night-dresses, three months later the section was closed and the work transferred to another factory.

Trouble at t'works?

The constraints imposed on the small textile manufacturer, Sew & Son, by a much larger retail company clearly generated instability in the former's employee relations. Conflict, in this instance, was manifest in the very high levels of labour turnover. Even at Marks & Spencer, however, where the dependency of small firms is used to pay for and protect the conditions of M&S staff, everything is not always 'sweetness and light'. In 1989, for example, the company introduced a telephone 'hotline' to management to enable employees to inform on colleagues suspected of shoplifting. The scheme was widely criticised for being open to abuse by the unscrupulous, and received a negligible response from staff. Both John Lewis and Tesco rejected similar schemes (Hamil, 1993:43). Later, in April 1991, M&S announced 850 redundancies which, in some quarters, was seen to herald 'the end of Marks & Spencer's unofficial commitment to its staff of a job for life' (ibid:41). As Lord Sieff (1990:64–5) makes clear, any such commitment on the part of M&S was always implicit rather than explicit, but the effect on the staff concerned was nonetheless traumatic. 'The Baker Street headquarters in London was gripped by gloom and confusion', wrote the *Financial Times* (30 April 1991), while City analysts predicted 'the transition from a safe, job-for-life type organisation into a meritocracy. To a certain extent, M&S has always been carrying a lot of fat and it is the first time that it has gone on a diet' (ibid).

Marks & Spencer was keen to quash any rumours that the company planned to cut welfare, adopt a less caring approach or change its culture (*Financial Times*, 11 May and 18 May 1991), but in July 1996 the company stopped providing free breakfasts (on the grounds that not all staff enjoyed this 'perk') and the very notion of a full-time employee was abolished (staff are now paid for hours worked rather than a set monthly salary). It must be recognised that M&S has always demonstrated 'a ruthlessness, manifested in a relentless pursuit of corporate objectives, which some commentators have characterised as authoritarian, albeit benevolently so' (Hamil, 1993:43). In other words, benevolence and authoritarian management have never been alternatives but rather part and parcel of the company's human relations policy. The contradictions between these two characteristics, however, have only become apparent in the face of very severe external pressures, most notably the intensification of competition in the mid to late 1990s in both high quality clothing (e.g. from Next, Gap, and Hennes & Mauritz) and discount clothing (e.g. from Primark and Matalan), as well as competition in high quality foods (e.g. from Tesco Finest). M&S was slow to react, believing that its traditional approach would ensure that the company weathered the storm. Indeed, many observers regarded senior management as arrogant and conceited, more concerned with their own position than the fortunes of the company and its workforce (see Eaton, 2001; and Mellahi *et al.*, 2002:23). Sir Richard Greenbury, the company's former Chairman, seemed to dismiss criticism rather than address the company's underlying problems: 'A crisis in women's outerwear? Nonesense. Trouble at t'works council? Balderdash. Too much competition in food? Rubbish' (quoted in Eaton, 2001:187). As a result,

> By the late 1990s . . . there were two M&S's. One, as perceived by its management, a world-class retail company with an exemplar management; the other, that seen by outsiders (industry observers and the City) and customers, was a company ill-adapted to the new circumstances and losing its market position and image very quickly. (Mellahi *et al.*, 2002:24)

Inertia led to falling sales and profits. Redundancies inevitably followed, which in their turn created fatalism which fed onto this inertia (ibid:25). One response was to 'Energise' staff through a customer care programme, launched in 1999, 'which teaches teamwork and positivity, [the programme] aims to mould staff thought processes and body language to create a more welcoming environment for customers' (*The Grocer*, 16 June 2001). More importantly, M&S recruited a new Executive Chairman from outside the company to shake up (and rationalise) the inward looking management team. Luc Vandevelde, a Belgian accountant, came to M&S with extensive experience in retail. He echoed the views of the City and industry observers, noting that 'no one here knew what our market share was or what the competition did' (*The Guardian*, 26 May 2001).

Mr Vandevelde's approach to 'human relations' quickly earned him the nickname 'Muscles from Brussels' (older readers might appreciate his other nickname, 'Cruel Hand Luc') (*The Guardian*, 26 May 2001). He acknowledged that morale was extremely low at all levels in the organisation (Vandevelde, 2003:28) but was determined to reduce costs by sourcing from cheaper overseas suppliers, resulting in the indirect loss of thousands of textile jobs in the UK; cutting overtime rates for new recruits; and closing all 38 of the company's Continental European stores along with the company's direct mail operation in Warrington. This resulted in the direct loss of 4400 jobs and led to further doubts about the meaning of 'good human relations'. In particular, the company only informed the employees of the impeding closures 5 minutes before the opening of the London Stock Exchange, which the French courts determined to be illegal (M&S was fined and ordered to withdraw the closure plans until it had properly consulted the workforce) (see Fulton, 2001; and *Labour Research*, October 2001). Unions were recognised at the company's European stores and while they were unable to prevent the closures they did negotiate more favourable redundancy packages or 'social plans' than their non-union UK counterparts (e.g. a 40-year-old worker with 4 years service at M&S

received 9 months salary in compensation for job loss in Belgium, 6 months salary in Spain, 3.2 months plus £640 for every dependent child in Germany, and just 10 weeks pay in the UK) (ibid). M&S has now restored its annual turnover to the levels achieved in 1997–98 and profits are climbing once more. The company still proclaims its commitment to people and good human relations, but it seems M&S will no longer err so heavily on the side of generosity.

Non-unionism's growing ranks

Even using the most flattering (for trade unions) measure of union density (based on civilian employees in employment), less than 30 per cent of the workforce now belong to a trade union (see Chapter 5). With non-unionism now dominant in the UK, numerically at least, the former labour editor of the *Financial Times* expressed some surprise that this had been all but ignored in texts on industrial relations, although he did suggest a reason why: 'you know how to find the TGWU: it's there, it's tangible. By contrast, non-unionism is amorphous, de-centralised, inaccessible' (Bassett, 1988:45; see also Blackburn and Hart, 2002; McLoughlin, 1996:301; and Terry, 1999). While this may be true of the vast majority of (small) non-union companies, it is certainly not true of them all. Indeed, as Bassett (1988:47) and others (e.g. Legge, 1995:36–7) note, the new role models for British employee relations are no longer Ford or ICI but IBM, Hewlett Packard, and other large multinationals such as Black & Decker, Gillette, Mars, Polaroid, Texas Instruments, Nestlé, and of course Marks & Spencer. Very large non-union companies are the exception rather than the rule (see Bacon, 2001). Nevertheless, the employment and other policies of these non-union companies are increasingly well-known and more widely publicised. Many are strongly associated with the US 'excellence' literature, for example (Peters and Waterman, 1982), which in turn has informed much of the recent writing on human resource management (see Boxall and Purcell, 2003; Guest, 1990; and Legge, 1995). At the risk of over-generalisation, the generic characteristics of these non-union companies tend to be a sense of caring, combined with carefully chosen plant locations and working environments, market leadership, high growth and healthy profits, employment security, single status, promotion from within, an influential personnel department (and a high ratio of personnel staff to employees), competitive pay and benefit packages, profit sharing, open communications, and the meticulous selection and training of management, particularly at the supervisory level (see, for example, Beaumont, 1987:117–19; and Foulkes, 1981). As with Marks & Spencer, the inevitable question that trade unions confront from employees in such organisations is, 'Why should I join a union?'

Of course, not all large non-union companies are benevolent, and for those which are benevolence is an act of business (to make a profit), not an act of charity. Some large non-union companies, such as McDonald's, are distinctly *anti*-union. Mrs Thatcher once said that 'we must expect that a lot more of our jobs will come from the service sector – from the McDonald's and the Wimpeys', but the neon lights of the hamburger economy 'hides a reality that is more like the slum industries of yesteryear' (Lamb and Percy, 1987:15). Labour costs at McDonald's outlets must not rise above 15 per cent of sales, such that if sales decline then staff numbers are cut back and work intensified. The company employs those with few other opportunities, typically women, ethnic minorities and youths (two-thirds of staff are less than 21 years old), and although annual labour turnover is around 200 per cent, labour is cheap and flexible (three-quarters are part-time) and tasks can be learnt in a day. In fact, workers' skills have effectively been eliminated (there are no chefs), and computerised machines do all the cooking. The more important ingredients are tight labour control and a team grading system that keeps workers smiling for the customers, but at each other's throats (ibid:15–17; see also Goffee and Scase, 1995:123–4; and Royle, 2000).

Clearly, then, not all large non-union companies are alike. Moreover, small non-union companies are different again. More importantly, there is a major discrepancy between the popular image and the reality of working in small firms. The popular image was articulated by a Committee of Enquiry on Small Firms back in the early 1970s:

> In many respects the small firm provides a better environment for the employee than is possible in most large firms. Although physical working conditions may sometimes be inferior in small firms, most people prefer to work in a small group where communications present fewer problems: the employees in the small firm can easily see the relation between what they are doing and the objectives and performance of the firm as a whole. Where management is more direct and flexible, working rules can be varied to suit the individual. (Bolton, 1971:23)

According to this account, employees choose small firms because of the non-economic rewards they offer. Not surprisingly, the predicted outcomes are greater moral involvement, organisational attachment, and of course industrial harmony. As the Conservative Party document *Moving Forward* (1983) claimed,

> One of the advantages that small businesses do, in fact, enjoy is the generally good state of relations between the owners and managers and their employees. There is a sense of partnership based on the willingness to work for a clearly perceived common purpose from which everyone benefits. (quoted by Goss, 1991:154)

Thus, the 1980s became the decade of 'small business revivalism' and the 'enterprise culture' (Burrows and Curran, 1989:527). Under Mrs Thatcher, the small firm was 'taken up as the articulating principle of right-wing reaction to economic crisis'

(Curran and Burrows, 1986:274), and the entrepreneur cast in the role of 'dynamic saviour of a moribund economy' (Rainnie, 1989:1). 'No longer reviled as a tax dodger or exploiter of cheap labour, small business exemplifies most of the [Conservative] Government's ideals, whether small shop (thrift, independence) or fast expanding Thames Valley electronics concern (risk taking, ambitious, profit orientated)' (*Financial Times*, 12 June 1984, quoted by Rainnie, 1985b:141–2). New Labour has continued to promote SMEs, establishing a Small Business Service under the auspices of the DTI to champion the interests of these firms. Mr Blair's government regards entrepreneurship as an important source of efficiency, innovation, opportunity, and even the renewal of the poorest and most marginalized communities and localities in the UK (SBS, 2003b). In short, '[s]mall is supposed to be not only beautiful, but also dynamic, efficient, competitive and perhaps most important, a source of new jobs' (Rainnie, 1989:1).

For both Conservative and Labour governments, then, the promotion of small firms is not only a key element of economic policy but also employee relations policy. The apparent industrial harmony of small firms is usually attributed to the absence of trade unions, minimum state intervention and, as a result, a more direct employer-employee relationship uncontaminated by 'outside' interference (Goss, 1991:152). For many policy makers, '[t]his combination of factors is claimed to reveal the employment relationship as it should be: a relationship between equals in the market (one the buyer and one the seller of labour) with a mutual interest in the success of the enterprise' (ibid). The reality, on *all* counts, however, can be very different. For example, an increasing number of studies have revealed employment relations in SMEs to be more akin to a 'black hole' or 'bleak house', characterised by poor conditions of employment, low pay, the absence of good (or any) personnel practices, little or no opportunity for employee voice, and enforced compliance rather than active employee commitment (see, for example, Guest and Conway, 1999; and Sisson, 1993).

Likewise, there is another side to the employment effects of SMEs. Although the number of small firms has increased in recent years, and although small firms have increased their share of total employment and created a great many new jobs (Dale and Kerr, 1995; and SBS, 2003b), they also contribute more than their fair share to the ranks of the unemployed (Daniel, 1985; and Rainnie, 1989:2 and 23). The death rate of small firms is almost as high as the birth rate (Daly, 1990), with one in ten currently failing in the first 12 months and a third going out of business within 3 years (www.sbs.gov.uk). Self-employed workers in the UK are far less likely to employ additional workers than their counterparts in the EU, with only 29 per cent of the self-employed in the UK hiring employees compared to 51 per cent in Germany, over 47 per cent in Austria, almost 46 per cent in Denmark and well over 40 per cent in Ireland (Cowling, 2003). As a result, micro firms (0–9 employees) often fail to grow into small businesses (10–49 employees) and these firms in particular find it difficult to grow into medium-sized firms (50–249 employees) (see

Gallagher *et al.*, 1990:95–6), suggesting that most small businesses are likely to remain small (Hakim, 1989a and 1989b). Such companies find it difficult to change from an informal to a more formal management structure, especially when dealing with employee relations (see Wilkinson, 1999).

The more important deficiency of the popular account of small firms, however, is that size *per se* is not a *necessary* characteristic of an organisation but a *contingent* one (Burrows and Curran, 1989:530). Size is an important variable in employee relations because of the very clear correlation between size and a number of key industrial relations indicators: as establishment size increases, organisations display more elaborate management structures (differentiated hierarchically and functionally), they devote more resources to personnel matters, and they are more likely to have formal management procedures for issues such as discipline and dismissal; bigger establishments are also more likely to recognise a trade union, have shop stewards present and experience strikes (see, for example, Cully *et al.*, 1999; and Millward *et al.*, 2000). But size plays a role in the functioning of an organisation *only* in relation to other factors (Curran, 1990:129). As Rainnie (1991:177) notes, 'to say that smallness *per se* is a characteristic that, alone, will determine the internal operation and external relations of this unit is bizarre'. The more important variables to consider *in relation to size* are industrial sector, technology, locality, labour and product markets (see Wilkinson, 1999:214). In their study of 397 small firms, for example, Scott *et al.* (1989) found it more useful to sub-divide the sample into four broad industrial groups, namely traditional manufacturing, high-tech manufacturing, traditional services and high-tech services. Size, in itself, could not account for the differences between firms.

Thus, 'what constitutes smallness will be very much contextual – dependent upon economic sector, market size and the like' (Burrows and Curran, 1989:530). As the small firm sector extends from the corner shop to the high-tech firms of the M4 corridor and Silicon Glen in Scotland, such a heterogeneous collection of organisations demands, first, a *relational* conceptualisation of their activities, and secondly the identification of those factors which, in general and in combination, determine why a great many firms, and the majority of small firms, are non-union. As in the case of Sew & Son and many other small clothing manufacturers producing *St Michael* branded goods, the (dependent) relationship with its major customer, Marks & Spencer, plays a crucial role in shaping employer-employee relations (see also Barrett and Rainnie, 2002; and Rainnie, 1984 and 1985a). Equally, the structural characteristics of the workplace and the composition of the workforce, the informal nature of employee relations, and the (unitarist) attitude of the owner/manager can combine to produce an environment unconducive to trade union membership. Each of these variables is analysed in turn. Finally, the problems of trade union recruitment, organisation and representation are analysed in more detail. Is it realistic to anticipate that the seeds of trade unions revival can be planted in the 'never unionised' sectors of the economy?

Small firms, big firms

The nature of employee relations in any organisation can only be fully understood in the context of, and in relation to, wider socio-economic, political and legal structures (see Chapter 2). Inter-organisational relations play an important part (Chapter 3), especially in the case of small firms whose relationship with much bigger firms can have a major bearing on their own labour process characteristics (Rainnie, 1991). Simply put, 'large capital determines not only the field of play, but also the rules of the game that small firms are engaged in' (Rainnie, 1985b:165). For this reason, 'Size *qua* size ... is secondary to the relationship with the wider economy and it is these which determine the organisational and social frameworks of the enterprise' (Curran, 1990:130). In the case of Marks & Spencer, for example, the highly competitive nature of the retail sector, and the uncertainty of market trends and changing fashions, has led to a relationship with suppliers described as 'benevolent dictatorship' (Salmans, 1980:68). Retailers such as M&S did not create a highly competitive, small-scale clothing sector, but they have certainly taken advantage of it. And in doing so they ensured that this situation would continue (Rainnie, 1984:153). In other words, a major reason why the clothing sector is characterised by low technology, ease of entry (and exit), and therefore small, predominantly non-union firms employing cheap female labour is because a dependent small-firm sector is necessary to the continuation of large-scale enterprise in retailing (Curran and Burrows, 1986:274).

> Briefly, the advantages to companies like Marks and Spencer of formally independent, but in reality utterly dependent small suppliers, are enormous and can be summed up as cheap flexibility, crucial at a time of increased competition. The existence of the *individual* small firm is not important, the continued existence of a *number* of them is vital. (Rainnie, 1985b:157, original emphasis)

As early as the mid 1920s, M&S pioneered a relationship with suppliers that allowed the company to decide *what they wanted to sell*, rather than would simply have to buy from what the manufacturers had produced. As Tse (1985:75) notes, 'Marks & Spencer has *dictated* a new type of relationship between the manufacturer and the retailer' (emphasis added). This account is somewhat at odds, however, with the more popular accounts of the harmonious, collaborative relationship that M&S enjoys with its suppliers. Tse (1985:76–7), for example, also talks of the relationship as a 'marriage', while Lord Sieff himself provides details of the technical support that M&S provides and the long-term partnership the company has enjoyed with many suppliers, adding that M&S encourages all its suppliers (who are required to sign a 'code of conduct') to offer similar terms and conditions of employment for their own workers (Sieff, 1986:161). Of particular concern to Lord Sieff was always the condition of the supplier's toilets, which he appeared to regard as a barometer of the state of employee relations at supplier companies (ibid). But the companies that 'Dan, Dan the lavatory man', as he was sometimes called (ibid), discusses are all larger companies with whom Marks & Spencer would have more of a *mutually dependent*, rather than dominant relationship (see, for example, Sieff, 1990:93–111). With smaller companies, such as Sew & Son, M&S has always displayed much less compunction about switching contracts or playing one supplier off against another (see Rainnie, 1984 and 1985b). That said, when competition intensified in the late 1990s and profits fell for the first time in 30 years, M&S revised its 'buy British' policy and its relationship with larger suppliers. Contracts with large clothing companies such as William Baird were cancelled, in this instance ending a 30 year relationship and wiping out 40 per cent of Baird's total business. Whereas M&S used to source almost 90 per cent of its clothing from UK suppliers, by 1999 this was down to 55 per cent and is expected to fall to just 30 per cent (*Financial Times*, 10 March 2001). The company now has 1500 suppliers in over seventy countries.

Although the strategies of large firms play a crucial role in the restructuring of economic relations in general and those with, and within, small firms in particular (e.g. Shutt and Whittington, 1987), this should not divert attention away from the small-firm sector itself. What is often suggested, for example, is that the relationship between small and large firms is simply one of *dependence*, with consequent implications for employee relations. The general argument, as Goss (1991:160) points out, is that 'small firms – directly or indirectly – are generally in a dependent position, a dependence which is frequently reflected in patterns of industrial relations as employers seek to maintain a competitive edge through rigorous exploitation of labour'. In many respects this is undeniably true: the appalling conditions of many (sweat shop) firms bears testament to this (e.g. Byrne, 1986; Hoel, 1982; Phizacklea, 1987; Pond, 1983; Toynbee, 2003; Wills, 2002; and www.nosweat.org.uk). But as Rainnie (1991:187) points out, it is important to consider the relationship between small and large firms more directly and in more detail, since there are at least four very different relationships which can be identified:

- *Dependent* small firms complement and service the activities of larger firms (e.g. sub-contracting). Labour costs must be minimised and flexibility is essential.
- *Dominated* small firms compete with large firms through the more intense exploitation of machinery and especially labour. Hyper-exploitation of labour is not uncommon.
- *Isolated* small firms operate in specialised and/or geographically discrete markets, the niches of demand that are unlikely to be touched by large capital. Living off the crumbs from the large firms' table, however, entails a hand-to-mouth existence and invariably sweat shop conditions for the workforce.

- *Innovative* small firms compete in (or even develop) specialised markets, but are always open to the potentially fatal attractions of large firms. Flexibility and innovation are essential, and attractive pay and conditions may be necessary to attract highly skilled workers (see Rainnie, 1989:85 and 1991:188).

In the clothing sector, small firms generally find themselves in a *dependent* relationship with their larger customers, with obvious implications for employee relations. Tight supervision, authoritarian management and payment systems that tie the workers to their machines are just some of the outcomes cited by Rainnie (1985a:218; see also Taplin *et al.*, 2003). These are not universal or inevitable features of the clothing industry *per se*, but rather reflect *the relationship with the customer*. As Ram (1991:607–11 and 1994) demonstrates in a study of clothing firms in the West Midlands where output went to intermediaries rather than direct to the retailers, supervision was not so tight, the workers tended to work at their own pace and controlled effort levels, and there was extensive negotiation, and re-negotiation, over the rate for the job. The difference between the outerwear section and the M&S work at Sew & Son bears out a similar point. At the same time, however, in either case, there appears in practice to be very little room for manoeuvre: the field of play is determined by the customer, and while the *precise* rules of the game may be subject to interpretation (negotiation), the large firm can always move the goalposts or take the ball elsewhere to play.

Among the *dominated* and *isolated* groups of small firms are to be found those which depend largely on second-hand machinery and cheap labour (Rainnie, 1991:188), the 'chaff' of yesterday's harvest rather than the 'green shoots' of future growth. These small firms operate in established markets (e.g. general printing) and/or those now populated by a large number of self-employed people (e.g. craft-related occupations) (see Cowling, 2003). Moule (1998), for example, discusses a small company supplying buttons to clothing manufacturers and large retailers such as M&S. Operating in a niche market, competition was limited but customers demanded very rapid turnaround of orders. While all work was 'urgent', deadlines were especially tight for key customers such as M&S – 'These initials were a byword for URGENT. Workers in all departments recognised their significance' (ibid:642). In this way, even isolated firms, and in particular their workforces, feel the presence of large firms.

Finally, among the *innovative* small firms we at last encounter those businesses that perhaps epitomise the 'enterprise culture' of the 1980s and 1990s, the high-tech firms of the electronics, computer and related sectors (Rainnie, 1991:191–4; and Scase, 2003:483–6). Contrary to popular belief, however, many of these companies are in fact unionised. In a survey of Scottish electronics plants, for example, 70 per cent of employees worked in establishments where trade unions were recognised (Sproull and MacInnes, 1987:335). In a more comprehensive study using data from the second Workplace Industrial Relations Survey (1984), Beaumont and Harris

(1988a:833–4) found that the extent of union recognition was actually *higher* in 'high tech' than 'non-high tech' industries for domestically-owned establishments (both for manual and non-manual employees). In the case of foreign-owned companies, however, the reverse was true, especially in relation to manual employees (ibid). In the media, most notably television, unions might seem alien in the new 'virtual world' of freelance engineers, camera crews and other staff who sell their skills and innovative talents to broadcasting companies who are little more than commissioning agents for programmes made by small-scale enterprises (Davis and Scase, 2000; and Scase, 2003:483). But unions such as BECTU have been quite effective in retaining membership among freelance workers and skill shortages have encouraged some broadcasters and programme makers to bring such workers back 'in-house' (see Saundry, 2001). In general, employer responses to union organising activity tends to be more positive when directed at professional as opposed to (skilled) manual workers or machine operatives (Heery and Simms, 2003). Moreover, given that many small, innovative (non-union) companies in high-tech sectors or the media are subject to predatory take-over by larger (unionised) companies, the effect of small-firm/large-firm relationships, over time, is perhaps more likely to result in unionisation among the innovative small-firm sector, rather than a perpetuation of non-union status (as in the previous three groups identified).

While Rainnie's fourfold categorisation of dependent, dominated, isolated and innovative firms allows us to distinguish a greater variety of relationships that SMEs experience, Curran (1990:130) argues that there is still a tendency, overall, for observers to suggest a subordinate or subservient role. Put differently, autonomy may in practice be greater than is often assumed among the small-firm sector (see also Ram, 1991 and 1994). This can be illustrated by the juxtaposing of Atkinson's (1984) model of the 'flexible firm' and Piore and Sabel's (1984) model of 'flexible specialisation'. In the former, small firms are seen as part of the periphery, involved in a dependent relationship with large firms for whom they provide numerical flexibility or lower costs as a result of 'distancing' (the replacement of an employment contract with a commercial contract, possibly via self-employment and labour-only sub-contracting). In the 'flexible specialisation' model, in contrast, small, craft-based firms are presented as a *complement to* or even an *alternative to*, rather than an appendage of, large firms, able to compete with the mass production techniques of large firms through the use of new technology (which lowers minimum efficient scale) and co-operative (network) relations with other small firms in the locality. Thus, a shift from a Fordist to a post-Fordist model of production (purportedly) implies a symbiotic and co-operative relationship between large (buyer) and small (supplier) firms (as opposed to a competitive and dependent relationship) (see Barrett and Rainnie, 2002:421). Although there are both conceptual and empirical problems with both models (see Pollert, 1988), the contrast between the subordinate, peripheral firm (more likely to be non-union) and the craft-based firm (more likely to be unionised) serves to highlight still further the possible roles and relationships that can influence employee relations in small firms. The skills of the workforce, for example, is just one of the characteristics that plays a key role in non-union employee relations (see, for example, Scase, 2003:478).

The structural characteristics of non-union firms and the composition of the workforce

Although 'single shot' pictures taken from cross-sectional surveys are, in many respects, unsatisfactory for the analysis of dynamic and diachronic processes of employee relations, they nevertheless provide a rich source of data on the *general* characteristics of non-union firms. This enables us to say whether, on the whole, non-union firms are more likely to be, for example, large or small, and employ predominantly manual or non-manual workers, men or women, full-time or part-time staff. Data from the Workplace Employee Relations Survey (1998) confirms the results of previous surveys that indicate that, *ceteris paribus*, non-union establishments are more likely to be small, single-plant rather than multi-establishment undertakings, and located in the private sector (and especially private services) rather than the public sector. For example, less than 40 per cent of workplaces with 25–49 employees recognise a trade union compared with 78 per cent of workplaces with 500 or more employees (Cully *et al.*, 1999:92; see also Cully and Woodland, 1996:223; Millward *et al.*, 1992:64; and Scott *et al.*, 1989:17). It is hardly surprising, then, that union membership is extremely low in industries such as clothing where over 50 per cent of firms employ fewer than twenty-five workers and nearly 90 per cent of all firms employ fewer than 125 workers (Rainnie, 1989:89–9). Likewise, in hotels and restaurants only 7 per cent of workplaces recognise a trade union (Cully *et al.*, 1999:92). Data from all three WIRS and WERS98 are presented in Table 9.1. A particularly interesting result from these surveys is that, as expected, older workplaces are more likely to recognise trade unions and have a higher union density (independent of size) but the rate of recognition among new workplaces has been much lower (see Disney *et al.*, 1995), indicating a 'cohort effect' (i.e. new businesses established during the 'Thatcher years' are far less likely to recognise unions) (Cully *et al.*, 1999:24). This effect has persisted, with the likelihood of recognition substantially less in 1998 than in 1990 (Millward *et al.*, 2000:101–3).

Locality also plays an important part in union or non-union status. The latter establishments, for example, are more likely to be located in areas of high unemployment (Millward *et al.*, 1992:63–4). Geographical sub-systems are generally overlooked in the study of industrial and employee relations, although it is often suggested that the decline of major conurbations – the heartland of union

Table 9.1 Non-unionism by sector and size

(a) Sector – percentage of establishments that do not recognise a trade union for collective bargaining (and percentage of establishments with no union members)

	1980	1984	1990	1998
All establishments	36 (27)	34 (27)	47 (36)	55 (46)
Private manufacturing	35 (23)	44 (33)	56 (42)	* (58)
Private services	59 (50)	56 (47)	64 (54)	* (65)
Public sector	6 (1)	1 (–)	13 (1)	5 (3)

Note: * 75% of all private sector establishments did not recognise a union in 1998

(b) Size: non unionism in private sector establishments (percentage of establishments that do not recognise a trade union)

	1980	1984	1990	1998
Workplace size				
25–49 employees	59	60	70	84
50–99 employees	51	51	60	77
100–199 employees	35	38	52	61
200–499 employees	25	34	31	46
500 or more employees	8	14	25	36

Source: Calculated from Cully *et al.* (1999:68 and 240) and Millward *et al.* (2000:85).

organisation and industrial militancy – and the growth of industry in new towns or semi-rural areas (Mason, 1991:74–6) can have a significant impact on employee relations (e.g. Handy, 1984:85; Lane, 1982; Massey, 1984; and Chapter 3). Bassett (1988:46), for example, notes that in Milton Keynes, the UK's fastest growing town in the mid to late 1980s, two-thirds of the local companies employed fewer than ten workers, two-thirds of all jobs were in the service sector, and around 80 per cent of all companies were non-union, a fact boldly advertised by the town's development corporation. Similarly, in a study of 411 companies in three new towns in Scotland (Glenrothes, Irvine and Livingston), over 86 per cent were non-union, a figure much higher than manufacturing in general (Beaumont and Cairns, 1987:14–15). On a regional basis, there is essentially a North-South divide when it comes to union membership and recognition. In 2002, for example, union density among full-time employees was 44 per cent in Wales and 43 per cent in the North East compared to just 23 per cent in the South East. If part-time workers are included then density levels fall to 40 per cent in Wales, 38 per cent in the North East and 21 per cent in the South East (*Labour Market Trends*, July 2003). Union recognition is also much higher in the North and lower in the South, and it is no coincidence that London and the South East have more small businesses and more rapid growth in the small business sector (SBS, 2003a).

Workforce characteristics are also notably different between union and non-union firms. The latter are more likely, *ceteris paribus*, to employ relatively fewer manual workers, more women, and a higher proportion of part-time staff (Cully *et al.*, 1999:254; and Millward *et al.*, 1992:63–4). In the clothing industry, for example, almost 88 per cent of the workforce is female (Rainnie, 1989:90). However, while trade unionism in the 1980s largely reflected a male-dominated labour market and work culture, with male-dominated private sector workplaces more likely to have union members than female-dominated workplaces, union presence in male-dominated workplaces plummeted between 1980 and 1998 whereas in female-dominated workplaces it stayed more or less constant (Millward *et al.*, 2000:85–6). In fact, by 1998 the differences between them had reversed in the private sector, with female-dominated workplaces more likely to have union members. As Millward *et al.* (2000:86) observe, 'Workplaces that had formed the bedrock for union membership in earlier decades, male-dominated workplaces, had not just become less common – they had also lost their appetite for unionism'.

Many non-union companies also rely on family or kin, who are often placed in key positions within the company (e.g. Moule, 1998:638; and Ram, 1991:609). In the small firms studied by Scott *et al.* (1989:47), almost half the workforce could be tied by bonds of kinship, thereby constituting a 'core' group of employees that the owner/manager could rely on. Family pressures are often brought to bear on the workers of small firms in a different way:

> Management in the clothing industry feels the necessity, but also the freedom, to impose discipline in their workers, particularly married women, from the word go. Taking advantage of the pressures on women brought to bear in trying to reconcile the dual roles of wife/mother and worker, management rely on this situation making women less likely to leave in response to poor wages and conditions. (Rainnie, 1989:119)

In other SMEs, management deliberately promote a 'family culture' to deter unionisation as well as control the labour process (see, for example, Dundon *et al.*, 1999).

Poor wages and conditions are a principal characteristic of small, non-union firms (McNabb and Whitfield, 2000). The owner/managers of small firms take a *deliberate* decision to pay lower wages (Craig *et al.*, 1985; and Phizacklea, 1987), recognising that there is a trade-off between lower pay and higher labour turnover but reconciling this trade-off through the employment of disadvantaged groups such as married women (e.g. Rainnie, 1989:119), ethnic minorities (e.g. Ram, 1991:605 and 1994:158–9) or young workers (Curran and Stanworth, 1981b:144), who are more stable, in employment terms, at lower levels of pay (due to their limited opportunities elsewhere) (see Cully *et al.*, 1999:254). Goss (1988 and 1991), for example, draws a contrast between non-union instant print shops that employ low-skilled, low-paid, predominantly younger workers, and unionised colour printing where skills are vital and the workforce older. Another important variable that distinguishes different types of small firms is ownership, with small, stand-alone firms more likely to pay low wages than establishments that are part of a larger organisation (small multiples) (see McNabb and Whitfield, 2000). The former are also far less likely to employ a personnel specialist on site, to recognise unions or use formal communication systems (Cully et al., 1999:257–68). More detailed studies of specific industrial sectors confirm these differences. Brown and Crossman (2000:215), for example, found that independently-owned hotels were significantly more likely to follow a short-term, cost minimisation strategy than hotels owned by national or international chains.

The idea, then, that workers deliberately choose to work for non-union companies because 'convenience of location, and generally the non-material satisfactions of working in them, more than outweigh any financial sacrifice involved' (Bolton, 1971:21), begins to appear somewhat suspect. As Curran and Stanworth (1981b:145) note, 'small firm workers did not so much self-select themselves into jobs as a result of possessing certain stable motivational patterns but rather developed a market situation in which their job choices were often highly circumscribed'. Many employees in non-union firms, for example, are unable to develop stable employment patterns when they are forced to work on a casual or seasonal basis, as in the hotel and catering industry (e.g. Macaulay and Wood, 1992:21), or even work 'off the cards' so that the employer can avoid statutory employment laws and national insurance contributions (e.g. Ram, 1991:605–6; and Scott et al., 1989:24–5 and 92). 'Voluntary resignations' are much higher in small private establishments, especially in hotels and restaurants where, on average, almost two-fifths of all employees leave their job every year (Cully et al., 1999:127–8). Self-employment may be the only option available to many seeking employment, and it comes as no surprise that ethnic minorities, married people and women with dependent children are more likely to be self-employed, or that many of the self-employed have a second job as an employee (see Daly, 1991; and Chapter 3).

All these characteristics of non-union firms and non-union workers are invariably set within a highly informal working environment. Informality begins with recruitment and extends right through the organisation, from communications and grievance handling to pay determination and the highly personalised, day-to-day relations between management and labour (Gilman et al., 2002; and Scott et al., 1989). In a large scale survey of SMEs, for example, Matlay (1999: 288) found that 92 per cent of micro business managers favoured an informal management style compared to 68 per cent of small business managers and just 24 per cent of managers working for medium-sized firms. For management, and of course the advocates of small non-union firms, the absence of bureaucracy is seen as a positive advantage, not least as reflected in very low levels of strike activity. The key advantage lies, however, not in the extent to which informality allows for more direct and flexible arrangements to suit the individual, but in the extent to which such arrangements serve to obscure the conflicts of interest inherent in the employment relationship – not least those prevailing in the small non-union firm. In fact, as Curran (1990:137–8) notes, employer-employee relations in small firms are based on a contradiction likely to lead to *permanent* instability: small firms find themselves in largely dependent relations with big firms and are therefore more susceptible to (i.e. less able to control) the external, competitive environment; yet within the firm, relations tend to be highly personalised such that when change and conflict cannot be contained or handled through such informal relations, 'it erupts with an intensity that is absent in more formal, procedurally regulated relationships' (Scott *et al.*, 1989:61). Is the absence of strike activity, then, an indication of industrial harmony or employee powerlessness in small, non-union firms?

Informality and industrial harmony in the non-union sector

Collective action requires collective organisation (see Kelly, 1998). Working without unions has therefore enabled many large non-union companies to remain 'strike free' (see Bassett, 1986:161; and Sieff, 1990:84). Just as there has been little incentive for workers in companies such as Marks & Spencer, IBM or Hewlett Packard to join a trade union, there is little incentive to strike. But the idea of industrial harmony in non-union firms is associated more directly with smaller firms, where it is assumed that better communications, easier working relations, personal ties, job satisfaction, employee involvement and a greater awareness of individual needs serve to overcome any inherent tension between capital and labour. Low levels of union membership and very few strikes combine to suggest that 'small is beautiful'. As far as small-firm employee relations are concerned, however, this would seem to be a 'modern myth' (Rainnie 1985a:213–16 and 1989) that arises from a confusion of image and reality. The image presented by the Conservative Party, for example, in their pamphlet *Small Firm, Big Future*, is that,

> Working relationships are easier and happier in small companies. Many of the problems that arise in large enterprises are unknown in firms where the owner is known to all his employees. (quoted by Rainnie, 1985b:148)

Unfortunately, there is virtually no empirical evidence to support such claims (Goss, 1988:115; and Scase, 1995), and that which does exist (e.g. Ingham, 1970) is methodologically suspect (Curran and Burrows, 1986; Curran and Stanworth, 1981a; and Rainnie, 1989:156–70). Invariably, the suggestion that the firm is 'one big happy family' is derived from the opinions of owners/managers, rather than from the workforce (Curran and Stanworth, 1981a:14–15; and Goss, 1988:115, and 1991:158). In general, managers express a more positive (i.e. favourable) view on the 'climate' of employee relations in their organisation than either union representatives or employees (see Cully *et al.*, 1999:277; see also Bryson, 2001c). Moreover, managers seem to equate 'good employee relations' with outcomes such as financial performance and higher labour productivity (i.e. where the organisation achieves the latter then managers are more likely to proclaim 'good employee relations') whereas workers are more likely to view employee relations in a positive light if they feel secure, have some influence over their work and are committed to their job, and in particular if they are 'fairly' treated (Cully *et al.*, 1999:277–81). It is well established that union members tend to be less satisfied with their jobs and pay than non-union members, but most of this satisfaction differential can be accounted for by differences in the demographic, job and workplace characteristics of the two groups (Bryson *et al.*, 2002). As Gilman *et al.* (2002:62) discovered, many non-union workers are 'not necessarily satisfied in some absolute sense, but given their skills and labour market options, they had found some consolation'. Thus, quiescence need not imply individual deference, nor does the absence of strike activity imply the eradication of industrial conflict (see Chapter 10). It is essential, therefore, to delve further into the social relations of production within small, non-union firms, and in particular to elicit the opinions of the workforce.

One of the most striking features of small, non-union firms, as already intimated, is the informality of employee relations. In their study of 397 small firms, for example, Scott *et al.* (1989:16) found that 61 per cent had no regular meetings with workforce representatives, and 44 per cent had no arrangements for informing or consulting employees through informal meetings or internal memos (see also Cully *et al.*, 1999:257–8; Matlay, 1999:288; and Millward *et al.*, 1992:364–5). Informality is, of course, a dynamic rather than a fixed characteristic of small firms (i.e. it is a matter of degree, rather than the total absence of formality) and it is highly context specific (see Cully *et al.*, 1999:272; and Ram *et al.*, 2001:846). Nonetheless, as Gunnigle and Brady (1984:23) conclude from their study of 25 small manufacturing firms, 'there seems to be a dangerous perception of complacency about communications and consultation in small firms. Owner/managers place emphasis on the frequency of employer/employee contact rather than on the quality of such contacts'. If problems arise, these will also be settled informally, as less than a third of the firms studied by Scott *et al.* (1989:16), for example, had a formal, written grievance procedure (see also Millward *et al.*, 1992:364). As expected, larger firms were more likely to have formal procedures, as were those that were unionised (Scott *et al.*, 1989:16–17; see also Earnshaw *et al.*, 2000:63–4). In sum, procedural informality characterises the small, non-union sector to a much greater extent than either the unionised or large, non-union sector. Figure 9.1 summarises the principal differences between union and non-union, large and small firms (see also Millward *et al.*, 1992:236–9).

The notion of small firms being 'one big happy family' is, of course, a cliché, 'and yet as with all clichés it contains a grain of truth' (Scott *et al.*, 1989:51). The significant presence of family members within small firms has already been noted.

Figure 9.1 Pay, benefits and working arrangements in union versus non-union finances

	UNION		NON-UNION	
	Large	**Small**	**Large**	**Small**
Pay system	Formalised system	Industry agreement	Formalised system	Informal
Differentials	Continuous and extensive pay hierarchy, few on industry minimum	Relatively continuous	Wide differentials, many pay 'industry standard' or above	Discontinuous, narrow differentials, now pay National Minimum Wage
Sick pay/ Pensions	Common, non-discretionary	Pensions uncommon, sick pay mainly for key staff	Common, but often restricted to specific groups	Pensions uncommon, sick pay for key staff
Holidays	Industry standard or better	Industry standard	Industry standard or low minimum entitlement increasing with grade/ service	Low entitlement for all grades, often below industry standard
Job guarantees	Collective agreement at industry or local level	Industry agreement/ statutory measures	None (statutory measures only)	None (statutory measures only)
Staffing agreements	Formal/informal deals	Industry agreement/ informal bargaining	Determined by management prerogative	Determined by management prerogative
Training systems	Formal (linked to state schemes)	Recruit skilled workers externally or formal (linked to state schemes)	Formal (linked to state schemes)	Recruit externally trained or informal/firm-specific training

Source: Adapted from Rubery (1987:62–3).

More generally, personal relations tend to become employee or industrial relations in small firms. In the building industry, for example, where market conditions are highly unstable, employers frequently adopt a *fraternal* strategy with few overtly hierarchical relations. Instead, the employer will adopt an 'all workers together' attitude, for example working alongside his employees on the job (see Goffee and Scase, 1982; and Scase, 1995:587–8). Thus, it is the *particularistic* relations that develop between employer and employee that demand attention. Like family relations, feelings of 'good' and 'ill' tend to be more intensely held in small firms (Holiday, 1995:157; and Scott *et al.*, 1989:42 and 51), as Rainnie (1989:127–8) illustrates:

> Management stress on the 'family' nature of their own firm and relationships within it, not only points to the way in which a particular social formation is used to legitimate power structures (manager-as-father allowed to discipline the children/workers), but also the way that disagreement can be termed pathological. The ideological power of the family is such that attacking this sacred institution is almost unthinkable within the ruling consensus. Likewise, anybody breaking the managerially defined boundaries of decent behaviour in a family firm, by definition steps out of the bounds of acceptable action.

The appearance of industrial harmony thus begins to appear somewhat suspect once the reality of (authority) relations between employer and employee within small, non-union firms is analysed more closely. When workers in small firms are questioned about relations with their employer, for example, they invariably report 'socially distant' relations (Curran and Stanworth, 1981b:148; see also Goss, 1988 and 1991; and Moule, 1998). Relations are often not overtly hostile, but 'it would be wrong to see such relations as necessarily tokening deep and strong affective relations between workers and bosses' (Curran and Stanworth, 1981b:149). Rather, 'friendship' and easy-going relations are simply the easiest way to deal with others in a closed environment. Conflict may therefore be 'submerged' in small firms due to the need to manage inter-group conflicts on a personal basis (Stephenson *et al.*, 1983:33). But herein lies the source of instability: such relations may achieve a degree of integration and a veneer of industrial harmony, but 'if the basis of legitimacy is relationships other than those stemming purely from the employment relationship, their continuance is threatened by change. Change of many types can pull back the veil of obscurity and reveal the unmediated effect of the employment relationship' (Scott *et al.*, 1989:48–9).

Even the 'happy family' owner/manager will change his tune when confronted by external pressures or internal dissent. Scott *et al.* (1989:50), for example, refer to one manager who boasted of his caring, paternalistic approach which he illustrated by reference to two older workers allowed to stay on at the firm beyond their retirement age. At a subsequent interview, however, he referred to these two workers in less affectionate terms. In the interim period, profits had fallen and the company had gone into the red for the first time. The result had been redundancies, including the two older workers who were now described in terms of 'getting rid of the shit'. As this and other examples cited by Scott *et al.* (1989:50) illustrate, it is not uncommon for the advantages of family and affective ties to turn into their opposites, into feelings which can border upon enmity (ibid:52). If an employee is not performing satisfactorily, for example, the owner/manager is initially just as likely to have a word with the employee's friend or a family member in order to put pressure on the offending party. Scott and his colleagues even cite the case of one employer who had a quiet word with an employee's husband at the local pub! If this approach fails, however, the owner/manager may not apply disciplinary action; instead, problems are often left to fester until critical rather than corrective action is taken (i.e. dismissal rather than discipline) (ibid:92; see also Earnshaw *et al.*, 2000). Most small employers are (blissfully) ignorant of workers' individual employment rights – most appear to operate on a 'need to know' basis (e.g. when they need to dismiss a worker or when an employee brings a claim of unfair dismissal) (see Blackburn and Hart, 2002). Disciplinary sanctions and dismissals are much lower in unionised firms compared to non-union firms (Cully *et al.*, 1999:128; Knight and Latreille, 2000; and Millward *et al.*, 1992:364). In 1998, the average workplace in the hotels and restaurant sector had dismissed a quite astonishing 5.9 employees in every 100 during the previous year (compared to the average for all workplaces of 1.5 dismissals per 100 employees and just 0.6 in education) (Cully *et al.*, 1999:128). In many cases, non-union employees in small workplaces are dismissed without statutory notice or even fair grounds (see Dickens *et al.*, 1985; and Earnshaw *et al.*, 2000). The burgeoning number of work-related complaints made to Citizens' Advice Bureaux come predominantly from non-unionists, mainly those employed in small workplaces (see Abbott, 1998:259–60).

For this reason, and of course the generally poorer conditions of work and pay in small, non-union firms, there is a good deal of 'churning' among the workforce (Cully *et al.*, 1999:128; and Scott *et al.*, 1989:30). Numbers may be fairly stable, but there is a high rate of entry and exit. In the clothing industry, for example, labour turnover is high where firms deliberately adopt a 'like it or leave' approach (Rainnie, 1985a). As at Sew & Son, many decide, or are forced, to leave. Many more have little alternative but to stay. Exit and/or silence, then, rather than voice, is the most likely scenario. Most employees in small, non-union firms lack the articulateness and self-confidence to challenge, or even question, the self-assured, and often highly opinionated owner/manager (Cully *et al*, 1999:257–8; and Goss, 1991:165), and even if they do, managers either fail to listen or do nothing about it (Scott *et al.*, 1989:45). Knowing this, many employees see it as pointless to complain. This powerlessness is often combined with enforced compliance which in some companies 'is made an explicit condition of continued employment, and the threat of dismissal kept ever-present' (Goss, 1991:161). As Scott *et al.* (1989:39) note, 'those who did not support management aims and policy were seen not only to be unreasonable, but also as being in some way treacherous'. The language may be strong (non-compliance as treachery), but such views are deeply held by many owners/managers of small businesses.

As a result, conflict is usually manifested in individual, invariably unorganised forms, such as absenteeism or high labour turnover. Edwards and Scullion's (1982:107, and 1984:561–2) account of two clothing firms is a case in point (see also Chapter 10). In some instances, workers' discontent is vented on other individuals, or groups of workers, rather than through direct confrontation with its source, the company or proprietors (see Moule, 1998:645). Such forms of 'displaced resistance' or 'lateral conflict' (Burawoy, 1979) are all the more likely in the absence of collective (trade union) support as individuals are understandably reluctant to challenge management directly (e.g. Goss, 1991:165; and Rainnie, 1985a:219), especially as they will almost inevitably be labelled as 'troublemakers'. Owners/ managers blame so-called 'troublemakers' for virtually all their labour ills, ranging from high turnover (unsettling staff), provoking unfair dismissal cases and encouraging absenteeism (Gunnigle and Brady, 1984:22; and Scott et al., 1989:42). More generally,

> The notion of the 'trouble maker' appears far too often to be dismissed merely as an interesting but insignificant feature of management accounts of the nature of their workforce. Rather, the importance of this notion is that it serves as an element within a *conflict neutralisation* technique. (Scott et al., 1989:42, original emphasis)

In other words, the unitary perspective adopted by management serves to *personalise* conflict within the organisation (problems are attributed to individuals, not to inherent antagonisms that exist between management and labour in *all* organisations). While most managers are unitarist in outlook (see Chapter 4), such views appear to be more deeply held by the owner/managers of small firms. Since they fail to recognise or accept *any* conflicts of interest as being legitimate, such attitudes play an important role in both the determination of management style in non-union firms and the (in)ability of trade unions to organise such companies.

Management style in non-union firms

One of the problems which besets many discussions of non-union firms and workers is that they tend to be studied predominantly from the perspective of the propensity of workers to unionise and/or the differences in management practice *vis-à-vis* unionised firms. Consequently, 'the very term non-unionism becomes a limiting definition of workplaces' (Guest and Hoque, 1994:2) which tend to 'fall' into one of either two principal 'types': 'traditionalists' who display outright hostility towards trade unions, or 'sophisticated paternalists' whose management policies effectively 'substitute' for union presence (see Turnbull and Wass, 1997b). As Purcell and Sisson (1983:113) point out, sophisticated paternalists might refuse to recognise trade unions, 'but do not take it for granted that their employees accept the company's objectives or automatically legitimise management decision-making; they spend considerable time and resources ensuring that their employees have the right approach'. Sew & Son would obviously be counted as a 'traditionalist' whereas Marks & Spencer is often cited as the archetypical 'sophisticated paternalist'. The distinction between *anti*-union (suppression) and *non*-union (substitution) firms, however, is a somewhat false dichotomy. Sophisticated paternalists display an apparent indifference towards trade unions because, first, they can afford to, and secondly because they rarely face any challenge from organised labour. If they are challenged, however, management are always quick to act and firm in their resolution to remain non-union.

In the IBM recognition vote in the UK in 1977, for example, which Bassett (1986:162–4) cites as evidence of both employee indifference towards trade unions and the effectiveness of the company's employee relations policies, IBM spent £10 000 on an advertising campaign to secure a 'NO' vote (Beaumont, 1987:121; see also Oliver and Wilkinson, 1992:125–6), a fact which Bassett fails to acknowledge, or perhaps conveniently overlooked. According to Dickson *et al.* (1988), even IBM employees may not be permanently lost to the trade union movement, a point perhaps reinforced by the company's recent troubles. McDonald's is another case in point (Royle, 1999 and 2000). M&S recently faced an organising campaign by USDAW among warehouse staff following the imposition of a three-year pay freeze. This was to bring the salary of (predominantly female) sales staff into line with those of (predominantly male) warehouse staff (by increasing the former by 26.5 per cent and freezing the latter), following an 'equal pay for work of equal value' case at Sainsbury's in November 1989. M&S accepted the right of warehouse staff to join a union but would not grant recognition, and certainly would not countenance the workers' claim to have their pay freeze cancelled. USDAW has accused M&S of victimising union members in one of its Glasgow depots by introducing 'unworkable shifts', with start times too early for employees to use public transport, an allegation M&S vigorously disputed (Hamil, 1993:43). M&S recognised trade unions in their European stores, however, which the company attributed to employment legislation and industrial relations practices in these countries which 'required' M&S to deal with trade unions (Salsbury, 1993:569). Industrial action at the company's stores in Dublin over pay, shift patterns and consultation procedures, however, suggests that 'internal' rather than purely 'external' factors are at work, illustrating yet again the highly *contingent* nature of management style discussed in Chapter 4.

If faced with a challenge, then, sophisticated paternalists can display vehement opposition to union organisation. It is at such times that the asymmetry of the employment relationship is revealed. As Hamil (1993:43) notes, few other companies would have the power to impose the kind of deal implemented at M&S in response to the equal value case, at least not without significant employee opposition. Management policy is clearly directed towards the maintenance of an employee relations system that does not include trade unions, which is one thing that the sophisticated paternalists have in common with the traditionalists. In the case of M&S and other 'sophisticated paternalists', however, management thinking is effectively pluralist to the extent that management recognise the need to manage employee relations *as if* the workforce has divergent interests. In this way, management is able to identify concerns, allay fears, satisfy workers' aspirations *and stay non-union*. Actual policies, of course, are to all intents and purposes unitary in both composition and purpose, but are founded on a deeper management understanding of the employment relationship. At companies such as Sew & Son, in contrast, management thinking is unashamedly unitarist, but employee relations policies are often imposed *against* the express wishes of the workforce. Given that actual policies are often implemented through coercion, it is more appropriate to label the management style as 'authoritarian': if all the organisation's members are on the 'same side' and part of a team, as the unitary perspective holds, then surely management would only need to *inform* employees of its policies, not enforce them.

Such characteristics of management style among small, non-union firms in the clothing industry are not uncommon (Rainnie, 1985a, and 1989:168). Likewise, in hotels and restaurants, management style tends to be highly autocratic and strongly anti-union (Brown and Crossman, 2000; Hoque, 2000; Macaulay and Wood, 1992:21; and Macfarlane, 1982:33–4). Variation obviously exists across different hotels, and in particular between the large chains and smaller independent hotels, but there is a common framework within which different management styles function, namely 'a framework which is reluctant to accept the legitimacy of employees taking any meaningful part in the influence or control of their working conditions or environment' (Macfarlane, 1982:34; see also Millward *et al.*, 1992:365). More general studies of non-union firms confirm management attitudes to be a mixture of unitarism, paternalism and authoritarianism (e.g. Gilman *et al.*, 2002; Gollan, 2001; Gunnigle and Brady, 1984:21–2; Matlay, 1999; Scase, 2003:481; and Scott *et al.*, 1989). The former has already been discussed at some length in Chapters 2 and 4. Paternalism, as the nomenclature suggests, has traditionally been based on a transfer of family/domestic relations into the workplace, with face-to-face relations between management and labour characterised by deference and indulgency (workers were treated as children to be looked after, rewarded and disciplined by their employer as a parent would a child) (Wray, 1996:702; see also Ackers, 1998). This benevolent form of despotism is typical of many small firms (see Scase, 1995:285; and Wray, 1996:702). To sustain paternalistic relations as firms grow in size, formal consultation and communication procedures are adopted and indulgency is maintained by corporate largesse through profit-sharing schemes and other benefits (at M&S, for example, benefits include subsidised meals, medical care, hairdressing, store discount cards and the like). Sophisticated paternalism thereby remains loyal to the familial culture of traditional paternalism, but only in an attempt to maintain employee subordination (Wray, 1996:703–4). At the heart of all forms of paternalism, in other words, is a over-riding desire to perpetuate managerial authority.

The principal reason for unitarist attitudes and paternalistic and/or autocratic management practices in small firms appears to be possessiveness. Owner-managers in particular regard *their* company as unique and regard themselves as benign, fair, even-handed and reasonable (Scott *et al.*, 1989:36). 'Typically the business is seen as his possession to do as he wishes – and especially where the owner/manager is also the founder. It is important to realise that for many owner/managers the business is essentially an extension of their ego' (ibid:91). Many members of the UK's 'petty bourgeoisie' (broadly defined as those who own small-scale capital which is used for productive purposes in conjunction with the proprietor's and, often, others' labour) (Scase, 1982:148), 'show strong psychological inclinations towards notions of autonomy and independence, and this is often translated into an organisational form to ensure their maximisation' (Curran and Burrows, 1986:270; see also Ford, 1982:45–6). As Cully *et al.* (1999:257–8) found, almost three-quarters of small business managers, and especially owner-managers, strongly believe that 'those at the top are best placed to make decisions about this workplace'. Not surprisingly, these managers are more likely to favour direct forms of control (ibid). In short, owners/managers not only believe in, but often impose their primacy over the labour process (Scott *et al.*, 1989:93). The implications for employee relations are immediately apparent. Not only will the personality of the owner/manager have a major impact on management style, but the owner's/manager's desire for independence and autonomy 'often result in ill-defined organisational structures with poorly defined roles, a high level of centralised decision-making and little forward planning. For employees the result may be feelings of lack of security and involvement' (Curran, 1990:138).

Generally, management policy in small firms is not formulated in a self-conscious way, relying instead on informal routinisation. This is especially true of labour relations policies, where there is little evidence of pre-planning: 'The dominant approach is one that stresses that as long as the workers are working there is no problem' (Scott *et al.*, 1989:34). There is some evidence that, in hotels at least, some managers have embraced a more strategic approach to HRM (Hoque, 2000) and many more have been compelled by the introduction of a National Minimum Wage (NMW) to think more strategically (Brown and Crossman, 2000:210). However, the dominant response has been one of cost minimisation, combined with numerical flexibility and union avoidance (ibid), and most small firms operate with sufficient indeterminacy to allow them to absorb the costs of the NMW (Arrowsmith *et al.*, 2003; and Gilman *et al.*, 2002:54). This helps to explain the apparent 'paradox' of an increase in wages (via the NMW) resulting in only modest employment effects (ibid).

Differences between small, non-union firms will of course be inevitable. Guest and Hoque (1994), for example, differentiate (newly-established) non-union firms according to whether or not the company has a human resource strategy on the one hand, and the nature of human resource policy and practice, on the other. This gives rise to a four-fold classification of 'good' non-union employers that have a clear human resource strategy and positive human resource management policies; 'lucky' non-union companies that have opportunistically followed the latest 'fads and fashions' of human resource management; 'bad' non-union companies that have no strategy and a low uptake of human resource policies; and the 'ugly' face of non-unionism represented by employers who (strategically) deprive workers of their rights and exploit their labour. In a sample of 122 non-union firms studied by Guest and Hoque, only 8 could be described as 'ugly' whereas 56 were 'good' employers. The comparatively high number of 'good' employers, in marked contrast to the picture suggested by successive WIRS and WERS98, is no doubt partly attributable to the 'self-selecting', rather than representative, nature of the sample. One might expect 'good' non-union firms with more sophisticated employee relations policies to be small 'high tech' firms in the 'innovative' group identified by Rainnie (1989:85, and 1991:188), but in fact most tended to be found in the non-financial service sector rather than manufacturing (Guest and Hoque, 1994:6–7). A major deficiency of this study, however, is that employees were not asked whether their employer was good, bad, or ugly.

In a specific study of high-tech companies, McLoughlin and Gourlay (1992:673–4) consider management style along two different dimensions, namely individualism-collectivism (as discussed in Chapter 4) and the extent of 'strategic integration' (essentially the extent to which company policies achieve a 'tight coupling' between strategic intent, management attitudes and actual behaviour or, at the other extreme, are largely informal, idiosyncratic, unco-ordinated or even contradictory). McLoughlin and Gourlay were concerned to establish the extent to which a sophisticated human resource management (HRM) strategy, such as that deemed to characterise companies such as IBM and Hewlett Packard, was pursued by non-union companies in this sector. The picture that emerged from a detailed study that included 23 non-union companies was that the companies most closely approximating to such an approach all employed fewer than 500 workers, employed predominantly non-manual labour (less than 20 per cent were manual workers in 8 of the 10 companies in this group), half had been established since 1979, and the majority were non-assembly/manufacturing plants (ibid:679). Overall, the conclusion was that 'non-union status was likely to be the result of straightforward avoidance or opportunism as any HRM-derived sophisticated substitution strategy designed to obviate a perceived need for union representation on the part of employees' (ibid:685). Put differently, companies such as M&S and IBM are very much the exception rather than the rule among non-union firms: most non-union firms do not *need*, nor could the majority *afford*, to adopt a substitution strategy.

Given the market position of most sophisticated paternalists, these companies are improbable 'role models' for most managers. Equally for trade unions in the UK, companies such as M&S and IBM remain an attractive, but unlikely prize. The reality that trade unions must confront, and the problems they must overcome if they want to organise the growing ranks of non-union employees, are those that characterise the more traditional firms such as Sew & Son. Whether such companies are non-union as a result of deliberate avoidance or simply pragmatic opportunism (or indeed lack of attention by union recruiters), the question that remains to be answered is whether employees in such companies would be receptive to unionisation.

Organising the unorganised

As the debate on the future of trade unionism shifts from analysis of decline to prognosis for growth, attention has focused on the prospects for new union strategies to organise in the expanding service sector of the economy (see Chapter 5). During the 1980s, the structure of trade unions in the UK was exposed as seemingly inappropriate, or incapable, of dealing with many of the changes thrown up by economic restructuring and recession, government legislation and employer hostility. This was especially so in the service sector, the new towns and the small-firm sector where union organising attempts were often duplicated (and diluted) and where unions were often unable to present potential members with a single, and clearly identifiable 'appropriate' union (Winchester, 1988:509). In hotels and catering, for example, the T&GWU and the Hotel and Catering Workers' Union (HCU) (a specialist union spawned by the GMB in 1980) competed for members. But within the T&GWU, hotels came under the Food, Drink and Tobacco division and officials simply did not know enough about the industry to recruit effectively. The HCU, on the other hand, adopted a 'softly, softly', non-confrontational approach, trying to build up membership by persuasion and establishing some confidence in the union among the management of larger hotel chains (Macaulay and Wood, 1992:22–3; and Macfarlane, 1982:35). Inappropriate structures and an ineffective approach to recruitment have led to the unions' role being characterised as one of 'studied invisibility', and it comes as no surprise that very few employees (only 15 per cent in one study) could even name the appropriate unions involved in the industry (Macaulay and Wood, 1992:23–5).

To recruit non-union members in the vast majority of non-union firms will require what Kelly and Heery (1989:198–9) classify as a 'distant expansion' recruitment strategy (see Chapter 5 for a more detailed review). Such firms are not covered by recognition agreements (unlike distribution, for example, where union membership is low but there is at least union recognition in place), and are outside most unions' traditional areas of recruitment (unlike non-union white-collar staff in manufacturing). This presents a much wider, and more difficult, range of problems that unions must overcome if they are to attract new members. Obstacles to expanding membership in new job territories include high rates of labour turnover, the small size of many establishments, their geographical dispersion, and in particular employer opposition (ibid:199; see also Dundon *et al.*, 1999:262; Gall and McKay, 2001; Gollan, 2001; Green, 1992:456; Heery and Simms, 2003; Macaulay and Wood, 1992:27; and Turnbull, 1997 and 2003:505). In hotels and restaurants, for example, employer antipathy puts trade unions 'in a Catch 22 situation where, in order to appear a credible source of representation to employees, they must demonstrate an ability to participate meaningfully in the process of job regulation, but this can only be achieved where the employer has conceded sufficient recognition rights' (Macfarlane, 1982:30). The latter is now regulated by a statutory recognition procedure (see Chapters 5 and 6), but many studies have still found that 'Everything turns ... on the orientation of employers' (Colling, 2003:387; see also Heery and Simms, 2003).

Without recognition from the employer, union effectiveness is more difficult (though not impossible) to establish and certainly more costly to maintain. As Willman (1989:263) argues, pre-recognition representation is more expensive as the union is at best only allowed individual representation rights (e.g. in discipline or dismissal cases). Recognition allows some of the representation costs to be shifted on to the employer, which means that unions typically seek to operate in *two* markets, one for members and one for employers. In small firms the market for employers is particularly important since access to employees is more difficult to secure and the union must establish independent workplace organisation (participative self-organisation) if it operates only in the membership market (see Chapter 5). Invariably, therefore, 'unions will not seek to organise employees where they see no prospect of gaining bargaining rights, since they must deal only with individual issues which are costly' (ibid). Thus, unions seek to offer something to the employer as well as the employee, as Figure 9.2 demonstrates.

Willman (1989) argued that 'market share unionism', where unions compete for a declining membership base in already organised sectors, rather than expand their membership in areas such as the private services sector (distant recruitment), was inevitable given the hostility of employers, the costly nature of such recruitment, the financial weakness of most British unions and the absence of legal recognition procedures that unions could use to force recognition on a recalcitrant employer. Even though a statutory union recognition procedure is now in place (Employment Relations Act, 1999), a considerable number of employers continue to resist union organising and recruitment campaigns, and some 'are prepared to resort to nakedly unethical behaviour to prevent workers forming unions' (Heery and Simms, 2003:6). Moreover, employers continue to exploit competition between unions, responding to union organising campaigns by inviting other (more pliant) unions to put forward a counter-proposal (ibid).

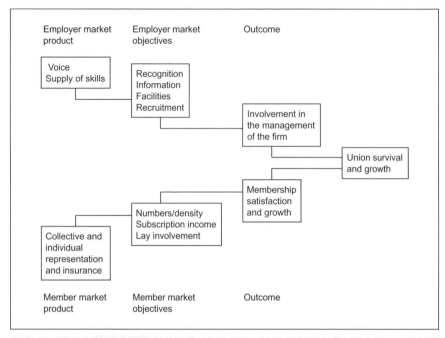

Source: Willman (1989:264).

Figure 9.2 The market for trade unionism

Although the 'logic' of market-share trade unionism continues to frustrate union revival, it is, of course, inherently *illogical* for the labour movement as a whole to have destructive competition for membership. This can be overcome, because the 'logic' of market-share unionism rests on two preconditions. The first is an absence of structures, procedures or a central body with sufficient authority to effect co-ordination and co-operation between individual unions. A good illustration of these problems was the Special Review Body (SRB) set up by the TUC in 1987. Under the auspices of the SRB, Congress conducted six pilot studies of local labour markets in order to facilitate new membership recruitment. These studies revealed striking deficiencies in the internal information systems of many unions, limited knowledge of the key organisational and workforce characteristics of non-union firms, and strictly limited attempts to recruit many non-union workers (see Beaumont and Harris, 1990:276). But while the diagnosis of the problem was accepted by the major unions, they were not prepared to accept a more 'intrusive' (proactive or co-ordinating) role on the part of the TUC.

In some respects, the authority of the TUC has declined in recent years (Ackers *et al.*, 1996:27), although the 'relaunch' of the TUC in the mid 1990s has resulted in a more strategic approach to a series of campaigns based on 'partnership' and the building of supporting coalitions. Thus, instead of simply seeking greater control and direction over affiliates, the TUC has become a networking organisation

(Heery, 1998:346). Equally important, under the *New Unionism* initiative launched in 1996 an Organising Academy has been established by the TUC to train union organisers in the techniques of the organising model discussed in Chapter 5. Dedicated organisers will target non-union workplaces and non-union workers, particularly women, young workers and ethnic minorities, disseminate 'best practice', and above all promote an 'organising culture' where recruitment and organising are regarded by everyone in the labour movement as a key priority. Private service sector workers, where union membership is lowest, are a key target. As Korczynski (2002) points out, there are particular features of service sector work that must be acknowledged and incorporated into the organising model if it is to prove successful, especially for the recruitment of 'front-line' (customer-contact) workers. In particular, the unions' role must not simply be 'anti-employer' as it is often perceived to be when unions follow the organising model (see Chapter 5), but also 'pro-customer'. As Table 9.2 highlights, unions should seek to civilise

Table 9.2   Three union approaches to organising front-line service workers

	Partnership approach	**Organising approach**	**Organising on the front line**
Who to organise?	Focus recruitment efforts on core workers in organisations in which unions have a presence	Bring in members from occupations and workplaces with little union presence, target both core and contingent workers	Recognise limited union presence in many service firms, focus on non-union workers and workplaces
What interests to prioritise?	Common interests with management, e.g. pay to hire and keep good workers, training and development	Issues of conflict with management, e.g. low pay, safety, work intensification	Issues of direct concern to front-line workers, e.g. definitions of 'customer care' or 'emotional labour'
How to organise and represent interests?	Representative democracy; relatively passive members with union official engaged in bargaining and 'back-stage' discussions with management	Participative democracy; active role for members at workplace level in mobilising to force concessions from management	Build union organisation around centralised nodes of consumption; use company rhetoric of customer service to mobilise customer support
The ideology of unionism	'Stakeholder' in the organisation and wider society	Class and community organisations	Civilising force in both production and consumption

Source: Adapted from Korczynski (2002:179).

production *and* consumption, thereby connecting more directly with the interests of front-line workers (ibid:188–9).

The second precondition for the logic of market-share trade unionism to prevail is a dependence on employers. One of the dilemmas facing all trade unions is that, over time, organisational survival is increasingly separated from, and is largely independent of, the motivation, mobilisation, solidarity and 'willingness to act' of the rank-and-file membership. In effect, the union substitutes external guarantees of survival – employer recognition and check-off arrangements, statutory recognition procedures and strong political ties to social democratic parties – for internal dependence on its members. As Offe and Wiesenthal (1980:107) point out, unions invariably develop bureaucratic structures in order to maximise the independence of the union's officials and their control over internal decision-making on the one hand, and a more 'individualistic' relationship with rank-and-file members on the other, emphasising individual incentives to join (for a review of these developments in the UK, see Heery and Kelly, 1994). The problem which then arises, of course, is that once the relative independence of the organisation from its members' 'willingness to act' has been achieved, 'the organization *no longer has any capacity to resist attempts to withdraw external support* and the externally provided legal and institutional status' (Offe and Wiesenthal, 1980:108, original emphasis). To date, previously non-union employers in the UK appear to have taken their lead from the change in public policy effected by the Employment Relations Act (1999) and have accepted union organising (Heery and Simms, 2003), but it must be acknowledged that statutory provisions can equally be used *against* trade unions. Certification law in the USA, for example, which is very similar to the new recognition procedure in the UK, was likewise passed originally to facilitate union organising and promote collective bargaining, but it frequently has the opposite effect as managers use the provisions of the law to derecognise existing unions or resist new recognition campaigns (see Adams, 2002; Brody, 2001; and HRW, 2000).

Even if unions can avoid or overcome these problems, two important questions still remain: will non-union workers want to join, and will non-union employers surrender their autonomy and authority? The answer to the first question is a resounding 'YES', *but only if unions can make a difference in the workplace*. The answer to the second question is a resounding 'NO'.

Workers in the UK want union representation. Around 40 per cent of non-union employees say they would join a union if one were available at their workplace (CEP, 2002; Charlwood, 2002:464; and TUC, 1996a). Moreover, the demand for union membership is highest in precisely those industries (e.g. wholesale and retail) where union density is lowest (CEP, 2002; see also Gallie, 1996; and Macaulay and Wood, 1992:26). Likewise, many part-timers (Labour Research Department, 1996:17; and Sinclair, 1996) and young people would like to join a union (TUC, 1996b). However, there is a profound lack of awareness of trade unions among many groups of workers, especially young people (ibid; and Roberts, 2003a), due in large part to the fact that they are simply never actively recruited or asked to join a union (see Cully et al., 1999; and Green, 1990). Other workers might be aware of unions and the benefits union membership might bring, but unions lack 'appeal' in terms of their structure, organisation and activities. Women, for example, 'benefit' considerably from union membership in terms of their wage premium (the union-negotiated 'mark-up' over comparable non-union jobs) and other benefits, unlike their male counterparts (Machin, 2001), but unions must do more than 'sell' these benefits to female workers if they are to increase their membership – they must also change their own gendered organisational structures and culture (Colgan and Ledwith, 2002; Cunninson and Stageman, 1995; Heery and Kelly, 1989; and Ledwith and Colgan, 1996). The most important constraint on union revival, however, appears to be workers' uncertainty about whether unions can 'deliver' (see Diamond and Freeman, 2001).

There is a significant difference between 'demand' (an expressed desire for unionism) and 'effective demand' (a 'willingness to pay' for union protection, benefits or services) (see Troy, 2001:254). Employer opposition can heavily weight the cost side of the equation, leaving workers to question whether the union can secure benefits in the face of the hostility of their employer. To be sure, once they become members, workers tend to support their union (see, for example, Diamond and Freeman, 2001:19) and the majority believes that their union does a good job and responds positively to their needs (Bryson, 1999:81). Data from WERS, for example, indicate that 46 per cent of trade unionists in Britain believe that unions 'make a difference to what it is like to work here' (compared to 30 per cent of non-unionists and 26 per cent of ex-unionists) (Cully et al., 1999:212–13) and data from the BSAS reveal that 49 per cent of respondents believe that the removal of union representation at their workplace would make things worse (Bryson, 1999:83). But this counts for nothing if unions cannot persuade workers to unionise or the employer to recognise. Many non-union workers are simply resigned to the fact that, while they might like to join a union, their employer would not 'allow' them.

Many workers continue to face victimisation by their employer when they attempt to form a union (Heery and Simms, 2003; see also Chapter 5). This is a particular problem when unions attempt to organise small, owner-managed firms (ibid; see Rainnie, 1989:219; and Scott et al., 1989:72–3). In the hotel and catering industry, for example, employees are well aware of management hostility towards trade unionism, and 'employees' perception of this hostility has a role in forming apparent psychological barriers to acceptance of the likely benefits of union membership and plays some part in generating a sense of both resignation and of the immutability of hotel and catering workers' lot in life' (Macaulay and Wood, 1992:27). Given the unitary outlook of the owners/managers of small firms, it is hard to imagine that many would voluntarily decide to grant union recognition. The majority would simply not countenance such a challenge to their cherished independence and authority.

Perhaps, however, we should not paint too bleak a picture. There have always been some non-union employers who are more receptive to union organising, if approached (see Abbott, 1993:310), and the Employment Relations Act (1999) does appear to have tempered employer hostility to unionisation (Diamond and Freeman, 2001:2; Heery and Simms, 2003; and Oxenbridge et al., 2003). In many respects, 'small firms and unions each need on the one hand to be far less wary. On the other hand, there might be positive benefits from co-existence' (Scott et al., 1989:83). Handling disciplinary matters and the management of change in small, non-union firms are examples of areas where such firms might benefit from more formal, collectively-determined procedures which provide rights of representation for the workforce (see also Freeman, 1995). As already noted, one reason why small firms do not grow, and therefore do not create the jobs that successive governments have longed for, is their inability to move from an informal employee relations system based on personal relations to a more formalised procedure: a principal reason why owners/managers do not expand their business is precisely because they perceive potential problems with staff. More formal procedures in the internal labour market should not, then, be equated automatically with inefficiency or a lack of flexibility but rather, if anything, their opposite (see Chapter 3). At the same time, and equally important, an independent organisation can protect and promote employee rights. Unionisation, in other words, need not be a 'zero sum' process for the owner/manager. At present it is not only the non-union employee that suffers from management hostility and the apathy of many trade unions, but also the economy itself wherein small, non-union firms fail to stimulate economic growth.

Conclusion

Now that 'non-unionism has come out of the closet' (Flood and Turner, 1993:54), it has been suggested that 'the influence by example of non-union companies of excellence (e.g. IBM, Marks & Spencer) ... may be factors working to bring about changes in management attitudes towards unions through the course of time' (Beaumont, 1986:33). This might account for some of the growing interest in HRM and 'high commitment' management practices discussed in Chapter 4, but this is clearly not the situation in the majority of non-union firms. Nonetheless, it is often assumed that all is well in the majority of non-union firms because their small size allows for close working relationships, flexible working practices, and employee satisfaction. This is reflected in public policy, with successive governments seeking to remove unwelcome 'restrictions' (including those imposed by trade unions) on SMEs in order to encourage 'enterprise'. However, instead of being 'burdened by the law', especially employment law, many small firms are genuinely ignorant of their obligations or else deliberately choose to flout the law (see, for example, Blackburn and Hart, 2002; Earnshaw et al., 2000; and Scott et al., 1989:90).

Unfortunately, *unorganised* employment is often *unregulated* employment (Dickens and Hall, 1995:271).

New Labour has gone some way towards enhancing the individual employment rights of workers and the rights of employees to collective representation at work (see Chapters 5–8), but this has not yet closed the 'representation gap' (Towers, 1997b) which leaves millions of workers in the UK without an effective voice at work. The UK is one of the few exceptions (along with the United States) to the pattern of 'dual representation' (i.e. collective bargaining and statutory works councils) found in most advanced industrialised economies (see Rogers and Streeck, 1994; and Chapter 8) and there are now far fewer workers covered by collective agreements in the UK than anywhere else in the European Union (see Chapter 7). Moreover, the 'institutional' (UK and US) approach to workers' right to freedom of association, based on a majority vote in a democratic election, presents an additional hurdle for unions to overcome and a formal opportunity for employers to put their anti-union cards on the table and resist organisation (e.g. by victimising union activists and warning employees of the dangers of 'outside interference' in the affairs of the business). This approach is very different from European practice where employment policy respects the constitutional right of employees to join a union (or refrain from doing so) while at the same time ensuring the human right of all employees to a collective voice at work. The 'prerogative' approach to workers' freedom of association is based on the principle that no majority should have the power to deny a minority from acting collectively (see Leader, 2002:130–1). In contrast, as with collective bargaining and other forms of joint regulation (discussed in Chapters 7 and 8) the UK approach encourages a culture of 'minimal compliance' with the law, especially on the part of SMEs, rather than active engagement with a new set of social norms, values and institutions designed to protect and promote workers' rights *as well as* the efficiency of firms.

In liberal market economies, it is widely assumed that any diminution of the 'social constraints' on self-interested rational action will enhance efficiency and entrepreneurial activity. However, as we have already noted (Chapters 1–3), economies that rely excessively on 'free markets' encounter problems of social justice and fairness (see Boyer and Hollingsworth, 1997:440). Moreover, socially institutionalised (and therefore accepted) constraints on firms' behaviour may actually enhance market performance (Streeck, 1997). If nothing else, such constraints would foreclose exploitative forms of cost minimisation that characterise the employee relations of many SMEs. The UK needs a new approach to the statutory regulation of employee relations and a much wider recognition and acceptance of the potential benefits of joint regulation (especially, it must be said, among the owners and managers of small firms). To be sure, not all workers want trade union organisation or even legislated works councils (Diamond and Freeman, 2001:3), but workers should not have to surrender rights they enjoy as citizens as soon as they walk through the office door or factory gates. At the most elementary level, more formalised procedures in SMEs would benefit workers *and* manage-ment: it would not only help to stabilise employee relations, but facilitate managed growth. As Scott *et al.* (1989:90) argue, 'it would be useful to dispel the myth that formalised, stable employment relationships … represent creeping bureaucratisa-tion, the death of enterprise and damage to employment growth'. In sum, many non-union employees need effective collective representation. A great many owners and managers would benefit as well. So too, it must be added, would the economic and social health of the nation.

10

The dynamics of industrial conflict

The firefighters' strike 2002–3

A battle for public support

'How many more have to die?' ran *The Sun's* headline on 15 November 2002, reporting the death of Evan Davies an 86-year old man from Halesowen, West Midlands, who died in his third floor flat following a fire which took the military fire crews twenty minutes to reach – though Mr Davies lived only half a mile from a fire station. The UK's firefighters had embarked on only their second national strike in their union's 84-year history, and were immediately embroiled in a battle for public opinion to convince the public of the 'justness' of their cause. And, to a critical extent, public opinion could be expected to hinge on whether the strike was seen to cause people to die unnecessarily in fires. It had been a similar story in the first firefighters' national strike in 1977–8 when the death of two children in Liverpool during the nine-week strike was seen as a contributory factor in the Fire Brigades Union (FBU) decision to end the action and agree a pay settlement with their employers.

The FBU was highly sensitive to the importance of public and media support during the 2002–3 dispute. Indeed, the local authority employers and the government, as well as the FBU, knew that public opinion towards the striking firefighters would be a crucial variable in the progress and outcome of the strike. Strikes in public services by definition cause disruption to the public. At the same time, public support (or the lack of it) is an important factor in maintaining solidarity and morale among the strikers, and bringing pressure to bear on the government and public sector employers to reach a settlement to restore the availability of the service. The FBU decision in 2002 to pursue a 40 per cent pay claim by staging a series of short strikes, rather than an indefinite, all-out stoppage, may be seen partly as a recognition of the greater difficulty of maintaining public support (and by extension, striker morale and solidarity) during an indefinite strike.

In general, the fire service is held in high esteem by the general public, an esteem further reinforced after the 11 September 2001 terrorist attack in New York, in which over three hundred US firefighters lost their lives. In the UK, both newspaper headlines and public opinion polls displayed early support for the firefighters' cause during their dispute. On 5 September 2002, for example, a *Guardian* leader was headed 'Burning Grievance: Avoid a Battle with the Firefighters', with the paper commenting that 'no-one who looks at the pay rates and structures for firefighters can deny that they have a legitimate grievance about being left behind'. Four days later, a headline in *The Sun* proclaimed 'Our Hero Firefighters Deserve Decent Wage'; on 23 October a *Daily Star* headline read 'Just Give 'Em the Flaming Money'; and on 27 October, the *Mail on Sunday* ran an article under the heading 'Striking firefighters deserve our backing'.

Opinion polls similarly indicated a substantial level of initial support for the firefighters' claim. In the months leading up to the first stoppage (in November 2002), the level of support did fall, but a majority continued to think that the pay claim was justified: in September 2002, 68 per cent of those questioned thought the pay claim was justified; by November this had dropped to 53 per cent, with support significantly higher among women questioned (60 per cent) than men (46 per cent) (*The Guardian*, 26 September 2002 and 19 November 2002).

In the end, after a number of one-, two- and eight-day strikes had taken place, the main factor that swung public (and particularly media) opinion away from the firefighters' cause was not deaths occurring during strike periods, but the extended preparations for military action against Iraq (which took place in early 2003). The consensus in the press was that the nation's military forces were being sidetracked by their continued role as emergency firefighters. Newspaper headlines expressed this from the time of the first strike onwards. *The Sun*, for example, used: 'Fire Union Chiefs are Saddam Stooges' (14 November, 2002), 'We Can't Fight Fires and Iraq' (21 November, 2002), and 'Fire Boss Gilchrist is Traitor to Our Troops' (18 March, 2003). The FBU responded by suspending strike action as military action approached. This proved to be a key factor in the fire dispute, with the FBU campaign losing momentum and union representatives ultimately voting to accept a pay rise far short of their initial demand. More importantly, the impending war in Iraq had drawn the FBU even deeper into open conflict with the Government, crossing the (already grey) line between an industrial and a political dispute.

A smouldering dispute

The FBU claim (first tabled in May 2002) for a 40 per cent pay rise for firefighters and control room staff, reflected a growing feeling that the relative pay of firefighters had fallen far behind what these emergency workers deserved. A generation earlier, the 1977–8 firefighters' strike (which followed the rejection of a 30 per cent pay claim) had been settled partly by a 10 per cent pay increase, but importantly also by the establishment of a pay formula that linked future firefighters' pay increases to the top quarter of adult male manual workers' earnings. For many years, this formula was widely seen to serve the firefighters well and was closely guarded by the union. In the early 1990s, for example, when employers were seeking to introduce changes to firefighters' terms and conditions, Darlington's (1998:67) study of the Merseyside fire brigade noted the importance given to 'a vigorous local publicity campaign, with the threat of national strike action, in support of the FBUs defence of the national pay formula'.

In more recent years, however, the FBU and many of its members have voiced a growing dissatisfaction with the pay formula, a dissatisfaction which culminated in the 2002 pay claim to give firefighters £30 000 a year rather than their existing £21 531. Partly, this dissatisfaction with the pay formula reflected the effects of compositional changes in the male manual workforce since the 1970s. The 1978 settlement came at a time when highly paid manual groups such as coal miners and steel workers bolstered the manual worker pay index, particularly the upper quartile of that index, to which firefighters' pay was linked. By the late 1990s, however, these highly paid manual occupations had drastically reduced in size, making the firefighters' link with manual earnings less financially rewarding.

Closely linked to the firefighters' pay claim was a second factor exacerbating the dispute – the intensified search within the service for cost efficiencies, primarily through organisational changes and a restructuring of work arrangements, in order to meet government targets for improved performance. In this regard, the fire service is no different from other areas of the UK public sector where funding and performance have been increasingly scrutinised over the past two decades, first by Conservative governments seeking to subject more of the public sector to market forces, and latterly by Labour governments that have placed the emphasis instead on performance management to achieve greater cost efficiency. In practice, this has taken the form of public service expenditure and performance being monitored more closely via target-setting, inspection and audit procedures, backed by future funding being tied to measured improvements and organisational reforms (Bach, 2002).

With labour costs representing around 85 per cent of total fire service expenditure (Fitzgerald and Stirling, 1999:50), the search for financial savings has focused primarily on the personnel budget. As a consequence, many of the proposed areas of reform have directly challenged long-established work arrangements and conditions of service, many secured by the FBU for their members in the past. The areas targeted for reform, including working time patterns, crewing levels and job duties for example, have, not surprisingly, met with considerable criticism and resistance from employees and the Union, reflected in a growing number of local disputes and industrial action as the 1990s progressed.

In part, the reforms sought by Chief Fire Officers and other fire service managers employed across the UK's 58 Fire Authorities, reflect the unusual work pattern of firefighters. A large majority (95 per cent) of firefighters have a work pattern of four days working (two day shifts and two night shifts) followed by four days off. On average, during their working periods, firefighters spend only around 5 to 10 per cent of their time actually fighting fires (Audit Commission, 1995). The remainder of their time is spent on other duties such as appliance checks and maintenance, training (including physical keep fit training), vehicle cleaning and a minimum of 29 per cent 'stand down' time – that is time during which firefighters respond to emergencies only and are able to use the time for resting (Bain, 2002:21).

In some brigades, the pattern of labour utilisation and deployment is further affected by the degree of cover the fire service provides in a particular area. Depending on their composition, geographical areas are placed in one of several fire risk categories; the higher the category, the more appliances and firefighters respond to callouts. For example, any callout in a top ('A' risk) category area is answered by three pumps with a five-minute limit for the arrival of the first two pumps. A category 'C' risk area, in contrast, is answered by one pump, with an eight- to ten-minute maximum response time (Audit Commission, 1995). Fire stations are constantly staffed to the level of their risk category area (a system known as constant crewing), despite the fact that the incidence of fires is not spread evenly across the 24 hours (most fires occur in the early evening and night) and that many areas have fluctuating rather than constant levels of actual risk (for example, most office blocks that are full of people during the day are virtually empty at night, whilst in contrast, commuter areas that have a small population during the day fill up with returning commuters at night and at weekends).

For fire service management, the outcome of these various factors has been judged to be an inefficient rigidity in their utilisation of labour:

> Managers are not free to manage: they are squeezed between national standards of fire cover which no longer protect people adequately, and national terms and conditions designed for working conditions of a generation ago. (Bain, 2002:29)

Several attempts to introduce changes in working arrangements during the 1990s met with significant resistance from firefighters and the FBU, and this reflects a third factor in the 2002–3 strike: a growing union militancy in the period running up to the national strike. The 1990s witnessed growing levels of protest and militancy across many parts of the Fire Service. In the 1995–7 period, for example, local protest action took place in ten brigades, ballots for strike action were held in five other brigades and strike action occurred in three further brigades. The most protracted conflict involved the Merseyside brigade where strike action in 1995–6 was followed in 2001 by an eight-day strike over plans to alter the recruitment policy to allow 'direct entry' into more senior posts, rather than filling these by promotion from below (Herbert, 2001). Against this background, it is not surprising that the incoming General Secretary of the FBU in the late 1990s, Andy

Gilchrist, displayed a significantly more militant approach to union strategy than his predecessor.

This growing militancy represents efforts by the FBU and its members to resist changes to the nature and (non wage) terms and conditions of fire service jobs. In mobilising their membership to exercise greater militancy, two additional factors have been important for the Union. First, the FBU has grown substantially during the period since the previous national strike in 1977. Whilst the overall membership of TUC-affiliated public service unions declined by over 11 per cent between 1979 and 1996, the FBU grew by a third (33 per cent) (Mathieson and Corby, 1999:204). By 1997, the level of union density in the Fire Service had reached 86 per cent, a rise of 25 per cent since 1977 (Fitzgerald and Stirling, 1999:54–5).

Second, the structure of work organisation in fire stations acts to increase the sense of solidarity among firefighters. In each station, every firefighter is a member of one of four teams or watches (differentiated by colours: red watch, green watch and so on); the firefighters stay in their watch, which becomes a close-knit community. The combination of working and living in close proximity over extended periods, and relying on each other in dangerous situations, helps to build a strong collectivist spirit within the watches:

> You spend a massive amount of time together with people on your watch in both work and play, and so people become very familiar with each other and that helps build very close relationships. (Merseyside FBU representative quoted by Darlington, 1998:63)

> We're like family. It's not like going to work to make widgets then going home again. We eat together, room together, train together. We know each other's strengths and weaknesses and cover each other's backs. (London firefighter quoted in Morrison, 2003:2)

Darlington (1998) and Fitzgerald and Stirling (1999) both comment that the discipline that is integral to the firefighter's job, and the way the watch operates in emergencies, also act to bolster loyalty and discipline towards the Union. These authors further comment on the important degree to which the watch structure not only builds solidarity among firefighters but also increases the degree of interest and involvement in matters affecting the watch members, strengthening the connection with local Union issues and providing additional support for the Union. As one local FBU official commented in relation to the watch and Union strength,

> I think it's the insular sense of the watch, you've got a union activist on that watch and he has the ears (of the members) and therefore our message is easier to get over. It's something they've been talking about at the tea table, they live together. (quoted by Fitzgerald and Stirling, 1999:57)

In addition to growing dissatisfaction with the pay formula, increased employer efforts to cut labour costs, and growing militancy at local level, the intervention of the state, whether direct or indirect, played a crucial role throughout the long-running dispute. As the controller of Fire Service (and other public service) funding, the state established the broad parameters within which the Service operates, including the determination of firefighters' terms and conditions of employment. What became increasingly apparent during the dispute was the Government's determination to 'keep a lid' on public sector pay settlements and defeat (or at least not concede ground to) one of the increasing number of left-wing union leaders dubbed the 'awkward squad' by the press (the 'awkward squad' includes Andy Gilchrist/FBU, Bob Crow/RMT, and Mick Rix/ASLEF, although some commentators would add other recently-elected left-wing union leaders to the list, including Tony Woodley/T&GWU, Kevin Curran/GMB, Derek Simpson/ Amicus and Dave Prentice/Unison). Behind the firefighters were several other (public sector) groups awaiting a pay settlement and 'lining up' for a possible confrontation with the Government, including railway workers, postal workers and health service employees, all determined to restore flagging public sector pay levels. Mr Blair insisted that he was not trying to 'do a Maggie' (i.e. provoke, square up to and defeat a militant public sector group of workers) (*The Guardian*, 26 November 2002), but it was clear that, for the Government, the firefighters' dispute was not only an important one to settle in its own right, but also important in potentially setting a precedent for other, much larger public sector groups.

Industrial action

Following the rejection by the FBU of a 4 per cent pay offer made by the local Fire Authority employers in the summer 2002, an FBU representatives' meeting in September agreed unanimously to ballot the membership on industrial action in support of their 40 per cent pay claim. This ballot yielded an almost nine-to-one (87.6 per cent) vote in favour of industrial action. Subsequently, in October 2002, 36 strike days were announced.

While negotiations continued, the Government (following a proposal from the Fire Service employers, but not supported by the FBU) established a wide-ranging Review of the Fire Service to be conducted under the chairmanship of Sir George Bain (former Chair of the Low Pay Commission and Vice-Chancellor of Queen's University, Belfast) to inquire into 'the future organisation and management of the Fire Service' including consideration of pay and conditions of service (Bain, 2002:1). Just before the first strike in November 2002, the Bain committee issued a 22-page interim report, recommending a pay deal worth 11 per cent over two years (4 per cent in year one, 7 per cent in year two) but with the rise tied to acceptance of far-reaching 'modernisation' changes designed to create greater 'flexibility' in working practices, relating for example to shift patterns, part-time working and crewing levels at different times of day. Many of these changes had also been recommended by an earlier 1995 Audit Commission report, but had not been advanced in the intervening period. The Bain recommendations, however, were rejected outright by the FBU, and both the interim and main report (published in December 2002) failed to act as the basis of a settlement.

At 1800 hours on Wednesday 13 November 2002, firefighters belonging to the FBU walked out of their fire stations to begin a 48–hour strike in support of their pay claim. It was to be the first of 15 days of strike action over the next three months. This first strike saw the return of troops to the UK's streets to act as emergency firefighters. Code-named Operation Fresco, 18 500 service personnel and 827 'Green Goddesses' (so-named because of their colour) took on the national role of emergency fire cover in a way they had previously done in the last national fire strike in 1977. In 2002, the Green Goddesses epitomised, even more than they had a generation earlier, the difference between normal and emergency fire cover. These unsophisticated fire tenders, many dating back to the 1950s, lack all forms of advanced equipment (even radios) and are restricted to very slow speeds because of their tendency to roll over on bends due to their instability when transporting water to fires.

With negotiations continuing, and several nominated strike dates put back by the FBU to allow talks to progress, it became evident that the Union and employers could reach a settlement (based on a staged pay rise amounting to 16 per cent) that the Union indicated would be sufficient to avoid further strike action. However, this offer was effectively blocked by the Government, with Ministers such as Nick Raynsford (the Minister responsible for the Fire Service) and John Prescott (the Deputy Prime Minister given a separate responsibility for trying to resolve the dispute) arguing that the costs involved in funding the deal were unacceptable and would be 'hyper-inflationary'.

In the following impasse, other strikes followed, most notably an eight-day stoppage in late November 2002, followed by shorter stoppages in January 2003. When further strike action was suspended by the FBU in the period leading up to the military conflict in Iraq, protracted negotiations continued. The two sides came closer to a deal based on a 16 per cent pay rise over thirty months but tied to radical reforms (the cost savings from which would pay for a large part of the pay rise). These 'strings' attaching to the pay deal were, however, unacceptable to an FBU delegate conference, until a further concession was brokered whereby some more radical reform proposals were shelved. It was also agreed that the reforms to crewing levels and working arrangements would be introduced by 'consensus' and negotiation, rather than merely 'consulted' over by Fire Service management. A proposal for a new pay formula linking fire crews' pay to that of other skilled staff, rather than manual workers' earnings, was also agreed together with an agreement to pay part-time ('retained') firefighters the same hourly rate as their full-time counterparts.

With the industrial action having lost momentum and a good deal of public support, due in important part to the pending war in Iraq; with a clear signal from the Government that if the deal was rejected then the Deputy Prime Minister John

Prescott was poised to use emergency powers to impose a pay and reform package; and with the key concession that reform would be subject to further negotiation, the package was endorsed (by a majority of 12-to-6) by the FBU executive, and subsequently approved by a majority of three-to-one at a special conference in Glasgow of station representatives drawn from over a thousand fire stations located across the 58 separate UK Fire Authorities.

Counting the cost

So who won the dispute? To answer this, we need to consider the bargaining objectives and outcomes for all the parties involved – the Government, employers and Fire Service management, the FBU and ordinary firefighters, and the general public. In terms of outcome for the Government, it has been estimated that the cost to the Exchequer (or more accurately, the tax-payer) of fighting the FBU was £125 million (*The Guardian*, 13 June 2003) but this sum pales against the cost of a 40-per-cent pay deal that might have set a precedent for other public sector workers. Thus, worried that public sector pay flood-gates would be opened if a large rise, with no reform conditions, had been conceded, the Government was clearly determined that such an outcome would not prevail and that if necessary emergency measures would be taken to impose a settlement. The compromise settlement may have fallen short of the Government's vision for a 'modern' fire service, but crucially the dispute did not spark a round of public sector militancy similar to that which proved to be the downfall of the 1974–9 Labour government.

The FBU secured a substantially bigger pay rise for its members than the 4 per cent offered before the action took place. The Union also won a key concession to negotiate any further changes. But the Union had raised expectations of its members very high. So a feeling prevailed amongst the membership that striking had not gained what had been hoped for, and in terms of the actual pay settlement agreed in June 2003, was little different from the one being discussed by employers and the FBU in the previous November. It is often noted that strikes 'don't pay' in terms of significantly increasing real wages, especially when loss of earnings incurred during the dispute is included in the calculation (Metcalf *et al.*, 1993), but strikes do change the future conduct of employee relations and can produce more favourable wage settlements in the future *without* resort to strike action (see, for example, Cohn, 1993).

In fact, the firefighters and control room staff achieved a pay rise much above what other employees (though not directors and senior executives) were securing in 2002–3, and in the longer term a pay formula that will probably raise their (relative) earnings still further. But even though the rise was significantly higher than was being offered in 2002, it was not the 'quantum leap' they might have hoped for, and certainly believed that they deserved. Still, many would probably agree with Paul Moss, a firefighter on red watch at the Low Hill fire station in Liverpool who commented that in the end they felt that they had no choice but to accept: 'In my opinion it is the best offer out of a bad deal', he told a *Guardian* correspondent (Carter, 2003).

Fire Service management may ultimately have gained comparatively little from the settlement. True, they settled an end to the strike and secured a pay deal that fell far short of that initially demanded. But what the employers failed to achieve was a guaranteed path to reform that would deliver desired cost savings and agreed performance targets. Throughout the 1990s, both local and national FBU representatives demonstrated an ability to fend off reforms that were regarded as 'unacceptable'. By 'dodging' the issue of reform, to a considerable extent, in order to resolve the dispute, management will have to contend with the legacy of past difficulties as well as the new agenda for reform. The (partial) resolution of the 2002–3 dispute has thereby 'set the scene' for the management of employee relations for may years to come.

Finally, if the press are to be believed, the real losers in any public sector dispute, especially one involving the emergency services, is the general public. Only time will tell whether the public will be better served by a better paid and (following further negotiations) a more 'modern' fire service. As regards the impact of the strike days themselves, a number of deaths did occur during the dispute. But deaths from fires are all too frequent occurrences in the UK, whether firefighters are on strike or not: in an average year around a dozen people die in fires each week (in 2000, for example, 595 people died in fires in the UK, 447 of these in their own homes). There is little evidence that the level of fatalities was significantly higher during the strike days than on other days in 2002–3. Indeed, the extra safeguards that the public were urged to take during the strike periods probably prevented a number of serious fires that would otherwise have occurred.

The UK's changing strike pattern

Strikes are inherently complex, and often dramatic, events. Specific strikes, especially those in the public sector, invoke media and political comment, with employees and their trade unions usually apportioned the blame. This was clearly evident during the firefighters' dispute, although on this occasion the rhetoric of the Government and the way it was seen to handle the dispute at times backfired in terms of its effect on public opinion. Most disputes, however, pass without press, let alone political comment. Local disputes over budget cuts in the fire service during 1998, for example, rarely made the headlines, although *The Sun* (25 August 1998) gave full page coverage to Melanie Blatt and Shaznay Lewis of All Saints when they appeared on stage at a V98 gig wearing T-shirts sporting the Adidas logo and a message that read: 'FBU FIREFIGHTERS AND CONTROL STAFF have **adinuff** Essex Strike 1998'. This particular story, however, appeared on the 'bizarre showbiz' page. When industrial disputes do make the front pages or are debated in the House, they are quickly forgotten. Invariably, all they leave behind for public scrutiny is a statistical entry in *Labour Market Trends* or other government publications. The firefighters' strike in 2002–3, for example, was registered as just one of 146 stoppages that began in 2002, contributing to the loss of over 1.3 million working days and involving more than 940 000 workers (*Labour Market Trends*, June 2003). The wider significance of the firefighters' strike – most notably as a demonstration of public sector discontent – was thus submerged along with 145 other disputes that took place in 2002, both big and small, long and short, in public and private sectors, and involving white-collar, blue-collar or pink-collar workers. One consequence of collapsing such diverse activity into just three figures, as Shalev (1978:1) points out, is that strike data have become 'some of the most over-abused and least understood of man's [*sic*] many attempts to freeze and condense richly dynamic social events into static, artificial, and misleadingly accurate arithmetic'.

Through the artificial, and somewhat anaesthetic process of measurement and recording, we often lose sight of the actors involved in industrial disputes, their motives, the meanings they attach to such behaviour, and the immediate outcomes and wider ramifications of industrial action for management, labour or the state. And yet we cannot ignore the aggregate statistics. At best, they are one of the few widely available measures of the trends in industrial conflict over time. At worst, they are seized upon by the press and politicians alike as some kind of barometer for the general health of employee relations, be it good (few strikes) or bad (many strikes) (see, for example, DTI, 2001). The firefighters' strike, for example, was seen to be part of a wider expression of public sector discontent. Days lost in 2002 were more than double both the total for the previous year and the average of the previous ten years. But other statistics counter the view of any return of the 'British disease'. The final number of recorded stoppages in 2002, at only 146, was the lowest annual total on record (records began in 1891).

It is not uncommon for strike levels to fluctuate from one year to another. The number of working days lost is particularly susceptible to the influence of a few major strikes (just sixteen disputes in 2002, for example, accounted for 94 per cent of all working days lost). As already indicated, however, statistics can be used to discern trends in the number (frequency), duration (working days lost) and breadth (workers involved) of strikes over time. Thus, the late 1960s and 1970s may be seen as a period of heightened industrial unrest compared with earlier post-war years or the 1980s and especially the 1990s and early years of the twenty-first century. For some, the decline in strike activity in recent years represents not only a vindication of Conservative governments' employment law and labour market policies (law and policies that have remained largely intact under New Labour; see Chapter 6), but also indicates that 'strikes themselves are inefficient and outdated means of bargaining. The strike is ill-suited to advanced societies in which workers have valuable skills to sell in an efficiently functioning labour market' (Hanson and

Mather, 1988:27). This interpretation must be rejected, however, on empirical, analytical and theoretical grounds. *Empirically*, there is the well-known problem of incomplete data: not all strikes are recorded (e.g. short disputes involving just a few workers). Equally important, official statistics exclude all industrial action short of a work stoppage (such as a work-to-rule) and there are numerous studies that indicate an increase in such expressions of discontent in recent years.

Analytically, there is the problem of imputing behaviour from statistical data: the causes of behaviour cannot be inferred simply from a statistical datum (e.g. strikes have declined, *ipso facto* they are inefficient and no longer necessary) without empirical observation of the actual 'data' themselves (strikes and those taking part in strikes). When the data under examination are human beings, the manifestations of individual and collective actions cannot simply be assumed, if only because workers have the ability to learn and modify their behaviour in response to varying stimuli. Crucially, strikes themselves can shape both the patterns and parameters of future industrial action: if strikes bring success, workers may be encouraged, or at least less reticent, about withdrawing their labour in subsequent disputes with their employer. As Cohn (1993) demonstrates, when unions develop a reputation for striking, employers are more likely to offer generous settlements. In fact,

> Winning or losing is less important than generating a reputation for militancy. Such a reputation can be obtained by showing a willingness to strike for striking's sake, even to the point of engaging in kamikaze assaults. (ibid:28)

This strategy is only successful, however, in relation to short (*blitzkrieg*) strikes (ibid:216–18). When unions lose major (siege) disputes, the impact can be widespread demoralisation and greater reluctance to strike in the immediate future.

Theoretically, it is implicit in Hanson and Mather's (1988) argument that if strikes are unnecessary or pathological, then conflict can simply be attributed to misunderstanding or mischief. As the latter is usually attributed to shopfloor activists or trade unions, these authors argue for the abolition of *all* trade union immunities, placing them under common law jurisdiction, on the assumption that this would lead to a further diminution of strike action (see Chapter 6). The only 'cause' of strikes would then be mistakes, misunderstandings or misfortune. As Graham Mather has argued elsewhere, 'In a few years' time the strike will be seen as a distortion, an error and an unnecessary feature of any sensible bargaining relationship' (*Independent on Sunday*, 30 July 1995). Indeed, it is not uncommon for management themselves to explain strikes in these terms. But such an explanation ignores *underlying* causes of unrest (morale, status, parity and insecurity, for example, that are evident in many instances of industrial conflict). The same criticism applies to similar arguments about the general decline of strikes, in which Hanson and Mather (1988), among others, not only ignore the diverse character of strike activity but more importantly the (unchanged) structural base of industrial conflict between employer and employee (discussed in Chapter 2).

Attention to such detail and the underlying causes of unrest produces a very different interpretation of recent trends. One of the most notable developments of recent years, for example, has been a shift in the locus of strike activity from the private to the public sector. Many of these disputes, including the recent firefighters' strike, are clearly political with a small 'p'. If nothing else, public opinion and the 'national interest' will tend to play a more prominent role in such disputes. But the most notable feature of the past decade is that behind the statistics published in the pages of *Labour Market Trends* lie some of the most intense and bitter struggles of recent memory. Thus, to extrapolate from a decline in the number of strikes to predict the eradication of industrial unrest is clearly facile. As many authors have noted (e.g. Durcan *et al.*, 1983:404–24; and Hyman, 1989b:197), it is possible to 'explain' strike trends over time, and the decline of strike activity during recent years, through the analysis of such *proximate* variables as the changing economic environment, the role of product and labour markets, bargaining structures and institutions, management initiatives, and the changing relationship between employees, their unions and the state. But the *underlying* causes of industrial conflict – the structural realities of economic relations within capitalist systems, the nature of the labour process, the division and distribution of income and wealth, and relations of power and control within and beyond the workplace – have remained fundamentally unaltered. Indeed, changes to the distribution of income, the growing number of workers on low wages, the decline of trade union influence and many of the other developments outlined in previous chapters suggest that, if anything, the bases of conflicts of interest have been heightened over the past two decades. What needs to be explained are the various *manifestations* of such conflicts, including non-strike forms of dissension.

A central aim of this chapter, therefore, is to consider the dimensions, trends and character of strikes over the post-war period, with particular emphasis on the period since the late 1960s. By exploring the various explanations of strikes within this broader historical context and by examining non-strike forms of conflict, it is possible to offer a more balanced evaluation of the nature of industrial conflict and its persistence in the face of state policy aimed at curbing strike activity. In doing so, the distinction between proximate or precipitating causes of strikes and the underlying causes of industrial unrest will be emphasised. Not only does this cast the 1980s and 1990s in a rather different light from that shed by many previous reviews of recent strike patterns, it also illustrates that strikes are not the only, or even the most important, form of industrial conflict. As Kornhauser *et al.* (1954:13) pointed out many years ago,

> A true understanding of industrial strife ... demands consideration of related, less spectacular manifestations as well. It may even be suggested that the general object of study is not the labor dispute, the strike, or the lockout, but the total range of behavior and attitudes that express opposition and divergent orientations between industrial owners and managers on the one hand and working people and their organizations on the other hand.

In order to encapsulate such a wide range of behaviour it is necessary to move from the bases of conflict (why is conflict inevitable?) to specific forms of work organisation (why do patterns of conflict and accommodation vary across firms, industries and occupations?) and the meanings attached to any specific manifestation of industrial conflict by the parties involved (see Edwards, 1986:17; and Hyman, 1989b:71–5). In other words, it is essential to go beyond the study of trends and statistics, and simple (mono-causal) explanations of strikes, to consider the actual *processes* of industrial conflict, especially at the workplace level where employees seek to achieve a degree of control over their working lives. First, however, we must consider the most (ab)used of all indicators of industrial conflict, the strike statistic.

Strikes: measurement and trends

Strikes have been defined as 'a temporary stoppage of work by a group of employees in order to express a grievance or enforce a demand' (Griffin, 1939:20). Thus, the action involves those who sell their labour – *employees* rather than employers; the employees intend to return to work after the strike is concluded (the stoppage is *temporary*); the workers have withdrawn their labour (a strike is a *stoppage* of work, unlike an overtime ban, work-to-rule or go-slow where labour is partially withheld); the action is collective (involving a *group* of employees); and it is purposive or calculative (to *express* a grievance or *enforce* a demand). It is interesting and important to note that the involvement of trade unions is not seen as a defining characteristic, despite the commonplace association of unions and strikes. Strikes can, and do, occasionally involve non-union workers, although the mobilisation of collective interests is often difficult in the absence of union organisation (see Kelly, 1998).

In order to measure strike activity, as opposed to defining it as a form of social activity, the Office for National Statistics (ONS) records as a strike any stoppage of work due to an industrial dispute (i.e. connected with the terms and conditions of employment) between employers and employees (or between one group of employees and another), which involves at least ten employees for at least one day, or which involves the loss of at least one hundred working days. Industrial disputes thus include strikes over such issues as pay, the duration and pattern of working hours, redundancy questions, working conditions and supervision, staffing and work allocation, dismissal and other disciplinary measures, and trade union matters such as demarcation disputes. Although the ONS uses these categories to define the 'principal cause' of a strike, in recognition of the fact that most strikes are multi-causal, in many cases a more appropriate term would be 'reason given for striking'. For example, the dominance of pay disputes in the official statistics is perhaps a reflection of the fact that, in a liberal market economy, work is in important part a means to an end (that end being income). Further, in a dispute with several contributory causes it is often easier to simplify and articulate the discontent in monetary terms, thereby providing a common denominator to mobilise opposition to fight for improved wages rather than more diffuse goals such as better working conditions, less stringent supervision or more acceptable work allocation procedures. Thus, in the firefighters' strike, proposed changes to working arrangements and duties had been key issues for several years, but in the event their grievance was expressed in pounds and pence, with wages used to 'represent a badge of status' (Hyman, 1989b:123).

Although the firefighters' strike had significant political ramifications, it was nonetheless an 'industrial' dispute as defined by the ONS. In general, strikes that have explicitly political *ends*, rather than political implications, are excluded from official statistics, though the dividing line is not always clear cut. Also excluded are many small/short disputes, or what Knowles (1952:xiv) described as 'the frontier incidents of industrial life'. Thus, as the criteria for counting strikes reflect, not all strikes are recorded by the ONS, even when official data are available on small/ short disputes (between 1949–73, for example, the National Dock Labour Board recorded over 3100 strikes on the waterfront but less than 2300 were entered in the official statistics) (see Turnbull *et al.*, 1996:722). Further, a proportion of those strikes which actually qualify as such under the government's definition go unrecorded. For example, in a study of fifty plants, Kelly and Nicholson (1980:27) found that of 183 known stoppages that met the official criteria, only 88 (43 per cent) were actually recorded in the *Employment Gazette*, while a further 91 stoppages lasting less than one day or involving fewer than ten workers were officially excluded. Major workplace industrial relations surveys have also demonstrated that official statistics miss around a third of all stoppages (Brown, 1981:97–101), a shortfall not only attributable to the very small size/duration of some strikes but also the fact that the data reported to the ONS come from management sources (and there is no statutory obligation to report stoppages). In the first Workplace Industrial Relations Survey in 1980, for example, if only management reports of strikes among manual workers were counted then 27 per cent of all establishments recorded a stoppage over the previous year, compared with 34 per cent if strikes reported by either management or union respondents were counted (Daniel and Millward, 1983:215–16). Although the incidence of industrial action is now much lower, data from WERS98 reveals that there is still a significant discrepancy between the accounts of management and worker representatives (Cully *et al.*, 1999:208). No doubt, on occasion, management simply forget or cannot be bothered to inform the relevant government department of a strike. On other occasions, however, management may be concerned about the company's public image (with the press, shareholders and the government) if it makes known each and every dispute (e.g. a strike over a company violation of health and safety standards).

Two further issues relating to the statistics are worthy of note. First, disputes which do not result in a stoppage of work, such as an overtime ban or a work-to-rule, are not included in the statistics. When England's top rugby union players decided to wear their shirts and tops inside-out in a dispute with the Rugby Football Union (RFU), so that sponsors' names could not be seen, this did not 'count' in the official statistics as there was no actual stoppage of work (or, in this case, play). To reinforce the point made earlier, the data refer to strikes and *not* industrial conflict, where the latter might also include sabotage, the restriction of output, absenteeism, labour turnover and even accidents. Thus, if we want to follow Kornhauser and his colleagues (1954:13) and explore the *total* range of behaviour and attitudes that express opposition and divergent interest between management and labour, we must look beyond the official statistics.

Secondly, although the official statistics include 'lock-outs' (that is, where the employer prevents employees working by locking the place of work), no distinction is made between strikes and lock-outs in the actual statistics. In other words, we do not know *who* caused the stoppage of work. Almost invariably, however, stoppages are attributed to employees in general and 'troublemakers' or trade unions in particular. When England's rugby players announced a strike in November 2000, for example, Clive Woodward (the team manager) expressed his amazement that the players had rejected the remuneration package on offer, highlighting the role of 'three or four strong characters' among the senior players. 'They've made a big mistake', said Mr Woodward. 'A lot of the younger guys will be driving home now, panicking and wondering what the hell they've just done' (*The Guardian*, 22 November 2000). The players, however, who had voted unanimously for strike action, blamed the RFU. They were particularly critical of the RFU's approach to negotiations, which in the words of Martin Johnson (the England captain) were conducted by 'old fashioned, patronising and arrogant officials' (*The Guardian*, 22 November 2000; Will Carling, a former England captain, famously described the senior RFU officials as a bunch of 'old farts'). Thus, although the 'problem' of industrial conflict is invariably defined in managerial terms, it is not uncommon for workers to attribute blame (the cause) for strikes to management action (Batstone *et al.*, 1978:47–8). In the firefighters' dispute, for example, this centred on management's perceived inability to persuade the government of the case for underwriting an offer which would have avoided strike action taking place.

Media accounts of industrial action, however, tend to cast unions as the villains while employers simply exercise 'managerial prerogative'. England's rugby players, for example, were accused of 'betraying their country' and were dismissed from the team's training camp before any industrial action on their part had taken place. Players were told to spend the evening 'examining their consciences'. Mr Woodward telephoned all the players to ask them to 'come to their senses', but also to inform them that he would select a fresh squad if the players did not report for training the following day (*The Independent*, 22 November 2000). Is this just, and justly, the exercise of managerial prerogative, or is it tantamount to employer conflict with the employee? As Hyman (1989b:184) notes,

> as well as the lock-out, conflict with the *employee* can take the form of plant closure, sackings, victimization, blacklisting, speed-ups, safety hazards, arbitrary discipline and so on. The routine practices of employers do not *count* as 'industrial conflict'; they are part of the normal, repressive reality of work. (original emphasis)

Bullying, it seems, is just one of the 'routine' management practices that employees must endure. A recent nationwide study of the NHS, for example, found that three-in-five people had witnessed bullying at work during the previous 2 years. Four-out-of-five people who had not reported bullying told the researchers it was because 'the bully is my boss' (*The Observer*, 12 May 2002).

The use of official data must therefore be treated with caution, both as a measure of the extent and causes of industrial unrest, especially in an international context (see McCarthy, 1970). For example, of the OECD countries for which strike statistics are readily available, only two, the UK and the United States, exclude political strikes. Denmark and Germany impose a similar qualifying restriction of at least one hundred working days lost, whereas Austria, Belgium, Italy, the Netherlands and Turkey impose no restrictions on size, while Finland, Greece and Spain require only that the dispute last one hour or more. In an international comparison for 1995, the UK had the fourth lowest strike rate (days lost per 1000 employees) out of 24 countries, but at least 15 of these countries count disputes that would not be recorded in the UK (Sweeney and Davies, 1997). In a national context, however, official strike statistics provide a reasonable indication of trends over time, given that the criteria for inclusion have remained fairly constant, the accuracy of reporting strikes is unlikely to have changed (at least not on a systematic basis), and significant year-on-year variations tend to even out over the longer run. The statistics for the frequency, breadth and duration of strike activity are presented in Table 10.1 (pp. 334–5). This illustrates the magnitude of these longer-term variations, especially with respect to the number of workers involved and working days lost. For the post-war period as a whole, it is possible to identify at least nine distinct phases or patterns of strike activity, each of approximately six years' duration.

The post-war peace, 1946–52

With the exception of 1951, there was a downward trend in strike activity during this period, and a virtual absence of national, large-scale official stoppages. Coal mining accounted for around a third of all days lost, half the number of workers involved and over 60 per cent of all stoppages. Eight other industries accounted for over half the remaining stoppages and nearly 70 per cent of the remaining time lost and workers involved (Durcan *et al.*, 1983:26–57). The socio-economic consensus constructed by the Labour government (as discussed in Chapter 6) no doubt contributed to the post-war peace, but this was also a period still characterised by a 'depression mentality', possibly because many of the trade union leaders of the time had first come to office during the inter-war years. Union leaders, through the TUC, held together a firm anti-strike policy (Coates and Topham, 1988:234–5), which in many respects failed to meet up to the expectations of the rank-and-file (Cronin, 1979:138; and Hyman, 1989b:197).

The return of the strike, 1953–9

The downward trend of strikes was reversed during 1953, with the number of stoppages exceeding 2000 in 1955 and remaining above that level for the rest of the 1950s. This period also witnessed the return, after a 20-year absence, of the 'set-piece' strike: industry-wide stoppages conducted with the support of the national trade union(s) concerned. There were two national strikes in engineering and one each in shipbuilding and printing during this period. There was also a marked increase in the concentration of strike activity, with the eight most strike-prone industries, which collectively employed 20 per cent of all employees, accounting for 55 per cent of all stoppages and 84 per cent of all workers involved and working days lost (Durcan et al., 1983:58–91).

The shopfloor movement, 1960–8

This period was marked by a growth in the number of stoppages at the shopfloor level, with non-mining strikes passing the 1000 mark for the first time (1166 in 1960) and then almost doubling by the end of the period (2157 in 1968). Strike frequency had been dominated by the coal mining industry up to the late 1950s, after which the proportion of mining strikes fell from around three-quarters of the total to less than 10 per cent by the end of the 1960s. A further indication of the 'contagion' rather than the 'concentration' of strike activity in this period was that no industries were completely strike free during the 1960s, as had been the case in previous periods. The strike pattern itself was now dominated by small, short, unofficial stoppages arising from shopfloor issues, with the virtual disappearance, yet again, of the national, official macro-stoppage (Durcan et al., 1983:92–131). The latter, it appeared, 'took on some of the characteristics of a conjuror's prop: Now you see it, now you don't' (ibid:403). The prominence of the large-scale strike was to return thereafter, however, since which time it has rarely been out of the limelight.

The formal challenge, 1969–74

Legal controls had been imposed on pay increases in the mid 1960s, and by the end of the decade there were demands (and plans) for legislative restrictions on strikes

Table 10.1 Post-war strikes

Year	Frequency (number of strikes beginning in year)	Breadth (number of workers involved, 000s)	Duration (number of working days lost, 000s)
1946	2 205	526	2 158
1947	1 721	623	2 433
1948	1 759	426	1 944
1949	1 426	434	1 807
1950	1 339	303	1 389
1951	1 719	379	1 694
1952	1 714	416	1 792
Average 1946–52	**1 698**	**444**	**1 888**
1953	1 746	1 374	2 184
1954	1 989	450	2 457
1955	2 419	671	3 781
1956	2 648	508	2 083
1957	2 859	1 359	8 412
1958	2 629	524	3 462
1959	2 093	646	5 270
Average 1953–59	**2 340**	**551**	**3 950**
1960	2 832	819	3 024
1961	2 686	779	3 046
1962	2 449	4 423	5 798
1963	2 068	593	1 755
1964	2 524	883	2 277
1965	2 354	876	2 925
1966	1 937	544	1 428
1967	2 116	734	2 787
1968	2 378	2 258	4 690
Average 1960–68	**2 372**	**1 323**	**3 189**
1969	3 116	1 665	6 846
1970	3 906	1 801	10 980
1971	2 228	1 178	13 551
1972	2 497	1 734	23 909
1973	2 873	1 528	7 197
1974	2 922	1 626	14 750
Average 1969–74	**2 924**	**1 589**	**12 872**

Source: *Employment Gazette* and *Labour Market Trends*.

Year	Frequency (number of strikes beginning in year)	Breadth (number of workers involved, 000s)	Duration (number of working days lost, 000s)
1975	2 282	809	6 012
1976	2 016	668	3 284
1977	2 703	1 166	10 142
1978	2 471	1 041	9 405
1979	2 080	4 608	29 474
Average 1975–79	**2 310**	**1 658**	**11 663**
1980	1 330	834	11 964
1981	1 338	1 513	4 266
1982	1 528	2 103	5 313
1983	1 352	574	3 754
1984	1 206	1 464	27 135
1985	887	791	6 402
Average 1980–85	**1 274**	**1 213**	**9 806**
1986	1 053	720	1 920
1987	1 004	887	3 546
1988	770	790	3 702
1989	693	727	4 128
1990	620	298	1 903
Average 1986–90	**828**	**684**	**3 040**
1991	357	176	761
1992	240	148	528
1993	203	385	649
1994	203	107	278
1995	232	174	415
1996	244	364	1 303
Average 1991–96	**247**	**226**	**656**
1997	216	130	235
1998	166	93	282
1999	205	141	242
2000	212	183	499
2001	194	180	525
2002	146	943	1 323
Average 1997–2002	**190**	**278**	**518**

from both major political parties (see Chapter 6). The turbulent period 1969–74 saw first the abandonment and then the reintroduction of legal controls on pay, the introduction and failure of the Industrial Relations Act 1971, and a significant increase in strike activity. Strikes spread to previously 'strike free' groups such as teachers, refuse collectors, hospital workers and postal workers, while long-quiescent groups in the steel, clothing and glass industry also took up the strike (see Coates and Topham, 1988:238). Not only did the macro-strike reappear, but the public rather than the private sector 'became the battleground for set piece confrontations' (Durcan *et al.*, 1983:132). With the introduction of incomes policies, the majority of strikes were now wage rather than non-wage disputes (from 1955 to 1964 the proportion of wage disputes was 47 per cent of the total, whereas from 1965 to 1974 it rose to 56 per cent), while greater legal intervention in employee relations sparked an unprecedented wave of political strikes involving around 6 million workers and accounting for the loss of over 6 million working days (ibid:170 and 438; and Wigham, 1976:156–80). These strikes, which were excluded from official statistics, serve to highlight the intensity of formal trade union opposition and worker militancy towards government policy during this period. Working days lost had exceeded 6 million on only one previous occasion during the post-war years, in 1957, but surpassed this total in every year between 1969 to 1974. With the exception of 1976, this trend continued throughout the rest of the 1970s.

Containment and resurgence, 1975–9

With the election of a Labour government in 1974 and the establishment of a Social Contract with the trade unions, the TUC agreed to rigid pay restraint in 1975. More importantly, this policy was broadly supported at the workplace level. Strikes declined by almost a third in the space of two years, and in 1976 there were fewer pay than non-pay strikes for the first time since 1967. However, incomes policies upset comparability and notions of fairness, especially among public sector workers where pay policy is invariably enforced more tightly. As Davies (1979:220) has demonstrated, incomes policies tend to reduce pay disputes but increase non-pay strikes, and reduce pay strikes only at the expense of an upsurge when the policy is removed. Ultimately, the Labour government's incomes policy was not so much removed as destroyed by a resurgence of conflict during 1977–9, especially in the winter of 1978–9. With real wages falling during a period of high inflation, a 'revival of struggle' was almost inevitable following the government's parsimonious pay limit of 5 per cent imposed in the autumn of 1978 (Hyman, 1989b:198–9).

Coercive pacification, 1980–5

During the first half of the 1980s, unemployment doubled, the Conservative government initiated a biennial legislative programme more restrictive than the

Industrial Relations Act 1971, and many employers (with full state support) took on the unions. Many of the strikes which occurred were 'defensive' in character, often against redundancy, attacks on trade union organisation, speed-up at work, or the erosion of real income (Hyman, 1989b:199–202). One illustration of this was that pay disputes declined from 58 per cent of the total during 1974–9 to 44 per cent during 1980–5. In manufacturing, the number of strikes halved between 1979–80, and the number of pay strikes fell by 60 per cent (compared to a 34 per cent decline in non-pay disputes). As a result, 60 per cent of the *total* reduction in strike activity between 1979–80 was attributable to the reduction in pay strikes in manufacturing (Lyddon, 1994). Year after year in the early 1980s, major battles in the public sector were fought and invariably lost by the unions (steel in 1980, railways in 1982, water in 1983, coal in 1984–5), along with several major private sector disputes (e.g. print workers in 1983 and 1984). 'Major' disputes (involving 500 000 or more working days) accounted for a much higher proportion of total days lost in the 1980s than during the 1970s (*Employment Gazette*, May 1992), and largely account for the fact that 'days lost' declined to only the level of the 1960s (a time of increasing concern about the UK's 'strike problem').

The defeats for the trade unions, however, combined with the decline of pay disputes in the face of severe cash limits in the public sector, represent 'evidence of an erosion of the will to resist' (Hyman, 1989b:212). With the balance of power now firmly in the employers' favour, strikes appeared to have little chance of success. Unlike the 'contagion' effect of strikes in the 1960s and 1970s, the 1980s witnessed a 'negative demonstration' effect, especially after the miners' strike of 1984–5, which 'systematically undermined most workers' collective strength and confidence' (ibid:226). Yet conflict was never far from the surface. There was evidence of workers increasingly indulging in 'cut price' forms of industrial action such as the overtime ban (Edwards, 1992:378; Milner, 1993). If workers did strike, it was increasingly for a shorter period, with a marked increase in what might be termed 'token stoppages' lasting no longer than a day.

Calculative bargaining, 1986–90

In 1985, the number of strikes fell below 1 000 for the first time in the post-war period. But as unemployment declined and the economy enjoyed a mini (inflationary) boom, strikes once again rose above 1 000 in both 1986 and 1987. Pay disputes continued to decline as a proportion of the total (now below 40 per cent), while the number of strikes lasting less than one day increased to almost half the total. At the same time, a number of major set-piece confrontations continued to take place (for example in telecommunications in 1987, postal workers in 1988, dockers and council workers in 1989, and engineering workers in 1990). Record bankruptcies, however, and the fear of unemployment clearly played a role in the overall 'damping down' of overt conflict, but so too did the rise of average earnings

Table 10.2 Industrial action in workplaces* with recognised unions, 1980–98 (all workplaces, percentages)

	1980	1984	1990	1998
None	75	69	80	96
Non-strike action	10	8	4	2
Strike action	9	11	11	2
Both strike and non-strike action	7	11	5	–

*workplaces with 25 or more employees where recognised trade unions present.
Source: Millward *et al.* (2000:178).

(for those in employment), suggesting that many workers did not 'need' to strike. Nevertheless, data from the third Workplace Industrial Relations Survey revealed that there was an increase in the proportion of employees who took strike action for the first time during this period, despite the decline in both strike and non-strike action during the latter part of the decade (Millward *et al.*, 1992:292–4). The number of workplaces with recognised trade unions affected by strike and non-strike action in each of the Workplace Industrial Relations Surveys (and WERS98) is reported in Table 10.2.

Legislation also played a part in the decline in strike activity. However, although the aim of successive Conservative governments was to curb trade union activities in general and strikes in particular, the evidence on the effectiveness of the law during the late 1980s was by no means clear-cut (see Chapter 6). Secondary action, which was expressly targeted by legal restrictions, almost disappeared by the end of the 1980s (Millward *et al.*, 1992:358–9), and in a number of major disputes the law was used to great, if not decisive, effect (Evans, 1985, 1987; and *Labour Research*, September 1990). The dock strike of 1989 is a good example (see Blyton and Turnbull, 1998:140–7; and Turnbull *et al.*, 1992). In the 1989 ambulance workers' dispute the employers sought, and obtained, injunctions prohibiting action in five separate regional health authorities (see Blyton and Turnbull, 1998:280–6; Kerr and Sachdev 1992; *Labour Research*, April 1990; and Nichol, 1992). In other cases, union representatives called off strike action after employers threatened to use the law, and union members have, in some cases, been unwilling to strike through fear of entanglement with the law (*Labour Research*, September 1990). But in the majority of cases it appeared that employers were reluctant to use (as opposed to threaten to use) the law.

Equally, it has been argued that the law has not only had a limited overall impact on the level of strike activity, but may have acted to increase worker solidarity in the event of a strike, given that the action will have been approved by a majority of the workforce in a democratic vote (Brown and Wadhwani, 1990; Elgar and Simpson, 1993; and Martin *et al.*, 1991). What is often overlooked is that ballots allow both parties to put their position to a vote without a strike taking place. Indeed, with ballots becoming increasingly integrated into trade union bargaining strategies and consultation with members (Millward *et al.*, 1992:298–301), they are available for use as a bargaining counter: once a ballot has been called and strike action approved, employers find the alternative of meeting the union's demand or facing a strike difficult to counter (see Edwards, 1995b:455–6; Kessler and Bayliss, 1992:222; Martin *et al.*, 1991:202–3; and Undy *et al.*, 1996:240). In this context, then, strikes might be viewed as an indicator of union weakness as more powerful unions do not need to strike to secure their objectives: the threat of action is sufficient. Not only were more and more strikes preceded by a ballot, but in an increasing proportion the vote was in favour of strike action. And yet in a majority of cases there was ultimately no strike action. For example, in 89 per cent of the YES ballots in 1986 there was no strike action. Thus, as Brown and Wadhwani (1990) demonstrate, there may be a decline in overt disruption but not necessarily a diminution in the impact of the strike *threat*. This is supported by the absence of any significant decline in the proportion of CBI member organisations who cited the threat of industrial action as an important factor in determining their annual wage increase. In short, a decline in strike activity is neither indicative of a decline in industrial conflict nor of the demise of trade union power.

Economic pacification and legal (self) restraint, 1991–96

In the early 1990s, Britain's strike pattern changed yet again, with the number of disputes, workers involved and working days lost all recording new post-war lows. Changes to the composition of the labour force, as documented in Chapter 3, most notably the decline of (former) strike-prone industries such as vehicle manufacturing, the virtual demise of coal mining, and the substitution of non-union/casual labour for registered dockers on the waterfront, clearly contributed to the decline in strike activity (see Edwards, 1995b:449–54). Moreover, there was only one very large dispute involving the loss of more than 500 000 working days (a pay dispute in the transport sector in 1996 which resulted in the loss of 789 200 working days) and very few national disputes in this period. In fact, the decentralisation of collective bargaining (Chapter 7) and privatisation of whole swathes of the public sector (Chapter 6) rendered the logistics and legality of national, official macro-stoppages problematic to say the least. In addition to these structural changes, two factors appear to have been instrumental to the diminution of industrial disputes in the early 1990s, namely economic forces and legal constraints. As in the early 1980s, the economic recession of the early 1990s had a significant impact on workers' willingness to strike. Unlike the Thatcher recession of 1980–1, however, the Major recession of 1990–3 had a more widespread impact on the south as well as the north of the country, and on white-collar as well as blue-collar workers. Thus, whereas strikes in public services increased significantly in the 1980s compared to the 1970s, the number of disputes tumbled in the mid 1990s. More generally, the proportion of working days lost in pay disputes declined from three-quarters of all days lost in the late 1980s to less than 53 per cent between 1991 and 1996 (this proportion falls to less than 40 per cent for 1991–95, largely because of two major pay disputes in 1996). Disputes over redundancy questions accounted for 43 per cent of all working days lost at the height of the recession between 1991 and 1993.

The reticence of workers to strike is illustrated by an increase in the proportion of short (token) stoppages (over half the total number of stoppages lasted just one day or less), and an increase in the number of collective conciliation cases undertaken by ACAS. As in the late 1980s there were far more ballots for industrial action than actual strikes, which raises once more the question of the role of the law in employee relations. Following the introduction of the Trade Union Reform and Employment Rights Act 1993 (see Chapter 6), ballots for industrial action must now be conducted through an independent body. In the two years following the introduction of the Act, 5487 ballots were conducted by the Electoral Reform Society and Unity Security Balloting Services, of which 73 per cent were in favour of strike action. Thus, while there were just 435 strikes in 1994–5 there were over 4000 votes in favour of strike action, continuing the pattern of calculative bargaining established in the late 1980s. However, the cumulative, and coercive, effects of the law cannot be discounted. Gall and McKay (1996), for example, have demonstrated that, while the total number of injunctions brought against trade unions may be relatively few in number (just 169 between 1983 and March 1996), there was a relatively high frequency of injunctions related to the main provisions of each new Act immediately after its introduction. A decline in the *resort* to injunctions by employers, therefore, cannot be equated with a decline in the general *deterrence* effects of the body of statutory and case law established during the years of Conservative government: 'employers have experimented with each of the provisions of a new Act ... to obtain the remedy *they* required' (ibid:569, emphasis added), thereby setting the parameters and possibilities of 'lawful' industrial action. As Gall and McKay (1996:575) conclude,

> much of the 'real' influence of employment law may be, as it were, 'inside the minds' of union members and officials ... the cautious attitudes of trade unionists and the threats to and use of the employment laws by the employers, have led to an atmosphere of self-imposed restraint.

Public sector discontent 1997–2002

The first Labour Government appeared to enjoy something of a 'honeymoon' period with the labour movement as all measures of strike activity fell to a post-war low. Strike frequency was just 199 disputes per annum between 1997 and 2001, the number of workers involved averaged just 145 000, and working days lost averaged 357 000 per annum. With New Labour committed to the previous government's spending targets it is perhaps surprising that more strikes did not take place in the public sector, but the unions seemed reluctant to 'rock the boat'. In addition, many of the factors contributing to the reduction in strike frequency during the 1980s and early 1990s (see above) continued to be influential. Calculative bargaining, for example, was still very much in evidence. Thus, in the year to May 2001 there were 1926 ballots for industrial action, with workers voting in favour of action in 81 per cent of all ballots, but very few ballots translated into strike action (in fact, only 13 per cent of these ballots were for strike action as opposed to other forms of industrial action). One example of how conflicts unfolded was the dispute involving the Professional Footballers' Association (PFA) over the union's share of TV revenues. The PFA held a ballot of its 3500 members and all but 22 of 2315 returned votes were in favour of strike action (to be held in December 2001). In the face of such unanimity a deal was reached and televised games went ahead as scheduled. As in the early 1990s, when strikes did take place they were often 'token' or 'demonstration' events (around half of all strikes lasted one day or less). In response, employers turned increasingly to the threat of litigation (*Labour Research*, February 2002).

Strike action has been dominated by public sector disputes in the most recent period. Statistically, this is almost inevitable as disputes in the public sector tend to involve greater numbers. Thus, with historically low levels of strike activity even moderate-sized public sector disputes exert a disproportionate influence on the breadth and duration of total strike activity. Nonetheless, there was a growing sense of disquiet during Labour's first term in office which erupted following the Party's re-election in 2001. While the firefighters' dispute has been the most prominent public sector dispute in recent years, at least in terms of media coverage, many more public sector workers have been involved in strike action (e.g. education, public administration, local authority, health and social workers). In 2001, over half (57 per cent) of all days lost were due to stoppages in public administration, health and social work, while in 2002 over three-quarters (76 per cent) of days lost were due to stoppages in the public services. Causes of these public sector disputes included pay, and in particular the gap between public and private sector pay, cuts in service, privatisation, the introduction of new contracts and the threat of redundancy. Above all, perhaps, public sector disputes reflect a growing discontent on the part of public sector unions with 'their' government and the zeal with which New Labour has pressed ahead with the reform of public services, despite the objections of staff at all levels (see Chapter 6). This discontent recently (September 2003) led to the Prime Minister to agree to the establishment of a Public Services Forum that will enable union leaders and Government ministers to discuss public service issues on a more regular and more formal basis.

Overview

Although the pattern of strike activity in the post-war period may be sub-divided into these (apparently) distinct periods, it should be borne in mind that in practice these phases both overlap and display contradictory tendencies (Hyman, 1989b:198–9; see also Lyddon, 1998, who sub-divides recent strike data into different periods). Again, our analogy of a spiral is useful (see Chapter 1), emphasising the interplay of both continuity and change, of movement and return within the cycle. In 2002, for example, although the total number of disputes was at an historically low level, the number of working days lost increased sharply over the previous year. As we write, in late 2003, other potentially major disputes are smouldering, in the Post Office and elsewhere. Thus, in contrast to the idea of a gradual demise of strike action (Hanson and Mather, 1988), various other authors have noted that, over the long run, strikes have tended to occur in waves, reflecting the fact that strike

> Movements in various industries have generally been in the same direction and of at least comparable magnitude, as if orchestrated to one basic rhythm. That rhythm itself is unique: periodic explosions of militancy, or strike waves, have predominated over the long-term trajectory and short-term fluctuations. (Cronin, 1979:49)

Each wave, however, is unique, an indicator 'of qualitative changes in the relations between workers and employers' (ibid:47). The fact that strikes tend to fluctuate over time, both in the short and long term, suggests that, among other things, the state of the economy exerts a significant impact on strike activity. But while the root cause of strike waves may be economic, their effects are deeply political:

> Strike waves are the nexus of the strategic interaction between workers, employers, and the state. The financial and legitimation crisis provoked by strike waves requires solutions at *both* the economic and political levels. Reactions by employers and the state to strike waves set the terms of class relations for years to come. (Franzosi, 1995:347, original emphasis).

The object of study, then, is not simply the strike (statistic) but the changing nature of employment relations and the manifestation of (class) conflict in its many different guises.

Theories of strikes

Long-run waves in the pattern of strike action have been linked to the 'Kondratieff cycle' of industrial output consisting of a long period of rapid growth, lasting 20 to 30 years, followed by an equally long phase of stagnation. Evidence from a number of countries suggests that strike waves correspond to the downturn of the Kondratieff cycle (as in 1968–74) when workers' expectations are still rising while employers face a crisis of profitability (Franzosi, 1995:339–40; Kelly, 1998; and Screpanti, 1987). During the period of economic upswing, strikes are more frequent (workers are more confident) but of shorter duration (employers are often more willing to concede). The downswing, in contrast, is often a period in which industrial conflict evolves in a very irregular form, 'with high, short and scattered peaks of intensity emerging over a floor of depressed moods' (Screpanti, 1987:112). As Coates and Topham (1988:249–50) have observed,

> severe, large, prolonged strikes are associated with periods of economic dislocation and nascent slump, a time when workers' organizations are still strong, undefeated in major conflicts, and often when workers are most conscious of what they have to lose, in terms of living standards and job security.

At the same time, it is in such periods that employers will be fighting for survival and the protection of profit margins.

Although the economic cycle is widely acknowledged as impacting upon both the level and the character of strike action, the influence of economic variables is rarely straightforward. For example, when unemployment is low, workers are likely to feel more confident and be prepared to strike more often, but equally employers might be more willing to concede to union demands without a strike. When unemployment is high and rising, workers are likely to be less confident, but in the face of employer initiatives to cut costs they may have more reason to strike, and if they do so may display considerable solidarity. As a result, it is often argued that the general economic environment is more important as a 'background' variable. At a more disaggregated level, for example, it is evident that while the same macro-economic conditions prevail across the economy, some industries experience an increase in strike activity while others display a decline (Durcan et al., 1983:404–5). Cronin (1979:179–87), however, illustrates that it is the interplay of labour *and* (international) product markets which is the crucial variable, as the strike-prone industries are generally those that are 'thoroughly entangled' with economic fluctuations; those with a moderate strike-propensity are merely 'jostled' by the market; while those industries with very few strikes are largely 'sheltered' from the international market, producing mainly for domestic demand.

It has long been recognised that some industries and occupations are more prone to strike activity than others. While Cronin highlights the importance of international product markets in creating uncertainty and change, others have stressed the location of the worker in society. In a study of 11 countries Kerr and Siegel (1954) noted that miners, dockers, sailors, loggers and, to a much lesser extent, textile workers displayed the highest strike rates among different occupational/industrial groups. For Kerr and Siegel (1954:191–2) these workers,

> form isolated masses, almost a 'race apart'. They live in their own separate communities: the coal patch, the waterfront district, the logging camp, the textile town. These communities have their own codes, myths, heroes, and social standards. There are few

neutrals in them to mediate the conflicts and dilute the mass. All people have grievances, but what is important is that all the members of each of these groups have the same grievances.

Furthermore, these groups tend to have strong union organisation, 'a kind of working-class party or even government for these employees, rather than just another association', while the strike itself 'is a kind of colonial revolt against far-removed authority, an outlet for accumulated tensions, and a substitute for occupational and social mobility' (ibid:193).

Over the years, however, this theory has been much discredited. In their study of strikes in France, for example, Shorter and Tilly (1974:349) demonstrate that most French strikers were not, by and large, marginal workers on the periphery of society: 'the most militant, effective workers are precisely those in the middle of the heterogeneous, swirling metropolis, not the isolated proletarians of the civic community'. Likewise, the idea of strikes as a 'colonial revolt' explains little about the day-to-day conflicts over the wage-effort bargain that traditionally characterise the activity of strike-prone occupational groups such as miners and dockers. In a powerful critique, Edwards (1977) casts doubt on the measure of strike propensity used by Kerr and Siegel; the value of a typology, or more precisely a description of polar cases, which runs along two separate continua ('individual-mass' and 'isolation-integration') but leaves the 'middle ground' unresolved; and the fact that even among isolated masses such as miners and dockers, strike propensity varies considerably both within and between countries. As Turnbull *et al.* (1996) demonstrate, while dockers may have a deserved reputation for militancy, strike activity within the port transport industry was characterised by persistent disputes in a minority of major ports, which dominated the industry's overall strike pattern, and relative quiescence in the majority of ports where dockers, like colliers in a previous era (Church *et al.*, 1990) and their contemporaries in manufacturing (*Employment Gazette*, 1976:1219), rarely struck work.

In an international context, as Kerr and Siegel (1954) noted, dockers are usually found to be 'strike prone' when compared to other workers in the same country, but compare the strike record of Dutch and British dockers: between 1970 and 1979, Dutch ports recorded a yearly average of 2196 working days lost per 1000 employees compared to just 32 working days per 1000 employees in manufacturing (Smit, 1992:105), but this is almost entirely the result of two wildcat strikes at the port of Rotterdam at either end of the decade (a 2-week strike in 1970 and a 4-week strike in 1979); the port of London, in contrast, recorded a yearly average of almost 9000 working days per 1000 men on the payroll over the slightly longer period of 1967 (fourth quarter) to 1979 (first quarter), the result of almost 18 strikes per annum (Turnbull *et al.*, 1996:704). Kerr and Siegel (1954) utilise a ranking of industries based on days lost and employment to identify those that are 'strike prone', such that an industry with a days-lost ranking significantly higher than its employment ranking is defined as strike prone. But this focuses attention on *between*-industry rather than *within*-industry variation in strike activity, leading Kerr and Siegel to the (erroneous) conclusion that strike propensity is determined by *industry-level* variables such as the isolation of the dockland community, the nature of dock work, and the type of people who work on the waterfront (see Turnbull and Sapsford, 2001:232–3).

Notwithstanding these evident shortcomings, it is not unusual for commentators to fall back on the isolated mass theory, or a variant of it, to explain, for example, the decline of strike activity during the 1980s:

> The work organization and work culture of manual labour in mine and mill, dock and railway, shipyard and engineering factory, were relatively conducive to a 'spontaneous' sense of solidarity. Shops and offices, schools and hospitals are significantly different work milieu, with labour processes which are often fragmented and isolated. Clerks and typists, nurses and teachers, supervisors and technicians, typically respond to a complexity of interests and pressures; and their responses are rarely informed by a reflex commitment to the ethics and traditions of the labour movement. (Hyman, 1989b:229)

This is not to say that such workers will not strike. In fact, whereas almost 2.8 million workers employed in administration, health and banking were involved in strike action during the 1970s (including the Winter of Discontent), the comparable figure for the 1980s was 3.5 million (*Labour Research*, June 1992; and Lyddon, 1994). Rather, it is the character and meaning of such strikes, for those involved, that is different.

Despite the criticisms, the idea of community and the sense of common purpose this can engender cannot be simply dismissed. Arguably, 'community' should not be invoked to explain strike *incidence* but rather to help understand the character of workplace relations, the connections between work and non-work activities, and ultimately the *processes* involved in strike action (Edwards, 1988; Turnbull, 1992; and Turnbull *et al.*, 1996). Such factors clearly play a role in the ability of some groups of workers both to mobilise and sustain collective solidarity. Among dock workers, for example, once a decision had been taken to strike the dockers traditionally would accept this decision to a man, even if they disapproved of strikes in general or the particular issue at stake (Turnbull, 1992:299). On the waterfront, the connections between work and community were felt most forcibly by the blackleg, who would face ostracism and 'contrived accidents' at work while his family would share the same fear of opprobrium (ibid:299–300). During a particularly bitter and long-running dispute in the port of Liverpool (1995–8), for example, the names and addresses of 'scabs' who crossed the picket line were displayed in local pubs, and the wives of dockers dismissed by Mersey Docks & Harbour Company distributed leaflets to the neighbours of working dockers and regularly held vigils outside their homes.

Such militant solidarity was inextricably linked to the second factor identified by Kerr and Siegel (1954:195) in accounting for the inter-industry propensity to strike, namely the character of the job and the worker. Again, strikes cannot simply be explained by the nature of technology (the monotony of the assembly line, the hazards of the pit, the ergonomics of the office) (see Edwards, 1983:224; and Gallie, 1978), but this is not to say that such factors are unimportant. In general, work which is either skilled or dangerous, and especially both, often produces a high degree of emotional involvement in the work tasks. If workers see themselves in terms of their occupational role – because this offers the highest status and most flattering self-image available – and/or subscribe to a value system which is set by their occupation, they are likely to develop a strong occupational culture (Turnbull, 1992:298). In the firefighters' strike, for example, it was clear that bonds of solidarity within each watch, combined with the dangers of the job, strengthened the resolve of the workforce and sustained a shared sense of injustice even when public opinion began to fade and the press turned against them. As with the notion of community, then, occupational culture helps to explain how strikes may be sustained by traditions of solidarity or occupational identity, rather than necessarily explaining why strikes take place or why the frequency of industrial action varies over time and place. The latter requires much closer attention to bargaining structures and institutions, management initiatives and worker responses.

A clear illustration of the importance attaching to bargaining structures and institutions can be found in the work of the Royal Commission on Trade Unions and Employers' Associations (Donovan, 1968). One of the major conclusions of the Commission was that:

> The shortcomings of the industrial relations system emphasises how important and how general a failure there has been to devise institutions in keeping with changing needs. Unofficial strikes and other types of unofficial action are above all a symptom of this failure. This conviction is borne out by consideration of circumstances in all four industries which suffer most from unofficial strikes – coalmining, docks, shipbuilding and ship-repair and motors. In all these industries work group organisation is exceptionally strong, fragmented bargaining has been the rule, and wage structures have been notoriously anarchic. (1968:108)

Simply put, strikes will be more prevalent where employees possess the *means*, the *motivation* and the *opportunity* to strike (Clegg, 1979:272–9). In the docks, for example, despite the fact that unofficial action was discouraged by the T&GWU, and despite too the fact that neither management nor the T&GWU recognised shop stewards until after the introduction of permanent employment contracts in 1967 (known as 'decasualisation'), dockers had always been able to act independently, and effectively, on the wharf, where any delay to shipping could be very costly (the means); as a result of casual employment and the irregular arrival of shipping, attributable to the trade cycle, seasonal variation and the vagaries of wind and wave, dockers' weekly earnings fluctuated widely (the motivation); and with work organised around small gangs, paid at a piece-rate on jobs where no two cargoes were ever exactly alike (in respect of ship, gear, packaging, sequence of discharge, gang composition, and ultimately weather), there was ample scope for the negotiation and renegotiation of the wage-effort bargain (the opportunity) (see Turnbull and Sapsford, 1991; Turnbull, 1992; and Turnbull *et al.*, 1996). Similar features were evident in coal mining (Church *et al.*, 1990 and 1991; and Durcan *et al.*, 1983:240–71) and the car industry (ibid:312–51; and Turner *et al.*, 1967). Firefighters, in contrast, might possess the means to strike but there are fewer opportunities under national bargaining arrangements and their motivation to strike, for many years, was dulled by a pay formula that was widely regarded as acceptable. Moroever, firefighters display a strong commitment to public service. Indeed, many firefighters, such as Tony Jones, believed their action in 2002–03 was 'immoral' and only justifiable because of an ever-widening pay gap with those they served:

> while I accept strike action may be morally wrong, is it not also morally indefensible for firefighters who take such severe personal risk, so regularly, to be paid so little? For us to enter hazardous chemical plants, when those running the other way are often better paid? (Jones, 2002)

As with many other explanations, this particular theory – focusing on the means, opportunity and motivation to strike – has a certain intuitive appeal and empirical purchase, at least for the strike-prone industries. Thus, the movement from piece-rates to a national day-wage system in the mining industry, most notably the National Powerloading Agreement of 1966, was associated with a decline in short, small, pit-level disputes. But while management reform initiatives clearly had an impact on at least one dimension of the strike pattern in coal mining, they met with far less success in other industries (Durcan *et al.*, 1983:412). Indeed, industrial relations reform in many industries exacerbated rather than resolved conflicts of interest, suggesting that the initial explanation was inadequate (Edwards, 1983:224; and Turner *et al.*, 1977) and highlighting the importance of worker response to management initiatives. Put differently, strikes are not simply the outcome of various structural characteristics and economic conditions, as agency (the mobilisation of discontent by union activists) plays a crucial intervening role (see Kelly, 1998). As Edwards (1992:386) has argued, it is essential to consider the strategies of the two sides, the interaction between strategy and resources, and in particular the processes whereby background conditions become defined as resources that can be actively employed.

By linking the processes of strike action to the structural conditions of the economy and industry in general, and the workplace in particular, it is possible to construct an integrated analysis of the level and character of strike activity in specific industries (ibid:385–6; and Turnbull *et al.*, 1996). As previously discussed in

Chapter 5, Batstone (1988) has provided a useful framework for looking at the power resources of capital and labour, and on the labour side he identifies three principal resources: disruptive capacity in the production process; scarcity value in the labour market; and political influence within the political arena. The extent to which workers possess and can wield these resources depends in turn on the structures and strategies of their trade union(s). The level of union membership and density and the sophistication of union organisation will play a key role (sophistication here refers to the number and quality of union representatives, especially at the shopfloor level, their relations with members and the resources and facilities available to them). Finally, the power resources of the parties are influenced by a series of contextual factors, namely the nature of labour and product markets, the form of the production process and its technology, the institutions of employee relations and the role of the state.

In the case of coal mining, rising oil prices during the 1970s enhanced the disruptive potential of the miners, while changes to collective bargaining arrangements and state involvement in industrial relations placed the National Union of Mineworkers (NUM) in a position of considerable political influence. These power resources were wielded with great effect in the first national coal strikes since the General Strike of 1926. In addition, the disruptive and political influence of the NUM in 1972 and 1974 was backed up by effective union organisation and strategy, most notably the use of mass and flying pickets who were able to close power stations and seriously disrupt electricity supply. In the recent firefighters' dispute, in contrast, crews had the power to disrupt the production process but the presence of the military, and volunteer fire cover in rural areas, ensured the continuation of a fire-fighting capability during the strike days. Nonetheless, firefighters were able to wield significant political influence, especially for a comparatively small group. This could be attributed, in no small measure, to the (occupational) solidarity of the rank-and-file and the considerable support that firefighters enjoyed from the (voting) public.

Given that no two strikes are ever identical, a more integrated analysis of the level and character of strike activity across industries, occupations and individual workplaces allows not only the processes but also the meanings attached to such action to be analysed. Clearly, a one-day strike in a factory or office differs markedly from a long-running dispute in an emergency service or a year-long pit strike. For some workers, striking is *part of* the day-to-day struggles of industrial life, for others it is almost *separate from* those struggles, a rare event entered into with considerable fear and trepidation. The docks (Turnbull et al., 1996) and a small minority of manufacturing plants (Smith et al., 1978:55) were formerly good examples of the former, while many white-collar and professional occupations, along with highly competitive industries such as clothing and, to a lesser extent, the health service and essential services, are examples of the latter. The processes of industrial conflict will therefore vary from one organisation to another. Each will have a 'negotiated order', the outcome of a dialectical interaction between social structure and social consciousness, but in some situations this will engender a high level of stability, in others it will lead to heightened levels of conflict (Hyman, 1989b:71).

It is essential, therefore, to consider workplace relations in more detail, but in so doing to consider *all* manifestations of industrial conflict. Strikes in practice are part of a continuum of behaviour, albeit the most visible or manifest example of industrial conflict. But they are not the only manifestation. In coal mining, for example, not only did the expression of strike action change over time (small, short, pit-level disputes giving way to large, protracted, national stoppages), but there was an increase in absenteeism at precisely the same time. Thus, absenteeism in coal mining was believed to have 'replaced strike action to some extent as the most reliable index and manifestation of discontent' (Handy, 1968:45). Although Handy linked the sharp increase in absenteeism to the impact of pit closures on morale, there is also a clear link to changes in the structure of collective bargaining and the movement away from piecework payment systems negotiated at the pit level (Sapsford and Turnbull, 1993). As Hyman (1989b:58) has observed, 'attempts to suppress specific manifestations of conflict, *without removing the underlying causes of unrest*, may merely divert the conflict into other forms' (original emphasis). In other words, as one opportunity to express discontent was closed off (the short, small, pit-level strike), others were used more frequently (national, industry-wide strikes and individual absence). Similar trends are evident across the UK economy as a whole during the 1980s and 1990s, with employee relations managers forced to 'switch their attention from dealing with collective conflict to dealing with its individualised alternatives' (Millward *et al.*, 2000:226). As Clark Kerr pointed out many years ago, 'the manifestation of hostility is confined to no single outlet. Its means of expression are as unlimited as the ingenuity of man [*sic*]' (1964:170–1).

The forms and theory of industrial conflict

The bases of industrial conflict within capitalist economies – the structural antagonism that exists between employer and employee, both in the workplace and beyond – have been examined in some detail in Chapter 2. The fundamental characteristics and tensions of the employment relationship, such as hierarchy and control, exploitation and resistance, need not be repeated here. Whatever else may have changed over the past decade or so, the defining characteristics of the employment relationship remain unaltered. Thus, the basic conflicts of interest that exist between employer and employee have neither been eroded nor eradicated. Indeed, there is not even any evidence of 'them and us' attitudes having significantly weakened, either among workers (D'Art and Turner, 1999; Edwards and Whitston, 1993:30–1; Kelly, 1998; and Kelly and Kelly, 1991) or management (Waddington and Whitston, 1995b:416). What *has* changed, however, are the manifestations of industrial conflict. The growth of 'cut price' forms of collective action has already been noted. But what about individual or 'unorganised' forms of conflict? What about employer conflict with the employee, such as the intensification of work in the office (Lane, 1988:77), the hospital (Bach, 1989) and elsewhere (Edwards and Whitston, 1991; Green, 2001; and Waddington and Whitston, 1995b), which in some industries has been accompanied by an increase in accident rates and even deaths (Beaumont, 1995:42; Grunberg, 1986; *Labour Research*, September 1990 and June 1991; and Nichols, 1990)? As has been noted, 'the tensions generated by a given work situation may cause workers either to go on strike, stay at home, hit the foreman, or smash (or be smashed by) the machine' (Hyman, 1982:403).

A major distinction drawn between the many forms of industrial conflict is that absenteeism, turnover, sabotage and the like are regarded as forms of 'unorganised' conflict, where:

> workers typically respond to the oppressive situation in the only way open to them *as individuals*: by withdrawal from the source of discontent, or, in the case of certain forms of sabotage or indiscipline, by reacting against the immediate manifestation of oppression. (Hyman, 1989b:56, original emphasis)

More specifically, such action is usually spontaneous, reactive, and above all not born out of any calculative strategy. 'Organized conflict, on the other hand, is far more likely to form part of a conscious strategy to change the situation which is identified as the source of discontent' (ibid). In reality, however, the dividing line between organised and 'unorganised' conflict is rarely so clear cut. How does one classify, for example, 'blue flu', a situation where all the officers of the New York Police Department report in sick on the same day? Prison officers at Wormwood Scrubs recently employed a similar tactic. As Plowman *et al.* (1981:27) note, such action can prove to be a very effective substitute for the strike. Conversely, some spontaneous strikes display little calculative intent, with concrete demands only formulated *after* the walkout (the unofficial walkout by BA check-in staff in July 2003 at London Heathrow is a good example). Such stoppages, according to Hyman (1975:187), are more akin to mass absenteeism as the 'withdrawal from work' aspect predominates. Likewise, absenteeism may not only be a purposive and positive path to various sorts of personal goals (Nicholson, 1977:238), but 'a stratagem in intergroup relations ... a defensive or aggressive act in intergroup conflict' (Chadwick-Jones *et al.*, 1982:1). The fact that virtually every organisation has a known and accepted 'absence norm' suggests that absenteeism may be determined, or at least the boundaries defined, by cultural norms related to the social organisation of the workplace (that is, shared understandings about 'absence legitimacy', the custom and practice of employee behaviour and its control). In other words, such behaviour may, to some extent, be organised by the work group (see Turnbull and Sapsford, 1992:293–6).

Of course, absence from work may reflect many things other than conflict, and in general does not represent deliberate defiance. Again, however, whether such forms of behaviour can be taken as an expression of conflict with the employer will depend both on the meanings attached to such behaviour (is absence, sabotage, pilfering, unco-operative behaviour, *inter alia*, viewed as a way of 'getting back' at management?), and on the structure of employer-employee relations (in any given workplace, the expression of industrial conflict, in its many different forms, will be contingent on the pattern of labour control). On the world's airlines, for example, apparently innocuous and imperceptible behaviour such as the type of shoes being worn, the amount of jewellery, and even the colour of eye-shadow or underwear can all represent an expression of conflict and a means of 'getting back' at management as all these have been specified in the employee's contract (Hochschild, 1983:102–3 and 126). More explicit is the effect of employer–employee relations and the pattern of labour control on the cabin crew's facial expressions:

> in the flight attendant's work, smiling is separated from its usual function, which is to express a personal feeling, and attached to another one – expressing a company feeling. The company exhorts them to smile more, and 'more sincerely', at an increasing number of passengers. The workers respond to the speed-up with a slowdown: they smile less broadly, with a quick release and no sparkle in the eye, thus dimming the company's message to the people. It is a war of smiles. (ibid:127; see also Linstead, 1995)

For other employees it is a war of words. Telephone sales personnel, for example, who are increasingly required to 'charm' customers over the phone, may proffer misleading information and a false name, leaving customers to ring back for 'Mike Hunt' or his brother, 'Eric'. Instead of a charm offensive the company's employees indulge in offensive charm as a way of 'getting back' at management. Sixty employees who work for 118–118, the telephone directory enquiry service, were fired in 2003 for deliberately giving out wrong numbers, although in this case the motivation was to complete the call in 40 seconds and thereby qualify for bonus pay.

Unfortunately, 'unorganised' conflict, and the relationship between organised and unorganised conflict, has received remarkably little attention in either industrial sociology or industrial relations (Edwards and Scullion, 1984:547). While organised conflict is seen to be both formal and collective, and unorganised conflict both informal and individual, there is a considerable grey area in between. However, there is sufficient research on absenteeism, sabotage, pilfering and other forms of employee behaviour such as turnover to locate such action along a continuum, illustrated in Figure 10.1, and to develop a theory of industrial conflict focused on the characteristics of workplace relations and the negotiation of the wage-effort bargain.

At the collective end of the continuum, strikes are the most notable form of action organised by workers and/or their unions (on a more or less formal basis). Often as effective can be the work-to-rule, as such action can cause considerable disruption to production and frustration for management, while the workforce

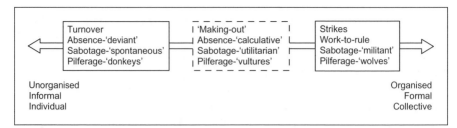

Turnover	'Making-out'	Strikes
Absence-'deviant'	Absence-'calculative'	Work-to-rule
Sabotage-'spontaneous'	Sabotage-'utilitarian'	Sabotage-'militant'
Pilferage-'donkeys'	Pilferage-'vultures'	Pilferage-'wolves'

Unorganised   Organised
Informal   Formal
Individual   Collective

Figure 10.1   Forms of industrial conflict

continue to receive wages. Such action is commonplace (see, for example, Coyne and Bartram, 2000:40; and Harris and Ogbonna, 2002:169) and often precedes wage negotiation or strike action (Batstone *et al.*, 1978:41). During wage negotiations, it is not uncommon for workers to indulge in 'bureaucratic sabotage', choking the company's grievance and disputes procedures with numerous claims (many of which may be bogus) in order to put pressure on management to reach a more favourable pay settlement. Although most people associate sabotage with the wilful destruction of machinery (throwing a spanner into the works), Dubois (1979:14) defines sabotage as *any* form of action, even 'working without enthusiasm', that results in a loss of production, lower quality output or an inferior service. Thus, sabotage might be active or passive, offensive or defensive, individual or collective, open or covert, spontaneous or organised (ibid:21; see also Ackroyd and Thompson, 1999). Harris and Ogbonna (2002), for example, describe 'service sabotage' as 'employee behaviour that is deliberately intended negatively to affect service standards'. In their survey of almost 200 staff in the hospitality industry, 85 per cent of customer contact staff admitted to some form of service sabotage behaviour during the previous week.

At the extreme, 'militant sabotage' – which is open, invariably collective, and usually well-organised – may be rare, but it has been actively and effectively deployed by some workers to exact concessions or exert control over the work process. Redundant textile workers in the French town of Givet, for example, recently released 5600 litres of sulphuric acid into a channel leading to the river Meuse as the first step of a four-stage action that was to culminate in blowing up their factory unless the government paid enhanced severance of two-years' salary and an £8000 lump sum. The French government conceded, at a cost of £5 million to the taxpayer. In the Italian port of Genoa, private employers recently conceded exclusive rights to a dockers' co-operative to supply any 'supplementary labour' required during cargo handling operations, following a prolonged period of industrial action that included arson attacks (see Turnbull, 2000:379). Such action is not only a direct challenge to managerial authority, but aims to restructure social relationships and redistribute power. As Taylor and Walton (1971:243) point out, however, attempts to assert control through sabotage (as at the Fiat car plant in Turin, Italy, in 1969) are more often found where 'restrictions are placed upon the expression of dissatisfaction in industries with a history of militant activity'. Thus, sabotage (ibid), and in particular absenteeism (Knowles, 1952:221), are often viewed as *alternatives* to strike activity, although some evidence suggests they may be *complementary* or *additive* forms of dissent (e.g. Bean, 1975; P.K. Edwards, 1979; and Turnbull and Sapsford, 1992).

For some workers, however, apparently individual acts such as absenteeism are in fact highly organised and controlled on a collective basis (Noon and Blyton, 2002:86–7). Not without reason, then, absence from work has been described as 'the silent strike' (Cook, 1990). In numerical terms absence from work is certainly as significant as strikes. There are in fact many more working days lost from absence than from strikes (Jones, 1971:12; and Nicholson, 1977:237); around 5–7 per cent of available working time for manual workers is lost due to absence (Edwards and Whitston, 1989:2) compared to much less than 1 per cent due to strikes. Absence among professional and white-collar workers has increased significantly in recent years, and it has been estimated that absence from work was costing British business around £11bn per annum by the late 1990s (CBI, 1997 and 2001). But is non-attendance an expression of conflict, either for the workforce as a whole or for specific work groups and/or individuals? The major cause of absence in the UK is short-term minor illness, and most employers are satisfied that the vast majority of sickness absence is genuine (CBI, 2001:6). But as the CBI (2001:6) asked, if this is the case then why are absence rates significantly different between the public and private sectors, and in particular between organisations of similar size in the same industrial sector?

Although a distinction is usually drawn between absence and absenteeism, where the former represents all permissible or excusable non-attendance while the latter implies deliberate or wilful non-attendance, in reality the distinction between the two is often blurred. The more important points, from the employers' perspective, are that, first, workers see absence through a very different 'moral lens', endorsing a range of types of absence that managers typically regard as illegitimate (Edwards and Whitston, 1993:45 and 48). Secondly, *any* form of 'avoidance behaviour' challenges managerial control. Absenteeism represents 'a refusal to accept managerial logic and an assertion by the worker of control over when his or her labour power shall be expended' (Edwards and Scullion, 1982:128). For management, then, absenteeism is at best a minor (logistical) impediment to the efficient organisation of production, at worst a direct challenge to managerial control and the viability of the organisation itself (Turnbull and Sapsford, 1992:294).

For employees, 'avoidable' absence is rarely a *deliberate* policy of resistance. More usually it is a means of relieving tension and frustration with the work situation, rather than any attempt to change that situation, let alone to restructure power relations. However, at times, and for some workers, absenteeism does represent an attempt to assert a greater degree of control over the labour process, a purposive activity which represents a direct challenge to managerial authority rather than simply a negative reaction to work pressures. Both forms of absence may represent conflict with the employer, but they have qualitatively different meanings for those involved, and qualitatively different behavioural consequences.

Where there are strong lateral ties between employees (strong horizontal integration) based on a strong 'occupational culture', as found among dockers, miners, shipbuilders or train drivers (see Edwards and Whitston, 1989:19; Nicholson and Johns, 1985:399; and Turnbull, 1992), and where hierarchical (low-trust) relations exist between management and workforce (weak vertical integration), it is not uncommon for workers to regard voluntary absence as an 'entitlement'. Moreover, such workers will defend their *right* to 'have one off' even in the face of managerial discipline (Turnbull and Sapsford, 1992:295; see also Noon and Blyton, 2002:87). Absence, in other words, is defiance of managerial control. Dockers, for example, traditionally engaged in highly organised forms of absence, taking it in turns to 'have one off', and would resist managerial attempts to discipline any one individual (gang member) for absenteeism on the argument that such action constituted random victimisation. The same would apply to pilfering, which among dockers was also a highly organised activity (Mars, 1974). As with absence, dockers would steal in groups, according to *their* rules, and would penalise their own deviants. Like refuse collectors, dock gangs display considerable order and internal control, maintained through a well-established hierarchy, earning the label 'wolves' as they work (hunt) and steal (kill) in packs (Mars, 1982:31–2; see also Ackroyd and Thompson, 1999:36–7, 81–5).

As with absenteeism, pilfering is arguably more costly than strikes. In fact, pilfering and fiddling was estimated in the early 1990s to cost UK companies £14m a day, or £5bn per annum (*The Independent*, 8 August 1992). In the retail sector, 25 000 incidents of theft by staff were reported in 1999 (an increase of 32 per cent on 1998) (Weait, 2001:57) and around 30 per cent of the costs of all retail crime (theft, fraud, burglary, and so on) is perpetrated by employees (Coyne and Bartram, 2000:38). Highly organised, collective forms of pilfering, however, are comparatively rare. More commonplace are situations where employees need the support of the group in order to steal, but like vultures they act on their own when at the feast (Mars, 1982:2). Travelling salesmen and bread roundsmen are good examples, relying on information and support from colleagues in order to 'work the fiddle', but acting in isolation for much of their actual work. A recent example that came to light involved British Airways cabin crew who were substituting counterfeit goods (e.g. replica Raymond Weil watches, Gucci sunglasses and Chanel perfumes) for in-flight duty free items on long-haul flights. Opinion was divided on how prevalent, and how well organised, such practices were within the organisation, but they were estimated to cost the company as much as £3 million per annum (*Sunday Times*, 12 September 1999).

Such cases clearly take us into the grey (middle) area of Figure 10.1 and presents considerable analytical problems (see Edwards, 1986:255). The boundary or dividing line between organised and unorganised, formal and informal activity is particularly difficult to locate. In order to protect piece-rates, for example, workers might establish output norms and discipline 'rate busters'. Controls are informal and individuals might refuse to conform, even when 'sent to Coventry'. More stringent collective controls are difficult to impose, however, as it is 'illegitimate' to discipline somebody for producing too much. The more significant point about such activity is that it is contrary to management control and direction of the labour process. Factory workers are often adept at deceiving management regarding the maximum effort or pace of work possible and are therefore able to 'make out' (Burawoy, 1979; and Noon and Blyton, 2002:237–42).

Output control, in its many guises, is essentially a calculative activity, an attempt to shift the wage-effort bargain in the employee's favour. Similarly, absence from work can take on 'calculative' overtones, especially in a low-trust work environment where employees' involvement in their work is limited to an essentially economic exchange (time versus money). The absence culture that develops will therefore be determined, in large part, by calculation (Nicholson and Johns, 1985:402–3), as will acts of sabotage. Again, the narrow conception of sabotage as a form of destruction is too limited as it can also include the production of goods below acceptable levels of quality (Dubois, 1979; and Edwards, 1986:249). In other words, workers might indulge in illicit or illegal activities to facilitate the work process, such as running machines above recommended speeds or using improper tools or materials, in order to increase output and earn more money, but such activity is against the interests of management as it can result in costly machine downtime and/or sub-standard production. Organisation, and even the connivance of supervisors, is implicit in such activity (see Taylor and Walton, 1971), although it will be *individuals* who are punished, or even dismissed, for such actions.

Thus, an important distinction between organised and (supposedly) unorganised forms of conflict is that, whatever the degree of organisation involved, in the latter case it is ultimately the individual that will be subject to discipline, and any group support for the individual concerned is more likely to be implicit rather than explicit. The employee's union, for example, is unlikely to condone the destruction of machinery, calculative absence, pilferage or even making out. At the extreme, where conflict is almost entirely unorganised, informal and individual, it is more than likely that unions will not be represented at all. The absence of union organisation, as was demonstrated in the case of Sew & Son and other non-union firms discussed in Chapter 9, is a key feature of many workplaces characterised by high levels of employee turnover (quits) (see Cully *et al.*, 1999:127–8). The physical isolation of employees at such companies makes organised activity difficult, as does the imposition of direct forms of control and the strict adherence to management rules. Thus, for supermarket check-out operators, shop assistants and many (female) machinists, patterns of isolation and subordination in their work are reflected in, for example, the nature of fiddling, where employees indulge in such activity on their own initiative and receive no group support either to perform such acts or if detected. The only collective dimension of such 'donkey' jobs (so-called because they are generally arduous, monotonous, repetitive and isolated) is that employees rarely accuse each other of fiddling. Beyond that, as a supermarket cashier cited by Mars (1982:68) pointed out, 'there are absolutely no alliances or anything like that'.

It is also commonplace for employee resentment at the impositions created by working in a supermarket or other repetitive jobs to be expressed through sickness and absence, which tend to be higher than normal (Hill and Trist, 1962:38; and Mars, 1982:31). According to Nicholson and Johns (1985:402–3), where management rules prevail, or where there is a dependent or paternalistic culture, voluntary absence from work is regarded as a form of deviant behaviour (consistent, of course, with the unitarist attitude of most managers). But it is difficult to distinguish between avoidable and unavoidable absence as non-attendance is more usually a means of relieving tension and frustration at work. Likewise, it is difficult to distinguish between accidental and intentional acts of sabotage. Such spontaneous acts of resistance can still be purposeful and positive for the employee – to let off steam or take a break – and at the same time can present considerable problems for management (see, for example, Harris and Ogbonna, 2002:171 and 178).

Running throughout this analysis of industrial conflict has been a focus on the on-going process of negotiation over the wage-effort bargain, the frontier of control which exists in all organisations. As employees attempt to redefine the wage-effort bargain or redraw the frontier of control, they come into conflict with their employer. Clearly, the pattern of negotiation and confrontation will differ markedly from one organisation to the next, with important consequences for the different forms of overt conflict – be it strikes, a work-to-rule, sabotage, pilferage, absenteeism, or whatever – and whether such action is organised or unorganised, collective or individual. In order to differentiate the many possible patterns, Edwards (1986:226–7) classifies workplaces according to three characteristics of workers' approaches and organisation:

- *Militant* – the extent to which workers perceive themselves as having interests which are opposed to, or are inconsistent with, the interests of management, and act accordingly.
- *Collective* – the degree to which an individual or collective orientation exists.
- *Organisation* – the extent to which a collective orientation is translated into collective organisation.

Using these characteristics, Edwards identifies four possible types of workplace, listed in Table 10.3.

As with other classifications, Table 10.3 comprises idealised and simplified types. Some cases will therefore fall between types, and there is a good deal of variation

Table 10.3 Classification of characteristics of workplace relations

	Militant	Collective	Organisational
TYPE 1	NO	NO	NO
TYPE 2	YES	NO	NO
TYPE 3	YES	YES	NO
TYPE 4	YES	YES	YES

TYPE 1 – is very common, especially in organisations that compete in highly competitive industries. Many of these industries employ female labour and have a strict system of supervision (direct control), as at Sew & Son (Chapter 9), but the key feature is the absence of resources among workers to make their demands effective against the demands of management. Also in this group, however, are organisations where sophisticated paternalism is the dominant management style, as at Marks & Spencer or IBM.

TYPE 2 – these workplaces are often characterised by militant individualism, where workers negotiate with management over rates of pay and assert their right to plan their own work (thereby exercising considerable influence over effort).

TYPE 3 – in these workplaces there is collective negotiation over the effort bargain (unlike Type 1), but controls are often informal or limited to exploiting managerial leniency. In other words, negotiation rarely develops into organised pressure to shift the frontier of control in workers' favour on a more permanent basis.

TYPE 4 – where the workforce exercises substantial control over the effort bargain, sustained through tight union organisation, control is exercised against management and over the workers as well (as on the docks).

Source: Adapted from Edwards (1986:227–34).

within each type. Nonetheless, there is a clear synergy between, for example, a Type 1 workplace and 'donkey' fiddles, 'spontaneous' sabotage, and absence which reflects an attempt to relieve the frustrations of work. Strikes in these organisations, if they do occur, are more likely to be *separate from* rather than an integrated part of day-to-day struggles. At the other end of the spectrum, one finds a synergy between a Type 4 workplace and 'wolf pack' fiddles and collectively imposed absence norms. For workers in such organisations, strikes are more likely to be *part of* the day-to-day struggle over the wage-effort bargain. Within Type 2 and 3 workplaces more calculative forms of pilferage, absence and sabotage may be found, but the fact that significant variation exists across these two types is indicative of the problems encountered in defining, and delineating, the different forms of conflict located in the grey (middle) area of Figure 10.1.

In each and every case, however, once it is recognised that the wage-effort bargain is indeterminate, as was demonstrated in Chapter 2, then it must be acknowledged that the struggle for control is an inevitable condition in *all* workplaces. That struggle may take the form of peaceful bargaining, or it may erupt into long and bitter strikes. The first step in the understanding of industrial conflict is therefore to recognise its many and varied forms. The second is to identify the meanings and purposes attached to workplace behaviour by the workers involved in order to determine whether such behaviour can be construed as an expression of conflict. Finally, just as 'to admit the rationality of strikes is to accept that strikers have a case: that genuine deprivations underlie industrial conflict' (Hyman, 1989b: 118–19), the same can be said of all other forms of conflict. To throw a spanner in the works or to go absent may not be as rational as to strike, since it brings only temporary relief and is unlikely to change either the immediate work situation or the frontier of control, except perhaps in the short term. But in some situations it may be the only option available and as such the most rational thing to do in the circumstances. Workers in the hospitality industry, for example, regard their predominantly individual acts of sabotage as 'rational' and entirely justifiable (Harris and Ogbonna, 2002:178). To restate the point made earlier, it is facile to argue that industrial conflict has abated in recent years without first undertaking not only a more detailed look at the strike statistics themselves but also, of equal, if not more importance, to consider the many other possible expressions of dissatisfaction and dissent in the workplace.

Conclusion

To seek an understanding of the nature of conflict within work organisations is to grapple with a complex phenomenon. While much analysis focuses on strike statistics which provide a ready 'index' of conflict, these data can offer a misleading picture. In recent years, for example, there has been a tendency to equate the decline in officially recorded strikes with a decline (or even demise) of industrial conflict. Not only does this ignore the intensity of conflict and bitterness of feelings invoked in many strike situations, it ignores the diverse nature of both strikes and other forms of industrial conflict. The firefighters' strike, for example, was just one of many prolonged and bitter public sector disputes over the past two decades. Prior to the strike, the firefighters had used an overtime ban and local protests to express their discontent. The subsequent failure of the strike either to gain even half of the pay demand or prevent radical changes from appearing on employers' or governmental agenda (Roberts, 2003b) suggests a continuation of discontent in the coming period. In this chapter we have therefore cautioned against any suggestion that industrial conflict has 'withered away', emphasising instead the many and varied forms of industrial conflict, the importance of both attitudes and behaviour, and the influence of a diverse range of structural, contextual and individual factors, both within the workplace and beyond. In particular, we have argued for a greater appreciation of the underlying (and continuing) sources of tension and conflict within contemporary work organisations, and an awareness that the business cycle, collective bargaining structures, pay systems and the like are as much a consequence as a cause of industrial conflict.

part 4

Summary and conclusions

11

The future direction of employee relations

Employee relations in transition

With more than half a million enterprises in the UK, spread across scores of industries, any attempt to draw general conclusions about the current state, and possible future direction, of employee relations, must necessarily be a cautious activity. In the foregoing chapters, however, we have sought to take account of some of the main aspects of this diversity. The case studies, for example, have purposely been drawn from public, private, and recently privatised sectors, from service and manufacturing activities, unionised and non-unionised settings and, in our case of Sew & Son in Chapter 9 and the discussion of union recruitment activities by the T&GWU and GMB in Chapter 5, smaller as well as larger establishments. What these cases and the wider analysis underline are the dangers of drawing too simple or over-generalised conclusions.

In practice, as we have seen, the colours in the landscape of employee relations run into one another: policies and practices are diverse, with developments taking place at different speeds and often in different directions. Tradition and a reluctance to change are represented in many employee relations practices, just as new departures and breaks with the past are evident. This should not take us by surprise. Employee relations are, after all, arrangements constructed and conducted by people, and the diverse characteristics of human nature – the presence of inertia, fear, reluctance and resistance to change, as well as forthrightness, risk and a desire to move on – will be reflected in the social arrangements that groups of people establish. What is more, those same social arrangements derive from an employment relationship whose essential characteristics are enduring: there remains an asymmetry of power, an indeterminacy surrounding the wage–effort contract, and an interdependency between the parties. The ensuing patterns of conflict, accommodation and co-operation produce both underlying continuities, while at the same time offer both opportunities and constraints to all the principal actors in employee relations. In many respects, employee relations, and in particular the context in which those relations take place, have been transformed in recent years. This transformation has been documented throughout the text. And yet there is still no coherent system of human resource management (HRM) or employee relations to replace the former reliance on collective bargaining and union-based channels of employee-interest representation. This reflects the fact that periods of transformation are characterised by experimentation with new practices and procedures, but also reflects the structural characteristics of capitalist employment relations in general and the (liberal-market) nature of the UK economy in particular. Thus, in a very real sense, nothing changes yet everything is different: as we twist around the spiral of capitalist economic development we experience progression and return, not a return to the same point but always to a place that has familiar features.

The developments and continuities evident in patterns of employee relations practice are of interest in their own right, but also as possible signposts to future trends. To illustrate these it is not necessary to rehearse all the arguments of the previous chapters, but it will be useful to summarise key developments for the main actors in employee relations and explore likely trajectories in coming years. In the following sections, we undertake this for management, trade unions, the national state and – in recognition of the growing importance of developments beyond national boundaries – the trans-national state.

Management, unions and the national and trans-national state

Management

In terms of management's role in employee relations over the past two decades, a persistent theme has been their attempt to reconstruct forms of labour control and develop a new employee-relations style. This has included attempts to ring-fence the power of the trade union voice – particularly the national union organisation – within the company. This objective can be seen to underlie, for example, debates within the union movement on the most appropriate relationship (co-operation or confrontation) between management and labour (see Chapter 5), in the way many companies (including Tesco, Chapter 8) have sought to (re)define the role of employee representatives in consultative rather than bargaining terms, and in the way (as in Corus, Chapter 7) attempts have been made to reduce or eliminate the significance of national collective bargaining frameworks (and national union influence) in favour of more localised activity, where attention is focused much more directly on plant performance. In addition, there has been a renewed emphasis on communicating the company's 'message' directly with employees. Compared to the 1970s, however, an increasing number of managers are keen to define this message and its operational implications as suitable topics for information and possibly even consultation, but not as a subject for joint regulation. Changes brought about in the nature of collective relations, and in particular the decline in collective bargaining coverage and a tendency for consultation to replace negotiation as the *modus operandi* of remaining union–management arrangements when dealing with work-related issues, coupled with a burgeoning of new forms of communication activity directly involving employees, reflect this management view.

Yet while important changes in management's attitude and approach to employee relations can be identified, this is not to deny that, in several respects, the way management handles employee relations has undergone little (and insufficient) change. This is partly the outcome of the continued reliance on a pragmatic and opportunistic approach to employee relations that elicits compliance rather than active co-operation from the workforce. The fact that management increasingly desire the latter but usually secure the former does not reduce the significance of co-operation in contemporary workplaces. In fact the opposite is true. For the language of 'customer care', 'continuous improvement' and 'total quality management' to be translated into meaningful activity, this requires the active co-operation, contribution, and knowledge of the workforce. Similarly, in such dictums as 'employees are our most valuable asset', the rhetoric, if not yet the reality, of HRM represents an acknowledgement that it is only through the active co-operation of the workforce that productivity, quality and ultimately profitability, can be sustained. Hence, in this key respect, the central managerial problematic – that of securing a surplus product *and* the co-operation of the workforce – remains all the more pressing today than in the past. Management's basic objective in any employee-relations policy remains the securing and maintenance of a predictable, productive and cost-effective labour force.

At various points throughout the book we have examined the different ways in which management rely on workforce co-operation and the various ways in which employee-relations policies and procedures are used to secure that co-operation. In our study of British Airways (Chapter 4), we examined how, in a growing number of contexts, management's need for co-operation has gone beyond the requirement to secure simply manual or mental labour, to a need to also elicit emotional labour: the self-subordination of employees' own emotions in the interests of 'customer satisfaction'. Clearly, the requirement for employees to suppress their emotions during the performance of their work role is not a new phenomenon. What *is* new, however, is the emphasis now placed on customer care as a particular source of competitive advantage. Indeed, in an industry where all airline staff greet their customers with a 'genuine' smile, it becomes *imperative* that management secure an active emotional contribution from their own workforce. Elsewhere too, the importance of employee co-operation and contribution is a prominent feature of our other cases: the importance of employee suggestions within Tesco, for example, and teamworking activities within Corus. Over the years, Marks & Spencer appears to have been adept at securing such co-operation from its workforce, although as we have seen the foundations for such co-operation are extremely high levels of dependency on the part of M&S employees and the subordination of employee interests at supplier companies.

To reiterate, at one level there appears to be a widespread recognition among management of the need to gain greater commitment and secure the active co-operation of its workforce in 'partnership' relations to achieve organisational success. At another level, however, management has failed to realise high levels of co-operation through the consolidation of employee relations on a more stable and longer-term footing. This may be illustrated by the way in which management in the UK, compared to some of their European counterparts, have sought to pursue greater workforce flexibility in recent years. The search for flexibility in the UK has been essentially 'defensive': it is primarily an *ad hoc*, short-term and low labour cost response to fluctuations in demand. The use of temporary and short-term contracts, hire and fire practices, and high rates of overtime working may be seen to typify this response. In contrast, 'offensive' or long-term flexibility strategies are characterised by greater proactivity, with an emphasis on achieving an adaptable, rather than a low-cost labour force. Training, re-training and the multi-skilling of employees are central to these notions of long-term flexibility. The deficiency of training provision in the UK, coupled with an emphasis on cost reduction (rather than productivity enhancement) as a central competitive strategy, are among the factors bolstering a continued reliance on short-term rather than longer-term flexibility strategies.

The short-term horizon of most flexibility strategies in the UK reflects a broader preoccupation with the short, rather than the longer term, and in particular the primacy of short-term financial performance as the measure of organisational success. It is often noted that UK companies display a unique form of financial myopia, in stark contrast to European firms. One survey, for example, found that UK (and US) managers ranked the importance of profitability for shareholders first and employee satisfaction last, whereas in western Europe (in particular Germany and France) the opposite was true (*The Observer*, 23 June 1996). This is just one of the many characteristics of liberal market economies (LMEs) compared to co-ordinated market economies (CMEs). The (over-)reliance on markets rather than institutions lies at the heart of poor productivity performance and many of the deleterious outcomes of employee relations in the UK (e.g. low wages, income inequality, the under-provision of training and low trust relationships between management and employees). In more recent years, macroeconomic stability, changes to corporate governance and new employment laws have gone some way to addressing some of the causes of short-termism. But these changes are insufficient to break the vicious spiral of cost-cutting which plagues UK industry. Stakeholding, as opposed to shareholding, where property rights are qualified by a mutual set of claims from employees, government, suppliers, customers and other interested parties (e.g. local communities), requires a legal and financial 'architecture' that allows companies to develop bonds of trust and co-operation with the various stakeholders in the company. If trust between management and labour does not evolve organically (as all the data from BSAS and other sources appears to suggest) then greater regulation of the labour market and labour management is called for.

The problem of short-termism in approaches to flexibility and other management policies is that they are self-reinforcing. For example, if labour is not only treated on an insecure and expendable basis but is also paid a comparatively low wage (such that it is always likely to be dissatisfied and in search of improved remuneration elsewhere), there is an increased likelihood that management will be discouraged from investing in high levels of training. For any specialist skills they require they will prefer, where possible, to 'poach' employees from elsewhere rather than train up their own workers or new recruits. The outcome, therefore, is inadequate training, both in quantity and quality. For capital as a whole, such a policy is inherently irrational, as firms face labour shortages for skilled labour even in the midst of high unemployment; but for individual capital*ists* it is evidently rational given the prevailing socio-economic context. Put differently, management often adopt irrational policies for rational reasons. This is perhaps the greatest failing of deregulation and HRM in a liberal market economy, namely the assumption that firms are 'islands' and that as long as top executives are committed to progressive personnel policies then everything will fall into place. But unless other firms in the same industry, sector or region adopt similar policies, firms that invest in their human resources run the risk of losing skilled labour. To prevent such 'free rider' and 'market failure' problems requires, first, a view of the workforce as a long-term investment and an important stakeholder in the future of the organisation; secondly, a degree of co-ordination between the actors (e.g. via collective bargaining, employers associations, and the TUC); and thirdly, an element of compulsion. The state can facilitate all three, via more proactive employment policies in the public sector (a return to the 'good employer' model), statutory support for collective bargaining and works councils, and compulsory training for all firms (perhaps via a training levy or similar policies).

Long-term commitment and motivation on the part of workers will be more likely to be secured if management are prepared to offer jobs that are stable, well paid, interesting and ones in which employees' views are adequately represented. Considerable lip-service has been paid by management to the importance of building long-term relationships grounded on partnership, trust and commitment, but in reality the reciprocity required to build a genuine improvement in employee relations has often been more notable by its absence. Managers have been clearer about what they require from employees (productivity, commitment, contribution) and the means to secure those outcomes (work intensification, cost minimisation, marginalisation of trade union influence, performance-related pay, teamwork, direct communications and the like) but are far less convincing when it comes to what they are offering in return, other than a job and a wage. And if the defining features of many jobs continues to be insecurity, low pay, inadequate representation, poor training and unsatisfying work, then any attempt to build employee commitment and more stable employee relations will be undermined by shallow foundations. It is little wonder that most UK firms have been unable to establish a coherent and consistent employee relations style, nor that they should encounter workforce opposition when they attempt to increase efficiency.

The argument here, then, is that there is a greater need for consistency and reciprocity in managerial policy towards employees and employee relations. In the longer term, the securing of high-quality, productive work from motivated employees will be more likely via the creation of a highly-skilled workforce afforded greater discretion and employed in better-paid jobs, than by continued adherence to a cost-minimisation strategy based on low-skilled, low-paid work. Indeed, the trajectory of international competition is increasingly towards non-price factors such as quality, specification, and service, which requires regulation, not deregulation, of labour markets (see Figure 3.5, p. 86). Although the UK's cost base may now be more competitive by world standards than in the 1970s, UK firms are still failing to develop new products and services at a sufficiently rapid rate. The 'hole in the heart' of UK manufacturing, and much of its service industry, is management who, though better trained now than previously (Storey and Tate, 2000), are failing to turn technology into competitive products.

These flaws in UK industry will take decades to remove, and will not be redressed without proactive labour market policies. Central to this must be higher levels of education and training, both for management and the workforce. For today's markets, productivity-enhancing, rather than cost-minimising approaches to service delivery and manufacturing are more likely to deliver high-value-added goods. Competitive edge, in other words, can be constructed on the basis of workers' skills, flexibility, innovation and adaptability, creating a matrix of high value added products, high wages, high productivity and high levels of investment (in both physical and human assets). Trade unions can play a positive role in such a matrix.

Trade unions

The challenges facing trade unions are widely recognised, both within and outside the labour movement: a decline in membership, a managerial attack on the role of unions within the workplace, increased legal circumscription of trade union action and internal organisation, political exclusion, and the need to appeal to new sections of the workforce. Recognition of these problems is one thing, action and resolution is another. Thus, just as management struggle to control the social relations of production in the face of a persistent (and inherent) tension with labour and the instability created by competition, so too do the very forces that have undermined trade union power, most notably economic recession and management hostility, have made the task of union renewal all the more difficult. If nothing else, the drain on union finances has put them in a Catch 22 situation: unions desperately need to recruit more members, but do not have sufficient resources to mount truly effective organising and recruitment campaigns, especially in those industries and firms where the potential for membership growth is greatest.

What has exacerbated the challenges facing trade unions is the evident lack of co-ordination within sections of the union movement itself. In part, this reflects the historic weakness of the TUC as a confederating body – a weakness which contrasts, for example, with the corresponding confederations in some European countries such as Austria, Germany, and Scandinavia (Traxler *et al.*, 2001) (though even in these, several union confederations in Norway, Sweden and elsewhere have weakened since the 1980s, with a growing proportion of union members belonging to organisations not affiliated to the central confederation). More significant in the UK, however, is the continued problem of inter-union competition over potential members, a problem which derives largely from historical structure and the absence of any 'industrial logic' in many union mergers. This has exacerbated the overall lack of co-ordination within the union movement, and renders organisation and recruitment in the non-union sector ('distant expansion') all the more problematic. The short-termism which bedevils managerial policy and practice in the UK, is thus echoed in trade union strategies for membership recovery, in particular the efforts being put into merger discussions and single-union recognition deals, rather than more concerted efforts in campaigning for membership recruitment and organising workers in new areas of employment and hitherto poorly-organised industries. Admittedly, these latter activities are riskier, and far more expensive in terms of union time and money; but in the longer run they are likely to create a more enduring basis for independent trade union organisation. As we discussed in Chapter 5, the adoption of an 'organising model' is designed precisely to circumvent some of these long-standing problems, but by its very nature is a time-consuming and resource-intensive process.

The impact of managerial strategies on trade union activity and action is more pervasive than is often appreciated. Most notably, the emphasis on cost minimisation contributes to the unions' problem of dwindling finances. Higher wage levels, particularly if coupled with an increased willingness to devote a higher proportion of wages to union subscriptions, could enable unions to establish more effective provision in such areas as membership enquiries, training of representatives, the buying-in of outside expertise and the funding of adequate research departments to facilitate, among other things, the development of more pro-active policies on work-related issues. The benefits of greater financial resources on the research capability of individual trade unions in Germany such as IG Metall (Jacobi, 2003:214), as well as the activities of the main German confederated body, the

Deutscher Gewerkschaftsbund (DGB), attest to the possibilities and potential of a more adequately resourced trade union movement. In the absence of significantly higher subscription income, an even greater premium is placed on unions deploying their resources effectively. This will not be achieved by competing with other unions for the same groups of workers, nor primarily by redistributing existing memberships by mergers and amalgamations, but rather by determining how unions can organise and work co-operatively to gain membership and influence in new areas of employment and develop their role in areas where recognition has already been secured. Currently, there are a great many employees who would benefit from union representation, particularly those employed by small, non-union companies. Moreover, the evidence suggests that many would actually join a union if given the opportunity (either by the union engaging in recruitment activity or the employer being willing to grant recognition). In a democratic society, employees should not be denied this right.

International research suggests that if trade unions in the UK could combine central and decentral organisation – effective representative structures at both national and workplace levels – then their prospects for the future would doubtless improve (see, for example, Boyer, 1995; Hancké, 1993; Hyman, 2001b; and Traxler *et al.*, 2001). While the organising model discussed in Chapter 5 might redress weaknesses at the workplace level, signs at the national level are less promising. In the late 1990s, unions were hoping to be led out of the political wilderness by the incoming Labour Government and thereby re-assert greater national-level influence. But as we saw in Chapter 6, so far this has not happened. In their efforts to remain 'business friendly' and to keep clear water between themselves and the trade union movement (in order to demonstrate to the electorate their independence from union leaders), Labour has enacted a programme of very specific rights at a minimum level, rather than a broader-based programme of reform. The unions have certainly not been invited back to the key policy-forming tables. If the UK is to move from a 'liberal' to a 'co-ordinated' economic system – as reflected in Labour's (partial) commitment to the 'social market' – then such a move, as depicted in Figure 6.1 (p. 185), will be predicated on a weak trade union movement, a 'pure' rather than a 'bargained' form of corporatism.

The national state

The UK state's general approach to employee relations has been characterised by a similar short-termism to that pervading management and, to a lesser extent, trade union thinking on employee relations. Of course these outlooks are not unrelated; management and unions are functioning in a labour market and an economy shaped by public policy and national economic management. In Chapter 6, we examined how the state's guiding principle throughout the 1980s and much of the

1990s was one of deregulating labour markets and removing 'obstacles' to the free operation of market forces. The main 'obstacle' to be removed or diminished was seen to be that of trade union influence, leading to an erosion by legislative action, strike defeats, unemployment and the termination of the union's role in policy-making bodies. As we noted, the competitive strategy advanced by successive Conservative governments centred on cost reduction, particularly the achievement and maintenance of the lowest possible labour costs. In turn, an emphasis on cost reduction rather than productivity enhancement drove a set of other policies: for example, a lack of priority given to the public funding of education, training and re-training provision. The upshot was the reinforcement of a comparatively low-skill, low-productivity, low-wage, and technologically backward economy, particularly in comparison with most of the UK's western European competitors.

This is the legacy that Labour inherited in 1997. While many changes in policy and direction are apparent since that time, the evidence reviewed in Chapter 6 also underlined the reticence that the Labour government has shown towards radically shifting the relative power of capital and labour within UK society. It is certainly not a shortage of parliamentary majority that has been the brake on radical change. More influential has been the desire to remain business friendly – to be seen as the first Labour government that gains and keeps the support of business. As a result, in many areas of public policy, only marginal revisions to the Thatcherite agenda have been introduced since 1997.

One of the most notable features of the UK's economic management is the degree to which key aspects of policy and practice are out of step with CMEs on the European mainland – countries that by most criteria are performing more successfully than is the case currently in the UK. While countries such as the Netherlands and Germany have built up extensive social protection and legal rights for employees, including rights to organise, bargain, receive information and take strike action, the UK in the 1980s and first half of the 1990s moved in the opposite direction, removing statutory protections from particular groups of workers, opposing European proposals aimed at safeguarding the interests of various (and often vulnerable) groups of workers, and weakening trade unions' ability adequately and effectively to represent the interests of employees. In the same way, while the vast majority of European countries operate with either minimum wage legislation or full coverage collective bargaining, in the UK significant sections of the workforce remained unprotected until the recent introduction of the National Minimum Wage. The result has been a wider dispersion of wages in the UK than in any of its European Union counterparts, and a higher proportion in low-paid employment (see Chapter 3). The Labour Government has, of course, signed the Social Chapter and introduced a statutory union recognition procedure, as well as enhanced employment rights and protections for individual workers. But Labour has also remained committed to retaining much of the previous Tory governments' employment and trade union legislation and, as a result, the UK still has some of the toughest labour laws in the western world. This is central to the Labour Government's commitment to labour market flexibility as a means of creating jobs, attracting inward investment, and holding down wage costs.

However, despite the attraction of the UK as a low-cost, off-shore location for overseas investment, in a world characterised by increased global trade and the trans-national organisation of service and goods production, a competitive strategy based on cheap labour costs in any Northern European country seems a likely act of folly. The Conservatives failed to recognise either the inability of UK capital to compete on labour costs with many newly-industrialising countries, or the centrality of identifying areas of potential competitive advantage and growth from a better-trained, more skilled workforce. The Labour Government has gone further in acknowledging the limitations of a cost-based strategy, but levels of skills development and utilisation remain disappointing (see Chapter 3). The main shortcoming of the state's labour market strategy during the 1980s and 1990s was not that it led to the UK becoming 'the Taiwan of Europe' as some observers suggested, but that it was impossible to maintain even this position in the face of the strong cost-based competition from Taiwan itself. There is no long-term security in a competitive strategy based on low-investment, low-cost, low-skill, low-technology, and low-value-added products. There will invariably be countries that can manufacture and export mass-produced, low-technology goods to the market cheaper than the UK. The same is true of much service activity, particularly involving lower skill, repetitive work, such as much call centre operations and data administration. It is alarming that the structure of the UK economy in key respects has come to resemble that of a semi-peripheral country, specialising in sectors that are not research intensive.

While the Labour government has prioritised education and training, fairness at work and company-based partnership, there remains serious doubt as to whether (functional) flexibility, productivity, and committed work relationships can germinate in soil which remains exhausted by neo-liberal economic policies and labour market deregulation. Outside the UK, in co-ordinated market economies, it has been more widely recognised that a truly adaptable workforce stems from secure rather than insecure employment relationships (see Figure 3.5, p. 86). According to Dore (1986), for example, the life-time employment system enjoyed by (a proportion of) workers in Japan, while appearing a potential source of rigidity, in practice yields high levels of flexibility, due to the reciprocal exchange of job security for acceptance of internal mobility and flexibility within the organisation. Similar arguments are evident in Europe, signalled for instance in the support for the EU Directive on 'atypical' workers designed to improve the rights of part-time and temporary workers (see Chapter 6). The previous Conservative government opposed this European Union initiative on the grounds that it would inhibit employers' flexibility, whereas other countries supported it on the grounds that a better-paid and better-protected part-time workforce would be more committed and more willing to be flexible: a flexibility based on the foundation, rather than the absence, of fairness and security.

In the UK, the widespread absence of high trust relationships in employee relations acts as a profound obstacle to the more effective development of those relations. It is difficult to see how that trust can develop and endure given attitudes that denigrate or at least marginalise collectivism as a component of employee relations, something to be discouraged wherever possible. As we have discussed, collectivism *is* compatible with efficiency, as European examples attest, and the EU has exerted a growing influence on employee relations in the UK in recent years. New Labour has signed the Social Chapter, but has not fully embraced the European agenda, exemplified by their reluctance to implement the Information and Consultation Directive (see Chapter 6). The so-called 'Third Way' – attempting to steer a path between liberal and co-ordinated market economics – has produced a vague and at times contradictory set of policies. For example, advocating partnership and fairness at work whilst retaining (external) labour market flexibility and Tory employment laws on union governance and strike action, two of the key channels for effective union and employee 'voice' within organisations. In contrast, the typical situation in Europe (though the precise position varies somewhat from country to country) is that these employee rights are seen by the state as legitimate and indeed *necessary* elements to the effective functioning of employee relations.

The trans-national state

Many of the structural features that shape and constrain employee relations in the UK – from the globalisation of capital and the dominance of shareholder over other stakeholder interests, to the nature and functioning of labour markets and the historical legacy of union organisation – will continue to exert a powerful influence in coming years. An increasingly significant factor in this coming period, however, will be that of further European integration. The precise extent of the European agenda will depend, in important part, on the way that governments, employers and trade unions respond to European initiatives. As we will see, so far the response from UK leaders in the twenty-first century demonstrates many of the shortcomings of their 1980s and 1990s forebears. By adopting a minimalist and at times hostile response to European initiatives, the UK could miss an important opportunity to put employee relations on a sounder footing to respond successfully to the transformed economic conditions that the economy now faces.

Any analysis and prediction of the influence of increasing European integration on employee relations within Member States and individual companies is far from straightforward. Not only has the UK government's orientation to Europe oscillated considerably during the time it has been an EU member, but in addition the attitudes of EU Member States as a whole towards the Union's social agenda lacks uniformity, with contrasting arguments being put forward regarding the merits of, on the one hand, establishing minimum levels of protection for employees within the EU and, on the other hand, the competitive dangers of failing to lower social charges and increase labour flexibility within the Union. With a further ten states joining the EU in 2004, the ability to predict the direction and pace of further European integration in general, and its social and employment policy in particular, is further complicated.

Under the Conservative government of John Major, the UK had 'opted out' of the social policy aspects of the Maastricht Treaty which limited the application of regulations introduced under the Social Chapter programme to the other Member States. During the period that the UK opt-out was in force, two employment-related Directives were introduced, concerning the introduction of European Works Councils in 'Community-scale undertakings', and the provision of parental leave. The incoming Labour Government expressed greater commitment to the philosophy underlying the Social Chapter, which it signed up to (cancelling the UK's opt-out) soon after gaining power in 1997. This meant that the terms of the European Works Council and Parental Leave Directives became applicable in the UK (together with subsequent Directives on part-time and fixed-term workers as well as the Information and Consultation Directive and other Directives in the pipeline on discrimination). In addition to these Directives, which have their origin in the European Commission, the European Court of Justice has made a number of significant judgements affecting employee rights in the UK, for example in relation to work of equal value and the access of part-time workers to statutory employment rights. Overall, and incrementally, these various provisions represent increasingly significant additions to basic employee rights and protections in Europe in general, and the UK in particular.

Yet, these various developments notwithstanding, it is also important to note that to date, the track record of the European Union in the area of employment and employee relations has been, at best, modest. In areas such as employee rights to information, for example, it has taken over two decades for proposals to make serious headway, and in the process many initial proposals concerning employee rights to information and consultation have been significantly diluted. Concerted employer opposition (voiced both by employers' associations and major trans-national corporations), the weakening of Directives in order to reach agreement, and (even then) the failure of individual Member States and companies to comply with EU regulations, signal the need for caution in being over-optimistic regarding any future scale and pace of development. Further, the overall level of economic activity, and in particular the level of unemployment both inside and outside the European Union, will exert an important influence on future developments.

Clearly, the power of organised labour to secure greater influence at organisational, national and supra-national levels is (and has been) undermined by slow economic growth. The continuing high level of unemployment in several

EU states, most notably Germany, will also affect the degree to which European Union institutions prioritise employment-generation issues, compared to defining and protecting the rights of those already in employment. Also, in spite of greater interaction between trade unions within Europe and the growth in the 1990s of the trade union 'Euro-demo' in Paris, Brussels and elsewhere against company closure announcements, unemployment levels in general, and related issues of job protection in particular, are likely to stimulate a greater degree of inward-looking (and thereby less of a pan-European) orientation among trade unions and employees within individual Member States: what one writer has termed 'the chronic vulnerability of unions to nationalism' (Ramsay, 1991:548). Thus, for both the EU institutions and the various trade union organisations, the level of attention given to extending employee rights and representation within the Union is likely to be greater during periods of low or declining unemployment, compared to when unemployment is high and/or increasing.

Yet, despite the only modest pace of development and the different factors impeding the pursuit of a strong employee relations agenda, incrementally the trans-national state is playing a growing role in employee relations. A brief review of one major form that this has taken in Europe – the creation of European Works Councils (EWCs) – indicates both the potential for development, and the scale of the task that lies ahead. Under the terms of the 1994 European Works Council Directive, trans-national organisations with at least 1000 employees across the Member States, and at least 150 employees in each of two or more States, are required to establish a European Works Council to act as the basis for informing and consulting with employee representatives on the company's plans and any proposals relevant to employee interests. Trans-national companies are required to provide information to their EWC on developments in the company's structure, its economic and financial situation, probable developments in the business, its current and likely future employment situation, and investment prospects. Consultation is required where management proposals are likely to entail serious consequences for the interests of employees.

According to figures from the ETUC, 639 trans-national companies had established EWCs by October 2002. Though a very substantial number, the ETUC points out that this represents only just over one-third of the estimated 1865 companies that fall within the scope of the Directive (Waddington and Kerckhofs, 2003:325). Just as this compliance rate to date may be seen as disappointing, assessment of the activity being undertaken by EWCs generally indicates the modest contribution that they have thus far made to the conduct of employee relations in trans-national firms. For example, the vast majority of EWCs meet only once a year, the minimum frequency under the Directive (ibid: 330; see also Weber *et al.*, 2000:14). Overwhelmingly, EWC meetings are management-led and principally used by management to communicate and consult over such areas as company performance, financial situation and investment, production and sales issues, new working methods, technology and employment (Waddington and Kerckhofs, 2003:330; see also Cressey, 1998). It is extremely rare for EWCs to go beyond information and consultation and undertake any joint decision-making activity (Carley, 2002). Even the extent of consultation and joint exchange can be highly restricted. At a recent EWC attended by one of the authors, for example, all questions from the employee representatives were required to be submitted four weeks in advance of the meeting to give management time to gather relevant information. The upshot was that the actual meeting was highly formalised and stultified: a series of managerial presentations, set answers and 'position statements' to the questions posed, with limited scope for further response. It is little wonder that the experience of most employee representatives at EWC meetings is one of disappointment with the conduct and outcomes of the meetings, particularly on key issues such as possible plant closures (Stirling and Fitzgerald, 2001:16). Little wonder too that given the restricted nature of the activity, studies have found no evidence that EWCs have any impact on company performance (Addison and Belfield, 2002).

The issue of consulting over closures highlights the shortcomings of the EWC structure. This was epitomised by the car-maker Renault who, in February 1997, announced the closure of its Vilvoorde plant near Brussels, without having consulted its 3100-strong workforce or their union representatives. This action was judged to contravene the 1975 EC Directive on collective redundancies (relating to the information and consultation rights of workers in the case of collective redundancies) and the European Works Councils Directive regarding employees being consulted and informed prior to the company's decision to close the plant. However, while Renault was found guilty of having contravened the Directives the maximum fines that might be imposed were trivial (for breaching the collective redundancies procedures, for example, the maximum was 4 million Belgian francs, around £66 000) and insignificant compared to either the 850 million French francs (over £90 million) which Renault announced it would save by transferring the production to other Renault plants (in fact no fines were applied by the Belgian court) (EIRR, 1998:22–3). Other trans-national corporations display a similar antipathy towards EWCs, as do the governments (or significant elements of the government) of some Member States.

To date, trans-national corporations have shown a clearer preference for 'divide and rule' policies towards workforces in different European locations, with attempts to control unions via 'coercive comparisons', threats of relocation, and unwillingness to divulge disaggregated financial information. This strategy is clearly facilitated by differences in national legislation, the tendency for some countries to be dominated by multi-employer industry bargaining arrangements (in contrast to others, such as the UK, where bargaining is more decentralised), the ideological conflicts between different union confederations in Europe, and the incipient nationalism of many employees and unions (particularly when faced with economic insecurity). Nonetheless, the EWC Directive may be seen to have a particular symbolic importance: not only does the Directive reflect the importance of worker rights to information and consultation within the Union, it also highlights the inter-related interests of employees working for trans-national organisations, and underlines the ability of firms to develop new (albeit restricted) forms of trans-national employee relations. More important, perhaps, are the possibilities for greater assistance, exchange of information and even international solidarity between trade unions, both at the EU level and within specific industries and trans-national firms. EU-wide consultative forums are already well-established in many industries (within the European Commission), such that for many unions EWCs will complement these activities and provide new opportunities for employee-interest representation.

In addition to any direct effects from EWCs or other Directives arising from the UK's termination of its 'opt-out' policy, European integration may gradually exert a more indirect, 'demonstration' effect on employee relations in the UK. Over the past two decades, the major demonstration effects on employee relations in the UK have come from Japan and North America. In part these have been imported via direct inward investment from these countries (by major companies such as Nissan, Sony, Toyota, Hewlett Packard, IBM and McDonald's). In addition, however, much of the managerial language that has become commonplace in recent years has drawn heavily on experiences and examples from these countries: for example, in the thinking behind TQM and JIT in Japan and in the language and practice of HRM in the United States. The influence of these ways of thinking is evident in recent UK employee relations – not least in the way that US-style HRM is seen to be consistent with an emphasis on individualism rather than collectivism in employee relations, or the emphasis on communications and involvement rather than bargaining and joint decision-making.

However, examples from Europe demonstrate that collectivism and social protection on the one hand, and economic success and efficiency on the other, are not mutually exclusive, and that such policies can operate successfully in systems where collectivism rather than individualism is still regarded as a central organising principle for employee relations. CMEs such as Germany demonstrate a greater acceptance of trade unions as legitimate members of the national body-politic, with works councils as highly regarded 'social partners' within the enterprise. The significance of works councils in Germany attests to the ability of management to work successfully with collective bodies that have rights to co-determination as well as consultation and information. Further, countries such as Germany and Sweden demonstrate that high levels of social protection are not an inevitable hindrance to efficiency, as appears to have been the view of recent UK governments and employers. On the contrary, employment security and social protection within CMEs acts as a 'positive constraint' on the activities of organisations, protecting workers interests *and* promoting the efficiency of the enterprise. If they could co-ordinate their efforts, this approach would be far more beneficial to workers, management and the state when compared to the short-term, cost-driven approach that characterises much employee relations practice in the UK.

A final word

A common adage is that management gets the trade unions and the employee relations it deserves. This maxim has been demonstrated at numerous points in the foregoing chapters. If the employment relationship is characterised by insecurity and mistrust, this hardly augurs well for employee relations. Add to this the attempts over much of the last two decades to undermine collective rights and representation, then the foundations of employee relations look shaky indeed. For seeking to reject collectivism is to disregard one of the fundamental characteristics of the employment relationship – namely the common experience of work within any organisation and the interdependencies that exist between workforce and management. The strident individualism of the 1980s and early 1990s is now widely seen as an historic failure. There is growing recognition of not only the legitimacy but also the efficacy of collective interest representation, both within the UK and in the pan-European context. That two decades of attack on trade unions did not break them is testament both to their resilience as organisations and the asymmetry inherent in the employment relationship, which gives rise to collective interests and the need for those to be articulated through independent representation.

In the past, too many employees have suffered from inadequate trade union support, poor management policies and the state's economic mismanagement. Unless the principal actors in employee relations adopt a longer-term perspective, recognise the legitimacy of collective representation, the benefits of an expanded floor of employee rights, and the value of much wider involvement and joint regulation of the employment relationship, then many employees will continue to be the victims of low-paid and unrewarding work. This situation is surely unsustainable for the state, unsatisfactory for management, and unacceptable for millions of employees.

Bibliography

Abbott, B. (1993) 'Small Firms and Trade Unions in Services in the 1990s', *Industrial Relations Journal*, 24(4): 308–17.

Abbott, B. (1998) 'The Emergence of a New Industrial Relations Actor – The Role of the Citizens' Advice Bureaux?' *Industrial Relations Journal*, 29(4): 257–69.

Ackers, P. (1998) 'On Paternalism: Seven Observations on the Uses and Abuses of the Concept in Industrial Relations, Past and Present', *Historical Studies in Industrial Relations*, 5(1): 173–93.

Ackers, P. (2002) 'Reframing Employment Relations: The Case for Neo-Pluralism', *Industrial Relations Journal*, 33(1): 2–19.

Ackers, P. and Payne, J. (1998) 'British Trade Unions and Social Partnership: Rhetoric, Reality and Strategy', *International Journal of Human Resource Management*, 9(3): 529–50.

Ackers, P. and Wilkinson, A. (2003a) 'Introduction: The British Industrial Relations Tradition – Formation, Breakdown, and Salvage', in P. Ackers and A. Wilkinson (eds), *Understanding Work and Employment: Industrial Relations in Transition*, Oxford: Oxford University Press, 1–27.

Ackers, P. and Wilkinson, A. (eds) (2003b) *Understanding Work and Employment: Industrial Relations in Transition*, Oxford: Oxford University Press.

Ackers, P., Marchington, M., Wilkinson, A., and Goodman, J. (1992) 'The Use of Cycles? Explaining Employee Involvement in the 1990s', *Industrial Relations Journal*, 23(4): 268–83.

Ackers, P., Smith, C. and Smith, P. (1996) 'Against All Odds? British Trade Unions in the New Workplace', in P. Ackers, C. Smith and P. Smith (eds), *The New Workplace and Trade Unionism: Critical Perspectives on Work and Organization*, London: Routledge, 1–40.

Ackroyd, S. and Thompson, P. (1999) *Organzational Misbehaviour*, London: Sage.

Adams, R. (1998) 'Taking on Goliath: Industrial Relations and the Neo-Liberal Agenda', in T. Wilthagen (ed.), *Advancing Theory in Labour Law and Industrial Relations in a Global Context*, Amsterdam: North Holland, 11–20.

Adams, R.J. (1995) *Industrial Relations Under Liberal Democracy*, Columbia: University of South Carolina Press.

Adams, R.J. (2002) 'The Wagner Act Model: A Toxic System Beyond Repair', *British Journal of Industrial Relations*, 40(1): 122–7.

Adams, R.J. and Meltz, N.M. (1993) *Industrial Relations Theory: Its Nature, Scope and Pedagogy*, Metuchen: IMLR Press.

Addison, J.T. and Belfield, C.R. (2002) 'What Do We Know About the New European Works Councils? Some Preliminary Evidence From Britain', *Scottish Journal of Political Economy*, 49(4): 418–44.

Adeney, M. and Lloyd, J. (1986) *The Miners' Strike, 1984–85: Loss Without Limit*, London: Routledge & Kegan Paul.

AEA (2002) *Association of European Airlines – Yearbook 2002*, Brussels: AEA.

Ahlstrand, B. and Purcell, J. (1988) 'Employee Relations Strategy in the Multi-Divisional Company', *Personnel Review*, 17(3): 3–11.

Aldington, Lord (1986) 'Britain's Manufacturing Industry', *Royal Bank of Scotland Review*, (151): 3–13.

Allen, M. (1998) 'All Inclusive', *People Management*, 4(12): 36–41.

Amin, A. and Dietrich, M. (1990) 'From Hierarchy to Hierarchy: The Dynamics of Contemporary Corporate Restructuring in Europe', Paper presented at the European Association for Evolutionary Political Economy Conference, Florence.

Andrews, M. and Naylor, R. (1994) 'Declining Union Density in the 1980s: What Do Panel Data Tell Us?', *British Journal of Industrial Relations*, 32(3): 413–31.

Appelbaum E. Bailey, T. Berg, P. and Kallenberg, A. (2000) *Manufacturing Advantage:Why High-Performance Work Systems Pay Off*, Ithaca, NY: ILR Press.

377

Armstrong, P. (1984) 'Competition Between the Organisational Professions and the Evolution of Management Control Strategies', in K. Thompson (ed.), *Work, Employment and Unemployment*, Milton Keynes: Open University Press, 97–120.

Arrowsmith, J. (2001) 'Pacts for Employment and Competitiveness in the Airline Sector', *Transfer*, 7(4): 629–35.

Arrowsmith, J., Gilman, M.W., Edwards, P. and Ram, M. (2003) 'The Impact of the National Minimum Wage in Small Firms', *British Journal of Industrial Relations*, 41(3): 435–56.

Ascher, K. (1987) *The Politics of Privatisation: Contracting Out Public Services*, Basingstoke: Macmillan.

Ashworth, M. and Forsyth, P. (1984) *Civil Aviation Policy and the Privatisation of British Airways*, Report Series No.12, London: Institute for Fiscal Studies.

Atkinson, J. (1984) 'Manpower Strategies for Flexible Organisations', *Personnel Management*, August: 28–31.

Audit Commission (1995) *In the Line of Fire*, London: HMSO.

Auerbach, S. (1990) *Legislating for Conflict*, Oxford: Clarendon Press.

Avis, R. (1990) 'British Steel: A Case of the Decentralization of Collective Bargaining', *Human Resource Management Journal*, 1(1): 90–9.

Bach, S. (1989) 'Too High a Price to Pay? A Study of Competitive Tendering for Domestic Services in the NHS', Warwick Papers in Industrial Relations, No.25, IRRU, University of Warwick.

Bach, S. (2002) 'Annual Review Article 2001. Public-Sector Employment Relations Reform Under Labour: Muddling Through or Modernization?', *British Journal of Industrial Relations*, 40(2): 319–39.

Bach, S. and Winchester, D. (2003) 'Industrial Relations in the Public Sector', in P. Edwards (ed.), *Industrial Relations: Theory and Practice*, 2nd edition, Oxford: Blackwell, 285–312.

Bacon, N. (1999) 'The Realities of Human Resource Management', *Human Relations*, 52(9): 1179–87.

Bacon, N. (2001a) 'Case 7.1: The UK's Largest Private Sector Employers', in T. Redman and A. Wilkinson (eds.), *Contemporary Human Resource Management: Text and Cases* Dorset: Pearson Education, 206.

Bacon, N. (2001b) 'Competitive Advantage Through Human Resource Management: Best Practice or Core Competencies?', *Human Relations*, 54(3): 361–72.

Bacon, N. (2003) 'Human Resource Management and Industrial Relations', in P. Ackers and A. Wilkinson (eds), *Understanding Work and Employment: Industrial Relations in Transition*, Oxford: Oxford University Press, 71–88.

Bacon, N. and Blyton, P. (2000) 'High Road and Low Road Teamworking: Perceptions of Management Rationales and Organizational and Human Resource Outcomes', *Human Relations*, 53(11): 1425–58.

Bacon, N. and Blyton, P. (2001) 'Management Practices and Employee Attitudes: A Longitudinal Study Spanning Fifty Years', *Sociological Review*, 49(2): 254–74.

Bacon, N. and Blyton, P. (2003a) 'The Impact of Bargaining Processes and Strategies on the Outcomes of Workplace Restructuring', Paper presented at BUIRA Annual Conference 2003, University of Leeds.

Bacon, N. and Blyton, P. (2003b) 'The Influence of Working Time Arrangements Accompanying the Introduction of Teamworking: Evidence from Four Sites', mimeo, Cardiff Business School.

Bacon, N. and Storey, J. (1996) 'Individualism and Collectivism and the Changing Role of Trade Unions', in P. Ackers, C. Smith and P. Smith (eds), *The New Workplace and Trade Unionism: Critical Perspectives on Work and Organization*, London: Routledge, 41–76.

Bacon, N. and Storey, J. (2000) 'New Employee Relations Strategies in Britain: Towards Individualism or Partnership?' *British Journal of Industrial Relations*, 38(3): 407–27.

Bailey, R. (1994) 'Annual Review Article 1993: British Public Sector Industrial Relations', *British Journal of Industrial Relations*, 32(1): 113–36.

Bailey, R. (1996) 'Public Sector Industrial Relations', in I. Beardwell (ed.), *Contemporary Industrial Relations: A Critical Analysis*, Oxford: Oxford University Press, 121–50.

Bain, G.S. (1970) *The Growth of White Collar Unionism*, Oxford: Clarendon.

Bain, G.S. (1986) 'Introduction to a Symposium on the Role and Influence of Trade Unions in a Recession', *British Journal of Industrial Relations*, 24(2): 157–9.

Bain, G.S. (2002) *The Future of the Fire Service: Reducing Risk, Saving Lives*. The Independent Review of the Fire Service. London: HMSO.

Bain, G.S. and Clegg, H.A. (1974) 'Strategy for Industrial Relations Research in Great Britain', *British Journal of Industrial Relations*, 12(1): 91–113.

Bain, G.S. and Elsheikh, F. (1976) *Union Growth and the Business Cycle*, Oxford: Blackwell.

Bain, G.S. and Elsheikh, F. (1980) 'Unionisation in Britain: An Inter-Establishment Analysis Based on Survey Data', *British Journal of Industrial Relations*, 18(2): 169–78.

Bain, G.S. and Price, R. (1983) 'Union Growth: Dimensions, Determinants and Destiny', in G.S. Bain (ed.), *Industrial Relations in Britain*, Oxford: Blackwell, 3–33.

Bank of England (2000) 'The International Environment', *Bank of England Quarterly Bulletin*, August: 233–46.

Bannock, G. and Daly, M. (1990) 'Size Distribution of UK Firms', *Employment Gazette*, May: 255–8.

Barney, J. (1991) 'Firm Resources and Sustained Competitive Advantage', *Journal of Management*, 17(1): 99–120.

Barrett, R. and Rainnie, A. (2002) 'What's So Special About Small Firms? Developing an Integrated Approach to Analysing Small Firm Industrial Relations', *Work, Employment & Society*, 16(3): 415–31.

Barsoux, J-L. and Manzoni, J-F. (2002) 'Flying into a Storm: British Airways (1996–2000)', INSEAD Cases, Fontainebleau, France.

Barton, H. and Turnbull, P. (1999) *End of Award Report: Labour Regulation and Economic Performance in the European Port Transport Industry*, (ESRC Award R000235425), www.regard.ac.uk.

Barton, H. and Turnbull, P. (2002) 'Labour Regulation and Competitive Performance in the Port Transport Industry: The Changing Fortunes of Three Major European Seaports', *European Journal of Industrial Relations*, 8(2): 133–56.

Bassanini, A. and Scarpetta, S. (2001) 'Does Human Capital Matter for Growth in OECD Countries? Evidence from Pooled Mean-Group Estimates', OECD Economics Department Working Paper No.289, Paris: OECD.

Bassett, P. (1986) *Strike Free: New Industrial Relations in Britain*, London: Macmillan.

Bassett, P. (1988) 'Non-Unionism's Growing Ranks', *Personnel Management*, March: 44–7.

Bassett, P. and Cave, A. (1993) *All for One: The Future of the Unions*, London: Fabian Society.

Bate, P. and Murphy, A.J. (1981) 'Can Joint Consultation Become Employee Participation?', *Journal of Management Studies*, 18(4): 389–409.

Bates, T. (1990) 'Entrepreneur Human Capital Inputs and Small Business Longevity', *Review of Economics & Statistics*, 72(4): 551–9.

Batstone, E. (1986) 'Labour and Productivity', *Oxford Review of Economic Policy*, 2(3): 32–43.

Batstone, E. (1988) 'The Frontier of Control', in D. Gallie (ed.), *Employment in Britain*, Oxford: Blackwell, 218–47.

Batstone, E., Boraston, I. and Frenkel, S. (1977) *Shop Stewards in Action: The Organization of Workplace Conflict and Accommodation*, Oxford: Blackwell.

Batstone, E., Boraston, I. and Frenkel, S. (1978) *The Social Organisation of Strikes*, Oxford: Blackwell.

Bean, R. (1975) 'The Relationship Between Strikes and Unorganised Conflict in Manufacturing Industries', *British Journal of Industrial Relations*, 17(1): 95–8.

Beardwell, I. (1996) 'How Do We Know How It Really Is? An Analysis of the New Industrial Relations', in I. Beardwell (ed.), *Contemporary Industrial Relations: A Critical Analysis*, Oxford: Oxford University Press, 1–10.

Beaumont, P.B. (1986) 'Management Opposition to Union Organisation: Researching the Indicators', *Employee Relations*, 8(5): 31–8.

Beaumont, P.B. (1987) *The Decline of Trade Union Organisation*, London: Croom Helm.

Beaumont, P.B. (1990) *Change in Industrial Relations*, London: Routledge.

Beaumont, P. B. (1992a) 'Annual Review Article 1991', *British Journal of Industrial Relations*, 30(1): 107–25.

Beaumont, P.B. (1992b) *Public Sector Industrial Relations*, London: Routledge.

Beaumont, P.B. (1995) *The Future of Employment Relations*, London: Sage.

Beaumont, P.B. and Cairns, L. (1987) 'New Towns - A Centre of Non-Unionism?', *Employee Relations*, 9(4): 14–15.

Beaumont, P.B. and Harris. R.I.D. (1988) 'High Technology Industries and Non-Union Establishments in Britain', *Relations Industrielles*, 43(4): 829–46.

Beaumont, P.B. and Harris, R.I.D. (1990) 'Union Recruitment and Organising Attempts in Britain in the 1980s', *Industrial Relations Journal*, 21(4): 274–86.

Beaumont, P.B. and Harris, R.I.D. (1992) 'Double-Breasted Recognition Arrangements in Britain', *International Journal of Human Resource Management*, 3(2): 267–83.

Beck, U. (1992) *Risk Society*, London: Sage.

Becker, B. and Gerhart, B. (1996) 'The Impact of Human Resource Management on Organizational Performance: Progress and Prospects', *Academy of Management Journal*, 39(4): 779–801.

Belanger, J. (1987) 'Job Control After Reform: A Case Study of British Engineering', *Industrial Relations Journal*, 18(1): 50–62.

Bellemare, G. (2000) 'End Users: Actors in the Industrial Relations System', *British Journal of Industrial Relations*, 38(3): 383–405.

Beynon, H. (1984) *Working for Ford*, 2nd edition, Harmondsworth: Penguin.

Beynon, H., Grimshaw, D., Rubery, J. and Ward, K. (2002) *Managing Employment Change: The New Realities of Work*, Oxford: Oxford University Press.

BHC (2002) *Annual Report and Accounts 2001*, Belfast: Belfast Harbour Commissioners.

Bird, D., Kirosingh, M. and Stevens, M. (1992) 'Membership of Trade Unions in 1990', *Employment Gazette*, April: 185–90.

Bitner, M.J. Booms, B.M. and Stanfield Tetreault, M. (1990) 'The Service Encounter: Diagnosing Favorable and Unfavorable Incidents', *Journal of Marketing*, 54(1): 71–84.

Black, O. Herbert, R. and Richardson, I. (2003) 'Jobs in the Public Sector, June 2002', *Economic Trends*, 598: 30–47.

Blackburn, R. A. (1990) 'Small Firms and Sub-Contracting: What is it and Where', Paper Presented at the Conference on Self-Employment, Essex.

Blackburn, R. and Hart, M. (2002) 'Small Firms' Awareness and Knowledge of Individual Employment Rights', DTI Employment Relations Series No.14, London: Department of Trade and Industry.

Blair, T. (1998) *The Third Way: New Politics for the New Century*, London: Fabian Society.

Blanchflower, D.G. and Oswald, A.J. (2004) 'Well-Being Over Time in Britain and the USA', *Journal of Public Economics*, (forthcoming).

Blyton, P. (1980) *Organizing Heterogeneous Employees Within A White Collar Union*, Unpublished PhD Thesis, Sheffield University.

Blyton, P. (1981) 'Cross National Currents in Joint Consultation', in R. Mansfield and M. Poole (eds), *International Perspectives on Management and Organization*, Farnborough: Gower, 59–66.

Blyton, P. (1989) 'Working Population and Employment', in R. Bean (ed.), *International Labour Statistics*, London: Routledge, 125–43.

Blyton, P. (1992) 'Steel: A Classic Case of Industrial Relations Change in Britain', *Journal of Management Studies*, 29(5): 635–50.

Blyton, P. (1993) 'Steel', in A. Pendleton and J. Winterton (eds), *Public Enterprise in Transition: Industrial Relations in State and Privatized Corporations*, London: Routledge, 166–84.

Blyton, P. and Bacon, N. (1997) 'Re-casting the Occupational Culture in Steel: Some Implications of Changing from Crews to Teams in the UK Steel Industry', *The Sociological Review*, 45(1): 79–101.

Blyton, P. and Turnbull, P. (eds) (1992) *Reassessing Human Resource Management*, London: Sage.

Blyton, P. and Turnbull, P. (1994) *The Dynamics of Employee Relations*, 1st edition, Basingstoke: Macmillan.

Blyton, P. and Turnbull, P. (1998) *The Dynamics of Employee Relations*, 2nd edition, Basingstoke: Macmillan.

Blyton, P., Martínez Lucio, M., McGurk, J. and Turnbull, P. (1998) *Contesting Globalisation: Airline Restructuring, Labour Flexibility and Trade Union Strategies*, London: International Transport Workers' Federation.

Blyton, P., Martínez Lucio, M., McGurk, J. and Turnbull, P. (2001) 'Globalisation and Trade Union Strategy: Industrial Restructuring and Human Resource Management in the International Civil Aviation Industry', *International Journal of Human Resource Management*, 12(3): 445–63.

Blyton, P., Nicholson, N. and Ursell, G. (1981) 'Job Status and White Collar Members Union Activity', *Journal of Occupational Psychology*, 54(1): 33–45.

Böheim, R. and Taylor, M.P. (2001) 'Option or Obligation: The Determinants of Labour Supply in Britain', Institute for Social and Economic Research, Working Paper 2001–05, University of Essex.

Bolton, J. (1971) *Report of the Committee of Enquiry on Small Firms*, Cmnd 4811, London: HMSO.

Booth, A.L. and Bryan, M.L. (2001) 'The Union Membership Wage-Premium Puzzle: Is There a Free Rider Problem?' Working Paper 2001–09, Institute for Social and Economic Research, University of Essex.

Booth, A.L., Dolado, J.J. and Frank, J. (2002a) 'Symposium on Temporary Work: Introduction', *The Economic Journal*, 112(480): F181–F188.

Booth, A.L., Francesconi, M. and Frank, J. (2002b) 'Temporary Jobs: Stepping Stones or Dead Ends?' *The Economic Journal*, 112(480): F189–F213.

Booth, C. (1902) *Life and Labour of the People in London*, London: Macmillan.

Bosch, G. (1990) *Retraining - Not Redundancy: Innovative Approaches to Industrial Restructuring in Germany and France*, Geneva: International Institute for Labour Studies.

Bosch, G. (2001) 'Working Time: From Redistribution to Modernisation', in P. Auer (ed.), *Changing Labour Markets in Europe*, Geneva: International Labour Organisation, 55–115.

Bosworth, D. (2000) 'Empirical Evidence of Management Skills in the UK', *Skills Task Force Research Paper*, London: DTI.

Bowles, S. (1985) 'The Production Process in a Competitive Economy: Walrasian, Neo-Hobbesian, and Marxian Models', *American Economic Review*, 75(1): 16–36.

Boxall, P. (1996) 'The Strategic HRM Debate and the Resource-Based View of the Firm', *Human Resource Management Journal*, 6(3): 59–75.

Boxall, P. and Purcell, J. (2003) *Strategy and Human Resource Management*, Basingstoke: Palgrave/Macmillan.

Boyer, R. (ed.) (1988) *The Search for Labour Market Flexibility*, Oxford: Clarendon Press.

Boyer, R. (1995) 'The Future of Unions: Is the Anglo-Saxon Model a Fatality, or Will Contrasting National Trajectories Persist?', *British Journal of Industrial Relations*, 33(4): 545–56.

Boyer, R. and Hollingsworth, J.R. (1997) 'From National Embeddedness to Spatial and Institutional Networks', in J.R. Hollingsworth and R. Boyer (eds), *Contemporary Capitalism: The Embeddedness of Institutions*, Cambridge: Cambridge University Press, 433–84.

Boyne, G., Kirkpatrick, I. and Kitchener, M. (2001) 'Introduction to the Symposium on New Labour and the Modernization of Public Management', *Public Administration*, 79(1): 1–4.

Bradley, J. and Hamilton, D. (1999) 'Making Policy in Northern Ireland: A Critique of Strategy 2010', *Administration*, 47(3): 32–50.

Brannen, P., Batstone, E., Fatchett, D. and White, P. (1976) *The Worker Directors: A Sociology of Participation*, London: Hutchinson.

Braverman, H. (1974) *Labor and Monopolgy Capital: The Degradation of Work in the Twentieth Century*, New York: Monthly Review Press.

Brecher, J. and Costello, T. (1994) *Global Village or Global Pillage: Economic Reconstruction from the Bottom Up*, Boston, Mass: South End Press.

Brewster, C.J., Gill, C.G. and Richbell, S. (1983) 'Industrial Relations Policy: A Framework for Analysis', in K. Thurley and S. Wood (eds), *Industrial Relations and Management Strategy*, Cambridge: Cambridge University Press, 66–72.

Brody, D. (2001) 'Labour Rights as Human Rights: A Reality Check', *British Journal of Industrial Relations*, 39(4): 601–5.

Brook, K. (2002) 'Trade Union Membership: An Analysis of Data from the Autumn 2001 LFS', *Labour Market Trends*, July: 343–55

Brown, D. and Crossman, A. (2000) 'Employer Strategies in the Face of a National Minimum Wage: An Analysis of the Hotel Sector', *Industrial Relations Journal*, 31(3): 206–19.

Brown, R.K. (1988) 'The Employment Relationship in Sociological Theory', in D. Gallie (ed.), *Employment in Britain*, Oxford: Blackwell, 33–66.

Brown, W. (ed.) (1981) *The Changing Contours of British Industrial Relations: A Survey of Manufacturing Industry*, Oxford: Blackwell.

Brown, W. (1983) 'British Unions: New Pressures and Shifting Loyalties', *Personnel Management*, October: 48–51.

Brown, W. (2000) 'Annual Review Article. Putting Partnership into Practice in Britain', *British Journal of Industrial Relations*, 38(2): 299–316.

Brown, W. and Nolan, P. (1988) 'Wages and Labour Productivity: The Contribution of Industrial Relations Research to the Understanding of Pay Determination', *British Journal of Industrial Relations*, 26(3): 339–61.

Brown, W. and Wadhwani, S. (1990) 'The Economic Effects of Industrial Relations Legislation', *National Institute Economic Review*, (131): 57–70.

Brown, W. and Walsh, J. (1991) 'Pay Determination in Britain in the 1980s: The Anatomy of Decentralization', *Oxford Review of Economic Policy*, 7(1): 44–59.

Brown, W. and Wright, M. (1994) 'The Empirical Tradition in Workplace Bargaining Research', *British Journal of Industrial Relations*, 32(2): 153–64.

Brown, W., Marginson, P. and Walsh, J. (2003) 'The Management of Pay as the Influence of Collective Bargaining Diminishes', in P. Edwards (ed.), *Industrial Relations: Theory and Practice*, 2nd edition, Oxford: Blackwell, 189–213.

Brown, W. Deakin, S. Hudson, M. Pratten, C. and Ryan, P. (1998) *The Individualisation of Employment Contracts in Britain*, Department of Trade and Industry Employment Relations Research Series 4, London: Department of Trade and Industry.

Brown, W., Deakin, S., Nash, D. and Oxenbridge, S. (2000) 'The Employment Contract: Form Collective Procedures to Individual Rights', *British Journal of Industrial Relations*, 38(4): 611–29.

Brown, W., Marginson, P. and Walsh, J. (1995) 'Management: Pay Determination and Collective Bargaining', in P. Edwards (ed.), *Industrial Relations: Theory and Practice in Britain*, Oxford: Blackwell, 123–50.

Bruch, H. and Sattelberger, T. (2001) 'Lufthansa's Transformation Marathon: Process of Liberating and Focusing Change Energy', *Human Resource Management*, 40(3): 249–59.

Bryson, A. (1999) 'Are Unions Good for Industrial Relations?' in R. Jowell, J. Curtice, A. Park and K. Thompson (eds), *British Social Attitudes: The 16th Report*, Aldershot: Dartmouth, 65–95.

Bryson, A. (2001a) 'Employee Voice, Workplace Closure and Employment Growth', Discussion Paper 6, London: Policy Studies Institute.

Bryson, A. (2001b) 'The Foundation of Partnership? Union Effects on Employees Trust in Management', *National Institute Economic Review*, 176(April): 91–104.

Bryson, A. (2001c) 'Union Effects on Managerial and Employee Perceptions of Employee Relations in Britain', Discussion Paper 494, Centre for Economic Performance, London School of Economics.

Bryson, A. (2001d) 'Union Effects on Workplace Governance 1983–1998', Discussion Paper 8, London: Policy Studies Institute.

Bryson, A., Cappellari, L. and Lucifora, C. (2002) 'Why so Unhappy? The Effect of Union Membership on Job Satisfaction', London: Policy Studies Institute.

Buchanan, R.T. (1992) 'Measuring Mergers and Concentration in UK Unions, 1910–1988', *Industrial Relations Journal*, 23(4): 304–15.

Bullock Committee of Inquiry (1977) *Report on Industrial Democracy*, London: HMSO.

Burawoy, M. (1979) *Manufacturing Consent: Changes in the Labor Process Under Monopoly Capitalism*, Chicago: University of Chicago Press.

Burchell, B.J., Day, D., Hudson, M., Ladipo, D., Mankelow, R., Nolan, J.P., Reed, H., Wichert, I.C. and Wilkinson, F. (1999) *Job Insecurity and Work Intensification*, London: Joseph Rowntree Foundation.

Burrell, G. (1992) 'Back to the Future: Time and Organization', in M. Reed and M. Hughes (eds), *Rethinking Organization*, London: Sage, 165–83.

Burrows, R. and Curran, J. (1989) 'Sociological Research on Service Sector Small Businesses: Some Conceptual Considerations', *Work, Employment and Society*, 3(4): 527–39.

Byrne, D. (1986) *Waiting for Change*, London: Low Pay Unit.

CAA (1996) *UK Airlines: Annual Operating, Traffic and Financial Statistics*, London: Civil Aviation Authority.

Cabinet Office (1999) *Modernising Government*, London: HMSO.

Caldwell, R. (2003) 'The Changing Roles of Personnel Managers: Old Ambiguities, New Uncertainties', *Journal of Management Studies*, 40(4): 983–1004.

Cameron, K.S. (1994) 'Investigating Organizational Downsizing – Fundamental Issues', *Human Resource Management*, 33(2): 183–88.

Campbell, J. (1997) *The Rose and the Blade: New and Selected Poems 1957–1997*, Belfast: Lagan Press.

Campbell, J. (1999) *Corner Kingdom*, Belfast: Lagan Press.

Campbell, M. and Daly, M. (1992) 'Self-Employment into the 1990s', *Employment Gazette*, June: 269–92.

Campbell-Smith, D. (1986) *The British Airways Story: Struggle for Take-Off*, London: Coronet Books.

Cappelli, P. (1985) 'Theory Construction in IR and some Implications for Research', *Industrial Relations*, 24(1): 90–112.

Cappelli, P. (1995a) 'Rethinking Employment', *British Journal of Industrial Relations*, 33(4): 563–602.

Cappelli, P. (ed.) (1995b) *Airline Labor Relations in the Global Era*, Ithaca: ILR Press.

Cappelli, P. and Crocker-Hefter, A. (1996) 'Distinctive Human Resources Are Firms' Core Competencies', *Organizational Dynamics*, 24(Winter): 6–23.

Carley, M. (1995) 'Talking Shops or Serious Forums?', *People Management*, 13 July: 26–31.

Carley, M. (2002) 'European-level Bargaining in Action? Joint Texts Negotiated by European Works Councils', *Transfer*, 8(4): 646–53.

Carlzon, J. (1987) *Moments of Truth*, New York: Harper and Row.

Carruth, A. and Disney, R. (1988) 'Where Have Two Million Trade Union Members Gone?', *Economica*, 55(1): 1–19.

Carter, B. (2000) 'Adoption of the Organising Model in British Trade Unions: Some Evidence from Manufacturing, Science and Finance (MSF)', *Work, Employment & Society*, 14(1): 117–36.

Carter, B. and Cooper, R. (2002) 'The Organizing Model and the Management of Change: A Comparative Study of Unions in Australia and Britain', *Relations Industrielles*, 57(4): 712–42.

Carter, H. (2003) 'Red Watch Bows to the Inevitable', *The Guardian*, 13 June: 10.

Casey, B. (1992) 'Redundancy and Early Retirement: The Interaction of Public and Private Policy in Britain, Germany and the USA', *British Journal of Industrial Relations*, 30(3): 425–43.

CBI (1997) *Managing Absence in Sickness and in Health*, London: Confederation of British Industry.

CBI (2001) *Pulling Together: 2001 Absence and Labour Turnover Survey*, London: Confederation of British Industry.

CBI/TUC (2001) *The UK Productivity Challenge: CBI/TUC Submission to the Productivity Initiative*, London: Confederation of British Industry/Trades Union Congress.

CEP (2002) *The Future of Unions in Modern Britain: Annual Report 2001*, London: Centre for Economic Performance, London School of Economics.

Chadwick, M.G. (1983) 'The Recession and Industrial Relations: A Factory Approach', *Employee Relations*, 5(5): 5–12.

Chadwick-Jones, J.K., Nicholson, N. and Brown, C. (1982) *Social Psychology of Absenteeism*, New York: Praeger.

Chan, D. (2000a) 'Beyond Singapore Girl: Grand and Product/Service Differentiation Strategies in the New Millennium', *Journal of Management Development*, 19(6): 515–42.

Chan, D. (2000b) 'The Story of Singapore Airlines and the Singapore Girl', *Journal of Management Development*, 19(6): 456–72.

Charles, R. (1973) *The Development of Industrial Relations in Britain 1911–1939*, London: Hutchinson.

Charlwood, A. (2002) 'Why Do Non-Union Employees Want to Unionize? Evidence From Britain', *British Journal of Industrial Relations*, 40(3): 463–91.

Child, J. (1997) 'Strategic Choice in the Analysis of Action, Structure, Organizations and Environment: Retrospect and Prospect', *Organization Studies*, 18(1): 43–76.

Church, R., Outram, Q. and Smith, D.N. (1990) ' British Coal Mining Strikes 1893–1940: Dimensions, Distribution and Persistence', *British Journal of Industrial Relations*, 28(2): 329–49.

Church, R., Outram, Q. and Smith, D.N. (1991) 'The Isolated Mass Revisited: Strikes in British Coal Mining', *Sociological Review*, 39(1): 55–87.

Clark, J. (ed.) (1993) *Human Resource Management and Technical Change*, London: Sage.

Clarke, J. and Newman, J. (1993) 'The Right to Manage: A Second Managerial Revolution', *Cultural Studies*, 7(3): 427–41.

Clausing, K.A. (2000) 'Does Multinational Activity Displace Trade?', *Economic Inquiry*, 38(2): 190–206.

Clegg, C., Nicholson, N., Ursell, G., Blyton, P. and Wall, T. (1978) 'Managers' Attitudes Towards Industrial Democracy', *Industrial Relations Journal*, 9(3): 4–17.

Clegg, C.W., Wall, T.D., Pepper, K., Stride, C., Woods, D., Morrison, D., Cordery, J., Couchman, P., Badham, R., Kuenzler, C., Grote, G., Ide, W., Takahashi, M., and Kogi, K. (2002) 'An International Survey of the Use and Effectiveness of Modern Manufacturing Practices', *Human Factors and Ergonomics in Manufacturing*, 12(2): 171–91.

Clegg, H.A. (1976) *Trade Unionism Under Collective Bargaining*, Oxford: Blackwell.

Clegg, H.A. (1979) *The Changing System of Industrial Relations in Great Britain*, Oxford: Blackwell.

Clegg, H.A. (1985) *A History of British Trade Unions Vol.2: 1911–33*, Oxford: Oxford University Press.

Clegg, H.A. (1990) 'The Oxford School of Industrial Relations', Warwick Papers in Industrial Relations, No.31, IRRU, University of Warwick.

Clegg, H.A., and Chester, T.E. (1954) 'Joint Consultation', in A. Flanders and H.A. Clegg (eds), *The System of Industrial Relations in Great Britain*, Oxford: Blackwell, 323–64.

Clegg, H.A., Fox, A. and Thompson, A.F. (1964) *A History of British Trade Unionism Since 1889*, Vol.1, Oxford: Clarendon Press.

Cliff, T. (1970) *The Employers' Offensive*, London: Pluto.

Coates, D. (1980) *Labour in Power?* London: Longman.

Coates, D. (1994) *The Question of UK Decline: The Economy, State and Society*, Hemel Hempstead: Harvester Wheatsheaf.

Coates, D. (2000) *Models of Capitalism: Growth and Stagnation in the Modern Era*, Cambridge: Polity Press.

Coates, D. and Hillard, J. (eds) (1986) *The Economic Decline of Modern Britain: The Debate Between Left and Right*, Brighton: Wheatsheaf Books.

Coates, K. (ed.) (1976) *The New Worker Cooperatives*, Nottingham: Spokesman Books.

Coates, K. and Topham, T. (1988) *Trade Unions in Britain*, London: Fontana.

Coates, K. and Topham, T. (1991) *The Making of the Transport and General Workers' Union Volume One: The Emergence of the Labour Movement*, Oxford: Blackwell.

Cohn, S. (1993) *When Strikes Make Sense – And Why: Lessons From Third Republic French Coal Miners*, New York: Plenum.

Cole, G.D.H. (1923) *Workshop Organisation*, Oxford: Clarendon Press.

Colgan, F. and Ledwith, S. (eds) (2002) *Gender, Diversity and Trade Unions: International Perspectives*, London: Macmillan.

Collard, R. and Dale, B. (1989) 'Quality Circles', in K. Sisson (ed.), *Personnel Management in Britain*, Oxford: Blackwell, 356–77.

Colling, T. (1995a) 'Experiencing Turbulence: Competition, Strategic Choice and the Management of Human Resources in British Airways', *Human Resource Management Journal*, 5(5): 18–32.

Colling, T. (1995b) 'Renewal or Rigor Mortis? Union Responses to Contracting in Local Government', *Industrial Relations Journal*, 26(2): 134–45.

Colling, T. (2003) 'Managing Without Unions: The Sources and Limitations of Individualism', in P. Edwards (ed.), *Industrial Relations: Theory and Practice*, 2nd edition, Oxford: Blackwell, 368–91.

Commons, J.R. (1919) *Industrial Goodwill*, New York: Arno Press.

Compa, L. (2002) 'Author's Reply to Wheeler-Getman-Brody Papers', *British Journal of Industrial Relations*, 40(1): 114–21.

Conyon, M.J. (1995) 'Directors' Pay in the Privatized Utilities', *British Journal of Industrial Relations*, 33(2): 159–71.

Cook, F.G., Clark, S.C., Roberts, K., and Semeonoff, E. (1975) 'White and Blue Collar Attitudes to Trade Unionism and Social Class', *Industrial Relations Journal*, 6(4): 47–58.

Cook, P. (1990) 'The Silent Strike: Causes and Solutions', Address to the Conference on Absenteeism and Employee Turnover, Centre for Industrial Relations and Labour Studies, University of Melbourne.

Corby, S. and White, G. (eds) (1999) *Employee Relations in the Public Services*, London: Routledge.

Corke, A. (1986) *British Airways: The Path to Profitability*, London: Frances Pinter.

Cornwall, J. (1977) *Modern Capitalism, Its Growth and Transformation*, Oxford: Martin Robertson.

Corus (2002) *Report and Accounts 2002*, London: Corus plc.

Council for Excellence in Management & Leadership (2002) *Managers and Leaders: Raising Our Game*, London: Council for Excellence in Management & Leadership.

Cowling, M. (2003) *The Contribution of the Self-Employed to Employment in the EU*, London: Small Business Service.

Coyne, I. and Bartram, D. (2000) 'Personnel Managers' Perceptions of Dishonesty in the Workplace', *Human Resource Management Journal*, 10(3): 38–45.

Crafts, N. and O'Mahoney, M. (2001) 'A Perspective on UK Productivity Performance', *Fiscal Studies*, 22(3): 271–306.

Craig, A. (1986) *The System of Industrial Relations in Canada*, 2nd edition, Scarborough, Ont: Prentice-Hall.

Craig, C., Garnsey, E. and Rubery, J. (1985) *Payment Structures and Smaller Firms*, Research Paper No.48, London: Department of Employment.

Cressey, P. (1998) 'European Works Councils in Practice', *Human Resource Management Journal*, 8(1): 67–79.

Cressey, P. and MacInnes, J. (1980) 'Voting for Ford: Industrial Democracy and the Control of Labour', *Capital & Class*, 11(Summer): 5–33.

Crompton, R. (2002) 'Employment, Flexible Working and the Family', *British Journal of Sociology*, 53(4): 537–58.

Cronin, J.E. (1979) *Industrial Conflict in Modern Britain*, London: Croom Helm.

Crouch, C. (ed.) (1979) *State and Economy in Contemporary Capitalism*, London: Croom Helm.

Crouch, C. (1982a) *The Politics of Industrial Relations*, 2nd edition, London: Fontana.

Crouch, C. (1982b) *Trade Unions: The Logic of Collective Action*, London: Fontana.

Crouch, C. (1995) 'The State: Economic Management and Incomes Policy', in P. Edwards (ed.), *Industrial Relations: Theory and Practice in Britain*, Oxford: Blackwell, 229–54.

Crouch, C. (2003) 'The State: Economic Management and Incomes Policy', in P. Edwards (ed.), *Industrial Relations: Theory and Practice*, 2nd edition, Oxford: Blackwell, 105–23.

Cully, M. and Woodland, S. (1996) 'Trade Union Membership and Recognition: An Analysis of Data for the 1995 Labour Force Survey', *Labour Market Trends*, May: 215–24.

Cully, M., Woodland, S., O'Reilly, A. and Dix, G. (1999) *Britain at Work: As Depicted by the 1998 Workplace Employee Relations Survey*, London: Routledge.

Cunnison, S. and Stageman, J. (1995) *Feminising the Unions: Changing the Culture of Masculinity*, Aldershot: Avebury.

Curran, J. (1990) 'Re-thinking Economic Structure: Exploring the Role of the Small Firm and Self Employment in the British Economy', *Work, Employment & Society*, 4(Special Issue): 125–46.

Curran, J. and Burrows, R. (1986) 'The Sociology of Petit Capitalism: A Trend Report', *Sociology*, 20(2): 265–79.

Curran, J. and Stanworth, J. (1981a) 'Size of Workplace and Attitudes to Industrial Relations in the Printing and Electronics Industries', *British Journal of Industrial Relations*, 19(1): 14–25.

Curran, J. and Stanworth, J. (1981b) 'The Social Dynamics of the Small Manufacturing Enterprise', *Journal of Management Studies*, 18(2): 141–58.

Currie, R. (1979) *Industrial Politics*, Oxford: Clarendon Press.

D'Art, D. and Turner, T. (1999) 'An Attitudinal Revolution in Irish Industrial Relations: The End of Them and Us?' *British Journal of Industrial Relations*, 37(1): 101–16.

Dabscheck, B. (1983) 'Of Mountains and Routes Over Them: A Survey of Theories of Industrial Relations', *Journal of Industrial Relations*, 25(4): 485–506.

Dahrendorf, R. (1956) *Class and Class Conflict in Industrial Societies*, London: Routledge & Kegan Paul.

Dale, I. and Kerr, J. (1995) 'Small and Medium-Sized Enterprises: Their Numbers and Importance to Employment', *Labour Market Trends*, December: 461–66.

Daly, M. (1990) 'The 1980s – A Decade of Growth in Enterprise', *Employment Gazette*, November: 553–65.

Daly, M. (1991) 'The 1980s – A Decade of Growth in Enterprise', *Employment Gazette*, March: 109–29.

Daniel, W.W. (1985) 'The First Job Taken by the Unemployed Compared with those they Lost', *Policy Studies*, 6(1): 38–58.

Daniel, W.W. (1987) *Workplace Industrial Relations and Technical Change*, London: Frances Pinter.

Daniel, W.W. and Millward, N. (1983) *Workplace Industrial Relations in Britain: The DE/PSI/SSRC Survey*, London: Heinemann.

Darlington, R. (1994) *The Dynamics of Workplace Unionism: Shop Stewards' Organization in Three Merseyside Plants*, London: Mansell.

Darlington, R. (1998) 'Workplace Union Resilience in the Merseyside Fire Brigade', *Industrial Relations Journal*, 29(1): 58–73.

Dastmalchian, A., Blyton, P. and Adamson, R. (1991) *The Climate of Workplace Relations*, London: Routledge.

Davies, G. (1999) 'The Evolution of Marks and Spencer', *Service Industries Journal*, 19(3): 60–73.

Davies, R.J. (1979) 'Economic Activity, Incomes Policy and Strikes – A Quantitative Analysis', *British Journal of Industrial Relations*, 17(2): 205–23.

Davies, R.J. (1983) 'Incomes and Anti-Inflation Policy', in G.S. Bain (ed.), *Industrial Relations in Britain*, Oxford: Blackwell, 419–55.

Davis, H. and Scase, R. (2000) *Managing Creativity: The Dynamics of Work and Organizations*, Milton Keynes: Open University Press.

Dawson, P. and Webb, J. (1989) 'New Production Arrangements: The Totally Flexible Cage?', *Work, Employment & Society*, 3(2): 221–38.

DED (1999) *Strategy 2010: Report by the Northern Ireland Economic Development Strategy Review Steering Group*, Belfast: Department of Economic Development.

Delaney, J.T. and Godard, J. (2001) 'An Industrial Relations Perspective on the High-Performance Paradigm', *Human Resource Management Review*, 11(4): 395–429.

Delbridge, R. (1998) *Life on the Line in Contemporary Manufacturing*, Oxford: Oxford University Press.

Delbridge, R. and Turnbull, P. (1992) 'Human Resource Maximization: The Management of Labou under Just-in-Time Manufacturing Systems', in P. Blyton and P. Turnbull (eds), *Reassessing Human Resource Management*, London: Sage, 56–73.

Delbridge, R., Turnbull, P. and Wilkinson, B. (1992) 'Pushing Back the Frontiers: Management Control and Work Intensification Under JIT/TQM Factory Regimes', *New Technology, Work and Employment*, 7(2): 97–106.

Deming, W.E. (1982) *Quality, Productivity and Competitive Position*, Cambridge, Mass: MIT Press.

Deming, W.E. (1986) *Out of Crisis*, Cambridge: Cambridge University Press.

Demos (1995) *The Time Squeeze*, London: Demos Quarterly.

Dempsey, P.S. (1989) *The Social and Economic Consequences of Deregulation: The Transportation Industry in Transition*, New York: Quorum Books.

Denman, J. and McDonald, P. (1996) 'Unemployment Statistics from 1881 to the Present Day', *Labour Market Trends*, January, 5–18.

Department of Employment (1991) *Industrial Relations in the 1990s – Proposals for Further Reform of Industrial Relations and Trade Union Law*, CM 1602, London: HMSO.

Desai, T., Gregg, P., Steer, J. and Wadsworth, J. (1999) 'Gender and the Labour Market', in P. Gregg and J. Wadsworth (eds), *The State of Working Britain*, Manchester: Manchester University Press, 168–84.

DETR (2000) *Modern Ports: A UK Policy*, London: Department of the Environment, Transport and the Regions.

Dex, S. and Smith, C. (2002) *The Nature and Pattern of Family-Friendly Policies in Britain*, York: Joseph Rowntree Foundation.

DfEE (2000) *Work-Life Balance 2000 Baseline Survey*, London: Department for Education and Employment.

Diamond, W. and Freeman, R.B. (2001) *What Workers Want from Workplace Organisations: A Report to the TUC's Promoting Trade Unionism Task Group*, London: Trades Union Congress.

Dicken, P. (1998) *Global Shift: The Internationalization of Economic Activity*, 3rd edition, London: Chapman.

Dickens, L. (1994) 'The Business Case for Women's Equality: Is the Carrot Better than the Stick?' *Employee Relations*, 16(8): 5–18.

Dickens, L. (1999) 'Beyond the Business Case: A Three-Pronged Approach to Equality in Action', *Human Resource Management Journal*, 9(1): 9–19.

Dickens, L. and Hall, M. (1995) 'The State: Labour Law and Industrial Relations', in P. Edwards (ed.), *Industrial Relations: Theory and Practice in Britain*, Oxford: Blackwell, 255–303.

Dickens, L. and Hall, M. (2003) 'Labour Law and Industrial Relations: A New Settlement?', in P. Edwards (ed.), *Industrial Relations: Theory and Practice*, 2nd edition, Oxford: Blackwell, 124–156.

Dickens, L., Jones, M., Weekes, B. and Hart, M. (1985) *Dismissed: A Study of Unfair Dismissal and the Industrial Tribunal System*, Oxford: Blackwell.

Dickmann, M. (2003) 'Implementing German HRM Abroad: Desired, Feasible, Successful?' *International Journal of Human Resource Management*, 14(2): 265–84.

Dickson, B. (2003) 'Northern Ireland's Experience', *Can Human Rights Save Society?* Liberty Annual Conference, London.

Dickson, T., McLachlan, H.V. Prior, P. and Swales, K. (1988) 'Big Blue and the Unions: IBM, Individualism and Trade Union Strategy', *Work, Employment & Society*, 2(4): 506–20.

Disney, R. (1990) 'Explanations of the Decline in Trade Union Density in Britain: An Appraisal', *British Journal of Industrial Relations*, 28(2): 165–78.

Disney, R., Gosling, A. and Machin, S. (1995) 'British Unions in Decline: Determinants of the 1980s Fall in Union Recognition', *Industrial & Labor Relations Review*, 48(3): 403–19.

Dobson, A.P. (1995) *Flying in the Face of Competition*, Aldershot: Avebury.

Docherty, C. (1983) *Steel and Steelworkers: The Sons of Vulcan*, London: Heinemann.

Doganis, R. (2001) *The Airline Business in the 21st Century*, London: Routledge.

Donovan. (1968) Royal Commission on Trade Unions and Employers' Associations 1965–68, *Report*, Cmnd 3623, London: HMSO.

Doogan, K. (2001) 'Insecurity and Long-Term Employment', *Work, Employment & Society*, 15(3): 419–41.

Dore, R. (1986) *Flexible Rigidities*, London: Athlone.

Dore, R. (1988) 'Rigidities in the Labour Market', *Government & Opposition*, 23(4): 393–412.

Dore, R. (1989) 'Where are We Now: Musings of an Evolutionist', *Work, Employment & Society*, 3(4): 425–46.

Dore, R. (2000) *Stock Market Capitalism – Welfare Capitalism: Japan and Germany Versus the Anglo Saxons*, Oxford: Oxford University Press.

Drucker, P. (1974) *Management: Tasks, Responsibilities, Practice*, London: Heinemann.

DTI (1998) *Fairness at Work*, Cm 3968. London: Stationery Office.

DTI (2000) 'Trade Union Recognition Procedure Begins', *DTI News Release*, 5 June: 1–2.

DTI (2001) *UK Competitiveness Indicators: Second Edition*, London: Department of Trade & Industry.

DTI (2002) *Productivity and Competitiveness Indicators: Update 2002*, London: Department of Trade & Industry.

DTI (2003) *Flexible Working: The Business Case. 50 Success Stories*, London: Department of Trade & Industry.

Dubois, P. (1979) *Sabotage in Industry*, Harmondsworth: Penguin.

Duffield, M. (2002) 'Trends in Female Employment 2002', *Labour Market Trends*, 110(11): 605–616.

Dundon, T. Curran, D. Ryan, P. and Maloney, M. (2003) 'Employee Information and Consultation in a Changing Economy', Paper presented at the 4th HRM International Workshop, University of Cadiz, Spain.

Dundon, T., Grugulis, I. and Wilkinson, A. (1999) 'Looking Out of the Black Hole: Non-Union Relations in an SME', *Employee Relations*, 21(3): 251–66.

Dunlop, J.T. (1958) *Industrial Relations Systems*, New York: Holt.

Dunn, S. (1990) 'Root Metaphor in the Old and New Industrial Relations', *British Journal of Industrial Relations*, 28(1): 1–31.

Dunn, S. and Metcalf, D. (1996) 'Trade Union Law Since 1979', in I. Beardwell (ed.), *Contemporary Industrial Relations: A Critical Analysis*, Oxford: Oxford University Press, 66–98.

Dunn, S. and Wright, M. (1994) 'Maintaining the Status Quo? An Analysis of the Contents of British Collective Agreements, 1979–1990', *British Journal of Industrial Relations*, 32(1): 23–46.

Dunning, J.H. (1976) *United States Industry in Britain*, London: Wilton House.

Durcan, J.W., McCarthy, W.E.J. and Redman, G.P. (1983) *Strikes in Post-War Britain: A Study of Stoppages of Work Due to Industrial Disputes, 1946–73*, London: George Allen & Unwin.

Dyer, L., Lipsky, D. and Kochan, T. (1977) 'Union Attitudes Towards Management Co-operation', *Industrial Relations*, 16(2): 163–72.

Earnshaw, J., Marchington, M. and Goodman, J. (2000) 'Unfair to Whom? Discipline and Dismissal in Small Establishments', *Industrial Relations Journal*, 31(1): 62–73.

Eaton, J. (2001) 'Management Communication: The Threat of Groupthink', *Corporate Communications: An International Journal*, 6(4): 183–92.

EDF (2002) *Working Together for a Stronger Economy*, Belfast: Economic Development Forum.

Edgeworth, F.Y. (1881) *Mathematical Psychics*, London: Kegan Paul.

Edwardes, M. (1983) *Back from the Brink*, London: Collins.

Edwards, P.K. (1977) 'A Critique of the Kerr-Siegel Hypothesis of Strikes and the Isolated Mass: A Study of the Falsification of Sociological Knowledge', *Sociological Review*, 25(3): 551–74.

Edwards, P.K. (1979) 'Strikes and Unorganised Conflict: Some Further Considerations', *British Journal of Industrial Relations*, 13(1): 95–8.

Edwards, P.K. (1983) 'The Pattern of Collective Industrial Action', in G.S. Bain (ed.), *Industrial Relations in Britain*, Oxford: Blackwell, 209–34.

Edwards, P.K. (1986) *Conflict at Work: A Materialist Analysis of Workplace Relations*, Oxford: Blackwell.

Edwards, P.K. (1988) 'Patterns of Conflict and Accommodation', in D. Gallie (ed.), *Employment in Britain*, Oxford: Blackwell, 187–217.

Edwards, P.K. (1992) 'Industrial Conflict: Themes and Issues in Recent Research', *British Journal of Industrial Relations*, 30(3): 361–404.

Edwards, P.K. (1995a) 'From Industrial Relations to the Employment Relationship: The Development of Research in Britain', *Relations Industrielles*, 50(1): 39–65.

Edwards, P.K. (1995b) 'Strikes and Industrial Conflict', in P. Edwards (ed.), *Industrial Relations: Theory and Practice in Britain*, Oxford: Blackwell, 434–60.

Edwards, P.K. (2003) 'The Employment Relationship and the Field of Industrial Relations', in P. Edwards (ed.), *Industrial Relations: Theory and Practice*, 2nd edition, Oxford: Blackwell, 1–36.

Edwards, P.K. and Scullion, H. (1982) *The Social Organisation of Industrial Conflict*, Oxford: Blackwell.

Edwards, P.K. and Scullion, H. (1984) 'Absenteeism and the Control of Work', *Sociological Review*, 32(3): 547–72.

Edwards, P.K. and Whitston, C. (1989) 'Industrial Discipline, the Control of Attendance, and the Subordination of Labour: Towards an Integrated Analysis', *Work, Employment & Society*, 3(1): 1–28.

Edwards, P.K. and Whitston, C. (1991) 'Workers are Working Harder: Effort and Shopfloor Relations in the 1980's', *British Journal of Industrial Relations*, 29(4): 593–601.

Edwards, P.K. and Whitston, C. (1993) *Attending to Work: The Management of Attendance and Shopfloor Order*, Oxford: Blackwell.

Edwards, P.K. and Wright, M. (1998) 'Human Resource Management and Commitment: A Case Study of Teamworking,Total Quality Management and Employee Involvement in Practice', *Organization Studies*, 18(5): 799–819.

Edwards, P.K. and Wright, M. (2001) 'High-Involvement Work Systems and Performance Outcomes: The Strength of Variable, Contingent and Context-Bound Relationships', *International Journal of Human Resource Management*, 12(4): 568–85.

Edwards, P.K., Hall, M., Hyman, R., Marginson, P., Sisson, K., Waddington, J. and Winchester, D. (1992) 'Great Britain: Still Muddling Through', in A. Ferner and R. Hyman (eds), *Industrial Relations in the New Europe*, Oxford: Blackwell, 1–68.

Edwards, R. (1979) *Contested Terrain: The Transformation of the Workplace in the Twentieth Century*, London: Heinemann.

Edwards, T., Rees, C. and Coller, X. (1999) 'Structure, Politics and the Diffusion of Employment Practices in Multinationals', *European Journal of Industrial Relations*, 5(3): 286–306.

EEF (2001) *Catching Up with Uncle Sam*, London: Engineering Employers' Federation.

EIRR (1998) 'The Repercussions of the Vilvoorde Closure', *European Industrial Relations Review and Report*, 289: 22–25.

Elgar, J. and Simpson, B. (1993) 'The Impact of the Law on Industrial Disputes in the 1980s', in D. Metcalf and S. Milner (eds), *New Perspectives on Industrial Disputes*, London: Routledge, 70–114.

Elger, T. (1990) 'Technical Innovation and Work Reorganisation in British Manufacturing in the 1980s: Continuity, Intensification or Transformation', *Work, Employment & Society*, 4(Special Issue): 67–101.

Elliott, J. (1978) *Conflict or Cooperation: The Growth of Industrial Democracy*, London: Kogan Page.

Emerson, M. (1988) 'Regulation or Deregulation of the Labour Market', *European Economic Review*, 32(2): 775–817.

Emmott, M. (2001a) 'Forward', in D. Guest and N. Conway, *Employer Perceptions of the Psychological Contract*, London: CIPD.

Emmott, M. (2001b) 'Woeful in Whitehall', *People Management*, 8 February, 39–40.

Enright, S. (2002) 'Preface', in G. Harvey and P. Turnbull, *Contesting the Crisis: Aviation Industrial Relations and Trade Union Strategies After 11 September*, London: International Transport Workers' Federation.

Equality Commission (2000) *Corporate Plan 2000–2003*, Belfast: Equality Commission for Northern Ireland.

Erickson, C.L. and Kuruvilla, S. (1998) 'Industrial Relations System Transformation', *Industrial & Labor Relations Review*, 52(1): 3–21.

ERM Economics (1999) *Privatisation of Belfast Port: Strategy Issues*, Report for the Department of Environment for Northern Ireland, Belfast: ERM Economics.

Estevez-Abe, M., Iversen, T. and Soskice, D. (2001) 'Social Protection and the Formation of Skills: A Reinterpretation of the Welfare State', in P.A. Hall and D. Soskice (eds), *Varieties of Capitalism: The Institutional Foundations of Comparative Advantage*, Oxford: Oxford University Press, 145–83.

European Commission (1997) *Partnership for a New Organisation of Work*, Green Paper, COM(97), Luxembourg: Office for Official Publications of the European Communities.

European Commission (2001) *Employment in Europe 2001*, Luxembourg: Office for Official Publications of the European Communities.

Eurostat (2000) *European Social Statistics – Labour Force Survey Results 2000*, Brussels: Eurostat.

Evans, S. (1985) 'The Use of Injunctions in Industrial Disputes', *British Journal of Industrial Relations*, 23(1): 133–7.

Evans, S. (1987) 'The Use of Injunctions in Industrial Disputes, May 1984–April 1987', *British Journal of Industrial Relations*, 25(3): 419–35.

Evans, S. (1990) 'Free Labour and Economic Performance: Evidence from the Construction Industry', *Work, Employment & Society*, 4(2): 239–52.

Ewing, K.D. (1989) *Britain and the ILO*, London: Institute of Employment Rights.

Ewing, K.D. (1991) *The Right to Strike*, Oxford: Clarendon Press.

Ewing, K.D. (1998) 'The State and Industrial Relations: "Collective Laissez-Faire" Revisited', *Historical Studies in Industrial Relations*, 5(1): 1–31.

Ewing, K.D. (2003) 'Labour Law and Industrial Relations', in P. Ackers and A. Wilkinson (eds), *Understanding Work and Employment: Industrial Relations in Transition*, Oxford: Oxford University Press, 138–60.

Fairbrother, P. (1983) *The Politics of Union Ballots*, London: Workers' Educational Association.

Fairbrother, P. (1996) 'Workplace Trade Unionism in the State Sector', in P. Ackers, C. Smith and P. Smith (eds), *The New Workplace and Trade Unionism: Critical Perspectives on Work and Organization*, London: Routledge, 110–48.

Fairbrother, P. (2000) *Trade Unions at the Crossroads*, London: Mansell.

Fairbrother, P. (2002) 'Unions in Britain: Towards a New Unionism?' in P. Fairbrother and G. Griffin (eds), *Changing Prospects for Trade Unionism: Comparisons Between Six Countries*, London: Continuum, 56–92.

Farnham, D. and Giles, L. (1995) 'Trade Unions in the UK: Trends and Counter-Trends Since 1979', *Employee Relations*, 17(2): 5–22.

Farnham, D. and Pimlott, J. (1990) *Understanding Industrial Relations*, 4th edition, London: Cassell.

Fells, R.E. (1989) 'The Employment Relationship, Control and Strategic Choice in the Study of Industrial Relations', *Labour & Industry*, 2(3): 470–92.

Felstead, A. (1993) *Franchising At Work*, London: Routledge.

Felstead, A. and Jewson, N. (2000) *In Work, At Home*, London: Routledge.

Felstead, A. Jewson, N. Phizacklea, A. and Walters, S. (2002) 'Opportunities to Work at Home in the Context of Work-life Balance', *Human Resource Management Journal*, 12(1): 54–76.

Ferner, A. (1989) 'Ten Years of Thatcherism: Changing Industrial Relations in British Public Enterprises', Warwick Papers in Industrial Relations, No.27, IRRU, University of Warwick.

Ferner, A. (1991) 'Changing Public Sector Industrial Relations in Europe', Warwick Papers in Industrial Relations, No.37, IRRU, University of Warwick.

Ferner, A. (2003) Foreign Multinationals and Industrial Relations Innovation in Britain' in P. Edwards (ed.), *Industrial Relations: Theory and Practice*, second edition, Oxford: Blackwell, 81–104.

Ferner, A. and Colling, T. (1991) 'Privatization, Regulation and Industrial Relations', *British Journal of Industrial Relations*, 29(3): 391–409.

Ferner, A. and Colling, T. (1995) 'Privatization and Marketization', in P. Edwards (ed.), *Industrial Relations: Theory and Practice in Britain*, Oxford: Blackwell, 491–514.

Ferner, A. and Varul, M. (2000) 'Vanguard Subsidiaries and the Diffusion of New Practices: A Case Study of German Multinational', *British Journal of Industrial Relations*, 38(1): 115–40.

Fernie, S. and Gray, H. (2001) 'It's a Family Affair: The Effects of Union Recognition and Human Resource Management on the Provision of Equal Opportunities in the UK', Centre for Economic Performance Working Paper No.1178, London School of Economics.

Fevre, R. (1987) 'Subcontracting in Steel', *Work, Employment & Society*, 1(4): 509–27.

Filipcova, B. and Filipec, J. (1986) 'Society and Concepts of Time', *International Social Science Journal*, (107): 19–32.

Fine, B. (1990) 'Scaling the Commanding Heights of Public Enterprise Economics', *Cambridge Journal of Economics*, 14(2): 127–42.

Fine, B. (2002) ' "Economic Imperialism": A View from the Periphery', *Review of Radical Political Economics*, 34: 187–201.

Fine, B. and Harris, L. (eds) (1985) *The Peculiarities of the British Economy*, London: Lawrence & Wishart.

Fine, B. and O'Donnell, C. (1985) 'The Nationalised Industries', in B. Fine and L. Harris (eds), *The Peculiarities of the British Economy*, London: Lawrence & Wishart, 147–66.

Finegold, D. and Soskice, D. (1988) 'The Failure of Training in Britain: Analysis and Prescription', *Oxford Review of Economic Policy*, 4(3): 21–53.

Fiorito, J. (2003) 'Union Oragnizing in the United States', in G. Gall (ed.), *Union Organizing: Campaigning for Trade Union Recognition*, London: Routledge, 191–210.

Fitzgerald, I. and Stirling, J. (1999) 'A Slow Burning Flame? Organisational Change and Industrial Relations in the Fire Service', *Industrial Relations Journal*, 30(1): 46–60.

Flanders, A. (1964) *The Fawley Productivity Agreements: A Case Study of Management and Collective Bargaining*, London: Faber.

Flanders, A. (1965) *Industrial Relations: What is Wrong with the System?* London: Faber.

Flanders, A. (1975) *Management and Unions: The Theory and Reform of Industrial Relations*, London: Faber & Faber.

Flanders, A. and Clegg, H.A. (1954) *The System of Industrial Relations in Great Britain*, Oxford: Blackwell.

Flint, P. (1999) 'The Flight to Quality', *Air Transport World*, 36(9): 5.

Flood, P. and Turner, T. (1993) 'Human Resource Strategy and the Non-Union Phenomenon', *Employee Relations*, 15(6): 54–66.

Fombrum, C., Tichy, N. and Devanna, M. (eds) (1984) *Strategic Human Resource Management*, New York: Wiley.

Ford, J. (1982) 'Who Breaks the Rules? The Response of Small Businesses to External Regulation', *Industrial Relations Journal*, 13(3): 40–9.

Forde, C. (2001) 'Notes and Issues – Temporary Arrangements: The Activities of Employment Agencies in the UK', *Work, Employment & Society*, 15(3): 631–44.

Forrester, V. (1999) *The Economic Horror*, London: Polity Press.

Forth, J. and Millward, N. (2000) 'The Determinants of Pay Levels and Fringe Benefit Provision in Britain', Discussion Paper 171, National Institute of Economic & Social Research, London.

Foster, D. and Scott, P. (1998) 'Competitive Tendering of Public Services and Industrial Relations Policy: The Conservative Agenda Under Thatcher and Major, 1979–97', *Historical Studies in Industrial Relations*, 6(Autumn): 101–32.

Foulkes, F.K. (1981) 'How Top Nonunion Companies Manage Employees', *Harvard Business Review*, September-October: 90–6.

Fournier, V. and Grey, C. (2000) 'At the Critical Moment: Conditions and Prospects for Critical Management Studies', *Human Relations*, 53(1): 7–32.

Fox, A. (1966) 'Industrial Sociology and Industrial Relations', *Royal Commission Research Paper No.3*, London: HMSO.

Fox, A. (1974) *Beyond Contract: Work, Power and Trust Relations*, London: Faber.

Fox, A. (1985) *History and Heritage*, London: Allen & Unwin.

Franz, H.W. (1991) 'Quality Strategies and Workforce Strategies in the European Steel Industry', in P. Blyton and J. Morris (eds), *A Flexible Future? Prospects for Employment and Organization*, Berlin: Walter de Gruyter, 259–73.

Franzosi, R. (1995) *The Puzzle of Strikes: Class and State Strategies in Postwar Italy*, Cambridge: Cambridge University Press.

Fredman, S. and Morris, G. (1989) 'The State as Employer: Setting a New Example', *Personnel Management*, August: 25–9.

Freeman, R. and Pelletier J. (1990) 'The Impact of Industrial Relations Legislation on British Union Density', *British Journal of Industrial Relations*, 28(2): 141–64.

Freeman, R.B. (1995) 'The Future for Unions in Decentralized Collective Bargaining Systems: US and UK Unionism in an Era of Crisis', *British Journal of Industrial Relations*, 33(4): 519–36.

Freeman, R.B. and Rogers, J. (1999) *What Workers Want*, Ithaca: Cornell University Press.

Frege, C. and Kelly, J. (2003) 'Introduction: Union Revitalization Strategies in Comparative Perspective', *European Journal of Industrial Relations*, 9(1): 7–24.

Friedman, A.L. (1977) *Industry and Labour: Class Struggle at Work and Monopoly Capitalism*, London: Macmillan.

Friedman, S. and Wood, S. (2001) 'Employers' Unfair Advantage in the United States of America: Symposium on The Human Rights Watch Report on the State of Workers' Freedom of Association in the United States: Editors' Introduction', *British Journal of Industrial Relations*, 39(4): 586–90.

Fulton, L. (2001) 'Marks and Spencer's Closure Plans and Trade Union Responses', *Transfer*, 3: 525–29.

Gall, G. (1994) 'The Rise of Single Table Bargaining in Britain', *Employee Relations*, 16(4): 62–71.

Gall, G. (2003a) 'Marxism and Industrial Relations', in P. Ackers and A. Wilkinson (eds), *Understanding Work and Employment: Industrial Relations in Transition*, Oxford: Oxford University Press, 316–24.

Gall, G. (2003b) 'Employer Opposition to Union Recognition', in G. Gall (ed.), *Union Organizing: Campaigning for Trade Union Recognition*, London: Routledge, 79–96.

Gall, G. (2003c) 'Introduction', in G. Gall (ed.), *Union Organizing: Campaigning for Trade Union Recognition*, London: Routledge, 1–18.

Gall, G. and McKay, S. (1994) 'Trade Union Derecognition in Britain, 1988–1994', *British Journal of Industrial Relations*, 32(2): 433–48.

Gall, G. and McKay, S. (1996) 'Research Note: Injunctions as a Legal Weapon in Industrial Disputes', *British Journal of industrial Relations*, 34(4): 567–82.

Gall, G. and McKay, S. (1999) 'Developments in Union Recognition and Derecognition in Britain, 1994–1998', *British Journal of Industrial Relations*, 37(4): 601–14.

Gall, G. and McKay, S. (2001) 'Facing Fairness at Work: Union Perception of Employer Opposition and Response to Union Recognition', *Industrial Relations Journal*, 32(2): 94–113.

Gallagher, C., Daly, M. and Thomason, J. (1990) 'The Growth of UK Companies 1985–87 and their Contribution to Job Generation', *Employment Gazette*, February: 92–8.

Gallie, D. (1978) *In Search of the New Working Class: Automation and Social Integration within the Capitalist Enterprise*, Cambridge: Cambridge University Press.

Gallie, D. (1996) 'Trade Union Allegiance and Decline in British Urban Labour Markets', in D. Gallie, R. Penn and M. Rose (eds), *Trade Unionism in Recession*, Oxford: Oxford University Press, 140–74.

Gallie, D. and Rose, M. (1996) 'Employer Policies and Trade Union Influence', in D. Gallie, R. Penn and M. Rose (eds), *Trade Unionism in Recession*, Oxford: Oxford University Press, 33–64.

Gallie, D., Penn, R. and Rose, M. (1996) 'The British Debate on Trade Unionism: Crisis and Continuity', in D. Gallie, R. Penn and M. Rose (eds), *Trade Unionism in Recession*, Oxford: Oxford University Press, 1–32.

Garrahan, P. and Stewart, P. (1992) *The Nissan Enigma: Flexibility at Work in a Local Economy*, London: Cassell.

Geary, J. (1993) 'New Forms of Work Organisation and Employee Involvement in Two Case Study Sites: Plural, Mixed and Protean', *Economic and Industrial Democracy*, 14: 511–34.

Geary, J. (2003) ''New Forms of Work Organization: Still Limited, Still Controlled, but Still Welcome?', in P. Edwards (ed.), *Industrial Relations: Theory and Practice*, 2nd edition, Oxford: Blackwell, 338–67.

Gennard, J. and Dunn, S. (1984) *The Closed Shop in British Industry*, London: Macmillan.

Gennard, J. and Kelly, J. (1997) 'The Unimportance of Labels: The Diffusion of the Personnel/HRM Function', *Industrial Relations Journal*, 28(1): 27–42.

Georgiades, N. and Macdonell, R. (1998) *Leadership for Competitive Advantage*, New York: Wiley.

Gerlach, M. (1992) *Alliance Capitalism: The Social Organization of Japanese Business*, Berkeley: University of California Press.

Gershuny, J. (2002) 'Beating the Odds (1): Intergenerational Social Mobility from a Human Capital Perspective', Institute for Social and Economic Research, Working Paper 2002–17, University of Essex.

Giles, A. (2000) 'Globalisation and Industrial Relations Theory', *Journal of Industrial Relations*, 42(2): 173–94.

Gilman, M., Edwards, P., Ram, M. and Arrowsmith, J. (2002) 'Pay Determination in Small Firms in the UK: The Case of the Response to the National Minimum Wage', *Industrial Relations Journal*, 33(1): 52–67.

Gintis, H. (1976) 'The Nature of Labor Exchange and the Theory of Capitalist Production', *Review of Radical Political Economics*, 8(2): 36–54.

Glass, J. L. and Estes, S. B. (1997) 'The Family Responsive Workplace', *Annual Review of Sociology*, 23(August): 289–313.

Goffee, R. and Scase, R. (1982) 'Fraternalism and Paternalism as Employer Strategies in Small Firms', in G. Day, L. Caldwell, K. Jones, D. Robbins and H. Rose (eds), *Diversity and Decomposition in the Labour Market*, Aldershot: Gower, 107–24.

Goffee, R. and Scase, R. (1995) *Corporate Realities: The Dynamics of Large and Small Organisations*, London: Routledge.

Gofton, K. (2000) 'Putting Staff First in Brand Evolution', *Marketing*, 3 February: 29–30.

Gollan, P.J. (2001) 'Tunnel Vision: Non-Union Employee Representation at Eurotunnel', *Employee Relations*, 23(4): 376–400.

Goodman, J. (1984) *Employment Relations in Industrial Society*, Oxford: Philip Allan.

Goodman, J. (1996) 'Annual Review Article 1995', *British Journal of Industrial Relations*, 34(1): 151–69.

Goodman, J., Earnshaw, J., Marchington, M. and Harrison, R. (1998) 'Unfair Dismissal Cases, Disciplinary Procedures, Recruitment Methods and Management Style', *Employee Relations*, 20(6): 536–50.

Goodstein, L.D. (1990) 'A Case Study in Effective Organizational Change Toward High Involvement Management', in D.B. Fishman and C. Cherniss (eds), *The Human Side of Corporate Competitiveness*, Newbury Park CA: Sage, 171–200.

Gordon, D.M. (1976) 'Capitalist Efficiency and Socialist Efficiency', *Monthly Review*, (3): 19–39.

Gordon, D.M., Edwards, R. and Reich, M. (1982) *Segmented Work, Divided Workers: The Historical Transformation of Labor in the United States*, Cambridge: Cambridge University Press.

Gorz, A. (1999) *Reclaiming Work: Beyond the Wage-Based Society*, London: Polity Press.

Gospel, H.F. (1992) *Markets, Firms, and the Management of Labour in Modern Britain*, Cambridge: Cambridge University Press.

Gospel, H.F. and Palmer, G. (1993) *British Industrial Relations*, 2nd edition, London: Routledge.

Gospel, H.F. and Wood, S. (eds) (2003) *Representing Workers: Union Recognition and Membership in Britain*, London: Routledge.

Goss, D.M. (1988) 'Social Harmony and the Small Firm: A Reappraisal', *Sociological Review*, 36(1): 114–32.

Goss, D.M. (1991) 'In Search of Small Firm Industrial Relations', in R. Burrows (ed.), *Deciphering the Enterprise Culture: Entrepreneurship, Petty Capitalism and the Restructuring of Britain*, London: Routledge, 152–75.

Grant, D. and Oswick, C. (1997) 'Of Believers, Atheists and Agnostics: Practitioner Views on HRM', *Industrial Relations Journal*, 29(3): 178–93.

Grant, D. and Shields, J. (2002) 'In Search of the Subject: Researching Employee Reactions to Human Resource Management', *Journal of Industrial Relations*, 44(3): 313–34.

Gray, H. (2001a) 'Family Friendly Working: What a Performance! An Analysis of the Relationship Between the Availability of Family Friendly Policies and Establishment Performance', Centre for Economic Performance Working Paper No.1135, London School of Economics.

Gray, H. (2001b) 'It Pays to be Family Friendly', *CentrePiece*, 6(3): 2–5.

Green, F. (1990) 'Trade Union Availability and Trade Union Membership in Britain', *Manchester School of Economic and Social Studies*, 58(4): 378–94.

Green, F. (1992) 'Recent Trends in British Trade Union Density: How Much of a Compositional Effect?', *British Journal of Industrial Relations*, 30(3): 445–58.

Green, F. (2001) 'It's Been a Hard Day's Night: The Concentration and Intensification of Work in Late Twentieth-Century Britain', *British Journal of Industrial Relations*, 39(1): 53–80.

Gregg, P. and Wadsworth, J. (1995) 'A Short History of Labour Turnover, Job Tenure, and Job Security. 1975–93', *Oxford Review of Economic Policy*, 11(1): 73–90.

Gregg, P. and Yates, A. (1991) 'Changes in Wage-Setting Arrangements and Trade Union Presence in the 1980s', *British Journal of Industrial Relations*, 29(3): 361–76.

Griffin, J.I. (1939) *Strikes*, New York: Columbia University Press.

Griffith, J.A. (1981) *The Politics of the Judiciary*, 2nd edition, London: Fontana.

Grugulis, I. and Wilkinson, A. (2002) 'Managing Culture at British Airways: Hype, Hope and Reality', *Long Range Planning*, 35(2): 179–94.

Grunberg, L. (1986) 'Workplace Relations in the Economic Crisis: A Comparison of a British and French Automobile Plant', *Sociology*, 20(4): 503–30.

Guest, D. (1990) 'Human Resource Management and the American Dream', *Journal of Management Studies*, 27(4): 377–97.

Guest, D. (1997) 'Human Resource Management and Performance: A Review and Research Agenda', *International Journal of Human Resource Management*, 8(3): 263–90.

Guest, D. (1999) 'Human Resource Management – The Workers' Verdict', *Human Resource Management Journal*, 9(3): 5–25.

Guest, D. (2001) 'Industrial Relations and Human Resource Management', in J. Storey (ed.), *Human Resource Management: A Critical Text*, London: Thomson Learning, 96–113.

Guest, D. (2002) 'Human Resource Management, Corporate Performance and Employee Well-Being: Building the Worker into HRM', *Journal of Industrial Relations*, 44(3): 335–58.

Guest, D. and Conway, N. (1999) 'Peering into the Black Hole: The Downside of New Employment Practices in the UK', *British Journal of Industrial Relations*, 37(3): 367–89.

Guest, D. and Conway, N. (2001) *Employer Perceptions of the Psychological Contract*, London: CIPD.

Guest, D. and Hoque, K. (1993) 'The Mystery of the Missing Human Resource Manager', *Personnel Management*, June: 40–1.

Guest, D. and Hoque, K. (1994) 'The Good, The Bad and the Ugly: Employment Relations in New Non-Union Workplaces', *Human Resource Management Journal*, 5(1): 1–14.

Guest, D. and Peccei, R. (2001) 'Partnership at Work: Mutuality and the Balance of Advantage', *British Journal of Industrial Relations*, 39(2): 207–36.

Guest, D., Michie, J., Sheehan, M., Conway, N. and Metochi, M. (2000) *Employment Relations, HRM and Business Performance*, London: CIPD.

Guest, D., Michie, J., Conway, N. and Sheehan, M. (2003) 'Human Resource Management and Corporate Performance in the UK', *British Journal of Industrial Relations*, 41(2): 291–314.

Guille, H. (1984) 'Industrial Relations Theory: Painting by Numbers', *Journal of Industrial Relations*, 26(4): 484–95.

Gunderson, M. (2001) 'Economics of Personnel and Human Resource Management', *Human Resource Management Review*, 11(4): 431–52.

Gunnigle, P. and Brady, T. (1984) 'The Management of Industrial Relations in the Small Firm', *Employee Relations*, 6(5): 21–4.

Hakim, C. (1989a) 'Identifying Fast Growing Firms', *Employment Gazette*, January: 29–41.

Hakim, C. (1989b) 'New Recruits to Self-Employment in the 1980s', *Employment Gazette*, June: 286–97.

Hakim, C. (1990) 'Core and Periphery in Employers' Workforce Strategies: Evidence from the 1987 ELUS Survey', *Work, Employment & Society*, 4(2): 157–88.

Hall, M. Broughton, A., Carley, M., and Sisson, K. (2002) *Works Councils for the UK? Assessing the Impact of the EU Employee Consultation Directive*, London: Industrial Relations Services/Industrial Relations Research Unit.

Hall, P.A. and Soskice, D. (2001) 'An Introduction to Varieties of Capitalism', in P.A. Hall and D. Soskice (eds), *Varieties of Capitalism: The Institutional Foundations of Comparative Advantage*, Oxford: Oxford University Press, 1–68.

Hamel, G. and Prahalad, C.K. (1994) *Competing for the Future*, Boston, Mass: Harvard Business School Press.

Hamil, S. (1993) *Britain's BEST Employers? A Job Hunter's Guide*, London: Kogan Page.

Hamilton, G. and Biggart, N. (1988) 'Markets, Culture and Authority: A Comparative Analysis of Management and Organization in the Far East', *American Journal of Sociology*, 94(Supplement): S52–S94.

Hamilton, P.M. (2001) 'Rhetoric and Employment Relations', *British Journal of Industrial Relations*, 39(3): 433–49.

Hancké, B. (1993) 'Trade Union Membership in Europe, 1960–1990: Rediscovering Local Unions', *British Journal of Industrial Relations*, 31(4): 593–613.

Handy, C. (1984) *The Future of Work*, Oxford: Blackwell.

Handy, L.J. (1968) 'Absenteeism and Attendance in the British Coal-Mining Industry: An Examination of Post-War Trends', *British Journal of Industrial Relations*, 6(1): 27–50.

Hanson, C.G. and Mather, G. (1988) *Striking Out Strikes: Changing Employment Relations in the British Labour Market*, Hobart Paper 110, London: Institute of Economic Affairs.

Harbison, F.H. (1954) 'Collective Bargaining and American Capitalism', in A. Kornhauser, R. Dubin, and A.M. Ross (eds), *Industrial Conflict*, New York: McGraw-Hill, 270–79.

Harding, R. (2002) *Global Entrepreneurship Monitor: United Kingdom 2002*, London: London Business School.

Hardwidge, C. (2002) 'Jobs in the Public and Private Sectors', *Economic Trends*, 583: 39–52.

Harper, K. (2000) 'Frustrations of the World's Favourite Airline', *Management Today*, January: 42–46.

Harris, C. (1988) *Redundancy and Recession in South Wales*, Oxford: Blackwell.

Harris, L. (1986) 'Working-Class Strength: A Counterview', in D. Coates and J. Hillard (eds), *The Economic Decline of Modern Britain: The Debate Between Left and Right*, Wheatsheaf Books, 264–6.

Harris, L.C. and Ogbonna, E. (2002) 'Exploring Service Sabotage: The Antecedents, Types and Consequences of Frontline, Deviant, Anti-service Behaviors', *Journal of Service Research*, 4(3): 163–83.

Hart, T.J. (1993) 'Human Resource Management - Time to Exorcize the Militant Tendency', *Employee Relations*, 15(3): 29–36.

Hartley, J., Kelly, J. and Nicholson, N. (1983) *Steel Strike: A Case Study in Industrial Relations*, London: Batsford.

Harvey, C. (ed.) (2001) *Human Rights, Equality and Democratic Renewal in Northern Ireland*, Oxford: Hart Publishing.

Harvey, G. and Turnbull, P. (2002) *Contesting the Crisis: Aviation Industrial Relations and Trade Union Strategies After 11 September*, London: International Transport Workers' Federation.

Hassel, A. (1999) 'The Erosion of Industrial Relations in Germany', *British Journal of Industrial Relations*, 37(3): 483–505.

Hassel, A. (2002) 'The Erosion Continues', *British Journal of Industrial Relations*, 40(2): 309–17.

Hayek, F.A. (1979) *Law, Legislation and Liberty*, London: Routledge & Kegan Paul.

Hayek, F.A. (1984) *1980s Unemployment and the Unions*, London: Institute of Economic Affairs.

Haynes, P. and Allen, M. (2001) 'Partnership as Union Strategy: A Preliminary Evaluation' *Employee Relations*, 23(2): 164–87.

Heery, E. (1993) 'Industrial Relations and the Customer', *Industrial Relations Journal*, 24(4): 284–95.

Heery, E. (1998) 'The Relaunch of the Trades Union Congress', *British Journal of Industrial Relations*, 36(3): 339–60.

Heery, E. (2002) 'Partnership versus Organising: Alternative Futures for British Trade Unionism', *Industrial Relations Journal*, 33(1): 20–35.

Heery, E. and Adler, L. (2004) 'Organizing the Unorganized', in C. Frege and J. Kelly (eds), *Labour Movement Revitalization in Comparative Perspective*, Oxford: Oxford University Press (forthcoming).

Heery, E. and Kelly, J. (1989) ' "A Cracking Job for a Woman" – A Profile of Women Trade Union Officers', *Industrial Relations Journal*, 20(3): 192–202.

Heery, E. and Kelly, J. (1994) 'Professional, Participative and Managerial Unionism: An Interpretation of Change in Trade Unions', *Work, Employment & Society*, 8(1): 1–22.

Heery, E. and Salmon, J. (eds) (2000) *The Insecure Workforce*, London: Routledge.

Heery, E. and Simms, M. (2003) *Bargain or Bust? Employer Responses to Union Organising*, London: Trades Union Congress.

Heery, E., Simms, M., Delbridge, R., Salmon, J. and Simpson, D. (2000) 'The TUC's Organising Academy: An Assessment', *Industrial Relations Journal*, 31(5): 400–15.

Heery, E., Delbridge, R. and Simms, M. (2003a) *The Organising Academy – Five Years On*, London: Trades Union Congress.

Heery, E., Simms, M., Delbridge, R., Salmon, J. and Simpson, D. (2003b) 'Trade Union Recruitment Policy in Britain: Form and Effects', in G. Gall (ed.), *Union Organizing: Campaigning for Trade Union Recognition*, London: Routledge, 56–78.

Hendry, C. (1990) 'The Corporate Management of Human Resources under Conditions of Decentralization', *British Journal of Management*, 1(2): 91–103.

Hendy, J. (2000) 'Article 11 and the Freedom to Strike', in K.D. Ewing (ed.), *Human Rights at Work*, London: Institute of Employment Rights, 113–41.

Hennessy, P. (1994) *The Hidden Wiring: Unearthing the British Constitution*, London: Indigo.

Herbert, I. (2001) 'Firefighters Issue an Ultimatum on National Strike', *The Independent*, 25 July: 7.

Herzberg, F. (1966) *Work and the Nature of Man*, Cleveland: World Publishing.

Hibbett, A. (1991) 'Employee Involvement: A Recent Survey', *Employee Gazette*, December: 659–64.

Hickson, D.J., Butler, R.J., Cray, D., Mallory, G.R. and Wilson, D.C. (1985) *Top Decisions: Strategic Decision-Making in Organisations*, Oxford: Blackwell.

Higginbottom, K. (2003) 'Mind Your Own Business', *People Management*, 1 May: 32–5.

Hildreth, A. (1999) 'What Has Happened to the Union Wage Differential in Britain in the 1990s?' *Oxford Bulletin of Economics & Statistics*, 61(1): 5–31.

Hill, C.W.L. and Pickering, J.F. (1986) 'Divisionalisation, Decentralisation and Performance of Large UK Companies', *Journal of Management Studies*, 23(1): 26–50.

Hill, J.M.M. and Trist, E.L. (1962) *Industrial Accidents, Sickness and Other Absences*, London: Tavistock Institute.

Hill, S. (1991) 'Why Quality Circles Failed but Total Quality Management Might Succeed', *British Journal of Industrial Relations*, 29(4): 541–68.

Hinton, J. (1973) *The First Shop Stewards Movement*, London: Allen & Unwin.

Hirst, P. and Thompson, G. (1996) *Globalization in Question*, London: Polity.

HM Treasury (1998) *Persistent Poverty and Lifelong Inequality: The Evidence*, Occasional Paper 10, London: HM Treasury.

HM Treasury (2000) *Productivity in the UK: The Evidence and the Government's Approach*, London: HM Treasury.

HM Treasury/DTI (2001) *Productivity in the UK: Enterprise and the Productivity Challenge*, London: HMSO.

HM Treasury/DTI (2003) *Balancing Work and Family Life: Enhancing Choice and Support for Parents*, London: HMSO.

Hochschild, A.R. (1983) *The Managed Heart: Commercialization of Human Feeling*, Berkeley: University of California Press.

Hoel, B. (1982) 'Contemporary Clothing Sweatshops', in J. West (ed.), *Work, Women and the Labour Market*, London: Routledge & Kegan Paul, 80–98.

Hoerr, J.P. (1988) *And The Wolf Finally Came: The Decline of the American Steel Industry*, Pittsburgh: University of Pittsburgh Press.

Hoffer Gittell, J., von Nordenflycht, A. and Kochan, T.A. (2001) 'Mutual Gains or Zero Sum? Labor Relations and Stakeholder Outcomes in the Airline Industry', mimeo, Harvard Business School, USA.

Holiday, R. (1995) *Investigating Small Firms: Nice Work?* London: Routledge.

Hollingsworth, J.R. (1997) 'Continuities and Changes in Social Systems of Production: The Cases of Japan, Germany, and the United States', in J.R. Hollingsworth and R. Boyer (eds), *Contemporary Capitalism: The Embeddedness of Institutions*, Cambridge: Cambridge University Press, 265–310.

Hollingsworth, J.R. and Boyer, R. (1997) 'Coordination of Economic Actors and Social Systems of Production', in J.R. Hollingsworth and R. Boyer (eds), *Contemporary Capitalism: The Embeddedness of Institutions*, Cambridge: Cambridge University Press, 1–47.

Holmes, J. (1986) 'The Organization and Locational Structure of Production Subcontracting', in A.J. Scott and M. Storper (eds), *Production, Work and Technology*, London: Allen & Unwin, 80–106.

Höpfl, H. (1992) 'Death of a Snake-Oil Salesman: The Demise of the Corporate Life-Lie', Paper presented at the Employment Research Unit Annual Conference, Cardiff Business School.

Höpfl, H. (1993) 'Culture and Commitment: British Airways', in D. Gowler, K. Legge and C. Clegg (eds), *Case Studies in Organizational Behaviour and Human Resource Management*, London: Paul Chapman, 117–38.

Höpfl, H., Smith, S. and Spencer, S. (1992) 'Values and Valuations: The Conflicts Between Cultural Change and Job Cuts', *Personnel Review*, 21(2): 24–38.

Hoque, K. (2000) *Human Resource Management in the Hotel Industry: Strategy, Innovation and Performance*, London: Routledge.

Hoque, K. (2003) 'All in All, It's Just Another Plaque on the Wall: The Incidence and Impact of the Investors In People Standard', *Journal of Management Studies*, 40(2): 543–71.

Hoque, K. and Noon, M. (2001) 'Counting Angels: A Comparison of Personnel and HR Specialists', *Human Resource Management Journal*, 11(3): 5–22.

Hotopp, U. (2002) 'Teleworking in the UK', *Labour Market Trends*, 110(6): 311–8.

House of Lords (1985) *Report from the Select Committee on Overseas Trade*, London: HMSO.

Houseman, S.R. (1991) *Industrial Restructuring with Job Security: The Case of European Steel*, Cambridge, Mass: Harvard University Press.

Howell, C. (1995) 'Trade Unions and the State: A Critique of British Industrial Relations', *Politics & Society*, 23(2): 149–83.

Howells, D. (1981) 'Marks and Spencer and the Civil Service: A Comparison of Culture and Methods', *Public Administration*, 59(3): 337–52.

HRW (2000) *Unfair Advantage: Workers' Freedom of Association in the United States Under International Human Rights Standards*, Washington DC: Human Rights Watch.

Hubbard, N. and Purcell, J. (2001) 'Managing Employee Expectations During Acquisitions', *Human Resource Management Journal*, 11(2): 17–33.

Hudson, R. and Sadler, D. (1989) *The International Steel Industry: Restructuring, State Policies and Localities*, London: Routledge.

Hutton, W. (1996) *The State We're In*, London: Vintage.

Hutton, W. (1997) *The State to Come*, London: Vintage.

Hyman, J. and Mason, B. (1995) *Managing Employee Involvement and Participation*, London: Sage.

Hyman, R. (1975) *Industrial Relations: A Marxist Introduction*, London: Macmillan.

Hyman, R. (1978) 'Pluralism, Procedural Consensus and Collective Bargaining', *British Journal of Industrial Relations*, 16(1): 16–40.

Hyman, R. (1981) 'Green Means Danger? Trade Union Immunities and the Tory Attack', *Politics and Power*, (4): 128–45.

Hyman, R. (1982) 'Pressure, Protest, and Struggle: Some Problems in the Concept and Theory of Industrial Conflict', in G.B.J. Bomers and R.B. Peterson (eds), *Conflict, Management and Industrial Relations*, Boston: Kluwer Nijhoff, 401–22.

Hyman, R. (1987a) 'Strategy or Structure? Capital, Labour and Control', *Work, Employment & Society*, 1(1): 25–55.

Hyman, R. (1987b) 'Trade Unions and the Law: Papering Over the Cracks?', *Capital & Class*, (31): 93–113.

Hyman, R. (1989a) *The Political Economy of Industrial Relations: Theory and Practice in a Cold Climate*, London: Macmillan.

Hyman, R. (1989b) *Strikes*, 4th edition, London: Macmillan.

Hyman, R. (1991) 'Trade Unions and the Disaggregation of the Working Class', mimeo, IRRU, University of Warwick.

Hyman, R. (1992) 'Industrial Relations Research: The European Dimension', Research Review, *IRRU Newsletter*, 10, Spring: 6–9.

Hyman, R. (1994) 'Theory and Industrial Relations', *British Journal of Industrial Relations*, 32(2): 165–80.

Hyman, R. (2001a) 'The Europeanisation – or the Erosion – of Industrial Relations', *Industrial Relations Journal*, 32(4): 280–94.

Hyman, R. (2001b) *Understanding European Unionism: Between Market, Class and Society*, London: Sage.

Hyman, R. (2003) 'The Historical Evolution of British Industrial Relations', in P. Edwards (ed.), *Industrial Relations: Theory and Practice*, 2nd edition, Oxford: Blackwell, 37–57.

Hyman, R. and Elger, T. (1981) 'Job Controls, the Employers' Offensive and Alternative Strategies', *Capital & Class*, (15): 115–49.

Ibbs, R. (1988) *Improving Management in Government: The Next Steps*, London: HMSO.

Ichniowski, C., Kochan, T., Levine, D., Olson, C. and Strauss, G. (1996) 'What Works at Work: Overview and Assessment', *Industrial Relations*, 35(3): 299–333.

IDE (1981) *Industrial Democracy in Europe*, Oxford: Clarendon Press.

IDS (1998) *Partnership Agreements*, IDS Study 656, London: Incomes Data Services.

IEA (1978) *Trade Unions: Public Goods or Public 'Bads'*, London: Institute of Economic Affairs.

ILO (1992) *Recent Developments in the Iron and Steel Industry*, Geneva: ILO.

ILO (2001) *Reducing the Decent Work Deficit – A Global Challenge*, Report of the Director-General, Geneva: International Labour Organisation.

Ingham, G. (1970) *Size of Industrial Organisation and Worker Behaviour*, Cambridge: Cambridge University Press.

Ingram, P.N. (1991) 'Changes in Working Practices in British Manufacturing Industry in the 1980s: A Study of Employee Concessions Made During Wage Negotiations', *British Journal of Industrial Relations*, 29(1): 1–13.

Ingram, P.N., Wadsworth, J. and Brown, D. (1999) 'Free to Choose? Dimensions of Private-Sector Wage Determination, 1979–1994', *British Journal of Industrial Relations*, 37(1): 33–49.

IPA (1998) 'Tesco Deal Heralds New Era of Employee Consultation', *IPA Magazine*, April: 2.

IPA (2001) 'The History of Partnership', London: Involvement Participation Association, www.partner-ship-at-work.com.

IRRR (1992) 'Single Union Deals in Perspective', *Industrial Relations Review and Report*, (523): 7–15.

IRRR (1993) 'Single Union Deals Survey: 1', *IRS Employment Trends 528*, January: 3–15.

IRS (1999) 'Partnership Delivers the Goods at Tesco', *IRS Employment Trends*, 686, 4–9.

ISER (2001) *ISER Report 2000/1*, Institute for Social and Economic Research, University of Essex.

ISR (1996) *Employee Satisfaction: Tracking European Trends*, London: International Survey Research.

Jackson, M.P. (1991) *An Introduction to Industrial Relations*, London: Routledge.

Jackson, M.P., Leopold, J.W. and Tuck, K. (1993) *Decentralization of Collective Bargaining: An Analysis of Recent Experience in the UK*, Basingstoke: Macmillan.

Jacobi, O. (2003) 'Union Recognition in Germany', in G. Gall (ed.), *Union Organizing: Campaigning for Trade Union Recognition*, London: Routledge, 211–27.

Jenkins, J. (2002) 'Patterns of Pay: Results of the 2001 New Earnings Survey', *Labour Market Trends*, March: 129–39.

Jones, R. M. (1971) *Absenteeism*, Manpower paper no. 4, London: HMSO.

Jones, T. (2002) '£30K: Because We're Worth it', *The Guardian*, 11 November.

Joseph, Sir Keith (1986) 'Solving the Union Problem is the Key to Britain's Recovery', in D. Coates and J. Hillard (eds), *The Economic Decline of Modern Britain: The Debate Between Left and Right*, Brighton: Wheatsheaf Books, 98–105.

Juran, J.M. (1979) *Quality Control Handbook*, New York: McGraw Hill.

Juran, J.M. (1988) *Juran on Planning for Quality*, New York: Free Press.

Kahn-Freund, O. (1954) 'Legal Framework', in A. Flanders and H.A. Clegg (eds), *The System of Industrial Relations in Britain*, Oxford: Blackwell, 42–127.

Kahn-Freund, O. (1959) 'Labour Law', in M. Ginsberg (ed.), *Law and Opinion in England in the 20th Century*, London: Stevens, 215–63.

Kahn-Freund, O. (1972) *Labour and the Law*, London: Stevens & Sons.

Kaldor, N. (1966) *Causes of the Slow Rate of Growth in the United Kingdom*, Cambridge: Cambridge University Press.

Katz, H. and Darbishire, O. (2000) *Converging Divergencies: Worldwide Changes in Employment Systems*, Ithaca, NY: ILR Press.

Kaufman, B.E. (1989) 'Models of Man in Industrial Relations Research', *Industrial & Labor Relations Review*, 43(1): 72–88.

Kaufman, B.E. (1993) *The Origins and Evolution of the Field of Industrial Relations in the United States*, Ithaca, New York: ILR Press.

Kaufman, B.E. (1999) 'Expanding the Behavioral Foundations of Labor Economics', *Industrial & Labor Relations Review*, 52(3): 361–92.

Kaufman, B.E. (2001) 'Human Resources and Industrial Relations: Commonalities and Differences', *Human Resource Management Review*, 11(4): 339–74.

Kaufman, B.E. (2003) 'Industrial Relations in North America', in P. Ackers and A. Wilkinson (eds), *Understanding Work and Employment: Industrial Relations in Transition*, Oxford: Oxford University Press, 195–226.

Kaufman, B.E. and Taras, D.G. (eds) (2000) *Nonunion Employee Representation: History, Contemporary Practice, and Policy*, New York: M.E. Sharpe Inc.

Kay, J. (1997) 'Stakeholding', *CentrePiece*, 2(1): 22–4.

Keenoy, T. (1985) *Invitation to Industrial Relations*, Oxford: Blackwell.

Keenoy, T. (1991) 'The Roots of Metaphor in the Old and New Industrial Relations', *British Journal of Industrial Relations*, 29(2): 313–28.

Keenoy, T. (1992) 'Constructing Control', in J.F. Hartley and G.M. Stephenson (eds), *Employment Relations: The Psychology of Influence and Control at Work*, Oxford: Blackwell, 91–110.

Keenoy, T. (1997) 'Review Article: HRMism and the Language of Re-Presentation', *Journal of Management Studies*, 34(5): 825–41.

Keenoy, T. and Noon, M. (1992) 'Employment Relations in the Enterprise Culture: Themes and Issues', *Journal of Management Studies*, 29(5): 561–70.

Keep, E. (2000) 'Learning Organisations, Life-Long Learning and the Mystery of the Vanishing Employers', ESRC Centre on Skills, Knowledge and Organisational Performance (SKOPE), University of Warwick.

Keep, E. and Rainbird, H. (2003) 'Training', in P. Edwards (ed.), *Industrial Relations: Theory and Practice*, 2nd edition, Oxford: Blackwell, 392–419.

Kelly, J. (1988) *Trade Unions and Socialist Politics*, London: Verso.

Kelly, J. (1990) 'British Trade Unionism 1979–89: Change, Continuity and Contradictions', *Work, Employment & Society*, 4(Special Issue): 29–65.

Kelly, J. (1994) 'Does the Field of Industrial Relations Have a Future?', mimeo, London School of Economics.

Kelly, J. (1996) 'Union Militancy and Social Partnership', in P. Ackers, C. Smith and P. Smith (eds), *The New Workplace and Trade Unionism: Critical Perspectives on Work and Organization*, London: Routledge, 77–109.

Kelly, J. (1998) *Rethinking Industrial Relations: Mobilization, Collectivism and Long Waves*, London: Routledge.

Kelly, J. (1999) 'Social Partnership in Britain: Good for Profits, Bad for Jobs and Unions', *Communist Review*, 30(3): 3–10.

Kelly, J. and Bailey, R. (1989) 'British Trade Union Membership, Density and Decline in the 1980s: A Research Note', *Industrial Relations Journal*, 20(1): 54–61.

Kelly, J. and Heery, E. (1989) 'Full-time Officers and Trade Union Recruitment', *British Journal of Industrial Relations*, 27(2): 196–213.

Kelly, J. and Heery, E. (1994) *Working for the Union: British Trade Union Officers*, Cambridge: Cambridge University Press.

Kelly, J. and Kelly, C. (1991) 'Them and Us: Social Psychology and The New Industrial Relations', *British Journal of Industrial Relations*, 29(1): 25–48.

Kelly, J. and Nicholson, N. (1980) 'Strikes and Other Forms of Industrial Action', *Industrial Relations Journal*, 11(5): 20–31.

Kelly, J. and Waddington. J. (1995) 'New Prospects for British Labour', *Organization*, 2(3/4): 415–26.

Kerckhofs, P. (2002) *European Works Councils – Facts and Figures*, Brussels: European Trade Union Institute.

Kerr, A. and Sachdev, S. (1992) 'Third Among Equals: An Analysis of the 1989 Ambulance Dispute', *British Journal of Industrial Relations*, 30(1): 127–43.

Kerr, C. (1964) *Labor and Management in Industrial Society*, New York: Doubleday.

Kerr, C. and Siegel, A. (1954) 'The Interindustry Propensity to Strike – An International Comparison', in A. Kornhauser, R. Dubin and A.M. Ross (eds), *Industrial Conflict*, New York: McGraw Hill, 189–212.

Kessler, I. and Purcell, J. (1995) 'Individualism and Collectivism in Theory and Practice: Management Style and the Design of Pay Systems', in P. Edwards (ed.), *Industrial Relations: Theory and Practice in Britain*, Oxford: Blackwell, 337–67.

Kessler, I. and Purcell, J. (2003) 'Individualism and Collectivism in Industrial Relations', in P. Edwards (ed.), *Industrial Relations: Theory and Practice*, 2nd edition, Oxford: Blackwell, 313–37.

Kessler, I. and Undy, R. (1996) *The New Employment Relationship*, London: Institute of Personnel and Development.

Kessler, I., Purcell, J. and Shapiro, C. (2000) 'New Forms of Employment Relation in the Public Services: The Limits of Strategic Choice', *Industrial Relations Journal*, 31(1): 17–34.

Kessler, S. and Bayliss, F. (1992) *Contemporary British Industrial Relations*, London: Macmillan.

Kessler, S. and Bayliss, F. (1995) *Contemporary British Industrial Relations*, 2nd edition, London: Macmillan.

Kilpatrick, A. and Lawson, T. (1980) 'On the Nature of Industrial Decline in the UK', *Cambridge Journal of Economics*, 4(1): 85–102.

Kinnie, N. (1992) 'From IR to HR? Change and Continuity in Industrial Relations – A Longitudinal Case', paper presented to Employment Research Unit Conference, Cardiff Business School, September.

Kinnie, N., Hutchinson, S. and Purcell, J. (1998) 'Downsizing: Is it Always Lean and Mean?', *Personnel Review*, 27(4): 296–311.

Klein, J. (1989) 'The Human Cost of Manufacturing Reform', *Harvard Business Review*, March-April: 60–6.

Kleinknecht, A. and ter Wengel, J. (1998) 'The Myth of Economic Globalisation', *Cambridge Journal of Economics*, 22(5): 637–67.

Klikauer, T. (2002) 'Stability in Germany's Industrial Relations', *British Journal of Industrial Relations*, 40(2): 295–308.

Knight, K.G. and Latreille, P.L. (2000) 'Discipline, Dismissals and Complaints to Employment Tribunals', *British Journal of Industrial Relations*, 38(4): 533–55.

Knowles, K.G.J.C. (1952) *Strikes: A Study in Industrial Conflict*, Oxford: Blackwell.

Kochan, T., Orlikowski, W. and Cutcher-Gershenfeld, J. (2002) 'Beyond McGregor's Theory Y: Human Capital and Knowledge-Based Work in the 21st Century Organization', mimeo, MIT.

Kodz, J., Davis, S., Lain, D., Sheppard, E., Rick, J., Strebler, M., Bates, P., Cummings, J., Meager, N., Anxo, D., Gineste, S., and Trinczek, R. (2002) *Working Long Hours in the UK: A Review of the Research Literature, Aanalysis of Survey Data and Cross-National Organizational Case Studies (Executive Summary)*, Employment Relations Research Series No.16, London: DTI.

Korczynski, M. (2000) 'The Political Economy of Trust', *Journal of Management Studies*, 37(1): 1–21.

Korczynski, M. (2002) *Human Resource Management in Service Work*, Basingstoke: Palgrave.

Kornhauser, A., Dubin, R. and Ross, A.M. (eds) (1954) *Industrial Conflict*, New York: McGraw Hill.

Kumar, N. (1997) 'The Revolution in Retailing: From Market Driven to Market Driving', *Long Range Planning*, 30(6): 830–35.

Labour Research Department (1996) *Part of the Union: The Challenge of Recruiting and Organising Part-Time Workers*, London: Trades Unions Congress.

Lamb, H. and Percy, S. (1987) 'Big Mac is Watching You', *New Society*, 82(1293): 15–17.

Lane, C. (1988) 'New Technology and Clerical Work', in D. Gallie (ed.), *Employment in Britain*, Oxford: Blackwell, 67–101.

Lane, T. (1982) 'The Unions: Caught on the Ebb Tide', *Marxism Today*, September: 6–13.

Lawler, E. (1986) *High Involvement Management: Participative Strategies for Improving Organizational Performance*. San Francisco, CA: Josey-Bass.

Layard, R. (2003) 'What is Happiness and Are We Getting Happier?' http://cep.lse.ac.uk/events/lectures/layard

Lazear, E. (2000) 'Economic Imperialism', *Quarterly Journal of Economics*, 115(1): 99–146.

Lazonick, W. (1978) 'The Subjection of Labor To Capital: The Rise of the Capitalist System', *Review of Radical Political Economics*, 10(1): 1–31.

Lazonick, W. (1991) *Business Organization and the Myth of the Market Economy*, Cambridge: Cambridge University Press.

Leader, S. (2002) 'Choosing an Interpretation of the Right to Freedom of Association', *British Journal of Industrial Relations*, 40(1): 128–37.

Lebrecht, D. (1999) 'Effects on Airline Employees of Growing Competition', London: British Airways, paper presented at the Airline Industrial Relations Conference, SMi Group.

Ledwith, S. and Colgan, F. (eds) (1996) *Women in Organisations: Challenging Gender Politics*, London: Macmillan.

Legge, K. (1995) *Human Resource Management: Rhetorics and Realities*, Basingstoke, Macmillan.

Legge, K. (2001) 'Silver Bullet or Spent Round? Assessing the Meaning of the High Commitment Management/Performance Relationship', in J. Storey (ed.), *Human Resource Management: A Critical Text*, 2nd edition, London: Thompson, 21–36.

Lehrer, M. (2001) 'Macro-Varieties of Capitalism and Micro-Varieties of Strategic Management in European Airlines', in P.A. Hall and D. Soskice (eds), *Varieties of Capitalism: The Institutional Foundations of Comparative Advantage*, Oxford: Oxford University Press, 361–86.

Leopold, J.W. (1986) 'Trade Union Political Funds: A Retrospective Analysis', *Industrial Relations Journal*, 17(4): 287–303.

Leopold, J.W. (1997) 'Trade Union Political Fund Ballots and the Labour Party', *British Journal of Industrial Relations*, 35(1): 23–38.

Lewin, D. (2001) 'IR and HR Perspectives on Workplace Conflict: What Can Each Learn from the Other?' *Human Resource Management Review*, 11(4): 453–85.

Lewis, B. (1999) 'Managing Service Quality', in B.G. Dale (ed.), *Managing Quality*, 3rd edition, Oxford: Blackwell. 181–97.

Lewis, P. (1989) 'The Unemployed and Trade Union Membership', *Industrial Relations Journal*, 20(4): 271–9.

Lewis, R. (1983) 'Collective Labour Law', in G.S. Bain (ed.), *Industrial Relations in Britain*, Oxford: Blackwell, 361–92.

Lewis, R. (1991) 'Reforming Industrial Relations: Law, Politics and Power', *Oxford Review of Economic Policy*, 7(1): 60–75.

Lewis, R. (ed.) (1986) *Labour Law in Britain*, Oxford: Blackwell.

Lewis, R. and Simpson, B. (1981) *Striking a Balance? Employment Law After the 1980 Act*, Oxford: Martin Robertson.

Linstead, S. (1995) 'Averting the Gaze: Gender and Power on the Perfumed Picket Line', *Gender, Work & Organisation*, 2(4): 192–206.

Littler, C. and Salaman, G. (1984) *Class at Work*, London: Batsford.

Lockwood, D. (1966) 'Sources of Variation in Working Class Images of Society', *Sociological Review*, 14(3): 249–67.

Low Pay Commission (2000) *The National Minimum Wage: The Story So Far*, Cm 4571, London: Stationery Office.

LSC (2003) *Skills in England*, London: Learning and Skills Council.

Lyddon, D. (1994) 'Recent British Strike Trends', British Universities Industrial Relations Association, mimeo, University of Keele.

Lyddon, D. (1998) 'Rediscovering the Past: Recent British Strike Tactics in Historical Perspective', *Historical Studies in Industrial Relations*, 5(1): 107–51.

Lyddon, D. (2003) 'History and Industrial Relations', in P. Ackers and A. Wilkinson (eds), *Understanding Work and Employment: Industrial Relations in Transition*, Oxford: Oxford University Press, 89–118.

Mabey, C., Skinner, D. and Clark, T. (eds) (1998) *Experiencing Human Resource Management*, London: Sage.

Macaulay, I.R. and Wood, R.C. (1992) 'Hotel and Catering Industry Employees' Attitudes Towards Trade Unions', *Employee Relations*, 14(3): 20–8.

Macfarlane, A. (1982) 'Trade Union Growth, the Employer and the Hotel and Restaurant Industry: A Case Study', *Industrial Relations Journal*, 13(4): 29–43.

Machin, S. (2000) 'Union Decline in Britain', *British Journal of Industrial Relations*, 38(4): 631–45.

Machin, S. (2001) 'Does it Still Pay to be a Union Member?' Working Paper 1180, Centre for Economic Performance, London School of Economics.

MacInnes, J. (1987) *Thatcherism at Work: Industrial Relations and Economic Change*, Milton Keynes: Open University Press.

Marchington, M. (1980) *Responses to Participation at Work*, Farnborough: Gower.

Marchington, M. (1987) 'A Review and Critique of Research on Developments in Joint Consultation', *British Journal of Industrial Relations*, 25(3): 339–52.

Marchington, M. (1989) 'Joint Consultation in Practice', in K. Sisson (ed.), *Personnel Management in Britain*, Oxford: Blackwell, 378–402.

Marchington, M. (1992) *Managing the Team*, Oxford: Blackwell.

Marchington, M. (1994) 'The Dynamics of Joint Consultation', in K. Sisson (ed.), *Personnel Management: A Comprehensive Guide to Theory and Practice in Britain*, Oxford: Blackwell: 662–93.

Marchington, M. (1995) 'Involvement and Participation', in J. Storey (ed.), *Human Resource Management: A Critical Text*, London: Routledge, 280–305.

Marchington, M. (2000) 'Teamworking and Employee Involvement: Terminology, Evaluation and Context', in S. Proctor and F. Mueller (eds), *Teamworking*, Basingstoke: Macmillan, 60–80.

Marchington, M. (2001) 'Management-Union Partnerships in Britain: Who Gains What?' Working Paper, Manchester Business School.

Marchington, M. and Grugulis, I. (2000) '"Best Practice" Human Resource Management: Perfect Opportunity or Dangerous Illusion?', *International Journal of Human Resource Management*, 11(6): 1104–24.

Marchington, M. and Harrison, E. (1991) 'Customers, Competitors and Choice: Employee Relations in Food Retailing', *Industrial Relations Journal*, 22(4): 286–99.

Marchington, M. and Parker, P. (1990) *Changing Patterns of Employee Relations*, Hemel Hempstead: Harvester Wheatsheaf.

Marchington, M. and Wilkinson, A. (2000) 'Direct Participation', in S. Bach and K. Sisson (eds), *Personnel Management*, 3rd edition, Oxford: Blackwell, 340–64.

Marchington, M., Goodman, J., Wilkinson, A., and Ackers, P. (1992) *New Developments in Employee Involvement*, Research Series No.2, Sheffield: Employment Department.

Marginson, P. and Sisson, K. (1996) 'Multi-national Companies and the Future of Collective Bargaining: A Review of the Research Issues', *European Journal of Industrial Relations*, 2(2): 173–97.

Marginson, P. Edwards, P.K., Martin, R., Purcell, J. and Sisson, K. (1988) *Beyond the Workplace: Managing Industrial Relations in Multi-Plant Enterprises*, Oxford: Blackwell.

Marginson, P., Armstrong, P., Edwards, P.K., Purcell, J. and Hubbard, N. (1993) 'The Control of Industrial Relations in Large Companies: An Initial Analysis of the Second Company Level Industrial Relations Survey', Warwick Papers in Industrial Relations, No. 45, IRRU, University of Warwick.

Marglin, S. (1974) 'What do Bosses do? The Origins and Function of Hierarchy in Capitalist Production', in A. Gorz (ed.), *The Division of Labour*, Brighton: Harvester Press, 13–54.

Markey, R., Gollan, P., Hodgkinson, A., Chouraqui, A. and Veersama, U. (2001) *Models of Employee Participation in a Changing Global Environment: Diversity and Interaction*, Aldershot: Ashgate.

Mars, G. (1974) 'Dock Pilferage', in P. Rock and M. McIntosh (eds), *Deviance and Control*, London: Tavistock, 109–28.

Mars, G. (1982) *Cheats At Work: An Anthropology of Workplace Crime*, London: George Allen & Unwin.

Marsden, D. (1999) *A Theory of Employment Systems: Micro-Foundations of Societal Diversity*, Oxford: Oxford University Press.

Marsden, D. and Thompson, M. (1990) 'Flexibility Agreements and their Significance in the Increase in Productivity in British Manufacturing Since 1980', *Work, Employment & Society*, 4(1): 83–104.

Marsden, R. (1982) 'Industrial Relations: A Critique of Empiricism', *Sociology*, 16(2): 232–50.

Marsh, A. (1982) *Employee Relations Policy and Decision Making*, London: Confederation of British Industry.

Marshall, A. (1930) *Principles of Economics*, 8th edition, London: Macmillan.

Martin, R. (1999) 'Mobilization Theory: A New Paradigm for Industrial Relations?' *Human Relations*, 52(9): 1205–16.

Martin, R. (2003) 'Politics and Industrial Relations', in P. Ackers and A. Wilkinson (eds), *Understanding Work and Employment: Industrial Relations in Transition*, Oxford: Oxford University Press, 161–75.

Martin, R., Fosh, P., Morris, H., Smith, P. and Undy, R. (1991) 'The Decollectivisation of Trade Unions? Ballots and Collective Bargaining in the 1980s', *Industrial Relations Journal*, 22(3): 197–208.

Martin, R., Smith, P., Fosh, P., Morris, H. and Undy, R. (1995) 'The Legislative Reform of Union Government 1979–94', *Industrial Relations Journal*, 26(2): 146–55.

Martínez Lucio, M., Turnbull, P., Blyton, P., and McGurk, J. (2001) 'Using Regulation: An International Comparative Study of the Civil Aviation Industry in Britain and Spain', *European Journal of Industrial Relations*, 7(1): 49–70.

Marx, K. (1972) *Contribution to the Critique of Political Economy*, Chicago: Charles H. Kerr.

Marx, K. (1976) *Capital*, Vol.1, Harmondsworth: Penguin.

Marx, K. and Engels, F. (1975) *Articles on Britain*, Moscow: Progress Publishers.

Maslow, A.H. (1943) 'A Theory of Human Motivation', *Psychological Review*, 50: 370–96.

Mason, B. and Bain, P. (1991) 'Trade Union Recruitment Strategies: Facing the 1990s', *Industrial Relations Journal*, 22(1): 36–45.

Mason, B. and Bain, P. (1993) 'The Determinants of Trade Union Membership in Britain: A Survey of the Literature', *Industrial & Labor Relations Review*, 46(2): 332–51.

Mason, C. (1991) 'Spatial Variations in Enterprise: The Geography of New Firm Formation', in R. Burrows (ed.), *Deciphering Enterprise Culture: Entrepreneurship, Petty Capitalism and the Restructuring of Britain*, London: Routledge, 74–106.

Massey, D. (1984) *Spatial Divisions of Labour*, London: Macmillan.

Massey, D. (1988) 'What's Happening to UK Manufacturing?', in J. Allen and D. Massey (eds), *The Economy in Question*, London: Sage, 45–90.

Mathieson, H. and Corby, S. (1999) 'Trade Unions: the Challenge of Individualism?', in S. Corby and G. White (eds), *Employee Relations in the Public Services*, London: Routledge, 199–223.

Matlay, H. (1999) 'Employee Relations in Small Firms: A Micro-Business Perspective', *Employee Relations*, 21(3): 285–95.

Matraves, C. (1997) 'German Industrial Structure in Comparative Perspective', *Industry & Innovation*, 4(1): 37–51.

Mayhew, K. (1991) 'The Assessment: The UK Labour Market in the 1980s', *Oxford Review of Economic Policy*, 7(1): 1–17.

Mayo, E. (1933) *The Human Problems of an Industrial Civilisation*, New York: Macmillan.

McCall, A. (ed.) (2002) *The Sunday Times 100 Best Companies to Work For*, London: Times Newspapers (published with the *Sunday Times*, 24 March 2002).

McCarthy, T. (1988) *The Great Dock Strike 1889*, London: Weidenfeld & Nicolson.

McCarthy, W.E.J. (1967) *The Role of Shop Stewards in British Industrial Relations*, Royal Commission on Trade Unions and Employers' Associations, Research Paper No.1, London: HMSO.

McCarthy, W.E.J. (1970) 'The Nature of Britain's Strike Problem: A Reassessment of Arguments in the Donovan Report and a Reply to H.A. Turner', *British Journal of Industrial Relations*, 8(3): 224–36.

McCarthy, W.E.J. (1991) *Towards 2000: A Consultative Document*, London: Trades Union Congress.

McCarthy, W.E.J. (1992) 'Time to Move On: Or Reflections on Forty Years of Industrial Relations Research', Research Review, *IRRU Newsletter*, 10, Spring: 2–5.

McCarthy, W.E.J., Parker, P.A.L., Hawes, W.R. and Lumb, A.L. (1971) *The Reform of Collective Bargaining at Plant and Company Level*, London: Department of Employment/HMSO.

McGregor, D. (1960) *The Human Side of Enterprise*, New York: McGraw-Hill.

McIlroy, J. (1988) *Trade Unions in Britain Today*, Manchester: Manchester University Press.

McIlroy, J. (1995) *Trade Unions in Britain Today*, 2nd edition, Manchester: Manchester University Press.

McIlroy, J. (1998) 'The Enduring Alliance? Trade Unions and the Making of New Labour, 1994–1997', *British Journal of Industrial Relations*, 36(4): 537–64.

McIlroy, J. (2000) 'The New Politics of Pressure – The Trades Union Congress and New Labour in Government', *Industrial Relations Journal*, 31(1): 2–16.

McKay, S. (2001) 'Annual Review Article 2000. Between Flexibility and Regulation: Rights, Equality and Protection at Work', *British Journal of Industrial Relations*, 39(2): 285–303.

McKersie, R. and Hunter, L. (1973) *Pay, Productivity and Collective Bargaining*, London: Macmillan.

McKittrick, D. (2003) 'Not Everyone is Weeping as the Last Ship Leaves Titanic Town', *Independent on Sunday*, 16 March.

McLoughlin, I. (1996) 'Inside the Non-Union Firm', in P. Ackers, C. Smith and P. Smith (eds), *The New Workplace and Trade Unionism: Critical Perspectives on Work and Organization*, London: Routledge, 301–23.

McLoughlin, I. and Gourlay, S. (1992) 'Enterprise Without Unions: The Management of Employee Relations in Non-Union Firms', *Journal of Management Studies*, 29(5): 669–91.

McNabb, R. and Whitfield, K. (2000) 'Worth So Appallingly Little: A Workplace-Level Analysis of Low Pay', *British Journal of Industrial Relations*, 38(4): 585–609.

McVey, J. (1996) 'Public Views and Experiences of Fair Employment and Employment Equality', in J. McVey and N. Hutson (eds), *Public Views and Experiences of Fair Employment and Equality Issues in Northern Ireland*, Belfast: Standing Advisory Commission on Human Rights, 1–14.

Mellahi, K., Jackson, P. and Sparks, L. (2002) 'An Exploratory Study into Failure in Successful Organizations: The Case of Marks & Spencer', *British Journal of Management*, 13(1): 15–29.

Mellor, M., Hannah, J. and Stirling, J. (1988) *Worker Co-operatives in Theory and Practice*, Milton Keynes: Open University Press.

Melman, S. (1958) *Decision-Making and Productivity*, London: Blackwell.

Metcalf, D. (1989) 'Water Notes Dry Up: The Impact of the Donovan Reform Proposals and Thatcherism at Work on Labour Productivity in British Manufacturing Industry', *British Journal of Industrial Relations*, 27(1): 1–31.

Metcalf, D. (1991) 'British Unions: Dissolution or Resurgence?', *Oxford Review of Economic Policy*, 7(1): 18–32.

Metcalf, D. (1999) 'The British National Minimum Wage', *British Journal of Industrial Relations*, 37(2): 171–201.

Metcalf, D., Wadsworth, J. and Ingram, P. (1993) 'Do Strikes Pay?' in D. Metcalf and S. Milner (eds.), *New Perspectives on Industrial Disputes*, London: Routledge, 179–93.

Milberg, W.S. (1998) 'Globalization and its Limits', in R. Kozul-Wright and R. Rowthorn (eds), *Transnational Corporations and the Global Economy*, Basingstoke: Macmillan, 69–94.

Miliband, R. (1969) *The State in Capitalist Society*, London: Weidenfeld & Nicolson

Miller, P. (1987) 'Strategic Industrial Relations and Human Resource Management – Distinction, Definition and Recognition', *Journal of Management Studies*, 24(4): 347–61.

Millward, N. and Stevens, M. (1986) *British Workplace Industrial Relations 1980–84*, Aldershot: Gower.

Millward, N., Bryson, A. and Forth, J. (2000) *All Change at Work: British Employment Relations 1980–1998, as Portrayed by the Workplace Industrial Relations Series*, London: Routledge.

Millward, N., Forth, J. Bryson, A. (2001) *Who Calls the Tune at Work? The Impact of Trade Unions on Jobs and Pay*, York: York Publishing Services.

Millward, N., Stevens, M., Smart, D. and Hawes, W.R. (1992) *Workplace Industrial Relations in Transition*, Aldershot: Dartmouth.

Milner, S. (1993) 'Overtime Bans and Strikes: Evidence on Relative Incidence', *Industrial Relations Journal*, 24(3): 201–10.

Minford, P. (1985) *Unemployment: Cause and Cure*, 2nd edition, Oxford: Blackwell.

Monks, J. (2001) 'The Union Renaissance', www.tuc.org.uk/*leedslecture*.

Morgan, J., Genre, V. and Wilson, C. (2001) 'Measuring Employment Security in Europe Using Surveys of Employers', *Industrial Relations*, 40(1): 54–72.

Morris, T. and Wood, S. (1991) 'Testing the Survey Method: Continuity and Change in British Industrial Relations', *Work, Employment & Society*, 5(2): 259–82.

Morrison, B. (2003) 'Eight Days in the Life of a Strike', *The Guardian*, 21 January: 2.

Moule, C. (1998) 'Regulation of Work in Small Firms: A View from the Inside', *Work, Employment & Society*, 12(4): 635–53.

Mueller, F. (1996) 'Human Resources as Strategic Assets: An Evolutionary Resource-Based Theory', *Journal of Management Studies*, 33(6): 757–85.

Murphy, A. and Armstrong, D. (1994) *A Picture of the Catholic and Protestant Male Unemployed*, Employment Equality Review Research Report 2, Belfast: CCRU.

NACAB (1993) *Job Insecurity: CAB Evidence on Employment Problems in the Recession*, London: National Association of Citizens Advice Bureaux.

Neale, A. (1992) 'Are British Workers Pricing Themselves out of Jobs? Unit Labour Costs and Competitiveness', *Work, Employment & Society*, 6(2): 271–85.

Neumark, D. (2002) 'Drawing the Lines: Comment on *Living in America: A Blueprint for the New Labor Market* by Paul Osterman et al', *Industrial & Labor Relations Review*, 54(4): 716–23.

Newell, H. (1993) 'Exploding the Myth of Greenfield Sites', *Personnel Management*, January: 20–3.

Nichol, D. (1992) 'Unnecessary Conflict: NHS Management's View of the 1989–90 Ambulance Dispute', *British Journal of Industrial Relations*, 30(1): 145–54.

Nichols, T. (ed.) (1980) *Capital and Labour: Studies in the Capitalist Labour Process*, London: Fontana.

Nichols, T. (1986) *The British Worker Question: A New Look at Workers and Productivity in Manufacturing*, London: Routledge & Kegan Paul.

Nichols, T. (1990) 'Industrial Safety in Britain and the 1974 Health and Safety at Work Act: The Case of Manufacturing', *International Journal of the Sociology of Law*, 18(3): 317–42.

Nicholson, N. (1977) 'Absence Behaviour and Attendance Motivation: A Conceptual Synthesis', *Journal of Management Studies*, 14(3): 231–52.

Nicholson, N. and Johns, G. (1985) 'The Absence Culture and the Psychological Contract – Who's in Control of Absence', *Academy of Management Review*, 10(3): 397–407.

Nicholson, N., Ursell, G. and Blyton, P. (1980) 'Social Background, Attitudes and Behaviour of White-Collar Shop Stewards', *British Journal of Industrial Relations* 18(2): 231–39.

Nickell, S., Jones, P. and Quintini, G. (2002) 'A Picture of Job Insecurity Facing British Men', *The Economic Journal*, 112(476): 1–27.

Nolan, P. (1983) 'The Firm and Labour Market Behaviour', in G.S. Bain (ed.), *Industrial Relations in Britain*, Oxford: Blackwell, 291–310.

Noon, M. and Blyton, P. (2002) *The Realities of Work*, 2nd edition, Basingstoke: Palgrave-Macmillan.

North, D.C. (1990) *Institutions, Institutional Change and Economic Performance*, Cambridge: Cambridge University Press.

Northern Ireland Assembly (1999) *Report of the Ad Hoc Committee (Port of Belfast)*, London: The Stationery Office.

O'Mahoney, M. and de Boer, W. (2002) *Britain's Relative Productivity Performance: Updates to 1999*, Final Report to DTI/Treasury/ONS, London: National Institute of Economic and Social Research.

Oakland, J.S. (1989) *Total Quality Management*, Oxford: Butterworth-Heinemann.

OECD (1994) *Economic Outlook*, July, Paris: Organisation for Economic Cooperation and Development.

OECD (1996) *Economic Outlook*, July, Paris: Organisation for Economic Cooperation and Development.

OECD (1999) *Employment Perspectives*, Paris: OECD.

OECD (2000a) *OECD Economic Outlook*, No. 67, Paris: Organisation for Economic Cooperation and Development.

OECD (2000b) *OECD Employment Outlook 2000*, Paris: Organisation for Economic Cooperation and Development.

OECD (2000c) *OECD in Figures*, Paris: Organisation for Economic Cooperation and Development.

OECD (2001) 'Balancing Work and Family Life: Helping Parents into Paid Employment', in *OECD Employment Outlook 2001*, Paris: Organisation for Economic Cooperation and Development, 130–166.

OECD (2002a) *OECD in Figures*, Paris: Organisation for Economic Cooperation and Development.

OECD (2002b) 'Taking the Measure of Temporary Employment', *OECD Employment Outlook*, Paris: OECD, 129183.

OECD (2002c) *The Sources of Economic Growth in OECD Countries*, Paris: OECD.

OECD (2002d) 'Women at Work: Who Are They and How are They Faring?', *OECD Employment Outlook*, Paris: OECD, 63–125.

OECD (2003) Measuring Globalisation Dataset 2003 release 01. <URL: http//www.sourceoecd.org [Accessed 6 March 2003].

Offe, C. and Ronge, V. (1982) 'Theses on the Theory of the State', in A. Giddens and D. Held (eds), *Classes, Power and Conflict*, London: Macmillan, 249–56.

Offe, C. and Wiesenthal, H. (1980) 'Two Logics of Collective Action: Theoretical Notes on Social Class and Organisational Form', *Political Power and Social Theory*, 1: 67–115.

Ogbonna, E. (1992) 'Organisational Culture and Human Resource Management: Dilemmas and Contradictions', in P. Blyton and P. Turnbull (eds), *Reassessing Human Resource Management*, London: Sage, 74–96.

Ogbonna, E. and Harris, L.C. (2002) 'Institutionalization of Tipping as a Source of Managerial Control', *British Journal of Industrial Relations*, 40(4): 725–52.

Ogbonna, E. and Wilkinson, B. (1988) 'Corporate Strategy and Corporate Culture: The Management of Change in the UK Supermarket Industry', *Personnel Review*, 17(6): 10–14.

Ogbonna, E. and Wilkinson, B. (1990) 'Corporate Strategy and Corporate Culture: The View from the Checkout', *Personnel Review*, 19(4): 9–15.

Ogden, S. (1981) 'The Reform of Collective Bargaining: A Managerial Revolution?', *Industrial Relations Journal*, 12(4): 30–42.

Ogden, S. (1982) 'Bargaining Structure and the Control of Industrial Relations', *British Journal of Industrial Relations*, 20(2): 170–85.

Ogden, S. (1994) 'The Reconstruction of Industrial Relations in the Privatized Water Industry', *British Journal of Industrial Relations*, 32(1): 67–84.

Ogden, S. (1995) 'Transforming Frameworks of Accountability: The Case of Water Privatization', *Accounting, Organizations & Society*, 20(2/3): 193–218.

Ogden, S. and Watson, R. (1996) 'The Relationship Between Changes in Incentive Structures, Executive Pay and Corporate Performance: Some Evidence from the Privatised Water Industry in England and Wales', *Journal of Business Finance & Accounting*, 23(5/6): 721–51.

Oliver, N. and Wilkinson, B. (1992) *The Japanization of British Industry*, 2nd edition, Oxford: Blackwell.

Organising Works (1995) *Organising Works*, No.2, Melbourne: Organising Works.

Organising Works (1996) *Organising in Everything We Do – A Manual on the Craft of Organising and Recruitment*, Melbourne: Organising Works.

Osterman, P. Kochan, T.A., Locke, R.M. and Piore, M.J. (2001) *Working in America: A Blueprint for the New Labor Market*, Cambridge, Mass: MIT Press.

Oswald, A.J. (1997) 'Happiness and Economic Performance', *The Economic Journal*, 107: 1815–31.

Oulton, N. (1996) 'Competition and the Dispersion of Labour Productivity Amongst UK Companies', Discussion Paper 103, London: National Institute of Economic and Social Research.

Oulton, N. (2001) 'Why do Foreign-Owned Firms in the UK Have Higher Labour Productivity?' in N. Pain (ed), *Inward Investment, Technological Change and Growth: The Impact of Multinational Corporations in the UK Economy*, Basingstoke: Palgrave, 122–61.

Oum, T. and Yu, C. (1998) *Winning Airlines: Productivity and Cost Competitiveness of the World's Major Airlines*, Boston: Kluwer.

Owen Smith, E. (1971) *Productivity Bargaining: A Case Study in the Steel Industry*, London: Pan.

Owen, N. (1998) *Differences in Companies' Performance: British Industry's Under-Performing Tail*, London: Department of Trade & Industry.

Oxenbridge, S. and Brown, W. (2002) 'The Two Faces of Partnership? An Assessment of Partnerships and Co-operative Employer/Trade Union Relationships', *Employee Relations*, 24(3): 262–76.

Oxenbridge, S., Brown, W., Deakin, S. and Pratten, C. (2003) 'Initial Responses to the Statutory Recognition Provisions of the Employment Relations Act 1999', *British Journal of Industrial Relations*, 41(2): 315–34.

Pain, N., Ashworth, P., Holland, D., Hubert, F. and te Velde, D.W. (2000) 'The World Economy', *National Institute Economic Review*, 172: 33–61.

Palmer, G., Rahman, M. and Kenway, P. (2002) *Monitoring Poverty and Social Exclusion 2002*, York: Joseph Rowntree Foundation/York Publishing Services.

Panitch, L. (1981) 'Trade Unions and the Capitalist State', *New Left Review*, (125): 21–43.

Parasuraman, A., Berry L. and Zeithmaml, V. (1991) 'Understanding Customer Expectations of Service', *Sloan Management Review*, 32(3): 39–48.

Parkin, F. (1971) *Class, Inequality and Political Order*, London: MacGibbon & Kee.

Parsons, T. (1952) *The Social System*, London: Routledge & Kegan Paul.

Pateman, C. (1970) *Participation and Democratic Theory*, London: Cambridge University Press.

Patterson, M., West, M., Lawthorn, R. and Nickell, S. (1997) *Impact of People Management Practices on Business Performance*, London: Institute of Personnel and Development.

Pearson, P. and Quiney, M. (1992) *Poor Britain: Poverty, Inequality and Low Pay in the Nineties*, London: Low Pay Unit.

Pendleton, A. and Winterton, J. (eds) (1993) *Public Enterprise in Transition: Industrial Relations in State and Privatized Corporations*, London: Routledge.

Peters, T. and Waterman, R. (1982) *In Search of Excellence*, New York: Harper Row.

Pfeffer, J. (1998) *The Human Equation: Building Profits by Putting People First*, Boston, Mass: Harvard University Press.

Phizacklea, A. (1987) 'Minority Women and Economic Restructuring', *Work, Employment & Society*, 1(3): 309–25.

Piore, M. and Sabel, C. (1984) *The Second Industrial Divide: Prospects for Prosperity*, New York: Basic Books.

Plowman, D.H., Deery, S.J. and Fisher, C.H. (1981) *Australian Industrial Relations*, Sydney: McGraw Hill.

Pollert, A. (1988) 'Dismantling Flexibility', *Capital & Class*, 34(Spring): 42–75.

Ponak, A.M. and Fraser, C.R.P. (1979) 'Union Activists' Support for Joint Programs', *Industrial Relations*, 18(2): 197–209.

Pond, C. (1983) 'Wages Councils, the Unorganised and the Low Paid', in G.S. Bain (ed.), *Industrial Relations in Britain*, Oxford: Blackwell, 179–208.

Poole, M. (1981) *Theories of Trade Unionism*, London: Routledge & Kegan Paul.

Poole, M. (1986) 'Managerial Strategies and Styles in Industrial Relations: A Comparative Analysis', *Journal of General Management*, 12(1): 40–53.

Poole, M. (1988) 'Industrial Relations Theory and Management Strategies', *International Journal of Comparative Labour Law and Industrial Relations*, 4(1): 11–24.

Poole, M. and Jenkins, G. (1996) *Back to the Line? A Survey of Managers' Attitudes to Human Resource Management Issues*, London: Institute of Management.

Poole, M. and Mansfield, R. (1992) 'Managers' Attitudes to Human Resource Management: Rhetoric and Reality', in P. Blyton and P. Turnbull (eds), *Reassessing Human Resource Management*, London: Sage, 200–14.

Poole, M. and Mansfield, R. (1993) 'Patterns of Continuity and Change in Management Attitudes and Behaviour in Industrial Relations, 1980–1990', *British Journal of Industrial Relations*, 31(1): 11–35.

Poole, M., Mansfield, R., Blyton, P. and Frost, P. (1981) *Managers in Focus*, Aldershot: Gower.

Poole, M., Mansfield, R. and Mendes, P. (2001) *Two Decades of Management: A Survey of the Attitudes and Behaviour of Managers Over a 20 Year Period*, London: Institute of Management.

Porter, M.E. (1990) *The Competitive Advantage of Nations*, New York: Free Press.

Proctor, S. and Mueller, F. (eds) (2000) *Teamworking*, Basingstoke: Macmillan.

Prokesch, S.E. (1995) 'Competing on Customer Service: An Interview with British Airways' Sir Colin Marshall', *Harvard Business Review*, November-December: 101–12.

Purcell, J. (1987) 'Mapping Management Styles in Employee Relations', *Journal of Management Studies*, 24(5): 533–48.

Purcell, J. (1989) 'The Impact of Corporate Strategy on Human Resource Management', in J. Storey (ed.), *New Perspectives on Human Resource Management*, London: Routledge, 67–91.

Purcell, J. (1991) 'The Rediscovery of the Management Prerogative: The Management of Labour Relations in the 1980s', *Oxford Review of Economic Policy*, 7(1): 33–43.

Purcell, J. (1999) 'Best Practice and Best Fit: Chimera or Cul-de-Sac?' *Human Resource Management Journal*, 9(3): 26–41.

Purcell, J. (2001) 'The Meaning of Strategy in HRM', in J. Storey (ed.), *Human Resource Management: A Critical Text*, 2nd edition, London: Thompson, 59–77.

Purcell, J. and Ahlstrand, B. (1994) *Human Resource Management in the Multi-Divisional Firm*, Oxford: Oxford University Press.

Purcell, J. and Gray, A. (1986) 'Corporate Personnel Departments and the Management of Industrial Relations: Two Case Studies in Ambiguity', *Journal of Management Studies*, 23(2): 205–23.

Purcell, J. and Sisson, K. (1983) 'Strategies and Practice in the Management of Industrial Relations', in G.S. Bain (ed.), *Industrial Relations in Britain*, Oxford: Blackwell, 95–120.

Purcell, J., Marginson, P., Edwards, P. and Sisson, K. (1987) 'The Industrial Relations Practices of Multi-Plant Foreign-Owned Firms', *Industrial Relations Journal*, 18(2): 130–37.

Purcell, K., Hogart, T. and Simm, C. (1999) *Whose Flexibility? The Costs and Benefits of Non-Standard Working Arrangements and Contractual Relations*, York: Joseph Rowntree Foundation/York Publishing Services.

Rainnie, A.F. (1984) 'Combined and Uneven Development in the Clothing Industry: The Effects of Competition on Accumulation', *Capital & Class*, (22): 141–56.

Rainnie, A.F. (1985a) 'Is Small Beautiful? Industrial Relations in Small Clothing Firms', *Sociology*, 19(2): 213–24.

Rainnie, A.F. (1985b) 'Small Firms, Big Problems: The Political Economy of Small Businesses', *Capital & Class*, (25): 140–68.

Rainnie, A.F. (1989) *Industrial Relations in Small Firms: Small Isn't Beautiful*, London: Routledge.

Rainnie, A.F. (1991) 'Small Firms: Between the Enterprise Culture and New Times', in R. Burrows (ed.), *Deciphering the Enterprise Culture: Entrepreneurship, Petty Capitalism and the Restructuring of Britain*, London: Routledge, 176–99.

Ram, M. (1991) 'Control and Autonomy in Small Firms: The Case of the West Midlands Clothing Industry', *Work, Employment & Society*, 5(4): 601–19.

Ram, M. (1994) *Managing to Survive: Working Lives in Small Firms*, Oxford: Blackwell.

Ram, M., Edwards, P., Gilman, M. and Arrowsmith, J. (2001) ' The Dynamics of Informality: Employment Regulation in Small Firms and the Effects of Regulatory Change', *Work, Employment & Society*, 15(4): 845–61.

Ramsay, H. (1977) 'Cycles of Control', *Sociology*, 11(3): 481–506.

Ramsay, H. (1980) 'Phantom Participation: Patterns of Power and Conflict', *Industrial Relations Journal*, 11(3): 46–59.

Ramsay, H. (1983) 'Evolution or Cycle? Worker Participation in the 1970s and 1980s', in C. Crouch and F. Heller (eds), *Organisational Democracy and Political Processes*, London: Wiley, 203–226.

Ramsay, H. (1991) 'The Community, the Multinational, its Workers and Their Charter: A Modern Tale of Industrial Democracy?', *Work, Employment & Society*, 5(4): 541–66.

Ramsay, H., Pollert, A. and Rainbird, H. (1992) 'A Decade of Transformation? Labour Market Flexibility and Work Organisation in the United Kingdom', in Organisation for Economic Cooperation and Development (ed.), *New Directions in Work Organisation: The Industrial Relations Response*, Paris: OECD, 169–95.

Ramsay, H., Scholarios, D. and Harley, B. (2000) 'Employees and High Performance Work Systems: Testing Inside the Black Box', *British Journal of Industrial Relations*, 38(4): 501–31.

Redman, T. and Wilkinson, A. (2001) *Contemporary Human Resource Management: Text and Cases*, London: Prentice Hall.

Reynolds, L.G. (1956) *Labor Economics and Labor Relations*, Englewood Cliffs, NJ: Prentice-Hall.

Ricardo, D. (1817) *Principles of Political Economy and Taxation*, 1965 edition, London: Dent.

Ritzer, G. (1996) *The McDonaldization of Society: An Investigation into the Changing Character of Contemporary Life*, Thousand Oaks, CA: Pine Forge Press.

Ritzer, G. (1998) *The McDonaldization Thesis: Explorations and Extensions*, London: Thousand Oakes.

Roberts, Z. (2003a) 'Crossing the Divide', *People Management*, 11 September: 29–32.

Roberts, Z. (2003b) 'HR Central to Fire Reform', *People Management*, 10 July: 12.

Roche, W. (2000) 'The End of New Industrial Relations', *European Journal of Industrial Relations*, 6(3): 261–82.

Rogers, J. and Streeck, W. (1994) 'Workplace Representation Overseas: The Works Council Story', in R.B. Freeman (ed.), *Working Under Different Rules*, New York: Russell Foundation, 97–156.

Rose, M. (1975) *Industrial Behaviour: Theoretical Developments Since Taylor*, Harmondsworth: Penguin.

Rosenthal, P. Hill, S. and Peccei, R. (1997) 'Checking Out Service; Evaluating Excellence, HRM and TQM in Retaining', *Work, Employment & Society*, 11(3): 481–503.

Rowthorn, B. (1986) 'The Passivity of the State', in D. Coates and J. Hillard (eds), *The Economic Decline of Modern Britain: The Debate Between Left and Right*, Brighton: Wheatsheaf Books, 264–6.

Royle, T. (1999) 'The Reluctant Bargainers? McDonald's, Unions and Pay Determination in Germany and the UK', *Industrial Relations Journal*, 30(2): 135–50.

Royle, T. (2000) *Working for McDonald's in Europe: The Unequal Struggle*, London: Routledge.

Rubenowitz, S., Norrgren, F. and Tannenbaum, A.S. (1983) 'Some Social Psychological Effects of Direct or Indirect Participation in Ten Swedish Companies', *Organization Studies*, 4(3): 243–59.

Rubery, J. (1987) 'Flexibility of Labour Costs in Non-Union Firms', in R. Tarling (ed.), *Flexibility in Labour Markets*, London: Academic Press, 59–83.

Rubery, J. (1988) 'Employers and the Labour Market', in D. Gallie (ed.), *Employment in Britain*, Oxford: Blackwell, 251–80.

Rubery, J. (1994) 'The British Production Regime: A Societal-Specific System?', *Economy & Society*, 23(August): 335–54.

Rubery, J. and Edwards, P. (2003) 'Low Pay and the National Minimum Wage', in P. Edwards (ed.), *Industrial Relations: Theory and Practice*, 2nd edition, Oxford: Blackwell, 447–69.

Rubery, J., Earnshaw, J., Marchington, M., Cooke, F.L. and Vincent, S. (2002) 'Changing Organizational Forms and the Employment Relationship', *Journal of Management Studies*, 39(5): 645–72.

Rubery, J., Tarling, R. and Wilkinson, F. (1987) 'Flexibility, Marketing and the Organisation of Production', *Labour & Society*, 12(1): 131–51.

Rubinstein, S.A. (2000) 'The Impact of Co-Management on Quality Performance: The Case of Saturn Corporation', *Industrial & Labor Relations Review*, 53(2): 197–218.

Salmans, S. (1980) 'Mixed Fortunes at M&S', *Management Today*, November: 67–73.

Salsbury, P.L. (1993) 'Memorandum from Marks and Spencer', House of Commons Employment Committee of Inquiry, *The Future of the Unions*, London: HMSO.

Sapper, S. (1991) 'Do Members' Services Packages Influence Trade Union Recruitment', *Industrial Relations Journal*, 22(4): 309–16.

Sapsford, D. (1981) *Labour Market Economics*, London: George Allen & Unwin.

Sapsford, D. and Turnbull, P. (1993) 'Research Note: Organized and Unorganized Conflict in the British Coal-mining Industry, 1947–83', *International Journal of Manpower*, 14(9): 6–63.

Saundry, R. (2001) 'Employee Relations in British Television – Regulation, Fragmentation and Flexibility', *Industrial Relations Journal*, 32(1): 22–36.

Saundry, R. and Turnbull, P. (1997) 'Private Profit, Public Loss: The Financial and Economic Performance of UK Ports', *Maritime Policy & Management*, 24(4): 319–34.

Sayer, A. and Walker, R. (1992) *The New Social Economy: Reworking the Division of Labour*, Oxford: Blackwell.

SBS (2003a) *Small and Medium-Sized Enterprise (SME) Statistics for the Regions, 2001*, London: Department of Trade & Industry/Small Business Service.

SBS (2003b) *Small Firms: Big Business. A Review of Small and Medium Sized Enterprises in the UK*, London: Department of Trade & Industry/Small Business Service.

Scase, R. (1982) 'The Petty Bourgeoisie and Modern Capitalism: A Consideration of Recent Theories', in A. Giddens and G. Mackenzie (eds), *Social Class and the Division of Labour*, Cambridge: Cambridge University Press, 148–61.

Scase, R. (1995) 'Employment Relations in Small Firms', in P. Edwards (ed.), *Industrial Relations: Theory and Practice in Britain*, Oxford: Blackwell, 569–95.

Scase, R. (2003) 'Employment Relations in Small Firms', in P. Edwards (ed.), *Industrial Relations: Theory and Practice*, 2nd edition, Oxford: Blackwell, 471–88.

Schuler, R. and Jackson, S. (1987) 'Linking Competitive Strategies and Human Resource Management Practices', *Academy of Management Executive*, 1(3): 207–19.

Schumpeter, J. (1950) *Capitalism, Socialism and Democracy*, 3rd edition, New York: Harper.

Scott, A. (1994) *Willing Slaves? British Workers Under Human Resource Management*, Cambridge: Cambridge University Press.

Scott, M., Roberts, I., Holroyd, G. and Sawbridge, D. (1989) *Management and Industrial Relations in Small Firms*, Research Paper No.70, London: Department of Employment.

Screpanti, E. (1987) 'Long Cycles in Strike Activity: An Empirical Investigation', *British Journal of Industrial Relations*, 25(1): 99–124.

Sewell, G. (1998) 'The Discipline of Teams: The Control of Team-Based Industrial Work Through Electronic and Peer Surveillance', *Administrative Science Quarterly*, 43(2): 397–428.

Sewell, G. and Wilkinson, B. (1992) 'Employment or Emasculation? Shopfloor Surveillance in a Total Quality Organization', in P. Blyton and P. Turnbull (eds), *Reassessing Human Resource Management*, London: Sage, 97–115.

Shalev, M. (1978) 'Lies, Damned Lies, and Strike Statistics: The Measurement of Trends in Industrial Conflict', in C. Crouch and A. Pizzorno (eds), *The Resurgence of Class Conflict in Western Europe Since 1968*, Vol.1, National Studies, London: Macmillan, 1–19.

Shorter, E. and Tilly, C. (1974) *Strikes in France, 1830–1968*, Cambridge: Cambridge University Press.

Shutt, J. and Whittington, R. (1987) 'Fragmentation Strategies and the Rise of Small Units: Cases from the North West', *Regional Studies*, 21(1): 13–23.

Shuttleworth, I., Shirlow, P. and McKinstry, D. (1996) 'Vacancies, Access to Employment and the Unemployed: Two Case Studies of Belfast and Londonderry', in E. McLaughlin and P. Quirk (eds), *Policy Aspects of Employment Equality in Northern Ireland*, Belfast: Standing Advisory Commission on Human Rights, 27–49.

Sieff, M. (1984) 'How I See the Personnel Function', *Personnel Management*, December: 28–30.

Sieff, M. (1986) *Don't Ask the Price: The Memoirs of the President of Marks & Spencer*, London: Weidenfield & Nicolson.

Sieff, M. (1990) *Marcuss Sieff on Management: The Marks & Spencer Way*, London: Weidenfield & Nicolson.

Simpson, B. (1986) 'Trade Union Immunities', in R. Lewis (ed.), *Labour Law in Britain*, Oxford: Blackwell, 161–94.

Sinclair, D.M. (1996) 'The Importance of Gender for Participation in and Attitudes to Trade Unionism', *British Journal of Industrial Relations*, 27(3): 239–52.

Sisson, K. (1987) *The Management of Collective Bargaining: An International Comparison*, Oxford: Blackwell.

Sisson, K. (1993) 'In Search of HRM', *British Journal of Industrial Relations*, 31(2): 201–10.

Sisson, K. (2001) 'HRM and the Personnel Function – A Case of Partial Impact?' in J. Storey (ed.), *Human Resource Management: A Critical Text*, 2nd edition, London: Thompson, 78–95.

Sisson, K. (2002) 'The Information and Consultation Directive: Unnecessary Regulation or an Opportunity to Promote Partnership?', Warwick Papers in Industrial Relations No. 67, Industrial Relations Research Unit, Warwick University.

Sisson, K. (ed.) (1989) *Personnel Management in Britain*, Oxford: Blackwell.

Sisson, K. and Brown, W. (1983) 'Industrial Relations in the Private Sector: Donovan Re-visited', in G.S. Bain (ed.), *Industrial Relations in Britain*, Oxford: Blackwell, 137–54.

Sisson, K. and Marginson, P. (1995) 'Management: Systems, Structures and Strategy', in P. Edwards (ed.), *Industrial Relations: Theory and Practice in Britain*, Oxford: Blackwell, 89–122.

Sisson, K. and Marginson, P. (2003) 'Management: Systems, Structures and Strategy', in P. Edwards (ed.), *Industrial Relations: Theory and Practice*, 2nd edition, Oxford: Blackwell, 157–88.

Slichter, S.H. (1941) *Union Policies and Industrial Management*, Washington DC: Brookings Institute.

Smit, E. (1992) 'Theoretische Reflecties bij de Arbeidssociologische Studies over de Rotterdamse Haven', *Tijdschrift voor Arbeidsvaagstukken*, 8(2): 100–12.

Smith, C.T.B., Clifton, R., Makeham, P., Creigh, S.W. and Burn, R.V. (1978) *Strikes in Britain*, Department of Employment, Manpower Paper 15, London: HMSO.

Smith, M. (1986) 'UK Manufacturing Output and Trade Performance', *Midland Bank Review*, Autumn: 8–16.

Smith, P. and Morton, G. (1990) 'A Change of Heart: Union Exclusion in the Provincial Newspaper Sector', *Work, Employment & Society*, 4(1): 105–24.

Smith, P. and Morton, G. (2001) 'New Labour's Reform of Britain's Employment Law: The Devil is not only in the Detail but in the Values and Policy too', *British Journal of Industrial Relations*, 39(1): 119–38.

Smith, P., Fosh, P., Martin, R., Morris, H. and Undy, R. (1993) 'Ballots and Union Government in the 1980s', *British Journal of Industrial Relations*, 31(3): 365–82.

Snape, E. (1994) 'Reversing the Decline? The TGWU's Link-Up Campaign', *Industrial Relations Journal*, 25(3): 222–33.

Soskice, D. (1990) 'Wage Determination: The Changing Role of Institutions in Advanced Industrialized Countries', *Oxford Review of Economic Policy*, 6(4): 36–61.

Soskice, D. (2000) 'Macroeconomic Analysis and the Political Economy of Unemployment', in T. Iverson, J. Pontusson and D. Soskice (eds.) *Unions, Employers and Central Banks*, Cambridge: Cambridge University Press, 38–74.

Sproull, A. and MacInnes, J. (1987) 'Patterns of Union Recognition in Scottish Electronics', *British Journal of Industrial Relations*, 25(3): 335–8.

Stafford, A. (1961) *A Match to Fire the Thames*, London: Hodder & Stoughton.

Stephenson, G., Brotherton, C., Delafield, G. and Skinner, M. (1983) 'Size of Organisation, Attitudes to Work and Job Satisfaction', *Industrial Relations Journal*, 14(2): 28–40.

Stevens, J. and Mackay, R. (1991) *Training and Competitiveness*, London: Kogan Page.

Stewart, M.B. (1991) 'Union Wage Differentials in the Face of Changes in the Economic and Legal Environment', *Economica*, 58: 155–72.

Stewart, M.B. (1995) 'Union Wage Differentials in an Era of Declining Unionisation', *Oxford Bulletin of Economics & Statistics*, 57(2): 143–66.

Stirling, J. (2000) 'Britain at Work: Letting the Facts Speak for Themselves?' *Capital & Class*, 73(Winter): 173–9.

Stirling, J. and Fitzgerald, I. (2001) 'European Works Councils: Representing Workers on the Periphery', *Employee Relations*, 23(1): 13–25.

Storey, J. (1985) 'The Means of Management Control', *Sociology*, 19(2): 193–211.

Storey, J. (1992) *Developments in the Management of Human Resources: An Analytical Review*, Oxford: Blackwell.

Storey, J. (ed.) (1989) *New Perspectives on Human Resource Management*, London: Routledge.

Storey, J. (ed.) (2001) *Human Resource Management: A Critical Text*, 2nd edition, London: Thompson.

Storey, J. and Sisson, K. (1993) *Managing Human Resources and Industrial Relations*, Buckingham: Open University Press.

Storey, J. and Tate, W. (2000) 'Management Development', in S. Bach and K. Sisson (eds), *Personnel Management*, 3rd edition, Oxford: Blackwell, 195–217.

Storper, M. (1995) 'Boundaries, Compartments and Markets: Paradoxes of Industrial Relations in Growth Pole Regions in France, Italy and the United States', in S. Jacoby (ed.), *The Workers of Nations*, New York: Oxford University Press, 155–81.

Strauss, G. and Feuille, P. (1978) 'Industrial Relations Research: A Critical Analysis', *Industrial Relations*, 17(3): 259–77.

Streeck, W. (1988) 'Comment on Ronald Dore, Rigidities in the Labour Market', *Government & Opposition*, 23(4): 413–23.

Streeck, W. (1992) *Social Institutions and Economic Performance: Studies of Industrial Relations in Advanced Capitalist Economies*, London: Sage.

Streeck, W. (1997) 'Beneficial Constraints: On the Economic Limits of Rational Voluntarism', in J.R. Hollingsworth and R. Boyer (eds.), *Contemporary Capitalism: The Embeddedness of Institutions*, Cambridge: Cambridge University Press, 197–219.

Streeck, W. (1998) 'The Internationalization of Industrial Relations in Europe: Prospects and Problems', *Politics & Society*, 26(4): 429–59.

Sturdy, A., Grugulis, I. and Willmott, H. (eds) (2001) *Customer Service*, Basingstoke: Palgrave.

Suff, P. (2000) *Partnership at Work*, IRS Management Review 17, London: Industrial Relations Services.

Sullivan, O. (2000) 'The Division of Domestic Labour: Twenty Years of Change?', *Sociology*, 34(3): 437–456.

Supiot, A. (2001) *Beyond Employment: Changes in Work and the Future of Labour Law in Europe*, Oxford: Oxford University Press.

Sweeney, K. and Davies, J. (1997) 'International Comparisons of Labour Disputes in 1995', *Labour Market Trends*, April: 129–34.

Taplin, I.M., Winterton, J. and Winterton, R. (2003) 'Understanding Labour Turnover in a Labour Intensive Industry: Evidence from the British Clothing Industry', *Journal of Management Studies*, 40(4): 1021–46.

T&GWU (1995a) *Organising for Strength: Organisers' Manual*, London: Transport & General Workers' Union.

T&GWU (1995b) *The Administrative Report of the 36th Biennial Delegate Conference*, London: Transport & General Workers' Union.

T&GWU (1996) *Organiser's Bulletin*, Winter, London: Transport & General Workers' Union, Region 1.

Tate, B. (1991) 'Book Review – The Human Side of Corporate Competitiveness, by D.B. Fishman and C. Cherniss (eds)', *Human Resource Management Journal*, 1(4): 110–12.

Taylor, B., Elger, T. and Fairbrother, P. (1991) 'Work Relations in Electronics: What Has Become of Japanisation in Britain?', Paper presented to the 9th Annual Labour Process Conference, UMIST, 10–12 April.

Taylor, L. and Walton, P. (1971) 'Industrial Sabotage: Motives and Meanings', in S. Cohen (ed.), *Images of Deviance*, Harmondsworth: Penguin, 219–45.

Taylor, S. and Tyler, M. (2000) 'Emotional Labour and Sexual Difference in the Airline Industry', *Work, Employment & Society*, 14(1): 77–95.

Terry, M. (1983) 'Shop Steward Development and Managerial Strategies', in G.S. Bain (ed.), *Industrial Relations in Britain*, Oxford: Blackwell, 67–91.

Terry, M. (1999) 'Systems of Collective Employee Representation in Non-Union Firms in the UK', *Industrial Relations Journal*, 30(1): 16–30.

Terry, M. (2003) 'Employee Representation: Shop Stewards and the New Legal Framework', in P. Edwards (ed.), *Industrial Relations Theory and Practice*, 2nd edition, Oxford: Blackwell, 257–84.

Tesco (2002) *Report and Accounts*, London: Tesco plc.

Thelen, K. (2001) 'Varieties of Labor Politics in the Developed Democracies', in P.A. Hall and D. Soskice (eds), *Varieties of Capitalism: The Institutional Foundations of Comparative Advantage*, Oxford: Oxford University Press, 71–103.

Thirlwall, A. P. (1982) 'De-Industrialisation in the United Kingdom', *Lloyds Bank Review*, (144): 22–37.

Thomas, P. and Smith, K. (1995) 'Results of the 1993 Census of Employment', *Employment Gazette*, October: 369–377.

Thompson, P. and McHugh, D. (1990) *Work Organisations: A Critical Introduction*, London: Macmillan.

Thompson, P. and McHugh, D. (2002) *Work Organisations: A Critical Introduction*, 3rd edition, Basingstoke: Palgrave Macmillan.

Thornthwaite, L. (2002) *Work-Family Balance: International Research on Employee Preferences*, Working Paper 79, ACIRRT, University of Sydney, Australia.

Towers, B. (1997a) 'Collective Bargaining, Democracy and Efficiency in the British and US Workplace', *Industrial Relations Journal*, 28(4): 299–308.

Towers, B. (1997b) *The Representation Gap: Change and Reform in the British and American Workplace*, Oxford: Oxford University Press.

Towers, B. (1999) 'Editorial: ...The Most Highly Regulated Labour Market... The UK's Third Statutory Recognition Procedure', *Industrial Relations Journal*, 30(2): 82–95.

Toynbee, P. (2003) *Hard Work: Life in Low Pay Britain*, London: Bloomsbury.

Traxler, F. (1999) 'Employers and Employer Organisations: The Case of Governability', *Industrial Relations Journal*, 30(4): 345–54.

Traxler, F. (2003) 'Coordinated Bargaining: A Stocktaking of its Preconditions, Practices and Performance', *Industrial Relations Journal*, 34(3): 194–209.

Traxler, F. and Kittel, B. (2000) 'The Bargaining System and Performance: A Comparison of 18 OECD Countries', *Comparative Political Studies*, 33(9): 1154–90.

Traxler, F., Kittel, B. and Blaschke, S. (2001) *National Labour Relations in Industrialized Markets*, Oxford: Oxford University Press.

Troy, L. (2001) 'Twilight for Organized Labor,' *Journal of Labor Research*, 22(2): 245–59.

Truss, C. (2001) 'Complexities and Controversies in Linking HRM with Organizational Outcomes', *Journal of Management Studies*, 38(8): 1121–49.

Truss, C., Gratton, L., Hope-Hailey, V., McGovern, P. and Stiles, P. (1997) 'Soft and Hard Models of Human Resource Management: A Reappraisal', *Journal of Management Studies*, 34(1): 53–73.

Truter, G.M. (2003) *Implementing the Information and Consultation Directive in the UK: Lessons from Germany*, London: Institute for Employment Rights.

Tse, K.K. (1985) *Marks & Spencer: Anatomy of Britain's Most Efficiently Managed Company*, Oxford: Pergamon.

TUC (1996a) *A Five Million Strong Challenge*, London: Trades Unions Congress.

TUC (1996b) *Testament of Youth: A Manifesto for Young Workers*, London: Trades Unions Congress.

TUC (1999) *Response to McKinsey Productivity and Partnership*, London: Trades Union Congress (www.tuc.org.uk/partnership).

TUC (2001) *Trade Union Trends: Focus on Recognition*. Trade Union Trends Survey 00/1. London: Trades Union Congress.

TUC (2002) *Partnership Works*, London: Trades Union Congress.

TUC (2003a) *A Perfect Union?* London: Trades Union Congress.

TUC (2003b) *High Performance Workplaces*, London: Trade Union Congress.

TUC (2003c) 'Productivity Hit as UK Managers Fail to Consult Staff', Trades Union Congress Press Release, 28 August.

TUC (2003d) *Review of the Employment Relations Act 1999: TUC Response*, London: Trades Union Congress.

Turnbull, P. (1988a) 'The Economic Theory of Trade Union Behaviour: A Critique', *British Journal of Industrial Relations*, 26(1): 99–118.

Turnbull, P. (1988b) 'The Limits to Japanisation – Just-in-Time, Labour Relations and the UK Automotive Industry', *New Technology, Work & Employment*, 3(1): 7–20.

Turnbull, P. (1991a) 'Buyer-Supplier Relations in the UK Automotive Industry', in P. Blyton and J. Morris (eds), *A Flexible Future? Prospects for Employment and Organization*, Berlin: Walter de Gruyter, 169–89.

Turnbull, P. (1991b) 'Trade Unions and Productivity: Opening the Harvard Black Boxes', *Journal of Labor Research*, 12(2): 135–50.

Turnbull, P. (1992) 'Dock Strikes and the Demise of the Dockers' Occupational Culture', *Sociological Review*, 40(2): 294–318.

Turnbull, P. (1993) 'Docks', in A. Pendleton and J. Winterton (eds), *Public Enterprise in Transition: Industrial Relations in State and Privatized Corporations*, London: Routledge, 185–210.

Turnbull, P. (1997) 'Organising Works in Australia – Will it Work in Britain?', mimeo, University of Leeds.

Turnbull, P. (1999) 'Regulation, Deregulation or Re-regulation of Transport?' Discussion Paper No.4, Symposium on the Social and Labour Consequences of Technological Developments, Deregulation and Privatization of Transport, Geneva: International Labour Organisation.

Turnbull, P. (2000) 'Contesting Globalization on the Waterfront', *Politics & Society*, 28(3): 273–97.

Turnbull, P. (2003) 'Review Essay: What Do Unions Do Now?' *Journal of Labor Research*, 14(3): 491–527.

Turnbull, P. and Harvey, G. (2001) 'The Impact of 11 September on the Civil Aviation Industry: Social and Labour Effects', ILO Sectoral Working Paper No. 182, Geneva: International Labour Office.

Turnbull, P. and Sapsford, D. (1991) 'Why Did Devlin Fail? Casualism and Conflict on the Docks', *British Journal of Industrial Relations*, 29(2): 237–57.

Turnbull, P. and Sapsford, D. (1992) 'A Sea of Discontent: The Tides of Organised and Unorganised Conflict on the Docks', *Sociology*, 26(2): 291–309.

Turnbull, P. and Sapsford, D. (2001) 'Hitting the Bricks: An International Comparative Study of Conflict on the Waterfront', *Industrial Relations*, 40(2): 231–57.

Turnbull, P. and Wass, V. (1994) 'The Greatest Game No More – Redundant Dockers and the Demise of Dock Work', *Work, Employment & Society*, 8(4): 487–506.

Turnbull, P. and Wass, V. (1997a) 'Job Insecurity and Labour Market Lemons: The (Mis)Management of Redundancy in Steel Making, Coal Mining and Port Transport', *Journal of Management Studies*, 34(1): 27–51.

Turnbull, P. and Wass, V. (1997b) 'Marksist Management: Sophisticated Human Relations in a High Street Retail Store', *Industrial Relations Journal*, 29(2): 98–111.

Turnbull, P. and Wass, V. (2000) 'Redundancy and the Paradox of Job Insecurity', in E. Heery and J. Salmon (eds), *The Insecure Workforce*, London: Routledge, 57–77.

Turnbull, P. and Wass, V. (2001) 'Overview of Redundancy Data in WERS 1998', mimeo, Cardiff Business School, Cardiff University.

Turnbull, P. and Weston, S. (1993a) 'Cooperation or Control? Capital Restructuring and Labour Relations on the Docks', *British Journal of Industrial Relations*, 31(1): 115–34.

Turnbull, P. and Weston, S. (1993b) 'The British Port Transport Industry, Part 2. Employment, Working Practices and Productivity', *Maritime Policy & Management*, 20(3): 181–95.

Turnbull, P., Blyton, P. and Harvey, G. (2004) 'Cleared for Take-Off? Management-Labour Partnership in the European Civil Aviation Industry', *European Journal of Industrial Relations*.

Turnbull, P., Blyton, P., McGurk, J. and Martínez Lucio, M. (2001) 'Strategic Choice and Industrial Relations: A Case Study of British Airways', mimeo, Cardiff Business School.

Turnbull, P., Morris, J. and Sapsford, D. (1996) 'Persistent Militants and Quiescent Comrades: Intra-Industry Strike Activity on the Docks, 1947–89', *Sociological Review*, 44(4): 710–45.

Turnbull, P., Woolfson, C. and Kelly, J. (1992) *Dock Strikes: Conflict and Restructuring in Britain's Ports*, Aldershot: Avebury.

Turner, H.A., Clack, G. and Roberts, G. (1967) *Labour Relations in the Motor Industry*, London: George Allen & Unwin.

Turner, H.A., Roberts, G. and Roberts, D. (1977) *Management Characteristics and Labour Conflict*, Cambridge: Cambridge University Press.

Tyler, M. and Abbott, P. (1998) 'Chocs Away: Weight Watching in the Contemporary Airline Industry', *Sociology*, 32(3): 433–50.

Ulrich, D. (1997) *Human Resource Champions: The Next Agenda for Adding Value and Delivering Results*, Boston: Harvard Business School Press.

UNCTAD (2001) *World Investment Report: Promoting Linkages*, United Nations Conference on Trade and Development, New York and Geneva: United Nations.

Undy, R. (1999a) 'Annual Review Article: New Labour's Industrial; Relations Settlement: The Third Way?', *British Journal of Industrial Relations*, 37(2): 315–36.

Undy, R. (1999b) 'The British Merger Movement: The Importance of the 'Aggressive' Unions', *Industrial Relations Journal*, 30(5): 464–81.

Undy, R., Ellis, V., McCarthy, W.E.J. and Halmos, A.M. (1981) *Change in Trade Unions: The Development of UK Unions Since the 1960s*, London: Hutchinson.

Undy, R., Fosh, P., Morris, H., Smith, P. and Martin, R. (1996) *Managing the Unions: The Impact of Legislation on Trade Union Behaviour*, Oxford: Clarendon Press.

United Nations (1996) *Human Development Report*, Geneva: United Nations.

Ursell, G. (1983) 'The Views of British Managers and Shop Stewards on Industrial Democracy', in C. Crouch and F. Heller (eds), *Organisational Democracy and Political Process*, Chichester: Wiley, 327–52.

Ursell, G. and Blyton, P. (1988) *State, Capital and Labour: Changing Patterns of Power and Dependence*, London: Macmillan.

Ursell, G., Wall, T., Clegg, C., Lubbock, J., Blyton, P. and Nicholson, N. (1980) 'Shop Stewards Attitudes Towards Industrial Democracy', *Industrial Relations Journal*, 11(1): 22–30.

USDAW (1998) *Tesco-USDAW A Real Partnership*, London: Union of Shop, Distributive and Allied Workers.

Van Amelsvoort, P. and Benders, J. (1996) 'Team Time: A Model for Developing Self-Directed Work Teams', *International Journal of Operations and Production Management*, 16(2): 159–70.

Vandevelde, L. (2003) 'The Saturday Essay', *The Grocer*, 226(7593): 28.

Visser, J. (1998a) 'European Trade Unions in the Mid-1990s', *Industrial Relations Journal – European Annual Review*, Oxford: Blackwell, 113–30.

Visser, J. (1998b) 'Two Cheers for Corporatism, One for the Market: Industrial Relations, Wage Moderation and Job Growth in the Netherlands', *British Journal of Industrial Relations*, 36(2): 269–92.

von Nordenflycht, A. (2002) 'Alternative Approaches to Airline Labor Relations', American Academy of Management, Denver Colorado.

Waddington, J. (1992) 'Trade Union Membership in Britain 1980–1987: Unemployment and Restructuring', *British Journal of Industrial Relations*, 30(2): 287–324.

Waddington, J. (1995) *The Politics of Bargaining: The Merger Process and British Trade Union Structural Development, 1892–1987*, London: Mansell.

Waddington, J. (2003a) 'Annual Review Article 2002. Heightening Tension in Relations Between Trade Unions and the Labour Government in 2002', *British Journal of Industrial Relations*, 41(2): 335–58.

Waddington, J. (2003b) 'Trade Union Organization', in P. Edwards (ed.), *Industrial Relations: Theory and Practice*, 2nd edition, Oxford: Blackwell, 214–56.

Waddington, J. and Kerckhofs, P. (2003) 'European Works Councils: What is the Current State of Play?', *Transfer*, 9(2): 322–39.

Waddington, J. and Kerr, A. (2000) 'Towards an Organizing Model in UNISON: A Trade Union Membership Strategy in Transition', in M. Terry (ed.), *Redefining Public Sector Unionism: UNISON and the Future of Trade Unions*, London: Routledge, 231–62.

Waddington, J. and Whitston, C. (1995a) 'Trade Unions: Growth, Structure and Policy', in P. Edwards (ed.), *Industrial Relations: Theory and Practice in Britain*, Oxford: Blackwell, 151–202.

Waddington, J. and Whitston, C. (1995b) 'Work Intensification and Grievances at Unionised Workplaces in the UK', *Industrielle Beziehungen*, 2(4): 414–43.

Waddington, J. and Whitston, C. (1997) 'Why Do People Join Trade Unions in a Period of Membership Decline?' *British Journal of Industrial Relations*, 35(4): 515–46.

Wajcman, J. (2000) 'Feminism Facing Industrial Relations in Britain', *British Journal of Industrial Relations*, 38(2): 183–201.

Wall, T.D. and Lischeron, J.A. (1977) *Worker Participation: A Critique of the Literature and Some Fresh Evidence*, Maidenhead: McGraw Hill.

Walton, R.E. and McKersie, R.B. (1965) *A Behavioural Theory of Labor Negotiations*, New York: McGraw-Hill.

Walton, R.E., Cutcher-Gershenfeld, J. and McKersie, R.B. (1994) *Strategic Negotiations: A Theory of Change in Labor-Management Relations*, Boston, Mass: Harvard University Press.

Watson, M. and Hay, C. (2003) 'The Discourse of Globalisation and the Logic of No Alternative: Rendering the Contingent Necessary in the Political Economy of New Labour', *Policy & Politics*, 31(3): 289–305.

Weait, M. (2001) 'The Workplace Ethic: Is it a Crime?' *Management Today*, January: 52–7.

Webb, S. and Webb, B. (1920) *The History of Trade Unionism 1866–1920*, London: Longman.

Weber, T., Foster, P. and Egriboz, K.L. (2000) *Costs and Benefits of the European Works Council Directive*, Department of Trade & Industry, Employment Relations Research Series No. 9, London: DTI.

Wedderburn, Lord (1972) 'Labour Law and Labour Relations in Britain', *British Journal of Industrial Relations*, 10(2): 270–90.

Wedderburn, Lord (1989) 'Freedom of Association and Philosophies of Labour Law', *Industrial Law Journal*, 18(1): 1–38.

Weekes, B.C.M., Mellish, M., Dickens, L. and Lloyd, J. (1975) *Industrial Relations and the Limits of Law: The Industrial Effects of the Industrial Relations Act, 1971*, Oxford: Blackwell.

Welch, R. (1991) 'The Legal Mystification of Industrial Relations', *Employee Relations*, 13(4): 9–15.

West, M., Patterson, M. and Dawson, J. (1999) 'A Path to Profit? Teamwork at the Top', *Centrepiece*, 4(3): 6–11.

Wever, K.S. (1995) *Negotiating Competitiveness: Employment Relations and Organizational Innovation in Germany and the United States*, Boston, Mass: Harvard Business School Press.

Wheatcroft, P. (2000) 'Why Bob Ayling Fell Off the Wheel of Fortune', *Management Today*, September: 33.

Wheeler, D. (1997) *The Stakeholder Corporation*, London: Pitman.

Whipp, R. and Clark, P. (1986) *Innovation and the Auto Industry*, London: Frances Pinter.

Whitfield, K. and Strauss, G. (2000) 'Methods Matter: Changes in Industrial Relations Research and Their Implications', *British Journal of Industrial Relations*, 38(1): 141–51.

Whitfield, K. and Strauss, G. (eds) (1998) *Researching the World of Work: Strategies and Methods in Studying Industrial Relations*, Ithaca, NY: ILR Press.

Whitley, R. (1999) *Divergent Capitalisms: The Social Structuring and Change of Business Systems*, Oxford: Oxford University Press.

Whitston, C. and Waddington, J. (1994) 'Why Join a Union?', *New Statesman & Society*, 18 November, 36–8.

Whittington, R. (1989) *Corporate Strategies in Recession and Recovery: Social Structure and Strategic Choice*. London: Unwin Hyman.

Wigham, E. (1976) *Strikes and the Government, 1983–1974*, London: Macmillan.

Wilkinson, A. (1999) 'Employment Relations in SMEs', *Employee Relations*, 21(3): 206–17.

Wilkinson, A. and Willmott, H. (eds) (1995) *Making Quality Critical: New Perspectives on Organizational Change*, London: Routledge.

Wilkinson, A. Godfrey, G. and Marchington, M. (1997) 'Bouquets, Brickbats and Blinkers: in P. Sparrow and M. Marchington (eds), *Human Resource Management: The New Agenda*, London: Pitman: 272–85.

Wilkinson, B. and Oliver, N. (1990) 'Obstacles to Japanization: The Case of Ford UK', *Employee Relations*, 12(1): 17–21.

Wilkinson, F. and White, M. (1994) 'Product-Market Pressures and Employers' Response', in J. Rubery and F. Wilkinson (eds), *Employer Strategy and the Labour Market*, Oxford: Oxford University Press, 111–37.

Wilks, S. (1996) 'Regulatory Compliance and Capitalist Diversity in Europe', *Journal of European Public Policy*, 3(4): 536–59.

Williams, K., Williams, J. and Haslam, C. (1987) *The Breakdown of Austin Rover*, Leamington Spa: Berg.

Williams, K., Williams, J., Haslam, C. and Wardlow, A. (1988) 'Facing up to Manufacturing Failure', Aberystwyth Economic Papers, OP.15, University of Wales College of Aberystwyth.

Willis, P.E. (1977) *Learning to Labour*, London: Saxon House.

Willman, P. (1989) 'The Logic of "Market-Share" Trade Unionism: Is Membership Decline Inevitable?', *Industrial Relations Journal*, 20(4): 260–70.

Willman, P. (1996) 'Merger Propensity and Merger Outcomes Among British Unions, 1986–1995', *Industrial Relations Journal*, 27(4): 331–8.

Willman, P. (2001) 'The Viability of Trade Union Organization: A Bargaining Unit Analysis', *British Journal of Industrial Relations*, 39(1): 97–117.

Willman, P. and Cave, A. (1994) 'The Union of the Future: Super-Unions or joint Ventures?', *British Journal of Industrial Relations*, 32(3): 395–412.

Willman, P. and Morris, T. (1995) 'Financial Management and Financial Performance in British Trade Unions', *British Journal of Industrial Relations*, 32(2): 289–98.

Wills, J. (2002) *Union Futures: Building Networked Trade Unionism in the UK*, London: Fabian Society.

Wills, J. (2003) 'Organizing in Transport and Travel: Learning Lessons from TSSA's Seacat Campaign', in G. Gall (ed.), *Union Organizing: Campaigning for Trade Union Recognition*, London: Routledge, 133–52.

Winchester, D. (1983a) 'Industrial Relations in the Public Sector', in G.S. Bain (ed.), *Industrial Relations in Britain*, Oxford: Blackwell, 155–78.

Winchester, D. (1983b) 'Industrial Relations Research in Britain', *British Journal of Industrial Relations*, 21(1): 100–14

Winchester, D. (1988) 'Sectoral Change and Trade-Union Organization', in D. Gallie (ed.), *Employment in Britain*, Oxford: Blackwell, 493–518.

Winchester, D. and Bach, S. (1995) 'The State: The Public Sector', in P. Edwards (ed.), *Industrial Relations: Theory and Practice in Britain*, Oxford: Blackwell, 304–34.

Winkler, J.T. (1974) 'The Ghost at the Bargaining Table: Directors and Industrial Relations', *British Journal of Industrial Relations*, 12(2): 191–212.

Wiseman, J. (1996) 'A Kinder Road to Hell? Labor and the Politics of Progressive Competitiveness in Australia', in L. Panitch (ed), *The Socialist Register 1996: Are There Alternatives*, London: Merlin Press, 93–117.

Women and Equality Unity (2001) *Parents Perceptions of and Attitudes Towards Government Work-Life Balance Initiatives – A Survey*, London: Women and Equality Unit.

Wood, S. (1982) (ed.), *The Degradation of Work?*, London: Hutchinson.

Wood, S. (1999) 'Human Resource Management and Performance', *International Journal of Management Reviews*, 1(4): 367–413.

Wood, S. (2001) 'Business, Government, and Patterns of Labor Market Policy in Britain and the Federal Republic of Germany', in P.A. Hall and D. Soskice (eds), *Varieties of Capitalism: The Institutional Foundations of Comparative Advantage*, Oxford: Oxford University Press, 247–74.

Wood, S. and Godard, J. (1999) 'The Statutory Union Recognition Procedure in the Employment Relations Bill: A Comparative Analysis', *British Journal of Industrial Relations*, 37(2): 203–44.

Wood, S. and Kelly, J. (1982) 'Taylorism, Responsible Autonomy and Management Strategy', in S. Wood (ed.), *The Degradation of Work?*, London: Hutchinson, 74–89.

Worrall, L. and Cooper, C. (2000) *The Quality of Working Life: 2000 Survey of Managers' Changing Experiences*, Manchester: UMIST/Institute of Management.

Worrall, L., Cooper, C. and Campbell, F. (2000) 'The New Reality for UK Managers: Perpetual Change and Employment Instability', *Work, Employment & Society*, 14(4): 647–68.

Worrell, D. L., Davidson, W. N. and Sharma, V. M. (1991) 'Layoff Announcements and Stockholder Wealth', *Academy of Management Journal*, 34(3): 662–78.

Wray, D. (1996) 'Paternalism and its Discontents: A Case Study', *Work, Employment & Society*, 10(4): 701–15.

Wright, M. (1996) 'The Collapse of Compulsory Unionism? Collective Organization in Highly Unionized British Companies, 1979–91', *British Journal of Industrial Relations*, 34(4): 497–513.

Wright, P. and McMahon, G. (1992) 'Theoretical Perspectives for Strategic Human Resource Management', *Journal of Management*, 18(2): 295–320.

Wright, P.M. and Boswell, W.R. (2002) 'Desegregating HRM: A Review and Synthesis of Micro and Macro Human Resource Management Research', *Journal of Management*, 28(3): 247–76.

WTO (2002) *World Trade Organisation Annual Report 2002*, Geneva: WTO Publications.

Yeandle, D. and Clark, J. (1989) 'Growing a Compatible IR Set-up', *Personnel Management*, July: 36–9.

Yergin, D., Vietor, R.H.K. and Evans, P.C. (2000) *Fettered Flight: Globalization and the Airline Industry*, Cambridge, Mass: Cambridge Energy Research Associates.

Young, H. (1989) *One of Us*, London: Pan Books.

Author index

Rahman, M.   56
Rainbird, H.   55, 58, 59, 83, 84
Rainnie, A.F.   279, 288, 289, 290, 291–2, 293, 294, 296, 298, 301, 302, 305, 307, 313
Ram, M.   196, 292, 293, 296, 297, 299, 305, 306
Ramsay, H.   83, 84, 116, 255, 258, 270–1, 373
Redman, G.P.   234, 328, 332, 333, 336, 343, 347
Redman, T.   32, 103, 115
Reed, H.   46, 77, 78, 87
Rees, C.   52
Reich, M.   108
Reynolds, L.G.   227
Ricardo, D.   24
Richardson, I.   204, 208
Richbell, S.   111
Rick, J.   60
Ritzer, G.   52, 115
Roberts, D.   236
Roberts, G.   236, 347
Roberts, I.   289, 294, 296, 297, 298, 299, 301–2, 303, 305, 306, 313, 314, 316
Roberts, K.   261
Roberts, Z.   312, 358
Roche, W.   13, 14
Rogers, J.   156, 259, 260, 261, 315
Ronge, V.   178
Rose, M.   108, 144, 146, 147
Rosenthal, P.   250
Ross, A.M.   328, 331
Rowthorn, B.   184
Royle, T.   52, 115, 287, 304
Rubenowitz, S.   261
Rubery, J.   5, 14, 16, 58, 80, 82, 124, 125, 128, 195, 196, 296, 300
Rubinstein, S.A.   248
Ryan, P.   14, 241, 296, 309

Sabel, C.   293
Sachdev, S.   338
Sadler, D.   69
Salaman, G.   103
Salmans, S.   290
Salmon, J.   46, 78, 87, 132, 147, 164, 165, 168
Salsbury, P.L.   282, 304
Sapper, S.   166
Sapsford, D.   26, 330, 344, 345, 347, 348, 349, 350, 353, 354
Sattelberger, T.   98, 122
Saundry, R.   171, 173, 293
Sawbridge, D.   289, 294, 296, 297, 298, 299, 301–2, 303, 305, 306, 313, 314, 316
Sayer, A.   69
SBS   288, 295
Scarpetta, S.   58
Scase, R.   287, 292, 293, 294, 298, 301, 305, 306
Scholarios, D.   116
Schuler, R.   124

Schumpeter, J.   15
Scott, A.   40, 128
Scott, M.   289, 294, 296, 297, 298, 299, 301–2, 303, 305, 306, 313, 314, 316
Scott, P.   81
Screpanti, E.   343
Scullion, H.   303, 351, 353
Semeonoff, E.   261
Sewell, G.   269, 274
Shalev, M.   326
Shapiro, C.   103
Sharma, V. M.   76
Sheehan, M.   115, 117
Sheppard, E.   60
Shields, J.   6, 12
Shirlow, P.   176
Shorter, E.   344
Shutt, J.   83, 291
Shuttleworth, I.   176
Sieff, M.   278, 279, 280, 281, 282, 284, 290–1, 298
Siegel, A.   343–5, 346
Simm, C.   46, 73
Simms, M.   131, 132, 134, 145, 147, 164, 165, 168, 198, 293, 309, 312, 313, 314
Simpson, B.   190, 191, 192, 338
Simpson, D.   132, 147, 164, 165, 168
Sinclair, D.M.   312
Sisson, K.   52, 80, 100, 111, 113, 116, 117, 120, 126, 127, 227, 228, 231, 233, 237, 240, 267, 288, 303–4
Skinner, D.   12, 119, 128
Skinner, M.   301
Slichter, S.H.   226
Smart, D.   111, 145, 151, 161, 241, 243, 294, 296, 299, 302, 305, 338, 339
Smit, E.   344
Smith, C.   67, 310
Smith, C.T.B.   348
Smith, D.N.   344, 347
Smith, K.   63
Smith, M.   86
Smith, P.   149, 193, 194, 198, 310, 338, 339
Snape, E.   133
Soskice, D.   15, 16, 19, 44, 45, 46, 52, 56, 58, 59, 225, 245
Sparks, L.   285
Sproull, A.   292
Stafford, A.   23
Stageman, J.   313
Stanfield Tetreault, M.   105
Stanworth, J.   296, 297, 298, 301
Steer, J.   69
Stephenson, G.   301
Stevens, J.   59
Stevens, M.   111, 142, 145, 151, 160, 161, 241, 243, 294, 296, 299, 302, 305, 338, 339
Stewart, M.B.   244
Stewart, P.   163
Stiles, P.   119, 124
Stirling, J.   188, 256, 319, 321, 374

Subject index

British Steel Corporation (BSC)   217, 218–24,
    228, 229, 243
  employment   217–8
  Lump Sum Bonus (LSB) scheme   220–1, 223
  privatisation   221
  'Slimline'   219
  see also BS, Corus and steel industry
British Telecom (BT)   51
British Transport Docks Board   172
Broadcasting and Entertainments Trade Alliance
    (BETA)   160
  see also BECTU
Broadcasting, Entertainment, Cinematograph and
    Theatre Union (BECTU)   160, 293
Bryant & May   23
Brymon   102
BS   see British Steel
BSC   see British Steel Corporation
Bullock Committee   260, 263
Burger King   109

Cabin Crew '89   97, 102
Cable & Wireless   73, 207
call centres   370
capitalism   15, 21, 24, 33–5, 39, 44, 46, 101, 191,
    227, 362
  see also long waves of capitalist economic
    development
car industry   see automotive industry
Cathay Pacific   102
Cemex   50
Central Arbitration Committee (CAC)   133–4,
    157, 197
change (in employee relations)   8, 12–15, 18, 20,
    361–2
  see also transformation
Chartered Institute of Personnel and
    Development (CIPD)   39
Citizens Advice Bureau   302
civil service   178, 262
closed shop   see legislation and trade unions
clothing industry   290–2, 294, 296, 302, 303, 305,
    336, 348
  see also Sew & Son
coal mining
  employment   61
  National Powerloading Agreement
    (1966)   16, 347
  see also National Union of Mineworkers and
    strikes
collective agreements   see collective bargaining
collective bargaining   26, 30, 118, 183, 193,
    224–47, 357, 362, 365
  co-ordinated   235, 245, 246, 247
  coverage   150–1, 152, 198, 224–5, 229, 238–9,
    240–2, 246–7, 362–3
  decentralisation   238–42, 243, 244, 245, 339,
    362, 374
  definition   226
  form   229, 234, 235
  formal   234–5, 236

historical development   228, 230
industrial democracy   226, 230, 242, 243, 247
informal   235, 236, 237
local   229, 230, 232, 233–4, 236, 237, 238
managerial control   226–8, 236–7, 240, 243
national/industry-wide   229, 230–2, 233–4,
    235, 237, 240, 243, 245
procedural rules   226
scope   229, 233, 235, 237, 238, 241–2
single-employer   242, 243, 245
state, role of   231–2, 243, 246, 247
substantive rules   226, 234
  see also Donovan Commission
Comair   102
commitment   364, 365, 366
  see also high commitment management
communication   268, 273, 274, 276, 363
  see also joint consultation
Communication Workers' Union (CWU)   147
Compulsory Competitive Tendering (CCT)   206,
    208
Confederation of British Industry (CBI)   103,
    181, 246, 275, 339, 353
Confederation of Health Service Employees
    (COHSE)   160
  see also Unison
conflict   see industrial conflict
Connect   168
consent   41
control   103–110
Conservative governments
  1970–4   190, 191
  1979–97   20, 59, 87, 130, 141, 144, 152–3, 154,
    155, 180, 182, 185, 191, 202, 206, 208,
    210, 239, 243, 298, 326, 336–7, 340, 369,
    370, 372
  see also Thatcher, Margaret and Thatcherism
consultation   see joint consultation
Continental Airlines   105, 122, 123
continuity (in employee relations)   8, 12–15, 18,
    20, 361–2
co-operation   40–1, 101, 272–3, 361
co-ordinated market economies (CMEs)   45–6,
    56, 57, 58, 87, 104, 122, 156, 201, 225, 364,
    369, 370, 371, 375
corporatism   179, 181, 182, 184, 187, 203, 368
Corus   21, 47, 217–24, 228, 229, 243, 362, 364
  collective bargaining   218–24
  redundancies   76
  teamworking   222–4, 240
  see also BS and BSC and steel industry
Crofter Hand Woven Tweed v. Veitch (1942)   189
customer care   10, 21, 41, 274–5, 285, 363
customers   42, 62, 93, 106, 108–9, 119, 125, 209,
    250–1, 274, 292, 311–2

Dan Air   102
Delta Airlines   105
democracy   see industrial democracy
denationalisation   see privatisation
Deutscher Gewerkshaftsbund (DGB)   368

skill 55, 58–9, 64, 83, 85, 117, 365, 370
  de-skilling 40, 83, 108
  see also training
single union agreements *see* trade unions
small firms 287–9, 290, 291–4, 298–301, 305–7,
    313–14, 315, 316
  see also non-unionism
Smith, Adam 4, 24
Social Chapter *see* Europe
Social Contract 153–4, 179
Sony 375
Southwest airlines 122, 123
stakeholding 104, 364–5
Star Alliance 123
state 170–213
  and capitalism 178–9, 187
  definition 178
  economic manager 183–9
  employer 201–9
  employment policy 368–71
  and employment relationship 177–83
  see also government, legislation *and* public
      sector
steel industry 205, 217–24, 229, 230
  collective bargaining 218–24, 230
  employment 217–18
  national strike (1980) 219–20, 223, 336, 337
  output 217
  rationalisation 218
  redundancies 217–8
  sub-contracting 221
  see also BS, BSC *and* Corus
strategic business units (SBUs) 80–1
strikes 325–49
  ballots 338–9, 340, 341
  breadth (workers involved) 326, 334–5, 337,
      339, 341, 342, 345
  causes 327–8, 329–30, 331
  coal mining 332, 333, 337, 339, 344, 346, 347,
      348, 349
  dock strikes 338, 339, 344–5, 346–7, 348, 352
  definition 329
  duration (days lost) 326, 334–5, 339, 341, 342
  frequency 326, 334–5, 337–8, 339, 341, 342
  General Strike (1926) 190, 348
  inter-industry differences 333, 343–5
  measurement 329–30, 331
  pay 336–7, 340, 341
  political 328, 330, 336
  public opinion 317
  public sector 326, 328, 336, 337, 340–1
  recession 339–40, 343
  statistics 326–7, 329–32, 342
  theories 327, 342–9
  trends 328, 332–42
  unofficial 234, 333, 346, 350
  waves 342
  see also firefighters' strike, industrial conflict
      and legislation
sub-contracting 82–3, 206
Sun-Air 102

supermarkets 355–6
  see also under individual supermarket names
systems theory 27–31

teachers 149, 205–6, 242, 336
teamworking 21, 53, 84, 162, 269–70, 273, 275,
    364, 365
  extent 269
  forms 269
Tebbit, Norman 192
technology 60, 83, 84, 88, 307, 346, 348
telecommunications 50, 52, 337
television 293, 341
Tesco 21, 47, 117, 248–53, 261, 284, 362, 363
  customer service 250
  employment 248
  human resource strategy 250–1
  partnership agreement 248–9, 250, 251–2
  profit-sharing 250, 253
  staff forums 248, 249, 253, 255, 256, 259, 265
Texas Instruments 286
textiles 352
  see also clothing
Thai Airways 123
Thatcher, Margaret xii, 56, 184, 185, 191, 202
Thatcherism 13, 19, 20, 44–5, 133, 151, 180–1,
    200, 202, 209–10, 369
theory 21, 23–47
  see also Marxism, Oxford School, pluralism,
      systems theory *and* unitarism
Theory X 107, 109, 110
Theory Y 107, 109, 110
  see also human relations
'Third Way' xii, 45, 57, 181, 189, 200, 202, 208,
    371
time
  hours of work 60, 64, 65–7, 261, 364
  spiral 14–15, 146, 342, 362
T-Mobile 198
Total Quality Management (TQM) 21, 48, 54,
    84, 254, 272, 273–4, 275, 363, 375
Toyota 375
Trade Disputes Act (1906) 190
Trade Union Act (1984) 193, 211
Trade Union Reform and Employment Rights Act
    (1993) 212, 340
trade unions 26, 130–69, 366–8
  beauty contests 162
  check-off 97, 150–1, 161
  closed shop 150, 157, 263
  craft unionism 228–9
  density 142–3, 145–6, 348
  derecognition 145, 149, 241, 312
  'double breasted' arrangements 149
  finances 367–8
  full-time officers (FTOs) 168
  inter-union conflicts 367, 368
  inter-union co-operation 367
  member attitudes 143, 144, 166, 312, 313
  membership 138, 139–48, 156–7, 158, 169
  mergers 158, 159–61, 367